COLLECTING
TOY CARS & TRUCKS:
No. 1
A Collector's Identification & Value Guide

by Richard O'Brien

ISBN 0-89689-103-8

BOOKS AMERICANA
INC.

Toys on the cover from the collections of Don Hultzman, Ron Smith, and Bob and Alice Wagner.

TABLE OF CONTENTS

INTRODUCTION AND ACKNOWLEDGEMENTS

The reason for this book is simple. In the fifteen or so years I've been doing *Collecting Toys,* which is a price guide and reference to all sorts of collectible toys, I had noticed the most popular of all, perhaps even exceeding the electric train, is the vehicle. I had amassed a large amount of material on the subject that simply couldn't be squeezed into *Collecting Toys.* Accordingly, I suggested this new venture to my publisher, Books Americana's Dan Alexander, and he quickly agreed.

This kind of book is necessarily a community project. It quickly became obvious to me that the toy vehicles community is not only widespread, but extremely generous. **Everyone** I asked for help pitched in, and **mightily.** Many others, hearing of the project, sprang to offer their services, and were just as generous with their time and knowledge.

The two Smiths, Ron and Bob, were Herculean; Ron with Japanese Tin, Hot Wheels and Promotionals, Bob with a slew of company histories, listings, prices and corresponding photographs. Don Hultzman, an expert on battery-operated toys and tin wind-ups, was as helpful and zealous as ever, as were Courtland experts Joe and Sharon Freed. Motorcycles are fun, and no one thinks them more fun than Kent M. Comstock, who, through his knowledge and photographs, quickly agreed to share that feeling of joy with this book's readers. Two devotees of small cars, Gates Willard and Dave Leopard, promptly and exhaustively responded to the chance to get the news out to aficionados and incipient collectors. Thomas G. Nefos, a true expert on Hess, jumped at the chance to funnel that expertise to the public. Brian Seligman plunged into the swamp that used to be Wyandotte, emerging with the best history of the company I've seen, plus a better listing than I've been able to compile in fifteen years of keeping an eye on that company (as well as providing a host of tip-top photos). I was tipped about Vincent Rosa late in the game; despite the tight deadline, he came through with flying colors, as can be seen in his Brooklin section.

Two experts on the military, William H. Kilborn and Ed Poole, emerged victorious from their respective campaigns; military Dinky and IDs. Plastics buff Terry Sells provided a history of Pyro, plus a huge number of photos of his favorite vehicles, and Mary Gaeta was cheerfully willing to divulge all about a company known (till now) to few collectors: Peter-Mar. Smith-Miller and Doepke man Ray Funk also donated a huge array of catalogs he'd picked up in the 1950s and 60s, and Fred Maxwell graciously allowed me to use all the research he's come up with in years of investigating the makers of "slush" (lead alloy) toys.

Photos are the lifeblood of a book like this. In addition to the above-mentioned, providers of visual material include Bob and Alice Wagner, Calvin L. Chaussee, Chic Gast, Gary Linden, Islyn Thomas, Roger E. Canup, Ron Fink, Tim O'Callaghan, Ron Chojnacki, Stan Alekna, Roy Bonjour, Craig A. Clark, K. Warren Mitchell, Virginia Caputo and James S. Maxwell Jr., Perry R. Eichor, Heinz Mueller of Continental Hobby House, B.R. Blaydes, Bob Bard, Jeff Bub Auctions, Jerry Combs, Charles L. Jackson, Sotheby's New York, Max Heiss, the Lawrence Scripps Wilkinson Collection of the Detroit Antique Toy Museum, David Mapes Auctions, R.F. Sapita, Orville C. Britton, Jack Matthews, James Apthorpe, Christie's East, Charles D. Richards, Phillips, New York, The Graham Werkes, Don Hallock, Al Lane and Dick MacNary.

Thanks to all, and to Bill Lango, who tipped me onto Bill Kilborn and Vincent Rosa. Finally, thanks to whomever I've forgotten. I almost certainly have; to my dismay, I almost always do. But that doesn't make my gratitude a whit less heartfelt.

Richard O'Brien
February, 1994

CONDITION AND PRICING

Condition is all-important in a toy. Prices are based on condition, so it's important to understand what condition means to a collector or dealer. Thus the box on this page.

It's also important to remember that this book is a **guide**. It is **not** the absolute last word on the price of a toy. Nothing could be. Prices may inflate or deflate in the months it takes to compile and publish a book. Even on the same day a toy can vary in price, depending on the dealer, the buyer, the geographical area, and whether it's being offered in the first moments of a toy show or in the last, draggy minutes, when the dealer finds himself having to pack up all that stuff again. "Auction fever" can drive a toy to a ridiculous new height; or establish it as the new height. Employed by itself, *Collecting Toy Cars & Trucks* should at least prevent very serious mistakes being made. Used with the assistance of a few current prices found on lists or on dealer tables, it can get the prospective buyer or seller much nearer to the current (always fuzzily defined) market price. As for the notation "No Price Found"; I'm often asked what that means. All it really means that I or my contributors haven't found a price. It **could** mean the toy is rare. It could even mean it is rare **and** valuable (the two don't always go together). But so many toys were produced and so many bought and sold that often even a common toy doesn't surface on the lists or at shows for months or even years.

Finally, for those who wish to consider this field as an investment, and it can be a good one, it should be stressed that mint or near-mint condition provides considerably more financial safety than any of the other conditions, as this is the only condition sure to attract all collectors and dealers of any particular toy.

CONDITION OF A TOY
AND ITS RELATION TO PRICE

CONDITION CODE:

C6 - Good. Evident overall wear, well-played with, but acceptable to many collectors

C8 - Very Good Minor wear overall, very clean

C10 - Mint (like new)

Note: Mint in Box commands a higher price. Condition below C6 brings considerably lower prices

---

FAKES
by Rod Carnahan

Fakes can be a problem in toy collecting. Cast iron fakes have a thick cast, and pieces often don't fit together properly or evenly. The bottoms of many fake iron castings have break marks. The old toy makers, when the toys were taken from the molds, would file or machine away those marks, but this doesn't happen on most fakes because it could increase the cost of labor for a cheap product (many iron copies are made in countries like Taiwan, and are meant to be sold as copies, but often aren't).

Cast iron fakes also have a rougher feel, a blurring of details and a coarse and gritty look. Spot welds also hold many fake castings together (rather than with the steel rivet rod that has been peened on one end). Fake wheels are thicker, and often don't have enough spokes (as little as four where there should be nine). Some of the reproductions also have hollow rolled tubing for the axles, and screws to hold the castings together. Some people actually bury the fakes to "age" them; rust can be a giveway, when combined with some or all of the other aspects already mentioned. A too-cheap price can be another indication the toy isn't original.

The best protection is knowledge; getting around to as many shops and shows as possible helps develop an "eye". Research through books and collector publications can also be very helpful. Knowing the measurements of an original can also be helpful; reproductions are almost invariably a bit smaller. In the case of lead alloy toys, a heavier-than-expected weight suggests a recent casting, as the people who legitimately cast from the old molds usually make the toys heavier in order to keep them from breaking when shipped. Many plastic toys are being reproduced. In this case it helps to know what the original plastic looked like, and what its color was. Reproductions in general try to use a different color, and plastics today look different, because, due to the danger of some of the original components, a different plastic must be used.

A final tip; for insurance purposes it helps to videotape your collection. A computer software program helps to keep up with your investment.

A.C. GILBERT

Alfred Carlton Gilbert (1884-1961) is best known as the creator of the Erector set. However, Gilbert also produced some very attractive vehicles circa the early 1920s.

	C6	C8	C10
A.C. Gilbert Racer, 9'' long, windup	$300	$500	$700
A.C. Gilbert Stutz	500	800	1200
A.C. Gilbert ''U.S. Mail'' truck, copyright 1920	300	450	625

ACME

Acme seems to have produced only two toy vehicles, both in clockwork; a 1903 curved-dash Oldsmobile roadster and a delivery truck with a pressed-steel canopied roof. In 1905 Jacob Lauth, the owner of the Chicago firm, turned to production of the real thing, under the name Lauth-Juergens. Co.

	C6	C8	C10
Acme Curved Dash Olds, 11'' long, clockwork, c.1905	500	750	1000

A.S.

(Adolf Schumann, Nuremburg, Germany, 1910-1930s)
by Bob Smith

Schumann was making toys for about 20 years and as so many of the German toy companies, he went out of business in the middle 1930s. Not much is known about this small company, and their toys are considered rare. The A.S. trade mark is usually on the door of the car.

A.S. Touring Car. Red/black, c/w motor, glass windshield 9.0'' long, c.1915.	1250	1500	2000

Acme Curved Dash Olds, 11'' long.
Courtesy Wilkinson Collection, Detroit Antique Toy Museum

A.S. Touring Car, 9'' long, c.1915.
Photo by Bob Smith

ACME PLASTIC TOYS, INC.

Many, perhaps all, Acme vehicles are exactly like Thomas Toys. The reason is that Acme's Ben Shapiro was a financial partner in Thomas Toys, and Thomas Toys' Islyn Thomas made up toys for Shapiro at his request, with the Acme imprint substituted for that of Thomas. Acme's order sheets sometimes show the name Acme Plastic Toys, Inc., and at other times B.H. Shapiro & Co. In both cases the address was the same: 121 East 24th Street, New York, NY. Dates in parentheses indicate the year, where known, the items appeared in the firm's order sheets. Acme also made other toys: helicopters, planes, baby carriages and strollers, wagons, etc.

(continued)

	C6	C8	C10
No. 16 Truck & Trailer, 9" long (1947)....................	$14	$16	$18
No. 17 Jeep, 4½" long, movable windshield (1947)...........	10	12	14
No. 18 Truck, Streamlined, 5" long (1947)....................	10	12	14
No. 19 Jeep & Trailer, 8½" long (1947)....................	14	16	18
No. 26 Truck Wrecker, 5" long	12	14	16
No. 27 Sedan, 4⁵⁄₁₆" long (1947)	11	13	15
No. 29 Airline Limousine, 4½" long (1947)	8	10	12
No. 30 Coupe & House Trailer, 8¼" long (1947).............	20	22	24
No. 40 Texaco Gas Truck, 4" long (1947)....................	8	10	12
No. 41 Delivery Truck, 4" long (1947)....................	8	10	12
No. 42 Dump Truck, 5" long (1947)....................	12	14	16
No. 43 Esso Gas Truck (1947)..	No Price Found		
No. 48 Streamlined Utility Trailer, "fits items 27-29-40-41", 2½" long......................	6	8	10
No. 55 Limousine and Trailer, 6¾" long......................	12	14	16
No. 67 Police-Fire Chief Radio Car, each 4½" long, price per each	11	13	15
No. 72 Plastic Motorcycle & Rider, 4" long....................	20	25	30
No. 74 Merry-Go-Round Truck, 4¾" long....................	20	25	30
No. 77 Streamlined Sedan, 4½" long......................	11	13	15
No. 77 Streamlined Convertible Coupe, 4½" long (Acme used the same number for these toys on the same order sheet)....	11	13	15
No. 90 Service Motorcycle & Rider, 4⁷⁄₁₆" long..................	25	30	35
No. 125 Plated Motorcycle, 4" long	20	25	30
No.? Auto Carrier, 9" long	20	35	50

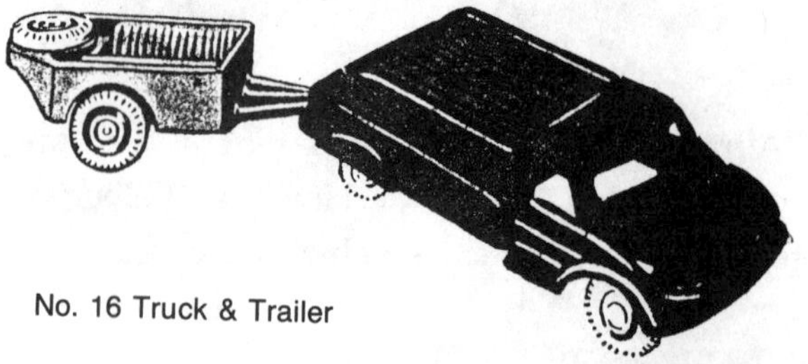

No. 16 Truck & Trailer

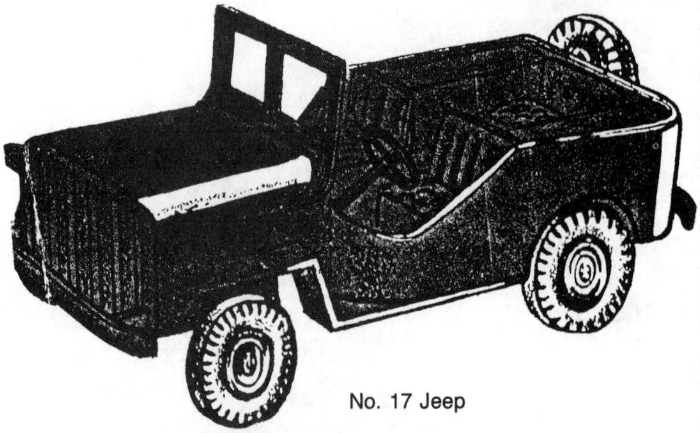

No. 17 Jeep

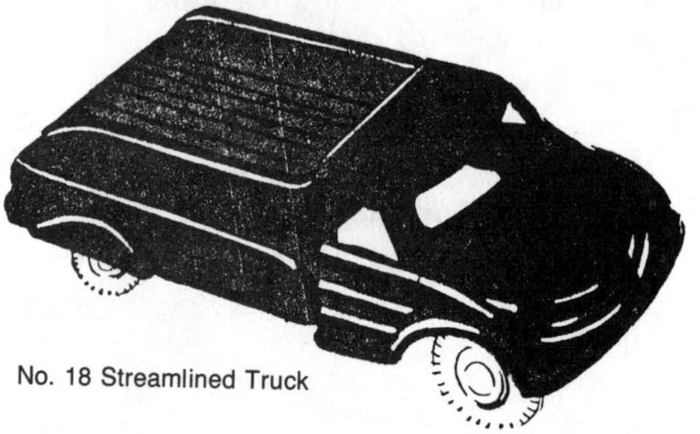

No. 18 Streamlined Truck

No. 19 Jeep & Trailer

No. 26 Truck Wrecker

ACME

No. 27 Sedan

No. 42 Dump Truck

No. 29 Airline Limousine

No. 30 Coupe & House Trailer

No. 43 Esso Gas Truck

No. 40 Texaco Gas Truck

No. 48 Streamlined Utility Trailer

No. 55 Limousine & Trailer

No. 41 Delivery Truck

No. 67 Police - Fire Chief Radio Car

5

No. 72 Plastic Motorcycle & Rider

No. 90 Service Motorcycle & Rider

No. 74 Merry-Go-Round Truck

No. 125 Plated Motorcycle

No. 77 Streamlined Sedan

Acme No. ? Auto Carrier.
Courtesy Bob & Alice Wagner

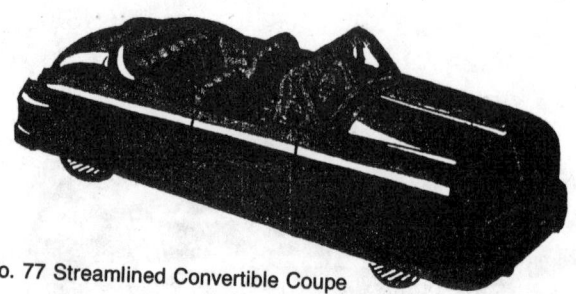

No. 77 Streamlined Convertible Coupe

AEROCAR

Aerocar PT 560 Made in U.S.A.	C6	C8	C10
Plas-Tex'', 7½'', plastic	30	45	60

"Aerocar PT560 Made in U.S.A. Plas-Tex"
Courtesy James S. Maxwell/Virginia Caputo
Photo by Virginia Caputo

ALL-AMERICAN

(Los Angeles, California)

''All American Hot-Rod'', 9'' long,	C6	C8	C10
sold in 1949	175	300	450

"All American Hot-Rod", 9" long, 1949.
Photo by Roger E. Canup

AL OTTO

(Chicago, 1940s-1950s)

Al Otto Stock Car Racer, 4½''			
long, early plastic	4	10	25

Al Otto Stock Car Racers.
These were made from 1949 till the present. They are still sold at some racetracks in dull modern plastic. The old ones are very smooth and very shiny, as shown.
Photo and caption courtesy Bob & Alice Wagner

ALL AMERICAN TOY COMPANY

All American was founded by Clay Steinke in Salem, Oregon about 1948. It continued till 1955, with its location the Jorgenson Building on Ferry Street. At its peak it employed 42 people and in its existence sold a total of 26,000 toys. Their most popular toy was the Timber Toter, despite its formidable 1950 price of twenty dollars. Bill Hellie purchased the defunct company; molds, dies, parts. All American now sells parts and is producing new limited editions (see Leading Collectors and Dealers).

All American C-5 Cattle Liner, 38''			
long.	$275	$400	$600
All American CL-8 Cargo Liner,			
38'' long.	400	650	925
All American D-3 Dyna-Dump,			
20'' long.	300	475	700
All American HD-6 Play-Loader,			
11'' long.	No Price Found		
All American Play-Dozer, 9'' long	No Price Found		
All American HH-9 Heavy Hauler,			
38'' long.	300	475	750

(continued)

ALL AMERICAN

	C6	C8	C10
All American L-2 Timber Toter, with logs, 38'' extended length	300	475	675
All American LJ-4 Timber Toter, Jr., 20'' long, with lumber . . .	150	250	375
All American MS Midget Skagit, 18'' long, battery-powered . . .	250	450	600
All American S-I Scoop-A-Veyor, 16'' long	240	360	480

AIR HORN STEERING

MODEL CL-8 CARGO-LINER
. . . top-selling "ride 'em" truck and semi. Easy Air Horn Steering for full maneuverability. Hauls just about anything a child can think of. 8"x8"x38".

MODEL L-2 TIMBER TOTER
. . . a rugged, adjustable-bed truck built just like the mammoth logging trucks that roar through Western mountains. Air Horn Steering. Truck 8"x8"x20". Combination truck and trailer adjustable to full 38". Logs are available at slight extra cost.

MODEL C-5 CATTLE-LINER
Open-top truck and semi is newest of big, tough "ride-'em" trucks. Strong steel sides are latticed. Air Horn Steering. 8"x8"x38".

ALL AMERICAN TOY COMPANY

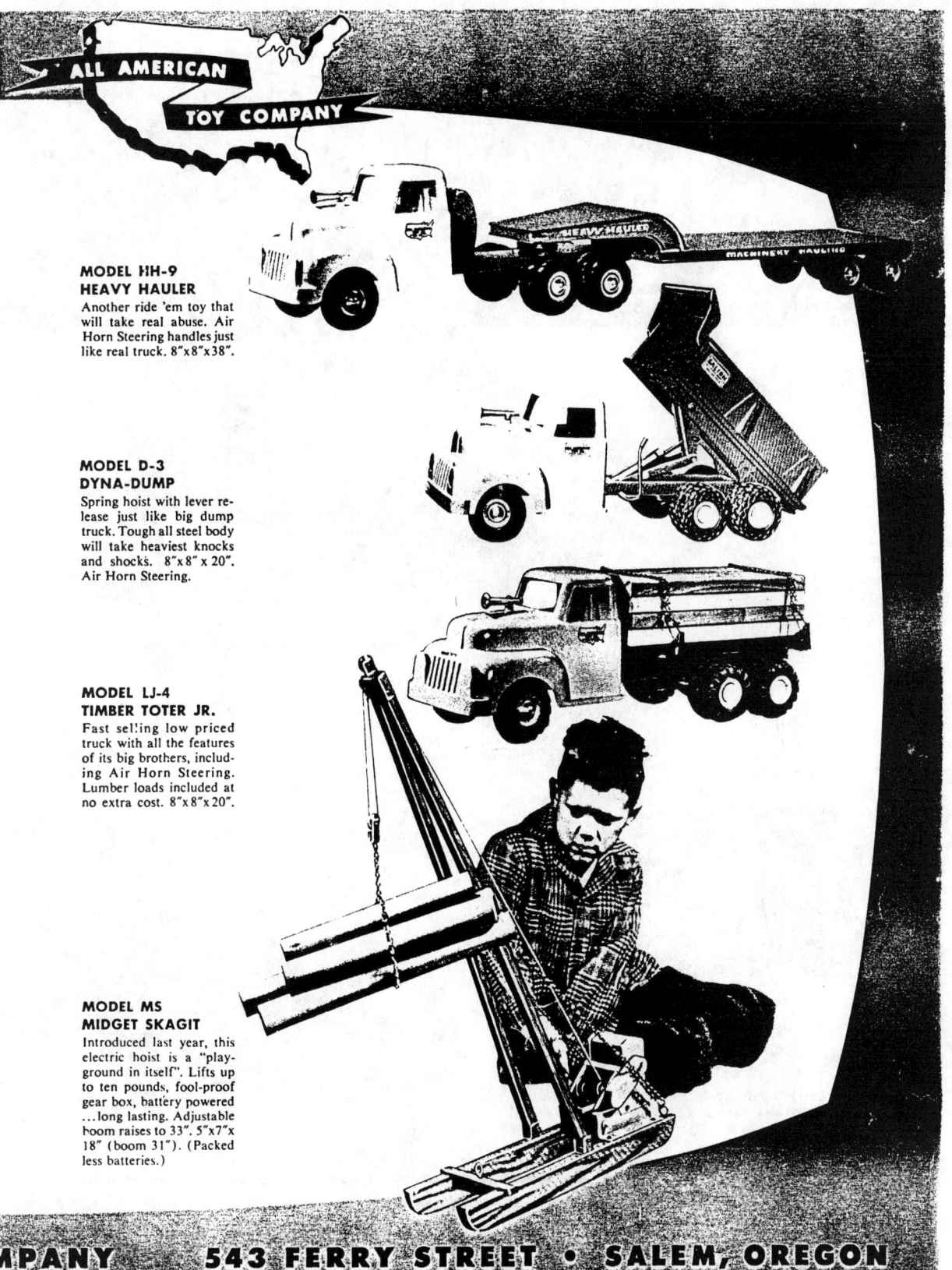

**MODEL HH-9
HEAVY HAULER**

Another ride 'em toy that will take real abuse. Air Horn Steering handles just like real truck. 8"x8"x38".

**MODEL D-3
DYNA-DUMP**

Spring hoist with lever release just like big dump truck. Tough all steel body will take heaviest knocks and shocks. 8"x8"x20". Air Horn Steering.

**MODEL LJ-4
TIMBER TOTER JR.**

Fast selling low priced truck with all the features of its big brothers, including Air Horn Steering. Lumber loads included at no extra cost. 8"x8"x20".

**MODEL MS
MIDGET SKAGIT**

Introduced last year, this electric hoist is a "playground in itself". Lifts up to ten pounds, fool-proof gear box, battery powered ...long lasting. Adjustable boom raises to 33". 5"x7"x 18" (boom 31"). (Packed less batteries.)

MPANY   543 FERRY STREET • SALEM, OREGON

NEW Big, Rugged, Low Cost
All American Toys with
Fast-Sell Buy Appeal

All American Toys are built to take rough, tough
treatment while giving full play value. These three new
toys are low in cost, make fine extras to go along
with their famous big brothers.

MODEL S-1 SCOOP-A-VEYOR. An action toy that works just like a real conveyor belt loader. Big scoop holds sand, dirt, pebbles and small objects while strong rubber belt hauls the load up and into truck. Welded steel frame, trailer hitch, spindle steering. Crank action. 6" x 10" x 16".

MODEL HD-6 PLAY-LOADER
A really play-full toy that scoops up its load, lifts it high, then dumps it, all under the easy control of the junior contractor. Positive lock action, caster steering. 5½" x 7½" x 11".

MODEL HD-7 PLAY-DOZER. Sturdy three-wheel tractor with a dozer blade that digs in, floats and raises to perform like a real bulldozer. Caster steering. 6½" x 5" x 9".

ALL AMERICAN TOY COMPANY

LITHO, U. S A.

ALL AMERICAN TOY CO., 543 FERRY ST., SALEM, ORE.

SALES REPRESENTATIVES

Alfred Hahn Company
200 Fifth Avenue
New York 10, New York

Sam Weiner
1433 Merchandise Mart
Chicago, Illinois

Donovan-Mercer Company
403B Merchandise Mart
Kansas City 8, Kansas

John Campbell and Associates
1077 Second Unit
Santa Fe Building
Dallas, Texas

Lou Frank Sales Company
704 Notre Dame Street West
Montreal 3, Canada

Du-Net Sales
H. R. Neathery
1388 Beach Haven Road N. E.
Atlanta, Ga.

All American Catalog

ALL-NU

All-Nu was founded by former Barclay sculptor Frank Krupp in 1937 or 1938 (incorporation was February 16, 1938). The original address was 55-58 Main Street, Yonkers, NY, with the firm having moved by the summer or fall of 1941 to 67 Irving Place in Manhattan. All-Nu's main products were soldiers and novelties. All-Nu's four lead vehicles are known only from the collection of Krupp's daughter. They would presumably be valuable if any reached the market (which seems likely, as the four examples seem to have come from finished molds), as All-Nu's very rare soldiers bring high prices.

	C6	C8	C10
All-Nu "Field Kitchen," approx. 2½" long, "Made in USA", lead	No Price Found		
All-Nu Searchlight, approx. 2¾" long, "Made in USA", lead	No Price Found		
All-Nu Sound Detector, approx., 2¾" long, "Made in USA", lead	No Price Found		
All-Nu Tank "USA", 3" long, "Made in USA", lead	No Price Found		

All-Nu cardboard vehicles:

	C6	C8	C10
All-Nu 150 Jeep	$3	$5	$7
All-Nu 151 Cannon	3	5	7
All-Nu 152 Wheeled AA Gun	3	5	7
All-Nu 153 Tank	3	5	7
All-Nu 154 Ambulance, Military	3	5	7
All-Nu 155 Army Troop Carrier	3	5	7

CONDITION OF A TOY
AND ITS RELATION TO PRICE

CONDITION CODE:

C6 - Good, Evident overall wear, well-played with, but acceptable to many collectors

C8 - Very Good Minor wear overall, very clean

C10 - Mint (like new)

NOTE: Mint in Box commands a high price. Condition below C6 brings considerably lower prices.

ALLIED MOLDING CORPORATION

Allied, of 126-02 Northern Boulevard, Corona, New York, seems to have made only plastic toys. It made a variety, from vehicles to pistols, boats, animals, a ferris wheel and a baby carriage.

	C6	C8	C10
Allied Cement Mixer, No. 197, 4" long	No Price Found		
Allied Dump Truck, Large, No. 174, 5½" long	No Price Found		
Allied Dump Truck, Small, No. 191, 4½" long	10	15	20
Allied Emergency Truck, 7" long	No Price Found		
Allied Enclosed Van, 6" long	10	15	20
Allied Fire Engine No. 125, 6½" long	No Price Found		
Allied Furniture Moving Van, Large, 5½" long, No. 208, clear trailer ("Viso Box"), price without original ten pieces of furniture	10	15	20
Allied Haulaway Truck & Trailer, No. 122, 10" long, 2 small cars, one large car	20	25	30
Allied Old Fashioned Car, 4½" long, No. 218	No Price Found		
Allied Pick-up Truck, 3½" long	8	10	15
Allied Racer No. 130, 4⅝" long	No Price Found		
Allied Stake Truck, 4½" long	10	15	20
Allied Stake Truck with Animals, No. 193, 9½" long, removable racks, 8 assorted farm animals	No Price Found		
Allied Station Wagon, 3½" long	8	10	15
Allied Steam Shovel Truck No. 134, 6" long	No Price Found		
Allied Taxi, 3½" long	8	10	15
Allied Tractor No. 30, 3" long	No Price Found		
Allied Construction Set No. 620: dump truck, cement truck, emergency truck with ladder, 15" long box	No Price Found		

Allied Emergency Truck, No. 129

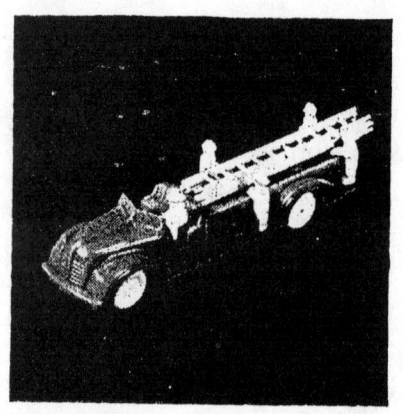

Allied Fire Engine, No. 125

Allied Old Fashioned Car No. 218

Allied Tractor, No. 30

Allied Stake Truck with Animals, No. 193

AMERICAN NATIONAL

American National, of Toledo, Ohio, produced a huge number of pedal cars in the 1920s and 1930s. It also had a line of pressed-steel toy trucks from the late 20s till the early 30s. It was founded by the Diemer brothers, William, Walter and Harry, about 1894.

	C6	C8	C10
American National Army Truck, Mack "Giant", 26½" long...	800	1400	2000
American National Cement Fire Truck, 28" long............	1000	1700	2300
American National Circus Truck, 27" long..................	800	1400	2000
American National Coal Truck..	1500	2500	4200
American National Duesenberg Bobtail Pedal Car, late 1920s .	3000	5500	7000
American National Dump Truck, 28" long..................	800	1400	2000

	C6	C8	C10
American National Fire Pedal truck, c.late 1920s	4000	7500	13000
American National "Juvenile Auto" dump truck pedal car, 57" long....................	2000	3500	5000
American National Moving Van, 28" long....................	800	1400	2000
American National Open Bed Truck, 29" long.............	700	1150	1700
American National Packard Coupe, 30" long, steerable front wheels.....................	900	1600	2200
American National Screenside Truck....................	1200	2200	3000
American National Sprinkler Truck	1400	2500	3500
American National Tanker......	1400	2500	3500

American-National-Automobiles

The premier line....exactingly modeled after the real cars....lustrous enamel finishes in flashy color combinations. Each with adjustable pedals

"WHIPPET"—Extreme length 32 in., American red enameled, blue & yellow trim, yellow number, 8 in. red enameled double spoke wire wheels, ⅝ in. rubber tires. EQUIPMENT—Cast steering wheel, gas lever, motor-meter, steel pedals. 1F820—1 in carton, 22 lbs...........Each $3.75

"DODGE"—Extreme length 35 in., American red enameled, chrome yellow trim, 10 in. wheels, ¾ in. rubber tires. EQUIPMENT—Cast steering wheel, gas lever, motor-meter, steel pedals. 1F824—1 in carton, 26 lbs.........Each $4.50

"CYCLONE"—Extreme length 35 in., dk. blue enameled, tangerine trim, 10 in. double disc wheels, ½ in. rubber tires. EQUIPMENT Gas lever, motor-meter, rubber pedals. 1F822—1 in carton, 33 lbs.........Each $5.50

"VELIE"—Extreme length 35 in., Falcon tan enameled, blue & yellow trim and stripes, spring chassis, 10 in. red enameled double disc wheels, ½ in. rubber tires. EQUIPMENT—Cast steering wheel, gas lever, nickeled motor-meter, metal headlights, horn, bumper, rubber pedals, oil can, oil. 1F833—1 in carton, 35 lbs.........Each $6.75

"ESSEX"—Extreme length 41 in. Chinese blue enameled, red, black & yellow trim, spring chassis, 10 in. red enameled disc wheels, 1 in. rubber tires. EQUIPMENT—Cast steering wheel, nickeled motor-meter, gas tank, rubber pedals, oil can, oil. 1F835—1 in carton, 40 lbs.........Each $7.95

"OAKLAND"— Extreme length 38½ in., Chrysler blue enameled, dk. blue & yellow trim and stripes, spring chassis, 10 in. red enameled disc wheels, ½ in. rubber tires. EQUIPMENT—Cast steering wheel, gas lever, adjustable windshield, nickeled motor-meter, metal headlights, license plate, rubber pedals, oil can. 1F837—1 in carton, 45 lbs. Each $9.75

"JEWETT"—Extreme length 41 in., Bolera cream enameled, blue & red trim, spring chassis, 10 in. blue enameled balloon type disc wheels, ¾ in. rubber tires. EQUIPMENT—Cast steering wheel, gas lever, horn, instrument board, adjustable windshield, nickeled motor-meter, metal headlights, license plate, gear shift, rubber pedals, oil can. 1F848—1 in carton, 50 lbs. Each $12.00

"MARMON" — Extreme length 41¼ in., Drake blue enameled, tangerine, yellow & aluminum trim, spring chassis, 10 in. tangerine balloon type disc wheels, 1 in. rubber tires. EQUIPMENT—Composition steering wheel, gas lever, horn, instrument board, adjustable windshield, nickeled motor-meter, metal headlights, license plate, gear shift, rubber pedals, oil can. 1F849—1 in carton, 50 lbs. Each $12.95

"REO"—Extreme length 44½ in., Ottawa tan enameled, amber, black, white & aluminum trim, Ottawa tan fenders, spring chassis, 10 in. cream enameled heavy wire wheels, 1¼ in. rubber tires. EQUIPMENT — Composition steering wheel, gas lever, French horn, instrument board, adjustable windshield, nickeled motor meter, metal headlights, rubber pedals. 1F850—1 in wire bound box, 65 lbs...............Each $14.75

"AMERICAN-NATIONAL" DUMP TRUCKS

End gate automatically opens and closes when box is raised or lowered by steel lever. Each with adjustable pedals. Sturdy trucks that are finding a tremendous and fast-growing market. And, in this field, it pays to sell the line children prefer....the name "American-National" is that line.

"BUICK"—Extreme length 46 in., deep maroon enameled, green, tangerine and yellow trim, aluminum bead, tangerine enameled fenders, full spring chassis, 10 in. maroon enameled balloon type disc wheels, 1 in. rubber tires. EQUIPMENT—Composition steering wheel, gas lever, French horn, instrument board, nickeled adjustable windshield, spotlight, nickeled motor-meter and radiator, metal headlights, license plate, gear shift, upholstered seat, rear trunk, rubber pedals, motor buzzer, oil can, oil. 1F853—1 in wire bound box, 79 lbs.........Each $19.75

"STUDEBAKER"—Extreme length 53 in., russet brown enameled, green, tangerine & yellow trim, aluminum bead on hood, black enameled fenders, full spring chassis, 12 in. green enameled roller bearing balloon type disc wheels, 1 in. rubber tires. EQUIPMENT—Composition steering rod, gas lever, French horn, instrument board, nickeled adjustable windshield, spotlight, nickeled motor-meter, metal lamps, license plate, gear shift, stationary hood, round bumper, heavy "die-form" fenders, rubber pedals, motor buzzer, oil can, oil. 1F854—1 in crate, 125 lbs. Each $23.00

"JUNIOR"—Extreme length 44 in., American red enameled body, black & yellow trim, black enameled dump box, 10 in. red enameled double disc wheels, ½ in. rubber tires. EQUIPMENT—Gas lever, license plate, horn, rubber pedals. 1F857—1 in wire bound box, 80 lbs...............Each $8.25

"SPEED" — Extreme length 44 in., Larchmont blue enameled body, red, black & yellow trim, black enameled dump box, 10 in. red enameled disc wheels, 1 in. rubber tires. EQUIPMENT—Composition steering wheel, gas lever, horn, radiator cap, rubber pedals. 1F858—1 in crate, 65 lbs. Each $10.75

American National pedal cars, as shown in a Christmas, 1929 Butler Bros. catalog.

	C6	C8	C10
American Precision Co. Allis-Chalmers "C" Model Tractor, diecast, 1950 ...	150	225	300
Andy Gard Brink's Armored Car, battery-operated	42	63	85

CONDITION OF A TOY
AND ITS RELATION TO PRICE

CONDITION CODE:

C6 - Good, Evident overall wear, well-played with, but acceptable to many collectors

C8 - Very Good Minor wear overall, very clean

C10 - Mint (like new)

NOTE: Mint in Box commands a high price. Condition below C6 brings considerably lower prices.

ANIMATE TOY CO.

In 1918 this firm was located at East 17th Street in New York City, and its president was L.T. Savage. By 1931 it had moved to 30 North 15th Street in East Orange, New Jersey, and employed ten men and forty women. In 1934 the president-vice president was George V. Turnbull and the secretary-treasurer was George H. Webb. Five men and eleven women made up the work force.

Animate Toy Tractor with Snow Plow, from a circa 1940-41 M.S. Young & Co. catalog

	C6	C8	C10
Animate Toy Co. "Baby Haymaker", 1916 tin push toy playset	$110	$165	$225
Animate Toy "Baby Tractor", friction, "patented June 20, 1916"	110	165	225
Animate Toy "Climbing Tractor", 9" long, 1929, windup	110	165	225
Animate Toy "U.S. Baby Tank", pat. 6/20/16, 2½" long, new in 1918, windup	37	56	75
Animate Toy Tractor and Dump Trailer, 15½" long, windup	No Price Found		
Animate Toy Tractor with Snow Plow, 13" long, windup	No Price Found		
Animate Toy Tractor with Sweeper, 12½" long, windup	No Price Found		
Animate Toy Tractor, windup, 8½" long	No Price Found		

Animate Toy Tractor with Sweeper, from a c.1940-41 M.S. Young & Co. catalog.

Animate Toy Tractor & Dump Trailer, from a 1940-41 L. Gould catalog.

Animate Toy "Baby Tractor"

Animate Toy "U.S. Baby Tank".
Photo by Ed Poole

ARCADE

Arcade is one of the great names in cast-iron toys; perhaps the most highly-regarded of all. It was founded in 1868 as the Novelty Iron Works, and was located from first to last in Freeport, Illinois. In 1884, when the firm was known as Arcade, it began to produce toy coffee mills from the left-over scraps of the "adult" mills it sold. However, it wasn't until 1921, when the firm struck a deal to produce Yellow Cabs that it made its mark in the toy world. The cab was an instant, overwhelming success, and led to a continuing line of cast-iron toy vehicles, as well as other toys. The firm's heyday was the 1920s, both financially and esthetically, but it continued to produce toys until the advent of World War Two.

Arcade AR68 as seen in Arcade catalog No. 26. Found in the archives of a rival company. It is hand-stamped "Received March 19, 1917".

An unlisted fire engine, as seen in Arcade catalog No. 26. Found in the archives of a rival company, the catalog is hand-stamped "Received March 19, 1917". No price found.

Two early Arcade cars, unlisted here, as seen in Arcade catalog No. 26. Found in the archives of a rival firm, the catalog is hand-stamped "Received March 19, 1917". No prices found.

	C6	C8	C10
(AR1) A.C.F. Bus, 1927, 11½'' long	$1500	$2500	$3700
(AR2) Allis-Chalmers Tractor and Trailer, 1936, No. 2650, 13'' long total length	125	200	275
(AR3) Allis-Chalmers Tractor and Dump Trailer, 1937, No. 2657, 12¾'' long with trailer	80	120	160
(AR3A) Allis-Chalmers Tractor and Dump Trailer, 1937, No. 2660, 8¼'' long	110	165	220
(AR4) Allis-Chalmers Tractor Trailer, 1937, No. 2650, 13'' long with trailer	200	300	400
(AR5) Allis-Chalmers "WC" Tractor, 1941, 7¾'' long	250	400	540
(AR6) Ambulance, 1932, No. 187, 7¾'' long	No Price Found		
(AR7) Ambulance, 1932, No. 188, 6'' long	375	562	750
(AR8) Ambulance, 1936, 4'' long, (white-painted version) of No. 2620X Chevrolet Panel Delivery Truck	No Price Found		
(AR9) Anthony Dump Truck, 1927, 8⅛'' long	1300	2200	3200
(AR10) Austin Autocrat Road Roller, 1928, No. 291, 7'' long	225	340	450
(AR11) Austin Delivery Truck, 1932, No. 173, 3¾'' long	50	75	100
(AR12) Austin Racer, 1932, No. 175X, 3¾'' long	50	75	100
(AR13) Austin Roadster, 1932, No. 174, 3¾'' long	No Price Found		
(AR14) Austin "Roll-A-Plane"	1200	2000	3000
(AR15) Austin Stake Truck, 1932, No. 176X, 3¾'' long	150	225	300
(AR16) Austin Wrecker, 1932, No. 177X, 3¾'' long	150	225	300
(AR17) Avery Tractor, 1923, 4½'' long, stack, no hood	30	45	60
(AR18) Avery Tractor, 1926, 4½'' long, has hood, no stack	125	188	250
(AR19) Borden's Milk Bottle Truck, 1936, 6¼'' long, No. 2640X	1000	1500	2500
(AR20) Brinks Express Truck, 1932, 11¾'' long	3000	5000	7500

	C6	C8	C10
(AR21) Buick Coupe, 1927, 8½'' long	2500	4500	6500
(AR22) Buick Sedan, 1927, 8½'' long	2000	3500	5500
(AR23) Bus, Double-Decker, 1929, No. 316X, 8½'' long	450	675	900
(AR24) Bus, Double-Decker, 1936, No. 317, "Chicago Motor Coach" stamp, 8¼'' long	450	675	900
(AR25) Car Carrier, 1931, No. 238, 24½'' long, cargo has four 25-cent cars or three 50-cent cars	800	1400	2000
(AR26) Car Carrier, 1932, No. 296, carries either 2 No. 114 Ford sedans and one 113X Ford Coupe, or one No. 213 Ford Stake Truck and one each of the others	800	1400	2000
(AR27) Car Transport, 1937, No. 3107, came with 2 No. 1501 sedans, No. 1502 stake truck and No. 1503 wrecker 18½ in. long	1500	2800	4000
(AR28) Car Transport, 1937, No. 2977, holds 2 sedans, 2 trucks, 11¼'' long	400	600	800
(AR29) Carry Car Truck and Trailer Set. 1934, No. 2970, 14¼'' long, carries Austin coupe, delivery and stake	700	1100	1500
(AR30) Caterpillar Tractor, 1930, No. 271, 7½'' long	700	1200	1600
(AR31) Caterpillar Tractor, 1931, No. 269X, 6⅞'' long	500	800	1100
(AR31A) Caterpillar Tractor, 1931, No. 268X 5⅝'' long	400	600	800
(AR32) Caterpillar Tractor, 1931, No. 267X, 3⅞'' long	50	75	100
(AR33) Caterpillar Tractor, 1931, No. 266X, 3'' long	50	75	100
(AR34) Caterpillar Tractor, 1936, No. 270Y, later 2700Y, 7¾'' long	700	1100	1500
(AR35) Century of Progress Bus, 1933, No. 3200, later No. 3250 (1934), 14½'' long	350	525	700
(AR36) Century of Progress Bus, 1933, No. 3210, 12'' long	300	475	650

Arcade AR3A

	C6	C8	C10
(AR37) Century of Progress Bus, 1933, No. 3220, 10½'' long ..	150	225	300
(AR38) Century of Progress Bus, 1933, No. 3230, 7⅝'' long....	175	263	350
(AR38A) Century of Progress Bus, 1933, approx. 5½'' long, won't pivot or detach.............	No Price Found		
(AR39) Checker Cab, 1923, 9'' long, paint variation of No. 1 Yellow Cab	700	1100	1500
(AR40) Checker Cab, 1932, No. 157, 9¼'' long (came with and without ''Checker'' on visor).	No Price Found		
(AR41) Chevrolet Coupe, 1929, No. 121X, 8¼'' long	1300	2000	2900
(AR42) Chevrolet Coupe, 1934, rumble seat, No. 1150X, 4⅜'' long......................	150	225	300
(AR43) Chevrolet Panel Delivery Truck, 1936, No. 2620X, 4'' long	125	188	250
(AR44) Chevrolet Sedan, 1929, No. 122X, 1929, 8¼'' long	800	1200	1800
(AR45) Chevrolet Sedan, 1934, No. 1170X, 4¼'' long	50	75	100
(AR46) Chevrolet Stake Truck, 1925, 9'' long	1000	1700	2400
(AR47) Chevrolet Stake Truck, 1936, No. 2610, 4¼'' long ...	No Price Found		
(AR48) Chevrolet Superior Roadster, 1925, 7'' long......	750	1125	1500
(AR49) Chevrolet Superior Sedan, 1925, 7'' long	No Price Found		
(AR50) Chevrolet Superior touring Car, 1925, 7'' long	800	1400	2000
(AR51) Chevrolet Utility Coupe, 1925, 7'' long	700	1100	1400
(AR52) Chevrolet Wrecker Truck, 1936, No. 2630X, 4¼'' long ..	150	225	300
(AR53) ''Chief'' Fire Chief Coupe, 1934, No. 1230, 6¾'' long ...	No Price Found		
(AR54) ''Chief'' Fire Chief Coupe, 1934, No. 1240, 5'' long	No Price Found		
(AR55) ''Coast To Coast GMC'' Transcontinental Bus, 1937, No. 4378X, 9'' long.............	450	675	925
(AR56) Corn Harvester, 1939, No. 702, 6½'' long	200	300	400

Arcade AR4

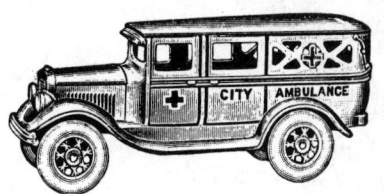

Arcade AR6

Arcade AR10
Courtesy David W. Mapes Auctions

	C6	C8	C10
(AR57) Corn Harvester, 1939, No. 4180, 5'' long	150	225	300
(AR58) Corn Planter, 1939, 4½'' long......................	62	93	125
(AR59) Coupe, ''1922'' on spare tire, 9'' long	No Price Found		
(AR60) Coupe, like above, no 1922 date on spare	1500	2250	3000

	C6	C8	C10
(AR61) Coupe, 1932, No. 109, 6″ long, no Arcade markings, rumble seat opens	175	263	350
(AR62) Deluxe Sedan, 1941, No. 1590X, same as Yellow Cab No. 1590Y, but with top lights and sun roof ground off. 8½″ long	350	525	700
(AR63) DeSoto Sedan, 1936, No. 1460X, 4″ long	180	270	360
(AR64) Double Decker Bus, 1939, No. 3180, 8″ long..........	450	675	900
(AR65) Dump Truck, 1936, No. 2320, 4½″ long	40	60	80
(AR66) Dump Truck, 1941, No. 3910X, 7″ long	550	950	1300
(AR67) Dump Truck Trailer, 1931, No. 234, 12⅞″ long	1200	2000	3000
(AR68) Dump Wagon, 1917, 7″ long, driver, no cab	475	725	1000
(AR69) Express Truck, 1929, No. 270X, 8″ long	No Price Found		
(AR70) Express Truck, 1929, No. 209X, 6″ long	No Price Found		
(AR71) Express Truck, 1929, No. 214X, 5″ long	No Price Found		
(AR72) Fageol Bus, 1925, 12″ long	500	750	1100
(AR73) Fageol Bus, 12½″ long .	500	700	1000
(AR74) Fageol Bus, 8″ long	250	375	500
(AR74A) Fageol Bus, 5″ long ...	150	225	300
(AR75) Farm Mower, 1939, No. 4210X, 4″ long	60	90	120
(AR76) Farmall "A" Tractor, 1941, No. 7050, 7½″ long	325	488	650
(AR77) Farmall "M" Tractor, 1941, No. 7070, 7¼″ long	300	450	600
(AR78) Farmall Tractor, 1929, No. 279, 6″ long	350	525	700
(AR79) Fire Engine, 1923, pumper, 7½″ long	No Price Found		
(AR80) Fire Engine, 1936, No. 1740, pumper, 9″ long	200	300	400
(AR81) Fire Engine, 1936, No. 1810, 6¼″ long	No Price Found		
(AR82) Fire Engine, 1936, No. 2340, 4½″ long	90	135	180
(AR83) Fire Engine, 1941, No. 6990, 13½″ long	700	1100	1600
(AR84) Fire Ladder Truck, 1936, No. 1820, 7″ long	200	300	400

Arcade AR17
Photo by Orville C. Britton

Arcade AR21
Courtesy Phillips New York

Arcade AR22
Courtesy James S. Maxwell/Virginia Caputo
Photo by Virginia Caputo

Arcade AR26

Arcade AR30

Arcade, L to R: AR45, AR42
Photo by Chic Gast

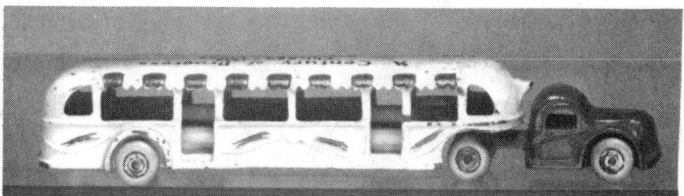

Arcade AR36
Courtesy Sotheby's NY

Arcade AR63

Arcade AR37
Courtesy Sotheby's NY

At right: Arcade AR64. The Mack stake truck is a Hubley, about 5'' long.

Arcade AR38
Courtesy Sotheby's NY

Arcade AR72

Arcade AR41
Courtesy James S. Maxwell/Virginia Caputo.
Photo by Virginia Caputo

	C6	C8	C10
(AR85) Fire Trailer Truck, 1934, No. 1940, ladder truck, 16¼'' long	500	750	1000
(AR86) Ford Carry Car Truck and Trailer, 1934, No. 2400	No Price Found		
(AR87) Ford Coupe, 1923, 6'' long	225	375	450
(AR88) Ford Coupe, 1924, 6½'' long	150	225	300

	C6	C8	C10
(AR89) Ford Coupe, 1934, No. 1610X, 6¾'' long, rumble seat opens	175	263	350
(AR90) Ford Coupe, 1930s, No. 1190X, 4¾'' long	100	150	200
(AR91) Ford Dump Truck, 1929, No. 219X, 7½'' long	200	300	400
(AR92) Ford Express Truck, 1929, No. 210X, 8¼'' long	No Price Found		
(AR93) Ford Fordor Sedan, 1924, 6½'' long, removable chauffeur	325	488	650
(AR94) Ford Sedan, 1923, 6½'' long	350	525	700
(AR95) Ford Sedan, 1934, No. 1620X, 6⅞'' long	No Price Found		
(AR96) Ford Sedan, 1934, ''Century of Progress'', 6⅞'' long	1000	1700	2400
(AR97) Ford Sedan, 1930s, No. 1200, 4¾'' long	150	225	300
(AR97A) Ford Sedan, 1934, ''Century of Progress'', 4¾'' long	No Price Found		
(AR98) Ford Sedan with Trailer, 1937, No. 1970, 12'' long (trailer 5½'' long)	1000	1600	2200
(AR99) Ford Stake Truck, 1925, 8¾'' long	1000	1600	2200
(AR100) Ford Stake Truck, 1927, 9'' long	No Price Found		
(AR101) Ford Stake Truck, 1934, No. 2010X 4¾'' long	No Price Found		

Arcade AR85, ladders missing.
Courtesy David Mapes Auctions

Arcade AR91

Arcade AR92

Arcade AR93

Arcade AR78, late wheels.
Photo by Perry R. Eichor

Arcade, top to bottom: AR96, AR97A.
Photo by John M. Ianuzzi

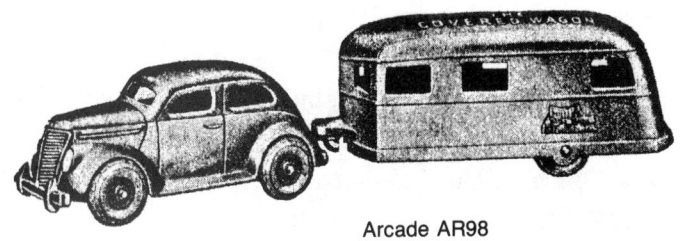

Arcade AR98

Arcade AR103
Courtesy James S. Maxwell/Virginia Caputo
Photo by Virginia Caputo

Arcade AR106

Arcade AR108-110

Arcade AR108A

	C6	C8	C10
(AR102) Ford Touring Car, 1923, 6½'' long	275	363	550
(AR103) Ford Touring Car Bank, 1923, 6½'' long	450	675	900
(AR104) Ford Tractor and Plow, 1941, No. 7220, tractor 6½'' long, overall length 8¾''	225	338	450
(AR105) Ford Truck, One-Ton Pickup, 1923, 8½'' long	1100	1700	2500
(AR106) Ford Wrecker, 1929, No. 215, 8¼'' length to end of hoist	700	1150	1600
(AR106A) Ford Wrecker, 1929, No. 217	300	450	600
(AR107) Ford Wrecker, 1930, No. 218, 4½'' long	125	188	250
(AR108) Fordson Tractor, 1923, 5⅜'' long	300	450	600
(AR108A) Fordson Tractor, No. 275, 1928	No Price Found		
(AR109) Fordson Tractor, 1928, No. 274, 4¾'' long	112	168	225
(AR110) Fordson Tractor, 1928, 3⅞'' long, No. 273	50	75	100
(AR111) Fordson Tractor, 1934, rubber wheels, No. 2730X, 3½'' long	75	112	150
(AR112) Greyhound Cruiser Coach bus, 1941, No. 4400, 9⅛'' long	285	430	575
(AR113) ''Greyhound Lines'' Bus, 1937, No. 3850 SP, 7¾'' long	250	375	500
(AR114) ''Greyhound Lines Great Lakes Exposition'', 1936, No. 437, 11'' long	800	1200	1600
(AR115) ''Greyhound Lines Great Lakes Exposition'', 1936, No. 436, 6¾'' long	450	675	900
(AR116) Greyhound Super Coach, 1937, No. 4380, 9'' long	375	525	750
(AR117) ''Ice'' Truck, c.1941, No. 1933, 6¾'' long	275	362	550

Arcade AR110
Courtesy Mapes Auctioneers

Arcade AR112
Courtesy Sotheby's NY

AR116
Courtesy Sotheby's NY

Arcade AR118
Courtesy James S. Maxwell/Virginia Caputo
Photo by Virginia Caputo

	C6	C8	C10
(AR118) International Delivery Truck, 1932, No. 226, 9¾'' long	1000	1500	2000
(AR119) International Delivery Truck, 1936, No. 3020 9½'' long	No Price Found		
(AR120) International Dump Truck, 1931, No. 236-0, 10¾'' long ..	700	1100	1600
(AR121) International Dump Truck, 1936, No. 3030, 10½'' long ..	1100	1800	2600
(AR122) International Dump Truck, 1937, No. 3710, 9½'' long ...	1000	1700	2400
(AR123) International Dump Truck, 1940, No. 1670, chassis and dump box are steel, 11⅝'' long	600	900	1200
(AR124) International Dump Truck, 1941, No. 7100, 11⅛'' long...	600	900	1200
(AR125) International Harvester Company Public Utility Truck, 1932, No. 197, 11¼'' long ...	No Price Found		
(AR126) International Pickup Truck, 1941, No. 7000, 9½'' long	1000	1500	2000
(AR127) International Stake Truck, 1931, No. 237-0, 12'' long....	750	1125	1500
(AR128) International Stake Truck, 1936, No. 3090, 12'' long	500	750	1100
(AR129) International Stake Truck, 1937, No. 2600, 9½'' long ...	No Price Found		
(AR130) International Stake Truck, 1941, No. 7090, 11½'' long .	700	1200	1600
(AR131) International Wrecker, 1940, No. 1650, 13'' long, wrecker crane body and crane are steel	400	600	800
(AR132) Ladder Truck, 1936, No. 1700, length with ladders 12½'' long	325	475	650
(AR133) Ladder Truck, 1936, No. 2350, 4¾'' long	75	112	150
(AR134) ''Mack'' Bus, 1929, No. 318, 13¼'' long	2000	3500	6000
(AR135) Mack Cement Mixer, 1931, 6¹¹⁄₁₆'' long, drum revolves ...	No Price Found		
(AR136) Mack Chemical Truck, 1928, fire engine No. 245R, 15'' long, has ladders	400	600	800
(AR137) Mack Chemical Truck, 1929, fire ladder truck, 15'' long	400	600	800
(AR138) Mack Chemical Truck, 1929, fire engine with ladders, 10'' long....................	No Price Found		

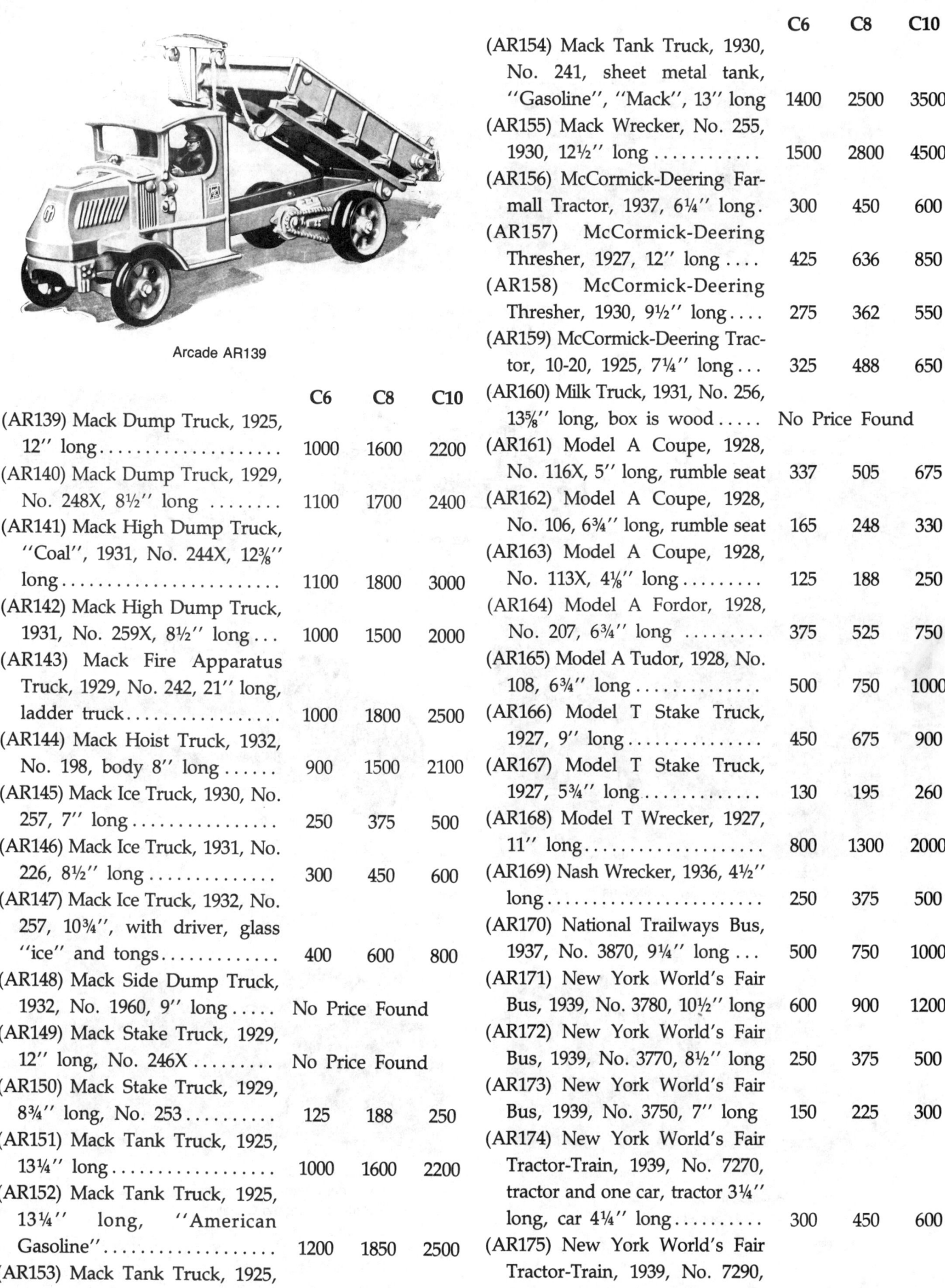

Arcade AR139

	C6	C8	C10
(AR139) Mack Dump Truck, 1925, 12" long	1000	1600	2200
(AR140) Mack Dump Truck, 1929, No. 248X, 8½" long	1100	1700	2400
(AR141) Mack High Dump Truck, "Coal", 1931, No. 244X, 12⅜" long	1100	1800	3000
(AR142) Mack High Dump Truck, 1931, No. 259X, 8½" long	1000	1500	2000
(AR143) Mack Fire Apparatus Truck, 1929, No. 242, 21" long, ladder truck	1000	1800	2500
(AR144) Mack Hoist Truck, 1932, No. 198, body 8" long	900	1500	2100
(AR145) Mack Ice Truck, 1930, No. 257, 7" long	250	375	500
(AR146) Mack Ice Truck, 1931, No. 226, 8½" long	300	450	600
(AR147) Mack Ice Truck, 1932, No. 257, 10¾", with driver, glass "ice" and tongs	400	600	800
(AR148) Mack Side Dump Truck, 1932, No. 1960, 9" long	No Price Found		
(AR149) Mack Stake Truck, 1929, 12" long, No. 246X	No Price Found		
(AR150) Mack Stake Truck, 1929, 8¾" long, No. 253	125	188	250
(AR151) Mack Tank Truck, 1925, 13¼" long	1000	1600	2200
(AR152) Mack Tank Truck, 1925, 13¼" long, "American Gasoline"	1200	1850	2500
(AR153) Mack Tank Truck, 1925, 13¼" long, "Lubrite"	2400	4200	5900

	C6	C8	C10
(AR154) Mack Tank Truck, 1930, No. 241, sheet metal tank, "Gasoline", "Mack", 13" long	1400	2500	3500
(AR155) Mack Wrecker, No. 255, 1930, 12½" long	1500	2800	4500
(AR156) McCormick-Deering Farmall Tractor, 1937, 6¼" long.	300	450	600
(AR157) McCormick-Deering Thresher, 1927, 12" long	425	636	850
(AR158) McCormick-Deering Thresher, 1930, 9½" long	275	362	550
(AR159) McCormick-Deering Tractor, 10-20, 1925, 7¼" long	325	488	650
(AR160) Milk Truck, 1931, No. 256, 13⅝" long, box is wood	No Price Found		
(AR161) Model A Coupe, 1928, No. 116X, 5" long, rumble seat	337	505	675
(AR162) Model A Coupe, 1928, No. 106, 6¾" long, rumble seat	165	248	330
(AR163) Model A Coupe, 1928, No. 113X, 4⅛" long	125	188	250
(AR164) Model A Fordor, 1928, No. 207, 6¾" long	375	525	750
(AR165) Model A Tudor, 1928, No. 108, 6¾" long	500	750	1000
(AR166) Model T Stake Truck, 1927, 9" long	450	675	900
(AR167) Model T Stake Truck, 1927, 5¾" long	130	195	260
(AR168) Model T Wrecker, 1927, 11" long	800	1300	2000
(AR169) Nash Wrecker, 1936, 4½" long	250	375	500
(AR170) National Trailways Bus, 1937, No. 3870, 9¼" long	500	750	1000
(AR171) New York World's Fair Bus, 1939, No. 3780, 10½" long	600	900	1200
(AR172) New York World's Fair Bus, 1939, No. 3770, 8½" long	250	375	500
(AR173) New York World's Fair Bus, 1939, No. 3750, 7" long	150	225	300
(AR174) New York World's Fair Tractor-Train, 1939, No. 7270, tractor and one car, tractor 3¼" long, car 4¼" long	300	450	600
(AR175) New York World's Fair Tractor-Train, 1939, No. 7290, same as above with three cars	400	650	900

Arcade AR143
Courtesy Phillips NY

Arcade AR144

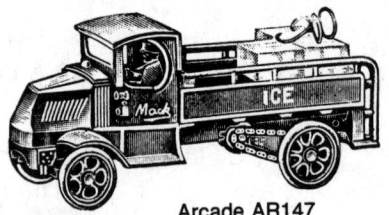

Arcade AR147

Arcade AR148

Arcade AR151
Courtesy David W. Mapes Auctions

Arcade AR154

Arcade AR153
Courtesy Sotheby's NY

Arcade AR155
Courtesy James S. Maxwell/Virginia Caputo
Photo by Virginia Caputo

Arcade AR156
Photo by Perry R. Eichor

Arcade AR172
Courtesy Sotheby's NY

Arcade AR173
Courtesy Sotheby's NY

Arcade AR157

Arcade AR162

Arcade AR170
Photo by Bob Smith

Arcade AR171
Courtesy Sotheby's NY

	C6	C8	C10
(AR176) Oliver Plow, 1923, 6½'' long	250	375	500
(AR177) Oliyer Plow, 1941, No. 4230X, 6¼'' long	125	188	250
(AR178) Oliver Superior Spreader, No. 7140, 1941, 10¼'' long	No Price Found		
(AR179) Oliver Tractor, 1937, No. 356, 7½'' long	750	1200	1800
(AR179A) Oliver Tractor, 1937, No. 359, 5½'' long	90	135	180
(AR180) Oliver Tractor, 1941, No. 3560, 7½'' long	75	112	150
(AR181) ''Plymouth'' Coupe, 1934, No. 1340X, 4½'' long	100	150	200
(AR182) ''Plymouth'' Sedan, 1934, No. 1330X, 4¾'' long	350	600	900
(AR183) ''Plymouth'' Stake Truck, 1934, No. 1840X, 4¾'' long	No Price Found		
(AR184) ''Plymouth'' Wrecker, 1934, No. 1830X, 4¾'' long	125	188	250
(AR185) Pontiac Sedan, 1934, No. 1350X, 4¼'' long	125	180	250
(AR186) Pontiac Sedan, 1935, 6½'' long	400	600	800
(AR187) Pontiac Stake Truck, 1935, No. 2390X, 6¼'' long	No Price Found		
(AR188) Pontiac Stake Truck, 1936, 2780X, 4¼'' long	No Price Found		
(AR189) Pontiac Wrecker, 1936, No. 2000X, 4¼'' long	125	188	250

Arcade AR191

Arcade AR196

Arcade AR197
Courtesy Phillips NY

Arcade AR198
Courtesy James S. Maxwell/Virginia Caputo
Photo by Virginia Caputo

	C6	C8	C10
(AR190) Racer, 1923, 7¾″ long .	No Price Found		
(AR191) Racer, Bullet Racer, 1931, No. 139X, 7⅝″ long	175	263	350
(AR192) Racer, 1931, No. 138X, 6¾″ long.	No Price Found		
(AR193) Racer, 1932, No. 140X, 10½″ long	No Price Found		
(AR194) Racer, 1932, No. 137X, 5⅝″ long	150	225	300
(AR195) Racer, 1937, No. 1440X, 8″ long.	No Price Found		
(AR196) Racer, 1937, No. 1457, 5¾″ long.	100	150	200
(AR197) Red Baby Dump Truck, 1923, No. 2, 10⅜″ long	500	750	1000
(AR198) Red Baby Truck, 1923, No. 1, 10¾″ long	700	1150	1600
(AR199) Red Baby "Weaver" Wrecker, 1929, 12″ long	675	1050	1500
(AR200) Reo Coupe, 1931, No. 1247, 9⅜″ long	3300	5900	8800
(AR201) Reo Coupe, 1931, smaller size	1200	2000	3000
(AR202) Sand Loading Shovel, 1932, No. 298 (later No. 299)	600	900	1200
(AR203) Scraper, 1929, No. 287, 8¼″ long.	42	63	85
(AR204) Sedan, 1937, No. 1501X, 4¾″ long.	100	150	200
(AR205) Sedan and Trailer, 1937, No. 1497X, car 5⅝″ long, trailer 2½″ long.	188	210	375
(AR206) Side Dump Trailer, 1932, No. 290, 7″ long, fastens to trucks or tractors	No Price Found		

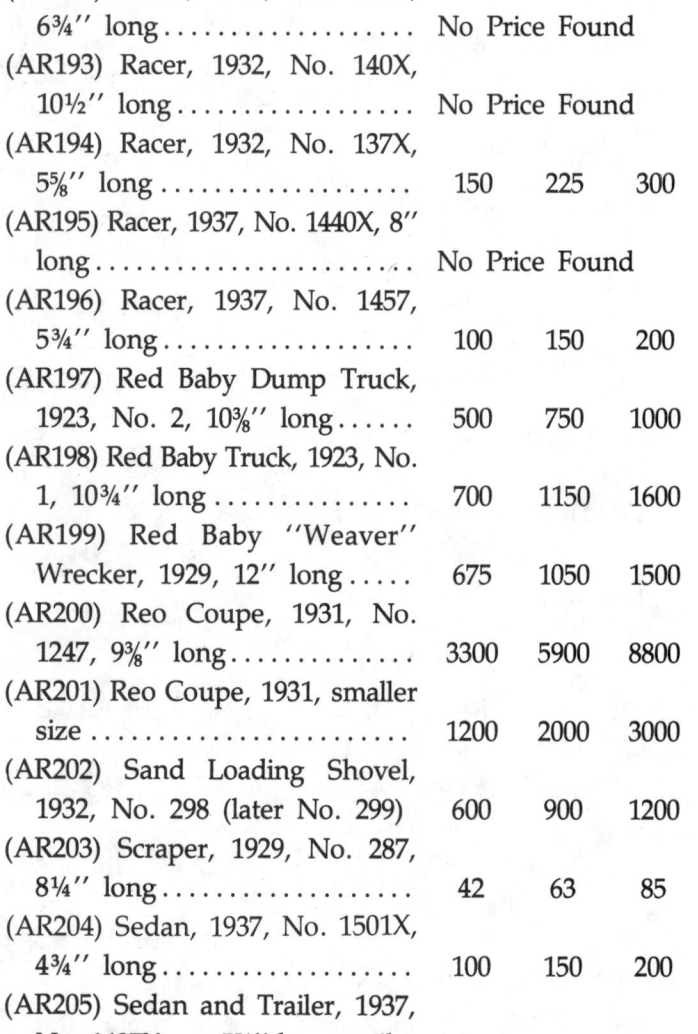

Arcade AR200

Arcade AR202

AR207

	C6	C8	C10
(AR207) "Silver Arrow", 1934, 7¼" long	350	525	725
(AR208) Stake Trailer Truck, 1931, No. 233, 11⁵⁄₁₆" long	1100	1800	2500
(AR209) Stake Truck, 1929, No. 208X, 6" long	225	345	450
(AR209A) Stake Truck, 1932, approx. 6" long	200	300	400
(AR210) Stake Truck, 1929, No. 213X, 5" long	125	188	250
(AR211) Stake Truck, 1932, No. 208, 6" long, no Arcade markings	300	450	600
(AR212) Stake Truck, 1937, No. 1502X, 4¼" long	200	300	400
(AR213) Steam Shovel, 1932, No. 292 Industrial Derrick, body 6" long	750	1125	1500
(AR214) Tandem Disc Harrow, 1939, No. 704, 6¾" long	60	90	120
(AR215) Tank, Army, 1937, No. 400, 8" long	450	675	900
(AR216) Tank, Army, 1941, No. 3960, 4" long, shoots	175	263	350
(AR217) Texas Centennial Bus, 1936 10¾" long (*Extremely Rare*)	700	1100	1600
(AR218) "Trac-Tractor", International Harvester, 1937, No. 277, 8¼" long	800	1300	1800
(AR219) Trac Tractor, 1941, No. 7120, 7½" long	900	1500	2200
(AR220) Unused			
(AR221) Unused			
(AR222) Tractor, 1941, No. 7200, 6½" long	No Price Found		
(AR223) Tractor, 1941, No. 4060X, 6¼" long, black rubber wheels	No Price Found		
(AR224) Tractor, 1941, No. 7341X, 6¼" long, wood wheels	No Price Found		
(AR225) Tractor, 1941, No. 7321X, 4¼" long	No Price Found		
(AR226) Tractor, 1941, No. 7260X, 3⅛" long, wooden wheels	No Price Found		
(AR227) Tractor, 1941, No. 7240X, 3⅛" long, rubber wheels	No Price Found		
(AR228) Tractor and Dump Trailer, 1941, No. 7300, 15½" long	No Price Found		

Arcade AR208
Courtesy James S. Maxwell/Virginia Caputo
Photo by Virginia Caputo

Arcade AR216
Photo by Ed Poole

	C6	C8	C10
(AR229) Trailer, farm, 1929, No. 286, 6⅜" long	40	60	80
(AR230) Trailer, farm, 1929, No. 288, 4⅝" long	35	52	70
(AR231) Trailer, farm, 1929, No. 289, 3¾" long	30	45	60
(AR232) Transport Trailer Truck, 1934, No. 1800, 7½" long	900	1400	1900
(AR233) W&K Truck Trailer, 1923, 8½" long	No Price Found		
(AR234) Two-wheeled Jack, 1932, No. 216, 5½" long	30	45	60
(AR234A) "Webaco Oil Co." truck, 13¼" long	2000	3500	5500
(AR235) White Bus No. 319, 1928, 13¼" long	2000	3200	4500
(AR236) White Delivery Truck, 1929, No. 252X, 8¼" long	1200	2000	3000
(AR237) White Delivery Van, 1929, No. 251, 13½" long	1500	2800	4500
(AR238) White Dump Truck, 1929, No. 249, 11½" long	1700	3000	5000
(AR239) White Dump Truck, 1931, No. 258X, 13½" long	No Price Found		
(AR240) White Tank Truck, 1931, No. 254X, 14⅛" long, "Gasoline"	1000	1500	2000

Arcade AR234A
Photo by Bob Smith

Arcade AR236
Courtesy James S. Maxwell/Virginia Caputo
Photo by Virginia Caputo

Arcade AR237
Courtesy James S. Maxwell/Virginia Caputo
Photo by Virginia Caputo

Arcade AR249
Courtesy Sotheby's NY

	C6	C8	C10
(AR241) Wrecker, 1929, No. 217 1928, body 8'' long	425	638	850
(AR242) Wrecker, 1932, No. 225, no Arcade markings	200	300	400
(AR243) Wrecker, 1934, No. 2020X, 7'' long	500	850	1200
(AR244) Wrecker, 1937, No. 1493X 6½'' long	150	225	300
(AR245) Wrecker, 1937, No. 1503X, 4¾'' long	100	150	200
(AR246) Wrecker, 1941, No. 3900X, 8½'' long	150	225	300
(AR247) Yellow Baby Wrecker, 1929, 12'' long	650	1100	1600
(AR248) Yellow Cab, 1922, No. 1, 9¼'' long	600	900	1200
(AR249) Yellow Cab, 1923, No. 2, 8'' long	600	900	1200
(AR250) Yellow Cab, 1927, No. 1, 9'' long	600	950	1300
(AR251) Yellow Cab, 1927, No. 05, 8½'' long	800	1400	2000
(AR252) Yellow Cab, 1927, No. 2, 8'' long	425	638	850
(AR253) Yellow Cab, 1927, No. 3, 5¼'' long	700	1050	1400
(AR254) Yellow Cab, 1934 Ford Sedan, 6⅞'' long	750	1125	1500
(AR255) Yellow Cab, 1936, No. 1580Y, 8¼'' long	1500	2500	3500
(AR256) Yellow Cab, 1941, No. 1590Y, 8½'' long	650	1000	1500
(AR257) Yellow Cab Bank, 1923, 8'' long	1000	1500	2200
(AR258) Yellow Cab Bank, 1927	750	1125	1500
(AR259) Yellow Cab Panel Delivery Truck, 1925, 8¼'' long, with driver	1200	2000	2800
(AR260) Yellow Coach Double-Decker bus, 1925, 14'' long ..	2000	3500	5500
(AR261) Yellow Parlor Coach Bus, 1926, 13'' long	1000	1600	2400
(AR262) Yellow Parlor Coach Bus, 1926, 9½'' long	800	1250	1800
(AR263) Andy Gump Car, 1920s, 7¼'' long	2250	3375	4500

Arcade AR250
Courtesy Wilkinson Collection, Detroit Antique Toy Museum

Arcade AR259. Side-mounted tire, original tires missing.
Courtesy James S. Maxwell/Virginia Caputo
Photo by Virginia Caputo

Arcade AR257
Courtesy James S. Maxwell/Virginia Caputo.
Photo by Virginia Caputo

Arcade AR263
Courtesy Christie's NY

Arcade AR258
Courtesy Chic Gast

Arcade set. No Price Found.
Photo by Bob Smith

ARCHER PLASTIC

(New York, NY)

Archer produced a number of space toys, beginning at least as early as 1949.

	C6	C8	C10
Archer A21 Rocket, Red, Yellow and Black, 13''.............	50	75	100
Archer A22 Futuristic Convertible, 10''......................	20	30	40
Archer A23 Futuristic Truck, 10''	20	30	40
Archer A24 Futuristic Coupe, 10''	20	30	40
Archer A25 Futuristic Coupe, 5''	10	15	20
Archer A26 Futuristic Sedan, 5''	10	15	20
Archer A27 Futuristic Truck, 5''	10	15	20
Archer A28 Futuristic Convertible, 5''......................	10	15	20
Archer A29 Raymobile........	No Price Found		
Archer A30 Scopemobile.......	No Price Found		
Archer A31 Searchmobile.......	No Price Found		
Archer A32 Futuristic Auto Carrier, 14'' long, No. 349, contains 4 of the 5'' futuristic vehicles.....	No Price Found		

Archer, Top, L to R: A22, A23, A24
Bottom L to R: A28, A26, A27
Photo by Bill Hanlon

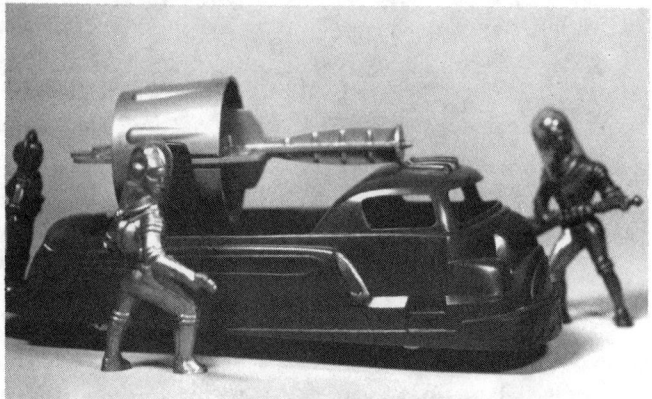

Archer A30
Photo by Terry Sells

Archer, A25, A26, A27, A29.
Photo by Bill Hanlon

ARGO

	C6	C8	C10
Argo ''Ambulance'', 4'' long, steel, 1955, bells ring.............	No Price Found		
Argo ''Chief'' fire car, 4'' long, steel, 1955, bell rings........	No Price Found		
Argo Hudson.................	15	22	30
Argo ''Police'' car, 4'' long, 1955, steel, guns rat-tat...........	No Price Found		
Argo ''Taxi'', 4'' long, 1955, steel, meters register fares.........	No Price Found		
Argo Sedan, 4'' long, steel, 1955, windshield wipers work.....	No Price Found		
Armored Truck bank, diecast, 1960s......................	9	13	18

ARNOLD

(German)

	C6	C8	C10
Arnold Packard Convertible, 10'' long.......................	90	135	180
Arnold A63 Motorcycle, windup, 8'' long, orange.............	200	325	450
Arnold A560 Motorcycle, windup, 7¾'' long, green............	200	325	450
Arnold Mac 700 Motorcycle, windup, black..................	300	450	600

Arnold, L to R: A63, A560.
Courtesy Kent M. Comstock

Astra Pharos (U.K.) Ordnance. Various Scales. L to R - Back Row: Pom-Pom, small searchlight, large AA gun, AA gun on pedestal.
Middle: AA gun and searchlight on trailer, AA gun on Y-mount, searchlight on large mount, searchlight small mount.
Front Row: AT gun with split trails, three versions of multiple barrel mortar (dual and single wheeled box trail and split trail), tandem wheeled AT gun with box trail.
Not shown: Pillboxes with cannons, at least two variants.
Photo by Ed Poole

Arnold Mac 700
Courtesy Kent M. Comstock

ASTRA PHAROS

This British company dates to before World War Two, with many of its toys particularly attractive to military collectors. Prices range from a few dollars to $100 or more for its large AA Gun. Its number 12 Mobile Unit would presumably run near that price.

AUBURN RUBBER

by Dave Leopard

For about 20 years (roughly 1935-1955), American kids enjoyed playing with rubber toys and Moms were told that these toys would not mar the furniture or floors. Then, almost as suddenly as they came on the market, they disappeared again, but left a rich legacy for toy collectors.

The Auburn Rubber Company of Auburn, Indiana was not the first to introduce rubber toys to the American market but they were no doubt the largest and had the greatest impact on the toy field. After introducing some toy soldiers in 1935, Auburn brought out its first vehicle in 1936 - a beautiful coffin-nosed Cord sedan. Today, the Auburn Cord is one of the most highly prized rubber toys and is seldom seen offered for sale. Auburn followed the Cord with a wealth of vehicles, including trucks, farm tractors and implements, motorcycles, racers, fire engines, military vehicles, aircraft, ships, and trains. In all, I have catalogued about 90 different varieties of Auburn rubber vehicles and I'm sure there are more than that. To my knowledge, 1952 was Auburn's last year of marketing rubber toys exclusively. The 1953 Auburn catalog contained a vinyl motorcycle, which I believe was their first vinyl toy. By 1955, their toy line was mostly vinyl with a few rubber varieties hanging on. The 1956 catalog is exclusively vinyl, except for two rubber fire engines, which were no doubt the last rubber toys to be marketed by Auburn. Auburn continued in the toy business in Auburn, Indiana and later in Deming, New Mexico until they went out of business in 1969.

Auburn AA01
Photo by Max Heiss

DAVE LEOPARD is a retired Air Force Colonel, now employed by the State of South Carolina Budget and Control Board, Division of Human Resource Management. Dave is a collector of small, American made toy cars and trucks and is an authority on rubber toys. He currently writes the "Little Wheels" column for *U.S. Toy Collector Magazine* and has completed his own book on rubber toy vehicles.

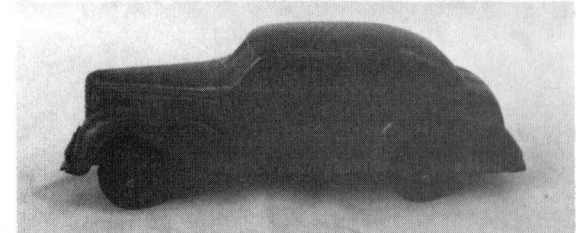

Auburn AA02
Photo by Dave Leopard

Auburn AA03
Photo by Dave Leopard

	C6	C8	C10
AA01 '36 Cord, four door coffin-nose sedan 6'' long	No Price Found		
AA02 '37 Olds, 4 door sedan, 4½'' long	20	25	35
AA03 '38 Olds, 4 door sedan, 5¾'' long	25	30	45
AA04 '40 Olds, 4 door sedan, open fenders, 6'' long	25	30	45
AA05 '40 Olds, 4 door sedan, fender skirts, 6'' long	25	30	45
AA06 '48 Buick, 2 door sedanette, fastback, 7¼'' long	40	50	65
AA07 '39 Buick, Y Job Experimental Roadster, 9¾'' long	No Price Found		
AA08 '35 Ford Coupe, 4'' long .	30	35	45
AA09 '35 Ford 2 door slantback sedan, 4'' long	30	35	45

Auburn, L to R: AA05, AA04
Photo by Dave Leopard

Auburn AA06
Photo by Dave Leopard

AUBURN

Auburn AA07. From a 1941 Butler Bros. catalog.

Auburn AA12. From a 1940 Butler Bros. catalog.

Auburn, L to R: AA13, AA14
Photo by Dave Leopard

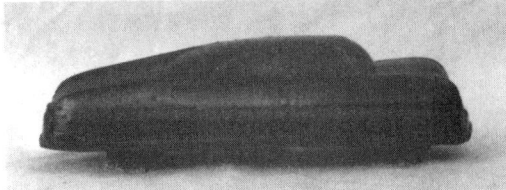

Auburn AA15
Photo by Dave Leopard

Auburn AA16
Photo by Tim O'Callaghan

Auburn AA17. From a 1941 Butler Bros. catalog.

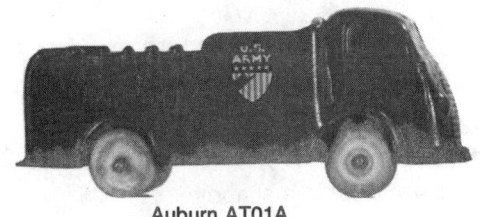

Auburn AT01A
Photo by Ed Poole

Auburn, L to R: AT01, AT03.
Photo by Dave Leopard

	C6	C8	C10
AA10 '50 Cadillac, 4 door sedan, 7¼'' long	40	50	65
AA11 '50 Cadillac, 4 door sedan, 5¾'' long	May Not Exist		
AA12 '39 Plymouth, 2 door trunkback sedan, 4¼'' long	20	25	35
AA13 '46 Lincoln convertible, 2 door, square headlights, 4½'' long	20	25	30
AA14 '46 Lincoln convertible, 2 door, round headlights, 4½'' long	20	25	30
AA15 Late 40s Futuristic Sedan, fin down back, 5'' long	20	25	35
AA16 Army Staff Car (AA04 in Khaki), ''U.S. Army'' label	30	35	50
AA17 Taxi, 6'' long	No Price Found		
AT01 '37 International cabover stake truck, 5⅜'' long	25	30	45
AT01A '37 Same as above, ''U.S. Army'' decal, khaki	30	35	50
AT02 Same as above with rounded bumper, minor variations	25	30	45
AT03 '37 International cabover stake truck, 4¼'' long	20	25	35
AT03A Same as above, khaki	25	30	40
AT04 Same as above with rounded bumper, minor variations	20	25	35
AT05 '37 International cabover stake truck, 3¾'' long	15	20	30
AT06 Same as above with rounded bumper, minor variations	May Not Exist		
AT07 '37 International cabover stake truck, milk version, 4¼'' long	No Price Found		
AT08 '37 International cabover stake truck, ambulance version	No Price Found		
AT09 Cab-Forward box truck, smooth sides, futuristic, 5½'' long	20	25	35

33

AT01A in two colors
Photo by Tim O'Callaghan

Auburn AT11
Photo by Dave Leopard

Auburn AT09
Photo by Dave Leopard

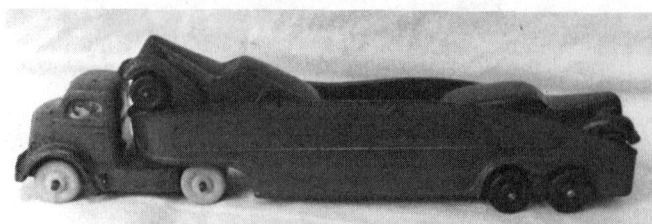

Auburn AT14
Photo by Dave Leopard

Auburn AT10
Photo by Dave Leopard

Auburn AT14A. From a 1940-41 L. Gould & Co. catalog.

Auburn AT15, from a 1940 Butler Bros. catalog.

	C6	C8	C10
AT10 Cabover box truck, smooth sides, futuristic, 4⅛'' long....	20	25	35
AT10A Army Truck, as above..	25	30	40
AT11 '47 Chevy Cab Forward Box Truck, 5¾'' long............	20	25	35
AT12 c. '50 Pickup truck, wheels outside fenders, 4½'' long...	20	25	35
AT13 c. '50 Pickup truck, wheels inside fenders, 4½'' long....	20	25	35
AT14 '38 GMC ''Carry Car'' Auto Transport, 11½'' long (no top)	45	55	75
AT14A Same as above, with rubber on top to carry cars.....	65	80	100
AT15 '38 GMC Cab/Open Squared-off Trailer, 9'' long..	40	50	65

	C6	C8	C10
AT16 Updated Carry Car Transport, cab changed, trailer same, 11¾'' long...........	No Price Found		
AT17 '35 Ford Stake Body Truck, 4¾'' long..................	No Price Found		
AE01 Ahrens-Fox Fire Engine, 5½'' long........................	No Price Found		
AE02 c. 40s Fire Engine, hose and ladders, 7¾'' long..........	35	40	50
AE03 c.40s Pumper, boiler, 7¼'' long......................	35	40	50
AE04 c.40s Fire Engine, ladders, no hose, 7¾'' long.............	35	40	50
AR01 Open racer, V-6, high fin, 10½'' long.................	50	60	80

AUBURN

Auburn AE01. From a 1940-41 L. Gould catalog.

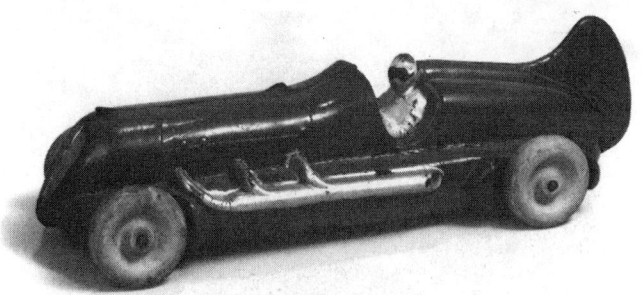

Auburn AR01
Courtesy David Mapes Auctions

Auburn AE02
Photo by Dave Leopard

Auburn AR02
Photo by Dave Leopard

Auburn AE03
Photo by Dave Leopard

Auburn AR03
Photo by Dave Leopard

Auburn AE04
Photo by Dave Leopard

Auburn AR04. From a c.1940-41 M.S. Young & Co. catalog.

	C6	C8	C10
AR02 Open racer, V-6, low fin, 10½'' long	40	55	75
AR03 Open racer, short, tapered tail, large tires, 10½'' long	40	55	75
AR04 Open racer, short, boat tail 6½'' long	40	50	65
AR05 Open racer, boat tail, 4¾'' long	30	40	50
AR06 Open racer, small fin, 6¼'' long	30	40	50

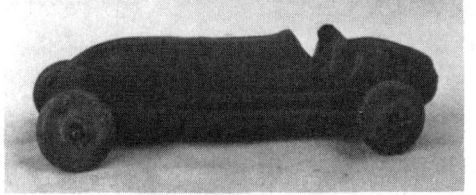

Auburn AR05
Photo by Dave Leopard

AUBURN

Auburn AR06
Photo by Dave Leopard

Auburn AF05
Photo by Dave Leopard

Auburn AR10

	C6	C8	C10
AR07 Open racer short, boat tail, early, 6½'' long	40	45	60
AR08 Open racer, no fenders, low fin, long back, 5¼'' long	20	25	35
AR09 Open racer, boat tail, no side pipes, 4¾'' long	40	50	60
AR10 Open racer, midget type, early, 5'' long	No Price Found		
AF01 Farm Tractor, John Deere ''A'', 5'' long	25	35	40
AF02 Farm Tractor, John Deere, 4¼'' long	May Not Exist		
AF03 Farm Tractor, Minneapolis-Moline ''Z'', 4'' long	25	30	40
AF04 Farm Tractor, Minneapolis-Moline ''R'', early style, 7½'' long	45	55	70

	C6	C8	C10
AF05 Farm Tractor, Minneapolis-Moline ''R'', later style, 7¼'' long	45	55	70
AF06 Farm Tractor, Oliver Row Crop ''70'', 8'' long	May Not Exist		
AF07 Farm Tractor, Oliver Row Crop ''70'', 6½'' long	45	55	70
AF08 Farm Tractor, McCormick-Deering IH Farmall ''M'', 4'' long	25	30	40
AF09 Farm Tractor, Graham-Bradley, 4¼'' long	30	35	45
AI01 Trailer, 2 wheel, Graham-Bradley, 5¾'' long	20	25	35
AI02 Trailer, 4 wheel, Graham-Bradley, 4¾'' long	20	25	35
AI03 Harvester, open top, 5½'' long	30	35	50
AI04 Manure Spreader, David Bradley, 4¾'' long	20	25	35
AI05 Reliable Front-Lift Seeder, 5'' long	20	25	35
AI06 Plow Seeder, 3½'' long . . .	No Price Found		
AI07 Side-Cutter Sickle Bar Mower, David Bradley, 3¾'' long	No Price Found		
AI08 Two Furrow Plow, David Bradley, 4¾'' long	20	25	35
AI09 Cultipacker (Disc Harrows?), David Bradley, 4⅜'' long	20	25	35
AI10 Harrow, 4½'' long	No Price Found		
AI11 Disc Harrows, 4½'' long . .	20	25	35
AI12 Plow with riding farmer . .	No Price Found		
AM01 Tank, Marmon-Harrington, 4½'' long	30	35	50

Auburn AF01. From a c.1940-41
M.S. Young & Co. catalog.

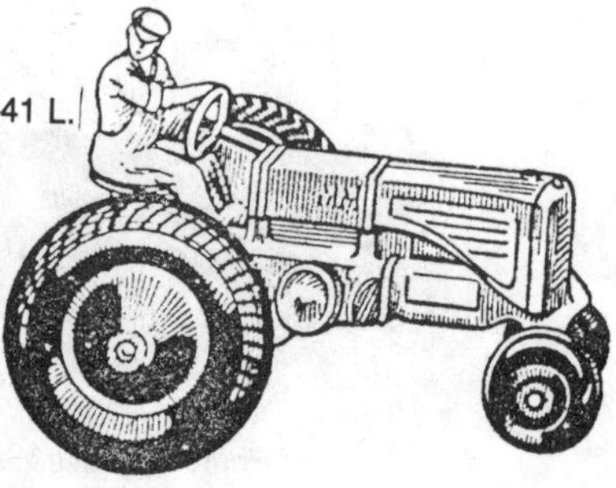

Auburn AF03. From a 1940-41 L.
Gould catalog

Auburn AF07. From a 1940-41 L. Gould catalog

Auburn AAM1
Courtesy K. Warren Mitchell

Auburn Rubber tractor and farm implements as seen in a 1940 Butler Bros. catalog

Auburn AMC1. From a 1941 Butler Bros. catalog.

Top, L to R: Auburn Howitzer, 155 mm, 7'' long, AM01 Tank. Bottom, L to R: AM02 Tank, Fieldpiece, 75mm, 7'' long
Photo by Ed Poole

AUBURN RUBBER VINYL

	C6	C8	C10
Army Recon Car No. 652	5	7.50	10
Army Truck No. 656	5	7.50	10
Bulldozer, 1960s	15	23	30
Cadillac Convertible, 5'' long . . .	10	15	20
Crane Shovel No. 356	40	65	100
Fire Truck No. 614	9	14	18
Fire Truck, 1960s	3	5	7
Jeep	7	11	15
Jeep with Cannon No. 654	10	15	20
Motorcycle	25	40	55
Motorcycle Cop, large	17	26	35
Motorcycle Cop, small	12	18	25
Motorcycle Cop, three-wheel, 4'' long	15	22	30
Ohio Dump, 6'' long	10	15	20
Racer, 7''	10	15	20
Steamroller, 1960s	15	22	30
Tank, Army No. 650	5	7.50	10
Telephone Truck No. 503	20	30	40
Truck	10	15	20
Utility Truck No. 508	12	18	25

	C6	C8	C10
AM02 Tank, Marmon-Harrington, 3¼'' long	20	25	35
AM03 Tractor and Cannon, 11½'' long, olive green	No Price Found		
AAM1 Ambulance, insert top . .	25	35	45
AMC1 Motorcycle Cop, 5'' long	25	38	50
AMC2 As above, in khaki	25	38	50
AMC3 Motorcycle soldiers with sidecar	25	38	50
AMC4 Army Motor Scout on motorcycle	25	38	50
AMC5 Motorcycle Cop, large, 5'' high	25	38	55

Auburn Vinyl Telephone Truck

Auburn Vinyl, L to R - top to bottom: Tank; Army Recon Car; Jeep with Cannon; Army Truck.

AUTOMATIC TOY COMPANY

	C6	C8	C10
Automatic Toy Company "Auto Speedway" c.1930 windup...	60	90	120
Automatic Toy Company "Cop 'N Car"; 4" long motorcycle, 8½" car, plastic with motor, siren, circa 1953..................		No Price Found	
Automatic Toy Company "Magic Crossroads" track, 2 windup cars, c.1950.................	85	125	170

Automatic Toy Company "Auto Speedway".
Courtesy Don Hultzman

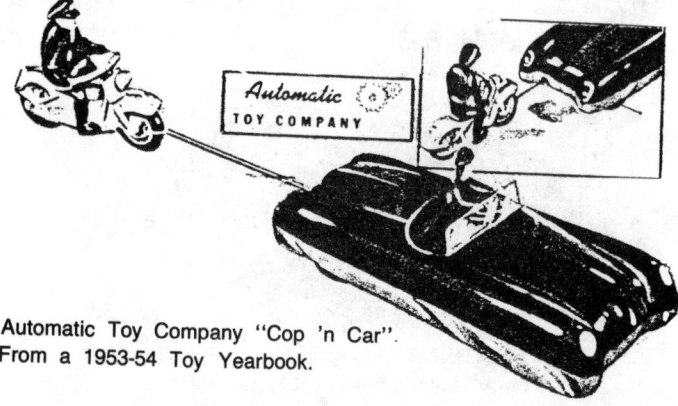

Automatic Toy Company "Cop 'n Car".
From a 1953-54 Toy Yearbook.

BANNER

Banner was begun by Emanuel M. Pressner (8/4/99-1/1/74) and Bernard Schiller (sp?) in 1945 or 1946 at 150 Bruckner Blvd. in the Bronx, New York. Pressner had been a toy importer before the war. When the war cut off imports, he went to work for Columbia Protektosite, which, among other things, cast Beton's plastic toy soldiers. (Though his family has no recollection of this, in 1942 Pressner was noted in a toy trade magazine as being secretary of Beton). Schiller was eventually edged out. Banner moved to 80 Beckwith Avenue in Paterson, New Jersey in 1950, where it remained. The firm's original toys seem to have been small plastic cars and trucks, with the leading items for years being tea sets and metalicized plastic forks, knives and spoons. Other items included plastic sand molds. The stamped steel Banner used was made up of "off-falls" - the blanks formed when holes were cut in steel to allow for car windows and television tubes.

The company, which at its peak periods had as many as 200 employees, went into Chapter 11 bankruptcy in 1965, came out of it, and then was sold in 1967 to Tal-Cap, a toy conglomerate in Minnesota. During its heyday, Banner produced at least tens of thousands of toys a week, according to former vice-president Joseph Stern. Banner got its name, according to Stern, because Pressner (his father-in-law) wanted a company with a name "high up in the alphabet".

	C6	C8	C10
Banner "Ambulance" (Army), 6" long, tin & plastic..........	12	25	40
Banner American Express Truck, tin, 11" long...............	300	450	600
Banner American Express Van..	50	75	100
Banner Buick Sedan, 4½" long.	7	11	14
Banner Clown Van, 4½" long, 1950s....................	12	25	40
Banner "Delivery" van, 4¼" long	8	12	25
Banner Dodge, 1950, 4" plastic.	8	15	25
Banner Dump Truck, plastic, 5¼" long......................	10	20	30
Banner Garbage Truck, Ford, plastic, 1954, 4".............	8	12	25
Banner Garbage Truck, 5½" long	15	22	30
Banner International Harvester Metro 1950 van, plastic, 4"	8	12	25
Banner Jewel Tea van..........	175	263	350

(continued)

Banner Clown Van
Courtesy Bob & Alice Wagner

	C6	C8	C10
Banner Side Dump Truck, 5¼'' long, plastic, 1950s	10	20	30
Banner Stake Truck, 4½'' long .	8	15	25
Banner Station Wagon, 1948 Oldsmobile, plastic, 4''	8	15	25
Banner Steamroller, 4'' long, plastic	7	11	14
Banner Steamshovel, 4'' long, plastic	10	15	20
Banner Tanker, plastic, 7'' long	15	22	30
Banner Trailer Steamshovel, 6¾'' long	15	25	35
Banner ''Toy Truck'' van, 9'' long	45	90	140
Banner Tractor, Wheelhorse, 3'' plastic	12	20	28
Banner ''U.S. Army'' truck, plastic & tin, 6'' long	12	25	40
Banner U.S. Mail truck, 11'' long	60	90	125
Banner Wonder Bread Truck, c.1950s 11'' long, tin litho ...	80	120	160

Banner ''Delivery'' van.
Photo by Terry Sells

Banner Garbage Truck, 5½'' long.
Photo by Terry Sells

	C6	C8	C10
Banner LaFrance Fire Truck, plastic, 4'', 1950	8	12	25
Banner North American Van Lines Truck & Trailer, 15'' long....	110	130	200
Banner Sedan, 4½'' long, plastic, 1950s	8	15	25
Banner Service Station (cardboard) with 3 plastic trucks, circa late 40s - early 50s	22	35	50

Banner Trailer Steamshovel.
Photo by Terry Sells

Banner, L to R: ''US Army'' truck, ''Ambulance''
Courtesy Roger Johnson & Charles Breslow

BARCLAY

In the 1930s and early 1940s, Barclay was the largest producer of lead alloy vehicles. The firm was in business in New Jersey as early as 1924, and probably not before that. It is best known for its toy soldiers, but in the early 1930s its largest seller was its tiny No. 53 racer (BV53). Barclay was originally co-owned by Leon Donze and Michael Levy, with Levy buying out Donze about 1928. The firm closed in 1971. It was located variously in West Hoboken, Union City and North Bergen.

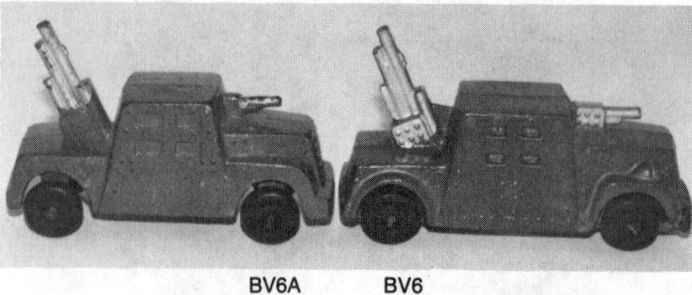

BV6A   BV6

BV6A has larger windows, no rivets up center, smaller front gun, no headlights, etc.
Photo by Stan Alekna

Barclay BV8
Photo by Stan Alekna

	C6	C8	C10
(BV 1) **Ambulance, No. 194,** 3½'' long, small cross	20	30	40
(BV 2) **Ambulance, No. 194,** 3½'' long, large cross	20	30	40
(BV 3) **Ambulance, No. 50,** 5'' long	25	38	50
(BV 4) **No. 151 Army Truck with Gun,** 2¾'' long	15	22	30
(BV 5) **No. 151 Army Truck with Anti-Aircraft Gun,** 2½'' long .	12	18	25
(BV 6) **No. 152 Armored Army Truck,** 2⅞'' long	12	18	25
(BV 6A) Same as above, with variations	12	18	25
(BV 7) **No. 197** Army tank truck, c.1935-36, 3⅛'' long.........	15	22	30
(BV 8) Army Car with two silver bullhorns, approx. 2½'' long (this may be same as BV86) .	22	33	44
(BV 9) Army Tractor (Minneapolis-Moline ''Jeep''), 2¾'' long ...	14	21	28
(BV 10) Austin Coupe, c.1931, 2'' long, No. 43	18	27	36
(BV 11) No. 330 Auto Transport Set, 4½'' long, 2 50s cars....	25	40	75
(BV 12) ''Beer'' truck, c.1940, **No. 376,** 4'' long, wood barrels ..	25	40	55
(BV 13) Beer Truck **No. 377,** with barrels.....................	25	40	55
(BV 14) Bus, futuristic, ''Made U.S.A.'', 3'' long	15	22	30

BV10

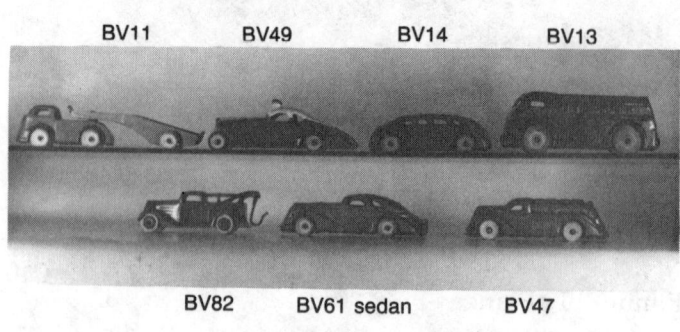

BV11   BV49   BV14   BV13

BV82   BV61 sedan   BV47

BV1   BV2   BV3
Photo by Craig A. Clark

40

In 1984, 45 plaster castings retained by Barclay's chief of maintenance when he cleaned out the shut-down factory in 1971 were shown to the author in the course of his research. Included were soldiers, Disney figures, vehicles and an autogiro, many never produced.

	C6	C8	C10
(BV 15) Cannon Car, 3⁵⁄₁₆'' long, gunner low	13	19	26
(BV 16) **No. 198, Anti-Aircraft Gun Truck,** in 1931 Barclay catalog, 3⅛'' long	20	30	40
(BV 17) Cannon Car, 3¼'' long, slight casting differences from headlight version	25	38	55
(BV 18) Cannon Car, battery-powered headlight, 3½'' long, in 1935 catalog	80	130	225
(BV 19) **No. 48 Anti-Aircraft Gun Truck,** 4'' long, one man	17	26	35
(BV 20) **No. 48, Anti-Aircraft Gun Truck,** 4'' long, two men	16	24	32
(BV 21) Cannon Truck, 4'' long, with moveable cannon	20	30	40
(BV 22) Unused			
(BV 23) Chrysler Airflow, 4'' long, c.1936	50	75	100
(BV 24) ''Coast to Coast'' 2⅞'' long diecast bus, ''Barclay Toy,'' two-piece, **No. 405**	40	50	85
(BV 25) Coupe, 1930s, ''Made in U.S.A.'' 3'' long	10	20	25
(BV 26) Coupe, 2½'' long, c. 1935 XXX	40	70	100
(BV 27) Coupe, 1934, 4¼'' long, XXX	40	60	80
(BV 28) Coupe, 2-piece, 1930s 2⅞'' long, ''Barclay Toy''	40	50	85
(BV 29) Unused			
(BV 30) Coupe, 1934, 4¼'' long, XXX	40	60	80

L to R: Barclay BV12, BV13
Photo by Craig A. Clark

BV15   BV6   RV4   BV9

BV56   BV19   BV20

Photo by Ed Poole

BV24

BV28

41

BV31

BV32

Barclay BV34 (tires in photo not correct)
Photo by James Apthorpe

	C6	C8	C10
(BV 31) **No. 40 Cord Front Drive Coupe,** c. 1931, 3⅝'' long....	20	30	40
(BV 32) **No. 302, Streamline Car,** c. 1936, 3⅛'' long?	25	38	50
(BV 33) ''Delivery'' Truck, **No. 309,** 2¹⁵⁄₁₆'' long, XXX	14	21	28
(BV 34) Double Decker Bus, 4''	35	52	70
(BV 35) (Unused)			
(BV 36) (Unused)			
(BV 37) ''Express'' stake truck, 1930s. 2¹⁵⁄₁₆'' long	22	33	45
(BV 38) Fire Engine No. 390?, moveable ladder, c.1950s	15	22	30
(BV 39) Field Kitchen, 2¼'' long	9	13	18

Barclay BV80

BV40

BV45. Photo from the Barclay files.
Courtesy *Toy Soldier Review*

BV32   BV33   BV41

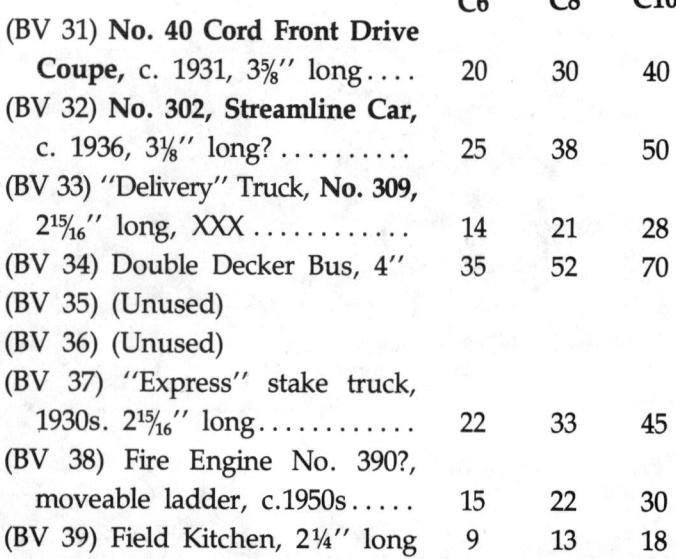

Photo by Bill Kaufman. Courtesy Evelyn Besser.

PARCEL DELIVERY

BV46

	C6	C8	C10
(BV 40) Fire Engine, 2 firemen, black metal wheels, 1930s, **No. 41,** 2¾''	25	38	50
(BV 41) Fire Engine, 4'' long, French-looking (Barclay often copied foreign toys), XXX....	25	38	50
(BV 42) Ford, 1931, 2¼''	15	22	30
(BV 43) ''Golden Arrow Racer'', 4½'' long, X?X	20	30	40
(BV 44) Mack Pick Up Truck, 3½''	15	22	30

BV47

BARCLAY

	C6	C8	C10
(BV 45) "Milk & Cream" truck, stamped **No. 377**, 3⅝" long, white rubber	35	52	70
(BV 45A) Milk Truck, **No. 377**, 3⅝" long, black rubber tires	22	33	45
(BV 46) Motorcycle with flat rider, full-dimensioned sidecar, **No. 55**, 2¾"	25	38	50
(BV 47) "Oil-Fuel" truck, c.1936, 3⁹⁄₁₆" long	12	18	25
(BV 48) "Parcel Delivery", 3⅝" long, slush lead, **No. 45**, c.1931	65	98	130
(BV 49) "Police" Car **No. 317**, slush mold, approx. 3⅝" long, c.1930s (Radio Police), 1939 Packard	35	53	70
(BV 49A) Police Car **No. 317**, diecast, 3⅝" long	15	22	30
(BV 50) Race Car, 3"	12	18	24
(BV 51) Racer, 5½", closed cockpit	17	26	35
(BV 52) Racer, closed cockpit, 7" long, c.1939	30	45	60
(BV 53) Racer, **No. 53**, early slush lead, 1920s-30s, approx. 2" long	25	38	50
(BV 54) Racer, two passengers, 4¼" long, XXX	50	75	100
(BV 55) Racer with tail fin, "Made U.S.A.", 3½" long	17	25	35
(BV 56) Renault Tank, c.1937, **No. 47**, 4" long	20	30	40
(BV 57) Searchlight Truck, white rubber tires, c.1940, 4¹⁄₁₆" long	87	130	175
(BV 57A) Searchlight Truck, second version	87	130	175
(BV 58) Sedan, 4 door, approx. 5" long, maybe Chrysler, c.1936	17	26	35
(BV 59) Sedan, two door, 3⅛" long, rubber wheels, slush lead, c. 1935, XX	35	55	75
(BV 60) Sedan, two-piece, **No. 401** 2-door, 1930s, "Barclay Toy", diecast, 2⅞" long	40	50	85
(BV 61) Sedan and "Tourist Trailer", "Made in U.S.A.", 1930s, 6½" long	35	52	70
(BV 62) Silver Arrow Race Car, 5½"	22	33	45

Barclay BV51
Photo by Craig A. Clark

BV52

BV53   BV71   BV49   BV87   BV74

BV46   BV4   BV6   BV68

BV54   BV30   BV81

BV57   BV21, cannon off   BV39

BV16   BV18   BV17
Photo by Ed Poole

BV57A
Photo by Ed Poole

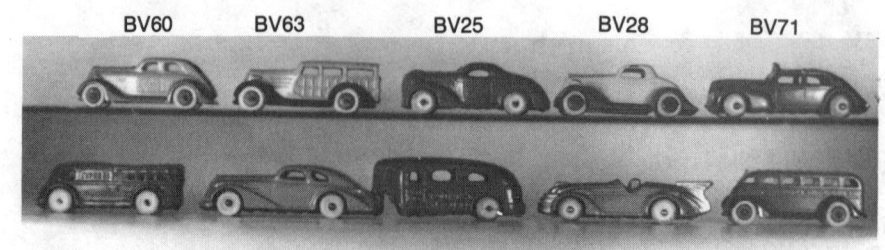

BV60 BV63 BV25 BV28 BV71

BV37 BV61 BV55 BV24

Barclay, L to R: BV63, BV24
Courtesy Alice & Bob Wagner

	C6	C8	C10
(BV 63) Station Wagon, **No. 404,** diecast, 1930s, 2-piece ''Barclay Toy'', 2¹⁵⁄₁₆'' long	37	55	75
(BV 64) Steam-Roller, 3¼'' long, traction type, slush lead with tin roof, **No. 44**	30	45	60
(BV 65) **No. 363 Large Streamline Racer,** in 1935 catalog, 6⅞'' long	45	68	90
(BV 66) Tank ''4562'' one man in turret, 3⅞'' long	17	26	35
(BV 67) Tank ''4562'' two men in turret, 3⅞'' long	17	25	35
(BV 68) Tank T41, 4¼'' long	15	22	30
(BV 69) Tank, 2⅝'' long, man in turret, diecast, black rubber tires	12	18	25
(BV 70) Tank 2½'' long (based on US M2 light tank)	9	13	18
(BV 71) Taxi, 3¼'' long, c.1940s, slush	12	18	25

	C6	C8	C10
(BV 71A) Taxi, **No. 318,** diecast, 3¼'' long	12	18	25
(BV 72) Tractor, approx. 2⅝'' long, caterpillar type, slush lead, XX	17	26	35
(BV 73) (Unused)			
(BV 74) Trailer Truck variously ''Railway Express'', or with Moving Company name, c.1950s	5	8	10
(BV 75) **Transport Set No. 330,** 2 cars, 1960s, 4½'' long	25	40	75
(BV 76) **No. 204 U.S. Army Truck,** 2½'' long, no hitch, red wood hubs	19	29	38
(BV 77) ''U.S. Army'' truck, white rubber wheels, 2½'' long, wire or peg hitch	10	15	20
(BV 78) Truck ''U.S. Motor Unit'', c.1940, white rubber tires, came 3 ways; no hitch, wire hitch, peg hitch, 3¼'' long	9	13	18
(BV 79) Wheel-A-Rific speedway track, two lead racers, black rubber wheels, 10' of plastic track, sold for $1.00 c.1970	6	9	12
(BV 80) **No. 46** wrecker, 3½'', c.1931	17	26	35
(BV 81) Wrecker, 3¹⁵⁄₁₆'' long, c.1934, XXX	55	82	110
(BV 82) Wrecker, two-piece, **No. 403,** diecast 1930s, ''Barclay Toy'', 2⅞'' long	40	50	85
(BV 83) Cannon Truck, moveable cannon, 4'' long	37	56	75

BV63 BV64 BV65

Photo by Craig A. Clark

BV64   BV72   BV40

BV66   BV67   BV68

Photo by Craig A. Clark

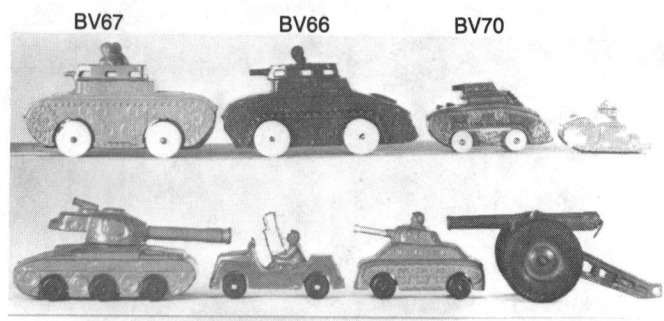

BV67   BV66   BV70

BV68   BV5   BV69   cannon, 4'' long
Post WWII

Photo by Ed Poole

BV69   BV70   BV71   BV71A

Photo by Craig A. Clark

Barclay, Top, L to R: Howitzer, 4 wheels, loop hitch horizontal, Howitzer, 4 wheels, loop hitch vertical, BV78 with wire hitch, BV78 with peg hitch; Bottom, L to R: BV7, BV77 peg hitch, BV77 wire hitch, BV76, no hitch.
Photo by Ed Poole

L to R: BV80-BV10, BV26, BV59

BV79
Courtesy *Toy Soldier Review*

BV82

Barclay BV83
Photo by Ed Poole

	C6	C8	C10
(BV 84) Milk truck in shape of bottle, **No. 567**	150	225	300
(BV 85) ''Milk'' Van truck, 2⅞'' long, bottle on side	17	26	35
(BV 86) Officer's car, 2½'' long with megaphone on top	22	33	44
(BV 87) Side dump, approx. 1½'' long	7	11	15

Barclay BV84
Courtesy Larry Burke

Barclay BV85

BV88

BV90, showing from Top to Bottom: BV140, BV145, BV144A.
Photo by Roger Sanders

Barclay BV90A
Photo by Perry R. Eichor

BV91. From the Barclay files.
Courtesy *Toy Soldier Review*

Paint and decal variations of Barclay BV91. Add five to ten dollars for
the Woolworth truck.
Photo by Stan Alekna

	C6	C8	C10
(BV 88) Convertible with vacationers	17	26	35
(BV 89) **100/4 Build & Paint Auto Set,** 6 vehicles, parts, paints, 1930s	No Price Found		
(BV 89A) **No. 5004** Build and Paint Auto Set, c.1934	No Price Found		
(BV 90) **2004 Build & Paint Set,** truck, coupe, sedan, parts, paints, early	180	270	360
(BV 90A) **2004 Build & Paint Set** same number, only 2 vehicles	No Price Found		
(BV 91) ''U.S. Mail'' truck, 1960s, approx. 2''	10	17	24
(BV 92) Moving Truck, c.1960s, approx. 2''	7	11	15
(BV 93) Log Truck, c.1960s, approx. 2''	7	11	15
(BV 94) Dump Truck, c.1960s, approx. 2''	7	11	15

Another variation of BV91
Photo by Stan Alekna

L to R: BV99, BV100, BV101, BV102
From the Barclay files
Courtesy *Toy Soldier Review*

L to R: BV92, BV93, BV94, BV87
Courtesy *Toy Soldier Review*

L to R: BV103, BV104, BV105, BV106
From the Barclay files.
Courtesy *Toy Soldier Review*

L to R: BV95, BV96, BV97, BV98
Courtesy *Toy Soldier Review*

	C6	C8	C10
(BV 103) U.S. Army truck, c.1968, approx. 2" long	7	11	15
(BV 104) Hospital Truck, c.1968, approx. 2" long	8	13	18
(BV 105) Army truck, open bed, c.1968, approx. 2" long	7	11	15
(BV 106) Army oil truck, c.1968, approx. 2" long	8	13	18
(BV 107) **Double Transport Set No. 440,** 4½" long, four cars on upper and lower racks, 1963 on, hinged for unloading	25	40	75
(BV 108) Two-door sedan, 1960s, 1⅝" long	3	5	7
(BV 109) **No. 203 Tractor,** 2⅛" long, peg hitch	11	16	22
(BV 110) Open coupe with driver in cap, early 30s	15	22	30
(BV 111) "Esso Gas" truck, 1930s, 5" long	20	30	40
(BV 112) **No. 361 Streamline Large Coupe**	17	26	35
(BV 113) 1935 DeSoto AirFlow, 5³⁄₁₆" long	17	26	35
(BV 114) Car Carr two small cars, early 1930s	25	38	50
(BV 115) **No. 371** Racing Car, large, 1930s, 4¼" long	16	24	32

	C6	C8	C10
(BV 95) Racing Car, c.1968, approx. 2"	5	8	10
(BV 96) "Police" car (like BV86 and BV97), approx. 2" long	5	8	10
(BV 97) "Chief" police car (like BV86 and BV96), approx. 2" long	5	8	10
(BV 98) Vintage Car, approx. 2" long	5	8	10
(BV 99) Oil Truck, c.1960s, approx. 2" long	8	13	18
(BV 100) Pepsi-Cola truck, 1960s, approx. 2" long	8	13	18
(BV 101) Racing car, c.1968, no fenders, approx. 2" long	5	8	10
(BV 102) Volkswagen, 1960s, approx. 2" long	10	17	24

BV107
From the Barclay files
Courtesy *Toy Soldier Review*

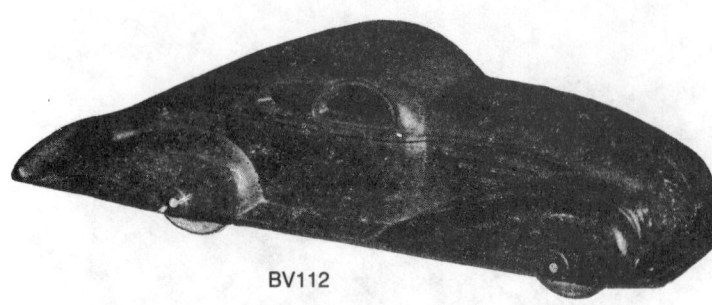

BV112

BV108
From the Barclay files
Courtesy *Toy Soldier Review*

BV113

BV114

BV109

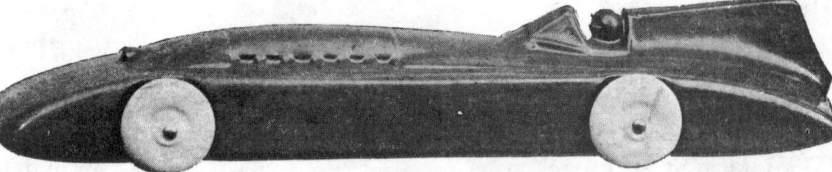

BV115

BV110

BV116

BV111

	C6	C8	C10
(BV 116) **No. 7** Tractor, c.late 20s early 30s	15	22	30
(BV 117) **No. 1105** (or 1705) "Towing Service" truck, large	20	30	40
(BV 118) 1929 Buick Sedan? 3¼" long	15	22	30
(BV 119) **No. 312** "Towing" truck, in 1936 catalog, 3⅜" long	17	26	35

BARCLAY

BV117

BV118

BV119

BV120

BV121

BV122

BV123

BV124

(BV 129) **No. 39 Imperial Chrysler**	C6	C8	C10
Coupe c.1931	15	22	30
(BV 130) **No. 5** Racer, in 1931 magazine, Golden Arrow	15	22	30
(BV 131) No. 206 Delivery Truck ''Bakery Fine Cake Pies'', c.1934, 3⅛'' long	50	75	100
(BV 132) **No. 51** Coupe, c.1931, 2³⁄₁₆'' long.	12	18	25
(BV 133) **No. 210** Fire Truck, c.1934, 3⅛'' long	12	18	25
(BV 134) **No. 209 Fire Engine,** c.1934, 3⅛'' long	12	18	25
(BV 135) **No. 311** Sedan, c.1936	12	18	25
(BV 136) **No. 309** ''Delivery'' truck, c.1936, 3½'' long	12	18	25
(BV 137) **No. 50** Fire Truck, c.1931, 2⅜'' long	22	33	45
(BV 137A) Like BV 137, but with gold hydraulics on both sides, wood hubs, rubber tires, 2⁷⁄₁₆'' long	25	38	50

	C6	C8	C10
(BV 120) **No. 306 Racer,** in 1936 catalog.	15	22	30
(BV 121) **No. 303 Streamline Racer,** 4⅜'' long	15	22	30
(BV 122) **No. 208 Hook and Ladder,** in 1935 catalog, 3'' long.	16	24	32
(BV 123) **No. 301 Coupe Streamline,** 3¼'' long	12	18	25
(BV 124) **No. 207 Stake Truck,** in 1935 catalog, 3⅛'' long.	40	60	85
(BV 125) **No. 362 Streamline Sedan Large,** in 1935 catalog	15	22	30
(BV 126) **No. 368** Fire Truck, 1930s, ''Fire Dept. No. 99'', 5¾'' long	20	30	40
(BV 127) **No. 1703** 1935 Chrysler Airflow sedan, large	17	26	35
(BV 128) **No. 42** small tractor, in 1931 magazine, 2³⁄₁₆'' long	12	18	25

BV125

BV133

BV126

BV134

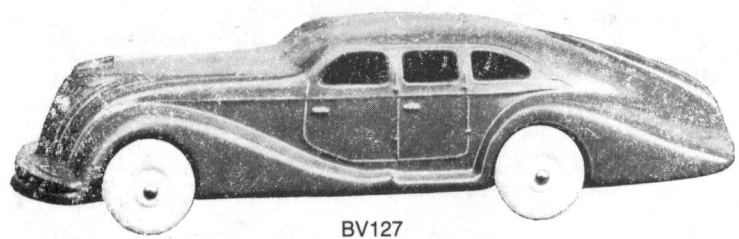

BV127

BV135

BV128

BV129

BV136

BV130

BV137

BV131 Delivery Truck

Barclay BV137A
Photo by Craig A. Clark

BV132

	C6	C8	C10
(BV 138) **No. 56** Double-Decker Bus, c.1931, 3¼" long	22	33	45
(BV 139) **No. 58** Auburn Speedster, c.1931	17	26	35
(BV 140) Sedan, c.1934	15	22	30
(BV 141) **No. 205 Tow Car,** in 1935 catalog, 3¹/₁₆" long	20	30	40

	C6	C8	C10
(BV 142) **No. 338 Contractor Set,** approx. 6¼'' long (has hole hitch for wire, unlike BV109's peg hitch), 1930s	No Price Found		
(BV 143) Large Streamline Coupe, 1930s	15	22	30
(BV 144) ''Gasoline'' Truck, small, c.1931, 2⁵⁄₁₆'' long, 3 tank top	30	45	60
(BV 144A) Gas Truck, c.1935, 200 series? 4 tank top, 3'' long ..	25	38	50
(BV 145) Coupe, cast rear tire, c.1935, 200 series?, 3⅛'' long .	42	63	85
(BV 146) Coupe, removable spare tire, in 1935 catalog, 4½'' long	75	113	150
(BV 147) Dump Truck, spring action, ratchet, in 1935 catalog, 4'' long......................	20	30	40
(BV 148) Sport Coupe, 2⅞'' long, removable spare tire, in 1935 catalog....................	40	60	80
(BV 149) Racing Car, large, raised exhaust pipe, driver, in 1935 catalog....................	17	26	35
(BV 150) Race Car, open, driver, 4'' long....................	70	105	140
(BV 151) Stake Truck, 4⅜'' long, in 1935 catalog..............	25	38	50
(BV 152) 2-Car transport set, approx. 4¾'' long............	42	63	85
(BV 153) 4-Car transport set, 10¼'' long, open-cab Mack Truck, (4) 2½'' cars, in 1935 catalog....	No Price Found		
(BV 154) Roadster, 4½'' long, open, driver, dummy spare tire on each side, in 1935 catalog	No Price Found		
(BV 155) Streamline Coupe, 5'' long, in 1937 catalog.......	No Price Found		
(BV 156) ''White Horse'' van, approx. 3'' long (some have sticker reading ''Welcome I.C.M.A. compliments THE WHITE MOTOR CO.'')	62	93	125
(BV 157) **No. 440 Double Decker Auto Transport,** earlier version of BV107, truck has one side window, 1939-1963	25	40	75
(BV 158) Hospital Truck, Cab over, approx. 2'' long............	8	13	18

BV138

BV139

BV141

BV142

BV144A

L to R: BV144, BV144A, BV145
Photo by Craig A. Clark

BV143

L to R: BV147, BV148, BV149
Photo by Craig A. Clark

L to R: BV148, BV147
Photo by Fred Maxwell

L to R: What appears to be Barclay BV154, somehow missing the driver; BV146. Each seem to have been painted by a child, rather than at Barclay.
Photo by Roy Bonjour

Barclay BV150
Photo by Craig A. Clark

L to R: BV155, BV156
Photo by Craig A. Clark

Barclay BV151
Photo by Craig A. Clark

Barclay, L to R: BV158, BV104
Photo by Stan Alekna

Barclay BV152
Photo by Craig A. Clark

Barclay, L to R: BV157, BV75
Courtesy Bob & Alice Wagner

Barclay BV153
Photo by David Leopard

	C6	C8	C10
(BV 159) Convertible Sports Car, c.1960, driver & passenger . . .	9	13	18
(BV 160) Volkswagen, c.1960s, slightly larger than BV102	12	18	26
(BV 161) Moving Truck, approx. 2" long, c.1960	8	13	18

325 TRAILER TRUCK

339 MINIATURE AUTOS

349 MINIATURE FOREIGN CARS

347 SPORTS CARS

At left, what seems to be a Barclay from the 1940s, though not yet verified. Values in C6, C8, C10: $15, 25, 35. At right No. 377 as a Delivery Truck. Values $45, 30, 20.
Courtesy Bob & Alice Wagner

Barclay Blister pack vehicles, c.1968. Value is about $35 in mint, except for the No. 339 pack of seven autos, which would go for about $55 in mint. Photo from the Barclay files.
Courtesy *Toy Soldier Review*

This 3'' long "Gasoline" truck appears to be Barclay. No value found.
Photo by Craig Clark

L to R: What appear to be a Barclay coupe and sedan, though neither has been verified as such. Sold in the 1930s and 1940s. Values in C6, C8, C10: $10, 20, 25.
Courtesy Bob & Alice Wagner

Barclays in "bottle" bubble packs. Value in mint about $25.
Courtesy *Toy Soldier Review*

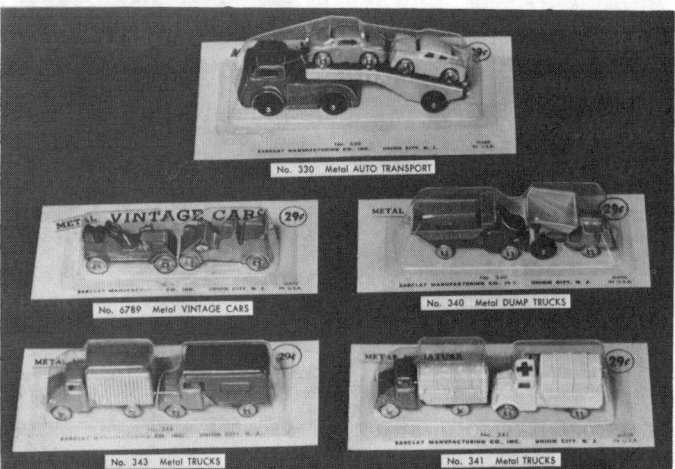

Barclay blister pack sets, c.1968. The no. 330 Auto Transport (BV75) is worth about $75 in mint. The others are worth about $35 in mint. Photo from the Barclay files.
Courtesy *Toy Soldier Review*

BARR RUBBER

Barr Rubber was located in Sandusky, Ohio. The following list, with its codings, was compiled by Dave Leopard. Vehicles are broken down by type.

	C6	C8	C10
BA01 '35 Ford Coupe, 4'' long .	25	35	45
BA02 '35 Ford 2 door slantback sedan, 4'' long	25	35	45
BT01 '35 Ford Stake Body Truck, 4¾'' long	25	35	45
BT02 '35 Ford Panel Truck/Ambulance, 4¼'' long	25	35	45
BT03 '35 Ford Army Truck, 4¾'' long	30	40	50

BEAUT MFG. CO.

Beaut Mfg. Co., North Bergen, New Jersey, was founded in 1946 by Eugene Buhler and Irving Reader, former machinist and salesman, respectively, for Barclay Mfg. Co. The company put out five toys: a taxicab, a police car, a fire engine, a sedan and a child's wagon. The company was successful at first, employing ten people, and selling to Woolworth's and many overseas buyers. It ceased its toy-making activities (it continued until 1982 as a general machine shop) around 1950, because of competition from plastic toys.

BEAUT "Police" car (left) and "Taxi" Photo by Bill Kaufman
Courtesy George Buhler.

	C6	C8	C10
BEAUT "Fire" Car, No. 4, approx. 3¾''	10	15	20
BEAUT "Police" car, approx. 3¾''	10	15	20
BEAUT Sedan, approx. 3¾''	10	15	20
BEAUT "Taxi", approx. 3¾'', No. 1	10	15	20

BEST TOY & NOVELTY FACTORY

By Fred Maxwell and Margaret Rice, With the assistance of members of the Best family, Perry Eichor, Kenneth Nudson and Ferd Zegel.

John M. Best, Sr., who founded Best Toy in Manhattan, Kansas, was an entrepreneur who stuck his neck out. Only senior citizens can understand how low our economy was in the 1930s, so starting a new business after watching other toy companies fail successively tells us something about John Best, and something about the perennial appeal of good toys. To Best, the molding of potmetal toys must have seemed a good risk for a second income as he was a printer who worked with metal alloys. And he probably had been following the ups and downs of "those TOYS with the NUMBERS" for he had lived in Clifton, the home of Kansas Toy Company.

It was started as a family hobby for his children, relatives, friends and neighbors according to Minnie Nelson, his daughter. Other employees we know of were John Best, Jr., and his family, and Conrad Morsch, a molder. For a "hobby" it grew into a respectable business, supplying toy distributors and dime stores; for the toys are readily found in today's toy markets. After several years of operation it was sold to Ralstoy, a Ralston, Nebraska company, in 1939.

At this point we are not certain when Best started or what "number" in the series was his first molding. Although contradictory, evidence from family members suggests purchase of the assets of a Clifton toy company occurred about 1933. Nor do we know whether he introduced any new patterns, although with his experience it is likely that he did. If he did not create, but only reproduced from old molds, then there is still a mystery-maker out there who also continued the Kansas Toy tradition. Regardless, it was an important chapter in the story of those wandering molds. (See history of Kansas Toy in this book).

Of great assistance was a donation from Dee Buchanan, Mrs. Nelson's granddaughter, of a faded copy of a Best Toy brochure. It appears to be a pre-publication printer's mockup, and undated; but its 42 illustrations (some shown here) were adequate to identify most of the Best and many of the Kansas toys in collections. With no paper trail to guide us previously, this was indeed a find; much of the hearsay errors and confusion of this family of toys was eliminated. Many thanks to all who helped and continue to help.

(O'Brien: Dee Buchanan, great granddaughter of John Best, Sr., also contributed a history in 1988 that may be of interest to readers: "About 55 years ago, John Milner Best, Sr. and his wife Roseana, purchased a company from Kansas Toy & Novelty Company* located in Vining*, Kansas - actually a suburb of Clifton. (*This is not confirmed by our Clifton sources). The Bests owned a newspaper, printing plant and book-bindery in Manhattan, Kansas. They moved the toy company to a building in back of their home at 530 Fremont Street, Manhattan. The family, in-laws and friends all worked making the lead cars produced by the toy company and were shipping them all over the world. There were also farm implements, tractors, airplanes, buses and trains as well as all types of cars. One of the Bests' grandchildren, Rosemary, remembers the Toy Factory well, as when she was about three years old and was playing about the factory she fell into one of the lead-melting pots head first. Very fortunately the lead was not hot - so she just had a bad bruise on her head; whereas if the lead had been hot and melted it would indeed have been a tragedy".)

Best Toy reproductions can usually be distinguished from those of earlier makes in the "numbers" dynasty if they have white rubber wheels or are embossed "Made in USA". However, some of their toys used the metal wheels (MW) of the Kansas Toy originals, or the later wood hubs with rubber tires (WHRT). In their first years the larger Best toys had realistic hard-rubber disk wheels, sometimes painted with black "tires". The soft-rubber white "balloon" wheel, often out of scale, was a Best standard. It is also possible that Best modified or rebuilt his molds to create variations.

Best molded a great number of designs. In order to reduce redundancy in this book we list them here but will not describe them in detail if they are adequately covered in Kansas Toy or Ralstoy lists. The following numbered toys and some unnumbered duplicates were found: #6, 10, 14, 17, 20, 25, 26, 27, 31, 32, 34, 35, 36, 37, 39, 40, 41, 42, 43, 45, 46, 47, 49, 51, 54, 55, 57, 58, 59, 60, 67, 70, 71, 72, 74, 76, 77, 78, 79, 80, 81. Higher numbered are described and illustrated.

BEST'S three different wheels, Top Row: BEV4, BEV7, BEV9a; Middle Row: BEV1, BEV8; Bottom Row: BEV11, BEV14, Courtesy of Fred Maxwell.

	C6	C8	C10
BEV1 Racer, "85", 4". Record car w/large square fin, driver, HO, VG, 12 exhaust ports, WHRT	10	15	20
BEV2 Sedan, "86", 4". Lincoln? 2 dr. fastback, slant grille w/grid pattern, HL, divided w/s, read wheel skirts	No Price Found		
BEV3 Sedan, "87". Brewster? . .	No Price Found		
BEV4 Sedan, "90", 3½". 2 dr. airflow, hood reaches front bumper w/no grille, 4 OW, hard rubber wheels	No Price Found		
BEV5 Sedan, "91", 3½". Cadillac? 2 dr. airflow, high style vee grille, faired front fenders	No Price Found		
BEV6 Coupe, "92", 3¾". Dodge? chopped top, Brewster-like heart shaped grille, HO, long streamlined front fenders	No Price Found		
BEV7 Coupe, "93", 3⅝" Cadillac?, streamlined, hood similar to #91, grid pattern grille, 2 OW, hard rubber wheels. (see illustration of #96)	16	24	32
BEV8 Large Sedan, "94", 4½". 2 dr. airflow, similar to #90, 4 OW, taxi lamp on roof	No Price Found		
BEV9a Sedan, "95", 3½". 2 dr. airflow similar to #94, with 3 headlamps, 4 OW, trunk, hard rubber wheels. Chrysler-Briggs show car?	No Price Found		

	C6	C8	C10
BEV9b Sedan, "95", 3½". Same as above with "Police Dept." shield on doors. Centered headlamp may be a siren. Other version have "Police" painted on roof	10	15	20
BEV10 Coupe, "96", 3½". Apparently same car as #93. Were both produced?	No Price Found		
BEV11 Large racer, "97", 4½". Bluebird record car, driver, large fin, 12 exhaust ports, hard rubber wheels, faired	10	15	20
BEV12 Coupe, "98"	No Price Found		
BEV13 Coupe, "99", 4". Pontiac?, streamlined, HO, rearmount .	No Price Found		
BEV14 Sedan, "100", 4". Pontiac, streamlined, 2 dr., HO, HG, 4 OW, trunk	No Price Found		

BEST TOY Tanker: BEV15, BEV16, Photo courtesy of Perry Eichor.

BEV15 Cab Unit, "101", 3¼". International ? sleeper cab, slanted grille, HO, 2 OW . . . . No Price Found

BEV16 Oil Transport, "No. 102", 4". Streamlined "Gasoline" semi-trailer to #101, 4 tanks, 4 storage compartments. Total length of cab-trailer - 6¾" . . . No Price Found

BEV17 ? Sedan, no #, 3⅞". DeSoto ? Airflow 2 door, HO, VG, HL, 4 OW, divided open windshield, bottom pan, Best? . . . . No Price Found

Top row: BEV7, BEV8
Bottom row: BEV9A, BEV9B (repro)
Courtesy Fred Maxwell

Best Toy racers: No. 76 BEV1
Photo courtesy of Perry Eichor

Top row: BEV7, BEV14
Middle row: BEV6 (repro), BEV2 (repro)
Bottom row: BEV5 (repro)
Courtesy of Perry Eichor

Box from a BEST TOYS Farm Set. All the Toys illustrated are from molds believed to have originated with Kansas Toys.
Photo by Perry Eichor. Courtesy Fred Maxwell

BEV 14, No. 100 - 4" long

BEV 13, No. 99 - 4" long

BEV 2, No. 86 - 4" long

BEV 10, No. 96 - 3½" long

BEV 5, No. 91 - 3½" long

BEV 9a, No. 95 - 3½" long

BEV 6, No. 92 - 3¾" long

BEV 4, No. 90 - 3½" long

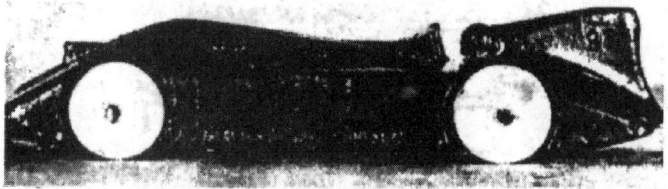

BEV 11, No. 97 - 4½" long

BEV 1, No. 85 - 4" long

No. 81 - 4½" long

No. 26 - 4" long

No. 76 - 4¼" long

No. 10 - Medium Racer

	C6	C8	C10
"Bico Bus to Joyville", open double-decker, passengers, driver	2000	3500	5000
Big Bang Army Tank No. 5T, 8⅛" long	35	50	100
Big Bang Motor Tank, No. 5T, 9½" long, c.1933	100	200	350
BIG BOY: See Kelmet			
BMC Pedal Car, c.1950s........	200	300	400
Boycraft Dump Truck..........	600	950	1400

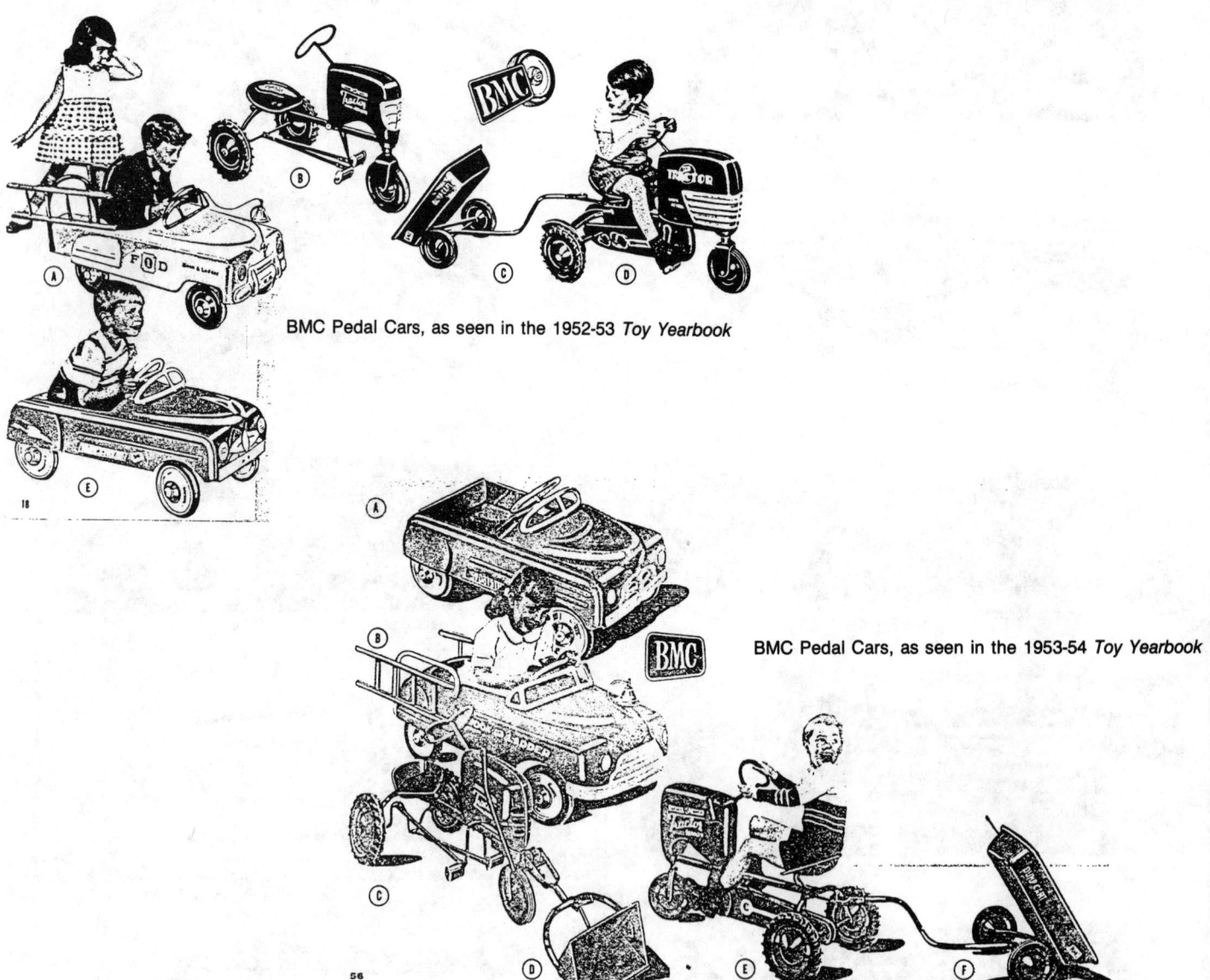

BMC Pedal Cars, as seen in the 1952-53 *Toy Yearbook*

BMC Pedal Cars, as seen in the 1953-54 *Toy Yearbook*

BING TOY WORKS

Nuremberg, Germany 1866-1933
by Bob Smith

Bing Toy Works started producing tin toys in the 1880s and by 1914 they employed over 5000 people. Business flourished through the 1920s until the great depression. In 1932, after falling to hard times, a receiver was assigned to the company. About two years later they ceased production of tin toys entirely. Karl Bub, another German toy manufacturer, took over the company soon after. Bing automobiles are somewhat hard to find and are held in high regard by most collectors. The Model T series came not only in solid black but in red, yellow, green and blue litho. The color litho versions are difficult to find.

Bing Garage with two open cars, c.1925.
Photo by Bob Smith

	C6	C8	C10
BING Garage, Raceabout and Limousine. Autos 5.5″ long, Garage 8″ W x 6.5″ D. Tin litho, c/w motor, c.1912......	500	675	850
BING Garage with two open cars. Garage 8″W, 6.5″D. Car length 5.5″. Tin litho, c/w motor. c.1925......................	450	600	750
BING Limousine. Blue/black litho. C/W motor, 9.5″ long, c.1915	900	1250	1750
BING "Model T" Ford Coupe. Red/black/cream tin litho. 6.5″· long, c/w motor. c.1924......	600	900	1300
BING "Model T" Ford Roadster. Red/black/yellow tin litho. 6.5″ long, c/w motor. c.1924......	600	900	1300

Bing Limousine, 9½″ long, c.1915.
Photo by Bob Smith

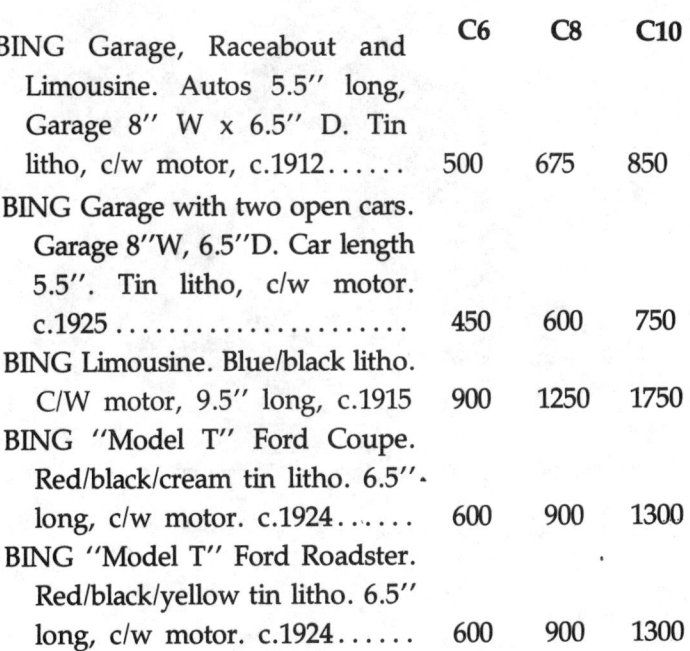

Bing Garage, Raceabout and Limousine. Autos 5½″ long. C.1912
Photo by Bob Smith

	C6	C8	C10
BING "Model T" Ford Sedan. Blue/black/cream tin litho. 6.5″ long, c/w motor. c.1924......	600	900	1300
BING "Model T" Ford Touring Car. Color tin litho, 6.5″ long, c/w motor. c.1924 (not pictured)	600	900	1300
BING "MODEL T FORDs". Sedan, Roadster, Touring, and Coupe, black paint. 6.5″ long, c.1923 each..................	350	500	700

	C6	C8	C10
BING Touring Car. Type 1 spoked wheels, c/w motor. red/black, male driver, 6'' long. c.1920	300	450	650
BING Touring Car. Type II - solid wheels, c/w motor. red/black, female driver. 6'' long. c.1923	300	450	650
BING ''Yellow Taxi''. Orange/black litho, c/w motor. 9'' long, c.1924	950	1100	1800

Bing ''Model T'' Ford Sedan, 6½'' long, c.1924.
Photo by Bob Smith

Bing ''Model T'' Ford Coupe, 6½'' long, c.1924.
Photo by Bob Smith

Bing ''Model T'' Fords, Sedan, Roadster, Touring and Coupe, 6½'' long, c.1923.
Photo by Bob Smith

Bing ''Model T'' Ford Roadster, 6½'' long, c.1924.
Photo by Bob Smith

Bing Touring Car, Type I, male driver, 6'' long c.1920.
Photo by Bob Smith

Bing Touring Car, Type II, female driver, 6" long, c.1923.
Photo by Bob Smith

Breslin Truck Pulling Cannon. Barry S. Josephs Collection
Courtesy Hank Anton

Bing "Yellow Taxi", 9" long, c.1924.
Photo by Bob Smith

Breslin, L to R: Tank, Motorized Machine Gunner.
Barry S. Josephs Collection
Courtesy Hank Anton

Brinks Truck Bank, 8" long.
Courtesy James S. Maxwell Jr./Virginia Caputo

BRESLIN

Breslin Industries of Toronto made a number of lead alloy toys, most or all of them copies, particularly of Barclay and Manoil. They can be easily distinguished from the originals as they usually read "Canada" or "Made In Canada".

	C6	C8	C10
Breslin Tank	30	40	50
Breslin Motorized Machine Gunner	30	40	50
Breslin Truck pulling Cannon . .	30	40	50
Brinks Armored Car, 9" long . .	250	375	575
Brinks truck bank, aluminum, 8" long	40	60	80

BRITAINS

Britains, of London, England, was originally owned by William Britain. In 1893 he introduced hollow-casting of toy soldiers. Britains is still in business and its soldiers are the most-collected military figures. It made, and continues to make, a number of vehicles. Understandably, many, perhaps the majority, are military. (Except where noted, photos by K. Warren Mitchell).

BRITAINS

	C6	C8	C10
BR27d Armored Car	No Price Found		
BR199 Motorcycle Machine Gun	40	75	110
BR200 Dispatch Rider	20	30	48
BR876 Bren Gun Carrier	35	65	85
BR1203 Tank (Carden Loyd Type)	110	155	230
BR1321 Armoured Car	185	360	450
BR1333 Lorry, Army, Caterpillar Type	125	200	300
BR1334 Lorry, Army, 4-Wheeled Type	105	130	210
BR1335 Lorry, Army, with Driver	135	190	260
BR1400 Speed Record Car, "The Blubird"	135	270	370

BR1334

BR1335

BR1400

Some Pre World War II Britains Ltd. Motor Vehicles (54mm Britains Armoured Corps Marching added for scale)
L to R, Back Row: 27d Armoured Car; 199 Motorcycle Machine Gun; 200 Dispatch Rider; 1321 Armoured Car, 1203 Tank (Carden Lloyd Type)
Front Row: 1335 Lorry, Army, six wheeled type; 1448 Car, Staff; 1462 Covered Lorry, Caterpillar Type (cover missing); 1512 Army Ambulance, Motor Type.
Photo by Ed Poole

Some of the Britains Ltd. Motor vehicles of the 1940s & 50s (Britains 54mm Tommy added for scale)
L to R, Back Row: 876 Bren Gun Carrier, 1334 Four Wheeled Army Lorry (towing 1717 Mobile unit, 2-pounder), 1335 six-wheeled Army Lorry, 1448 Staff Car, 1433 Covered Army Tender, caterpillar type (towing 1718 searchlight).
Front Row: 1512 Army Ambulance, 1877 Beetle Lorry (towing 1725 4.5" Howitzer and 1726 Regulation Limber), 1791 Dispatch Rider, 2102 Austin Champ (towing 2173 B.A.T. Gun).
Photo by Ed Poole

BR1413

	C6	C8	C10
BR1413 Police Car with Two Officers	350	600	900
BR1432 Army Tender, covered, 10-wheel	110	140	190
BR1433 Army Tender, covered, caterpillar type	95	150	200

BR1432

BR1433

BR1433 Post-War

BR1448, L to R: first and second versions

	C6	C8	C10
BR1448 Army Staff Car, officer and driver, first version smooth white tires, black fenders	180	320	400
2nd version - white tires, all khaki body	175	310	385
3rd version, 1948-50, rectangular windshield, rubber tires......	150	270	335
4th version, 1951-57, lead tires, painted gray, split windshield	155	290	360
5th version, 1958-59, black plastic tires	130	230	310

BR1448, 3rd version

BR1448, 4th version

	C6	C8	C10
BR1462 Covered Lorry, R.A. Gun, drivers.....................	160	365	470
BR1512 Army Ambulance, wounded man and stretcher, all doors open, 6" long.........	115	175	230
Post-War	95	150	210
BR1514 Corporation Motor Ambulance, driver, wounded and stretcher	365	580	840
BR1641 Underslung Heavy-Duty Lorry	210	365	575
BR1642 Heavy-Duty Lorry, driver, searchlight, battery and lamp	315	525	735
BR1643 Heavy Duty Lorry, underslung, with driver......	600	900	1200
BR1717 Mobile Unit, 2-pounder.	35	55	75
BR1718 Mobile Searchlight......	35	55	75
BR1725 4.5" Howitzer	15	22	32

BR1462

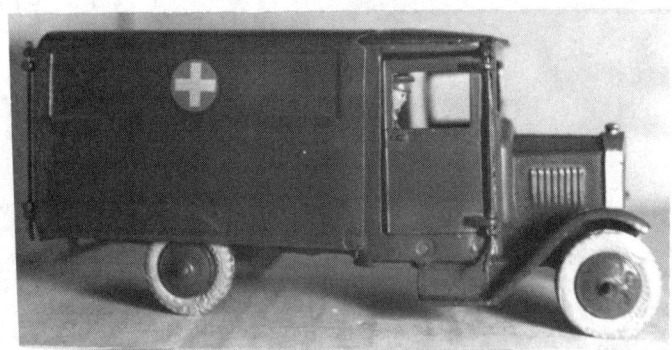

BR1512

BR1512 Post-War

BR1514

BR1642

BR1643

BR1727

	C6	C8	C10
BR1726 Regulation Limber......	15	22	27
BR1727 Complete Mobile Howitzer Unit, 4 pcs., with limber and caterpillar trailer............	315	570	780
BR1757 Balloon Barrage Unit (lorry, winch, balloon)..............	750	1100	1700
BR1791 Dispatch Rider.........	95	150	190

BR1757

Britains BR1877, Pre-War with box.
Photo by Ed Poole

BR1832

BR1877 Post-War

BR1833

BR1897

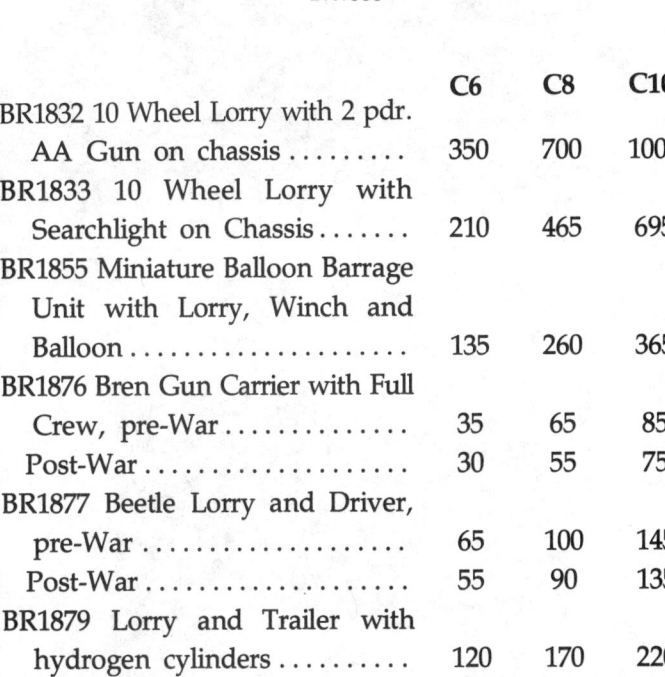

	C6	C8	C10
BR1832 10 Wheel Lorry with 2 pdr. AA Gun on chassis	350	700	1000
BR1833 10 Wheel Lorry with Searchlight on Chassis	210	465	695
BR1855 Miniature Balloon Barrage Unit with Lorry, Winch and Balloon	135	260	365
BR1876 Bren Gun Carrier with Full Crew, pre-War	35	65	85
Post-War	30	55	75
BR1877 Beetle Lorry and Driver, pre-War	65	100	145
Post-War	55	90	135
BR1879 Lorry and Trailer with hydrogen cylinders	120	170	220

	C6	C8	C10
BR1897 Motor Ambulance with doctor, wounded, nurses, orderlies, 18 pcs.	180	330	460
BR2024 Light Goods Van with Driver	260	470	630
BR2102 Austin Champ	35	55	70
BR2150 (also 9770) Centurion Tank	180	300	410
BR2154 Centurion Tank, painted for Desert Warfare	260	470	630
BR2173 (also 9720) Batallion Anti-Tank Gun	10	14	19
BR2175 (also 9748) 155mm Gun, Mounted on Centurion Tank Body	210	365	525

BR2102

BR2150

BR2175

	C6	C8	C1
BR172F Fordson Power Major Tractor, no driver	55	80	105
BR173F Three Furrow Plough	8	12	17
BR174F Muledozer	No Price Found		
BR175F Cultivator	No Price Found		
BR176F Acrobat Rake	No Price Found		

BR641

L to R: BR748, 750, 751

BR59F

BRITAINS FARM

	C6	C8	C10
BR641 Motorcycle with Sidecar	500	700	1250
BR748 Shell Gas Pump	12	20	27
BR749 Shellmax Gas Pump	11	17	23
BR750 BP Gas Pump	11	17	23
BR59F Lorry with Driver, 4 wheel	11	17	23
BR127F Fordson Tractor, metal wheels, driver	60	90	125
BR128F Fordson Major Tractor, driver, rubber tires	45	80	105
BR129F Timber Trailer with real log	25	50	75
BR134F Farmyard Display	40	55	75

BR128F

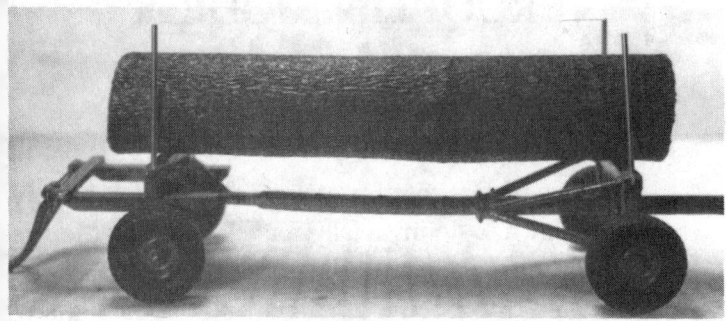

BR129F

BR134F

BR172F with attached 174F

BRITAINS LILLIPUT

	C6	C8	C10
LV/601 Open Sports Car	25	38	50
LV/602 Saloon Car	25	38	50
LV/603 Articulated Lorry	25	38	50
LV/604 Fordson Tractor with Driver	25	38	50
LV/607 Army Covered 3 ton truck, removable plastic top	25	38	50
LV/608 3 Ton Farm Lorry	No Price Found		

	C6	C8	C10
LV/609 Austin Champ, removable hood	No Price Found		
LV/610 Centurion Tank	25	38	50
LV/611 Sexton Self-Propelled Gun	30	45	60
LV/612 1½ Ton Army Truck with spare wheel	No Price Found		
LV/613 1½ Ton Covered Army Truck with spare wheel	No Price Found		
LV/614 Articulated Truck with Spare Wheel	No Price Found		
LV/615 Saracen Armoured Personnel Carrier	No Price Found		
LV/616 1½ Ton Farm or Civilian truck with spare wheel, measures 2¹³/₁₆" long	No Price Found		
LV/617 Local authority ambulance, cream, measures 3" long	10	18	25
LV/618 Army ambulance, measures 3" long	No Price Found		
LV/619 Post Office Royal Mail Van, measures 3" long	No Price Found		
LV/620 3 Ton open Army truck with spare wheel, measures 3¼" long	No Price Found		
LV/SA Boxed set containing: 1 LV/601, 1 LV/602, 1 LV/603, 1 LV/604 with driver, 1 LV/605 with Milkman, 1 LV/606, with accessories and Carter as listed in the 1951 Catalog Supplement	70	135	210
L7 Lilliput Display Box containing Saloon Car, tractor, tumbrel cart and milk float, farmer, farmer's wife, stable lad, farm girl and dog, horses, cows and calf, sheep and lamb, pig, geese, hurdles and tree, 28 pcs	80	160	260
L11 Lilliput Railway Personnel & Vehicles: saloon car, lorry, sports car, articulated lorries, Austin "Champ", motor cyclists, station trollies, packing cases, barrels, hampers, porters w/trollies, guards, station master, porters with luggage, newsvendor, general public asst., 43 pcs	No Price Found		

L to R: LV611, LV610

Britains Lilliput LV/SA

Britains Lilliput L-7

BROOKLIN MODELS

by Vincent Rosa
with some excerpts from his work
The Brooklin Collection Book © 1989

The love of cars, both prototype and model, are the reasons John and Jenny Hall created Brooklin Models Ltd., a firm that makes the finest 1:43 scale replicas of white metal model cars on the market today. Many collectors say that Brooklin models are the standard of the industry - very similar to the ''standard of the world'' description for Lionel toy trains or Britains toy soldiers. Brooklins today are known worldwide. The new Brooklin Collection includes some of the greatest and most controversial American motor cars made by U.S. manufacturers in the past five decades.

John Hall began humbly in the basement of his Canadian home in the early 1970s making models by hand with resin and no windows, using popcicle sticks ''woodburnt'' with the familiar early Brooklin Models logo to keep the resin casting from warping. Brooklin Models is named after a suburb of Ontario, Canada called Brooklin.

When the Brooklin company was in its infancy, it experienced the greatest changes in technology and process. Therefore, the early Canadian models reflect many different changes as John Hall, in an attempt to perfect his models, experimented with many forms of casting materials and color variations. 1974 was a pivotal year for John Hall. It was early that year that he decided to leave his teaching position at Durham College and devote full time to model making and designing equipment to create finished scale model cars. Most of the companies at this time were doing kits, not built-up models.

Meanwhile, back in the basement, John was dabbling in model making and scratch-building models for himself and other collectors. He helped form the Canadian Toy Collector's society with Ron Faithful and Tony Topley. Through the CTCS, John met many collectors from Canada and Buffalo where John went to his first toy show called ''Motoring in Miniatures''. At the show collectors persuaded him to make a Pierce Arrow. Thinking this was a good idea, John then made two master models out of resin. He then cast a total of 86 models at the laborious rate of 10 models per week. Thus, Brooklin Models began in 1974. The handpainted Pierce Arrow with resin base became car #1. The Pierce Arrow was retired in 1993.

In 1975, John felt he could raise money at the Canadian Plowing Match held in Toronto, by selling a model of a plow commemorating the event. Two thousand were produced, but only 200 were sold. The remainder were melted down. To say the least, it was **not** a financial success. Today, it is a rare and sought-after piece, as many Brooklin collectors have never seen one. There is one pictured in the hardcover *Brooklin Collection* Book by Vincent Rosa, ©1989.

Initially, John did everything to create a Brooklin Model. He carved the master, made the mold, cast the piece and assembled the models. Two employees helped assemble and paint. As business improved, more people were hired, until today, the business supports 25 or more employees, including Jenny Hall, who runs the business office, and John, who oversees the entire operation.

In October of 1979, John and Jenny decided to move back to the United Kingdom. This ceased all future production of Brooklin Models stamped "Made in Canada". They settled in Bath, England, a beautiful city filled with culture. The first factory was located in the Huggett Electrical building in Bath. John has used the Huggett's logo on many of his #16 Dodge models.

In England, new markets opened up and orders began to pour in. American cars are quite popular in Europe, so are Brooklin models. They have always been popular in America.

Today, John Hall continues his original idea - to manufacture only models of American cars. He has chosen some of the most controversial cars of the past five decades. Each is a legend or classic in its own right. When asked why he models only American cars, John replied, "I think being influenced by living and working in North America is the obvious reason. And, of course, the sheer outrageous design and ostentation of the American car calls out to be modeled."

At the new Brooklin factory in Bath, Brooklin manufacturers over 50,000 models a year. Since 1988, the models were marketed in a new box which includes the Statue of Liberty, the New York City skyline and an Edsel with an American flag banner. Gone are the old tan and brown logo boxes. These have been resurrected as of late for promotional issues, lending a nostalgic touch for the collector.

Bonnie & Vincent Rosa

BIOGRAPHY
Author Vincent Rosa

Author Vincent Rosa grew up in Brooklyn, New York and moved to Long Island where he attended Adelphi-Suffolk-Dowling College. He holds a Masters degree in History from Stony Brook University and looks forward to be working on his doctorate.

Vincent's hobbies include collecting Lionel® Trains and Toy Soldiers of the British Victorian period.

Vincent and his wife Bonnie both operate a business called "Model Cars and Trains Unlimited" of Blue Point, New York, a firm that specializes in the sale of collectible trains, die-cast model cars and toy soldiers of all types and varieties.

Vincent's hobby-related works include:
Greenbergs Guide to Lionel H.O. *for Greenberg Pub. Co. 1987, 1993. He has published his own copyrighted work.*

The Book Collection © *1989 and the* Official Brooklin Models Collector Guide © *1989. For all information call: Vincent or Bonnie at (516) 363-2134.*

John and Jenny Hall and Brooklin Models Ltd. have dedicated their craft to quality. And John Hall, the man, is he happy about his success - making his hobby his vocation? I would say yes. "I just wanted to make my cars", says John, "I've done what I set out to do. My greatest pleasure these days is watching the staff take over the skills and enthusiasm of the early days. Brooklin Models Ltd. is now a true company." Brooklin Models is still dedicated to three things - quality, quality and quality. They are the standard by which all 1:43 scale models are judged. That is why Brooklin Models will continue to be the collector's choice for years to come.

(NOTE: Prices are for **Mint In The Box**)

Brooklin Codes

Code I - All pieces built, assembled and decaled from the Brooklin factory in England. Also, those pieces produced in the factory, but, partially assembled/partially or totally decaled outside with total knowledge and approval of John Hall. These are considered 100% authentic Brooklin. For example, some C.T.C.S., C.P.C.T.S., and promotionals like Mobil and City of Toronto, Bay State Lobster, Model Auto Review, Coca Cola, et. al.

Code II - Altered or modified Brooklin models outside the factory, done with full approval of the company. At the present time, there are only a few such models that fall into this category. The first is the series of convertibles produced by the Model Car Shop. Their first car was the Burgandy 1953 Skylark with wire wheels and the second being the 1949 Red Mercury with wire wheels. The only other Code II piece at the present time is the plated (silver color) Edsel done by Danhausen.

Code III - Altered or modified Brooklin models outside the factory done without the approval of the company. There are many beautiful models in this category that can enhance your collection, but cannot be considered true Brooklin pieces. The excellent convertibles done by Jerry Rettig, the Orange County Fire Dept. Dodge Pickup done by TFC and the Yellow Corvette with wire wheels done by the Model Car Shop are some examples.

Prototypes - These are pieces which may have been cast differently or paint tested in color variation and were never intended for sale. These do not fall into any category above. There are many such models and the collector need not feel that his/her collection is incomplete without them. If however, these pieces were put up for sale by The Company or by an individual with permission of The Company then they would be Code I, such as the turquoise Mercury, and the eleven Tucker samples given to the Tucker Club so they could pick three promotional colors.

Discontinued Color/Style

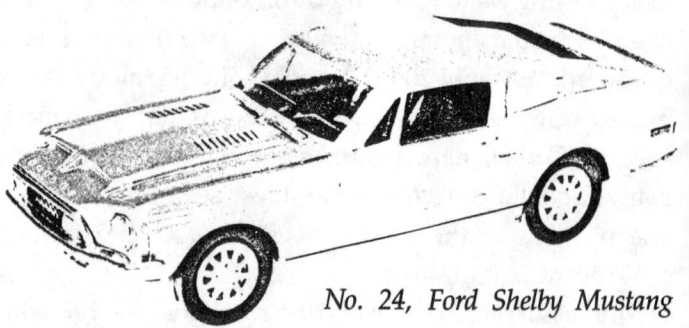

No. 24, Ford Shelby Mustang

Only 1,253 Shelby American G.T. 500 Fastbacks were built in 1968, making it one of the rarest cars in its class. It was the undisputed King of the 60s muscle cars.

NOTE: Numbers 1, 16a, 17, 26a and 31 were discontinued from the Brooklin Collection during 1992.

Brooklin 41
Courtesy Vincent Rosa

Brooklin 40
Courtesy Vincent Rosa

KEY

R	Regular Issue	5	One of a kind
D	Discontinued body style	6	First casting
C	Discontinued color	7	No gas cap
M	Made	8	With gas cap
W/C	With certificate	9	Numbered on baseplate
App.	Approximately	10	Smooth side
Int.	Interior	11	Small decals
Dk.	Dark	12	Rim linted sides
L	Means #14 in Tucker Canadian Issue		
Lt.	Light	13	No windows - van style
Med.	Medium	14	Large scale
M	Metallic	15	Last 250 made came with certificate
P	Promotional - Limited run	16	Gold trim
1	Resin baseplate	CPCTS	Canadian Pacific Coast Toy Show
2	No plastic windows	CTCS	Canadian Toy Collectors Society
3	Rare (not plentiful, hard to find, in demand)	CTCI	Classic Thunderbird Collectors International
4	Detailed chassis	PROTO	Prototype

MINT IN BOX - The only designation of trade as far as grading is concerned is MINT IN BOX.
NRS - No Reported Sales

CANADIAN ISSUES

Model No.	Year and Description	Key	Misc. Info.	Notes	
1	**1933 PIERCE ARROW**				
☐	Blue/Grey	D-5-3	All resin	First issue	No Price Found
☐	Brown/Cream	D-5-3	All resin	First issue	No Price Found
☐	Blue/Grey	D-1-2-3	App. 30 m.	Second issue	No Price Found
☐	Maroon/Grey	D-1-2-3	App. 3 m.	Second issue	No Price Found
☐	Green/Grey	D-1-2-3	App. 30 m.	Second issue	No Price Found
☐	Brown/Cream	D-1-2-3	App. 30 m.	Second issue	No Price Found
☐	Champagne	R	Maroon Int.	Third issue	350.00
☐	Champagne	—	Red Int.	Third issue	350.00
☐	White	D-1-2-5-3			
☐	Silver Grey	D-M-1-2-3		Third issue	350.00
☐	Medium Blue	M		Third issue	350.00
☐	Silver Grey	M		Third issue	350.00
2	**1949 TUCKER**				
☐	Medium Blue	D-2-6-2-L	Grey Int.		200.00
☐	Dark Blue	D-2-6-2-L	Grey Int.		200.00
☐	Very Dark Blue	D-2-6-2-L	Grey Int.		200.00
☐	Black	D-2-3-6-L	Beige Int.		200.00
☐	Black	D-2-3-6-L	Lt. Grey Int.		200.00
☐	Maroon	D-3		14m.	No Price Found
☐	Medium Blue	D-M			200.00
☐	Dark Blue	D-R-M	Grey Int.		200.00
3	**1930 FORD VICTORIA 2 DR.**				
☐	White top Beige body	D-M-2	Tan Int.	Cream wheels	250.00
☐	White/Olive	D-2	Grey Int.	White wheels	250.00
☐	White/Olive	D-4	Tan Int.	White wheels	250.00
☐	White/Med. Brown	D-4	Grey Int.	White/wheels	105.00
☐	Beige/Olive	D-4	Tan Int.	White wheels	90.00
4	**1937 CHEVY COUPE**				
☐	Buff Green	D-R			325.00
☐	Medium Green	D			325.00
☐	Dark Green	D			325.00
☐	Dark Green	D-4			325.00
☐	Black	D-4-3		App. 18 m.	Nrs.

(continued)

BROOKLIN

Model No.	Year and Description	Key	Misc. Info.	Notes	
5	**1930 MODEL A 2DR COUPE**				
☐	Black top/Brown body	D	Tudor body	Orange wheels	500.00
☐	Black top/Brown body	D-4	Tudor body	White wheels	500.00
☐	Black/Black	D-3	Tudor body	White wheels	500.00
6	**1932 PACKARD**				
☐	Dk. Beige Top Maroon Body		Grey Int.		
☐	Lt. Beige/Maroon		Grey Int.		
☐	White/Maroon		Grey Int.		
☐	Dark Grey/Maroon				325.00
☐	Lt. Grey/M. Grey		Maroon fenders	Grey Int.	325.00
☐	Lt. Grey/Lt. Grey		Blue grey fenders		
☐	Med. Grey/Med. Grey		Med. blue fenders		
7	**1934 CHRYSLER AIRFLOW**				
☐	Cream (Off White)	R			190.00
8	**1940 CHRYSLER NEWPORT 4DR**				
☐	Lt. Green	M-R	Lt. Brown Int.		175.00
☐	Med. Green	M-R	Lt Brown Int.		200.00
8A	**1941 CHRYSLER NEWPORT PACE CAR**				
☐	White - Dearborn Nat.				
☐	Car Convention	3	Red Int.	200 M.	475.00
9	**1940 FORD VAN**				
☐	Tan	P-3	Toledo Toy Show	213 m.	500.00
☐	Dark Blue	P-12-3	CTCS '79	60 m.	600.00
☐	Dark Blue	P-12-3	Marque	50 m.	600.00

ENGLISH ISSUES

Model No.	Year and Description	Key	Misc. Info.	Notes	
1	**1933 PIERCE ARROW**				
☐	Light Blue	R-M	Grey Int.		65.00
☐	Med. Blue	M	Grey Int.		
☐	Dark Blue	M	Grey Int.		
☐	Champagne	M		100 m.	350.00
☐	Lt. Silver	M	Grey Int.		350.00
☐	Dk. Silver	M	Grey Int.		350.00
☐	Silver	M-P	Harrah's	Blue Int.	200.00
2	**1948 TUCKER**				
☐	Lt. Maroon	D-R-M-7			195.00
☐	Lt. Maroon	D-R-M-8			195.00
☐	Maroon	D-2-M			195.00
☐	Dk. Maroon	D-R-M-8			
2A	**1948 TUCKER**				
☐	Gold	R-M	Tan Int.		65.00
☐	Dark Gold	R-M	Tan Int.		65.00
☐	Maroon	P-M-3	Tan Int.	500 m. Tucker Club	200.00
☐	Silver	P-M	Tan Int.	Harrah's	175.00
☐	Lt. Brown	P-M	Grey Int.	Harrah's	175.00
☐	Gold	P-M	Beige Int.	Harrah's	175.00
☐	Lazer Red	P-M	Paramount Pictures	Semi-limited 1000 m	200.00
☐	Stratus Silver	P-M	Paramount Pictures	Semi-limited 1000 m.	200.00
☐	Turquoise	P-M	Paramount Pictures	Semi-limited 1000 m.	200.00
☐	Green	5 Proto			No Price Found
☐	Sierra Beige	5 Proto			No Price Found
☐	Black	5 Proto			No Price Found
☐	Signa Amber	5 Proto			No Price Found
☐	Champagne	5 Proto			No Price Found
☐	Zircon Blue	5 Proto			No Price Found

(continued)

Model No.	Year and Description	Key	Misc. Info.	Notes	
☐	Jaguar Coral	5 Proto			No Price Found
☐	White	5 Proto			No Price Found
Bk 2 Bx	Lt. Blue T.A.C.A. 2nd issue	P	Tucker Club		150.00
3	**1930 FORD VICTORIA 2DR**				
☐	Beige top/Med. Gr. Body	D-R-4-15	Beige wheels	Lt. Br. Int.	150.00
☐	Beige/light green	D-C-4	Beige wheels	Lt. Br. Int.	150.00
☐	Beige/Tan	D-4	White wheels	Lt. Br. Int.	175.00
☐	Beige/Lt. Olive	D-4	Beige wheels	Lt. Br. Int.	150.00
4	**1937 CHEVY COUPE**				
☐	Dark Green	D-R-4-15	Beige wheels		160.00
☐	Dark Green	D-C-4	Beige wheels		160.00
☐	Blue	D-P-3-9	Ill. Toy Show '86	100 m.	400.00
☐	Beige	D-P-3	Webers 87	70 m.	No Price Found
☐	Red	D-P	James Leake 87	150 m. 15th Auc.	
☐	Bright Green	D-P	Toledo Toy Show 87	100 m.	
☐	Blue	P	Ill. Toy Show	100 m.	
☐	White	P	Brooklin Club England	275 m.	
☐	"Police"	P	Bay Brooklin Club		150.00
4	**MODEL A FORD 2DR COUPE**				
☐	Black top/Dk. Br. Body	D-3	Tudor body		100.00
☐	Black/Green	D-R-15			100.00
☐	Black/Lt. Green	D-C			100.00
☐	Black/Red	D-P	New Orleans Fire	100 m.	200.00
☐	Black/Red	D-P	Philly Fire	300 m.	300.00
☐	Black	D-P-3	Webers '86	69 m.	Nrs.
6	**1932 PACKARD STANDARD 8**				
☐	Lt. Brown top/Cream Body	R	Brown fenders	Lt. Br. Int.	125.00
☐	Blue-grey top silver	3	M. Lt. Blue fenders	Red Int.	200.00
☐	Grey Lt. Grey	3	Dk. grey fenders	Red Int.	200.00
☐	Tan/Lt. Grey	3	Brown fenders	Red Int.	200.00
7	**1934 CHRYSLER AIRFLOW**				
☐	Light Blue	R	Black wall tires		65.00
☐	Medium Blue	R	White wall tires		All Variants
☐	Medium Blue	R	Black wall tires		90.00 or more
☐	Dark Blue	R	White wall tires		
☐	Dk. Blue	R	Black wall tires		
8	**1940 CHRYSLER NEWPORT**				
☐	Yellow	R-D-15			110.00
8A	**1941 CHRYSLER PACE CAR**				
☐	White	R	Chrysler logo		65.00
☐	White	P	Motor Sport	140 m.	225.00
☐	White	P-3	Mtr. Sp. 60th Anv.	60 m.	300.00
9	**1940 FORD VAN**				**90.00**
☐	Black	D-R-12	Ford		75.00
☐	Black	R	Ford		550.00
☐	Red	P-12-3	CTCS '80	Beige Int. 125 m.	550.00
☐	Red	P-3-10	CTCS '80	Lt. Br. Int. 125 m.	550.00
☐	Blue	P	CPCTS '84	100 m.	350.00
☐	Lt. Blue	P	CPCTS '87	150 m.	250.00
☐	Yellow	P-12-11	Coke	"Drink"	325.00
☐	Yellow	P-11	Coke	"Drink"	325.00
☐	Yellow	P	Coke	"Enjoy"	325.00
☐	Yellow	P	Coke	"Drink"	325.00
☐	Black	P	James Leake '85	250 m. 13th Auc.	200.00
☐	Orange	P	James Leake '88	150 m. 16th Auc.	225.00
☐	Yellow	P	Danhausen	150 m. 1st Issue	225.00
☐	Grey	P	Danhausen, red wh.	150 m. 1st issue	225.00
☐	Tan	P	Danhausen	2nd issue	225.00
☐	Grey	P	Danhausen, grey wh.	2nd issue	200.00
☐	Red	P-3	Indian River Fire	50 m.	400.00
☐	White	P	Nutmeg Ambulance	300 m.	200.00

(continued)

Model No.	Year and Description	Key	Misc. Info.		Notes
☐	Red	P	Springfield Fire	100 m.	350.00
☐	Off White	P	Philly Ambulance	300 m.	350.00
☐	Maroon	P	Buchi Optik	60 m.	400.00
☐	Red	P	Old Toyland	100 m.	275.00
☐	Blue	P	Deaf Child Soc.	200 m.	220.00
☐	Dark Blue	P-3	BF Goodrich	50 m.	400-800.00
☐	White	P	Harrah's '85	400 m.	225.00
☐	Dark Brown	P	Hershey		375.00
☐	Maroon	P-3-9	J.U.N.K.	50 m.w.c.	800.00
☐	Beige	P-12-3	Lamberts	100 m.w.c.	650.00
☐	White	P-3	Mobil Bk. Tires	26 m.	No Price Found
☐	Beige	P-3	Model Auto	50 m.	450.00
☐	White	P-3	Maidenhead	150 m.	500.00
☐	Brown	P-3	Marque	50 m.	350.00
☐	Green	P-3	Randalls	50 m.	390.00
☐	Yellow	P	Shell-Model Garage	140 m.	175.00
☐	Cream	P	Spanish Armada	150 m.	200.00*
☐	Green	P-10	Toronto Works	50 m.	295-350.00
☐	Green	P-12	Toronto Works	50 m.	295-350.00
☐	Beige	P-3	Webers '84	67 m., Rare	No Price Found
☐	Maroon	P-3	Wessex Model	75 m., Rare	No Price Found
☐	Red	P	Yateley	150 m.	225.00
☐	Green	P	Huggett		110.00
☐	Red	P	Weeties		150.00
10	**1949 BUICK ROADMASTER**				
☐	Lt. Silver Grey	R-C	Beige Int.	w/o hood orn.	65.00
☐	Med. Grey	R	Beige Int.	w/o hood orn.	75.00
☐	Dark Grey	R	Beige Int.	w, w/o hood orn.	75.00
☐	Black	3	Autosatisfaction	100 m. w/o hood orn.	
☐	Black	3	Beige Int.	w/hood orn.	200.00
☐	Maroon	P	Beige Int.	Mini cars	70.00

*Sleeper

Model No.	Year and Description	Key	Misc. Info.		Notes
11	**1956 LINCOLN CONTINENTAL MARK II**				
☐	Lt. Blue	R-M	Grey Int.		65.00
☐	Med. Blue	R-M	Grey Int.		70.00
☐	Dark Blue	R-M-C	Red Int.		75.00
☐	Black	P	Maroon Int.	500 m.	125.00
☐	Black	P-9	Accent, First Issue	White Int.	195.00
☐	Black	P-9	Accent, Grey Int.	400 m.	150.00
☐	White	5-Proto			No Price Found
☐	Gold	P-3	Autosatisfaction	50 m., Rare	No Price Found
12	**1931 HUDSON BOATTAIL**				
☐	Orange/cream fenders	R			70.00
☐	Beige top black body	P	CTCS '81 Red Fenders	250 m.	550.00
13	**1956 FORD T-BIRD**				
☐	Red	R			
☐	Dark Red	R			
☐	Beige	R	CTCI '82	300 m.	350.00
☐	Tan	P	CTCI '82	?m.	350.00
☐	Green	P	CTCI '88	200 m.	200.00
☐	White	P-9	Ill. Toy Show '87	100 m. w/c Red Int.	350.00
☐	White	P	Mini Cars	Black Int.	80.00
14	**1940 CADILLAC V-16 CONVERTIBLE**				
☐	Gold-Bronze	R-M			65.00
☐	Dark Bronze-Brown	R-M			75.00
☐	White top/red body	P	CTCS '83	400 m.	375.00

BROOKLIN

Model No.	Year and Description	Key	Misc. Info.		Notes
15	**1949 MERCURY**				
☐	Cream	C-R	Red or Grey Int.		200.00
☐	Med. Green	R-M			65.00
☐	Dark Green	R-M			75.00
☐	Dark Blue	P-M-9	Ill. Toy Show '88	100 m. w/c	200.00
☐	Turquoise Blue	Proto		6 m.	NRS
☐	Maroon	P	CTCS		140.00
16	**1935 DODGE VAN**				
☐	Grey body/red fenders	R-C	Burma Shave	Black run bds.	90.00
☐	Grey body/red fenders	R-C	Burma Shave	Red run bds.	90.00
☐	Grey body/black fenders	3	Burma Shave	Apr. 50 m.	250.00
☐	White	P	Bay St. Lobster	J. Leake Redo 50 m.?	300.00
☐	(16A) Lt. blue/dk. blue	R	City Ice		65.00
☐	Orange/Brown	P-3	Avon Club	75 m.	395.00
☐	Blue	P	Argus De LaMiniature	100 m.	295.00
☐	Cream/Orange	P	Bayview Model	50 m.	500.00
☐	White/Red	P	Dr. Bernardo's	100 m.	300.00
☐	Brown/black	P	Bimbo	100 m.	300.00
☐	Blue/Black	P	Buchi Optik	100 m.	300.00
☐	Pea Green/Green	P-M	Calandre	100 m.	300.00
☐	Cream/Brown	P	Camel	75 m.	450.00
☐	Red/Black	P	Classic & Sport	200 m.	200.00
☐	Yellow/Black	P	Coca Cola		450.00
☐	Gold/Red	P-M-16	Collectors Gazette '86	24 K. Gold, 200 m.	425.00
☐	Maroon/Black	P	CPCTS '83	50 m.	400.00
☐	Silver/Black	P-M	CPCTS '85	w/logo 100 m.	200.00
☐	Grey/Black	P	CPCTS '85	w/o logo ? m.	200.00
☐	Beige/Brown	P	CTCS '82	250 m.	225.00
☐	Beige/Brown	P	Gems & Cobwebs	100 m.	275.00
☐	Brown/Black	P	Hershey		300.00
☐	Green/Grey	P	Huggett Elec. '83	w/c 100 m.	325.00
☐	Red/Red	P-3	Indian River	50 m.	495.00
☐	White/Red	P	ITT Kruse '87	150 m.	175.00
☐	White/Red	P	J. Leake '84	12th Auction	275.00
☐	Red	P	Litchfield Fire	200 m.	275.00
☐	Dark Red	P	Litchfield Fire	200 m.	275.00
☐	White/Blue	P	London Mtr. Fair '85	100 m.	300.00
☐	Dark Blue	P-3	Maidenhead	100 m.	300.00
☐	Dark Blue/Red	P	Merley Museum	100 m.	300.00
☐	Lt. Blue/Dark Blue	P	Mini Wheels of Midland	50 m.	395.00
☐	Dark Green/Lt. Green		Model Auto Review	100 m.	295.00
☐	Yellow/Red	P	Old Toyland '87	100 m.	295.00
☐	Goldish Green/Black	P-M	Passport Transport	150 m.	275.00
☐	Maroon/Black	P-R	Dr. Pepper	Semi ltd.	70.00
☐	Red/Red	P	Philly Fire	App. 300 m.	295.00
☐	Black/Black	P-R	Sears	Semi ltd.	70.00
☐	Cream/Green	P	St. Martins	App. 150 m.	295.00
☐	Gold/Black	P-M-16	Spielgoed Otten	100 m.	250.00
☐	Yellow/Black	P-3	Weber's '85	68 m.	No Price Found
☐	Maroon/Gold	P	Wessex	75 m.	
☐	Maroon	P	Wessex Silver Key		120.00
16X	**1935 DODGE PICK-UP**				
☐	Orange Body/Brown fenders	P	Avon	75 m.	400.00
☐	Green/Green	P	A.T.T. w pole	400 m.	350.00
☐	Green/Beige	P	CTCS '84	400 m.	300.00
☐	Yellow/Blue	P	CTCS '86	450 m.	290.00
☐	Burgundy/Cream	P	CPCTS '86	150 m.	300.00
☐	Blue/Cream	P-3	B.F. Goodrich	50 m.	600.00
☐	Green/Green	P-3	Huggetts	100 m.	300.00
☐	Orange/Brown	P	J. Leake '86	150 m. w/c 14th Auc.	300.00
☐	Blue/Black	P	Markham (250 made)	500 m.	185.00
☐	Red/Red	P	Orange Cty. Fire	400 m.	350.00

(continued)

Model No.	Year and Description	Key	Misc. Info.	Notes	
☐	Olive Green	P	New Eng. Telephone & Pole truck	400 m.	250.00
☐	Red	P	Yately	150 m.	285.00
☐	Yellow	P	Brasilia Press	700 m.	75.00
☐	Red/Black	P	Yateley's	150 m.	185.00
17	**1952 STUDEBAKER STARLIGHT**				
☐	Black	C-R	Grey Int.		110.00
☐	Grey	R	Grey Int.		65.00
☐	Grey	R	Red Int.		70.00
18	**1941 PACKARD CLIPPER**				
☐	Maroon	R			65.00
☐	Gold/Bronze	P-M	CTCS '85	400 m.	350.00
☐	Khaki/White Stars	P	Military Staff Car	160 m.	400.00
☐	Yellow	P	American Taxi	500 m.	140.00
19	**1955 CHRYSLER C-300***	**P**	**Brooklin Club Model, NRS (White)**		**65.00**
☐	Red	R		500 m.	70.00
☐	Black/Tan	P	Mini Cars	500 m.	70.00
20	**1953 BUICK SKYLARK**				
☐	Aqua	R-M			
☐	White Convertible	P	Ketchner Oct. Fest.	100 m.	350.00
☐	Maroon Conv.	Code 2	Produced for Model Car Shop - Now Model Cars and Trains unlimited blue, PT, NY, Very Rare	No Price Found	
21	**1963 CORVETTE**				
☐	Blue	C-R-M			
☐	Red/Grey Int.	P	Mini Cars		70.00
☐	Red	P	Ill. Toy Show	100 m.	No Price Found
☐	White	R	Red Int.		65.00
☐	Silver	P-M-3		350 m.	300.00
☐	Red	P	Ill. Toy Show '87 Bk. Int.	100 m.	375.00
☐	Red	P			400.00
22	**1958 EDSEL CITATION**				
☐	Pink	R	Gold Name Decal		150.00
☐	Pink	R	Black Name Decal		75.00
☐	Lavender-Pink	R-C	Gold Name		
22A	Green, Metallic	R	W/Cont. Kit		65.00
23	**1956 FORD FAIRLANE VICTORIA**				
☐	White top/Green body	R	Marked #22 in error		90.00
☐	White top/Green body	R			65.00
24	**1968 SHELBY MUSTANG**				
☐	Blue	D-R-M			
☐	Green	D-P-3	Model Expo	250 m? - How many are in the hands of collectors is not known - NRS	No Price Found
24A	**1968 FORD MUSTANG**				
☐	Red	R			
25	**1958 PONTIAC BONNEVILLE CONV.**				
☐	Black	R-3	Burgundy Int.	40 m.	150.00
☐	Black	R	Grey Int.		65.00
26	**1956 CHEVY NOMAD**				
☐	White top/Lt. Blue body	R			65.00
☐	White/Coral	P	CTCS '87	375 m.	275.00
26X	**1956 CHEVY NOMAD VAN**				
☐	Red	P	Fire Chief		75.00
☐	Black	P	CPCTS '88	150 m.	195.00
☐	Black	P	Webers '88	71 m.	No Price Found
☐	Black	P	Das Automobile	200 m.	250.00

76

(continued)

BROOKLIN

Model No.	Year and Description	Key	Misc. Info.	Notes	
☐	Dk. Blue	P	Cars Only	150 m.	275.00
☐	Maroon	P	Wessex		150.00
27	**1957 CADDY ELDORADO BROUGHAM**				
☐	Silver	R-M			
28	**1957 MERCURY TURNPIKE CRUISER**				
☐	Bronze-Tan	R-M			65.00
☐	Blue (Monarch)	P-M	CTCS '88	450 m.	300.00
1989					
29	**1953 KAISER MANHATTAN**		**Standard Issue**	**1989**	**65.00**
☐	Blue	R	500 Produced for Rotterdam Shoppe		275.00
29X	Black	P			275.00
30	**1954 Dodge 500 Convt.**		**Standard Issue**	**1990**	**65.00**

New releases since 1990 follow The most variations and collectible items since 1989 have appeared on the #31 Pontiac Van. Since Brooklin models has changed its policy on the number of promotionals produced a pattern for value has yet to be determined. Values tend to be regional and varied. The average production for promotionals tends to be 750 models. The days when Brooklin models would make 50 models for a toy shoppe are clearly over. The higher the production runs, the lower the after-market prices tend to be.

Lower prices attract more collectors since they have a chance to own at least one or more promotional items.

NEW RELEASES

Model No.	Year and Description	Key	Misc. Info.	Notes	
31A	1953 PONTIAC SEDAN DELIVERY	R	Orange Gulf regular issue		1990
31X	1953 Pontiac Sedan Delivery	P	Part of boxed set Brooklin Video #1		Silver w/tonneau cover (blue)
31A	Mobil Gas	R	1952		1992
31A	Sunoco	R	1953		
32	1953 Studebaker Commander	R	Light Green, Reg. Issue		1990
33	1938 Phantom Corsair	R	Black Body		
33A	Tan	D	Original Brochure color, mini grid		
34	Maroon	R	Regular Issue, Dark Maroon		1991
35	1957 Ford Skyliner	R	Tan/gold chrome enhanced		
36	1953 Hudson Hornet	R	Green, Tan Interior		1992
37	1960 Ford Sunliner	R	Purple metal flake, Maroon top, convt.		1992
38	1938 Graham Sharknose	R	Khaki Tan		1992
39	1953 Olds Fiesta	R	Blue and white 2-tone - a first for Brooklin models		1992
40	1948 Cadillac	R	Dk. Navy Blue, Red Int.		1992
41	1959 Chrysler Convt.	R	Gold - Regular Issue		
41A	Light Milky Gold	R	Mistake a Brooklin Factory Released		
B	Pale Gold	R	Variation - of Reg. Issue (Color only)		

PROMOTIONAL GROUPS

Accent	11-11	CTCI	13-13
Autosatisfaction	10-11	Ill. Toy Show	4-13-21-15
Avon	16-16X	Indian River	9-16
Buchi Optic	9-16	J. Leake	16-9-16X-4-9
Coke	9-(9)-(9)-(9)-16	Maidenhead	16-9
CPCTS	16-9-16-(16)-16X-9-26X	Marque	9-9
CTCS	9-9-(9)-(12)-16-14-16X-18-16X-26	Old Toyland	9-16
Danhausen	9-9-9-9	Philly Fire	5-9-16
Goodrich	9-16X	Toledo Toy	9-4
Harrah	1-2-2-2-9	Weber	9-16-5-4-26X
Hershey	9-16	Wessex	9-16
Huggett	16-16X	Yately	9-16X

NOTES

Changes for 1992:

No. 17A - 1952 Studebaker convt. replaced No. 17 Studebaker Champion Coupe.

No. 20 - 1953 Buick Skylark available in red (only) as of October 1991.

No. 22A - Reworked Edsel, Improved casting replaced No. 22A Edsel Citation

No. 31B - 1953 Pontiac Sedan Delivery "Gulf Oil" replaced by another Gas Co. livery Mobilgas - and then Sunoco making for an attractive oil co. Series Set ongoing yearly promotionals for the collector and service station enthusiast.

No. 33 1938 PHANTOM CORSAIR

No. 20 1953 BUICK SKYLARK

No. 34 1954 NASH AMBASSADOR

No. 17x 1952 STUDEBAKER INDY PACE CAR. LTD EDITION

No. 31a 1953 PONTIAC

No. 35 1957 FORD SKYLINER

Brooklins
Courtesy Vincent Rosa

78

	C6	C8	C10
BUCKEYE Semi Tractor	400	600	800

Buckeye Semi-Tractor
Photo by Calvin L. Chaussee

BUDDY "L"

Buddy "L": Buddy "L" toys were first manufactured by the Moline Pressed Steel Company, Moline, Illinois, in 1921, and were named after the son of the owner, Fred Lundahl. Lundahl had started the company about eight years earlier, manufacturing auto and truck parts (fenders, etc.). The toys were originally made as special items for his son, but as Buddy Lundahl's playmates began to clamor for similar toys of their own and their fathers began asking Lundahl senior to make duplicate toys for their sons, Lundahl went into the toy business. Buddy "L" toys were large, typically 21 to 24 or more inches long for trucks and fire engines. Construction was of very heavy steel, strong enough to support a man's weight. These were made until the early 1930s, when the line was modified and lighterweight materials were employed. Before this time, Fred Lundahl had died, having already lost control of the company. The company has changed names several times, being known as the Buddy "L", Corp., Buddy "L" Toy Co., etc., in recent years dropping the quotes around the L. Continuing to make toys till the present day, the company even put out a few wooden toys during World War II, when its main plant made nothing but war-related items. The early Buddy "L" trains are also popular, and tend to be worth even more than the vehicles. Buddy "L" material from the pre-1932 period is almost indestructible and as a consequence, 50% of the pieces found are either very rusty or have been repainted at some point. The basic metal seems to hold up forever, but repainting and rust drops the price well below "good".

Following is a list of pre-1932 Buddy "L" toys compiled by Thomas W. Sefton.

	C6	C8	C10
Large Trucks			
Buddy L 200 Express Truck 1921-31, auctioned in 1992, restored, for	$4400		
Buddy L 201 Dump Truck (Ratchet) 1921-30	600	900	1200
Buddy L 201 A Hydraulic Dump Truck 1926-31	800	1200	1600
Buddy L 202 Coal Truck 1926-31	1800	2900	4000
Buddy L 202A Sand & Gravel Truck 1926-31	1800	3000	4500
Buddy L 203 Stake Truck 1921-24, 1926-28	700	1050	1400
Buddy L 203A Lumber Truck 1925-30	1000	1500	2000
Buddy L 203B Baggage Truck 1929-31	3000	6000	9000
Buddy L 204 Moving Van 1924-30	800	1200	1600
Buddy L 204A Railway Express 1926-31	1300	2000	2800
Buddy L 206, 206B Street Sprinkler Truck 1924-31	1500	2300	3500
Buddy L 206A Oil Truck 1925-30	1500	2300	3000
Buddy L 207 Ice Truck 1926-31 .	1400	2100	2800
Buddy L 208 Coach 1928-31 (Lt. Green Motorbus), auctioned 1992, Excellent, for	$5720		
Buddy L 209 Auto Wrecker 1928-31 (Tow Truck)	1800	2900	4000
Fire Trucks			
Buddy L 205 Hook & Ladder 1924-31	1100	1700	2300
Buddy L 205A Pumper 1925-30 .	2000	3000	4200
Buddy L 205AB (Working) Pumper 1930-31	1800	2800	4000
Buddy L 205B Aerial Ladder 1926-30	900	1350	1800
Buddy L 205C Insurance Patrol 1926-30	650	1000	1350
Buddy L 205D Water Tower Truck (Working) 1930-31	2000	3200	4600
Model T Series			
Buddy L 210 Flivver Truck 1925-30	900	1400	1900
Buddy L 210A Flivver Roadster 1925-27	750	1050	1500

Buddy L 201 (restored).
Photo by Calvin L. Chaussee

Buddy L 205B

Buddy L 201A

Buddy L 203B

Buddy L 206A (restored)
Photo by Calvin L. Chaussee

Buddy L 204A

Buddy L 207

Buddy L 205

Buddy L 209

Buddy L 205AB

	C6	C8	C10
Buddy L 210B Flivver Coupe 1925-30	550	825	1100
Buddy L 211 Ford Dump Cart 1926-30	1500	2300	3300
Buddy L 211A Ford Dump Truck 1926-30	1000	1500	2000
Buddy L 212 Ford Express Truck 1929-30	1200	1900	2600
Buddy L 212A One-Ton Ford Delivery Truck 1929-30	1200	2000	3200
Construction Equipment			
Buddy L 220 Steam Shovel 1921-31	325	485	650
Buddy L 220A Heavy Steam Shovel 1929-30	600	900	1200
Buddy L 220AB Heavy Shovel (on Treads) 1929-30	3000	5000	7500
Buddy L 230 Sand Loader 1925-31	250	375	500
Buddy L 240 Small Derrick 1922-31	275	363	550
Buddy L 241 Large Derrick 1922-31	350	575	725
Buddy L 250 Overhead Crane 1924-27	750	1125	1500
Buddy L 250A Traveling Crane 1928-30	1200	1800	2500
Buddy L 260 Pile Driver 1926-28	1000	1500	2000
Buddy L 270 Dredge (Clamshell) 1926-30	700	1100	1400
Buddy L 270A Tractor Dredge (on Treads) 1929-30	3000	5000	7500
Buddy L 280 Concrete Mixer 1926-30	600	900	1200
Buddy L 280A Mixer (on Treads) 1929-31	1000	1500	2000
Buddy L 290 Road Roller 1929-31	1800	2900	4400
Buddy L 300 Sand Screener 1929-30	700	1050	1400
Buddy L 350 Hoisting Tower 1929-31	750	1125	1500
Buddy L 360 Aerial Tramway 1929-30	2000	3000	4500
Buddy L 400 Trencher 1928-31 . .	2200	3300	5000

End listing by Thomas W. Sefton

Buddy L 210A
Courtesy Wilkinson Collection, Detroit Antique Toy Museum

Buddy L 230

Buddy L 280 Concrete Mixer
Courtesy Thomas G. Nefos, Federal Shipping Network

Buddy L 300

Buddy L Aerial Ladder Truck, 25" long.
Photo by Calvin L. Chaussee

BUDDY L 1932 on

Buddy L Aerial Ladder Truck, 1933-34, 40" long	550	950	1300
Buddy L Aerial Ladder Truck, 25" long......................	100	150	200
Buddy L Aerial Ladder Truck, wooden, 32" long..........	800	1300	1800
Buddy L Airway Express Van No. 563.......................	115	172	230
Buddy L "Allied Van Lines" moving van No. 366, 31" long...	350	550	750
Buddy L "Allied Van Lines", wooden, 27" long..........	250	375	500
Buddy L Ambulance Truck.....	100	150	200
Buddy L Anti-Aircraft Air Force Blue Truck, GMC..........	42	63	85
Buddy L Army Combat Car, wooden....................	120	180	240
Buddy L Army Electric Searchlight Truck No. 5545, 1957........	138	208	275
Buddy L Army Half Track w/Cannon..................	138	208	275
Buddy L "Army Signal Corps" Truck, 1941-42, 12" long.....	120	175	260
Buddy L Army Supply Corps Truck, 12" long.............	100	150	200
Buddy L Army Tank, wood, 1943, 13" long....................	85	130	175
Buddy L Army Transport, 27" with towed cannon, 6-spoke wheels....................	100	150	200
Buddy L "Army Truck 21", c.1940, cloth top	120	180	240
Buddy L Army Truck No. 506, 20½" long.................	125	195	250
Buddy L "Army" truck, 13" long, wooden, canvas top	160	245	325

Buddy L Army Electric Searchlight Truck.
Courtesy Continental Hobby House

Buddy L "Army Supply Corps", 12" long.
Photo by Calvin L. Chaussee

Buddy L "Army Transport" truck, (missing canvas) 19½" long.
Photo by Calvin L. Chaussee

BUDDY L

Buddy L "Army" truck, 16" long, wooden, canvas top	100	150	200
Buddy L "Army Transport" truck, 19½" long	175	263	350
Buddy L Atlas Van Lines	250	375	500
Buddy L Automatic Tail-Gate Loader with steering handle, 25" long	240	360	480

Buddy L Automatic Tail-Gate Loader with steering handle, 25" long.
Photo by Calvin L. Chaussee

Buddy L Baggage Truck No. 11, 26½" long, 1933	225	385	500
Buddy L Baggage Truck No. 41	65	98	130
Buddy L Baggage Truck No. 203-B, 1930-32, 26" long, auctioned in 1992 in very good-excellent condition for $8800.			
Buddy L "Big Show Circus" truck, wood, 1947, No. 484, 25½" long	900	1400	1900
Buddy L Brinks Armored Truck	155	230	315
Buddy L Buick Convertible, wooden, 18" long	275	413	550
Buddy L Bus, 23½" long, early 1930s	375	525	750
Buddy L Camper, 1961	95	140	195
Buddy L Car Carrier, 1961	44	66	88
Buddy L Cattle Truck	105	158	210
Buddy L Chain Dump, 1920s	400	650	900
Buddy L Circus Tractor Trailer, 1960s	175	263	350
Buddy L City Baggage Dray No. 439, 1934, 19" long	185	278	370
Buddy L City Baggage Dray No. 839, 1939, 20¾" long	125	188	250
Buddy L Coca-Cola Truck, 14" long, 1950s	175	263	350
Buddy L Coca Cola Truck, wooden, 19" long, circa WWII, only 3 known, worth $4200 in mint 1984			
Buddy L Concrete Mixer, 1930s	200	300	400

Buddy L "Big Show Circus" truck, wood, 1947. No. 484.
Photo by William G. Floyd

Buddy L Bus, 23½" long, early 1930s.
Photo by Calvin L. Chaussee

Buddy L Coca-Cola truck, 14" long, 1950s. (Missing bottles in photo).
Photo by Calvin L. Chaussee

Buddy L Coca Cola truck, wooden, 19" long.
Photo by Dick MacNary

Buddy L Concrete Mixer, 1930s.
Photo by Calvin L. Chaussee

Buddy L Double Hydraulic Self-Loader-N-Dump Truck No. 5892.
Courtesy Thomas G. Nefos, Federal Shipping Network

Buddy L "Emergency Auto Wrecker".
Photo by Calvin L. Chaussee

	C6	C8	C10
Buddy L Concrete Mixer with Truck No. 54, 34½" long, 1937	100	150	200
Buddy L Concrete Mixer No. 832, 1950-51 with Motor Sound, 10¾" long	140	210	280
Buddy L Construction Truck, c.1960s	50	75	105
Buddy L Convertible, wooden, 18" long	210	320	425
Buddy L Country Squire Station Wagon, 15" long	90	135	180
Buddy L Curtiss Candy Truck	275	413	550
Buddy L Dairy Truck No. 2002 (Junior Line), 1930-32, 24" long	240	360	480
Buddy L Dandy Digger No. 33	120	180	240
Buddy L Delivery Truck Deluxe Rider No. 803, 1945-48, 22¾" long	60	100	145
Buddy L Double Hydraulic Self-Loader-N-Dump truck No. 5892	100	150	200
Buddy L Dump Truck No. 434, 1936	300	450	600
Buddy L Dump Truck No. 634, 20½" long	150	225	300
Buddy L Emergency Auto Wrecker No. 3317	100	150	200
Buddy L Engine No. 29, 1933-34, 25½" long	150	275	450
Buddy L Excavator Truck and Shovel Set No. 948, 27½" long, 1940	125	175	280
Buddy L Express Trailer Truck No. 35, 1934	450	750	1100

	C6	C8	C10
Buddy L Express Truck, screenside, 1932	1200	2000	3000
Buddy L Farm Machinery Hauler	65	98	130
Buddy L "Farm Supplies" Hi-Lift Dump Truck, 20" long, 1954	No Price Found		
Buddy L Fast Delivery Truck No. 3313	75	112	150
Buddy L "Fast Freight", 20" long	65	98	130
Buddy L Fire Chief's Car with Siren No. 483, wood, 1947, 19½" long	450	700	950
Buddy L Fire Hose Truck, 12" long	42	63	85
Buddy L Fire Ladder Truck, semi, rounded trailer fenders, 1960	160	240	325
Buddy L Fire Ladder Truck, wooden, 20" long	110	165	220
Buddy L Fire Pumper, c.1960s	45	68	90
Buddy L "Fire Station", wooden, 17x15", with wooden chief car and ladder truck. Auctioned in 1992 in near-mint condition for $4070			
Buddy L Freight Hauler, GMC, 1957	100	150	200
Buddy L Giraffe Truck	210	315	420

Buddy L ''Farm Supplies'' Hi-Lift Dump Truck, 20'' long, 1954.
Courtesy Islyn Thomas

Buddy L ''Hydraulic Highway Maintenance'' truck, 17'' long.
Photo by Calvin L. Chaussee

Buddy L Fire Chief's Car with Siren No. 483, wood, 1947.
Photo by William G. Floyd

Buddy L ''Ladder Truck'', 1930s.
Courtesy Continental Hobby House

Buddy L Fire Ladder Truck, Semi, rounded trailer fenders, 1960.
Photo by Calvin L. Chaussee

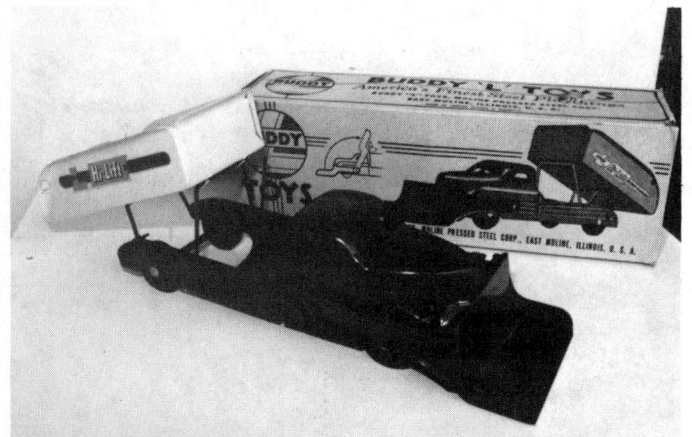

Buddy L Merry-Go-Round Truck No. 5429.
Courtesy Thomas G. Nefos, Federal Shipping Network

Buddy L ''Hi-Lift Scoop-A-Dump''.
Photo by Thomas G. Nefos, Federal Shipping Network

	C6	C8	C10
Buddy L Greyhound Bus, winds up, 16'' long	350	550	725
Buddy L Greyhound Bus with Bell No. 481, wooden, 18½'' long	250	375	500
Buddy L Grocery Truck	150	225	300
Buddy L Heavy Machinery Truck	120	180	240
Buddy L "Hi-Lift Scoop-A-Dump"	No Price Found		
Buddy L Hook and Ladder Truck No. 859, wooden, 21½'' long	150	225	300
Buddy L Horse Van, 18'' long	30	45	60
Buddy L Hose Truck No. 38, 1933, 21¾'' long	150	240	325
Buddy L Hot Rod Station Wagon	50	75	100
Buddy L Hydraulic Aerial Truck No. 27, 1933-34, 40'' long with ladders down	600	900	1200
Buddy L Hydraulic Dump Truck, 25'' long, 1932	1100	1700	2500
Buddy L Hydraulic Dump Truck No. 10, 23¾'' long, 1933-34	165	248	330
Buddy L Hydraulic Dump, 1938, 26'' long	900	1400	2000
Buddy L Hydraulic Dump, c.1960s	200	300	400
Buddy L "Hydraulic Highway Maintenance" truck, 17'' long	100	150	200
Buddy L Ice Cream Truck	65	98	130
Buddy L Ice Truck No. 12, 1933-34, 26½'' long	200	350	460
Buddy L International Delivery Truck No. 51, 1935, 24½'' long	200	300	400
Buddy L International Ice Truck, 28'' long, 1939	550	825	1100
Buddy L Jr. Airmail Truck, 22'' long	1500	2500	3500
Buddy L Jr. Baggage Truck, 22'' long	1800	3000	4500
Buddy L Jr. Cement Mixer	300	450	600
Buddy L Jr. Dairy Truck, 22'' long	1000	1800	2500
Buddy L Jr. Dump Truck, 22'' long	500	800	1200
Buddy L Jr. Milk Delivery Truck No. 2002	2000	3500	5000
Buddy L Jr. Oil Truck, 22'' long	1200	2000	2800
Buddy L Jr. Steam Shovel, treads, 24'' long	500	800	1100
Buddy L "Ladder Truck", 1930s	No Price Found		
Buddy L Long Distance Moving Van, wooden	275	415	550
Buddy L Lumber Truck, wooden, 30'' long	425	638	850

Buddy L Mister Buddy Ice Cream Van.
Courtesy Thomas G. Nefos, Federal Shipping Network

Buddy L "Railway Express Truck" No. 480, wooden, 1947. The pressed steel hand truck came with it.
Photo by William G. Floyd

Buddy L "Repair-It" (1953).
Courtesy Mapes Auctioneers

	C6	C8	C10
Buddy L Mack Tandem, 1969 ..	45	68	90
Buddy L Mack 30-Ton Dump ..	100	150	200
Buddy L Merry-Go-Round Truck No. 5429	70	105	140
Buddy L Milk Farms Truck, wooden	250	375	500
Buddy L Missile Launcher, GMC	90	135	180
Buddy L Mister Buddy Ice Cream Van	150	225	300
Buddy L Pepsi-Cola Truck, wooden, auctioned in 1992 for	$1595		
Buddy L "Popsicle" truck, wooden, 17" long	400	600	800
Buddy L "Pure Ice" truck, wooden, 16" long	112	178	225
Buddy L "Railway Express" truck, 1953, milk ad	350	525	700
Buddy L "Railway Express" truck No. 480, wooden, 1947, 16¼" long	275	363	550
Buddy L Red Baby Pickup, 26" long, doors open. Auctioned in 1992 for	$4620		
Buddy L Red Baby Pickup, 24" long	500	800	1200
Buddy L Repair-It, 24" long	140	210	280
Buddy L Ride-Em Dump	100	150	200
Buddy L Ride-Em Fire Truck ...	200	300	400
Buddy L "Riding Academy" No. 5455 truck, with 3 horses	112	168	225
Buddy L Robotoy Dump Truck with driver, operates on remote control	750	1200	1800
Buddy L Sand & Gravel Truck No. 3312	75	112	150
Buddy L "Sand & Stone" truck	No Price Found		
Buddy L Sanitation Truck, late .	90	135	180
Buddy L Scarab No. 211, no wind-up mechanism	250	375	500
Buddy L Scarab No. 711, winds up	270	405	540
Buddy L Scissors Dump	40	60	80
Buddy L Scoop Dump	75	112	150
Buddy L Searchlight Truck, GMC, 1950s	100	150	200
Buddy L Service Truck, 1953 ...	100	150	200
Buddy L "Shell" truck, 13½" long	140	210	280
Buddy L "Shell" truck, 17½" long, 1941	275	412	550
Buddy L Siren Pull-n-Ride	120	180	240

Buddy L "Riding Academy" No. 5455 truck.
Courtesy Thomas G. Nefos, Federal Shipping Network

Brand New! First Time Offered!
Remote Controlled Electric Dump Truck

Buddy L Robotoy Dump Truck, as shown in the October, 1932 Butler Bros. catalog.

Buddy L "Sand and Stone" truck.
Courtesy Continental Hobby House

Buddy L Scarab No. 711 (bumpers missing in photo).
Courtesy Heinz Mueller, Continental Hobby House

Buddy L Standard Oil Truck, 1933-34, 26" long	C6	C8	C10
	850	1300	2000
Buddy L Station Wagon, wooden, 19" long	200	300	400
Buddy L Steam Shovel and International Truck No. 16, 1937, 29½" long, 13½" high	110	165	225
Buddy L Steam Shovel, Mechanical, No. 30, 1935, 17½" long, 13½" high	200	325	450
Buddy L Steam Shovel on Treads (Junior Line) No. 2005, 1930-32, 24" long	150	275	400
Buddy L Store Delivery Truck	75	112	150

Buddy L Tank Truck, 27" long, 1930s (restored).
Photo by Calvin L. Chaussee

Buddy L "Super Market Delivery" truck.
Courtesy Continental Auctions

Buddy L "Texaco" tanker, 27" long.
Courtesy Calvin L. Chaussee

Buddy L "Super Market Delivery" truck	No Price Found		
Buddy L Super Motor Market Truck	315	472	635
Buddy L Supply Truck w/load	125	188	250
Buddy L Surf Truck, 12" long, 1953	60	90	120
Buddy L Tank Truck, 27" long, 1930s	500	775	1100
Buddy L Tank Truck No. 438, 19¼" long, 1935	200	325	480
Buddy L Tank Truck No. 938, 21½" long, 1941	200	325	450
Buddy L Telephone Truck, GMC	90	135	180
Buddy L Telephone Truck w/trailer	75	112	150
Buddy L "Texaco" Tanker, 27" long	112	170	225
Buddy L "Texaco" tanker, 25" long, promo sold at gas stations	80	120	160
Buddy L Towing Service Truck, late	50	75	100
Buddy L Traveling Zoo, post WWII	40	60	80

Buddy L Truck, open bed, 16' long, wooden.
Courtesy Charles D. Richards

	C6	C8	C10
Buddy L Truck, open bed, 16" long, wooden	No Price Found		
Buddy L U.S. Mail Truck, 21¾" long	225	338	450
Buddy L Utility Truck, GMC	82	124	165
Buddy L Utility Delivery Truck No. 946, 25" long, 1941-42	90	130	185
Buddy L Victory Jeep and Cannon, wood	100	150	200
Buddy L Water Tower, 1933-34, 48" long	1500	2500	3500

Buddy L "U.S. Mail" truck, 21¼" long.
Photo by Calvin L. Chaussee

Buddy L "Western Auto" semi, 25" long.
Photo by Calvin L. Chaussee

Buddy L Wild Animal Circus.
Courtesy Thomas G. Nefos, Federal Shipping Network

Buddy L "Wrigley's Spearmint" Railway Express truck, 1935.
Courtesy Rodney A. Heesacker

	C6	C8	C10
Buddy L Water Tower No. 28, 1936	800	1250	1800
Buddy L "Western Auto" semi, 25" long	75	112	150
Buddy L Wild Animal Circus Truck	175	263	350
Buddy L Wrecker No. 13, 31" long, 1933	1000	1700	3000
Buddy L Wrecker No. 37, 1933, 24" long	150	250	400
Buddy L Wrecker, 1936-37, 27" long	600	950	1300
Buddy L Wrecker, 1938, 26" long	1000	1700	2400
Buddy L Wrecker No. 813, 1938, 32" long	80	140	200
Buddy L Wrecker No. W37, 25¼" long, 1939	90	145	200
Buddy L Wrecker No. 437, 1934, 24" long	200	325	450
Buddy L Wrecker No. 503, 1940, 19¼" long, 1941-42	90	135	225
Buddy L No. 647, 1949, 26¼" long	110	165	200
Buddy L Wrecker, 16" long, c.1950s	112	168	225
Buddy L Wrecker, wooden, 18" long	162	245	325
Buddy L Wrecker, Emergency Towing Rider No. 903, 1949, 33" long	75	112	150
Buddy L Wrecker No. 903, 33" long, 1950, "Buddy L Emergency Towing"	100	160	225
Buddy L Wrecker No. 937, 1939, 25¼" long	130	180	285

	C6	C8	C10
Buddy L Wrecker No. 937, 1941-42 version, 25" long	50	95	135
Buddy L "Wrigley's Spearmint" Railway Express Truck No. 835, 25" long, 1938	700	1100	1500
Buddy L "Wrigley's Spearmint" Railway Express truck, 1935, headlights light up, 23⅛" long	400	600	800
Buddy L "Wrigley's Spearmint Railway Express Agency" truck No. 953, 1940	400	700	1000
Buddy L Zoo Truck	75	112	150

BUFFALO TOYS

Buffalo Toys, of Buffalo, New York, began in 1924. It produced a number of lightweight steel toys up until World War II. The firm, apparently no longer making toys, folded in 1968.

	C6	C8	C10
Buffalo Toys Blue Bird Racer	150	225	300
Buffalo Toys Mack Stake Truck, 25" long, electric lights, circa 1928	300	450	700
Buffalo Toys Silver Bullet Racer, 26" long	225	338	450
Buffalo Toys Silver Dash	175	263	350
Buffalo Toys Silver Streak	300	450	600

Buffalo Toys Mack Stake Truck, 25" long, electric lights, c.1928
Photo by Bob Smith

	C6	C8	C10
Buick, 1947, plastic, 5½" long	5	8	10

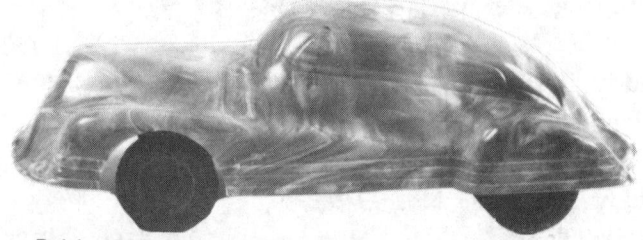

Buick, 1947, plastic, 5⅜" long
Courtesy James S. Maxwell/Virginia Caputo. Photo by Virginia Caputo

BUILT-RITE

Built-Rite, of Warren, Ohio, began in 1922 as a cardboard-box manufacturer. About 1934 it began to produce cardboard construction toys, with its apparent heyday in the late 1930s and World War Two. It is still in business, making card games, games and puzzles under the name of Warren.

	C6	C8	C10
Built-Rite No. 7 Private Garage, brick	30	40	50
Built-Rite No. 15 Commercial Garage	65	70	80
Built-Rite No. 17 Service Station	65	70	80
Built-Rite No. 20 Army Battery Set	80	100	125
Built-Rite No. 28 Garage and Super Service Station	65	75	85
Built-Rite No. 50 Army Raiders' Victory Unit, 28 pieces, truck, tank, AA gun, jeep, semitrack truck, 20 soldiers, WWII	65	75	85
Built-Rite No. 56 5 Miniature buildings, church, school, RR station, firehouse, drugstore	30	55	60
Built-Rite No. 83 Weapons Carrier	No Price Found		
Built-Rite No. 84 Armored Car	No Price Found		
Built-Rite No. 415 House, circa 1943, 13" x 20" boxed set with 19" house and garage, 27 pieces of furniture, sedan, baby buggy, shrubbery, etc.	75	90	100
Burdette Murray Express Truck	1600	2700	3800

Built-Rite No. 20
Photo by Ed Poole

BURNETT LIMITED

Birmingham/London, England
1900-1930s
by Bob Smith

Burnett started producing toy cars around the turn of the century. Their cars were said to have excellent quality. Burnett moved the business to London in 1914 where they would continue to make toys into the 1930s. The company was then purchased by Chad-Valley. Burnett toy cars have become quite rare.

	C6	C8	C10
Burnett limousine, Blue/black, c/w motor, driver, 8.0" long, c1925	550	750	1100
Burnett Cargo Truck, Maroon & black, c/w motor, driver, 8.5" long, c.1926	600	800	1150
Burnett Roadster, Green/black, c/w motor, driver, folding windshield, 7.5" long, c1925	600	800	1150

Burnett Cargo Truck, 8½" long, c.1926
Photo by Bob Smith

Bus, "Twin Coach, Buffalo, Niagara Lines", 15½" long, aluminum	C6	C8	C10
	2500	3500	6000

Bus, "Twin Coach, Buffalo, Niagara Lines", 15½" long, aluminum.
Courtesy James S. Maxwell/Virginia Caputo

Burnett Limousine, 8" long, c.1925
Photo by Bob Smith

BW MOLDED PLASTICS

What is known about BW Molded Plastics is that in 1954 it was located at 1346 East Walnut Street in Pasadena, California, and that it made a variety of plastic toys; musical instruments, tea sets, ships, vehicles, etc.

BW873B, 5-piece Auto Parade Set; pickup truck, convertible, coupe, ladder truck, racer	No Price Found
BW879 "Roly" The Steam Roller, "fully mechanized"	No Price Found
BW886 Jeep, 9¼" long	No Price Found
BW887 Tank, 10" long	No Price Found
BW888 Jaguar, 12½" long	No Price Found

Burnett Roadster, 7½" long, c.1925
Photo by Bob Smith

Top Row: BW873B, Middle Row: BW879, BV886, Bottom Row: BW887, BW888
BW Molded Plastics from their catalog

C.A.W. NOVELTY COMPANY

by Fred Maxwell and Ferd Zegel
with the assistance of the Clay Center Historical Society, Gary Franson, Arlan and Gerry Conrad.

It is remarkable indeed that collectors had not found this fine company until 1990. Charles A. Wood not only ran a substantial operation but he made some of the finest replica toys in the slushmold industry. Chic Gast, a collector, was perceptive when he wrote of unidentified toys as "orphans"; this company may have been the most invisible of those orphan companies. Ironically, Wood had one of the longest histories of the slushmold industry. Founded about 1925, his company was active until about 1940 when lead casting came to a halt with WWII. It was located in Clay Center, Kansas.

Wood's line was heavy with miniature airplanes for he was a pilot, an aviation mechanic and an air enthusiast. It was even reported he flew his toys to Eastern markets; this could have been true under special cir-

cumstances only, for in its best years (over 60 employees and 2 million toys) the company output would have been too large to "ship by air".

About 1940, Rod Hemphill found himself to be the last C.A.W. employee. With Howard Clevenger he bought Wood's assets, and set up business at 1610 So. Florrisant Road in St. Louis, Missouri, as C&H Mfg. Co. According to Mrs. Hemphill, C&H produced no new molds.

NEW LINE OF CAST TOYS

Of particular interest to jobbers and quantity buyers will be the announcement of the three new attractively colored cast metal toys which are being offered by

the Mid-West Metal Novelty Manufacturing Co. of Clay Center, Kan.

This manufacturer of novelties and art castings has instituted a new finish process enabling them to use lacquers which do not chip. Also by the use of plenty of metal, strength is obtained and breakage avoided. Each one of their toys, including the coupe illustrated here, moves on its own wheels and the toys are packed securely and neatly three colors to each carton. A wide variety of these colors is offered from which choice may be made. Cartons contain either half gross or gross.

These toys retail at popular prices and are particularly interesting as 10 cents to $1 merchandise.

Is this article about C.A.W.? It seems quite likely. From *Toys and Novelties*, August, 1929.

L to R: C.A.W. CWV1, CWV2
Photo by Fred Maxwell

C.A.W. CWV3
Courtesy of Gary Franson

C.A.W., L to R: CWV1, CWV?, 3" long.
Photo by Craig Clark

C.A.W. CWV5

C.A.W. CWV6
Photo by Craig Clark

C.A.W. CWV7
Courtesy of Gary Franson

C.A.W. CWV8
Courtesy of Gary Franson

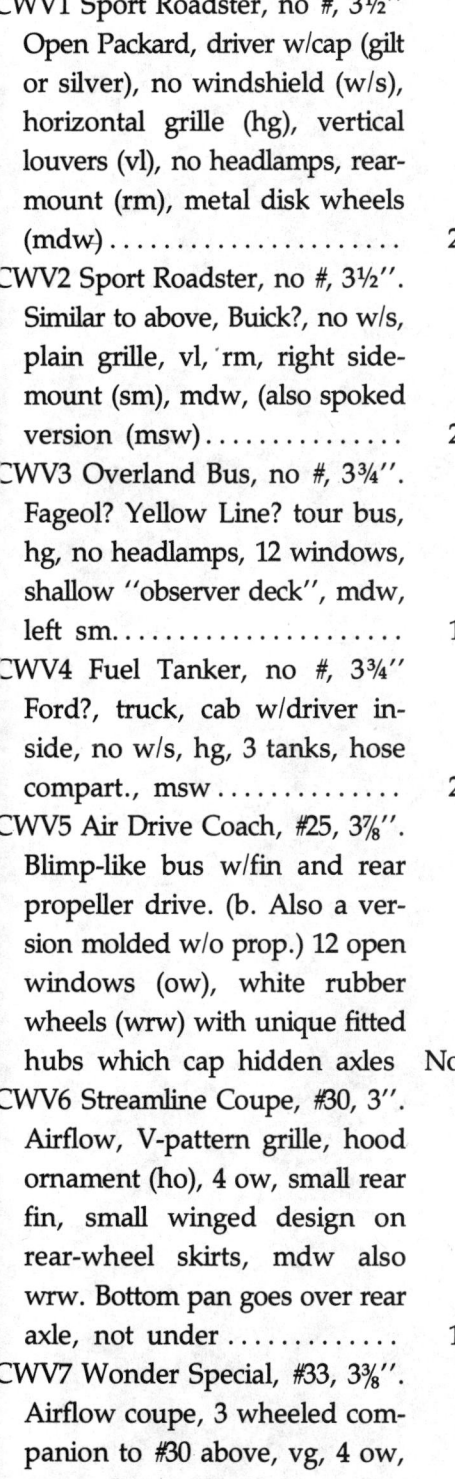

	C6	C8	C10
CWV1 Sport Roadster, no #, 3½" Open Packard, driver w/cap (gilt or silver), no windshield (w/s), horizontal grille (hg), vertical louvers (vl), no headlamps, rear-mount (rm), metal disk wheels (mdw)	20	30	40
CWV2 Sport Roadster, no #, 3½". Similar to above, Buick?, no w/s, plain grille, vl, rm, right side-mount (sm), mdw, (also spoked version (msw)	22	33	44
CWV3 Overland Bus, no #, 3¾". Fageol? Yellow Line? tour bus, hg, no headlamps, 12 windows, shallow "observer deck", mdw, left sm.	12	18	24
CWV4 Fuel Tanker, no #, 3¾" Ford?, truck, cab w/driver inside, no w/s, hg, 3 tanks, hose compart., msw	20	30	40

CWV5 Air Drive Coach, #25, 3⅞". Blimp-like bus w/fin and rear propeller drive. (b. Also a version molded w/o prop.) 12 open windows (ow), white rubber wheels (wrw) with unique fitted hubs which cap hidden axles   No Price Found

	C6	C8	C10
CWV6 Streamline Coupe, #30, 3". Airflow, V-pattern grille, hood ornament (ho), 4 ow, small rear fin, small winged design on rear-wheel skirts, mdw also wrw. Bottom pan goes over rear axle, not under	16	24	32
CWV7 Wonder Special, #33, 3⅜". Airflow coupe, 3 wheeled companion to #30 above, vg, 4 ow, wrw, front wheel skirts. Pan goes over front axle	16	24	32

CWV8 Marvel Racer, #31, 3⅝". Streamlined FWD Indy type, driver, torpedo tail with very small fin, V-grille pattern, 8 exhaust ports, alum. wheels. Also found in a modern bubble-pack, w/lucent hard plastic wheels, "Woodchuck Industries Metal Toys, Clay Center, Ks." This name may have been a new idea, part of a recent market test No Price Found

CWV9 Desoto Sedan, #32, 3⅞".
Airflow, divided windshield,
bow, hl, vg, ho, wrw . . . . No Price Found

CWV10 New Design Racer #38,
3⅜". Streamlined coupe,
rounded tail, 2 oval open windows show driver, hood ornament loop (stringpull?), wrw
w/hubs . . . . No Price Found

CWV11 Transparent Windshield
Racer, #39, 3". Indy FWD 2
man racer, v-shaped vg, dual
exhausts, boattail, unique hub-
tires as in #25 (also wrw). (Not
complete if divided plastic wind-
shield is missing (fragile) . . . . No Price Found

**CWV12 Three Piece Auto Set, #40,
as follows: a.** Midget coupe
racer, no #, 2¹⁄₁₆". Hg, hl,
divided open w/s, 2 ow, 2 colored body, mdw, headlamps
and cowl ventilators! . . . . No Price Found

b. Midget racer, no #, 2⅛". Gilt
driver, vl, hg, mdw. (easily con-
fused w/Barclay #53) . . . . No Price Found

c. Austin Bantam, no #, 2". 2 dr.
sedanette, 5 ow, hl, plain grille,
rm, mdw. (Easily confused with
other makers' Bantams) . . . . . . No Price Found

CWV13 Dump Truck, no #, 3⅛".
Ford?, hinged dump body,
divided open w/s, 2 ow, hg,
mdw . . . . No Price Found

CWV14 Tank Truck, no #, 3³⁄₁₆".
Ford ?, 3 fuel tanks, otherwise
matching above. Unusual 2 pc.
body connected by rear axle . No Price Found

C.A.W. CWV10
Courtesy of Gary Franson

C.A.W. CWV11B
Courtesy of Gary Franson

C.A.W., L to R: CWV12A; CWV4
Photo by Craig Clark

C.A.W. CWV12B
Courtesy of Gary Franson

C.A.W. CWV12C
Photo by Craig Clark

C.A.W. CWV9
Courtesy of Gary Franson

C.A.W. CWV13
Courtesy of Gary Franson

C.A.W. CWV14
Courtesy of Gary Franson

C.R.

(Charles Rossignol, Paris, France, 1868-1962)
by Bob Smith

Rossignol began making toy automobiles in 1895. The company became best known for the toy trains it produced in the nearly 100 years it was in business. In 1920 C.R. came out with a line of toy buses which lasted until the company closed its doors in 1962.

	C6	C8	C10
C.R. Dump Truck, Green/yellow, c/w motor, head lamps, dual side mount wheels, 16" long. c1935.	800	1200	1800

C.R. Dump Truck, 16" long, c.1935
Photo by Bob Smith

CARETTE, GEORGES

(Nuremburg, Germany, 1886-1917)
by Bob Smith

Born in France, Carette went to Nuremburg to start his toy factory in 1886. He has become a legend in the hobby since. Next to Marklin; Carette is the most desirable of German toy car makers. They are known for their fine detail and quality of materials. Carette

stayed in business until 1917. At the onset of World War I he fled to France and his company was taken over by Karl Bub. The Carette limousines were made in three general lengths, 9.0 inch (22cm), 12.5 inch (32cm), and 15.5 inch (40cm). The larger size is the most desirable and usually sells in the five figures.

	C6	C8	C10
CÀRETTE Limousine, White & green, 9" long, c/w motor, hand brake, head lamp, rubber tires, glass windows, c.1911	1400	1800	2500
CARETTE / BUB open car. Red/black, 6.7" long, c/w motor, Tin plate or cloth dressed driver, hand brake, forward & reverse gear. c1911	900	1300	1800

Carette/Bub Open Car, 6⁷/₁₀" long, c.1911
Photo by Bob Smith

Carette Limousine, 9" long, c.1911.
Photo by Bob Smith

CASS TOYS

(Athol, Massachusetts, 1890s to present)

	C6	C8	C10
Cass Station Wagon, wooden, 19″ long	60	90	120
Cass Tank, wooden	90	135	180
Cass Truck, wooden, 40″ long ridem	150	225	300

CHAMPION

The Champion Hardware Co., though in business from 1883-1954, produced toys only from 1930-36, as a Depression stopgas. As might be expected from a hardware firm, its toys were cast iron. During its toy years the Geneva, Ohio outfit was headed by C.I. Chamberlin.

	C6	C8	C10
Champion Airflow, 4¾″ long	No Price Found		
Champion Coupe, Plymouth type, rumble seat opens, 7½″ long	No Price Found		
Champion Coupe, Reo type, 7½″ long	400	600	800
Champion Gas and Motor Oil truck, 8″ long, cast iron, c.1930s	285	430	565
Champion four-casting nickeled radiator car, approx. 4″ long	175	262	350
Champion Mack Dump, 7″ long, c.1930s	375	563	750
Champion Mack Express Truck, 7½″ long	100	150	200
Champion Mack Stake truck, 4½″ long, c.1930	90	135	180
Champion Mack Stake Truck, 7½″ long	350	525	700

Champion, L to R: CM2, CM3.
Photo by Kent M. Comstock

Champion Wrecker, 7½″ long.
Photo by Bill Kaufman

CHAMPION MOTORCYCLES
(list by Kent M. Comstock)

	C6	C8	C10
(CM 1) Motorcycle, solo policeman rubber tires 5″	50	75	125
(CM 2) Motorcycle solo policeman nickel wheels 5″	75	100	150
(CM 3) Motorcycle solo policeman rubber tires 7¼″	150	250	400
(CM 4) Motorcycle solo policeman nickel wheels 7¼″	175	275	450
(CM 5) Motorcycle with sidecar, policeman, rubber tires, 3″	60	90	120
(CM 6) Motorcycle with sidecar policeman and passenger rubber tires 5″	150	225	350
(CM 7) Motorcycle with sidecar policeman and passenger, rubber tires 6″	200	300	450
Champion Panel delivery	750	1300	1800

Champion Mack Dump, 7″ long.
Courtesy Wilkinson Collection, Detroit Antique Toy Museum

96

Champion Race car, 2 riders, 5½''	125	188	250
Champion Race car, 6'' long, cast iron, detachable driver.......	100	150	200
Champion Race car, 9'' long, c.1930s	150	225	300
Champion Sedan, 5'' long	No Price Found		
''Champion'' Wrecker, 7½'' long, cast iron..................	250	385	550
Champion Wrecker, 4'' long ...	112	172	225

CHEIN

Chein (pronounced ''chain'') was founded in 1903 by Julius Chein. The New Jersey company specialized in lithographed metal toys, the majority of them mechanical. In 1918 it was located at 310 Passaic Avenue, Harrison, New Jersey, with 250 employees. In 1934 it had 55 male and 92 female workers. In a 1946-47 directory it listed 148 male and 132 female employees. Chein made toys until 1979, and is still in business today in Burlington, New Jersey.

	C6	C8	C10
Chein Army truck, cannon on back, 8½'' long, tin, early ...	75	111	150
Chein Army Truck, open bed, 8½'' long, tin, early	90	135	180
Chein ''Dan-Dee Dump Truck'' windup....................	200	300	400
Chein ''Greyhound'' bus, 9'' long windup....................	120	180	240

Chein Army Truck, open bed, 8½'' long.
Photo by Ed Poole

CHEIN HERCULES ''C'' CAB MACK TRUCKS
by Bob Smith

Bob Smith

Bob Smith began collecting toys in 1978 after being influenced by some old friends who were members of the Genesee Valley Antique Toy Association. Starting out by collecting Dinky Toys, he soon expanded his interests to Tootsie Toys, Early Hill Climber Vehicles, Pre-War Tin Cars and early wind-up toys. He joined the G.V.A.T.A. and became its president for 10 years. Bob retired from the automobile business in 1991 after 27 years in auto sales. He now devotes full time to the toy hobby and promoting his well known toy show in Rochester, NY. The RATS (Rochester Antique Toy Show) has grown to be one of the largest in the U.S. and is held twice a year in June and November. Bob's articles about old toys and his antique toy ads are seen in numerous collectors magazines which bring him in contact with collectors through out the world. Bob lives in Fairport, New York with his wife Roberta and their two sons Aaron and Evan.

Chein introduced the Hercules series vehicles in 1925, the first model being the Dump Truck. It was made entirely of light-weight stamped steel (heavy gauge tin). Chein made at least fourteen different Hercules models, the smallest being seventeen inches long and stretching to thirty inches with the C cab Bull Dog Mack mobile clam truck (including boom). These toys generally retailed between $1.00 and $1.25. They were manufactured up until the middle 1930s.

Chein Hercules Mack Coal Truck.
Courtesy Bob Smith

Chein Hercules Mack Army Truck.
Courtesy Bob Smith

Chein Hercules Mack Dump Truck.
Courtesy Bob Smith

Chein Hercules Mack Ice Truck.
Courtesy Bob Smith

Chein Hercules Mack Log Truck.
Courtesy Bob Smith

	C6	C8	C10
Chein Hercules Mack Army Truck, 19¾'' long. Brown with canvas cover	350	550	1100
Chein Hercules Mack Coal Truck, 20'' long, Black cab, chassis, green bed. Tin coal chute, chute door opens	550	800	1250
Chein Hercules Mack Dump Truck, 20'' long. Black cab, chassis, red dump body. Tailgate opens	300	450	750
Chein Hercules Mack Ice Truck, 19½'' long. Black cab, green cargo box, step plate at rear of bed	500	750	1200
Chein Hercules Mack Log Truck 18½'' long, all black	700	1000	1500
Chein Hercules Mack Mobile Clam Truck, 30'' long (including boom). Green, red, black	700	1000	1500
Chein Hercules Mack Motor Express Truck, 19½'' long. Black cab, orange stake bed	500	750	1200
Chein Hercules Mack Oil Tank Truck, 19'' long. Black and orange	500	750	1200
Chein Hercules Mack Ready-Mixed Concrete Truck, 17'' long. Deluxe model. Orange/black litho, rotating drum	750	1100	1600
Chein Hercules Mack Wrecking Truck, 23½'' long (including tow boom). Black cab, chassis, tow boom, red bed	500	750	1200

	C6	C8	C10
Chein Hercules No. 8 Racer, 20" long. Driver, spare tire (mounted on rear). Red with yellow trim	700	1000	1500
Chein Hercules Roadster, 18" long. Red & Black. Rumble seat, luggage rack	350	550	900
Chein Hercules "The Royal Blue Line" Pullman Bus, 18" long. Gray, red, black	750	1100	1600
Chein "Junior Truck", 1920s ...	60	90	120
Chein "Junior Oil Tank" truck, 8½" long, 1920s	62	93	125
Chein "Peanuts" bus, "Happiness Is An Annual Outing"	No Price Found		
Chein "Playland Whip" No. 340, 4 bumpem cars, windup.....	400	600	800
Chein "Racer No. 3", 1920s, 6½" long windup	120	180	240
Chein Racer "52"	60	90	120
Chein Roadster, tin litho, c. 1925, 8½" long	315	472	630
Chein "Royal Blue Line Coast to Coast Service"	600	900	1200
Chein Taxi, 7" long windup, 1920s	185	278	370
Chein Touring Car, tin litho, 7" long	250	375	500

Chein Hercules Mack Motor Express Truck.
Courtesy Bob Smith

Chein Hercules Mack Oil Tank Truck.
Courtesy Bob Smith

Chein Hercules Mack Ready-Mixed Concrete Truck.
Courtesy Bob Smith

Chein Hercules Mack Mobile Clam Truck
Courtesy Bob Smith

Chein Hercules Mack Wrecking Truck.
Courtesy Bob Smith

Chein Hercules No. 8 Racer.
Courtesy Bob Smith

Chein Hercules Roadster.
Courtesy Bob Smith

Chein Hercules "The Royal Blue Line" Pullman Bus.
Courtesy Bob Smith

Chein "Peanuts" bus.
Courtesy Continental Hobby House

CLARK, DAVID P. & CO.

(Dayton, Ohio, c.1898-1909)
by Bob Smith

D.P. Clark was the first manufacturer to use the heavy cast iron flywheel on friction drive Hill Climber toys, patented by Israel and Edith Boyer. The cars and trucks were made of heavy sheet metal, wood, and cast iron. Clark also made trains, animals, and other novelty toys with the friction mechanism. William Schieble, who was a partner in the company, bought Clark's half of the business in 1909. Schieble then changed the firm's name to the Schieble Toy and Novelty Co. Schieble filed bankruptcy in 1931.

Back on his own, Clark went on to begin a new business. Naming his company the "Dayton Friction Toy Works", Clark felt free to use the patents from the now Schieble Toy Co. Lawsuits followed, with Schieble being the winner. Clark sold the Dayton Toy Works to Nelson Talbot in 1924. He passed away soon after. The company managed to survive for eleven more years.

	C6	C8	C10
Clark Electric Runabout. Flywheel drive, two c.i. lady riders, wd., sheet mtl. & c.i. construction. Red/black/gold, 7.50" L, c.1902	550	800	1175
Clark Horseless Carriage. First toy with flywheel drive. Wood, tin & c.i. const. Blue/red, came lady passenger & driver, 11.5"L, c1898	650	900	1200
Clark Horseless Carriage push toy, Spring suspension no flywheel mechanism. Wood, tin & c.i. const. Green/red/yellow, 11" L. Possibly the first Clark toy. Patented November 2, 1897	550	800	1175
Clark Open Touring Car. Flywheel drive, tin head lamps, red, 8.0" c.1903	300	450	650
Clark Police Patrol, Flywheel drive, five riders, red/gold, 9.5" L, c.1900	500	750	1050
Clark Runabout, Flywheel drive, wood head lamps, red, 7.75" L. c.1902	325	475	675

	C6	C8	C10
Clark Runabout, Flywheel drive, wd., sheet mtl. & c.i. const. Red, 7.25'' L, c.1903.........	250	375	500
Clark Steam Pumper. Flywheel drive, gold/red, 11'' L., c.1908	350	500	700
Clark Steam Pumper. Flywheel drive. Wood, sheet metal & cast iron construction. Red, silver & gold, 10.25'' long, c.1903 ...	500	750	1050

Clark Police Patrol, 9½'' long, c.1900.
Photo by Bob Smith

Clark Horseless Carriage. First toy with flywheel drive. 11½'' long.
Photo by Bob Smith

Clark Runabout, 7¾'' long, c.1902.
Photo by Bob Smith

Clark Open Touring Car, 8'' long, c.1903.
Photo by Bob Smith

Clark Runabout, 7¼'' long, c.1903.
Photo by Bob Smith

Clark Steam Pumper, 11'' long, c.1908.
Photo by Bob Smith

Clark Horseless Carriage push toy. Possibly the first Clark toy. 11''
long.

Clark Steam Pumper, 10¼'' long, c.1903.
Photo by Bob Smith

Hill-Climbing Friction Toys

No. 10. "Automobile."
8½ inches long.
3½   "   wide.
7¼   "   high.
Imitation of our modern Runabouts.
Packed 2 dozen in case.
Price, Doz., List...$8.30

No. 15. "Pullman Car."
13   inches long.
3½   "   wide.
6   "   high.
Substantially made and nicely painted.
Carries 6 passengers.
Packed 2 dozen in case.
Price, Doz., List...$8.30

No. 25. "Automobile."
9   inches long.
4½   "   wide.
6   "   high.
A strong, durable toy.
Carries 3 passengers.
Attractively painted.
Packed 2 dozen in case.
Price, Doz., List...$8.30

No. 35. "Cruiser."
13   inches long.
3   "   wide.
7   "   high.
Constructed of sheet steel.
Equipped with 4 lifeboats.
Packed 2 dozen in case.
Price, Doz., List...$8.30

No. 40. "Scorcher."
11   inches long.
4   "   wide.
5½   "   high.
A perfect model of up-to-date racers.
Speedy machine.
Packed 2 dozen in case.
Price, Doz., List...$8.30

No. 20. Police Patrol.
10½ inches long.
4   "   wide.
7½   "   high.
Made of steel. Equipped with 2 hand-cuffed prisoners, officer and chauffeur.
Packed 2 dozen in crate.
Price, Doz., List...$8.30

No. 220. "Patrol."
10¼ inches long.
4   "   wide.
7½   "   high.
Very good design.
Two prisoners, 1 driver and 1 officer.
Packed 2 dozen in case.
Price, Doz., List. $11.50

No. 210. Combination.
13   inches long.
4   "   wide.
7   "   high.
May be used as Ambulance, Moving Van or Delivery.
Nicely painted.
Packed 2 dozen in case.
Price, Doz., List. $11.50

A page from a 1908 toy catalog showing D.P. Clark's Hill-Climbing
friction toys. The numbers and descriptions appear to be the
manufacturer's own.

Clark Electric Runabout, 7¾'' long, c.1902.
Photo by Bob Smith

Hill-Climbing Friction Toys

No. 250. Chemical Engine.

10¾ inches long.
4 " wide.
7½ " high.

Equipped with ladder and chemical reservoir.

Packed 2 dozen in case.

Price, Doz., List..**$11.50**

No. 96. Automobile.

12¾ inches long.
4¾ " wide.
7½ " high.

Miniature representation of latest style Automobile. Runs forward, backward or in a circle.

Packed 2 dozen in case.

Price, Doz., List..**$16.50**

No. 100. Battleship.

19 inches long.
4 " wide.
8¾ " high.

Made of Sheet Steel, and painted gray. Boat rocks while in motion to reproduce actual sailing.

Has 4 Guns and 2 Turrets.
Packed 2 dozen in case.

Price. Doz., List..**$16.50**

No. 4. Hook and Ladder.

19½ inches long.
3¼ " wide.
6¾ " high.

Equipped with 3 ladders, and may be used for scaling purposes. Automatic gong that rings while machine is in operation.

Packed 2 dozen in case.

Price. Doz., List..**$15.50**

No. 1. Locomotive.

21 inches long.
5½ " wide.
7⅞ " high.

Representation of large American Locomotive. Capable of pulling ten cars.

Automatic Bell.

Packed 2 dozen in case.

Price, Doz., List..**$16.50**

No. 2. Automobile.

10¼ inches long.
3¾ " wide.
7 " high.

Contains four Passengers.
Up-to-date equipment.

Packed 2 dozen in case.

Price, Doz., List..**$16.50**

No. 3. Fire Engine.

11½ inches long.
4 " wide.
8 " high.

Made of Sheet Steel. Automatic Gong that rings while engine is in motion.

Packed 2 dozen in case.

Price, Doz., List..**$16.50**

No. 310. Automobile.

17 inches long.
7 " wide.
11 " high.

Miniature reproduction of finest automobiles on the market. Carries six passengers.

Packed one-half dozen in case.

Price, Doz., List..**$72.00**

A second page from a 1908 toys catalog, showing D.P. Clark toys.

CLEVELAND TOY

Racer, aluminum, steel wheels, c. 1935, 13" long	C6	C8	C10
	175	262	350

Cleveland Toy Racer
Courtesy David W. Mapes Auctions

COHN

Cohn Fire Chief pull car, 1940s, metal	56	84	112
Cohn "Superior Sales Service" garage, tin	75	112	150

COMET-AUTHENTICAST

Comet-Authenticast, owned by the Slonim family, began toy-making (as Comet) about 1940 in Queens, New York. Though it began with only toy soldiers, it switched to making ID models for the government virtually as soon as the Second World War began. After the war it sold them as toys. It seems to have gone out of business in the early 1960s. Its vehicles appear to sell in the $8-$10 range, and probably more for something rare, like the Lee tank. In recent times, Quality Castings of Alexandria, Virginia has been reissuing these toys, using the original molds in a generally $4-$6 range.

1/108 Scale Metal Identification Models by Comet/Authenticast NY, NY. Russian Vehicles and Soldiers of World War II. L to R - Back Row: 5200 KV-1 Heavy Tank, 5201 KV-2 Heavy Tank, 5202 Josef Stalin, 5203 T34 Medium Tank.
Middle: Russian soldiers by Holger Erikson sold by Comet in sets R1 thru 8, the latter two containing tanks also. Standing figure offers scale for tanks at 20mm tall.
Front: 5204 T70 light tank, 5205 ST2 Armored Carrier, 5206 T34/85 medium tank, 5207 Josef Stalin III.
Photo by Ed Poole

1/108 Scale identification models of WWII Japanese tanks by Comet/Authenticast. Authenticast GI in photo is 23mm tall. L to R - Back Row: 5051 Amphibian Tankette, 5052 Tankette, 5053 Medium Tank.
Front Row: 5054 Medium Tank, 5055 Tankette, 5056 light tank, 5057 heavy medium tank.
Photo by Ed Poole

1/108 Scale identification models of WWII Germany vehicles by Comet/Authenticast. Also shown are Authenticast German soldiers up to 21mm tall. L to R - Back Row: 5100 PzKwIII, 5101 PzKwl, 5102 Panzerjager, 5103 PzKw IV G, 5104 PzKw IV F.
Middle: 5105 PzKw II, 5106 PzKw III, 5107 Tiger, 5108 8-Wheeled Armored Car.
Front: 5109 Pz35T, 5110 Panther, 5111 Sturmgeschutz, 5112 Half-Track.
Photo by Ed Poole

1/108 Scale identification models of WWII U.S. Vehicles Comet/Authenticast. Authenticast GI with Mine Detector is 20mm tall. L to R - Back Row: 5150 75mm Gun on Half Track, 5151 Heavy Tank M6, 5152 Sherman Tank, 5153 Greyhound Armored Car, 5154 Half-Track.
Middle: 5155 Hellcat, 5156 Priest, 5157 General Scott, 5158 General Stuart, 5159 Wolverine.
Front: 5160 Jeep, 5161 Weasel, 5162 Scout Car, 5163 Quack, 5164 King Kong
Photo by Ed Poole

1/108 U.S. ID Models by Comet/Authenticast. Soldiers were sculpted by Holger Eriksson; tallest 20mm. L to R - Back Row: 5165 General Pershing, 5166 General Chaffee, 5167 Slugger II, 5168 Slugger, 5169 76mm Sherman.
Front Row: 5170 Airborne Tank, 5171 Armored Car (Staghound), 5172 Armored Car (Twin 50), 5173 DUKW, 5174 M32 Tank Recovery.
Photo by Ed Poole

1/108 U.S. ID Models by Comet/Authenticast. Marching GIs are 20mm tall. Quality castings are shown in place of Authenticast 5177 and 5178. L to R - Back Row: 5175 LVTAA Amphibian Tank, 5176 LVT Amphibian, 5177 Utility Tank, 5178 Medium Tank 105mm.
Front: 5180 Walker Bulldog, 5179 General Patton, 5181 6X6 Truck, 5182 Command Car, 5183 Troop Carrier.
Photo by Ed Poole

1/108 Scale U.S. ID Models of the Cold War Era. Quality castings model is substituted for Authenticast 5189. Figures are 15mm tall. L to R - Back Row: 5184 Trailer, 5185 Weapons Carrier, 5186 M-47 Tank, 5187 M48 Tank, 5188 M103 Heavy Tank.
Front Row: 5189 Atomic Cannon
Photo by Ed Poole

Cold War U.S. 1/108 ID Models (cont'd). Standing figures 15mm tall. Quality castings models substituted for nos. 5193, 5195 and 5196. By now Comet was producing for collectors and so belatedly brought out 5192 M3 Medium Tank. L to R - Back Row: 5190 T98 S.P. 105mm Gun, 5191 S.P. 155mm Howitzer, 5192 M3 Tank, 5193 Hawk Missile - Transporter, Launcher and Mobile Radar with crew.
Front: 5194 Honest John Launcher and crew, 5195 Nike - Ajax Launcher and crew, 5196 M42 Duster Twin 40mm AA, 5197 Ontos S.P. Rocket Launcher.
Photo by Ed Poole

The 1/108 Series Continues: Quality Castings of Alexandria VA not only reproduces but upgrades the Authenticast line. Here are some of the original German pieces. L to R - Back Row: 4017 Wespe, 4018 7.5 PAK, 4023 Opel Blitz, 4026 88 Flak on bogie wheels and off.
Middle: 4027 2 CM FLAF on & off trailer, 4031 3.7 PAK, 4035 7.5 INF gun, 4036 Kubelwagen, 4037 BMW cycle with 4037A MB variant, 4041 Pz 38t.
Front: 4042 Wirblewing FLAK , 4044 Hetzer, 4045 Marder III, 4046 250/I Halftrack, 4049 Hummel, RFE Lost Silver DAK (added for scale 22mm tall).
Photo by Ed Poole

Quality Casting 1/108 German (continued). L to R - Back Row: 4051 5cm PAK, 4052 222 Armored Car, 4054 Brumbar, 4055 234/I Armored Car, 4058 Tiger II (Porsche Turret).
Front: 4061 7/2 Halftrack w/3.7 FLAK, 4062 2 cm QUAD FLAF and trailer, 4063 3.7 FLAK on trailer, 4064 88 PAK, 4065 105 Howitzer, 4066 Ferdinand, 4067 Elefant, 4068 250/7 Mortar Halftrack, over-size Authenticast (Erikson) GI 20mm tall for comparison. Quality makes many troops nearer to correct scale but squat and thick bodied.
Photo by Ed Poole

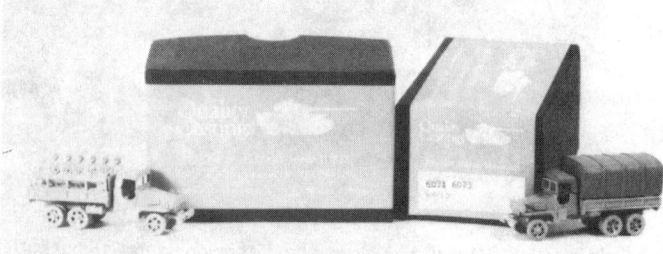

Quality Castings 1/108 Numbers 6033 (L) and 6031 (R) with boxes typically packed several kits each. These models replace old 6031 and 6033 which were Authenticast types 5181 and 5183 in the Quality line.
Photo by Ed Poole

Two Comet/Authenticast 1/108 Models and boxes. Comet address given as NY, NY and Authenticast as Richmond Hill, NY and both indicating "Design Copyrighted 1943". 5009 Cromwell on left. 5010 Churchill on right.
Photo by Ed Poole

CONVERSE

Beginning in 1878 Converse helped make Winchendon, Massachusetts "Toy Town U.S.A." It made wooden, tin and steel toys and was felled in 1934 by the Depression. It was originally owned by Morton E. Converse.

	C6	C8	C10
Converse Auto with fringe on top, 3-seat, 1905, painted, pressed steel, clockwork, rubber tires .	600	900	1200
Converse Fire Engine ladder truck, bell, wooden headlight, 10", 1915	1250	1875	2500
Converse Pick-Up Truck, very early, open cab	500	750	1000
Converse Touring Auto, open, four-seater	1100	1800	2600
Converse Touring Auto, 1910, pressed steel, canvas roof	1300	2200	3000
Converse Transitional Taxi, clockwork, 10½" long	525	770	1050

Converse Transitional Taxi, 10½" long
Courtesy Sotheby's NY

Conway Packard Convertible . . .	75	112	150

COR-COR

According to Margaret E. Holland (as reported by Ross Hermann in the July 27, 1992 *Antique News*), the granddaughter of Cor-Cor founder Louis A. Corcoran, this Washington, Indiana firm began on 21st Street in 1926, then expanded to East 3rd and Vantress, and after a fire, built its final plant on Front Street. At this latter location the company changed its name to Corcoran Metal Products. At its height, the firm employed up to 590 people (in 1939 Corcoran, for obvious reasons, was named his county's "most valuable citizen"). Corcoran retired in 1941 because of failing health, and died in 1945. His toys are marked "Cor-Cor" on the wheels.

	C6	C8	C10
Cor-Cor Airflow windup, electric lights, 18" long	900	1350	1800
Cor-Cor Army Truck	No Price Found		
Cor-Cor Bus, 23" long	300	500	700
Cor-Cor Chrysler Airflow	No Price Found		
Cor-Cor DeSoto Airflow	No Price Found		
Cor-Cor dump truck, dumps back or side to side, 23" long	200	300	400
Cor-Cor Fire Truck	No Price Found		
Cor-Cor Graham Paige sedan, 20" long, electric	1000	1550	2100
Cor-Cor Ice Truck	No Price Found		
Cor-Cor Semi Truck	No Price Found		
Cor-Cor Van, painted metal, c.1928, 23" long	250	380	525

CORGI

(Britain)

Corgi is the registered trademark of Playcraft Toys. Its vehicles first appeared in 1956. Since Corgis are generally sold mint in the box, those are the prices shown here.

	MIB
Corgi 10 Tank and Transporter	150
Corgi 34 David Brown 1412 Tractor & Trailer	80
Corgi 58 Beast Carrier	50
Corgi 61 Four Furrow Plow	15
Corgi 62 Farm Tipper Trailer	20
Corgi 64 Jeep FC150 Conveyor	145
Corgi 69 Massey Ferguson Tractor	95

	MIB
Corgi 73 Massey Ferguson tractor w/saw	110
Corgi 74 Ford Tractor with haybine scoop	125
Corgi 150 Vanwall	120
Corgi 152 BRM Formula 1	80
Corgi 152 Ferrari 312 B2 Formula 1	42
Corgi 153 Surtees T.S. 9b racer	50
Corgi 153 Bluebird	185
Corgi 154 Ferrari	45
Corgi 154 Lotus	85
Corgi 155 Shado racer	50
Corgi 156 Cooper Maserati	55
Corgi 156 Embassy Shadow racer	50
Corgi 158 Lotus Climax F 1	70
Corgi 158 Elf Tyrrell Ford F-1	45
Corgi 159 Patrick Eagle Indy Car	45
Corgi 160 Hesketh 308 Formula 1 Car	35
Corgi 161 Santa Pod Commuter Dragster	45
Corgi 162 Quartermaster Dragster	38
Corgi 164 Wild Honey Dragster	38
Corgi 166 Ford Mustang Organ Grinder Drag Funny	38
Corgi 167 U.S. racing buggy	20
Corgi 169 Arnold Sundquist's Jet Car	55
Corgi 200 Mini 1000	10
Corgi 202 Morris Cowley	110
Corgi 206 Hillman Husky	110
Corgi 210 Citroen D.S. 19	100
Corgi 211 Studebaker Golden Hawk	100
Corgi 215 Thunderbird	200
Corgi 217 Fiat 1800	75
Corgi 218 Aston Martin DB4	65
Corgi 220 Chevrolet Impala	100
Corgi 222 Renault FloRide	80
Corgi 224 Bentley Continental	90
Corgi 225 Austin Seven mini	80
Corgi 228 Volvo P1800	75
Corgi 229 Chevy Corvair	95
Corgi 232 Fiat 2100	75
Corgi 234 Ford Consul Classic	80
Corgi 235 Olds Super 88	75
Corgi 236 Motor School Car	125
Corgi 238 Jaguar Mark X	65
Corgi 239 VW Kharmann Ghia	70
Corgi 241 Ghia L6.4	55

	MIB		MIB
Corgi 245 Buick Riviera	80	Corgi 318 Lotus Elan	95
Corgi 247 Mercedes 600 Pullman	80	Corgi 319 GT Miura-Lamborghini	30
Corgi 248 Chevrolet Impala	92	Corgi 320 The Saint's Jaguar	95
Corgi 252 Rover 2000	72	Corgi 322 Rover 2000 Monte Carlo	150
Corgi 256 VW Safari	300	Corgi 323 Citroen DS19 Monte	
Corgi 258 The Saint's Volvo	150	Carlo	140
Corgi 259 Penguinmobile	52	Corgi 324 Ferrari Daytona	30
Corgi 260 007 Aston Martin	275	Corgi 325 Ford Mustang Fastback	88
Corgi 260 Metropolis Buick	60	Corgi 329 Mustang Mach	40
Corgi 260 Renault	35	Corgi 331 Ford Capri GT	40
Corgi 261 James Bond Aston		Corgi 332 Lancia Fulvia Sport	
Martin	275	Zagato	50
Corgi 262 Lincoln Continental	98	Corgi 334 Mini-Cooper Magnifique	70
Corgi 263 Rambler Marlin	85	Corgi 335 Jaguar E2X2	140
Corgi 263 Captain America		Corgi 336 007 Toyota 2000	375
Jetmobile	45	Corgi 337 Corvette Sting Ray	60
Corgi 264 Olds Toronado	65	Corgi 338 Chevy SS 350 Camaro	70
Corgi 266 Chitty Chitty Bang Bang	375	Corgi 339 Monte Carlo Mini	105
Corgi 267 Batmobile	280	Corgi 342 The Professionals Ford	
Corgi 269 James Bond Lotus Esprit	95	Capri	100
Corgi 272 James Bond Citroen 2CV	45	Corgi 342 Lamborghini	60
Corgi 273 Rolls Royce Silver		Corgi 343 Firebird	100
Shadow	90	Corgi 344 Ferrari 206 DinoSport	62
Corgi 274 Bentley Series T	90	Corgi 347 Chevy Astro	60
Corgi 276 Olds Toronado	70	Corgi 348 Vegas Thunderbird	85
Corgi 277 Monkeemobile	400	Corgi 358 Olds H.Q. Staff Car,	
Corgi 281 Rover 2000TC	60	Military	150
Corgi 281 Austin Metro Royal		Corgi 359 Army Field Kitchen	220
Wedding	25	Corgi 370 Ford Mustang	16
Corgi 283 DAF City Car	30	Corgi 372 Lancia Fulvia Sport	50
Corgi 284 Citroen sm	40	Corgi 373 VW 1200 Police Car	45
Corgi 285 Mercedes Benz 2400	20	Corgi 373 Peugeot 505	16
Corgi 285 Jaguar XJ12C	30	Corgi 378 Ferrari 308 GTS	15
Corgi 290 Kojak's Buick	80	Corgi 380 Alfa Romeo Pinin Farina	40
Corgi 291 AMC Pacer X	28	Corgi 381 GP Beach Buggy	50
Corgi 292 Starsky & Hutch Ford		Corgi 383 VW1200	50
Torino	90	Corgi 384 Renault 11 GTL	16
Corgi 293 Renault 5TS	15	Corgi 385 Mercedes 190E	22
Corgi 300 Chevrolet Stingray	100	Corgi 385 Porsche 917	35
Corgi 302 VW Polo	15	Corgi 386 Bertone Runabout	50
Corgi 303 Porsche 954	15	Corgi 392 Bertone "Shake" Buddy	45
Corgi 304 Mercedes Benz 300SL		Corgi 393 Mercedes Benz 350SL	55
Hardtop Roadster	100	Corgi 396 Datsun 240Z	50
Corgi 310 Corvette Sting Ray	75	Corgi 397 Can-Am Porsche 917	25
Corgi 311 Ford Capri 3 litre	50	Corgi 402 Ford Cortina Police Car	50
Corgi 312 Jaguar E. Competition	105	Corgi 405 Ford Transit Milk	20
Corgi 312 Marcos Mantis	40	Corgi 405 Chevrolet Ambulance	45
Corgi 314 Ferrari Berlinetta 250LM	90	Corgi 411 Lucozade Van	150
Corgi 315 Simca 1000 Competition	50	Corgi 413 Mazda Maintenance	
Corgi 316 N.S.U. Sport Prinz	75	Truck	50

	MIB
Corgi 414 Coast Guard Jaguar XJ	25
Corgi 418 Austin Taxi.........	85
Corgi 420 Ford Airborne Caravan	90
Corgi 421 Bedford "Evening Sandard"..................	200
Corgi 422 Riot Police Armored Car	25
Corgi 422 Corgi Toy Van	350
Corgi 425 Booking Office.......	420
Corgi 428 Mr. Softee Truck	300
Corgi 433 VW Delivery Van....	80
Corgi 435 Superman Van	48
Corgi 436 Spiderman Van......	45
Corgi 437 Cadillac Ambulance ..	92
Corgi 438 Land Rover	40
Corgi 445 Plymouth Sports Station Wagon	100
Corgi 448 Police Mini Van	75
Corgi 455 Karrier Bantam	165
Corgi 457 ERF Platform Lorry ..	100
Corgi 458 ERF Earth Dumper ..	90
Corgi 459 Raygo Rascal	40
Corgi 463 Commer Ambulance .	88
Corgi 468 Routemaster Bus, Outspan..................	50
Corgi 470 Forward Control Jeep	50
Corgi 471 Smith's Mobile Canteen "Joe's Diner"	165
Corgi 471 London Transport Silver Jubilee bus..................	30
Corgi 474 Walls Ice Cream (w/chimes)	220
Corgi 475 Safari	175
Corgi 477 Breakdown Truck....	65
Corgi 478 Hydraulic Tower Wagon	95
Corgi 482 Range Rover Ambulance	40
Corgi 490 VW Breakdown Van .	100
Corgi 491 Ford Estate Car......	70
Corgi 494 Bedford Tipper Truck	95
Corgi 497 Man From Uncle	275
Corgi 497 Ford Escort "Radio Rentals"	16
Corgi 500 Police Car...........	35
Corgi 501 Range Rover	9
Corgi 503 Giraffe Truck	125
Corgi 509 Porsche Targa Police Car	68
Corgi 511 Performing Poodles Truck....................	400
Corgi 524 Route Master Bus-Stevenson's	20

	MIB
Corgi 529 Route Master Bus-Graham Ward Calendar	20
Corgi 530 Route Master Bus-Yorkshire Post	20
Corgi 702 Breakdown Truck	20
Corgi 805 Hardy Boys Rolls Royce	250
Corgi 809 Dick Dastardly Car...	100
Corgi 811 J.B. Moon Buggy	195
Corgi 908 AMX Recovery Tank .	75
Corgi 1100 LowLoader	325
Corgi 1100 Mack Transcontinental	130
Corgi 1101 Warner & Swasey Hydraulic Crane.............	70
Corgi 1102 Crane Fruehauf Bottom Dumper	60
Corgi 1103 Chubb Pathfinder Crash Truck	95
Corgi 1105 Car Transporter.....	250
Corgi 1106 Decca Radar Van ...	250
Corgi 1106 Mack Container Truck "ACL"	75
Corgi 1107 Euclid Bulldozer	275
Corgi 1110 Mobile Gas Tanker..	300
Corgi 1110 JCB Crawler Loader .	85
Corgi 1111 MF Combine Harvester	325
Corgi 1123 Circus Cage Wagon .	135
Corgi 1126 Ecurie Ecosse Transporter	225
Corgi 1127 Simon Snorkel Fire Engine.....................	160
Corgi 1128 Priestman Cub Shovel	142
Corgi 1137 Ford Semi-Trailer Truck	212
Corgi 1138 Ford Car Transporter	185
Corgi 1142 Ford Holmes Wrecker	170
Corgi 1143 American LaFrance Fire Engine.....................	145
Corgi 1144 Berliet Wrecker Truck	50
Corgi 1145 Mercedes Unimog-Goose Dumper..............	50
Corgi 1146 Tri-Deck Car Transporter	185
Corgi 1147 Seammell Tractor & Trailer, "Ferrymasters"	125
Corgi 1150 Unimog Snow Plow.	50
Corgi 1152 Mack Tanker, "Esso"	75
Corgi 1154 Mack Crane Truck ..	150
Corgi 1159 Ford Car Transporter	75
Corgi 1160 Gulf Petrol Truck ...	85
Corgi 1163 Human Cannonball Truck........................	65

	MIB
Corgi 1192 Ford Van "Lucas" ..	15
Corgi 6547 Ford Tractor-Conveyor on Trailer	150
Corgi 9001 1927 Bentley	65
Corgi 9013 1915 Ford	70
Corgi 9031 1910 Renault	65

Courtland all-wood open high-side trailer. This may be a one-of-a-kind preproduction or designer's model as at present this is the only one known.
Courtesy Joe and Sharon Freed

COURTLAND MFG. CO.

WALT REACH

History based on information from Joe and Sharon Freed

Walter Reach, owner of Courtland, had a burning desire to be known as the second Louis Marx. Also functioning as designer, he began production in 1944 with two die-cut cardboard toys (a rabbit and cart and horse and cart). Reach turned to tin litho toys after the war, a number of them non-wind-ups. At its height, Courtland, located first in Camden, New Jersey, and later in Philadelphia, had 600 workers and in 1947 its sales exceeded 1.5 million. But success was short-lived, and the firm lasted just seven years.

Courtland Toys Listing by Joe and Sharon Freed

Courtland No. 610 Side Dump
Courtesy Joe and Sharon Freed

COURTLAND (WALT REACH) NON-POWERED VEHICLES

	C6	C8	C10
Courtland all-wood open high-side trailer. Prototype?	No Price Found		
600 Courtland Open Van tractor-trailer L-13", W-3" H-3¼" 1946 retail price 49¢	55	75	100
610 Courtland Side dump tractor-trailer, L-13", W-3", H-3¼", 1946 retail price 49¢	55	75	100
620 Courtland Log Truck tractor-trailer. L-13", W-3", H-3¼", 1946 retail price 59¢	65	85	125
700 Courtland Side dump tractor-trailer. L-13", W-3", H-3¼", 1946 retail price 49¢	55	75	100
900 Courtland Ice Cream Truck. L-9" W-3", H-2¾" 1946 retail price 39¢	75	100	150

620 Courtland (non-power)
Courtesy Joe and Sharon Freed

Courtland, L to R: 900 Fire Patrol Truck; 900 Moving and Storage Truck.
Courtesy Joe and Sharon Freed

	C6	C8	C10
900 Courtland Moving and Storage Truck. L-9", W-3", H-2¾", 1946 retail price 39¢	85	125	175
900 Courtland Fire Patrol No. 2 Truck, L-9", W-3", H-2¾", 1946 retail price 39¢	75	100	150
900 Courtland Express and Hauling Truck. L-9", W-3", H-2¾", 1946 retail price 39¢	75	100	150
1050 Courtland Logging Camp Train Set. L-26¾", W-3", H-3¼", 1946 retail price $1.79	No Price Found		
1060 Courtland Trailer Truck Parade. L-13", W-3", H-3¼", 1946 retail price $1.79	No Price Found		
1070 Courtland Big 4 Truck Parade. The four 900 L-9½", W-3¼", H-3", 1946 retail price $1.79 .	No Price Found		
1200 Courtland Side Dump tractor-trailer. L-13", W-3", H-3¼" .	75	100	150
Courtland tractor-trailer. Same tractor as No. 2000 except marked, "Loft-Fresh Candy" and no manufacturer markings. L-13", W-3", H-3¼". Punched to receive motor, but no motor ever installed. (Loft was a major purchaser of Courtland toys)	150	225	300

Courtland Tractor-Trailer, Same tractor as No. 2000 except marked "Loft-Fresh Candy".
Courtesy Joe and Sharon Freed

Courtland Non-Powered tractor-trailer marked "Loft - Fresh Candy".
Extremely Rare.
Courtesy Dutkins of Cherry Hill, NJ

COURTLAND (WALT REACH) FRICTION-POWERED VEHICLES

List by Joe and Sharon Freed

	C6	C8	C10
3875 Courtland Mechanical "Gulf" Gasoline tractor-trailer L-13", W-3", H-3¼"	150	200	250
4000 Courtland Woody Sedan, Red & Tan, L-7¼", W-3¼", H-2¾"	65	75	100
4000 Courtland Woody Sedan, Blue & Tan, L-7¼", W-3¼", H-2¾", Note: This is one of only four Courtland styled toys stamped "A Walt Reach Toy by Courtland Toy Co. Phila. Pa. Made in U.S.A." The only known Courtland-styled toys marked with the Courtland Toy Company, Philadelphia stamping is this No. 4000 sedan, a non-powered "Fire Chief" car, a private garage similar to No. 9075 and a mechanical parking meter bank	75	85	110
4000 Courtland "Fire Chief" Car, L-7¼", W-3¼", H-2¾"	75	125	150
As above, but sparking motor and red plastic bubble on hood ..	100	125	150
4050 Courtland FBI Riot Squad Car, similar to 7600 FBI Riot Squad Car, except for color ..	100	125	150
4060 Courtland Space Rocket Patrol Car. L-7¼", W-3¼", H-2¾", 1952 retail price 98¢ .	150	200	250

Courtland 3875 (Friction)
Courtesy Mapes Auctioneers

Courtland No. 4000 Woody Sedan
Courtesy Joe and Sharon Freed

Courtland No. 4000 "Fire Chief" car, first version.
Courtesy Joe and Sharon Freed

	C6	C8	C10
7500 Courtland Mechanical State Police Car with siren. L-7¼", W-3¼", H-2¾"	135	165	195
7500 Courtland Mechanical Fire Chief Car with siren. L-7¼", W-3¼", H-2¾"	135	165	195
XXXX Courtland Dump Truck w/dual rear wheels, L-10½", W-3", H-3⅜"	125	150	175
7600 Courtland FBI Riot Squad Car. L-7¼", W-3¼", H-2¾".	125	150	175
XXXX Courtland "Pop-Up" Ladder Fire Truck. L-13", W-3", H-3¼"	125	150	175
XXXX Courtland Mechanical Military Gun Car. L-7½", W-3¼", H-2½", painted gun shield	150	175	200
XXXX Variation of above, lithographed gunshield	150	175	200
Courtland Mechanical Gasoline Tractor-Trailer, similar to No. 2000 Gasoline Truck with Trailer. Marked "Gasoline-Motor Oils", Philadelphia, PA. L-13", W-3", H-3¼"	125	150	175

Courtland 4000 Fire Chief Car, red and white, with red plastic bubble on hood.
Courtesy Joe and Sharon Freed

Courtland "Pop-Up" Ladder Fire Truck
Courtesy Joe and Sharon Freed

Courtland Dump Truck with dual rear wheels
Courtesy Joe and Sharon Freed

Courtland Mechanical Military Gun Car, variation with litho gun shield
Courtesy Joe and Sharon Freed

COURTLAND VEHICLES WITH OPEN WIND-UP SPRING MOTORS

	C6	C8	C10
No. 1070 Mechanical Big 4 Truck Parade, 9'' long, 3'' wide, 2¾'' high, 1947 retail- $3.39.......	No Price Found		
No. 1200 Mechanical Trailer - Truck 13'' long, side dump, 3'' wide, 3¼'' high, 1947 retail - $1.00.....................	100	125	150
No. 1300 Mechanical Ice Cream Truck, 9'' long, 3'' wide, 2¾'' high, retail 79¢.............	125	150	175
No. 1300 Mechanical Moving and Storage Truck, 9'' long, 3'' wide, 2¾'' high, 1947 retail - 79¢	135	160	195
Same as above, with No. 130 lithographed on the sides of the truck bed..................	150	175	200
No. 1300 Mechanical Fire Patrol No. 2 Truck, 9'' long, 3'' wide, 2¾'' high, 1947 retail - 79¢ ..	135	160	175
No. 1300 Mechanical Express and Hauling Truck, 9'' long, 3'' wide, 2¾'' high, 1947 retail - 79¢	125	150	175
No. 1400 Mechanical ''Automatic Ladder'' Fire Truck, 9'' long, 3'' wide, 2¾'' high, 1947 retail - $1.00.....................	135	160	185
No. 1500 Mechanical Road Roller Truck, 9'' long, 3'' wide, 3¼'' high......................	150	200	250
No. 1600 Mechanical Dump Truck, 7'' long, 3'' wide, 2¾'' high .	45	60	85
No. 2000 Mechanical ''ESSO'' Gasoline tractor-trailer, 13'' long, 3'' wide, 3¼'' high....	150	225	300

Courtland 1600
Courtesy Joe and Sharon Freed

COURTLAND VEHICLES WITH ''Motor Guaranteed for Life''

	C6	C8	C10
No. 2000 Mechanical Gasoline tractor-trailer, 13'' long, 3'' wide, 3¼'' high............	125	150	175
No. 2050 Mechanical Milk tractor-trailer, 13'' long, 3'' wide, 3¼'' high, ''American Dairies''....	135	160	185

NOTE: *1951 catalog shows Milk trailer markings that read the same as above except 'Approved' is used in place of the words 'Vitamin D'. This variation is not known to have been produced.*

Courtland Motor Guaranteed for Life No. 2000 Mechanical Gasoline Tractor-Trailer (packed in individual boxes all with motor guarantee certificate).
Courtesy Joe and Sharon Freed

Courtland Motor guaranteed for life No. 2050 Mechanical Milk tractor-trailer.
Courtesy Joe and Sharon Freed

	C6	C8	C10
No. 2100 Mechanical Hook and Ladder tractor-trailer, 13'' long, 3'' wide, 3¼'' high	100	125	150
No. 2150 Mechanical Emergency Rescue Squad tractor-trailer, 13'', 3'' wide, 3¼'' high.....	100	125	150
No. 2200 Mechanical Logging tractor-trailer, 13'' long, 3'' wide, 3¼'' high............	100	125	150

Courtland Motor guaranteed for life No. 2100 Mechanical Hook &
Ladder tractor-trailer.
Courtesy Joe and Sharon Freed

Courtland Motor guaranteed for life No. 2150 Mechanical Emergency
Rescue Squad.
Courtesy Joe and Sharon Freed

Courtland 2300 Mechanical Open Van tractor-trailer
Courtesy Joe and Sharon Freed

	C6	C8	C10
No. 2300 Mechanical Open Van tractor-trailer, 13'' long, 3'' wide, 3¼'' high	100	125	150
No. 2350 Mechanical Open Van tractor-trailer, 13'' long, 3'' wide, 3¼'' high	110	135	160

	C6	C8	C10
No. 2375 Mechanical Heavy Duty Sand and Gravel tractor-trailer, 13'' long, 3'' wide, 3¼'' high	100	125	150
No. 2400 Mechanical Trailer Tow Truck, 13'' long, 3'' wide, 3¼'' high	100	125	150
No. 2600 Mechanical Freight Haulers tractor-trailer, 13'' long, 3'' high, 3¼'' wide	100	125	150
No. 2700 Mechanical Side Tipper tractor-trailer, 13'' long, 3'' high, 3¼'' wide	100	125	150

Courtland Motor guaranteed for life No. 2200 Mechanical Logging
tractor-trailer.
Courtesy Joe and Sharon Freed

Courtland 2375
Courtesy Joe and Sharon Freed

No. 2800 Assortment consists of 2
No. 2000 Gasoline Trucks, 2 No.
2050 Milk Trucks, 2 No. 2200
Log Trucks, 2 No. 2350 Open
Van Trucks, 2 No. 2600 Freight
Hauler Trucks and 2 No. 2700
Side Tipper Trucks - Wholesale
Assortment Only . . . . No Price Found

Courtland No. 3000 Mechanical Road Roller Truck
Courtesy Joe and Sharon Freed

	C6	C8	C10
No. 3000 Mechanical Road Roller Truck, 9″ long, 3″ wide, 3¼″ high	200	250	300
No. 3100 Mechanical Dump Truck, 7″ long, 3″ wide 3¼″ high .	100	125	150

Courtland, Top to Bottom: 3100 Mechanical Dump Truck; 1600 Dump Truck
Courtesy Joe and Sharon Freed

Courtland 3900
Courtesy Joe and Sharon Freed

	C6	C8	C10
No. 3200 Mechanical Stake Bed Truck, 7″ long, 3″ wide, 3¼″ high	100	125	150
No. 3800 Assortment consists of 6 No. 3200 Stake Bed Trucks and 6 No. 3100 Dump trucks. Wholesale Assortment Only	No Price Found		
3900 Courtland Mechanical Side Tipper Tractor-trailer, "Black Diamond Coal Company - 340", L-13″, H-3″, W-3¼″	100	150	175
No. 4000 City Meat Market Delivery Sedan, 7¼″ long, 3¼″ wide, 2¾″ high	75	125	150
No. 4000 Modern Bakery Delivery Sedan, 7¼″ long, 3¼″ wide, 2¾″ high	75	125	150
No. 4000 Fire Chief Car, 7¼″ long, 3¼″ wide, 2¾″ high, red & white	75	100	125
Same as above, all red	100	125	150
No. 4000 Checker Cab Car, 7¼″ long, 3¼″ wide, 2¾″ high, green and yellow	125	150	175
Same as above, green and white	135	160	185
No. 4500 Express Service Pick-up, 7¼″ long, 3¼″ wide, 2¾″ high	75	100	125
No. 4500 Country Produce Pick-up, 7¼″ long, 3¼″ wide, 2¾″ high	75	100	125
No. 4500 Modern Decorators Pick-up, 7¼″ long, 3¼″ wide, 2¾″ high	75	100	125
No. 5000 Mechanical Operating No. 51 Crane Truck 13″ long, 3⅝″ wide, 5″ high	135	165	200
No. 5100 Mechanical "Black Diamond" Coal Truck, 10½″ long, 3″ wide, 3⅜″ high	100	135	170
No. 5200 Mechanical No. 51 Steam Shovel, 15½″ long, 3¾″ wide, 9½″ high	76	100	125
No. 5300 Mechanical Combination Steam Shovel carried by low-boy tractor-trailer, 15½″ long, 3⅞″ wide, 10½″ high	150	200	250
No. 5800 Assortment consists of 3 No. 2300 Aluminum Open Van Trucks, 3 No. 2150 Emergency	(continued)		

115

Courtland No. 4000 City Meat Market Delivery Sedan
Courtesy Joe and Sharon Freed

Courtland 4000 "Modern Bakery"
Courtesy Continental Hobby House

Courtland No. 4000 Checker Cab Car
Courtesy Joe and Sharon Freed

Courtland "Motor Guaranteed for life" No. 5100 "Black Diamond" Coal Truck.
Courtesy Joe and Sharon Freed

	C6	C8	C10
Rescue Squad Trucks, 3 No. 2375 Sand and Gravel Trucks and 3 No. 2400 Towing Service Trucks - Wholesale Assortment Only	No Price Found		
No. 6000 Mechanical Farm Tractor w/scraper, rear tires are large rubber and front are small rubber tires 8¾'' long, 4¾'' wide, 4½'' high.................	85	115	145
No. 6050 Mechanical Farm Tractor w/o scraper. Rear tires are large rubber and front are small rubber tires, 7½'' long, 4¾'' wide, 4½'' high.................	75	100	125
No. 6075 Mechanical Farm Tractor w/o scraper, rear tires are large tin litho while the front are small rubber tires, 7½'' long, 4¾'' wide, 4½'' high........	150	200	250
No. 6100 Mechanical Caterpillar Tractor with rubber treads, 6'' long, 3'' wide, 4½'' high....	150	200	250

(continued)

Courtland 5300
Courtesy Joe and Sharon Freed

Courtland 6050
Courtesy Continental Hobby House

	C6	C8	C10
No. 6500 Mechanical Ice Cream Scooter, 6½″ long, 3″ wide, 4½″ high	175	250	325
No. 7000 Mechanical Fire Chief Car with siren, 7¼″ long, 3¼″ wide, 2¾″ high	125	175	225
No. 7500 Mechanical State Police Car with siren, 7¼″ long, 3¼″ wide, 2¾″ high	125	175	225

No. 7500 Mechanical Parking Meter and Bank, Base 6″ x 6″, 24½″ high. **NOTE:** *This is one of only four Courtland toys stamped "A Walt Reach Toy by Courtland Toy Co., Phila., Pa. Made in U.S.A." The only known Courtland styled toys marked with the Courtland Toy Company, Philadelphia stamping is this mechanical parking meter bank, a No. 4000 sedan, a non-power "Fire Chief" car, a private and a garage similar to No. 9075* . . . . . 75 . . 100 . . 125

	C6	C8	C10
No. 8500 Mechanical Chromed Trimmed Tow Truck, 8″ long, 3¼″ wide, 3½″ high, tow boom shows detail	125	175	225
No. 8500 Mechanical Chromed Trimmed Tow Truck, 8″ long, 3¼″ wide, 3½″ high, tow boom is solid color	125	175	225

End Courtland Windups

Courtland No. 8500.
Courtesy Joe and Sharon Freed

	C6	C8	C10

9050 Fire Department with automatic garage door. 7¾″ x 10⅛″ x 6¾″, found to have a non-powered fire chief car with the Courtland Toy Co., Phila. Pa., markings, it is quite possible that some of the 9050 garages were also manufactured in Philadelphia . . . 45 . . 55 . . 75

9075 Private Garage with automatic door, 7¾″ x 10⅛″ x 6¾″. Since the non-powered car which accompanies this garage is found with Courtland Toy Co., Phila. Pa. markings, it is quite possible that some of the 9075 garages were also manufactured in Philadelphia . . . 50 . . 75 . . 100

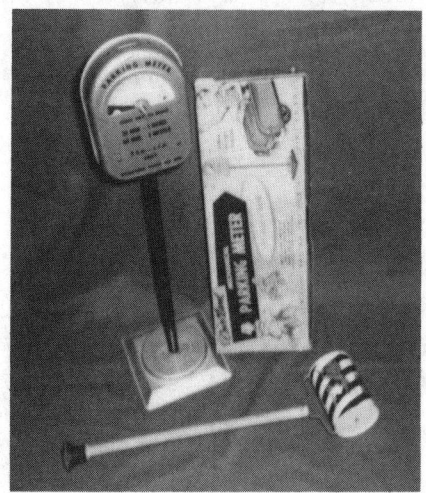

Courtland No. 7500.
Courtesy Joe and Sharon Freed

Courtland 9050.
Courtesy Joe and Sharon Freed

Courtland 9075 Private Garage.
Courtesy Joe and Sharon Freed

COX

(See also Thimbledrome)

	C6	C8	C10
Cox Ford GT-40 with gas motor	112	168	225
Cox Gas Dune Buggy	35	52	70

CRAFTOYS

by Fred Maxwell and Ron Eccles

Craftoy, a small Omaha, Nebraska firm, had a brief career casting slushmold vehicles before the War's need for lead brought the potmetal era to a long halt. We have discovered little more about the company other than it acquired some of the assets when Ralstoy was reorganizing about 1940.

For those readers accustomed to identifying by "those numbers", note: #92 sedan has the same number as a Best Toy coupe but they are not the same car. #100 racer is obviously not the same as Best #100 sedan. Older molds were also used for #78 mixer, #81 racer and #102 gasoline semitanker. #101 fire truck, #103 Speed car, #104

oil truck and #105 station wagon possibly come from Ralstoy. The ancestry of Kansas toy is evident in #17 tractor and the freight train set. The designs of the RR coal car, stock car and tank car are recent or new. Thus we come to the end of the line as "those toys with the numbers" roll into history. These catalog numbers may or may not be found on the toys.

Black rubber wheels are seen to be characteristic of this line, but they are not exclusive with Craftoy.

	C6	C8	C10
Craftoy Tractor, "17", 2½". "Fordson", "Made in USA" farm tractor, driver, rear wheels larger, visible engine	8	12	16
Craftoy Freight Train, "3600", 16½". Locomotive, 0-6-4, 4½", "KT&N RR"; cars 3¼"; caboose 2¾". "Made in USA". Value of indiv. cars	6	9	12
Craftoy Cement Mixer, "78", 3¾". 2 open windows, "Made in USA"	8	12	16
Craftoy Racer, "81", 4½". Miller FWD Indy racer, "Made in USA"	10	15	20
Craftoy Sedan, #92, 4". Streamlined 2 door sedan, 4 open windows, screen pattern grille	No Price Found		
Craftoy Racer #100, 4¼". Indy type, driver, removable tin hood, rounded nose	No Price Found		
Craftoy? Racer, no #, 3¾". Indy type, driver, removable tin hood, slanted nose	No Price Found		
Craftoy Fire Truck, #101, 4½". Hose truck or insurance patrol, 4 open windows	No Price Found		
Craftoy Tanker, "102", 6¾". 1938 International K-line ?, "gasoline" semi-trailer, 2 open windows	No Price Found		
Craftoy Speed Car, #103, 4¼" Streamlined closed racer, body trimmed in fantasy streamlines	No Price Found		
Craftoy Oil Truck, #104, 3¾". 1938 International ?, COE, "gas", "oil" tanker, 2 open windows	No Price Found		

(continued)

Craftoy Station Wagon, #105, 3¾''
Streamlined, 4 open windows No Price Found

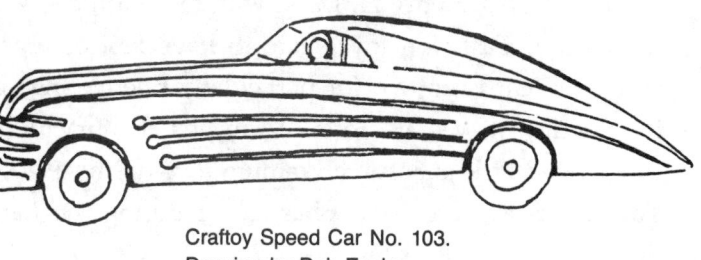

Craftoy Speed Car No. 103.
Drawing by Deb Eccles

End Craftoy

DAISY

	C6	C8	C10
Daisy ''Tank-Daisymatic No. 64 Rapid Fire Tank, 1960s, battery-operated, 8'' long, four actions	110	165	220
Daisy ''Tank-Daisymatic No. 80'', 1965, battery-operated, 8½'' long, five actions, with darts .	100	150	200

DAYTIME TOYS

	C6	C8	C10
Tractor Trailer	200	300	400

DAY TIME TOYS

	C6	C8	C10
Semi-Stake Truck, 18'' long, cast aluminum, c.1940s	300	425	600

Day Time Lines Semi-Stake Truck, 18'' long, cast aluminum, c.1940s.
Photo by Bob Smith

DAYTON FRICTION TOY WORKS

Dayton, Ohio (1909-1935)
See David P. Clark history

	C6	C8	C10
Dayton Armored Car, Flywheel drive, sheet metal const., red/gold, 11'' L, c.1909	250	375	500
Dayton Coal and Ice Truck, tin friction c.1920	200	300	400
Dayton Coupe, 12'', 1928, pressed steel	125	188	250
Dayton Coupe, 12½'' long, c.1920	600	900	1200
Dayton Coupe, friction, 17'' long, tin	No Price Found		
Dayton ''Dayton Friction, pressed steel, rubber tires, 1920s, 14½'' long	250	375	500
Dayton Delivery Van, friction . . .	250	375	500
Dayton Dump Truck	375	563	750
Dayton Fire Ladder Truck, 18'' long	185	278	370
Dayton Fire Ladder Truck, 22'' long, friction	225	338	450
Dayton Fire Pumper Truck, flywheel drive, sheet metal const., white/gold, 14¾'' long, c.1909	450	600	800
Dayton Seven-Passenger Touring Car. Flywheel drive, sheet metal const., red/gold, 13.25''L, patent date April 2, 1909.	450	600	800
Dayton touring car, 13½'' long, unpowered	350	525	700

Dayton Coupe, friction, 17'' long, tin.
Photo by Terry Sells

Dayton Fire Pumper Truck, 14¾" long, c.1909.
Photo by Bob Smith

Dayton Seven-Passenger Touring Car, 13¼" long, c.1909.
Photo by Bob Smith

DELUXE

(Richmond Hill, Queens, NY)

	C6	C8	C10
DeLuxe "DeLuxe Service Station", 1940s	40	75	100

DeLuxe "DeLuxe Service Station" with box.
Photo by Ron Fink

DENT HARDWARE COMPANY

Dent, of Fullerton, Pennsylvania, was in business from 1895-1973. Henry H. Dent, with four partners, was the owner. Cast iron toys seem to have first emerged in 1898. Dent is known for particularly fine castings in its vehicles. It was also one of the first manufacturers to try (with little success) aluminum toys (in the 1920s). Toys seem to have been phased out during the hard times of the Depression.

Dent marked few, if any, of its toys.

	C6	C8	C10
Dent "American Oil Co.", cast iron truck, approx. 10½" long	800	1200	1600
Dent "American Oil" truck, 15" long	1200	1900	2700
Dent Bus, cast iron, 6¼" long .	375	563	750
Dent "Bus Line"	400	650	900
Dent Coast to Coast Bus, 7½" long	125	187	250
Dent "Coast to Coast" bus, c.1925, 15" long	750	1000	1500
Dent convertible	400	700	1000
Dent Coupe, 5" long	125	188	250
Dent Dump Truck	250	400	600
Dent "Express J & B" stakebed truck, 14½", 1915, driver	500	800	1100
Dent Fire Pumper, 11" long, early, tiny driver	700	1200	1600
Dent Fire Pumper, 11" long, normal-sized driver, hose	500	850	1200
Dent fire truck, cast iron, 7" long	150	225	300
Dent fire ladder truck, 8½" long, with driver	450	675	900
Dent fire truck with ladder and men, cast iron, 18" long	900	1350	1800
Dent Fordson Tractor	250	375	500
Dent hose reeler with men, cast iron, large	500	750	1000
Dent "Interurban" bus, cast iron, 9" long	250	375	500
Dent "Junior Supply Co. New York Philadelphia", c.1923, 16" long	3000	5000	10,000
Dent La Salle, approx. 4" long .	200	300	400

Dent "American Oil Co." 10½" long.
Courtesy Phillips NY

Dent "Junior Supply Co. New York Philadelphia".
Courtesy Sotheby's NY

Dent "Police Patrol", approx. 8¾" long.
Courtesy Phillips NY

Dent "Public Service" Bus, 13½".
Courtesy Sotheby's NY

Dent La Salle Panel Truck	450	700	950
Dent Ladder truck, 10" long, two drivers.....................	250	375	500
Dent Mack Cement Truck, extremely rare, auctioned in 1992 in Good-Very Good condition for	47,300		
Dent Mack Dump Truck, 4½" c.1925, iron wheels	55	82	110
Dent Mack Express State Truck, auctioned in 1992 for	4400		
Dent Mack Express Van, auctioned in 1992 for	9900		
Dent Mack Tank Truck, auctioned in 1992 for	3960		
Dent Model T two door sedan, iron wheels, c.1925	125	187	250
Dent "Patrol", 6½" long, c.1920s	125	187	250
Dent "Pioneer" Fire Ladder Truck, driver	1200	2000	3000
Dent "Police Patrol", 8¾" long	750	1125	1500
Dent "Public Service" Bus, c.1926, 13½" long	1800	3000	4500
Dent Road Sweeper, auctioned in 1992 for	4400		
Dent Runabout, 6" long, driver, tiller	212	368	425
Dent Sedan, 7½" long, spare tire, has stop and go light, full bumpers on front	900	1350	1800
Dent Steam Roller, cast iron, 6" long......................	45	68	90
Dent Touring Car	500	7500	1000
Dent Yellow Cab, approx. 7¾" long......................	850	1275	1700

DINKY

Dinky toys were first made in England in 1932 under the name "Modeled Miniatures", later "Meccano Miniatures", and in 1934, "Dinky", which in England means "fetching".

CIVILIAN DINKY

Prices are for Mint in the Box, since that is how most Dinky civilian vehicles are sold.

	MIB
14c Coventry Fork Lift	150
22A Maserati Sport 2000	125
23G Cooper Bristol Racing Car	150
23H Ferrari Racer	100
23J H.W.M. Racer	150
24B Peugeot	75
24C Citroen DS19	75
24H Mercedes 190SL	150
24U Simca 9 Arnode	135
24X Ford Vedelle	80
24Y Studebaker	125
25 Ford Zodiac Police Car	85
25V Bedford Refuse Truck	60
27 Motorcart	150
27F 1948 Plymouth Station Wagon	200
30A Chrysler Airflow	250
30E Breakdown Lorry	No Price Found
33 Simca Glass Truck	150
33 AN Simca Bailly	150
34B Royal Mail	90
36A Log Lorry	190
36F British Salmson	120
36F Taxi	120
39A Unic Auto Transporter	210
42A Police Box	90
60Y Fuel Tender	400
61 Ford Prefect	No Price Found
62 Singer Roadster	125
64 Austin Lorry	75
66 Bedford Flat Truck	75
71 Dublo Volks Van	120
101 Sunbeam Alpine Sports Car	120
103 Austin-Healey 100 Sports Car	250
103 Spectrum Patrol	135
104 Spectrum Pursuit Vehicle	185
105 Triumph TR2	175
106 Austin Atlantic Convertible	90

	MIB
106 Thunderbird 2	185
106 "The Prisoner" mini moke	250
107 Sunbeam Alpine	150
110 Aston Martin	95
111 Triumph TR2 Competition	160
112 Purdy's TR7	55
113 MGB	95
122 Volvo 265	30
123 Princess 2200 HL Saloon	50
124 Rolls Royce Phantom V	50
127 Rolls Royce Phantom V	50
128 Mercedes Benz 600	50
129 VW Bug	95
130 Ford Consul Corsair	95
131 Cadillac	110
131 Jaguar Type E 2+2	100
131 Jaguar Type G	100
132 Ford 40-RV	70
132 Packard Convertible	225
138 Hillman Imp	50
139A 1949 Ford Sedan	60
140 Morris 1100	95
141 Vauxhall Victor	75
142 Jaguar	75
143 Ford Capri	120
146 Daimler 2½ litre V8	100
148 Ford Fairlane	95
150 Rolls Royce Silver Wraith	85
152 Rolls Royce Phantom V Limousine	85
156 Rover 75	125
156 Saab 96	135
157 Jaguar XK120	225
157 BMW 2000 Tilux	90
158 Rolls Royce Silver Shadow	80
161 Mustang Fastback	60
162 Ford Zephyr Saloon	140
162 Triumph 1130	90
163 Bristol 450 Sports Coupe	135
163 Volkswagon 1600 TL Fastback	75
164 Ford Zodiac	70
164 Vauxhall Crest Saloon	135
166 Sunbeam Rapier	130
168 Singer Gazelle	130
169 Ford Corsair 200E	65
169 Studebaker Golden Hawk	155
170 Lincoln Continental	95
171 Hudson Sedan	140

	MIB
172 Studebaker	220
173 Nash Rambler	55
173 Pontiac Parisenne	80
174 Ford Mercury Cougar	80
174 Hudson Hornet	165

Dinky, L to R: 174 Hudson Hornet Sedan, 172 Studebaker Land Cruiser.
Courtesy Phillips NY

Dinky, L to R: 157 Jaguar KX120 Coupe, 344 Estate Car.
Courtesy Phillips NY

176 Austin A105 Saloon, first Dinky with windows	140
176 N SU R 80	140
178 Mini Clubman	40
178 Plymouth Plaza	200
180 Packard Clipper Sedan	185
180 Rover 3H	40
182 Porsche 356A Coupe, deep pink	300
185 Alfa Romeo Coupe	120
186 Mercedes Benz	95
187 DeTomaso Mangusta	50
187 VW Karmann Ghia	125
188 Jensen FF	75
189 Lamborghini Marzal	50
189 Triumph Herald	85
190 Monteverdi 375L	75
190 Caravan	55
191 Dodge Royal Sedan	140
192 Desoto Fireflite Sedan	175
192 Range Rover	30
195 Fire Chief's Car	35
196 Holden Special	90
198 Rolls Royce Phantom V	125
199 Austin Countryman	110

	MIB
201 Plymouth Rally '76	40
202 Fiat Abarth 2000	50
208 VW Porsche 914	50
210 Alfa Romeo 33 LeMans	70
212 Ford Cortina Rally	85
217 Alfa Scarabo	40
220 Ferrari P5	60
222 Hesketh 308F	55
223 McLaren M8A CanAm	45
225 Lotus FI Racing Car	40
226 Ferrari 312	40
230 Talbot-Lago race car	135
232 Alfa Romeo race car	125
233 Cooper Bristol race car	135
236 Connaught racer	135
237 Mercedes racer	100
238 Jaguar racer	150
240 Cooper racer	60
242 Ferrari racer	60
242 Simca Versalles	90
243 BRM racer	60
250 Police Mini Cooper S	100
250 Streamlined Fire Engine	145
251 Pontiac Police Car	100
252 Pontiac RCMP Police Car	75
254 Austin Taxi	145
255 Zodiac Police Car	70
257 Canadian Fire Chief's Car	110
258 Desoto Police Car	125
260 Royal Mail Van	170
261 Telephone Service Truck	200
263 Airport Fire Rescue Tender	80
264 Ford Fairlane Police Car	125
266 ERF Fire Tender	80
267 Bedford Dump	75
268 Renault Dauphine mini car	150
268 Range Rover Ambulance	30
269 Jaguar Police Car	175
270 Ford Panda Police Car	55
271 Bedford Royal Van	40
271 Ford Fire Appliance	50
275 Brinks Truck	90
277 Superior Ambulance	95
278 Plymouth Yellow Cab	35
279 Diesel Road Roller	85
279 Plymouth Taxi	28
280 Observation Coach	150
282 Land Rover Fire Appliance	40

DINKY (MECCANO) MILITARY TOYS

1937-1980
by William W. Kilborn

GENERAL HISTORY:

When Dinky Toys were first issued in 1933, they were intended to add a touch of realism to the 'Hornby' train models. The first offering to the public was a set of six small accessories referred to as "MODEL MINIATURES" and were commonly known as the "22 SERIES". In the original 22 SERIES group of six die-cast vehicles one product is of particular interest to us who are military model collectors, this being NO. 22F which resembled an army tank of the era. It had two cast components, one large casting for the main body and side skirts and a smaller one for the turret, which actually rotated. A fair amount of attention was paid to the louvres and rivets on both castings. The tank was propelled by two large wheels on the outside and three smaller ones on the inside fitted to each side of the larger casting which in turn carried the rubber treads. The treads were originally manufactured in red rubber and later in green. The metal casting was originally green with an orange turret, which makes the tank non-believable in military terms, but later versions were painted drab grey with green treads which were sold as individual items. The original tank was available in

the boxed sets only and marked "Hornby Series Model Miniatures No. 22". In the later thirties the base was altered and stamped to read "Dinky Toy".

The reason I have taken the time to describe this piece under the company's history is that I personally feel that the tank was intended as part of a 'market feeler' to see where interest lay in future production of military toys, and from the records I have read, the tank led in production quantities and demand over the other five items produced in this original set.

The year 1937 saw the introduction of what developed into the finest range of mass market die-cast military toys ever produced until the birth of SOLIDO. The year 1938 saw further consolidation of the vehicle range which by then contained almost three varieties. During World War II the Dinky operations were interrupted by the war effort. One of the few new or adapted models during this period was a replica of a petrol tanker painted grey with the word 'POOL' in white on its sides. The unfortunate part of this period in the company's history was that many of the toy dies were lost during the equipment shuffling to make room for the wartime production. Christmas 1945 saw production get under way again and some 50 different toy models went out to the retailers for sale to the public. The hopes for a quick return to the pre-war status quo were, however, not to be fulfilled, as metal alloys were put to priority use for much-needed domestic products, and to feed the giant export projects on which the British economy now depended for its survival.

However, by 1952 the post-war boom was gathering momentum as railway accessories and model planes were re-introduced. New products flowed from the design studios to the production lines until finally in 1954 the production of the first new group of army vehicles arrived on the scene. Also one of the most significant events of that year for future collectors was the 'renumbering of all models'. The suffix system was no longer manageable, and a block number system was allocated to types of vehicles. The larger-scale 'Super Dinky Toys' in blue striped boxes with a white background were also introduced in the mid-fifties. It was 1958 before Dinky replied to the challenge of domestic competition from "CORGI", who entered the market in 1956, by fitting special features to their models. Pausing for a breath from the introduction of gimmicks to keep abreast of their competition, in 1961 the company produced 20 or so new models and changed over

rom plain to tread tires on all their vehicles (although
nilitary models had them since the mid 50s).

In June 1969 the company again made a significant
change in its vehicle products to attempt to stay with
the competition - this was the introduction of speed
wheels which were eventually to become standard on
everything. Six years earlier, after the take over by LINES
BROS., the name of the firm was changed to
"MECCANO-TRIANG LTD." A bad omen, for in 1971,
after a general recession in the toy trade, the company's
bank loans were recalled and the whole of the "LINES
GROUP" went into liquidation. The MECCANO assets
were transferred to a new company, "MAOFORD LTD."
which was subsequently named "MECCANO (1971)
LTD." New toys were desperately needed, and in 1972
the company went into the "KIT" business for the first
time in its career, reflecting "Airfix's" expertise, who
had put a lot of thought into designs to make castings
lighter and finer through the judicious use of plastic,
which made the production and assembly easier and
cheaper.

But by now, the hand of doom was resting on production and even the introduction of space toys would
not delay the inevitable, as the Binns Road factory was
effectively closed on November 30th, 1979. The closure
did not save the parent company, which was also having difficulty in the American market, and AIRFIX eventually had to call in the Receiver.

Although DINKY TOY continued to be produced
elsewhere for several years, the eventual low labour cost
and success of mass plastic extrusion manufacturing from
the Asian export market was the real culprit behind the
demise of one of the English-speaking world's finest toy
manufacturers, who in its heyday produced approximately 3000 varieties of transportation toys during a
marvellous history of almost 50 years in England, France
and India.

ESTABLISHING A VALUE:

Dollar values in today's world are always changing,
therefore I have always found it more beneficial to deal
in 'FORMULAS' when trying to establish fees or prices.
Thanks to Jack Wilson of "COLLECTORS PRESS", Brad-
ford, England I can now put forth our combined efforts
into my own hypothesis as follows:

Step #1 Mint Prices:

Mint boxed condition

A. Over 45 years old - original price x 75 = m/b

William W. Kilborn

NAME: William Kilborn
AGE: 57
OCCUPATION: Professor of Interior Design, Ryerson Poltechnical Institute, Toronto, Ontario, Canada
PUBLICATIONS: Contributing Editor *Toy Soldier Review* North Bergen, NJ; 10 years/Quarterly *Bill the Band Man*, Articles; Text Book - *Business Skills for Designers* 1990, Ryerson Press, Toronto, Ontario
COLLECTING: Marx Trains 20 Years, Member TCA 11 years; Toy Soldier Bands - 1975 to present; Military Dinky Toys - 1973 to present

The collection in the photographs is 'complete' with three exceptions and is over 85% mint in the box including the pre-war mechanized set #156. I have corresponded with collectors in the UK, France, Italy and Germany while attending toy shows in both Canada and the United States to acquire this collection. Other military collections include:

Solido - 'D' Day collection & complete 1992 military edition.

Barnes and Buller/English - 1985 production pieces

B & B Military/English - 1991 to present

B. Over 25 years old - original price x 40 = m/b
C. Over 15 years old - original price x 20 = m/b
D. Under 14 years old - original price x 5% per annum (not compounded)

The exceptions to the above formulas depend on - 1) amount of production and 2) the number of years in production; for example if an article was only made for one year, but had a production run of 90,000 units; the price applied to the above might only double. Therefore, the rarer the piece, the higher the price applied to the above formulas. Now we have established Mint Boxed value but only if you know the last original price while in production. Otherwise you will have to accept the selling price of dealers and collectors.

Step #2 Establishing Condition Price:

Taking a mint boxed model with an estimated value of $20.00 American the different values according to condition in military collecting are:

1. EXCELLENT (BOXED)—Shows some sign of play and moisture rust 20% off mint boxed price = $16.00

2. NEAR MINT (NO BOX) or EXCELLENT (BOXED)—Some rust, no scratches, all decals in place. 30% off mint boxed price = $14.00.

3. VERY GOOD (BOXED)—Some rust, scratched, all decals, no paint missing 45% of mint boxed prices = $11.00

4. VERY GOOD (NO BOX)—Some rust, scratches, no missing parts or paint 55% off mint boxed prices = $9.00

5. GOOD (NO BOX)—Rust, paint chipped, decals partially missing, no missing parts 60% off mint boxed = $8.00

6. FAIR (NO BOX)—Rusted wheels axle and base, scratches, and chipped, missing paint, decals gone, missing tires or chains but not broken, paint still good for the purpose of reconditioning (50% there). Negotiated price only below 60% of the original value.

Please note that all deductions are taken from the original mint box price and that my FORMULA does not deal with broken or missing components or with pieces having less than 40% of the original paint finish gone; such pieces have no real value to the collector unless reconditioned and then they should only bring 50% of excellent, not mint boxed! In addition it should also be noted that boxes can bring $3.00 to $50.00 depending on age and condition for which I have not worked out a formula as of this writing (perhaps someone else has).

Prices shown above are mainly based on my purchased price between 1979 and 1989 when I stopped collecting Dinky and went into other military lines; plus updates from the English monthly newspaper *Toy Collectors Gazette* circa 1992.

See chart next page

22S Searchlight Lorry.
W. Kilborn Collection

Meccano "Dinky" military vehicles issued pre WWII (standing Dinky figures at far left are 30mm tall. Figures shown are from sets 150 and post war descendants of sets 150 & 160)
L to R - Back Row: 22f Tank, 37c Royal Corps of Signals Dispatch Rider, 151a Medium Tank, 151d Water Tank trailer, 151c Cooker trailer, 151b Transport Wagon
Middle Row: 151b Transport Wagon, 152a Light Tank, 152b Reconnaissance Car, 152c Austin 7 Car.
Front Row: 161b AA Gun on trailer, 161a Searchlight on Lorry, 161c Gun, 162b Trailer, 162a Light Dragon.
Photo by Ed Poole

151A Medium Tank with Markings
W. Kilborn Collection

DINKY MILITARY PRODUCTION, PERIODS AND TYPES

British Vehicles Pre-War (1937-41) and re-issued (1945-50):

SERIES	ARTICLE	YEARS OF MFG	VALUE N/M	EX	VG
22F	Tank Grey or (orange)	1933 -	$200	$150	$75
22S	Search Light Lorry 6 to a box (small)	1935/41	$350	$250	$150
37C	Dispatch Rider RCS.	1938/41	$70	$40	$25
150A	Royal Tank Corp Officer	1937/41	$20	$15	$10
150B	Royal Tank Corp Private	1937/41 (seated)	$25	$20	$15
150C	Royal Tank Corp NCO	1937/41	$30	$20	$10
150D	Royal Tank Corp Driver	1937/41 (seated)	$20	$15	$15
151A	Medium Tank	1937/41	$300	$200	$100
151B	Transport Wagon (reissued)	1937/41, 1953-54*	$200	$150	$100
			*$100	$80	$50
151C	Cooker Trailer	1937/41	$125	$100	$80
151D	Water Tank Trailer	1937/41	$120	$90	$70
152A	Light Tank (reissued)	1937/41, 1954-55*	$100	$80	$60
			*$50	$40	$30
152B	Reconnaissance Car ('')	1937/41, 1954-55*	$100	$80	$60
			*$75	$50	$40
152C	Austin Staff Car	1937/41	$125	$100	$75
153A	U.S. Jeep white star	1954/55	$100	$80	$50
156 Set	Mechanized army set 12pc. 151 a,b,c,d-152, a,b,c	1937/41	$200m/b		
				$1500n/m boxed	
	161 a,b-162, a,b,c-				$1000 boxed
160	Ranco Seated Gunners (3)	1939/41	$60	$40	$30
160A	Royal Artillery NCO	1939/41	$20	$15	$10
160B	Royal Artillery Gunner	1939/41(seated)	$20	$15	$10
160C	Royal Artillery Gunlayer	1939/41	$25	$20	$15
160D	Royal Artillery Gunlayer	1939/41(standing)	$20	$15	$10
161 set	Mobile Anti-Aircraft Unit 161a,b,c,(with box prices)	1939/41	$1000m/b		
			$800	$600	
161A	Transport Lorry with Search Light	1939/41	$500	$300	$250
161B	AA Gun on Trailer		$125	$100	$75
	(reissued)	1939/41,1954/55*	$70	$50	$40
162A	Lt. Dragon Motorized Tractor (reissued)	1939/41,1954/55*	$100	$80	$65
			$75	$50	$35
162B	Ammunition Trailer ('')	1939/41,1954/55*	$50	$35	$25
			*$20	$15	$10
162C	18 PD. Gun (reissued)	1939/41,1954/55	$50	$35	$25
			*$20	$15	$10

SETS (Complete with boxes)

150	Royal Tank Corp. Personnel 150A,B,C,D,6 pcs.	1937/41	$120	$90	$60

(continued)

SERIES	ARTICLE	YEARS OF MFG.	VALUE		
			N/M	EX	VG
151	Royal Tank Corp. Medium Set 151A,B,C,D 4 pcs.	1937/41	$300	$200	$100
152	Royal Tank Corp Light Set 152A,B,C 3 pcs.	1937/41	$250	$200	$150
160	Royal Artillery Personnel 160A,B,C,D 6 pcs.	1939/40	$120	$90	$60

151A Medium Tank (without markings) 1932-41.
W. Kilborn Collection

152B Reconnaissance Car Reissue.
W. Kilborn Collection

151B Transport Wagon, 1937-41.
W. Kilborn Collection

152C Austin Staff Car, 1937 issue.
W. Kilborn Collection

152A Light Tank reissue.
W. Kilborn Collection

153A U.S. Jeep, postwar.
W. Kilborn Collection

DINKY

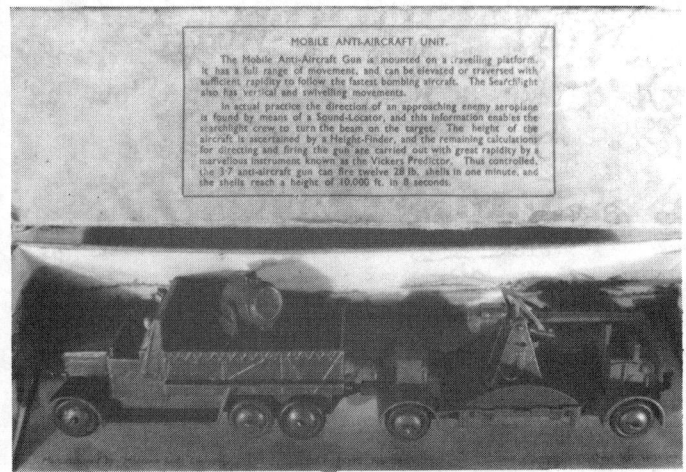

Set No. 161 Mobile Anti-Aircraft Unit.
W. Kilborn Collection

L to R: 601 Austin Paramoke, 673 Scout Car.
W. Kilborn Collection

L to R: 161A Transport Lorry with Searchlight, 1937, 151C Cooker,
151D Water Tanker, 1937.
W. Kilborn Collection

617 Volkswagon & Anti-Tank Gun Set.
W. Kilborn Collection

161B Anti-Aircraft Gun reissued.
W. Kilborn Collection

620 Berliet Missile Launcher Vehicle.
W. Kilborn Collection

162A, B, C. Lt. Dragon Set with 18 pounder, reissued.
W. Kilborn Collection

DINKY

NOTE: Early military Dinky except for boxed sets were sold in yellow boxes with black lettering, 6 or 12 pieces to the box, thus eliminating MINT/BOXED as a value or condition of the item. It should also be noted that pre-war items differed from re-issue as follows: 1) pre-war, smooth hub caps 2) post-war, rimmed hub caps British Vehicles post-war (1954-1977):

NUMBER	DESCRIPTION	YEAR	CONDITION	VALUE AM.
601	Austin Paramoke	1966/77	M/B	$37.00
603	Army Personnel Privates	1955/71	M/B	$50.00
621	3 Ton Army Wagon	1954/63	M/B	$50.00
622	10 Ton Army Truck	1954/64	M/B	$50.00
623	Army Covered Wagon	1954/63	M/B	$50.00
624	Daimler Ambulance #30H	1944/54	M/Box (4)	85.00 each
625	Austin Covered Lorry/30s	1948/54	M/Box (4)	$75.00 each
626	Military Ambulance	1956/65	M/B	$50.00
640	Bedford Army Truck #25w	1944/54	M/Box (4)	$50.00 each
641	1 Ton Cargo Truck	1954/62	M/B	$50.00
642	R.A.F. Pressure Fueller	1957/60	M/B	$120.00
643	Army Water Tanker	1958/64	M/B	$100.00
651	Centurion Tank	1954/70	M/B	$50.00
660	Tank Transporter	1956/64	M/B	$120.00
661	Recovery Tractor	1957/65	M/B	$110.00
665	'Honest John' Launcher	1964/76	M/B	$120.00
666	Missile Erector/Platform	1959/64	M/B	$320.00
667	Missile Service Platform	1960/64	M/B	$230.00
669	U.S. Army Jeep #405 sd/tr	1944/54	M/B	$50.00
341	Land Rover Trailer (army) sold with #669 Super Dinky set	1954	M/B	$40.00
670	Armoured Car	1954/70	M/B	$50.00
673	Scout Car	1953/62	M/B	$50.00
674	Austin Champ Jeep	1954/70	M/B	$25.00
674	Austin Champ "UN white"	1954/70	M/B	$300.00
675	Ford Fordor U.S. Army #139	1944/54	M/Box (4)	$100.00 each
676	Armoured Personnel Car	1955/62	M/B	$60.00
677	Armoured Command Vehicle	1952/61	M/B	$60.00
686	Field Artillery Tractor	1957/70	M/B	$90.00
687	Trailer and 25 Pdr.	1957/70	M/B	$90.00
688	Gun Set	1957/70	M/B	$90.00
689	Medium Artillery Tractor	1957/65	M/B	$65.00
692	5.5 Medium Gun	1955/62	M/B	$30.00
693	7.2 Howitzer	1958/67	M/B	$30.00

British Vehicles Military - Late Models (1977-1980):

NUMBER	DESCRIPTION	YEAR	CONDITION	VALUE AM.
602	Armoured Command Car	1980	M/B	$35.00
604	Landrover Bomb Disposal	1977	M/B	$30.00
609	U.S. 105mm Howitzer	1977	M/B	$70.00
612	Commando Jeep	1980	M/B	$40.00
616	AEC. Artic Transporter	1977	M/B	$100.00
617	Volkswagon Anti-tank gun	1977	M/B	$75.00

(continued)

DINKY

NUMBER	DESCRIPTION	YEAR	CONDITION	VALUE AM.
618	AEC. Artic Trans./Helicopter	1980	M/B	$100.00
619	Bren Gun Set	1980	M/B	$80.00
620	Berliet Missle Launch	1973	M/B	$100.00
622	Bren Gun Carrier	1977	M/B	$60.00
625	6 Pdr. Anti-tank Gun	1977	M/B	$50.00
654	155mm. Mobile Gun	1980	M/B	$50.00
654	155mm. Mobile Gun	1980 -	M/B	$50.00
656	Static 88mm. Gun	1980 -	M/B	$90.00
667	Armoured Patrol Car	1977 -	M/B	$20.00
668	Foden Army Truck	1980 -	M/B	$55.00
680	Ferret Armoured Car	1977 -	M/B677	$10.00
681	D.U.K.W.	1977 -	M/B677	$60.00
682	Stalwart Load Carrier	1977 -	M/B677	$30.00
683	Chieftan Tank	1980	M/B616	$80.00
687	Convoy Truck	1980 -	M/B	$15.00
690	Scorpian Tank	1979 -	M/B	$85.00
691	Striker Anti-tank Vech.	1979 -	M/B	$50.00
692	Leopard Tank	1980 -	M/B	$60.00
694	Hanomog Tank Destroyer	1980 -	M/B	$50.00
696	Leopard Anti-Aircraft T.	1979 -	M/B	$140.00
699	Leopard Recovery Tank	1977 -	M/B	$75.00
290	SNRG Hovercraft British	1979 -	M/B	$50.00
303	Helicopter Set #667 & 687	1977 -	M/B	$120.00

Top to Bottom: 622 Foden 10-ton Truck; 689 Artillery Tractor
W. Kilborn Collection

Top to Bottom: 623 Bedford Truck & 692 Medium Gun; 621 Bedford
Truck & 693 Howitzer.
W. Kilborn Collection

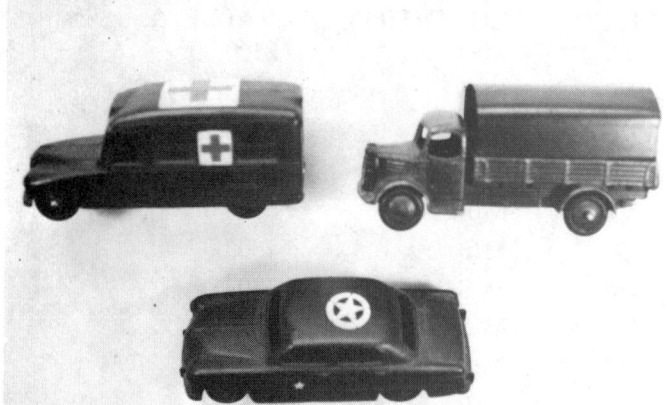

624 Daimler Ambulance, 625 Austin Lorry, 675 U.S. Ford.
W. Kilborn Collection

Top to Bottom: 642 RAF Tanker, 661 Recovery Tractor.
W. Kilborn Collection

640 Bedford Army Truck (two versions - black grille or chrome).
W. Kilborn Collection

660 Tank Transporter with 651 Centurion Tank.
W. Kilborn Collection

Top to Bottom: 641 1-ton truck, 677 Command Vehicle.
W. Kilborn Collection

665 Honest John Missile Launcher.
W. Kilborn Collection

666 Missile Erector Platform.
W. Kilborn Collection

669 Jeep sold with 341 Trailer as set.
W. Kilborn Collection

667 Missile Servicing Platform Vehicle.
W. Kilborn Collection

Top - L to R: 674 UN white Austin Champ, 674 Khaki. Bottom - L
to R: 643 Water Tanker, 626 Ambulance
W. Kilborn Collection

Top to Bottom: 668 Foden Truck, large scale; 604 Landrover Bomb
Disposal Unit, 687 Convoy Army Truck.
W. Kilborn Collection

Top to Bottom: 676 Personnel Carrier, 670 Armoured Car; 688 Tractor, 687 Gun Trailer, 686 Field Gun
W. Kilborn Collection

FRENCH MILITARY VEHICLES (1946-1977):

24 M	Willy's Jeep	1946/49	M/B	$300.00
80A	Panard EBR Tank	1957/63	M/B	$50.00
80B	Willy's Hotchkiss Jeep	1957/60	M/B	$50.00
80BP	Willy's Hotchkiss Jeep	1958/63	M/B	$50.00
80C	AMX13 Char Tank	1958/67	M/B	$50.00
80D	Berliet 6x6 Truck	1958/67	M/B	$45.00
80E	155mm. Fieldgun	1958/67	M/B	$35.00
80F	Renault Ambulance	1959/67	M/B	$40.00
800	Renault SINAPAR Radio Tk	1974	M/B	$45.00
802(819)	155mm. Fieldgun	1973/77	M/B	$40.00
808/2	GMC Wrecker Sahara	1972/73	M/B	$170.00
808/3	GMC Wrecker Khaki	1974 -	M/B	$150.00
807	Renault Ambulance Tous	1973 -	M/B	$70.00
809	GMC Truck 6x6	1970 -	M/B	$60.00
810	Dodge Command Car	1973 -	M/B	$60.00
813	AMX Self Propelled Gun	1965 -	M/B	$50.00
814	Panard AML Amoured Car	1962/67	M/B	$75.00
815	Panard EBR Tank	1962/67	M/B	$50.00
816	Berliet Gazelle Rkt. Launch	1969	M/B	$140.00
821	UNIMOG Covered Truck	1960 -	M/B	$60.00
822	M3 Half Track	1960 -	M/B	$150.00
823	Field Kitchen	1962/67	M/B	$30.00
823	GMC Tanker	1969 -	M/B	$320.00
824	Berliet Gazelle Truck	1963 -	M/B	$110.00
825	D.U.K.W. Amphibian	1964 -	M/B	$130.00
826	Berliet Wrecker	1963 -	M/B	$115.00
827	Panard FL10 Tank	1963 -	M/B	$70.00
828	Jeep/anti-tank Missles	1964 -	M/B	$30.00
829	Jeep with recoil rifle	1964 -	M/B	$30.00
883	AMX Bridge Layer	1964 -	M/B	$180.00
884	Brockway Bridging Truck	1962 -	M/B	$295.00
890	Berliet Tank Transporter	1960 -	M/B	$180.00
1406	Sinpar 4x4 Military Pol.	1977 -	M/B	$75.00
816/2	Hotchkiss Willy's Jeep	1958/59	M/B	$250 with tow hook

French Dinky, Top to Bottom: 80C AMX Tank RT No. 813 AMX Self-Propelled Gun, 80A Panhard EBR in box.
W. Kilborn Collection

French Dinky - Top to Bottom: 80D/818 Berliet Army Truck, 80E/819 Howitzer
W. Kilborn Collection

French Dinky, Top to Bottom: 80E 155m Fieldgun; 824 Berliet Gazelle.
W. Kilborn Collection

French Dinky, Top to Bottom: 808/2 GMC Wrecker Sahara, 808/3 Wrecker Khaki.
W. Kilborn Collection

French Dinky, Top - L to R: 80H/807 Ambulance; 820 Ambulance.
Bottom: 825 D.U.K.W. Amphibian
W. Kilborn Collection

French Dinky, Top to Bottom: 809 GMC Truck 6X6; 823 GMC Tanker reissue.
W. Kilborn Collection

French Dinky 800 Renault Sinpar Radio Truck.
W. Kilborn Collection

French Dinky, top L to R: 810 Dodge Car, 828 Jeep with missiles; bottom L to R: 829 Jeep with cannon, 815 Renault Sin Par.
W. Kilborn Collection

French Dinky, top to bottom: 814 Panhard Aml; L: 80B Hotchkiss Jeep, R: 80BP Hotchkiss Jeep.
W. Kilburn Collection

French Dinky 826 Berliet Crane.
W. Kilborn Collection

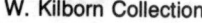

French Dinky, top to bottom: 815 Panhard EBR boxed; 890 Berliet Transporter.
W. Kilborn Collection

French Dinky 827 Panhard EBR.
W. Kilborn Collection

French Dinky, 821 Mercedes Benz Unimog; 823 Field Kitchen Trailer.
W. Kilborn Collection

French Dinky 883 AMX Bridge-Layer Tank.
W. Kilborn Collection

French Dinky 822 M3 Half Track.
W. Kilborn Collection

French Dinky 884 Brockway Bridgelayer Truck
W. Kilborn Collection

French Dinky 1406 Renault Sinpar set, Airforce colors with figures
W. Kilborn Collection

Some Dinky Military Vehicles made in France (French Dinky). Dinky
standing soldier is 30mm tall.
L to R, back row: 810 Dodge Command Car, 813 155mm Self Pro-
pelled Gun, 80A (Renumbered 815A) Panhard Armored Car - gun
barrel not original, 822 Half track M3 towing 923 Army Field Kitchen.
Front Row: 825 DUKW, 829 Gun-Carrier Jeep, 883 AMX Bridge-laying
Tank, 884 Brockway Bridge Truck (Bridge Rails & Pontoons Missing).
Photo by Ed Poole

2 in 1 for even greater playing power!

616
A.E.C. Artic.
with Chieftain Tank
318mm

618
A.E.C. Artic.
with Helicopter
318mm

Dinky 616 and 618, from U.S. catalog No. 12

DOEPKE "MODEL TOYS"
by Ray Funk

Doepke "Model Toys" advertised their toys as outlasting all others 3 to 1. The company's full title was the "Charles Wm. Doepke Mfg. Co., Inc." of Ross-moyne, Ohio. Each toy was an authorized replica of the actual thing and the decals and coloring were exactly as upon the real equipment or trucks, with the exception of the manufacturer having his own, in this case "Model Toys". At the end of the Second World War, the Doepke Corp. hit the market with five models, first in a line of heavy duty metal operating replicas, employing metal tread or authentic miniature tires, either Goodyear or Firestone, with authentic tread and name and tire sizes, exactly as on the real tires. This, to the best of my knowledge, has never been done so perfectly, even in the model kits of today.

Ray Funk is a leading collector and authority on trains and other toys, as well as a collector and authority on comic books and western literature.

These toys all had rubber smoke stacks, and received the approval of *Parents Magazine, P.T.A., Boy's Life Magazine*, and all other experts and advocates of good toys at that period. The first five numbers were 2000, 2001, 2002, 2006, 2007. Why not 3, 4, and 5, I cannot say. Perhaps Doepke had toys planned for these numbers that fell through. Following is a list of the Doepke vehicles.

No. 2000, Wooldridge H.D. Earth hauler, bright yellow, four huge tires, 25" long, and weighing 10 lbs. The actual manufacturer's address is listed as Sunnyvale, Calif. I'm sure most of you have seen the John Wayne movie, "The Fighting Seabees", which used several of these, along with caterpillar bulldozers and road graders.

These Wooldridge's caught my eye with their maneuvering ability, and could traverse the roughest terrain easily. Two long doors, the length of the bottom of the dirt-hauling area, could be released to deposit a load. Price was $14.75 new in 1945.

No. 2001, Barber-Greene high-capacity bucket loader, 13'' high, 10 lbs., dark green, all steel and rolling on steel tread, was designed as a toy to load earth haulers. Handcrank operated, operated exactly as the real thing. Price $14.75.

No. 2002, Jaeger concrete mixer, bright yellow, 15'' long, 8 lbs. on four wheels, steerable via draw bar (all model toys steered exactly like the real thing), though perhaps the best-detailed, was the poorest selling toy, as although you could, it wasn't feasible to really mix concrete in them, due to small amount received versus cleaning time. This toy was priced at $10.75 to $13.75.

No. 2006, Adams diesel road grader, dark orange, 26'' long, 14 lbs., all six wheels, three axles, and blade adjustable to all angles, exactly like the real thing, steerable via steering wheel, priced at $14.75.

No. 2007, Unit Mobile Crane, dark orange, 11½'' long, 19½'' boom, eight lbs. and eight ounces, adjustable side jacks, steered via a drawbar, with block and tackle, and removable operating clam shell as standard accessory. Priced at $14.75.

No number 2008, as the next year, No. 2009 was released and No. 2000 dropped. No 2009 was a Euclid earth-hauler truck, with uncoupling four-wheel tractor to use to tow other toys. 27'' long, 11 lbs., Euclid green, or light road-grader orange, the trailer dumped in the same way as the Wooldridge. Priced $14.75.

No. 2010, American-LaFrance pumper fire truck, 18'' long, 7 lbs., bright red with chrome trim, ladder, bell, fire extinguisher, hoses and nozzle, a reservoir that held water for hand-operated pressure pump. A beautiful toy at $16.75.

No. 2011, Heiliner earth scraper, 29'' long, 13 lbs., bright dark red, loaded and dumped and operated on four wheels as the Wooldridge did. Priced at $16.75.

No. 2012, Caterpillar D6 tractor and bulldozer, caterpillar yellow, 15'' long, 7 lbs., with real bulldozer treads for sharp realistic turning (removable only by using punch and hammer to remove connecting pin from between two of the pads) and adjustable bulldozer blade, plus heavy draw bar. Truly a beautiful toy at $13.75. Diesel motor was cast metal.

No. 2013 eliminated and replaced No. 2001. No. 2013, Barber-Green mobile high-capacity bucket loader, 22''

long, 12'' high, 10 lbs., buckets on chains and rubber conveyor belt, adjustable and steered by steering wheel, priced at $19.75.

No. 2014, American La-France aerial ladder truck, 23'' long, 42'' extended ladder height, 11 lbs., bright red and chrome, bell, red light, adjustable side jacks, single unit truck steered by steering wheel, priced at $20.75.

Doepke "Model Toys" were doomed to extinction by lower-priced, lighter-constructed imitators of lesser quality, some of which were started in the 1920s, and others that came into being in the 1950s, several of which are still around today, but none ever containing, before or after, the heavy-duty constructed realism and operating qualities as had the one and only "Model Toys".

Of the Doepke Model Toys that were mass produced, several had variations in their basic construction from time to time. Usually these changes were an elimination of the more intricate operating procedures, and had little or no effect on the toy's overall outward appearance.

In *Antique Toy World*, Philip Sayer wrote a two part article on the Doepke Co., and featured pictures of nearly all toys manufactured by the firm. The ones that were produced in such limited numbers (only one to a few), are mentioned and often times described. Also listed are nearly all of the slight changes in the mass produced toys, though I could not (perhaps overlooked it) find mention of the change in the D-6 Caterpillar. The first models to hit the market have the front axles held tightly forward by springs, so when being pushed forward and they strike a solid object to climb over, there is some give to absorb the shock and protect the tract pads. Later models eliminated this and opted for simple axle wells as in the rear wheels. Had I not had both types, this slight change would have easily gone unnoticed.

It would seem that the Doepke Co. would accept orders to make model toys of the real thing for the actual producers, and the toys with the most allure, playability, and feasible mass production design, and greatest entertainment to be provided to the child that received one, would be mass produced. Of the others that would not withstand rough handling by young hands, or because of cost and time required to produce them, there were only one to a few produced as previously mentioned. This is no doubt the explanation for the number gaps between the marketed items.

Among the scarcer articles produced, were even a few automobiles, avidly sought after by collectors that have delved into this company's past history to any depth. Of these, perhaps there were catalogs or brochures about them, though all I have seen are the ones dealing with the mass produced toys I have listed.

Clark AIRPORT TRACTOR and Trailers

Here's an exciting, new Model Toy that's loaded with customer appeal—a rugged scale miniature of the Clark Airport Tractor that hauls air freight and baggage!

Like all Model Toys, the AIRPORT TRACTOR and TRAILERS are wonderfully realistic in appearance and performance. Trailers bear the emblems of leading airlines—an authentic touch that will thrill and impress all youngsters.

Doepke 2015. Part of an ad in the May, 1954 *Hobby Merchandiser*
Courtesy Bob Bard

Doepke 2017, as seen in the May, 1954 *Hobby Merchandiser* magazine.
Courtesy Bob Bard

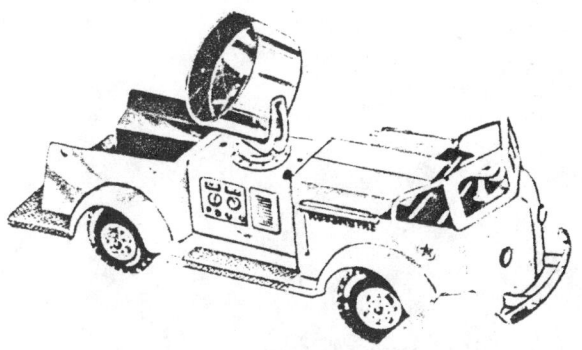

Doepke 2023 as seen in the 1955-56 *Toy Yearbook*

	C6	C8	C10
Doepke No. 2000 Wooldridge H.D. Earth Hauler, 25″ long	140	210	285
Doepke No. 2001 Barber-Greene high capacity bucket loader, 13″ high	175	263	350
Doepke No. 2002 Jaeger Concrete Mixer, 15″ long	175	263	350
Doepke No. 2006 Adams Diesel Road Grader, 26″ long	100	150	200
Doepke No. 2007 Unit Mobile Crane, 11½″ long	130	195	260
Doepke No. 2008 American La France Aerial Ladder Truck . .	240	360	480

Doepke No. 2000 Wooldridge
Photo by Ray Funk

Doepke 2006
Photo by Calvin L. Chaussee

Doepke 2001
Photo by Calvin L. Chaussee

Doepke No. 2007 Unit Mobile Crane
Photo by Ray Funk

Doepke 2008 as shown in Doepke catalog

Doepke 2002
Photo by Calvin L. Chaussee

Doepke 2009 in Doepke catalog.
Courtesy Ray Funk

DOEPKE

	C6	C8	C10
Doepke No. 2009 Euclid Earth Hauler Truck, 27'' long......	160	240	325
Doepke No. 2010 American-La France pumper fire truck, 18'' long..................	175	263	350
Doepke No. 2011 Heiliner Earth Scraper, 29'' long..........	150	225	300
Doepke No. 2012 Caterpillar D6 tractor and bulldozer, 15'' long	250	375	500
Doepke No. 2013 Barber-Greene mobile high-capacity bucket loader 22'' long............	225	338	450
Doepke No. 2014 American-La France aerial ladder fire truck 23'' long.................	250	375	500
Doepke No. 2015 Clark Airport Tractor and Baggage Trailers .	225	338	450
Doepke No. 2017 MG, 1954, 15'' long..................	225	338	450
Doepke No. 2018 Jaguar, 1955..	300	475	650
Doepke No. 2023 Searchlight Truck, 1955.................	500	850	1200

Doepke 2012
Photo by Calvin L. Chaussee

Doepke No. 2013 Barber-Greene.
Courtesy Thomas G. Nefos, Federal Shipping Network

Doepke catalog illustration of Model No. 2010
Photo by Bill Kaufman
Courtesy Ray Funk

Doepke 2011 as shown in a Doepke catalog.
Courtesy Ray Funk

Doepke 2013 on wheels

Doepke 2014 (Bell at middle).
Photo by Calvin L. Chaussee

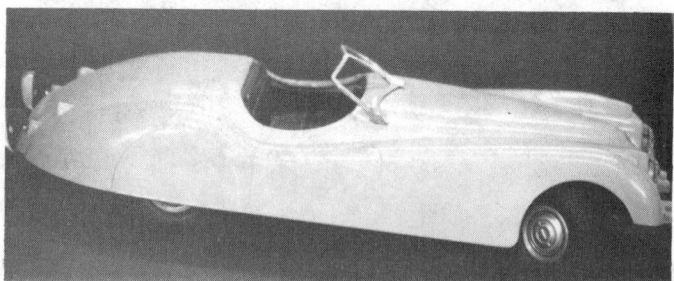

Doepke No. 2018 Jaguar
Photo by Calvin L. Chaussee

	C6	C8	C10
Dooling Brothers F Car, Hornet Powered	700	1100	1600
Drudge "Hyster" Lumber Carrier	175	263	350

Dooling Brothers Mercury "18" gasoline-powered racer. This was auctioned in Jan., 1993 for $1550. Made in California in limited quantities between 1939 and 1945.
Courtesy Jeff Bub Auctions

DUNWELL

Dunwell was the trade name given to its toys by Metal Products Co. of Clifton, New Jersey. Its trucks seem to have been sold circa 1953-58. Their line resembles Tonka's rather closely, and is rare.

	C6	C8	C10
Dunwell Auto Transport	162	243	325
Dunwell Dump Truck	65	98	130
Dunwell "Grain Hauler"	50	75	100
Dunwell Log Truck	150	225	300
Dunwell "Red Star Express Lines" truck	300	450	650
Dunwell "Snowcrop" Refrigerator Semi	200	300	400
Dunwell "Steel Carrier Co." semi	50	75	100
Dunwell Wrecker	150	225	300

Dunwell "Red Star Express Lines"; c.1953
Photo by Bob Smith

DYNA-MODEL PRODUCTS COMPANY
(Dyna-Mo)
by Fred Maxwell

Dyna-Model Products Co., 93 South Street, Oyster Bay, Long Island, New York, may have pioneered the scale models industry dominating today's markets with their "Dyna-Mo" brand of HO toys to be used in train layouts. They are rather high quality pot-metal toys, identified by their method of assembling body parts, clamping axles between small posts and the standardized appearance of the undersides of the whole line.

DYNA-MODEL

Probably produced in the 1930s, and perhaps in the post-war era, the toys were made by a coarse die-casting process. The earlier vintage cars were made into two to five parts, exclusive of wheels and axles, to be pinned, clamped or glued together; body, frame, steering wheel, top and windshield. Some were packaged as kits, with instructions printed on the box: "Pinch ends of axel (their spelling) after installing wheels" (R-26). The toys were factory painted in as many as 4 colors per toy.

Dyna Model, top L to R: D14, D20?, D12, Cadillac 2-door Sedan, 2⅜". Middle, L to R: D15, D18, D21. Bottom, L to R: D22, D23, D24. Photo by Fred Maxwell

	C6	C8	C10
D1 Dyna "R-26 HO Surrey, 35c": 1¾". Horseless carriage, tiller steering, 3 colors, 3 pc. body, kit	4	6	8
D2 Dyna Touring Car: 2" Antique Stanley Steamer, open tonneau, rt. hand steering, 4 colors, 4 pc.	4	6	8
D3 Dyna Speedster: 2". Antique Mercer, rt. hand steering, 4 colors, 3 pc.	4	6	8
D4 Dyna Roadster: 1⅞". Antique Buick? Open rt. hand steering, 4 pcs., 3 colors	4	6	8
D5 Dyna Touring Car: 1⅞". Antique. Realistic folded top attachable with hinge pins, left hand steering, 5 pcs., 2 colors	4	6	8

Dyna-Model, top L to R: D1, Ford T Roadster, 1⅞", D7, D3, Franklin steam touring 2⅛". Middle, L to R: D5, D6, D9, D10, D8. Bottom, L to R: D11, Cadillac Sedan 2", D23, D16. Photo by Fred Maxwell.

D6 Dyna "R-61 HO Model T Ford 1914 touring with top 60c": 1⅝". One piece body, top up, 3 colors. "Cut plastic windshield to fit, darken edges with ink or

	C6	C8	C10
paint and glue top and windshield in place, in slots provided"	4	6	8
D7 Dyna Touring car: 1¾". 1914 Ford, top down cast in one-piece body, glued windshield, 3 colors	4	6	8
D8 Dyna Roadster: 2". 1920's Packard convertible, top down, rumble seat, one piece body glued windshield, spoked wheels, 3 colors	6	9	12
D9 Dyna Roadster: 2". Packard, same as above, top up, 3 colors	6	9	12
D10 Dyna Touring: 2". Packard, same as above, top down, 3 colors	6	9	12
D11 Dyna Roadster: 2". Model A Ford? Top down, open rumble seat, disc wheels, one piece body, unpainted	2	3	4
D12 Dyna Sedan: 2". Buick sedan, 1930's. Open windshield and windows. 2 colors	4	6	8
D13 Dyna "R-68 HO Buick convertible 55c". 2⅜". Late 1930's. Open, 2 dr. sedan, top down, one piece body, solid cast windshield, disk wheels	6	9	12
D14 Dyna Sedan: 2⅜", Buick 2 dr. airflow, open windshield and windows	6	9	12

	C6	C8	C10
D15 Dyna Taxi: 2⅜''. Buick sedan, late 1930's. Open windshield and windows, 2 colors	6	9	12
D16 Dyna Convertible, 2⅜''. Cadillac 2 dr. sedan, late 1930's	6	9	12
D17 Dyna Sedan: 2⅜''. Cadillac 2 dr. sedan, open windshield and windows, incl. rear, late 1930's	6	9	12
D18 Dyna Taxi: 2⅜''. Cadillac sedan, late 1930's, open windshield and windows including rear, 2 colors	6	9	12
D19 Dyna Sedan: 2⅜''. Pontiac 4 dr. airflow, open windshield and windows incl. rear	6	9	12
D20 Dyna Limousine: 2½''. Cadillac, late 1930's, open windows as above	6	9	12
D21 Dyna Delivery Van: 2⅜''. Pontiac, late 1930's, open windshield and door windows	4	6	8
D22 Dyna Pickup Truck: 2½''. GMC?, late 1930's, open windows, spoked wheels, 2 piece, 3 colors	4	6	8
D23 Dyna Wrecker: 2¾'', GMC?, late 1930's, open windows, 3 piece, 4 colors	6	9	12
D24 Dyna Dump Truck: 2¾''. Open windows, hinged body with realistic load of coal. 3 pieces, 2 colors, dual rear wheels	8	12	16
D25 Dyna Pickup Truck: 2''. GMC?, 1930's, one piece, open windows, one color	4	6	8
D26 Dyna Pickup Truck: 2''. Mack? ''US Army'', Air Corps star decals, late 1930's, 2 pc. body, 2 colors	4	6	8
D27 Dyna Truck: 2''. Mack? Same chassis as above, but tarpaulin covered, 2 pc. body	4	6	8

ELDON

*(Los Angeles, CA
1010 E. 62nd St.)*

	C6	C8	C10
Eldon Aerial Ladder Truck, 21'' long	No Price Found		
Eldon Concrete Truck, 17'' long	44	66	85
Eldon Corvette, 14'' long	44	66	85
Eldon Dump Truck, 18'' long . .	30	45	60
Eldon Ford Lift Gate Truck, 18'' long	50	75	100
Eldon Road Race slot car set, 1965	35	55	70
Eldon Steam Shovel	20	30	40

Eldon Aerial Ladder Truck, 21'' long.
Photo by Terry Sells

ELMAR PRODUCTS COMPANY

(15 West 24th Street, NYC, c.1950s)

Elmar Rocket Shooting Tank, 3½'' long . . . . No Price Found

Elmar Rocket Shooting Tank.
Courtesy Islyn Thomas

EMPIRE FORCES

(Gardel Industries, 106 East 19th St., NYC, c.1943-44)

Empire Forces E5 Tank, composition (also in plaster) . . . . No Price Found

Empire Forces E6 Tank, composition (also in plaster) . . . . No Price Found

Erie EV09
Courtesy Bob & Alice Wagner

Empire Forces tanks.
L to R: E5, E6

ERIE

(Parker White Metal)
Listing by Dave Leopard

According to James Apthorpe, Erie toys were made by Parker White Metal Company, which apparently began in Erie, Pennsylvania, but moved to Fairview (West of Erie, Pa.) in the early 1960s. However, according to company officials he contacted, the firm made toys only prior to World War II. It printed no catalogs.

Erie EV20
Photo by James Apthorpe

	C10	C6	C8
EV01 Lincoln Zephyr sedan, 1936, 5½'' long, painted	40	50	60
EV02 Lincoln Zephyr sedan, 1936, 5½'' long, plated	45	55	65
EV03 Lincoln Zephyr sedan, 1936, 3½'' long, painted	25	30	35
EV04 Lincoln Zephyr sedan, 1936, 3½'' long, plated	30	35	40
EV05 Packard Roadster, 1936, 6'' long, painted	40	50	60
EV06 Packard Roadster, 1936, 6'' long, plated	45	55	65
EV07 Packard Roadster, 1936, 3½'' long, painted	25	30	35
EV08 Packard Roadster, 1936, 3½'' long, plated	30	35	40
EV09 Ford Pickup Truck, 1935, low sides, 5'' long, painted	40	50	60

	C6	C8	C10
EV10 Ford Pickup Truck, 1935, low sides, 5'' long, plated	45	55	65
EV11 Ford Pickup Truck, 1935, high sides, 5'' long, large rear window	40	50	60
EV12 Ford Pickup Truck, 1935, high sides, 5'' long, small rear window	40	50	60
EV13 Ford Ice Truck, 1935, ''Pure Ice Co.,'', 5'' long	50	60	70
EV14 Ford Tow Truck, 1935, ''Servel Body'', 5'' long	50	60	70
EV15 Cabover truck, c. 1937, no tail gate, 3¼'' long	20	25	30
EV16 Cabover truck, c. 1937, tailgate, updated, 3¼'' long . .	20	25	30
EV17 Tow Truck, c.1939, no chassis, 4¼'' long	30	35	40
EV18 Sedan, c.1939, futuristic, fin on trunk, no chassis, 4¼'' long	30	35	40
EV19 Coupe, c.1939, futuristic, no chassis, 4¼'' long	30	35	40
EV20 Sedan, c.1939, sharknose, no chassis, 4¼'' long	30	35	40

ERTL

Ertl was begun by Fred Sr. in 1945, working out of his Dubuque, Iowa home. As business expanded, the firm moved to Dyersville. Ertl had learned about using sand molds in his native Germany, and very early in the company's history began working directly from the original blueprints to make his toy tractors, trucks and other wheeled toys. Ertl's specialty is farm toys, with rights obtained from such manufacturers as International Harvester and John Deere. Today Ertl is the largest manufacturer of toy farm equipment in the world, and in addition makes a number of other toys, such as cars, trucks and airplanes.

	C6	C8	C10
Ertl Allis-Chalmers B-112 Tractor	70	110	165
Ertl Conoco Tanker	75	120	175
Ertl Fleetstar Hi-Side Dump Truck, red/wht	85	135	195
Ertl Fleetstar Tilt Bed, green	70	120	180
Ertl Fleetstar 10-Wheel Dump Truck, red	70	120	180
Ertl Ford 8000 Tractor, early	25	40	60
Ertl GE Truck, white	15	22	30
Ertl Gleaner C-280 w/corn picker	25	45	60
Ertl Grain Hopper, early	22	34	48
Ertl IHC Farmal 806, square fender	100	175	230
Ertl International Fleetstar Gravity Feed Truck	150	250	350
Ertl International Scout, maroon, or blue	85	135	195
Ertl John Deere 500 Bulldozer w/blade	40	70	100
Ertl John Deere 6600 Combine	60	100	140
Ertl Loadstar Box Van, lavender/white	200	375	575
Ertl Loadstar Concrete Truck, red/white	225	400	600
Ertl Loadstar Dump Truck	140	250	325
Ertl Loadstar Grain/Cattle stake truck	120	200	270
Ertl Loadstar Straight Cab & Chassis only	55	85	125
Ertl Loadstar Tilt Bed, green/gray	125	175	260
Ertl Loadstar Tow Truck, white/red	200	375	575
Ertl Mary Kay Cosmetics Trailer Truck	65	115	150
Ertl Mobile Tanker	40	65	88

	C6	C8	C10
Ertl Picker	25	40	60
Ertl Texaco Tanker No. 2	150	250	350
Ertl "Van Lines" Pup Trailer only, white	100	150	225
Ertl White Cab-Over Dump Truck, white/red	165	265	400

Ertl, L to R: "Ertl Van Lines" pup trailer, Loadstar straight cab and chassis.
Photo by Bob Smith

Ertl Fleetstar Dump Truck, 10 wheel
Photo by Bob Smith

Ertl Fleetstar Hi-Side Dump truck.
Photo by Bob Smith

Ertl Fleetstar Tilt Bed.
Photo by Bob Smith

Ertl Loadstar Box Van.
Photo by Bob Smith

Ertl International Fleetstar Gravity Feed Truck.

Ertl Loadstar Concrete Truck.
Photo by Bob Smith

Ertl International Scout (both).
Photo by Bob Smith

Ertl Loadstar Tilt Bed.
Photo by Bob Smith

Ertl Loadstar Tow Truck.
Photo by Bob Smith

Ertl White Cab-Over Dump Truck.
Photo by Bob Smith

	C6	C8	C10
Erwin, Ford w/windshield wipers	40	60	80
Erwin Race Car	55	82	110

F&F CEREAL PREMIUMS

by Dave Leopard

The toy vehicles that were included in Post cereals during the 50's-60's were made by the F&F Mold and Die Works of Dayton, Ohio, a company that specialized in manufacturing plastic premiums for the food industry. The "Fiedler and Fiedler" company was in business from 1945 until 1987 and their entire product line consisted of plastic premiums.

The small plastic vehicles, about 3 in. long, were included in Post Grape-Nut Flakes, Corn Flakes, Rice Krispies, etc. over a period of about 15 years, beginning in 1954. Most of the cereal premiums were cars, but they also made speedboats, which were marked "Century"; several versions of a tractor-trailer truck, which were marked "Ford" on the cab and "Fruehauf" on the trailer; and two versions of a Greyhound bus.

All of the F&F vehicles from 1954 to 1967 are clearly marked with their trademark. Two earlier Fords, a 1950 and a 1951 sedan, have magnets glued underneath the roof, are the same scale and are very similar to other F&F vehicles. Collectors disagree as to whether these early Fords are in fact F&Fs. Likewise, a series of 1969 Mercury's, identical to earlier F&F vehicles in scale, style, and materials, are marked "JVZ Co." Whether these Fords and Mercurys are properly identified as F&F or not, they are very similar and fit nicely with known F&F vehicles.

	C6	C8	C10
1950 Ford 4 Door Sedan	15	20	25
1951 Ford 4 Door Sedan	15	20	25
1954 Mercury XM-800 Show Car	8	10	15
1954 Mercury Monterray Convertible	8	10	15
1954 Mercury Monterray 4 Door Sedan	8	10	15
1954 Mercury Monterray 2 Door Sedan	8	10	15
1954 Ford Crestline Sunliner	8	10	15
1954 Ford Crestline Hardtop	8	10	15
1954 Ford Crestline 4 Door Sedan	8	10	15
1954 Ford Customline 2 Door Sedan	8	10	15
1954 Ford Customline Ranchwagon	8	10	15
1955 Ford Country Sedan (wagon)	8	10	15
1955 Ford Customline 2 Door Sedan	8	10	15
1955 Ford Fairlane Crown Victoria	8	10	15
1955 Ford Fairlane Sunliner	8	10	15
1955 Ford Thunderbird Convertible	8	10	15
1957 Ford Convertible	8	10	15
1957 Ford 4 Door Hardtop Sedan	8	10	15
1957 Ford Highway Patrol	8	10	15
1957 Ford Ambulance	8	10	15
1957 Ford Firechief Car	8	10	15
1959 Ford Thunderbird Hardtop	8	10	15
1959 Ford Thunderbird Convertible	8	10	15

	C6	C8	C10
1960 Plymouth Convertible	8	10	15
1960 Plymouth Hardtop Coupe .	8	10	15
1960 Plymouth Station Wagon . .	8	10	15
1961 Ford Thunderbird Convertible	8	10	15
1961 Ford Thunderbird Hardtop	8	10	15
1961 Ford Thunderbird Roadster (single seat)	10	15	20
1966 Ford Mustang Convertible .	6	10	12
1966 Ford Mustang Hardtop	6	10	12
1966 Ford Mustang Fastback	6	10	12
1967 Mercury Cougar Hardtop . .	6	10	12
1969 Mercury Cougar Hardtop . .	6	10	12
1969 Mercury Cyclone Fastback .	6	10	12
1969 Mercury 2 Door Hardtop . .	6	10	12
1969 Mercury 4 Door Sedan	6	10	12
Ford Tractor/Trailer (flatbed)	8	10	15
Ford Tractor/Trailer (lowboy) . . .	8	10	15
Ford Tractor/Trailer (moving van)	8	10	15
Ford Tractor/Trailer (enclosed trailer)	8	10	15
Ford Tractor/Trailer (oil tanker) .	8	10	15
Greyhound Bus	8	10	15
Greyhound Scenicruiser Double-Decker Bus	8	10	15

Fallows Toys, Frederick & Henry, Horseless Carriage with driver, 8'' long.
Courtesy Wilkinson Collection, Detroit Antique Toy Museum

F & F: Front, 1955 Ford Thunderbird Convertible. Rear, 1954 Mercury XM-800 Show Car, 1954 Ford Customline Ranchwagon.
Photo by Rick Lacaire
Courtesy Dave Leopard

	C6	C8	C10
Fallows Toys, Frederick & Henry, Horseless Carriage with driver, 8'' long, cast iron and tin, c.1905	900	1350	1800

FIRESTONE

The following list, with its codings, was compiled by David Leopard

	C6	C8	C10
FA01 '39 Mercury fastback 4 door sedan, 4¾'' long	60	75	90
FA02 '35 Ford 2 door humpback sedan, 4⅞'' long	50	60	75
FA03 '36 Ford 2 door humpback sedan, 4⅞'' long	50	60	75

Firestone FA-03 (both) with original box.
Photo by Ron Smith

FISCHER, HEINRICH & CO.

(Nuremburg, Germany, 1908-1931)
by Bob Smith

Fischer's easily recognized mark, a fish swimming through the letter A, is a unique trademark usually found on the rear of the car. The George Borgfeldt store of N.Y. City purchased many of the toys produced by Fischer for the U.S. market. Not all of the Fischer toys carried his mark however. "Nifty" toys for example, was one of the trademarks used by the company. The great comic character tin toy, "Toonerville Trolley", is one of the best known Fischer toys made under the Nifty trademark.

	C6	C8	C10
Fischer Limousine, Green/back, 9" long, c/w motor, back doors open, c.1915	600	875	1200
Fischer Limousine, Green/black, 7.5" long, c/w motor head lamps, windshield, c.1918	500	775	1100
Fischer Torpedo, Red/yellow tin litho., 8.0" long, c/w motor, c.1912	650	950	1300

Fischer Torpedo, 8" long, c.1912.
Photo by Bob Smith

FISHER-PRICE

Fisher-Price was founded by Herman Fisher and Irving Price on October 1, 1930 in East Aurora, New York. It made (and makes) quality wood toys for small children, colorfully lithographed.

	C6	C8	C10
Fisher-Price 7 Looky Fire Truck	85	125	170
Fisher-Price 234 Nifty Station Wagon	225	325	450
Fisher-Price 472 Peter Bunny Cart	225	275	375
Fisher-Price 745 Elsie's Dairy Truck	400	575	700

Fischer Limousine, 9" long, c.1915.
Photo by Bob Smith

Fischer Limousine, 7½" long, c.1918.
Photo by Bob Smith

Fisher-Price 7 Looky Fire Truck.
Courtesy John Murray

Fisher-Price 234 Nifty Station Wagon.
Courtesy John Murray

Fisher-Price 472 Peter Bunny Cart.
Courtesy John Murray

Fisher-Price 745 Elsie's Dairy Truck.

FREIDAG

According to a well-illustrated article by Fred MacAdam in the March, 1993 *Antique Toy World*, William Freidag formed Freidag Mfg. Co. and Foundry in Freeport, Illinois in 1920. He pronounced his last name "Friday". Freidag's cast iron toys are obscure but significant, and can easily be confused with those by another maker. Thus collectors might find it helpful to obtain a copy of the MacAdam article when they're uncertain about any cast iron toy c.1920-1932, when Freidag went out of business.

	C6	C8	C10
Freidag Taxi with black driver ..	900	1350	1800

	C6	C8	C10
Gama Cadillac................	350	550	850
Garland Red Flyer Hydraulic Dump (Made in Detroit).....	125	188	250

Garland Red Flyer Hydraulic Dump, 25" long.
Photo by Jerry Combs

	C6	C8	C10
Garton "Fire Department" ladder pedal car, 1949.............	700	1100	1600
Garton Hot Rod pedal car	400	650	900
Gendron Federal Knight Dump Truck, offered in "museum quality" in 1992 for $11,000..			
Gendron "Racer" pedal car, 38" long.......................	1300	2000	3000
Gendron/Sampson Army Truck, 27" long...................	800	1300	2000
Gendron/Sampson Chemical Fire Truck, 28" long............	1200	2000	2800
Gendron/Sampson Coal Truck, 26" long, steel.............	1000	1600	2500
Gendron/Sampson Dump Truck, 27" long, pressed steel......	850	1350	1900
Gendron/Sampson Screen Side Express Truck, 27" long.......	650	1100	1500
Gendron/Sampson Stake Truck, 26" long..................	1500	2300	3500
Gendron/Sampson Tank Truck, 29" long..................	800	1400	2000
Gibbs "Gibbs No. 701" truck..	150	250	350
Giftcraft (possibly only the distributor) TA01 Fastback Sedan, c.1946 Nash, solid rubber, 4" long...............	15	20	25

Giftcraft, TA01.
Photo by Dave Leopard

GILBERT

See A.C. Gilbert

GIRARD

Girard Model Works was founded by C.G. Wood in 1906, in Girard, Pa. His son Frank was soon made a partner. In 1918 they began making mechanical toys for an unidentified New York firm. In 1920 they sold them under their name: "Wood's Mechanical Toys". The business eventually passed into other hands, and had 1000 employees in 1931. In the Depression, Girard laid off its salesman, Louis Marx, who stalled Girard customers as he tried to get a plant of his own in business. Since Marx was better-known to buyers than the people at Girard, he emerged triumphant, and in 1934 Marx took over the firm. Girard remained in business till 1980, though its last toys seem to have been made in 1975.

Girard Pierce-Arrow Coupe, 14" long, c.1932.
Photo by Bob Smith

Girard Touring Bus.
Courtesy Mapes Auctioneers & Appraisers

	C6	C8	C10
Girard Army Truck, cloth top, c.1940	150	225	300
Girard Auto Transport, circa early 1930s, carries two trucks	275	413	550
Girard Bus with driver, 12½" long wind-up	188	282	375
Girard Coupe, 6" long	30	45	60
Girard Coupe, 14" long, battery operated headlights	350	525	700
Girard Fire Chief Car, 15" long	175	263	350
Girard "Fire Chief Siren Coupe", 14" long wind-up	350	525	700
Girard Fire truck, 12" long, 1920s	125	188	250
Girard "Gasoline" tanker, c.1939	85	128	170
Girard Pierce-Arrow Coupe, 14" long, c.1932, green, orange & cream, wind-up	275	400	600
Girard Pump Truck, battery operated, headlights, 10" long	100	150	200

	C6	C8	C10
Girard Race Car No. 2, 8" long wind-up	300	450	600
Girard Race Car, 1920s, pull rod	138	205	275
Girard Roadster, 14½" long, electrified	212	318	425
Girard Side Dump, 11½" long	175	263	350
Girard Stake Truck, 10" electric headlights	212	318	425
Girard Tank Truck, 11½" long, wood wheels	92	138	185
Girard Touring Bus, painted tin, c.1920, 12" long	150	225	300
Girard Truck with Trailer, 1930s, 17"	100	150	200
Glass Gas Pump, 1930s	200	325	450
Glass Motorcycle & Cop, 1930s	250	400	600

Girard "Fire Chief Siren Coupe".
Photo by Bill Kaufman

	C6	C8	C10
Gong Bell "Mickey Mouse Bus Lines - Walt Disney Stars" ..	250	375	500
Gong Bell Racer, 20" long, c.1930s	200	300	400

	C6	C8	C10
1954 DeSoto Station Wagon	10	12	15
1955 Ford Fuel Truck	10	12	15
American LaFrance Pumper	10	12	15
Military Jeep	10	12	15
Moving Van....................	10	12	15
Step Van	10	12	15
Land Speed Racer	10	12	15
Land Speed Racer (bubble fenders)	10	12	15

Gong Bell "Mickey Mouse Bus Lines - Walt Disney Stars".
Courtesy Wilkinson Collection, Detroit Antique Toy Museum

Goodee 1953 GMC Pick up, large and small versions.
Photo by Dave Leopard

GOODEE

by Dave Leopard

Goodee diecast vehicles were made by the Excel Products Company of East Brunswick, New Jersey. All of the prototypes for Goodee vehicles appear to be in the 1953-1955 range. It would seem that all Goodee vehicles were produced in two sizes - about 3 in. and about 6 in. - although I have listed only the ones I have actually seen. Some of the larger models had wind-up motors, which would increase their value.

	C6	C8	C10
Large Size:			
1953 GMC Pickup Truck	15	20	25
1953 Ford Police Cruiser	15	20	25
1954 DeSoto Station Wagon	15	20	25
1955 Ford Fuel Truck	15	20	25
American LaFrance Pumper	15	20	25
Military Jeep	15	20	25
Small Size:			
1953 GMC Pickup Truck	10	12	15
1953 Studebaker Coupe	12	15	20
1953 Lincoln Capri Hardtop	10	12	15
1953 Cadillac Convertible	10	12	15
1953 Ford Police Cruiser	10	12	15

GREY IRON

Grey Iron began in 1840 as the Brady Machine Shop in Mount Joy, Pa. Toymaking began as early as 1903, almost entirely in iron (only occasionally in lead and aluminum). Its best known products are toy soldiers. It is still in business today as Donsco-John Wright, located in Wrightsville, though still casting in Mount Joy.

	C6	C8	C10
Grey Iron, Convertible Midget, 1½" long..................	20	30	40
Grey Iron, Coupe Midget, 1½" long	20	30	40
Grey Iron, Delivery Truck, Midget, 1½" long	20	30	40
Grey Iron, Racer, Midget, 1½" long	20	30	40
Grey Iron, Sedan, Airflow Type, Midget, 1½" long	20	30	40
Grey Iron, Sedan, Older, Midget, 1½" long..................	20	30	40
Grey Iron, Sedan, 1927, 9" long	1000	1500	2000

Grey Iron "Midget" Vehicles, approx. 1" long.
Photo by Stan Alekna

Gunthermann Limousine, 12" long, c.1920.
Photo by Bob Smith

GUNTHERMANN

"SG". Nuremburg, Germany. 1887 to present
by Bob Smith

Gunthermann's toy business flourished well into the 1900s. S.G. Gunthermann passed away in 1890. His widow married the company manager, Adolf Weigel. Weigel's initials were added to the SG logo until his death in 1919. They were then removed and the logo was changed back to the original SG. The company was sold to Seimens in 1965 and is still in business today.

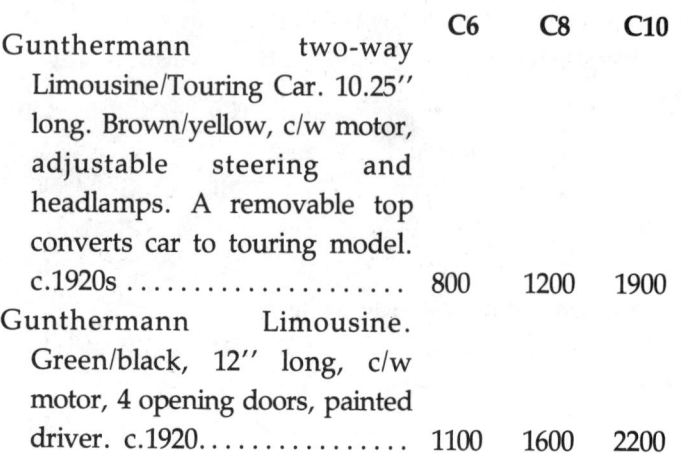

Guntherman two-way Limousine/Touring Car, 10¼" long, c.1920s.
Photo by Bob Smith

	C6	C8	C10
Gunthermann two-way Limousine/Touring Car. 10.25" long. Brown/yellow, c/w motor, adjustable steering and headlamps. A removable top converts car to touring model. c.1920s	800	1200	1900
Gunthermann Limousine. Green/black, 12" long, c/w motor, 4 opening doors, painted driver. c.1920.	1100	1600	2200

GYRO

Richard B. Munday became head of Dayton Friction Works in 1926, where he patented a horizontal flywheel and called his toys "Gyro" after the gyroscope. Gyro shut its doors in 1935. The author found no toys listed for sale specifically labeled "Gyro". However, for research and identification purposes, some illustrations of Gyro toys are run here.

FRICTION TOYS

"GYRO" FRICTION STEEL TOYS

Sturdy....powerful....flashy steel toys....each equipped with friction motor (no springs to get out of order)....dependable, powerful, lasting. All BIG sizes for the money. Beautiful enamel finishes in two and three colors.

Gyro toys, as seen in the Christmas, 1929 Butler Bros. catalog.

Happy Sam driving wood truck,	C6	C8	C10
c.1920s, 8" long............	80	120	160

Hafner, L to R: "Auto Express Co.", Runabout with upholstered driver's seat.
Courtesy Sotheby's NY

Mechanical Runabout.

Modeled a f t e r the popular American style Runabout seen on our streets. Made of sheet steel formed and clinched, finely painted and varnished and decorated with gold ornamentation. A plush cushioned seat is fitted to it, and will carry a doll as large as 12 inches. Fitted with steering gear which permits accurate adjustment to run in any circle or a straight line. Large rubber tires of ¼ inch in diameter make the running almost noiseless. Price..95¢

Hafner's Runabout, as shown in the 1903 Siegel Cooper Co. toy catalog.

HAFNER

Chicago's Hafner began in 1900 as the Toy Auto Company, though it may not have produced its first model till the following year. By 1904 the firm's name became W.F. Hafner. Hafner set off on his own in 1914 (the first company eventually evolving into American Flyer) with the Hafner Manufacturing Company, his son joining him in 1918. This latter outfit manufactured wind-up trains till it was purchased in 1950 by Wyandotte.

	C6	C8	C10
Hafner "Auto Express Co." truck, 8½" long, steel clockwork ...	450	675	900
Hafner Runabout with upholstered driver's seat, steel clockwork, 7" long......................	450	675	900
Hafner Touring Car, 10" long, pressed steel, clockwork	750	1125	1500

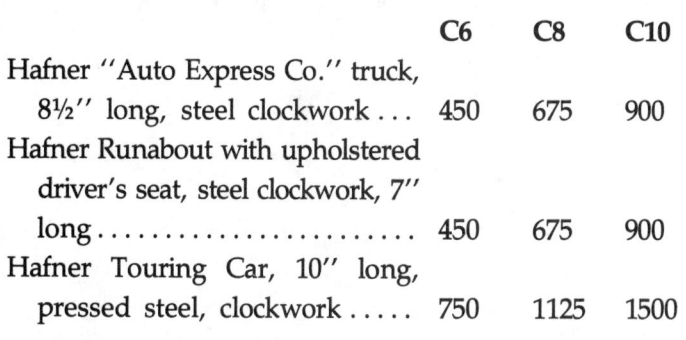

Hafner Touring Car, 10" long.
Courtesy Sotheby's NY

TRAILER PULL TOYS WITH BLOCKS

This line of pull toys packed with blocks of vivid colors gives real, double play value. All blocks contained in the trucks have rounded corners and are finished in harmless, brilliant enamels. Each truck individually packed.

No. 449—TRUCK WITH BLOCKS. Extreme length 11 inches, width 3 inches. Contains 10 only $1\frac{3}{16}$ inch blocks. Packed ¼ dozen sets in a package..................Per doz. $4.00

No. 450—TRUCK WITH BLOCKS. Extreme length 15½ width 3 inches. Contains 10 only $1\frac{5}{16}$ inch blocks. Packed ¼ dozen sets in a package..............Per doz. $4.00

No. 451—TRUCK WITH BLOCKS. Extreme length 17 inches, width 4 inches. Contains 24 only 1¾ inch blocks.

Per doz. $16.00

A Halsam trailer truck as shown in the September, 1934 Butler Bros. catalog.

HALSAM

Halsam is best known for its American Logs (similar to Lincoln Logs, but preferred by some collectors), which went into production in 1934. It was also well known for its blocks, and as can be seen by the accompanying illustrations, its trucks came with loads of them. No sales were found for any of Halsam's vehicles.

HARRIS

Harris Toy Company of Toledo, Ohio seems to have begun production of cast iron toys during the late 1880s. The firm, which also jobbed for Dent, Hubley and Wilkins, stopped making toys in 1913.

Harris Tiller Auto, driver....... No Price Found

HAUSER

Elastolin, Germany

	C6	C8	C10
Hauser Truck with Cannon, 11" long......................	350	525	700
Hauser Troop Carrier..........	175	263	350

Hauser (Elastolin), top to bottom: Troop Carrier; Truck with Cannon, 11" long.
Courtesy Sotheby's NY

HESS PROMOTIONAL TOYS
A Holiday Tradition

by Thomas G. Nefos

Thomas G. Nefos is Publisher & Editor of the National Toy Connection. This publication was developed to enhance the hobby of collecting transportation & promotional toys. He is also the author of several articles on Hess toys for two major magazines, a contributing writer to the book "The Hess Toy Collector" and publishes a price guide annually on this subject.

One can trace the roots of the Amerada Hess Corp. (formally Hess Oil & Chemical) back many years before a promotional toy was even considered. Hess entered retail gasoline marketing around 1958 with a minority purchase of the Meadville Corporation. Meadville operated clean, oversized service stations under the brands of Save Way & Safeway in some large Northeast cities. The Hess branch was introduced in 1959 and by 1962 the company operated approximately 28 stations under its own brand name. By 1965 several other fuel companies were bought into (Delhi-Taylor - Billups Eastern) and some of their stations were renamed as Hess. It wasn't until 1964 that the first toy tanker truck was sold at Hess stations. Almost every year since then (around Thanksgiving Day) a high quality plastic toy vehicle bearing their name has been offered. These highly detailed toys are said to be exact replicas of actual vehicles in the Hess fleet (from 1987 to present day the toys design was changed to reflect non-fleet vehicles). The toys are produced in limited quantities and over the past few years customers have been restricted to "two toys per customer" because of the great demand. Each vehicle is packaged in a very colorful box and batteries are included in the purchase price. A great deal of respect has been given to these toys by collectors in view of their limited production and quality construction. It's important to note that in order to maintain the value one must keep all the packaging that comes with the toy (box, inserts, battery card etc).

The 1964 toy truck commonly referred to as the B Mack was manufactured by Marx in Hong Kong and sold at the stations for $1.39. The cab of the truck was green with yellow fenders and red chassis. The tank trailer featured a green and white body with the Hess name applied to both sides of the tank and cab. The truck had operating head & tail lights powered by a battery located under the tank. It also came with a small red funnel which enabled the tank to be filled with liquid and a drain hose to empty it. This unique toy truck can be hard to find in completely original condition today.

Not commonly known by collectors, this same truck design was offered under the private labeling of several other fuel companies...**Billups Petroleum, Aetna** (which was the North Carolina-based Taylor Oil Co. operating under the Travelers Brand), **Wilco** (also on the Delhi-Taylor supply system), **Service** of North Carolina and **Gant.** Each of these marketers sold the B Mack toy truck in 1964. By 1965, the Billups brand name had been eliminated in the East and their stations sold to Hess. Hess continued the toy promotion the following year (1965) with the reissue of the B Mack.

1966 brought the only non-land vehicle to date in the Hess toy collection; the Hess Voyager. This replica of an oil tanker ship made by Marx in the U.S.A. was outfitted with battery-operated lights both on the bow and stern, as well as port and starboard. The Hess name appeared on the ship's stack and both sides of the bow. The toy came with a battery installation card inside the box and sold for $1.89.

During the holiday season of 1967 Hess offered a newly-designed semi-tanker truck often referred to as the "red velvet bottom". This term describes the box, not the truck. The "split window" (two-piece windshield) cab was done in the company colors of green, yellow and red, with the tank trailer being green and white. The box, which was only available that year, had a red velvet base on which the truck could be displayed and a card in the box explained the battery was already installed. This truck sold for $2.89 and was made by Marx in the U.S.A.

The 1968 and 1969 trucks sold for $1.49 and were basically a reissue of the 1967. This truck was manufactured by Marx, but in Hong Kong. Here are some guidelines to help you distinguish between the three years. In 1967 the velvet based box used clearly stated "Made in the U.S.A." and the Marx logo was not present. In 1968-69 the velvet box was not used, the box lid was marked "Made in Hong Kong" - "Hess Oil & Chemical Corp. Home Office Perth Amboy, NJ" and the Marx logo can be found on the battery cover of the truck.

The merger of Hess Oil and Chemical with Amerada Petroleum Corp. took place in 1969 producing the present day name of Amerada Hess. To commemorate this occasion the 1968-69 toy truck, relabeled with the new name, was given to the Hess employees. This extremely rare truck occasionally appears on the collector market even though it wasn't sold publicly.

As the 1970 holiday season approached, everyone wondered what Hess would offer next (this type of anticipation is still evident today). 1970 brought the first pumper-style fire truck ($1.69) with detachable hoses and ladder. The truck, made in Hong Kong by Marx, featured a revolving (motor driven) red emergency light instead of head and tail lights. The box featured a full-length picture of the truck, which came with a battery instruction card.

The same fire truck was reissued in 1971 ($1.69) with the box being the only difference. The '71 is referred to as the "Seasons Greetings" truck. The usual full color picture of the toy was not in this plain white cardboard box. Instead, a simple label stating "Hess - Seasons Greetings" was used. The reason is unclear. However, in this case the box makes a significant difference in the toy's value today.

1973 was the first year that Amerada Hess opted not to offer a toy promotion at their stations. However, another variation of the 1968 semi-tanker appeared in 1972-74. These two trucks do have slight modifications you should be aware of. The landing gear or "feet" on the trailer in 1968 were square while the 1972-74 are round. Additionally the 1972-74 box now reads "Amerada Hess Corporation". Selling prices: 1972 - $1.79 / 1974 - $1.89.

A new addition brings a new design in 1975. The first semi box truck with opening side and rear doors made its appearance. This truck carries the company colors of green, red and yellow on the cab. The box trailer is done in green, white, yellow and housed three miniature oil drums, along with battery powered head and tail lights. The truck sold for $1.99 and is stamped on the bottom "Made in Hong Kong" - "Amerada Hess Corporation". Although very rare, a "Marx - Made in the U.S.A." version of this same truck was manufactured. This version is identifiable by the stamp on the bottom of the trailer, and has a slightly larger box which reads "Made in the United States of America". Both trucks were packaged with different battery installation cards.

The 1975 truck was slightly modified and became the 1976 holiday promotion. In '75 the cab was fabricated in one piece as opposed to the 1976 version, which was made in two separate pieces (the fenders can be removed from the upper cab). The three miniature oil drums were still provided but Hess labels were added to them. This year's cost to the customer was $2.29.

In keeping with the times, a newly designed tractor was featured on the 1977 semi-tanker truck. Once again, the company colors were prominent, along with the traditional lighting system. The underside of the tanker was dated in roman numerals (1977) along with "Made in Hong Kong" and "Amerada Hess Corporation". The packaging included a battery installation card and the price tag was $2.39.

In 1978 ($2.49), with a minor change, the reissue of the 1977 truck appeared at the gas stations in time for the holiday season. The only difference is the size of the Hess label located on the rear of the tank trailer. In 1977 the label size was 1½" x 1" which makes the Hess name appear flatter. In 1978 the Hess label appeared a bit taller, measuring 1½" x ⅞".

1979 brought another void in the series with no promotional toy being offered. Amerada Hess, in maintaining high standards of service, provided training to its service station personnel on location by means of a modified GMC motor home. In 1980 a toy replica of the Hess Training Van was chosen as the holiday promotion. This van sold for $3.29 and featured an opening door, a pop-up TV antenna and operating lights. Its detail was so complete it sported miniature New Jersey license plates, windshield and sideview mirrors. The underside states "Made in Hong Kong" - "Amerada Hess Corporation". The copyright date of 1978 can be confusing, since the van was sold in 1980. A battery-installation card was included in the packaging.

1981 was the third and final year to date that Hess decided not to offer a holiday promotional toy. This decision didn't affect the toy's popularity when the 1982 truck ($4.69) made its debut. This replica of a 1933 Chevy home delivery oil tanker is said to be fashioned after the original truck that Leon Hess drove as a young man in the oil business. In fact, the box reads "The First Hess Truck". This '33 Chevy had operating lights, opening doors and a hose reel with a rubber hose located on the passenger side of the vehicle. Roman numerals dated the truck (1980) even though it wasn't offered until 1982. The underside was stamped "Made in Hong Kong" -

"Amerada Hess Corporation" with the operating instructions printed on the box.

A reissue of the '33 Chevy appeared in 1983 with a new feature: a savings bank. Hess advertised this popular toy as a "built-in bank in the tank" truck because of this unique addition. Your coin could be inserted into the top of the tank body and removed by turning one of the simulated filler caps. The selling price increased slightly to $5.29.

Continuing with the addition of the savings bank, 1984 brought a newly-designed semi-tanker similar to 1977-78 trucks, except for the addition of the bank. The underside of the truck was marked "Made in Hong Kong" - "Amerada Hess Corporation" and roman numerals dated (1984) the toy. Instructions were printed on the box, as well as a separate card in the packaging. Price $4.99.

Two previously offered trucks were used in 1985. Depending on your geographic location you could buy the 1933 Chevy in the Northeast or the 1984 tanker bank in the Southeast. To the best of my knowledge, this was the only time two different toys were offered in the same year.

The second fire truck in the Hess series was offered as a savings bank in 1986. This red aerial ladder truck included flashing emergency lights and head/tail lights. The white ladder could be fully rotated and extended, with the coin slot located under the ladder to the rear of the truck. Coins could be removed through a small trap door conveniently located in the back of the fire truck. Stamped on the underside "Made in Hong Kong" "Amerada Hess Corporation" and dated with roman numerals (1986), the toy sold for $5.49.

1987 brought an entirely new color scheme to the Hess toys; white & green. In previous years the actual company colors were used. The "18 Wheeler" box truck offered in 1987 had sliding cargo doors which concealed three miniature Hess-labeled oil drums, clearance lights were added to the traditional head and tail lights along with a savings bank. This truck was manufactured in two places and carries the name of origin on the truck & box - "Made in Hong Kong" or "Made in China" - The "Amerada Hess Corporation". Roman numerals (1987) were used to date the truck, which sold for $5.99.

The 1988 Hess toy truck and friction-powered racer sold for $6.95. The new white and green colors gave this toy a clean, crisp appearance and the customer two toys in one package for the first time. Once again the toy was produced in both Hong Kong and China, with operating instructions printed on the box.

A third fire truck ($8.99) was used for the 1989 promotion. The body of the truck was the same as 1986 but with a color change (white body - red aerial ladder). This year's toy featured a savings bank, lights and the addition of sound (dual sirens). It was dated by roman numerals (1989) and was manufactured in China.

1990 brought back the familiar semi-tanker truck (white & green). This truck boasted 36 working lights and dual sounds (air horns - back-up alarm.). The tanker, which was "Made in China", sold for $9.99.

As certain toys became more popular they were reissued. This was the case of the 1991 toy truck and friction-powered racer sold in that year. Looking much like its predecessor, it had a newly-designed race car and slightly larger truck cab. This edition was made in China and sold for $10.99.

Thanksgiving day 1992 will long be remembered for yet another advancement in an already outstanding promotional toy. The "18 Wheeler with Race Car" went on sale at the Hess gas stations. The white and green semi box truck was outfitted with clear side windows on the trailer to showcase a friction-powered car. The rear door opened to expose a movable ramp and the lighting system was enhanced to include the race car, which had battery-powered front and rear lights. Manufactured in China for Amerada Hess, the toy truck sold out quickly at $11.99.

PRICE GUIDE TO "HESS PROMOTIONAL TOYS"

(Original Selling Prices in Parentheses)

1964 'B Mack' Tanker
Courtesy Thomas G. Nefos National Toy Connection

1964 ($1.39) $1,850.00

B Model Mack Tanker truck made in Hong Kong

1965 SAME AS 1964

1966 ($1.89) $2,000.00

"Hess Voyager" Tanker Ship - Made in U.S.A.

1967 ($2.89) $2,200.00

Split Window Tank Truck with "Red Velvet" base on box - Made in U.S.A.

1967 'Red Velvet' Truck
Courtesy Thomas G. Nefos National Toy Connection

1968 ($1.49) $550.00

Same as 1967 except - no red velvet box - made in Hong Kong

1969 Same as 1968

1969 Never Sold Publicly $2,200.00

Split window tank truck **Amerada Hess** - Hong Kong

1970 ($1.69) $595.00

Red pumper fire truck Hong Kong by Marx

1st Truck in Series. 1970 Pumper F/T.

1971 ($1.69) $3,000.00

Same as 1970 except for box - "Season's Greetings"

1972 ($1.79) $250.00

Split window tanker truck same as 1968 with some minor changes

1973 No promotion offered

1974 ($1.89) $250.00

Split window tanker truck same as 1968 with some minor changes

1975 ($1.99) $295.00

Box-type tractor/trailer with 3 oil drums - no labels on drums - 1 pc. cab - made in both Hong Kong and the U.S.A.

1975 Box Truck
Courtesy Thomas G. Nefos National Toy Connection

1976 Box Truck
Courtesy Thomas G. Nefos National Toy Connection

1976 ($2.29) $285.00

Same as 1975 except - oil drums have "Hess" labels - 2 pc. cab - made in Hong Kong

1977 ($2.39) $135.00

Tanker tractor/trailer - made in Hong Kong - rear label is 1.5" x 1"

1977/78 Tanker Truck
Courtesy Thomas G. Nefos National Toy Connection

1982 '33 Chevy
Courtesy Thomas G. Nefos National Toy Connection

1978 ($2.49)   **$135.00**

Same as 1977 except the rear label is 1″ x ⅞″

1979 No promotion offered

1980 ($3.29)   **$200.00**

GMC training van - made in Hong Kong

1980 Hess Training Van
Courtesy Thomas G. Nefos National Toy Connection

1981 No promotion offered

1982 ($4.69)   **$55.00**

33 Chevy tanker delivery truck "first Hess truck" - Hong Kong

1983 ($5.29)   **$65.00**

Same as the 1982 except it was issued as a bank - made in Hong Kong

1984 ($4.99)   **$55.00**

Similar to 1977 except it was issued as a bank

1985 Reissue 1933 Chevy

Distributed in the North **Reissue 1984 Tanker** distributed in the South

1986 ($5.49)   **$65.00**

Red Aerial ladder fire truck made in Hong Kong - Bank

1987 ($5.99)   **$50.00**

Box-type tractor/trailer with 3 Hess labeled drums - made in both Hong Kong & China

1987 "18 Wheeler" Box Truck.
Courtesy Thomas G. Nefos National Toy Connection

1988 ($6.95)   **$48.00**

Race car transporter with friction powered car - made in both Hong Kong & China

1989 ($8.99)   **$28.00**

White aerial ladder fire truck dual siren sounds - bank made in China

1990 ($9.99)   **$20.00**

White semi-tanker truck with back-up/air horn sounds - made in China

1991 ($10.99)   **$20.00**

Reissue of 1988 with some slight changes - made in China

1992 ($11.99)

18 wheeler box truck with race car - made in China

WILCO PROMOS

1966   **$2,500.00**

B Mack Tanker Truck - Same color as the Hess 1964/65 Silver "W" tooled into grill

1967   **$650.00**

Split Window Tanker blue body with white trim

1968   **NO PRICE RECORDED**

Oil Tanker Ship - Green Body

"NO PROMOTIONAL TOYS IN THE 70's"

1985   **$95.00**

Semi Tanker Truck Bank - Blue body, white trim & red letters

1986   **$65.00**

'33 Chevy Tanker Bank - Blue body, white trim & red letters

1988   **$25.00**

Semi Box Truck - No barrels white body, blue trim with red/blue letters

1989   **$35.00**

Race Car Transporter - white body, blue trim, red/blue letters

1990   **$20.00**

Aerial Ladder Fire Truck - white body, blue trim with red letters

1991   **$15.00**

Semi-tanker truck - white body, blue trim, red letters

1992

Race Car Transporter

Hess 1989 Ladder Fire Truck
Courtesy Thomas G. Nefos Federal Shipping Network

1988, 1991, 1992 Hess Promos
Courtesy Thomas G. Nefos National Toy Connection

HESS TOY COMPANY

Nuremburg, Germany 1825-1934
by Bob Smith

Founded in 1825 by Matthieu Hess, making this company one of the oldest toy makers in Germany. Matthieu passed away in 1886, leaving the business to his son Johann Leonard, beginning the J.L.H. trademark. Most Hessmobile cars used a unique friction mechanism which had a power-lock on top of the cowl and a hand crank in the front. When cranking the handle a momentum would build up. You would then lift the power-lock, releasing the driveshaft to turn the rear wheels.

	C6	C8	C10
Hess Limousine, blue/black, 9" long, friction drive, c.1920 ...	800	1050	1400
Hess Limousine, Green/black, 7.5" long, friction drive, c.1920 ...	575	775	1000

Hess, from top: Limousine, 9" long, c.1920; Limousine, 7½" long, c.1920.
Photo by Bob Smith

The Hill Climber, with its unique style, is very easily recognized as an American made toy.
(Hill Climbers under the various above-named companies).

	C6	C8	C10
Hiller Comet race car, "3", fuel-powered, c.1940-42	800	1300	1800
Hiller Comet race car "4", non-powered, 18" long	500	800	1100

Hiller Comet Race Car "3"
Photo by William G. Floyd

	C6	C8	C10
Hoge Fire chief car, 15" long ..	225	400	550

HILL CLIMBER VEHICLES

by Bob Smith

Hill Climber Vehicles were first produced in the late 1800's. A patent was issued to Israel D. Boyer on November 2, 1897. This patent date is found on some Clark friction toys, though they were most likely produced after the turn of the century. The "Hill Climber" name was adopted by most of the friction toy manufacturers in the early 1900's. Four Companies in Dayton Ohio; the D.P. Clark Co., the Dayton Friction Toy Works, the Schieble Toy & Novelty Co., and the Republic tool Co. had a rivalry in the industry that lasted for 40 years. Research has found that the designers and engineers of Hill Climber toys were known to jump from one firm to another, bringing their trade secrets with them. This caused some similarities in color and style, making it difficult for the collector to recognize who made the toy. In the beginning all Hill Climber Vehicles had a primitive, husky look to them. They had wooden bodies, with cast iron wheels and buggy tops and pressed steel dash boards, and always a huge cast iron fly wheel to propel them up a hill. They were painted by hand in a dark green or blue color with accent striping of gold or yellow.

Hoge Fire Chief Car, 15" long
Photo by Bob Smith

HOLGATE

Holgate was founded by Cornelius Holgate in Philadelphia. About 1930 it began turning out educational wooden toys. It merged with Playskool in 1958; now owned by Hasbro.

	C6	C8	C10
Holgate Army Tank, 10 wheels, wooden, 12'' long..........	65	82	130
''Holmes Coal Co''. pressed steel delivery truck, 17½'' long....	400	600	800

''Holmes Coal Co.''
Courtesy Sotheby's NY

Hot Wheels - See Mattel

HUBLEY

The Hubley manufacturing company was founded at least as early as 1892 by John Hubley, and made iron toys from the start at its plant in Lancaster, Pennsylvania. All toys at the beginning were cast iron, and some early toys included coal ranges, circus wagons and mechanical banks. Hubley's cast iron toys were popular almost from the start, and have long been collector's items, as they were well-made and attractive. By 1940, however, the cast iron toy, due to the increased cost of freight and foreign competition, was slowly becoming a thing of the past. At this time, when Hubley was the largest producer of cast iron toys and cap pistols in the world, it began to introduce die-cast zinc alloy toys. During the Second World War, Hubley was 98% engaged in war production, turning out over five million M-74 bomb fuses, which the Hubley engineers played a large part in developing. Since the war, Hubley manufactures die-cast toys and plastic toys exclusively. In 1952, Hubley manufactured 9,763,610 toys and 11,184,878 cap pistols, about ten times the amount of toys and pistols they produced in 1930, but with a line of toys 80% smaller than in 1930. It is the combination of the relative scarcity (and multiplicity) of the older toys, plus the preference by collectors for cast iron over die-cast zinc alloy and plastic toys that makes the pre-World War II toys the most at-

tractive to collectors. Hubley was acquired by Gabriel Industries in late 1965, and puts out holster sets, cap pistols, vehicles, hobby kits and a number of other toys.

	C6	C8	C10
Hubley Air Compress Truck, 7'' long, c.1950s..............	37	56	75
Hubley Army Motor Truck No. 807 with driver, 15'' long.......	1100	1800	2400
Hubley Auto, 6½''...........	80	120	160
Hubley Auto, 7½'' long, No. 358, c.1928....................	150	225	300
Hubley Auto, 9'', 1922, Chevy?	400	600	800
Hubley Auto carrier, 10'' long, with three cars and one pickup truck, c.1939................	400	650	900
Hubley Auto Carrier, 1950s, 2 Packards....................	80	120	160
Hubley Auto Express, 9'' long, cast iron.....................	900	1450	2000
Hubley Avery tractor, 4¾'' long, very early..................	120	180	240
Hubley auto c.1950s, black plastic wheels, die-cast............	12	18	25
Hubley Bell Telephone Truck, 3¾'' long......................	150	235	310
Hubley Bell Telephone, 5¼''...	200	320	450
Hubley ''Bell Telephone'', 12'' long, with tools.............	100	150	210
Hubley Bell Telephone truck, 12½'' long, 1940s..........	175	263	350
Hubley Bell Telephone, truck 10'' long, 1931, with derrick and windlass, auger, trailer with 10'' pole, three digging tools, and two loose ladders...........	450	725	1050
Hubley as above, no equipment	300	550	700
Hubley ''Bell Telephone'', 13'' long, just ladders as equipment	250	375	500
Hubley Bell Telephone Truck, 9'' long, implements............	375	525	750
Hubley Bell Telephone Truck, 14'' long, 1950s, accessorites......	85	128	170
Hubley Bell Telephone, 24'' long, post WWII..................	90	135	185
Hubley Black & White cab, 1920s	1200	2000	3000
Hubley ''Borden's Milk Cream'', deluxe version, 7½'' long, rubber tires, clicker.............	1250	1875	2500

Hubley Bell Telephone, 24'' long, Post-War.
Courtesy Thomas G. Nefos, Federal Shipping Network

Hubley Bulldozer, 12'' long.
Photo by Calvin L. Chaussee

Hubley ''Borden's Milk Cream'', 7½'' long.
Courtesy Phillips NY

Hubley, Caterpillar, 3¼'' long.
Courtesy Mapes Auctioneers & Appraisers

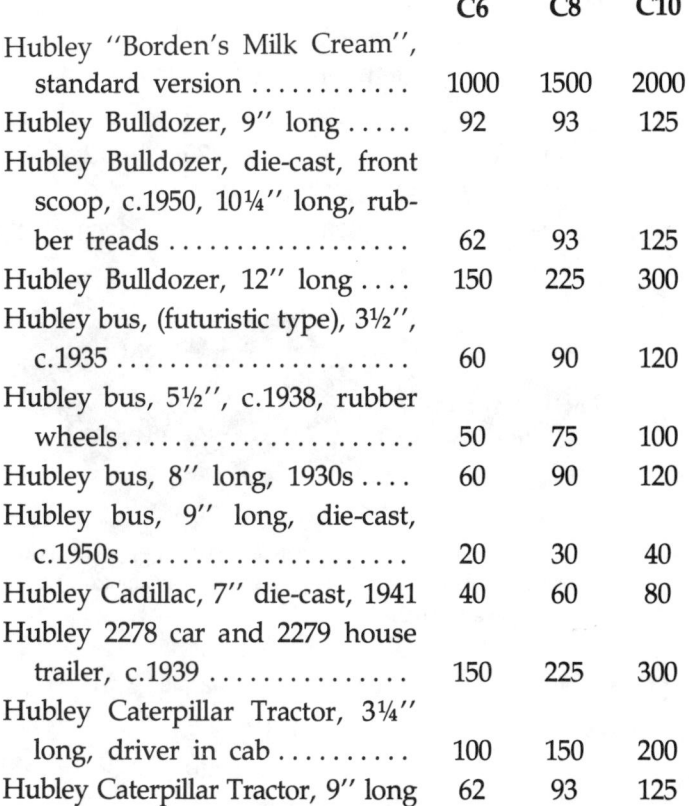

	C6	C8	C10
Hubley ''Borden's Milk Cream'', standard version	1000	1500	2000
Hubley Bulldozer, 9'' long	92	93	125
Hubley Bulldozer, die-cast, front scoop, c.1950, 10¼'' long, rubber treads	62	93	125
Hubley Bulldozer, 12'' long	150	225	300
Hubley bus, (futuristic type), 3½'', c.1935	60	90	120
Hubley bus, 5½'', c.1938, rubber wheels.....................	50	75	100
Hubley bus, 8'' long, 1930s	60	90	120
Hubley bus, 9'' long, die-cast, c.1950s	20	30	40
Hubley Cadillac, 7'' die-cast, 1941	40	60	80
Hubley 2278 car and 2279 house trailer, c.1939	150	225	300
Hubley Caterpillar Tractor, 3¼'' long, driver in cab	100	150	200
Hubley Caterpillar Tractor, 9'' long	62	93	125

Hubley Cattle Truck, plastic, 12'' long.
Photo by Terry Sells

	C6	C8	C10
Hubley Cattle Truck, plastic, 12'' long......................	45	68	90
Hubley Cement Mixer, 18'' long	400	600	800
Hubley Champion Stake Truck, 8½'' long, 1930s white rubber tires	140	210	280
Hubley Chemical Truck with ladders, 13'' long	200	300	400
Hubley Chevrolet 1932 Coupe, kit	15	22	30

	C6	C8	C10
Hubley Chevrolet 1932 Phaeton kit, 1960s	15	22	30
Hubley Chevrolet 1932 Roadster Kit, 1960s	15	22	30
Hubley Chrysler Airflow, 4½'' long, take-apart body	100	150	200
Hubley Chrysler Airflow, 6¾'' long, take-apart body	350	525	750
Hubley Chrysler Airflow, 8'' long, electrified, white rubber tires on wood hubs	600	900	1200
Hubley Chrysler Airflow racing car, c.1938	100	150	200
Hubley Coal Truck, cast iron, with driver, 16¾''	1200	1800	2500
Hubley ''Coast to Coast'' bus, cast iron, 1927, 13'' long	450	675	900
Hubley Compressor Truck	45	70	95
Hubley Convertible, 7'' long, die-cast & iron	100	150	200
Hubley Convertible, Hard Top, 1950s	50	75	100
Hubley Corvette	250	375	550
Hubley Coupe, 4½'' long, 1920s	100	150	200
Hubley Coupe, 3½'' long, 1930s	50	75	100
Hubley Coupe, 1933 Ford	90	135	180
Hubley Coupe roadster, rumble seat, 11'' long, rubber tires . .	125	187	250
Hubley De Soto Air flow, 4'' long	100	150	200
Hubley Diesel Low Boy w/grader	115	172	230
Hubley Diesel ''Road Roller'' . . .	200	300	400
Hubley Duesenberg Town Car, 9'' built-it model	25	38	50
Hubley Dump Truck, 5½''	50	75	100
Hubley Dump Truck, c.1938, 7½'' long	1000	1600	2400
Hubley Dump Truck, Mack, 1930s, 6 tires, 10¾'' long	1000	1800	2800

	C6	C8	C10
Hubley Dump Truck, plastic . . .	35	52	70
Hubley ''Elgin, The'' Street Sweeper, 8'' long, cast iron, 1931	3500	5000	7500
Hubley Fire Engine Pumper, c.1920, 12½'' long, cast iron, black rubber tires, driver, boiler-trailer	350	525	700
Hubley Fire Engine Pumper, 14'' long, two firemen, early, No. 554, auctioned in 1992 for $6820.			
Hubley Fire Engine pumper, early, No. 504	350	525	700
Hubley Fire Engine No. 526, 10½'' long, c.1936	175	263	350
Hubley Fire Engine, die-cast, white rubber tires with wooden rims, c.1941	40	60	80
Hubley Fire Ladder Truck, 7½'' long, early	130	195	260
Hubley Fire Ladder Truck, 8½'', early	250	375	500
Hubley Fire Ladder Truck, 14'' long, driver, c.early 1930s	500	800	1200
Hubley Fire Ladder Truck, 19½'' long	850	1400	1900
Hubley Fire Truck with searchlight, white rubber tires with wooden rims	55	82	110
Hubley Fire Truck, 5''	75	112	150
Hubley ''5 Ton Truck'', 17'' long, 8 wooden barrels, c.1920	750	1200	1700

Hubley Dump Truck, Mack, 1930s, 6 tires, 10¾'' long. Driver missing in photo. Courtesy James S. Maxwell/Virginia Caputo Photo by Virginia Caputo

	C6	C8	C10
Hubley Ford Coupe, 1936	40	50	80
Hubley Ford Model A Coupe Kit, 1960s	20	30	40
Hubley Ford Model A Phaeton Kit, 1960s	20	30	40

Hubley ''5 ton truck''
Courtesy Sotheby's NY

HUBLEY

	C6	C8	C10
Hubley Ford Model A Pickup Kit, 1960s	20	30	40
Hubley Ford Model A Station Wagon Kit, 1960s	20	30	40
Hubley Ford Model A Town Car Kit, 1960s	20	30	40
Hubley Ford Model A Victoria Kit, 1960s	20	30	40
Hubley Ford Tractor & Disc	85	128	170
Hubley Fordson Front-End Loader, cast iron, circa early 1930s	1000	1800	2700
Hubley Fuel Truck, cast iron, 5½" long	100	150	200
Hubley Grader	56	84	112
Hubley "General" steam shovel, 6" long	175	263	350
Hubley "General" steam shovel, 9" long	400	625	850

Hubley, Huber Road Roller, 8" long.
Courtesy Mapes Auctioneers & Appraisers

1F3159 — "Huber," 15 in. long, nickeled tank, scarifier lowers by lever, painted driver, steering wheel steers, can be used as a pull toy. ⅓ doz. in box................Doz $24.00

Hubley "Huber" Road Roller, 15" long, as shown in December, 1929 Butler Bros. catalog.

Hubley "General", 9" long.

	C6	C8	C10
Hubley "General" steam shovel, 10½" long	450	700	1000
Hubley "General" steam shovel, 15" long	450	700	1000
Hubley Hook & Ladder No. 463	28	42	56
Hubley Hook & Ladder No. 473	100	150	200
Hubley Hook & Ladder Truck, 19½" long, cast iron	200	300	400
Hubley Huber Road Roller, 4" long	110	165	220
Hubley Huber Road Roller, 8" long	450	700	1000
Hubley Huber Road Roller, 13" long	2500	3850	5000
Hubley Huber Road Roller, 14" long	1600	2500	3800
Hubley Huber Road Roller, 15" long	3000	4500	6000

"Hubley Tanker", plastic, 12½" long.
Photo by Terry Sells

	C6	C8	C10
Hubley "Hubley Tanker", plastic, 12½" long	No Price Found		
Hubley "Hubley Transport", plastic, 13" long auto carrier	No Price Found		
Hubley "Jaeger" Cement Mixer	475	712	950
Hubley Jaguar, 7½" long, die-cast	95	135	190
Hubley Jeep & Speedboat, late	25	38	50
Hubley Kiddietoy No. 432 MGTD Roadster, 6" long	110	165	220
Hubley Kiddietoy No. 5 "Taxi"	7	12	25
Hubley Kiddietoy No. 476 Dump Truck	70	105	140
Hubley Kiddietoy No. 510 series Dump Truck	125	188	250

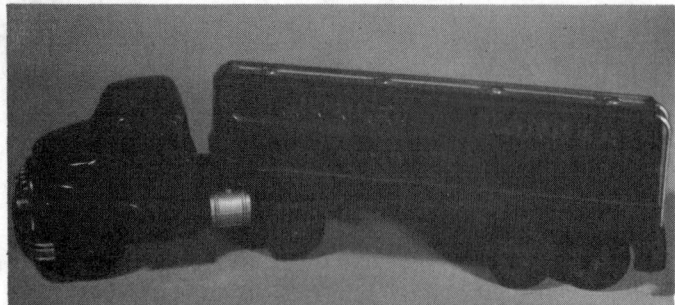

Hubley "Hubley Tanker", 12½" long.
Photo by Terry Sells

Hubley Kiddietoy Stake Truck No. 461.
Courtesy Alice & Bob Wagner

"Hubley Transport", plastic, 13" long.
Photo by Terry Sells

Hubley Kiddietoy No. 5 "Taxi".
Courtesy Bob & Alice Wagner

IF3111—"Jaeger" Concrete Mixer, 6¾ x6¼, yellow enameled chassis with motor front, blue enameled uprights, bright aluminum hopper, nickeled wheels, operated by turning crank & wheel. ½ doz. in box.
Doz **$11.50**

Hubley "Jaeger" Cement Mixer, 1929

L to R: Hubley, "Merchants Delivery", Arcade, Ambulance, "City Ambulance", 6" long.
Courtesy Chic Gast

Hubley Jaguar 7½" long, diecast.
Photo by Bob Smith

	C6	C8	C10
❮Hubley Kiddietoy No. 457 Racer, 6½" long, die-cast, rubber tires	27	41	55
Hubley Kiddietoy Stake Truck No. 461, Ford, 1946	45	90	170
Hubley Kiddietoy, "Patrol" stake truck, c.1937	27	41	55
Hubley Kiddietoy Wrecker, 8" long	67	105	135

	C6	C8	C10
Hubley Ladder Truck circa late 1930s, 5″	45	67	90
Hubley Ladder Truck, terraplane front, 1930s, 6″ long	70	105	140
Hubley Ladder Truck, 7″ long, c.1920s	175	263	350
Hubley Ladder Truck, 10″ long, 1930s	110	165	225
Hubley Ladder Truck, 13½″ c.1940	300	550	700
Hubley LaSalle, 1940, die-cast . .	90	135	180
Hubley Life Saver Truck, c.1930, hole in rear is large enough to hold pack of Life Savers	125	187	250
Hubley Life Saver Truck, small hole in rear, can't hold Life Savers	400	600	800
Hubley Limousine, 7″ long, six-door, 1920s	160	240	320
Hubley Lincoln Zephyr, 7¼″ long	200	300	400
Hubley Lincoln Zephyr and House Trailer, cast iron, 14″ long overall	400	600	800
Hubley Log Truck, 13″ long . . .	100	150	200
Hubley Log Truck, 16″ long . . .	70	105	140
Hubley Log Truck No. 469	45	100	200
Hubley Log Truck with five chained logs, black rubber tires, die-cast, approx. 19″ long . . .	70	105	140
Hubley Low Boy Hauler w/Road Grader	215	370	435
Hubley Low Boy truck, trailer, tractor	200	300	400
Hubley Mack Dump truck, 8½″ long	600	950	1400
Hubley Mack Dump truck, 11½″ long, with driver	900	1400	2200
Hubley Mack Gasoline truck, 13¼″ long, c.1925	550	900	1300
Hubley Mack Truck Steam Shovel-Digger, c.1920, nickel wheels and scoop, 7″ long	450	675	920
Hubley "Merchants Delivery" 1920s, approx. 6″ long	No Price Found		
Hubley MG, 9″ long	95	135	190
Hubley MG, 5¾″ long	24	36	48
Hubley Mighty Metal Power Shovel	100	150	200

Hubley MG, 9″ long, die-cast.
Photo by Bob Smith

Hubley "Milk Cream" truck.
Courtesy James S. Maxwell/Virginia Caputo
Photo by Virginia Caputo

	C6	C8	C10
Hubley "Milk Cream" truck, 1930s, cast iron, 3½″ long, white rubber tires	200	300	400
Hubley "Mr. Magoo Car", 1961, 9″ long, five actions, includes cloth roof top, battery op. . . .	150	225	300
Hubley Monarch tractor, 5½″ long	600	900	1200
Hubley Motor Express tractor and trailer, black rubber tires, 500 series, approx. 19″ long	145	218	290
Hubley 2287 "Motor Express" truck and trailer, 8″ long	200	300	400

Hubley Motorcycles

(list by Kent M. Comstock)

Kent M. Comstock

Hubley HM2, passenger missing.
Photo by Max Heiss

Hubley, L to R: HM8, HM7.
Photo by Kent M. Comstock

Kent M. Comstock, who has contributed photos, and much information, regarding motorcycles to various sections of this book, is a lifelong motorcycle enthusiast. It was his interest in antique motorcycles that got him interested in toys. He was at an Antique Motorcycle Club (AMC) meet in Wauseon, Ohio in 1985 when he saw small cast iron motorcycles trading for hundreds of dollars. He was hooked. He believes toy replicas are great collector pieces for motorcycle enthusiasts. "The Harleys, Indians and Hendersons made out of iron are very realistic and representative of their period. They were all authorized and very well detailed." He strongly advises new collectors to buy what they like, as they'll be able to continue to enjoy the toy even if it dips in price.

	C6	C8	C10
HM 1 Motorcycle solo, "Cop", rubber or nickel wheels 4" ..	50	75	100
HM 2 Motorcycle with sidecar "Cop" rider and passenger 4"	60	90	120
HM 3 Motorcycle racer "Speed" 4¼"	100	150	225
HM 4 Motorcycle tandem, "PDH" rubber or nickel wheels 4⅛".	100	150	250

Hubley HM1

	C6	C8	C10
HM 5 Motorcycle trike "Crash Car" rubber or nickel wheels 4¾"	50	75	125
HM 6 Motorcycle trike, traffic car nickel wheels, 3⅝"	75	125	200
HM 7 Motorcycle trike "Flowers" nickel wheels, blue, 3⅜".....	500	800	1200
HM 8 Motorcycle trike "Flowers" rubber or nickel wheels, blue 4½"	500	800	1200
HM 9 Motorcycle policeman "Harley Davidson", nickel wheels, 5½"	150	250	400
HM 10 Motorcycle policeman "Harley Davidson" swivel head, rubber or nickel wheels, 7¼"	300	450	700
HM 11 Motorcycle Hillclimber "HD-45" rubber or nickel wheels 6½"	325	475	750
HM 12 Motorcycle Racer, nickel wheels 5¾"	375	550	800

Right: Hubley HM9. The left is an unknown, but probably Hubley. It is 4¼" long, with removable rider and rubber tires. Price in C6, C8, C10: $50, 75, 125.
Photo by Kent M. Comstock

Hubley HM13
Photo by Kent M. Comstock

Hubley HM11
Photo by Kent M. Comstock

	C6	C8	C10
HM 13 Motorcycle civilian driver, rubber or nickel wheels, 6¼"	250	400	600
HM 14 Motorcycle with sidecar, civilian driver and passenger, 6½"	300	500	750
HM 15 Motorcycle policeman "PD" 1950's die-cast with plastic driver 8½"	200	300	500
HM 16 Motorcycle trike "Traffic Car" Indian, rubber tires, 9"	600	750	1000
HM 17 Motorcycle policeman, battery operated headlight, 6"	150	250	350
HM 18 Motorcycle with demountable cop, battery operated headlight 8½" red	600	750	1000

Hubley HM12
Photo by Kent M. Comstock

Hubley HM15
Photo by Kent M. Comstock

Hubley HM16
Courtesy Sotheby's NY

Hubley HM17
Photo by Max Heiss

Hubley HM19
Courtesy Sotheby's NY

	C6	C8	C10
HM 19 Motorcycle with sidecar, 2 demountable cops, battery-operated headlight 8½'' red..	700	950	1300

	C6	C8	C10
HM 20 Motorcycle with sidecar ''Harley Davidson'' 2 demountable cops 9'' Olive green......	700	1000	1400

Hubley HM20
Photo by Kent M. Comstock

Hubley HM21
Courtesy Sotheby's NY

	C6	C8	C10
HM 21 Motorcycle with sidecar ''Indian'' 2 demountable cops 9'' red......	700	1000	1400
HM 22 Motorcycle with detachable civilian rider ''Harley Davidson'' 9'' olive green, blue, or orange	1000	1750	2500
HM 23 Motorcycle with detachable cop, ''Harley Davidson'' 9'' olive green, blue, or orange..	600	900	1200
HM 24 Motorcycle with detachable cop, ''Indian'' nickel 4-cylinder motor, 9¼'' red, green, or yellow......	900	1200	1500

Hubley HM22
Photo by Kent M. Comstock

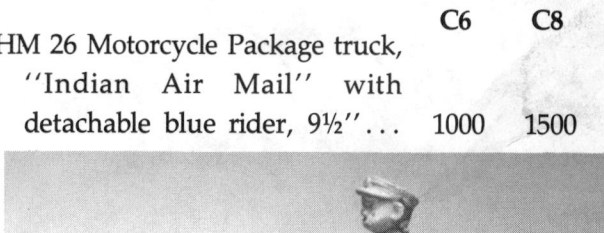

Hubley HM26
Courtesy Sotheby's NY

	C6	C8	C10
HM 26 Motorcycle Package truck, "Indian Air Mail" with detachable blue rider, 9½"...	1000	1500	2500

	C6	C8	C10
HM 27 Motorcycle trike "Indian Crash Car" demountable rider, axes and hose reel 11½"....	1500	2000	3000
HM 28 Motorcycle trike "Indian Traffic Car", demountable rider, 12" red and blue..........	1500	2000	3000
HM 29 Motorcycle with sidecar, "Indian Armored Car", 2 demountable cops, 8½", red...	1000	1500	2500
HM 30 Motorcycle, plastic Kiddietoy, 5" long..........	15	22	30

Hubley HM24
Photo by Kent M. Comstock

Hubley HM25
Courtesy Sotheby's NY

Hubley HM30
Photo by Terry Sells

	C6	C8	C10
HM 25 Motorcycle Package truck, "Harley Davidson Parcel Post" with detachable blue rider 9½"	1000	1500	2500

Hubley HM31
Courtesy Sotheby's NY

	C6	C8	C10
HM 31 Motorcycle, trike "Say It With Flowers", cast iron.....	No Price Found		
HM 32 Motorcycle, Harley-Davidson, with policeman, swivel head, 6½" long, early	500	750	1000
HM 32 Like above, later version	400	600	800

Hubley HM32
Courtesy David Mapes Auctions

	C6	C8	C10
Hubley Motorized Steam Pumper, 4" long, c.1930s............	50	75	100
Hubley Nite Coach, 3½" long, metal wheels, went on "Nu-Car" carrier, 1930s.........	30	45	60

Hubley HM32
Courtesy Wilkinson Collection, Detroit Antique Toy Museum

Hubley Nite Coach, 3½" long, metal wheels, went on "Nu-Car" carrier, 1930s.
Courtesy Chic Gast.

Hubley Packard Sedan, 5½" long, 1939-40s.
Courtesy Bob & Alice Wagner

HUBLEY

1F3109—"Packard," 11 in. long, green & black enameled body, stripped, hood and front doors open, imit. engine, disc wheels, imit. balloon gray tires, nickeled driver. ⅓ doz. in box.
Doz $14.00

Hubley Packard, 1929

	C6	C8	C10
Hubley "Nucar Transport" with trailer 17" long, 4 cars	500	900	1250
Hubley Packard sedan, 5½", 1939-1940s	25	40	75
Hubley Packard, 15 parts, 1929, 11" long	5000	7500	10,000
Hubley Packard, 1930 "Phaeton" Kit	25	38	50
Hubley Packard Roadster Kit	16	24	32
Hubley "Panama" Digger, approx. 3½" long (hard to find)	300	450	600
Hubley "Panama" digger, 9½" long	800	1200	1650

	C6	C8	C10
Hubley "Panama" digger, Mack, 13" long	1100	1650	2200
Hubley "Patrol", 15½" long, driver, policeman	1400	2100	2800
Hubley Pickup, 3½" long, cast iron	22	33	45
Hubley Pipe Truck No. 803, 9½" long, c.1950s	35	52	70
Hubley Power Shovel, 14"	87	130	175
Hubley Hubley Pumper, circa late 1930s	115	172	230
Hubley Pumper, Ahrens-Fox, 7" long	400	600	800
Hubley Pumper, Ahrens-Fox, 10" long	250	375	500
Hubley Pumper, terraplane front, 1930s, 6¼" long	185	275	370
Hubley Pumper w/Searchlight, 7" long, c.1950s	55	83	110

Hubley, Racer "1790"
Photo by Bill Kaufman

Hubley "Panama", 9½" long.

Hubley "Panama" digger, Mack, 13" long

	C6	C8	C10
Hubley Racer, "1790", 5" long, approx.	100	150	200
Hubley Racer, 5½" long, 1930s, 2 passengers	125	188	250
Hubley Racer, 6" long, driver, tail fin, 1930s	210	325	450
Hubley Racer, 6½" long, driver, 1930s	200	300	400
Hubley Racer, 6½" long, plastic	44	66	88
Hubley Racer, driver, 7" long	230	345	460
Hubley Racer, driver, 7" long, electric headlights	No Price Found		
Hubley Racer, 2241, 7½" long, 1930s	45	68	90
Hubley Racer, 8½" long, 1930s, tail fin, exhaust stacks, driver	650	1000	1500
Hubley Racer No. 5, early wheels	1400	2250	2900

	C6	C8	C10
Hubley Racer No. 5, painted and nickeled iron and aluminum, 9½″ long, raise hood-see motor	1250	1900	2700
Hubley Racer 629, 1936 6¾″ long	300	475	650
Hubley Racer No. 677, 8½″ long	700	1200	1600
Hubley Racer, Closed Cabin, 1930s, 8″ long	250	375	500
Hubley Racer, die-cast, 12″ long	65	93	130
Hubley Racer ″No. 1″, 8″ long	250	375	500
Hubley Racer, driver, rubber tires, 8″ long	125	188	250
Hubley Racer, die-cast, black rubber tires, 4″ long	25	38	50
Hubley Racer, animated exhaust stacks, 8″ long, driver	550	875	1250
Hubley ″Railway Express″ Truck, 5″ long, rubber tires	200	300	400

Hubley ″Railway Express″ truck, 5″ long.
Courtesy Mapes Auctioneers & Appraisers.

	C6	C8	C10
Hubley Road Grader, 12″	70	105	140
Hubley Road Grader, 15″ long, 1950s	40	60	80
Hubley Road Roller, late 1920s, 8″ long, driver	300	450	600
Hubley Road Scraper No. 481	37	52	75
Hubley Roadster, early 1920s, 7¼″ long, driver	300	450	650
Hubley School Bus	36	54	72
Hubley Sedan, 1920, cast iron, 7″ long	100	150	200
Hubley Sedan, 1928, cast iron, 7″ long	150	225	300

	C6	C8	C10
Hubley Sedan, 5″ long, sidemount tire, 1930s	225	338	450
Hubley Sedan, c.1938, 2-door, 3½″, looks like Ford, rubber wheels	60	90	120
Hubley Sedan, die-cast, 7″ long	62	93	125
Hubley Service Car, 4¼″ long	60	90	120
Hubley Service Car, 5″ cast iron, including wheels, 1930s	200	300	400
Hubley 726 Shovel Truck, 10″ long, c.1930	No Price Found		
Hubley Shovel Truck, 8½″ long, c.1938	550	900	1250
Hubley Speedster No. 6, early, 7″ long	225	350	435
Hubley Sport Car no. 485	70	105	140
Hubley Stake Dump, die-cast	30	45	60
Hubley Stake Truck, circa late 1930s	160	240	325
Hubley No. 614 Stake Truck, c.1930s	75	112	150
Hubley Stake Bed Truck, cast iron, 3½″ long	25	38	50
Hubley Stake bed truck, 7″ long	200	300	400

Hubley, Stake bed truck, 7″ long, Courtesy Mapes Auctioneers & Appraisers.

	C6	C8	C10
Hubley Stake Truck with trailer - No. 927. Two pieces, 21″ long	40	60	80
Hubley No. 452 stake-type truck, black rubber tires, circa post WWII	40	60	80
Hubley Station Wagon, c.1940s, 1950s	75	112	150
Hubley Steam Roller, 5″	150	225	300
Hubley Stock Truck, plastic, 12″ long	112	168	225

Hubley Elgin
Courtesy Chic Gast

Hubley "10 ton" stake truck, 7" long, cast iron.
Photo by Bob Smith

	C6	C8	C10
Hubley Studebaker Roadster, frame and body separate	300	450	600
Hubley Studebaker Stake Truck	20	30	40
Hubley Studebaker Touring Car, cast iron...................	325	518	650
Hubley Take-Apart Coupe, 6" long	No Price Found		
Hubley Take-Apart Sedan, 6" long, early 1930s	150	230	325
Hubley Take-Apart Stake Truck, 4¾" long.................	200	300	400
Hubley Take-Apart Station Wagon, 1920s...................	250	400	550
Hubley Telephone Truck, plastic	25	38	50
Hubley "10 Ton" Stake Truck, cast iron, 7" long	300	425	600
Hubley Thunderbird	120	180	240
Hubley Touring Auto, 1921, 11½" long......................	No Price Found		

	C6	C8	C10
Hubley Touring Auto, 1915, 9½" long, cast iron, chauffeur and rider	750	1125	1500
Hubley Tow Truck, 8¾" long, cast iron, c.1930s	140	210	280
Hubley Tow Truck, Ford, 9" long, die-cast....................	60	90	120
Hubley Tractor No. 472........	40	60	80
Hubley Tractor No. 490........	50	75	100
Hubley Tractor, Ford 6000......	80	120	160
Hubley Tractor, steam boiler in front, 4¾" long, c.early 1920s	125	187	250
Hubley Tractor, 5", 1930s......	250	450	600
Hubley Tractor, die-cast........	20	30	40
Hubley Tractor Loader No. 501, 11" long, 1950s	65	98	130
Hubley Tractor Trailer c.1950s ..	75	112	150
Hubley Tractor Trailer and Road Scraper No. 506.............	100	150	200
Hubley Trailer Truck, c.1936-38 .	100	150	200
Hubley Transitional Fire Patrol, 12" cast iron, driver, firemen, 1920......................	1000	1500	2000
"Hubley U.S.A." Airflow type, c.1937, approx. 3½" long....	20	30	40
Hubley Water Tower, early, 14" long, 2 drivers	850	1400	2000
Hubley Wrecker, chrome wheels, Service Car	45	68	90
Hubley Wrecker, 3½"	42	63	85
Hubley Wrecker, 4½", rubber wheels, 1930	65	100	135
Hubley Wrecker, 4¾"	75	112	150
Hubley Wrecker, 6" c.1940, white wheels on large hubs........	100	150	200
Hubley Wrecking Truck, 1930, cast iron, rubber tires, 7½" long .	150	225	300
Hubley Wrecker, 10" long, Ford, No. 474	82	123	165
Hubley Yellow Cab, 8" long, rear luggage rack folds down.....	300	450	600

Hubley Yellow Cab, rear luggage rack folds down.
Photo by Chic Gast

Ideal, L to R: Army Ambulance, Van, 6'' long.
Courtesy Bob & Alice Wagner

IDEAL

	C6	C8	C10
Ideal American LaFrance Aerial Ladder Truck	95	143	190
Ideal American LaFrance Fix-It Tow Truck w/1952 Pontiac car & tools	150	225	300
Ideal Army Ambulance, 5'' long	20	30	40
Ideal Army Van, 4'' long	20	30	40
Ideal Atomic Rocket Launching Truck, 12'' long	50	75	100
Ideal Barracuda Coupe, 1964, plastic, 4'' long	15	23	30
Ideal Cadillac, four door, 1948, plastic, 4'' long	25	38	50
Ideal Car Trailer, c.1945, plastic, 3'' long	20	30	40
Ideal Ideal Car Trailer, plastic, 4 cars, 27'' long	40	60	80
Ideal Carousel Truck	50	75	100
Ideal Cattle Truck, 13'' long	25	38	50
Ideal Coal Truck, 1949, 5½'' long	21	31	42
Ideal Corvette	55	83	110
Ideal Danger Patrol Truck, 1950s	40	60	80
Ideal ''Dairy Farm'' Van	10	25	60
Ideal Dragnet Talking Police Car	No Price Found		
Ideal Dump Truck	25	38	50
Ideal Emergency Van, 6'' long .	10	35	45
Ideal Fire Pumper	34	51	68
Ideal Ice Cream Truck, 5½'' long, 1948-54	30	60	100
Ideal Fix-It Sport Convertible, 13'' long	65	98	130

Ideal, back row: Van, sliding front door, ''Dairy Farm'' van. Front: Van, 6'' long.
Courtesy Bob & Alice Wagner

Ideal Dump Truck, plastic.
Photo by Dave Leopard

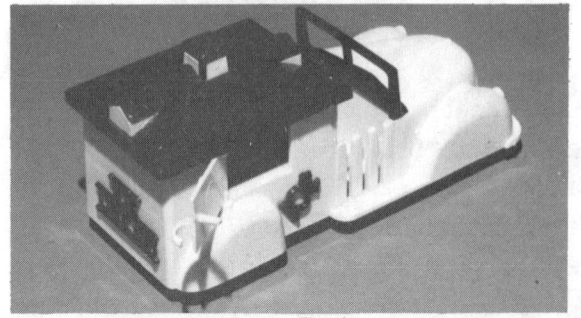

Ideal Ice Cream Truck.
Courtesy Bob & Alice Wagner

	C6	C8	C10
Ideal Fix-It Tow Truck and Car with Dented Fender, 20½" long, metal and plastic	No Price Found		
Ideal Fix-It Truck, 8½" long, with tools, plastic	No Price Found		
Ideal Ford Truck	40	60	80
Ideal Ford Wagon	40	60	80
Ideal "Gambles" semi truck, 12" long, plastic	36	54	72
Ideal Jeep, circa 1945	20	30	40

Ideal, L to R: Pick-up truck, streamlined, with canopy and gas tank filler, 4½", Pick-up truck, streamlined, 4½".
Courtesy Alice & Bob Wagner

Ideal Jeep, c.1945, on original box.
Photo by Terry Sells

Ideal Robert the Robot
Photo by Don Hultzman

	C6	C8	C10
Ideal Jet Racer	50	75	100
Ideal Mercedes Sedan, 9" long	35	52	70
Ideal Oldsmobile, 1954, 19" long	150	225	300
Ideal Pickup truck, American, 1948, 4" plastic	20	30	40
Ideal Pickup truck, Ford, 1940, 4" plastic	20	30	40
Ideal Pickup truck, streamlined, 4½" long, 1950s	4	10	20
Ideal Pickup truck, streamlined, with canopy and gas tank filler, 4½" long, 1950s	4	10	20
Ideal Race Car, 8" wind-up	60	90	120

	C6	C8	C10
Ideal Robert the Robot, battery-operated	150	225	300
Ideal Rocket Cycle, 6½" long	No Price Found		
Ideal Sanitation truck, 5½" long, plastic	20	35	50
Ideal Scooter, 4" long, plastic	No Price Found		
Ideal Sedan, 9¼" long, plastic	20	35	50
Ideal Semi, 12" long	26	39	52
Ideal Service Truck, 8" long	22	33	45
Ideal Service Van, 5" long	20	30	40
Ideal Shell Truck, 12½" long	25	38	50
Ideal Signal Corps truck, 5" long	20	30	40
Ideal Speed King Dream Racer, plastic, 13" long	50	75	100
Ideal Steam Shovel, 7½" long	40	60	80
Ideal "Television Repair" truck	70	105	140

Ideal Rocket Cycle
Photo by Terry Sells

Ideal Scooter
Photo by Terry Sells

Ideal Sedan, 9¼'' long.
Photo by Terry Sells

Ideal Shell truck
Photo by Terry Sells

Ideal Steam Shovel, plastic.
Photo by Dave Leopard

	C6	C8	C10
Ideal Tow truck, 17'' long, plastic and metal	100	150	200
Ideal tractor, 1948, plastic, 4'' long	20	30	40
Ideal Two-Car Garage..........	No Price Found		

Ideal Two-Car Garage, plastic.
Photo by Dave Leopard

Ideal Turbo-Jet Car	40	60	80
Ideal Van, 6'' long	10	35	45
Ideal Van, sliding front door, 4½'' long......................	10	25	60
Ideal Work truck	12	18	25
Ideal XP-600 Fix-It car or tomorrow	115	172	230

Ideal XP-600 Fix-It Car of Tomorrow. This originally sold for $6.

Ideal Fix-It Sport Convertible, as shown in the 1953-54 Toy Yearbook. .

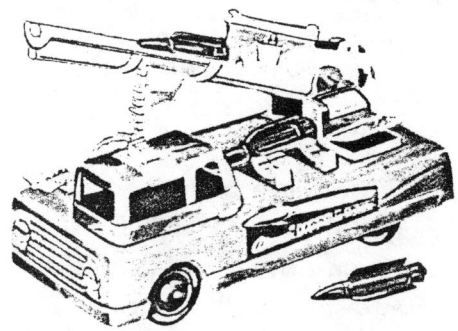

Ideal Atomic Rocket Launching Truck, as shown in a 1955-56 Toy Yearbook

Ideal Fix-It Truck, as shown in a 1952-53 Toy Yearbook.

D, Ideal Fix-It Tow Truck and Car with dented fender. 20½'' plastic and metal truck holds tools for chaning tires and fender. Also has battery-operated searchlight, crank-operated tow crane, ''fire extinguisher''. $9.95

E, Ideal Danger Patrol truck, 12¾'' long, of plastic and metal, with friction motor. Includes tool chest, ''oxygen'' tank, ladders, road block, control box with ''microphone'', etc. Red light flashes as truck moves. $3.98.

F, Ideal Dragnet Talking Police Car. Official 14½'' ''Dragnet'' plastic and metal car. Crank produces ''radio voice''. Has built-in swivel chair, table, battery-operated searchlight, camera, binoculars, rifles, etc. $3.98.

Illustration from the 1955-56 Toy Yearbook.

	C6	C8	C10
Ingap Mouse Car, wind-up, Italian, 6" long, eccentric wheels, arms extend........	1650	2475	3300

Ingap Mouse Car
Courtesy Christie's East

IRWIN TOY CORPORATION

Irwin was founded in 1922 by Irwin Cohn. Located at first in New York City, it began as a maker of celluloid baby rattles and pinwheels, soon becoming the largest manufacturer of pinwheels in the U.S. In the late 1940s it produced the first polyethelene toy, a seven-inch car. Irwin, which eventually moved to Leominster and Fitchburg in Massachusetts (with an additional plant in Nashua, New Hampshire), sold out to Miner Industries in 1973.

	C6	C8	C10
Irwin Army Bus..............	25	38	50
Irwin Barney Rubble Car.......	17	26	35
Irwin Buick Convertible, 1948, 5" long......................	10	15	20
Irwin Chevrolet Panel Delivery, 6" long......................	10	15	20
Irwin Chevrolet Pickup Truck, 5.3" long, 1952.................	10	15	20
Irwin Dream Car convertible, 16" long, metal	200	300	400
Irwin Ford Sunliner, 9" long, plastic friction..............	47	72	95

	C6	C8	C10
Irwin Ice Cream Truck, plastic..	50	75	100
Irwin Jaguar Roadster, 6" long.	35	52	70
Irwin Packard Sedan, friction, 9" long, 1952	25	30	35
Irwin Pontiac Hardtop Coupe, friction, 6" long, 1952..........	15	20	25
Irwin "Skipper" convertible, 1962	150	225	300
Irwin Steeraway Wonder Car...	95	143	190

Irwin Chevrolet Pick-Up Truck, 5.3" long.
Photo by Dave Leopard

Irwin Pontiac Hard-top Coupe, friction.
Photo by Dave Leopard

	C6	C8	C10
Ives horseless carriage runabout, 6½" long, 6" high to the top of jockey cap on driver.........	2500	3750	5000
Ives steamer, cast iron, 19½" long, two drivers	500	750	1000

JANE FRANCIS TOYS

(This history was prepared by Jane Francis in May, 1984)

In 1942, the scarcity of toys during the war started me making stuffed toys for a Pittsburgh hospital gift shop, Allegheny General, where I was a Medical Librarian. It wasn't long before I was making the "Gingham Dog", the "Calico Cat", and "Jumbo, The Elephant" for several hospital gift shops in the Pittsburgh area. The toy buyer at Gimbel's called one day and asked me to make 12 dozen stuffed toys. This was the real beginning of Jane Francis Toys.

I located a woman who had had a great deal of experience in an Eastern sewing factory. She agreed to sew in her own home. Twelve dozen were made and delivered one day ahead of schedule.

It wasn't long before other major department stores in Philadelphia, Baltimore and Washington were ordering and more sewers were found. A giraffe and a turtle were added to the line.

Pearce Woolen Mills in nearby Latrobe was manufacturing army blankets and we purchased the combings from the blankets to stuff the toys. The Association for the Blind took the contract to stuff the toys. Now we were off and running.

Home sewers were unable to meet production, so we found a sewing factory in Canton, Ohio to cut and sew the bodies. They were shipped back to Pittsburgh where they were stuffed and packed for shipment. After the first few weeks a string tab, saying "Jane Francis Toys" was attached to each animal. By this time we had a commissioned agent to handle sales. Their sales office was at 200 Fifth Ave., New York.

The war was winding down and my husband decided to join the operation and bring out a line of die-cast cars and trucks, spinning toys and a Gulf Service Station.

The die-cast line went well until the advent of plastic toys. At approximately the same time, a man by the name of Frank Snedden invented and patented the first automatic shut-off hose nozzle. He was about to retire from Westinghouse and decided to sell his patents and dies. A purchase was negotiated.

A fire at our location in Wilkinsburg (Pittsburgh) prompted us to move to Somerset. At that location, a partner was brought into the business. The partnership did not work out and in 1951 we started the A.W. Francis Co. to manufacture lawn and garden accessories.

(A shorter history by Jane Francis states her firm operated in Wilkinsburg from 1942 through 1946 and in Somerset from 1947 through 1949. The line of die-cast cars was introduced in 1945. The last Jane Francis toys were manufactured in 1949. Jane Francis Vanyo, the Francis' daughter, in 1993 stated that the successor company, A.W. Francis, was still in business in Somerset under the name Green Garden, Inc., producing lawn and garden accessories.)

	C6	C8	C10
JF01 Pickup truck, 6½" long . . .	30	40	50
JF02 Pickup truck, 5" long, No. 347	20	25	30
JF03 Pickup truck, 5" long, No. 447	20	25	30
JF04 Tow truck, 5" long, No. 447	30	35	40
JF05 Gulf truck, tin cover, 5" long, No. 447	30	40	50
JF06 Sedan, fastback, futuristic, 6½" long	25	30	40
JF07 Sedan, fastback, futuristic, 6½" long, with wind-up motor	30	40	50

Jane Francis JF02
Photo by Dave Leopard

Jane Francis JF05
Photo by Dave Leopard

Jane Francis JF04
Photo by Dave Leopard

Jane Francis produced this Gulf Service Station in the late 1940s. Robert H. Mauler of Jessup, Maryland secured a gross of these stations many years ago, in mint condition. The most recent price for one from Mr. Mauler was $1000.
Courtesy Barbara Francis Vanyo

JAPANESE BATTERY-OPERATED TOYS

by Don Hultzman

"Made in Japan" are the words toy collectors look for in their pursuit of high-quality mechanical tin toys.

Before World War II, these words were synonymous with cheap, poor quality, drab-looking toys made from re-cycled materials and ideas. Most of the toys were people-animal oriented with less emphasis on vehicle, nautical, or aircraft-type toys. They were powered either by a spring or a flywheel and didn't last too long or do too much as far as play-value goes. These inexpensive, poor quality toys kept Japan a third-rate toy manufacturing nation until after World War II, when Japan's surrender resulted in economic chaos for this industrial nation.

In their quest for economic recovery and to compete in a toy market already dominated by Germany and America, the Japanese knew they had to come up with a new, different, and exciting type of toy that would make them more desirable than their competitors.

The Japanese toy designers concentrated their technology on a different type of toy operation. Not satisfied with the limited action and short duration of spring-driven or flywheel-propelled toys, the toy engineers developed a small electric motor, powered by flashlight batteries. This mini-motor took up less room than other mechanisms, had a longer-running duration, and enabled the toy to perform more functions. This development opened up an entirely new dimension in toy design and introduced the concept of the battery-operated toy!

The Toy designers integrated this new concept into hundreds of automaton-like toys, capable of as many as eight different type of actions all in one cycle. These unique toys were an instant hit with the foreign market, expecially the USA. These clever, unusual and high-quality toys made Japan the dominant toy producer and exporter for the next 20-30 years.

Again, Japan flooded the market with these ingenious, well-made toys while quality control remained a high priority. These merits were not only apparent in their figural toys, but also in their vehicle line. Here, the Japanese toy makers concentrated on very fine detail and quality especially in their scale-model passenger cars, with the ultimate goal or making them look like the "real thing" and they succeeded. Their workmanship carried over into their other vehicle lines, such as motorcycles, emergency and construction vehicles as well as their novelty (silly) and comic character cars, trucks, and space toys.

No other nation was able to equal or surpass the impetus & determination of the Japanese toy makers until Japan relinquished its domination by re-aligning it's economy in the electronic-automotive field.

Now that they are approaching middle age, it is no wonder that these fine toys remain in great demand today and often very pricey!

DON HULTZMAN confesses he has always been a collector of toys, but didn't really get serious about the hobby until ten or so years ago, not only collecting but also repairing them. Born and raised in Cleveland, Ohio, he received a masters degree in Guidance and Administration at Kent State, and is currently employed by the Panama City School System as a school Counselor. He does free-lance writing as a science consultant to the encyclopedia department of World Publishing Co. and lives in Brunswick Hills, Ohio. Many of his tin wind up toys can be seen in the 1983 MGM movie "A Christmas Story".

CONDITION OF A TOY AND ITS RELATION TO PRICE

The value of a battery operated toy depends not only on its desirability, rarity and complexity, but very much on its condition. A toy in "mint" condition is generally worth twice as much as a toy in "good" condition. A toy in "very good" condition will be equally priced between "good" and "mint".

C-10—"Mint", means just that — the condition in which the toy was originally issued — **perfect** — regardless of age. It will also be in perfect mechanical condition, complete with all accessory parts when applicable, and will look "brand new". The cloth or fur (plush) covering on some battery toys may reveal some discoloration (yellowing) due to age, but this should not affect its value as a "mint" toy as long as it is clean. All toys in this category must be in perfect working condition. The original box in mint condition will significantly enhance the value of any "mint" toy.

C-8—"Very good", indicates the condition of a battery toy that has seen some use and is starting to show its age. It will still be in perfect working order and have all its accessory parts where applicable. It will have some age-soiling, but will have no rust or corrosion. Overall, it will have an appearance of "freshness" and still be highly desirable to the fussy collector.

C-6—"Good", applies to a battery toy that has seen considerable use, wear and tear, some age soiling, but still in perfect working condition with no missing parts of accessories. The "wet" toys may show some slight surface rust that can be easily removed. A toy in "good" condition is still a welcome addition to any toy collection, but will be targeted for upgrading by a piece in better condition.

Any battery toy below the condition of "good" will reflect a drastic reduction in value. Toys in good shape, but missing accessory parts, will not lose as much value as those that are severely rusted, corroded, painted over, have parts broken off and are totally inoperable. These "poor" toys are usually collected for their "scrap value" by the toy repairer and seldom are they worth more than $10.00.

The key to grading is to use common sense and avoid wishful thinking. Since grading the condition of a toy may be difficult at times, consulting with an expert in the field, if possible, could clear up any lingering doubts. (See back section of this guide for references of toy collectors.)

GUIDELINES FOR THE CARE AND REPAIR OF YOUR BATTERY OPERATED TOY

by Don Hultzman

Your prized battery toy needs T.L.C. and when it stops working, you now have a frustrating disaster on your hands. To avoid this, the following suggestions should be of some help:

Battery toys, like other mechanical toys, should be operated periodically to keep them loosened up. A lightweight spray lubrication now and then will help considerably if the mechanism is accessible. Do not over-lubricate as the excess may stain any cloth or fur covering on some battery toys.

A good quality car wax or polish will keep the lithographed and bare metal parts looking like new — especially on the "wet" toys. Always test an obscure lithographed area to make sure the polish doesn't soften or dissolve the paint. Care should be exercised when polishing metal parts adjoining any cloth or plush covering, as the substance may stain the coverings. Light surface rust usually disappears with a careful polishing. Nothing can be done for deep rust or corrosion without ruining the value of the toy. Repainting will only further reduce the value and is not recommended.

Should your battery toy fail to operate, the following steps might be helpful:

1. Make sure it is not gunked-up and that no moving parts are binding.

2. Make sure the battery contacts are not dirty or corroded —   if so then clean them with crocus cloth. ALWAYS USE FRESH BATTERIES!

3. Lightly tap the toy with your finger or **lightly** nudge one of the moving parts while the switch is "on".

If none of the above steps work, then your toy needs "major surgery". This means the toy must be completely torn down, repaired and reassembled. Most battery toys are repairable as long as they have not been destructively tampered with and no parts are missing or corroded beyond repair. This job is best left to an expert in toy repair and should never be attempted by one who doesn't know what he is doing. Expert repairs will not affect the value of a battery toy so long as the repair is **undetectable** and the toys looks and functions **exactly** as it did before the repair. Such repairs are acceptable in toy collecting circles. Expert repairs are also expensive but well worth the investment if it means the difference between a "mint" (and prized toy) and one below the grade of "good", since an inoperable toy is practically worthless, regardless of condition.

	C6	C8	C10
"American Circus Television Truck" 1950s, Exelo Co., 9¼" long, six actions, RARE, (includes detachable metal antenna) 450	675	900
"Anti-Aircraft Jeep," 1950s, "K" Co., 9½" long, five actions . .	100	150	200
"Anti-Aircraft Jeep", 1950s, T-N Co. 11" long, six actions, (includes detachable tin radar antenna)	250	375	500

Anti-Aircraft Jeep
Photo by Don Hultzman

Antique Gooney Car
Photo by Don Hultzman

	C6	C8	C10
"Antique Gooney Car," 1960s, Alps Co., 9" long, four actions	70	105	140
"Armored Attack Set", 1960s, Marx Co., jeep 6¼" long and tank 5¼" long, plus 15 2" plastic figures	150	225	300
"Army Radio Jeep - J1490", 1950s Linemar Co., 7¼" long, four actions	90	135	180
"Atom Motorcycle", 1950s, M-T Co., five actions, 11¾" long .	400	600	800

Atom Motorcycle
Photo by Don Hultzman

	C6	C8	C10
"Auto-top Ferrari Convertible", 1960s, Bandai Co., three actions, 11" long	450	675	900
"Automatic Toll Gate", 1955, Sears, 16"x17" base, six actions, (includes 8" tin Valiant)	150	225	300
"Batmobile," 1972 National Periodical Publications, ASC Co., 12" long, three actions .	200	300	400

Batmobile
Photo by Don Hultzman

	C6	C8	C10
"Big Ring Circus Truck", 1950s, M-T Co., 13" long, three actions	130	195	260
"Big Shot Cadillac," 1950s, T-N co., 10" long, four actions, Rare	200	300	400
"Big Wheel Coca Cola Truck", 1970s, Taiyo Co., three actions	80	120	160

Big Wheel Coca-Cola Truck
Photo by Don Hultzman

	C6	C8	C10
"Big Wheel Family Camper", 1970s, 10" long, three actions	80	120	160
"Big Wheel Ice Cream Truck", 1970s 10" long, three actions.	70	105	140
"Bulldozer", 1950s, T-N Co., 7½" long, five actions	80	120	160
"Bulldozer", 1950s, M-T Co., 11" long, six actions	90	135	180

Bulldozer, Shaking Old-Timer Car, Tractor.

	C6	C8	C10
"B-Z Porter" Baggage truck, 1950s, M-T Co., 7½" long, 6½" high, minor toy, includes three pcs. of luggage (tin)	150	205	300
"Cadillac" car, 1949, Ashai Toy Co., 10" long, three actions .	150	225	300

Caterpillar Tank M-1.
Photo by Don Hultzman

	C6	C8	C10
"Caterpillar Tank M-1", 1950s, M-T Co., five actions, 8½" long, 11" long with barrel extended	150	220	300
"Chaparral 2F," car, 1960s, Alps Co., 11" long, five actions . . .	90	135	180
"Chemical Fire Engine", 1950s, HTC Co., 10" long, four actions	110	165	220
"Circus Fire Engine", 1960s, M-T Co., 11" long, four actions . .	140	210	280
"Climbing Donald Duck On His Friction Fire Engine," 1950s Linemar Co., four actions, 12" long	400	600	800
"Clown Circus Car", 1960s, M-T Co., 8½" long, 9" high, five actions	130	195	260
"Coin Taxi", 1960s, Daiya Co., 6½" long, Minor toy	90	135	180
"Comic Hungry Bug", VW auto, 1970s, Tora (S-T) Co., 7¾" long, five actions	40	60	80
"Comic Musical Car", 1960s, T-N Co., four actions, 6" long, 8½" tall	70	105	140
"Comic Road Grader", 1950s, Bandai Co., 9" long, four actions	70	105	140
"Comic Road Roller", 1960s, Bandai Co., four actions, 9" long	70	105	140
"Corvair Bertone", 1970s, Bandai Co., four actions, 12" long . .	50	75	100

	C6	C8	C10
Corvette Sting Ray Sport Coupe, 1968, Eldon Co., 13½" long, Minor toy	100	150	200
"Cragstan Beep Beep Greyhound Bus", 1950s, Cragston Co., 20" long, three actions	120	330	240
Cragstan Firebird III, 1956, Alps Co., 11¾" long - 3 actions ..	400	600	800
"Crane Tractor", 1950s, SKK Co., 7½" long, 11½" high extended	70	105	140
"Crazy Car", 1950s, Marusan Co., five actions, 9" long........	70	105	140

Farm Truck, Alps.
Photo by Don Hultzman

Crazy Car
Photo by Don Hultzman

	C6	C8	C10
"Desert Patrol Jeep", 1960s, M-T Co., 11" long, four actions, includes turret gunner........	100	150	200
Dick Tracy Police Car, 1949, TN co., 9" long - 4 actions......	200	300	400
"Disney Fire Engine", 1950s, Linemar Co., 11" long, four actions....................	440	660	880
"Disneyland Fire Engine", 1950s, Linemar Co., 18" long, five actions....................	300	450	600
Dreamboat Hot-Rod - See Hot Rod			
"Dump Truck No. 7343", 1960s, T-N Co., 10¼" long, seven actions....................	70	105	140
"Electric School Bus", 1950s, M-T Co., 9½" long, minor toy ...	80	120	160
"Electro Special Racer", 1950s, Yonezawa Co., 10" long, three actions....................	100	150	200
"Electro Toy Racer", 1950s, Yonezawa Co., three actions, 10" long....................	1000	1500	2000

Farm Truck, T-N.
Photo by Don Hultzman

	C6	C8	C10
"Electronic Fire House", 1940s, Banner Co., 7" square, minor toy (includes plastic fire engine)	80	120	160
"Expert Motor Cyclist", 1950s, MT Co., 12" long, five actions ...	600	900	1200
"Farm Truck", 1960s, Alps Co., 11" long, three actions	120	180	240
"Farm Truck", 1950s, T-N Co., five actions, 9" long	100	150	200
"F.D. Fire Engine", 1960s, Y-M Co., 10" long, 12" high when ladder is extended, four actions	100	150	200
Ferris Wheel Truck, 1950s, T-N co., 11" long, four actions	400	600	900

F.D. Fire Engine, Fire Engine, Fire Chief Mystery Action Car, Police
Motorcycle Cop.
Courtesy Don Hultzman

	C6	C8	C10
"Fire Chief No. 8 Car", 1960s, Y Co., 11¼" long, three actions	90	135	180
"Fire Chief Mystery Action Car", 1960s, T-N Co., 9¾" long, four actions	120	180	240
"Fire Command Car", 1950s, T-N Co., five actions	170	255	340

Fire Command Car
Photo by Don Hultzman

"Fire Engine", 1950s, Marusan Co., four actions, 9" long	150	225	300
"Fire Engine", 1950s, T-N Co., (Electro Toy), three actions, 9" long-ladder extends 13"	150	225	300
"Fire Engine", 1950s, Y Co., 12" long, ladder extends 16", six actions	100	150	200
"Fire Engine", c.1950s, S-H Co., 3 actions, 8" long	100	150	200
"Firebird Racer", 1950s, Tomiyama Co., four actions, 14¼" long	300	450	600

	C6	C8	C10
"Ford Model T", 1950s, Nihonkogei Co., 10¼" long, four actions (includes detachable tin roof)	60	90	120
"Ford Mustang 2"x2", 1960s, Wenmac-AMF Co., four actions, 16" long	70	105	140
"Fork Lift Truck", 1960s, M-T Co., 10¼" high, Minor Toy	70	105	140

Fork Lift Truck
Photo by Don Hultzman

Go-Kart, M-T Co.
Photo by Don Hultzman

"Go Kart", 1960s, M-T Co., 6½" long, minor toy (includes control wire with steering key)	90	135	180
"Go Kart", 1950s, Rosko Co., 10" long, three actions, includes detachable head	100	150	200
"Go-Stop Benz Racer", 1950s, Marusan Co., three actions, 11" long	150	220	300

	C6	C8	C10
"Grand-Pa Car", 1950s, Y Co., 9" long, four actions	60	90	120
"Greyhound Bus", 1950s, KKK. Co., Minor Toy, 7¼" long...	100	150	200

Greyhound Bus
Photo by Don Hultzman

	C6	C8	C10
"Greyhound Bus-Scenicruiser", 1950s, I.Y. Metal Toy Co., 16" long, three actions	100	150	200
"Greyhound bus with Headlights", 1950s, Linemar Co., 10¼" long, three actions	120	180	240
"Handy Hank Mystery Tractor", 1950s, T-N Co., 9" long, four actions....................	60	90	120
"Happy Clown Car", 1960s, Y Co., 6½" long, three actions .	80	120	160
"Happy Tractor", 1960s, Daiya Co., 8" long, four actions ...	40	60	80
"Highway Drive", 1950s, T-N Co., 15½" long, three actions (includes tin magnetic car)	60	90	120
"Highway Patrol Police Special, 1960s, Y Co., five actions, 11½" long.....................	100	150	200
"Highway Patrol Jeep", 1950s, Daiya Co., 10" long, four actions....................	70	105	140
"Highway Skill Driving", 1960s, K Co., 13" long, three actions .	70	105	140
"Hot Rod" car, 1950s, T-N Co., 10" long, Minor Toy	200	300	400
"Hot Rod Custom 'T' Ford", 1960s, Alps Co., four actions, 10½" long.................	190	275	380

	C6	C8	C10
"Hot Rod Limousine", 1960s Alps Co., four actions, 10½" long .	200	300	400
"Ice Cream Truck", 1960s, Bandai Co., 10½" long, five actions .	150	225	300
"James Bond's Aston-Martin" - See "007 Aston Martin"			
"James Bond-007 Car-M101", 1960s, Daiya Co., 11" long, seven actions, includes ejectable driver - See "M101 Aston Martin"			
"Jeep-USA", 1950s, TKK Co., 12½" long, a minor toy	60	90	120
"Jeep No. 10560", 1950s, Cragstan, 5½" long, a minor action toy	70	105	140
"John's Farm Truck", 1950s, T-N Co., 9" long, seven actions ..	100	150	200

John's Farm Truck
Photo by Don Hultzman

	C6	C8	C10
"K-55 Electric Tractor", c.1950s, M-T Co., 3 actions, 7" long	70	105	140
"King Size Fire Engine", 1960s, Bandai Co., three actions, 12½" long......................	150	225	300
"Kissing Couple", 1950s, Ichida Co., 10¾" long, five actions	150	225	300
"Ladder Fire Engine", 1950s, Linemar Co., five actions, 13" long......................	170	255	340
"Love-Beetle-Volks", 1960s, K.O. Co., 10" long, three actions .	60	90	120
"M-101 Aston Martin Secret Ejector Car", 1960s, Daiya Co., 11" long, six actions, (includes ejectable passenger)	200	300	400

King Size Fire Engine
Photo by Don Hultzman

Kissing Couple
Photo by Don Hultzman

M-101 Aston-Martin Secret Ejector Car.

	C6	C8	C10
"Magic Action Bulldozer", 1950s, T-N Co., 9½" long, three actions	100	150	200
"Marvelous Car", T-Bird, 1956, T-N Co., three actions, 11" long	250	375	500
"Marvelous Fire Engine", 1960s, "Y" Co., 11" long, four actions	100	150	200

Marevelous Fire Engine
Photo by Don Hultzman

	C6	C8	C10
Melody Comping Car, 1970s, "Y" Co., 10" long, three actions	100	150	200
Merry-Go-Round Truck, 1950s, M.T. Co., 11" long, four actions	400	600	800
Merry Ice Cream Truck", 1960s, Bandai Co., 10½" long, five actions	90	135	180
"Mickey Mouse and Donald Duck Fire Engine", 1960s, M-T Co., 16" long, three actions	200	300	400
"Mickey Mouse Sand Buggy", 1960s M-T Co., 11" long, four actions	150	225	300
"Military Air Defense Truck", 1950s, Linemar Co., four actions, 15¼" long	100	150	200
"Military Command Car", 1950s T-N Co., five actions, 11" long	150	225	300
"Million Bus", 1950s, KKK Co., three actions, 12" long, RARE	1250	1875	2500
"Mobile Satellite Tracking Station", 1960s, Y Co., six actions, 9" long, (includes detachable antenna) RARE	400	600	800
"Monkee-Mobile", 1967, ASC Co., (Aoshin Co.) Minor Toy, 12" long	350	525	700

Merry Ice Cream Truck
Photo by Don Hultzman

Monkee-Mobile
Photo by Don Hultzman

Military Command Car
Photo by Don Hultzman

	C6	C8	C10
"Motorcycle Cop", 1950s, Daiya Co., 10½" long, 8¼" high, five actions	200	300	400
"Musical Cadillac Car", 1950s, Ir-co Co., 9" long, Minor Toy	300	450	600
"Musical Comic Jumping Jeep", 1970s, M-T Co., 12" long, six actions	90	135	180
"Mystery Fire Chief Car No. 81", 1950s, Sanshin Co., 9¼" long, three actions	120	180	240
"Mystery Police Car", 1960s, T-N Co., 9¾" long, 6" wide, 4" high, three actions	100	150	200

Mobile Satellite Tracking System.
Photo by Don Hultzman

Mystery Police Car
Photo by Don Hultzman

	C6	C8	C10
Newbuggy Crazy Car, 1970s, M-T Co., 10'' long, Minor Toy . . .	50	75	100
"News Service Car", 1960s, TPS Co., 10'' long, four actions . .	150	225	300
"Nutty Mads Car" (Drincar), 1960s, Marx Co., 9¼'' long, three actions	200	300	400
"007 Aston Martin", 1966, Gilbert Co., 11½'' long, eight actions, (includes ejectable passenger).	250	375	500
"007 Secret Agent's Car", (Impala), 1960s, Spesco Co., (Joy Toy), 15'' long, five actions . .	200	300	400
"Ol' MacDonald's Farm Truck", 1960s, Frankonia, four actions (includes plastic pig, cow and chicken)	110	165	220

"Ol' MacDonald's Farm Truck"
Courtesy Mapes Auctioneers & Appraisers

Old Fashioned Fire Engine
Photo by Don Hultzman

	C6	C8	C10
"Old Fashioned Fire Engine", 1950s, M-T Co., four actions, 12½'' long	110	165	220
"Old Fashioned Car", 1950s, S-H Co., 10'' long, four actions . .	50	75	100
"Old Ford Touring Car", 1950s, Z Co., 10'' long, four actions . .	50	75	100
"Old Time Automobile", 1950s, "Y" Co., 8¾'' long, three actions (includes detachable tin litho driver and steering wheel)	100	150	200
"Old Timer", Car, 1950s, Cragstan Co., 9'' long-three actions . . .	100	150	200

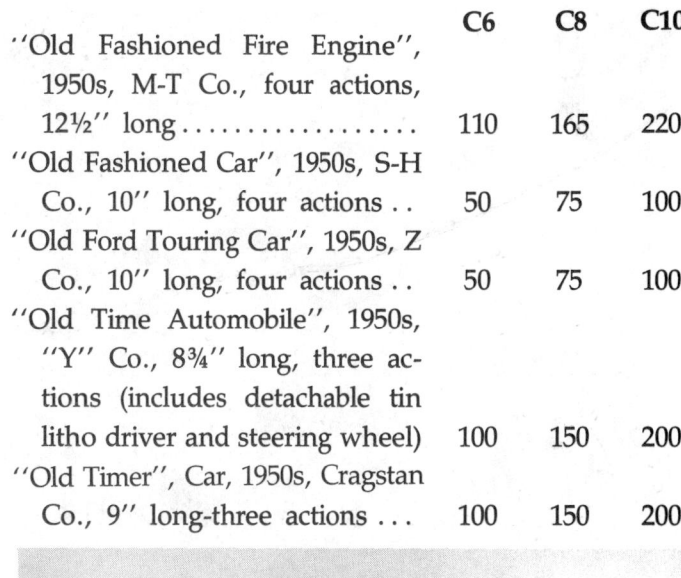

"Old Timer" car, Cragstan
Courtesy Mapes Auctioneers & Appraisers

	C6	C8	C10
"Oldtimer Automoball", 1950s, M-T Co., 10'' long, three actions, includes celluloid ball	90	135	180
"Oldtimer Sunday Driver", 1960s, Daiya Co., 9'' long, four actions	70	105	140
"Passenger Bus", 1950s, "Y" Co., 16'' long, four actions	300	450	600
"Patrol Auto-Tricycle", 1960s, T-N Co., 19'' long, 7½'' high, four actions	160	240	320
"P.D. No. 5 - Police Patrol Car", (Buick), 1960s, Askakusa Toy Co., 11½'' long, three actions	90	135	180
"Pick-Up Truck", T-N Co., 10'' long, four actions	90	135	180
"Piston Action Bulldozer", 1960s, Linemar Co., 7½'' long, two cycles	80	120	160
"Police Auto Cycle", 1960s, (motorcycle and plastic driver), Bandai Co., five actions, Remote Control	150	225	300

Police Auto Cycle
Photo by Don Hultzman

Police No. 5
Photo by Don Hultzman

Police Motorcycle
Photo by Don Hultzman

Power Shovel
Courtesy Don Hultzman

	C6	C8	C10
"Police Motorcycle", 1950s, M-T Co., 11¾" long, seven actions	160	240	320
"Police No. 5" Police Car, 1950s, T-N Co., four actions, 9½" long	100	150	200
"Police Patrol Jeep", 1960s, T-N Co., four actions, lights, bump & go, noise, smoke, 9¼" long	100	150	200
"Pom Pom Tank", 1950s, S&E Co., 12" long, five actions...	170	235	340
"Popcorn Vendor Truck", 1960s, T-N Co., 9" long, three actions	130	195	260
"Porsche With Visible Engine", 1964, Bandai Co., 10" long, three actions...............	90	135	180
"Power Shovel", 1950s, Alps Co., 15" long, extended, six actions	100	150	200

	C6	C8	C10
"RCA-NBC Mobile Color TV Truck", 1950s, Yonezawa Co., 9" long, four actions........	350	525	700
"Racecar #25", 1950s, Alps Co., three actions, 9" long, RARE	800	1200	1600
"Radar Jeep", 1950s, T-N Co., 11" long, four actions..........	150	225	300
"Reversible Diesel Electric Tractor", 1950s, Marx Co., Minor Toy.......................	60	90	120
"Road Construction Roller", 1950s, Daiya Co., 8½" long, four actions.....................	60	90	120
"Road Grader", 1960s, T-N Co., 12" long, three actions......	70	105	140
"Road Roller", 1950s, M-T Co., 9" long, four actions..........	70	105	140
"Robotank TR-2", 1960s, T-N Co., four actions, 5" high........	200	300	400

Road Roller
Photo by Don Hultzman

	C6	C8	C10
"Romance Car M-841", 1950s, "M" Co., 8" long, three actions	110	165	220
Santa Claus on Hand Car......	100	150	200

Santa Claus on Scooter
Courtesy Don Hultzman

	C6	C8	C10
"Santa Claus on Scooter", 1960s, M-T Co., 10" high, four actions	100	150	200
"School Bus", 1950s, Cragstan, 20½" long, a Minor Toy	60	90	120
Searchlight Jeep, 1950s, T-N Co., 16" long overall, (7½" Jeep & 8½" artillery, four actions ...	100	150	200
"Secret Service Action Car", (Green Hornet motif), 1960s, ASC Co., 11" long, four actions, RARE	250	375	500
"Shaking Classic Car", 1960s, T-N Co. 7" long, four actions .	60	90	120

	C6	C8	C10
"Shaking Old-Timer Car No. 2511-1", 1960s, T-N Co., 9" long, four actions, includes plastic driver................	70	105	140
"Sheriff Car", 1950s, T-N Co., four actions, 10" long	90	135	180
"Sight Seeing Bus", 1960s, Bandai Co., 14½" long, four actions	150	225	300
"Sight Seeing Bus", 1950s, Yonezawza Co., Minor Toy, 9" long	150	225	300
"Siren Fire Car", 1950s, M-T Co., 9" long, four actions	130	195	260
"Siren Patrol Car", 1960s, M-T Co., four actions, 12½" long .	80	120	160
"Siren Patrol Motorcycle", 1960s, M-T Co., three actions, 12" long	200	300	400
"Smoky Bill on Old Fashioned Car", 1960s, T-N Co., 9" long, four actions	110	165	220
"Smokey the Bear Jeep", 1950s, M-T Co., 10" long, four actions	250	375	500
"Smoking Bulldozer", 1960s, WKC Co., 9" long, four actions ...	80	120	160
"Smoking Volkswagen", 1960s, Aoshin Co., 10½" long, four actions......................	60	90	120
"Smoky Joe-Fancy Mobile", 1960s, T-N Co., four actions, smokes, lights, bump & go, noise, 9" long	90	135	180
"Sports Car Race Set", 1960s, TPS Co., Minor Toy, 8"x14" base, includes four plastic racecars .	100	150	200
"Steam Roller (Road Roller), 1950s, T-N Co., (Rosko), 12" long with trailer, four actions	90	135	180
"Steam Roller", 1950s, "Y" Co., 8" long, four actions (includes tin trailer	110	165	220
"Steerable Tank", 1950s, Linemar Co., 9" long, five actions	60	90	120
"Strange Explorer", 1960s, DSK Co., 7½" long, four actions ..	150	225	300

"Strange Explorer" with box Courtesy James S. Maxwell/Virginia Caputo.
Photo by Virginia Caputo

Sunday Driver
Photo by Don Hultzman

Sunbeam Jeep No. 1
Photo by Don Hultzman

	C6	C8	C10
"Sunbeam Jeep No. 1", 1940s, 10" long, unmarked, three actions	100	150	200
Sunbeam Side Car (Motorcycle) 1950s, Marusan Co., 9½" long, three actions	800	1200	1600
"Sunday Driver", 1950s, M-T Co., 10" long, four actions (includes detachable driver)	70	105	140
"Superman Tank", 1950s, Linemar Co., 10¼" long, three actions, RARE	700	1050	1400
"Surrey Jeep", 1960s, T-N Co., 11" long, three actions	90	135	180
"Talking Police Car-Mystery Action", 1960s, Y Co., 14" long, three actions	70	105	140

	C6	C8	C10
"Tank M-4 Combat Tank", 1960s, Taiyo Co., 11½" long, 13" with gun barrel extended, five actions	80	120	160
"Tank M-35", 1950s, HTC Co., 8" long, three actions	110	165	220
"Tank M-41", 1970s, J Co., 8¼" long, four actions	110	165	220
"Tank M-48-T", 1960s, T-N Co., 8¼" long, four actions	100	150	200
"Tank M-56", 1940s, M-T Co., 7½" long, wheel drive	100	150	200
"Tank M-71", 1950s, M-T Co., 5¾" long, five actions	100	150	200
"Tank M-81", 1960s, M-T Co., 8½" long, seven actions	100	150	200
"Tank M-103", 1950s, M-T Co., 7" long, three actions	90	135	180
"Tank M-107-US Army", 1950s, Y Co., 6" long, four actions, includes four missiles	110	165	220
"Tank M-X", 1950s, T-N Co., 8½" long, five actions	70	105	140
Tank T-5", 1950s, T-N Co., 8½" long, three actions, includes detachable radar antenna	120	160	240
"Tank X-3" (explorer defense), 1950s, Cragstan Co., 7¾" long, five actions, includes six cartridge shells	130	195	260

196

Tank (M-81), Tank (M-35), Tank (M-56), Tank (M-107)

Turn-O-Matic Gun Jeep
Photo by Don Hultzman

Twin Racing Cars
Photo by Don Hultzman

"Tank X-75", 1950s, M-T Co., 9" long, three actions, includes tin gun and darts 110 165 220

Tank - Daisymatic #64 .... 100 150 200

Tank - Daisymatic #80 .... 100 150 200

	C6	C8	C10
"Tank Robot" 1960s, S-H Co., five actions, 10" tall	250	375	500
"Taxi", (yellow cab), 1950s, Linemar Co., 7½" long, five actions	70	105	140
"Taxi Cab", 1950s, "Y" Co., 8½" long, five actions	70	105	140
"Taxi Cab", 1960s, "Y" Co., four actions, 9" long	80	120	160
"Teddy-Go-Kart", 1960s, Alps Co., 10½" long, four actions .	90	135	180
The Swinger (Mustang Mach I), c.1960s, T.P.S. Co. - 10½" long three actions	50	75	100
"Tiny Jeep", 1950s, WACO Co., 4¼" long, minor action	30	45	60
"Tiny Tank", 1950s WACO Co., 4¼" long, minor action	30	45	60
"Tom and Jerry Highway Patrol", 1960s, M-T Co., 8" long, three actions	120	180	240
"Tom and Jerry Jumping Jeep", 1960s, M-T Co., 9" long, three actions	150	225	300
"Tractor", 1950s, Showa Co., 7½" long, four actions, includes litho tin figure (driver)	110	165	220
"Tractor", 1960s, Y Co., 6" long, three actions	100	150	200
"Tractor On Platform", 1950s, T-N Co., tractor 9" long, trailer 7" long, minor toy	100	150	200
"Turn-O-Matic Gun Jeep", 1960s, T-N Co., 10" long, five actions	100	150	200
"Twin Racing Cars", 1950s, Alps Co., three actions, 7" long - 10" long with coupling rod)	400	600	800
"Visible Ford Mustang", 1960s, Bandai Co., 10" long, four actions	90	135	180
"Volkswagen Convertible", 1950s, T-N Co., three actions, 9¾" long	250	375	500
"Volkswagen-Eletrik", 1950s, Mignon Co., 8½" long, three actions	70	105	140
"Volkswagen No. 7653", 1960s, Bandai Co., 10" long, three actions	80	120	160

	C6	C8	C10
"Volkswagen With Visible Engine", 1960s, K.O. Co., 7" long, three actions	70	105	140
"Volkswagen with Visible Engine No. 4049", 1960s, Bandai Co., 8" long, three actions	90	135	180

J1

JAPANESE (ETC.) TIN CARS

by Ron Smith

Tin toy cars have been manufactured since the first horseless carriages roamed the streets of the United States and Europe. They ranged in size and price from the tiny one-inch penny toy to the 28" Eldorado which sold at the ten dollar mark. Although there are German, Spanish and French toy cars listed here, our concentration will be the 1950's Golden Era of Japanese tin toy cars. These examples enjoy much popularity today and prices have been raised by the limitlessness of some people's insanity. Keep one thing foremost in your mind when trying to sell a toy at the mint price; the person who paid that price already has one.

Ron Smith

Ron Smith has always loved toy cars and planes. He can still show you his first Dinky Toy bought for him in 1940 by his aunt in Fred Harvey's Toy Store inside Cleveland's Terminal Tower Building. Born and raised in Shaker Heights, Ohio, Ron served in the United States Navy, attended John Carroll University, and for the last 14 years has been employed by Arrow Distributing of Solon, Ohio. He has collected die-cast cars, trucks and planes, cast iron toys, plastic promotional cars and, for the last 10 years, specialized in tin plate cars and planes. Ron lives in Solon, Ohio with his wife Joan and their two cats, Trouble and Bogart.

All photos by Ron Smith except where noted

J2

J2C

J5

No.	Year	Model	Manufacturer	Power	Size	C6	C8	C10
J1	1960s	Aston-Martin DB5 (James Bond)	Gilbert	Friction	11½''	50	100	200
J2	1960s	Aston-Martin DB6	Asahi Toy Co.	Friction	11''	100	200	400
J2A	1959	Austin Healey 100 Six Coupe	Bandai	Friction	8''	40	80	150
J2B	1959	Austin Healey 100 Six Convertible	Bandai	Friction	8'	40	80	150
J2C	1960s	BMW1500	Ichiko	Friction	8''	90	150	275
J3	1953	Buick	Marusan	Friction	7''	75	125	250
J4	1954	Buick Station Wagon	Unknown	Battery	8''	75	150	200
J5	1955	Buick Roadmaster	Yoshiya	Friction	11''	200	300	400
J6	1958	Buick Century	Yonezawa	Friction	12''	400	600	1200
J7	1958	Buck Century	Bandai	Friction	8''	60	80	100
J8	1959	Buick	T.N.	Friction	11''	80	125	250
J9	1959	Buick	Ichiko	Friction	12''	100	250	300
J10	1960	Buick	Ichiko	Friction	17½''	150	250	600
J11	1961	Buick	T.N.	Friction	11''	50	100	175
J12	1961	Buick Emergency Car	T.N.	Friction	14''	50	95	125
J13	1963	Buick Wildcat	Ichiko	Friction	15''	125	250	400
J14	1966	Buick Le Sabre	Ashai Toy Co.	Friction	19''	100	200	400
J15	1968	Buick Sportswagon	Asakusa	Friction	15''	100	150	200
J16	1950	BMW 600 Isetta	Bandai	Friction	9''	150	200	250
J17	1950	BMW Isetta (three wheels)	Bandai	Friction	6½''	75	125	150
J17B	1960s	Coke Truck	Japan	Battery	12''	125	225	400

J6

J8

J7

J13

J17B

J18

No.	Year	Model	Manufacturer	Power	Size	C6	C8	C10
J18	1950	Cadillac	Marusan	Friction	11''	500	700	1200
J19	1950	Cadillac	Marusan	Battery	11''	500	800	1500
J20	1952	Cadillac	Alps	Friction	11½''	300	500	900
J21	1952	Cadillac	T.N.	Battery	13''	75	150	350
J22	1954	Cadillac	Gama	Friction	12''	200	300	500
J23	1954	Cadillac	Joustra	Battery	12''	200	300	500
J24	1959	Cadillac Sedan	Bandai	Friction	12''	75	100	200
J25	1959	Cadillac Convertible	Bandai	Friction	12''	75	100	200
J26	1960s	Cadillac	Bandai	Friction	17''	125	175	375
J27	1960	Cadillac	Yonezawa	Friction	18''	150	200	350
J28	1961	Cadillac 60	Unknown	Friction	9''	95	125	150
J29	1961	Cadillac Fleetwood	SSS	Friction	17½''	150	300	500
J30	1962	Cadillac	Yonezawa	Friction	22''	100	250	350
J31	1963	Cadillac	Bandai	Friction	17''	125	200	350
J32	1965	Cadillac	Ashahi Toy Co.	Friction	17''	100	200	300
J33	1965	Cadillac	Ichiko	Friction	22''	300	400	600
J34	1967	Cadillac	K.O.	Friction	10½''	100	150	300
J35	1967	Cadillac	Unknown	Friction	10¾''	75	100	125
J36	1967	Cadillac El Dorado	Ichiko	Friction	28''	200	400	700
J37	1953	Chevrolet Corvette	Bandai	Friction	7''	75	100	150
J38	1958	Chevrolet Corvette	Yonezawa	Friction	9½''	200	300	500
J39	1962	Chevrolet Corvette	Bandai	Friction	8''	40	60	80
J40	1965	Chevrolet Corvette	Bandai	Friction	8''	40	60	80
J41	1964	Chevrolet Corvette	Ichida	Battery	12''	150	225	350
J42	1968	Chevrolet Corvette	Taiyo	Battery	9½''	35	50	75
J43	1960s	Chevrolet Corvair	Bandai	Friction	8''	40	60	80
J44	1963	Chevrolet Corvair	Ichiko	Friction	9''	50	65	95
J45	1967	Chevrolet Camaro	Taiyo	Friction	9½''	10	20	30
J46	1967	Chevrolet Camaro	T.N.	Friction	14''	150	250	400
J47	1967	Chevrolet Camaro	Modern Toys	Friction	11''	25	50	75
J48	1971	Chevrolet Camaro Rusher	Taiyo	Battery	9½''	10	20	35
J49	1954	Chevrolet	Marusan	Friction	11''	500	800	1000
J50	1955	Chevrolet	Marusan	Battery	10¾''	500	900	1500
J51	1956	Chevrolet Station Wagon	Bandai	Friction	9½''	75	125	175
J52	1956	Chevrolet Pick Up	Bandai	Friction	9½''	75	125	175
J53	1956	Chevrolet Convertible	Bandai	Friction	9½''	100	150	225

J20

J24

J21

J25

J23

J25

J24

J29

J31

J38

J31

J41

J34

J42

J37

J46

J48

J50

J49

J57

No.	Year	Model	Manufacturer	Power	Size	C6	C8	C10
J54	1958	Chevrolet Red Cross Ambulance	Bandai	Friction	8″	20	30	50
J55	1958	Chevrolet Pick Up Truck	Bandai	Friction	8″	50	65	90
J56	1958	Chevrolet Convertible	Bandai	Friction	8″	60	90	125
J57	1958	Chevrolet Station Wagon	Bandai	Friction	8″	50	60	85
J58	1958	Chevrolet Sedan	Bandai	Friction	8″	75	100	125
J59	1959	Chevrolet Sedan/Convertible	SY	Friction	11½″	200	300	500
J60	1960	Chevrolet	Marusan	Friction	11½″	200	300	500
J60A	1960	Chevrolet H.T.	Japan	Friction	9″	100	150	200
J61	1959	Chevrolet Wagon	SY	Friction	12″	60	90	115
J62	1961	Chevrolet Impala Sedan	Bandai	Friction	11″	100	150	300
J63	1961	Chevrolet Impala Convertible	Bandai	Friction	11″	100	150	300
J64	1962	Chevrolet Secret Agent	Unknown	Battery	14″	50	75	125
J65	1962	Chevrolet	Unknown	Friction	11″	125	250	350
J66	1963	Chevrolet Impala	Unknown	Friction	18″	150	225	375
J67	1960	Citroen DS 19 Convertible	Bandai	Friction	12″	100	150	300
J68	1960	Citroen DS 19 Sedan	Bandai	Friction	12″	100	150	300
J69	1960	Citroen ID 19 Station Wagon	Bandai	Friction	12″	100	150	300
J70	1950	Chrysler	Guntherman	Friction	11″	100	200	500
J71	1955	Chrysler	Yonezawa	Friction	8″	100	200	300
J72	1957	Chrysler New Yorker	Alps	Friction	14″	500	700	1000 +
J73	1958	Chrysler	Unknown	Battery	13″	200	300	600
J74	1959	Chrysler Imperial convertible	Bandai	Friction	8″	75	90	125

No.	Year	Model	Manufacturer	Power	Size	C6	C8	C10
J75	1959	Chrysler Imperial Sedan	Bandai	Friction	8″	75	90	125
J76	1960	Chrysler Valiant	Bandai	Friction	8″	20	45	65
J77	1962	Chrysler Imperial	Asahi Toy Co.	Friction	16″	500	700	1000 +
J78	1960	DKW 1000 Convertible	Bandai	Friction	8″	90	125	200
J79	1960s	Datsun Bluebird 1200	Bandai	Friction	8″	60	75	125
J80	1950s	Divco Dugans Bakery Truck	Unknown, Japan	Friction	7½″	300	400	600
J81	1930s	DeSoto	Masudaya	Friction	8″	300	400	800
J81A	1950s	DeSoto H.T.	Japan	Friction	7″	50	75	150
J82	1958	Dodge Sedan	T.N.	Friction	11″	300	400	600
J83	1959	Dodge Truck	Unknown	Friction	24″	350	500	800
J84	1959	Dodge Pick Up	Unknown	Friction	18½″	350	500	800
J85	1968	Dodge Yellow Cab	T.N.	Friction	12″	90	125	175
J85A	1969	Dodge H.T.	Buddy L	X	13″	60	90	120
J86	1958	Edsel Convertible/Sedan	Haji	Friction	10½″	300	400	800
J87	1958	Edsel Wagon	Haji	Friction	10½″	200	300	400
J88	1958	Edsel Ambulance	Haji	Friction	11″	200	250	300
J89	1958	Edsel Station Wagon	T.N.	Friction	11″	150	200	300
J90	1958	Edsel H.T.	Asahi	Friction	10¾″	300	400	600
J91	1958	Edsel H.T.	Toy Nomura	Friction	8½″	100	150	250
J92	1958	Edsel	Yonezawa	Friction	10½″	300	400	600
J92A	1960s	Ferrari Berlinetta	Bandai	Friction	9½″	75	125	200
J92B	1946	Ford	Italy	Windup	10″	100	200	400

J59

J60A

J60

J62

J63

J64

J65

J66

J71

J72

J73

J74

J77

J86

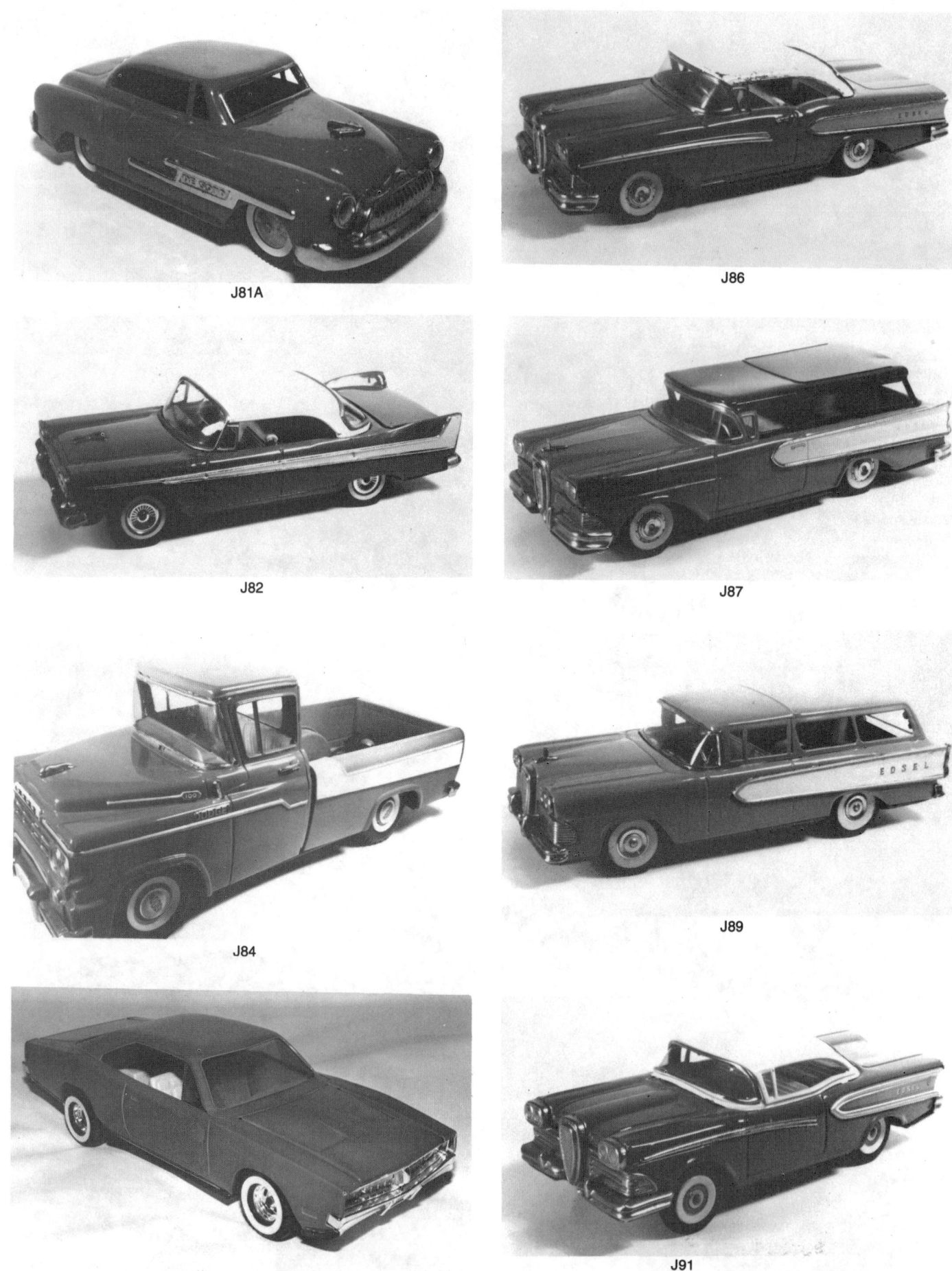

J81A

J86

J82

J87

J84

J89

J85A

J91

J92A

J92B

No.	Year	Model	Manufacturer	Power	Size	C6	C8	C10
J93	1949	Ford Sedan	Guntherman	Wind Up	11″	150	300	400
J94	1951	Ford Sedan	Guntherman	Wind Up	11″	150	300	400
J95	1950	Ford Good Humor Ice Cream Truck	KTS, Japan	Friction	10¾″	150	250	350
J95A	1954	Ford H.T.	Marusan	Friction	11″	125	175	350
J96	1955	Ford Pick Up	Bandai	Friction	12″	150	250	300
J97	1955	Ford Station Wagon	Bandai	Friction	12″	150	250	300
J98	1955	Ford Ambulance	Bandai	Friction	12″	150	250	300
J99	1955	Ford Panel Truck	Bandai	Friction	12″	200	400	600
J100	1955	Ford Convertible	Bandai	Friction	12″	300	500	700
J101	1956	Ford H.T.	Yonezawa	Friction	12″	300	500	800
J102	1956	Ford Convertible	Haji	Friction	11½″	400	600	1000
J103	1956	Ford Sedan	Marusan	Friction	13″	500	800	1000
J104	1956	Ford Wagon	Nomura	Friction	10½″	100	150	300
J105		Ford Fairlane Sedan	Ichiko	Friction	10″	100	200	300
J106	1957	Ford H.T.	T.N.	Friction	12″	100	200	300
J107	1957	Ford Sedan/Con./Wagon/Pick Up	Joustra	Friction	12″	200	250	300
J108	1957	Ford Sedan/Conv./Wagon/Pick Up	Bandai	Friction	12″	200	250	300
J109	1957	Ford Station Wagon	Nomura	Friction	7½″	60	80	100
J110	1958	Ford Retractable Top	K. Japan	Friction	10″	70	90	150
J111	1958	Ford Retractable Top	T.N.	Battery	11″	100	125	175
J112	1958	Ford Country Squire Station Wagon	Bandai	Friction	8″	40	60	80
J113	1958	Ford Fairlane H.T./Conv.	Bandai	Friction	8″	40	60	80
J114	1958	Ford Fairlane H.T./Conv.	Sankei Gangu	Friction	9″	90	115	125
J114A	1958	Ford H.T.	Japan	Battery	12″	150	250	475
J115	1959	Ford Fairlane Skyliner	Sankei Gangu	Friction	9″	90	115	125
J116	1950	Ford Station Wagon	T.N.	Friction	12″	100	150	200
J117	1959	Ford Retractable	T.N.	Friction	11″	100	150	200
J118	1960s	Ford Falcon	Bandai	Friction	8″	20	30	50
J119	1960	Ford	Haji	Friction	11″	200	300	400
J120	1961	Ford Country Sedan	Bandai	Friction	10½″	125	150	250
J121	1962	Ford Country Sedan	Asahi	Friction	12″	200	300	600
J122	1964	Ford H.T.	Ichiko	Friction	13″	125	150	200

(continued)

JAPANESE

No.	Year	Model	Manufacturer	Power	Size	C6	C8	C10
J123	1964	Ford H.T.	Rico	Friction	17″	200	400	600
J124	1964	Ford Convertible	Rico	Friction	17″	200	400	600
J125	1965	Ford Galaxie H.T.	MT	Friction	11″	125	150	250
J126	1968	Ford Torino	S.T.	Friction	16″	200	250	400
J127	1956	Ford Thunderbird	T.N.	Friction	11″	275	325	375
J128	1956	Ford Thunderbird H.T. Clear Top	T.N.	Friction	11″	275	325	375
J129	1956	Ford Thunderbird	T.N.	Battery	11″	275	350	400
J130	1959	Ford Thunderbird Sedan	Bandai	Friction	8″	50	60	80

J93

J97

J95A

J98

J96

J99

J100

J106

J102

J107

J103

J114A

J104

J116

J105

J117

J119

J126

J120

J127

J121

J129

J122

J134

J125

J134

No. Year	Model	Manufacturer	Power	Size	C6	C8	C10
J131 1959	Ford Thunderbird Convertible	Bandai	Friction	8''	50	60	80
J132 1961	Ford Thunderbird Retractable	Yonezawa	Battery	11''	90	120	150
J133 1962	Ford Thunderbird Retractable	Yonezawa	Battery	11''	90	120	150
J134 1963	Ford Thunderbird Retractable	Yonezawa	Battery	11''	90	120	150
J135 1964	Ford Thunderbird Convertible	Asahi	Friction	12½''	150	200	400
J136 1964	Ford Thunderbird H.T.	Asahi	Friction	12''	150	200	400
J137 1964	Ford Thunderbird	Ichiko	Friction	16''	100	200	400
J138 1965	Ford Thunderbird H.T.	Bandai	Friction	10¾''	60	85	125
J139 1965	Ford Mustang F.B.	Bandai	Friction	11''	45	65	90
J140 1965	Ford Mustang H.T./Conv.	Bandai	Fric/Bat.	11''	75	125	150
J141 1965	Ford Mustang (FBI)	Bandai	Friction	11''	75	100	125
J142 1965	Ford Mustang Convertible	Yonezawa	Battery	13½''	90	125	200
J143 1966	Ford Mustang F.B.	T.N.	Friction	17''	100	175	250
J144 1967	Ford Mustang	Bandai	Battery	13''	45	65	100
J145 1960s	Ford Taunus 17M Convertible	Bandai	Friction	8''	30	40	60
J146 1960s	Ford GT	Bandai	Battery	10''	65	85	125
J147 1957	Ferrari 250 G. Convertible	A.T.C.	Friction	9½''	100	250	400
J147B 1960s	#3 Ferrari	Bandai	Friction	8''	85	150	190
J148 1958	Ferrari	Bandai	Battery	11''	90	150	300
J149 1960	Ferrari Super America Coupe	Bandai	Friction	12''	100	200	300
J150 1960s	Ferrari Super America Convertible	Bandai	Friction	12''	100	200	300
J151 1960s	Fiat 600 Sedan	Bandai	Friction	8''	50	65	95
J152 1950s	International Cement Mixer	SSS	Friction	19''	275	300	400
J153 1950s	International Grain Hauler	SSS	Friction	23''	275	300	400
J154 1960	Jaguar XK150 H.T. Conv.	Bandai	Friction	9½''	75	125	200
J155 1960s	Jaguar XKE Convertible	T.T.	Friction	10½''	95	125	175
J156 1960s	Jaguar XKE Coupe	Lendolet Auto	Friction	10½''	75	100	125
J157 1960s	Jaguar XK140	Bandai	Friction	9½''	40	60	90
J158 1960s	Jaguar XKE	Bandai	Battery	10''	90	125	200
J159 1960s	Jaguar 3.4 Sedan	Bandai	Friction	8''	50	60	100
J160 1960s	Jaguar 3.4 Convertible	Bandai	Friction	8''	50	60	100
J161 1965	Jaguar XKE120	Alps	Friction	6½''	90	150	350
J161B 1950s	Lancia	Bandai	Friction	8''	50	90	150
J162 1954	Lincoln	Unknown	Friction	12''	175	275	375
J163 1955	Lincoln Sedan	Yonezawa	Friction	12''	250	325	500
J164 1956	Lincoln Continental Mark II	Linemar	Friction	12''	400	600	1000
J165 1956	Lincoln	Ichiko	Friction	16½''	150	250	375
J166 1959	Lincoln Continental Mark III Conv.	Bandai	Friction	12''	90	150	200
J167 1959	Lincoln Continental Mark III Sedan	Bandai	Friction	12''	90	150	200
J168 1960	Lincoln H.T./Convertible	Yonezawa	Friction	11''	100	150	300
J169 1964	Lincoln	Unknown	Friction	10½''	90	175	275
J170 1950s	Lotus Elite	Bandai	Friction	8½''	25	35	45
J170A 1960s	Lotus Ford Racer	Junior	Battery	16''	400	800	1000
J171 1960s	Land Rover "88" Station Wagon	Bandai	Friction	8''	30	40	60
J172 1950s	Mercedes Limousine	Tipp & Co.	Friction	14''	500	800	1000
J173 1950s	Mercedes Benz Racer	Line Mar	Friction	9½''	95	150	185
J174 1950s	Mercedes Benz Racer W196	Marusan	Battery	10''	150	200	250

(continued)

J136

J143

J137

J147B

J138

J155

J139

J161B

J140

J163

J164

J165

J166

J167

J168

J169

J170A
Photo by Strine

J176

JAPANESE

No.	Year	Model	Manufacturer	Power	Size	C6	C8	C10
J175	1960s	Mercedes	Ichiko	Friction	12½''	115	155	185
J176	1960s	Mercedes Benz 219 Sedan	Bandai	Friction	8''	50	80	100
J177	1960s	Mercedes Benz 219 Convertible	Bandai	Friction	8''	50	80	100
J178	1960s	Mercedes Benz 230 SL	Modern Toys	Battery	15''	175	210	250
J179	1960s	Mercedes Benz 230 SL	Alps	Battery	10''	65	75	95
J180	1960s	Mercedes Benz 230 SL	Yanoman	Battery	14½''	125	155	185
J181	1960s	Mercedes Benz 250 SE	Ichiko	Battery	13''	110	140	185
J182	1960s	Mercedes Benz 250 S	Daiya	Friction	14''	110	155	175
J183	1950s	Mercedes Benz 300 SL	T.N.	Battery	11''	125	150	200
J184	1950s	Mercedes Benz 300 SL	KS	Battery	7''	45	65	85
J185	1950s	Mercedes Benz 300 SL	Dist. Cragstan	Battery	9''	65	95	125
J186	1950s	Mercedes Benz 300 SL	Bandai	Friction	8''	65	95	125
J187	1957	Mercedes Benz 300 SL	Marusan	Friction	8½''	150	250	325
J188	1960s	Mercedes Benz 600	Unknown	Friction	10''	95	125	175
J189	1960s	Mercedes Benz Taxi	Bandai	Battery	10''	75	100	125
J190	1962	Mercedes Benz	SSS	Battery	12''	200	250	350
J191	1970	Mercedes Benz	Ichiko	Friction	24''	125	150	200
J192	1954	Mercury H.T.	Rock Valley Toys	Battery	9½''	100	125	150
J193	1956	Mercury H.T.	Alps	Friction	9½''	400	500	800
J194	1958	Mercury Station Wagon	Bandai	Friction	8''	60	80	100
J195	1958	Mercury H.T.	Yonezawa	Friction	11½''	250	325	400
J196	1967	Mercury Cougar H.T.	Taiyo	Battery	10''	25	45	65
J197	1967	Mercury Cougar H.T.	Asakusa Toys	Friction	15''	175	225	275
J198	1952	MG TF	Unknown	Friction	8½''	50	75	95
J199	1954	MG TD	SSS	Friction	6½''	35	65	85
J200	1955	MG TF	Bandai	Friction	8''	95	125	150
J200B	1955	MG	SSS	Friction	6''	50	70	100
J201	1957	MGA	A.T.C.	Friction	10''	175	250	400
J202	1960s	MG Magnette Mark III Sedan	Bandai	Friction	8''	95	125	150
J203	1960s	MG Magnette Mark III Convertible	Bandai	Friction	8''	95	125	150
J204	1960s	Messerschmitt 4 Wheels Convert.	Bandai	Friction	8''	200	250	300
J205	1960s	Messerschmitt 4 Wheels Sedan	Bandai	Friction	8''	200	250	300
J206	1950s	Nash	MSK	Battery	8''	40	70	90
J207	1956	Nash Ambassador	Sankei Gangu	Friction	8''	100	125	150
J207A	1952	Oldsmobile	Y	Friction	11''	150	350	500
J208	1956	Oldsmobile Sedan	Ichiko/Kanto	Friction	10½''	200	400	600
J209	1956	Oldsmobile Super 88 Sedan	Masudaya	Friction	16''	300	400	600
J210	1958	Oldsmobile Sedan	A.T.C.	Friction	12''	200	300	400
J211	1958	Oldsmobile Super 88 Sedan	A.T.C.	Friction	13''	250	325	425
J212	1958	Oldsmobile Sedan	Y	Friction	16''	300	400	700
J213	1959	Oldsmobile Sedan	Ichiko	Friction	12½''	75	125	175
J214	1961	Oldsmobile Convertible	Yonezawa	Friction	12''	75	125	175
J215	1966	Oldsmobile Toronado	Bandai	Battery	11''	65	110	150
J216	1968	Oldsmobile Toronado	Ichiko	Friction	17½''	300	400	500
J217	1950s	Opel Sedan	Yonezawa	Fric/Bat	11½''	70	90	125
J218	1954	Pontiac Star Chief	Asahi	Friction	11''	250	350	450
J218A	1954	Pontiac	Minister	Friction	11''	New Issue		15
J218B	1950s	Pontiac Conv.	KS	Friction	14''	150	300	450

J177

J200B

J193

J205

J195

J197

J207A

J208

J214

J209

J215

J210

J216

J213

J217

JAPANESE

No.	Year	Model	Manufacturer	Power	Size	C6	C8	C10
J218C	1950s	Pontiac Coupe	KS	Friction	14''	150	300	450
J218D	1956	Pontiac H.T.	TN	Friction	8''	150	300	500
J219	1967	Pontiac Firebird	Akasura	Friction	15½''	90	150	275
J220	1967	Pontiac Firebird	Bandai	Friction	10''	30	55	75
J221	1967	Pontiac Firebird (w/wipers)	Bandai	Battery	9½''	40	55	75
J222	1953	Packard Convertible/Sedan	Alps	Friction	16''	500	800	1500
J223	1957	Packard Hawk Convertible	Schuco	Battery	10¾''	300	400	500
J224	1956	Plymouth H.T.	Unknown	Friction	8½''	200	400	600
J225	1956	Plymouth H.T.	Alps	Battery	12''	300	400	600
J226	1957	Plymouth Fury H.T.	Y	Friction	11½''	300	400	600
J227	1958	Plymouth Fury	Bandai	Friction	8''	75	90	150
J228	1959	Plymouth Hardtop	A.T.C.	Friction	10½''	200	400	600
J229	1959	Plymouth Convertible	A.T.C.	Friction	10½''	250	400	600
J230	1961	Plymouth Sedan	Ichiko	Friction	12''	125	250	350
J231	1961	Plymouth Station Wagon	Ichiko	Friction	12''	125	165	195
J232	1961	Plymouth T.V. Car	Ichiko	Battery	12''	125	175	250
J233	1964	Plymouth Futy H.T.	Kusama	Friction	10''	60	80	100
J233B	1960s	Porsche	T.T.	Friction	9½''	75	125	200
J233C	1960s	Porsche	JNF (Ger.)	Wind Up	9''	200	400	600
J233D	1960s	Porsche	Geshia (Ger.)	W/W	9''	200	400	600
J234	1960	Porsche 911	Bandai	Battery	10''	65	95	125
J234B	1960s	Porsche 9115	T.T.	Friction	9½''	75	125	200
J235	1950s	Porsche Speedster	Distler	Battery	10½''	350	400	600
J235B	1960s	Rolls	HTC	Friction	6''	75	100	150
J235C	1960s	Rolls Royce Sedan	TN	Friction	10''	300	500	800
J236	1960	Rolls Royce "Silver Coupe" Conv.	Bandai	Friction	12''	100	150	200
J237	1960s	Rolls Royce "Silver Coupe" Sedan	Bandai	Friction	12''	100	150	200
J238	1960s	Rolls Royce (with Electric Lights)	Bandai	Battery	12''	100	200	300
J239	1960	Rolls Royce	T.N.	Friction	10½''	175	250	375
J240	1960s	Rambler Rebel Station Wagon	Bandai	Friction	12''	50	85	125
J241	1960	Renault	Bandai	Friction	7½''	95	150	200
J242	1960s	Studebaker Avanti	Bandai	Friction	8''	125	175	300
J243	1954	Studebaker	Yoshiya	Friction	9''	150	200	300
J244	1960s	Saab 93 B	Bandai	Friction	7''	40	60	80
J245	1960s	Subaru 360	Bandai	Friction	7''	75	100	125
J246	1960s	Triumph TR-3 Convertible	Bandai	Friction	8''	50	75	150
J247	1960s	Triumph TR-3 Coupe	Bandai	Friction	8''	50	75	150
J248	1960s	Toyopet Crown	Bandai	Friction	9''	40	50	75
J249	1960s	Toyota	Ichiko	Friction	16''	150	275	325
J250	1967	Toyota 2000 GT	A.T.C.	Friction	15''	150	275	325
J251	1960s	Vespa	Bandai	Friction	9''	50	75	125
J252	1960	VW Karmann-Ghia	Bandai	Friction	7''	100	150	250
J253	1960s	Volkswagen Bus	A.T.C.	Friction	12''	125	175	350
J254	1960s	Volkswagen Pick Up Truck	Bandai	Friction	8''	50	60	75
J255	1960s	Volkswagen Bus	Bandai	Friction	8''	50	60	75
J256	1960s	Volkswagen Bus	Bandai	Bat/Fric	9½''	75	125	175
J257	1950s	Volkswagen Bus	Tipp & Co.	Battery	9''	300	400	600

J218A

J220

J218B

J222

J218C

J223

J218D

J224

J219

J225

J226

J232

J227

J233B

J228

J230

J233C

J231

J233D

J234B

J235C   Rare

J235

J236

J237

J235B

J239

J240

J258

J242

J260

J243

J262A

J252

J264

JAPANESE

No.	Year	Model	Manufacturer	Power	Size	C6	C8	C10
J258	1950s	Volkswagen Convertible	T.N.	Friction	9½"	100	150	250
J259	1960s	Volkswagen Convertible	Bandai	Battery	7½"	50	70	90
J260	1960s	Volkswagen Convertible	Bandai	Battery	11"	110	145	185
J261	1960s	Volkswagen Convertible	Taiyo	Battery	10½"	25	45	90
J262	1960s	Volkswagen	Bandai	Friction	8"	25	40	60
J262A	1950s	Volkswagen	German	Wind Up	6"	75	150	300
J263	1960s	Volkswagen	Bandai	Battery	10½"	25	50	75
J264	1960s	Volkswagen	Bandai	Battery	11"	25	50	75
J265	1960s	Volkswagen with/without Sun Roof	Bandai	Friction	15"	60	90	125
J265A	1950s	Volvo	Sweden	Wind Up	11"	600	700	1800
J265B	1960s	Volvo	KS	Friction	7"	100	200	350
J266	1960s	Willys Jeep FC - 150 Pick Up	T.N. Toy Nomura	Friction	11"	50	75	95
J267	1950s	Zuendapp Janus	Bandai	Friction	8"	125	150	200
J268	1950s	Mazda Auto Tricycle K 360	Bandai	Friction	6"	75	100	200
J269	1950	Daihatsu Midget	Kokyu Shokai	Friction	5"	75	100	200
J270	1950s	Daihatsu Midget	Yonezawa	Friction	7"	75	100	200
J271	1950s	Mitsubishi Auto Tricycle Leo	Bandai	Friction	5"	75	100	200
J272	1950s	Mitsubishi Auto Tricycle	Bandai	Friction	11"	100	150	300
J273	1950s	Orient Auto Tricycle	Yonezawa	Friction	9"	75	100	200
J274	1950s	Mazda Auto Tricycle	Bandai	Friction	8"	75	100	200
J275	1950s	Daihatsu Auto Tricycle	Nomura	Friction	11"	100	150	300
J276	1950s	Buick Futuristic Le Sabre	Yonezawa	Friction	7½"	100	200	400
J277	1963	Corvair Bertone	Bandai	Battery	12"	75	150	200
J278	1950s	Dream Car Buick Phantom	Tipp & Co.	Friction	12"	300	400	600
J278A	-	Dream Car	Y	Friction	17"	600	800	1500
J279	1960s	Dream Car Firebird III	Alps	Friction	11"	100	200	300
J280	1960	Ford Gyron	Ichida	Battery	11"	75	100	150
J281	1956	GM's Gas Turbine Powered Firebird II	Ashahi	Friction	8½"	100	200	500
J282	1950s	Pontiac Dream Car	Mitsubishi	Friction	10"	100	200	500
J283		Atom Jet Car	Y	Friction	30"	300	500	1000
J284		Atom Car	Yonezawa	Friction	17"	200	400	800
J285	1950s	Record Racer NSU	Bandai	Friction	18"	100	150	200
J286	1950s	Agajanian Racer No. 98	Y	Friction	18"	500	800	2000
J287	1950s	Champion's Racer No. 98	Y	Friction	18"	500	800	1500
J288	1950	Champion Racer No. 42	Gem	Friction	18"	500	750	1200
J289	1950	Champion Racer No. 15	German	Friction	18"	500	750	1200
J290	-	Electrospecial #21	Y	Battery	10"	300	500	800
J291	-	Midget Special #6	Y	Friction	7"	300	500	700

J265

J265A

J265B

J284

J274

J286

J276

J287

J278A

J288

J289
Photo courtesy Sonny Glassbrener

JEP

J de P, Paris, France, 1899-1965
by Bob Smith

J de P was founded in 1899 as the "Societe Industrielle de Ferblanterie" (SIF). The name was changed to "Jouets de Paris" (J de P) in 1928 as the company introduced a new line of toy cars. Four years later the name was again changed to "Jouets en Paris" (JEP). This name stayed until 1965 when the company went out of business.

	C6	C8	C10
JEP (J de P) Delage Limousine. Green/black, c/w motor, horn, batt/op. spot light, full steering, 13.5" long c.1929............	1300	1700	2200
JEP (J de P) "Madeline-Bastille" 6 wheel Autobus. Green/cream, c/w motor, front/rear wheel steering, 10.25" long. c.1928 .	1200	1600	2100

J290

JEP Delage Limousine, 13½" long, c.1929.
Photo by Bob Smith

J291

JEP "Madeline-Bastile" Autobus, 10¼" long, c.1928.
Photo by Bob Smith

JONES

(NOTE: At presstime, it was discovered American Metal Toys of Chicago actually made these toys c.1937-1941)

	C6	C8	C10
Jones (JV1) Tank, throwing flame, flame touching hull..........	40	60	80
Jones (JV2) Tank, throwing flame, flame not touching hull......	45	67	90
Jones (JV3) Tank, throwing flame, "No. 25"	60	90	120
Jones (JV4) Tank, "22" on side.	50	75	100

L to R: JV2, JV1

Jones, L to R: JV3, JV4, JV2
Photo by Ed Poole

	C6	C8	C10
Jones & Bixler, "Express J & B" truck, 15½" long............	900	1350	1800

Jones & Bixler "Express J&B" truck.
Courtesy Sotheby's NY

THE JUDY COMPANY

History and listings by Dave Leopard

The Judy Company of Minneapolis, Minnesota made educational toys, including a farm set called "Happy's Farm Family" (patented in 1945) which included a solid rubber car, pick-up truck, and tractor, along with human and animal figures.

	C6	C8	C10
JA01 Sedan, 2 dimensional, (part of set), solid rubber, 5¼" long	15	20	25
JT01 Pickup Truck, 2 dimensional (part of set), solid rubber, 5¼" long.......................	15	20	25
JF01 Farm tractor, 2 dimensional (part of set), solid rubber, 3½" long.......................	15	20	25

Judy, L to R: JA01, JT01
Photo by Dave Leopard

KAHN

KAHN Cadillac & Trailer with furniture, bushes, c.1950, plastic   No Price Found

---

CONDITION OF A TOY
AND ITS RELATION TO PRICE

CONDITION CODE:

C6 - Good, Evident overall wear, well-played with, but acceptable to many collectors

C8 - Very Good Minor wear overall, very clean

C10 - Mint (like new)

NOTE: Mint in Box commands a high price. Condition below C6 brings considerably lower prices.

KANSAS TOY & NOVELTY COMPANY

By Fred Maxwell and Bob Condray
With the assistance of Lorene Sorell, L. D. Morgison
and the Clifton Historical Society

Arthur Haynes, an auto mechanic, started molding toys in his Clifton, Kansas shed for local stores in 1923. With clever hands and an artist's eye, he charmed his friends and local townspeople with his bright-colored toys. He made his patterns from advertising pictures, from local vehicles and probably from other makes of toys, such as Tootsietoy. He made his own production tools. His range was diverse, for he made miniatures of aircraft and autos then making international and national news, farm equipment and even a zeppelin; also a few animals, novelties and charms.

This was a town enterprise from the beginning. Jess Foster, News editor, helped with alloy mixtures; Mr. Hadsell, the Union Pacific agent (see #38, an early promotional?), suggested they send samples to Woolworth's in New York. Clayton D. Young, a traveling salesman, saw the toys, joined the company and built a profitable business with the chain stores, including Kress, Kresge and Sears-Roebuck; and became a partner. At its peak of international sales in the late 1920s they employed as many as 65 in two shifts during the X-mas order season.

They were young people who had grown up together, a happy gang who joked and sang at their work. This informality was reflected in the local name, "the Hoopie Factory". Two or three of their early toys, #26 and #33, were stripdowns - hoopies - probably raced locally. Whether "Whoopee", tractor toy #48, was a local spelling of this or whether it celebrated a fat, cheering order, is not known. Certainly a lot of happy whoopee-e-e-s must have floated from hoopie-land.

Teamwork there must have been, for a molder, according to Ernest Istas, could produce 2000 toys a day. Helen Istas was the secretary; Bill Haynes was another molder, showing the family nature of the work force, with its clippers (trimmers), painters, clampers (axles) and boxers. "Butch" Morgison, one of our sources, was each of these during his long career with the company. Haynes believed that he invented hollow-casting of metal toys, so he must have started with solid toys. One day he dropped his full mold, spilling its hot metal. To his delight he had a perfect, hollow auto toy, with promise of savings of metal and shipping costs.

Those "numbers" embossed on the toys may enhance realism on aircraft, racers, taxis and trains. On classic autos they may irritate adults although they couldn't have bothered the kids who eagerly collected them. The earliest Kansas toys were not numbered so it may have filled a need. It may have become a convenience between salesman and certain buyers when discussing orders without a catalog.

Although neither the first Kansas Toy nor the last have been firmly identified, we have great progress. But now that those numbers are better understood, what other clues should dealers and collectors rely on? If it has metal wheels and a number under #75 it is most likely KT&N, although a few pieces made by later owners had metal wheels. Look for simulated wire wheels and spoke wheels; the reverse sides of these are disks; tractor wheels are open spoked. These simulated wheels are exclusive with KT&N, but regular disk wheels were standard throughout the industry. Many of these toys had stringpull loops or knobs in the handcrank position. Bottom pans are not found; they were introduced by later owners. "Made in USA" labels were a late 1930s regulation. KT&N often issued the same design in two or three scales (5c, 10c & 15c?)

Generally the styles of the prototype will aid in dating; they may commemorate an event such as world speed records (#46). Toy experts will recognize the herd instinct which prompted toy makers to issue popular toys simultaneously. The first pieces were said to be unpainted; if so, few have survived. The first finish used was Egyptian (a U.S. brand name) lacquer, a japanning which applied thinly gave the toys a glittery look. Toys with this finish have been found up to #66. Later they used enamel in all colors including gold. The bodies usually had single colors with "tires" simulated in black. All rules have exceptions; in this case the towed farm implements, #61 to #65 made out of several moving parts. My harrow is in red, green and blue; disks and wheel spokes are unpainted but the rims are orange. A whimsical touch for such a down-to-earth toy.

During its good years KT&N created more designs and produced more toys than any in the industry, save Barclay. Mr. Young left the company in the late 1920s and retired in Kansas City. Whether it was the loss of his assets or the onset of the Depression, the company was in trouble by 1930. George Hoeffer (sp?) reorganized the company and moved the factory down the road, but his effort lasted only a few months. A happy era had come to an end for Clifton.

Fred Maxwell, collector and occasional author, has been collecting antique aircraft and vehicle toys for 25 years. This retirement hobby was started from scratch, for his lead soldiers were missing when he returned home from college. He founded Capital Miniature Auto Collectors Club 20 years ago to promote interest in the Central Atlantic states. He felt challenged by the lack of public knowledge and the ambiguity of that orphan category; Pot Metal or Slushmold Toys.

Fred Maxwell

Transitional Era - Following those Numbers

Where were those Hobo molds? During this period the molds and some of the employees too, were wandering but we don't know under whose roof they were producing. Hardly surprising, for during the 1930s the U.S. was full of wanderers, hoping to find a roof and a job. We called some of them "hobos".

This story is included here because the number series started by KTN will always be associated with its creator. It is not surprising that the series continued unbroken because the migrating assets included Ernest and Helen Istas and others with all their know-how. Today, the true story is elusive or contradictory and may continue so. To the average collector the real makers may not matter, for style, condition and supply may be more important in setting market value. For the serious collector I have included details and clues to maker and vintage lest much of it be lost to history.

Some believe that after Hoeffer failed in 1931 there was a second reorganization in Clifton. If this version sticks then the numbers from #75 to at least #85 were Clifton toys. Other insiders say that the assets moved to Ralston, Ne., but the Ralston historian, herself a Ralstoy ex-employee, says that the toy factory started in 1939. Next, it is said, the assets moved to Springfield, Mo. (a vague story with no evidence yet), and from there

to Manhattan, Ks. and the Best Toy Co. John Best, Sr. had lived in Clifton earlier and probably had been following those Hobo molds. The transitional era numbers may have gone as high as #102, for we have been unable to determine whether Best Toy created new patterns or just reproduced from old molds, or both.

Starting with #75 the new issues used wooden wheels, or hubs, and white rubber tires, a style popularized by Tootsietoy in 1932. This ended the era of metal wheels, although a few pieces, particularly farm toys, continued with metal wheels until 1940. Parallel with these wood wheels was another style, a white hard-rubber disk wheel, often found with black painted "tires". These have been found on numbers from #59 to #97 on both new toys and repros. They may have been used on early Best Toy production. Also during this area we find two-colored toy bodies, such as gilt grilles and trunks, or different-colored tops. Since these are rare, they may have been sales samples.

The transitional era included some of Best Toy. For this history see the Best section earlier in this book.

The following list has been carefully prepared but it is probably not yet complete. All cast numbers and labels are shown in quotes, i.e. "48".

For collectors who find variations useful, the following abbreviations are used:

HRDW	white hard rubber disk wheels	OW	open windows
HG	horizontal grille pattern	RM	rearmount spare
HL	horizontal hood louvers	SW	sidemount spare
HO	hood ornament, cap or motometer	SP	stringpull knob or loop, in front
LI	landau irons, on convertibles	T	trunk, external
MDW	metal disk wheels	UV	unnumbered version
MDSW	metal solid spoke wheels	VG	vertical grille
MSW	metal open spoke wheels	WS or W/S	windshield
MWW	metal simul. "wire" wheels	WV	windshield visor
		WHRT	wood hubs, rubber tires

	C6	C8	C10		C6	C8	C10
KTV1 Midget racer, no #, 3". No driver, torpedo tail, HO, SP, VL, HG, ⅝" MDW w/simulated lug nuts, lacquer finish. Some say this was their first toy; some say first had non-moveable wheels or was a large racer..	20	30	40	KTV2 Midget racer, no #, 3". Same as above, with driver, plain MDW, lacquer. Easily confused with another maker's copy. See #31 and #67.......	40	60	80
				KTV3 Large lady racer, no #, 6". Driver, boattail, HO, MDW, lacquer .... No Price Found			

	C6	C8	C10

KTV4 Coupe, no #, 3⅛". Crude, slant roof, shallow rear body, no fenders, hood similar to first racer above, lacquer. First "hoopie" or stripdown made? — No Price Found

KTV5 Sedan, no #, 3⅜". Crude limousine or stretch taxi, 6 windows, louvered rear quarters, HO, VL, HG, T, SP, large MDW, lacquer . . . . — No Price Found

KTV6 Coupe, no #, 2⅞". Convertible, LI, VL, HG, WV, SP, MDSW, lacquer . . . . — 30 / 45 / 60

KTV7 Coupe, "8", 3⅛". Convertible, LI, VL, HG, WV, SP, RM, MWW, no HO, no headlamps, enamel finish. Also UVs with "Chrysler", headlamps and HO; or with MDSW . . . . — 20 / 30 / 40

KTV8 Coupe, "8", 3⅛". Trunk convertible, T, HO, VG, SM, MDW . . . . — No Price Found

NOTE: #8 is the lowest numbered vehicle found. Its realistic, high quality signals the ending of a novice toymaker's experimental phase. The five coupes above have the same 1924 Chrysler hood and nice details like landau irons and kickplates, but not all had headlamps. The basic body expanded into this series of coupes, #14 roadsters, and sedans (all (?) unnumbered), lacquered or enameled, with 3 types of wheels: MDW, MDSW, and MWW. They were unnamed or named: Chrysler, Cadillac, Chevrolet. Any Fords out there? The large coupe, KTV9, is a scale-up of #8. Only 3 of these large pieces are known: the racer KTV3, John Deere tractor KTV19, and a mail-plane.

KTV9 Large coupe, no #, 5" Chrysler convertible, MWW and 2 golf club doors. Larger version of #8 . . . . — No Price Found

KTV10 Sedan, no #, 2⅞". "Chevrolet", 6 windows, LI, WV, VL, SP, RM, MWW . . . . — 16 / 24 / 32

KTV11 Sedan, no #, 3¼". "Chevrolet", as above, HG, HO, MSW . . . . — No Price Found

KTV12 Overland bus, "9", 3½". "Fageol", solid windows . . . . — No Price Found

KTV13 Overland bus, no #, 3½". "Fageol", 9 male passengers,

driver and "baggage" cast on windows, HG, RM, MDW. Also an UV w/various family passengers on windows, also w/comic characters (Kansas Toy?) . . . . — 26 / 39 / 52

KTV14 Indy racer, "10", 3⅛". Driver, boattail, exhaust right, VL, HG, HO, SP, MSW or MWW. Also UV . . . . — 6 / 9 / 12

KTV15 Roadster, "14", 3⅛". Open "Chrysler", solid W/S, plain grille, HO, VL, SP, RM, MDSW — 18 / 27 / 36

KTV16 Roadster, no #, 3⅛". Same as above, HG, 2 golfclub doors — No Price Found

KTV17 Farm tractor, "17", 2⅞". "Fordson", driver, HG, crank, no tow hook, large 1¼" and ¾" MDW with 4 holes in disks. Also found with same size 6 spoke wheels. See #57 . . . . — 35 / 52 / 70

	C6	C8	C10
KTV18 Farm tractor, no #, 2⅝". Same basic body as above, "Fordson", on radiator and crankcase, VG and towhook, with smaller, plain MDW....	No Price Found		
KTV19 Large farm tractor, no #, 4⅞". Deere Model D. A finely crafted replica in 2 colors, steering shaft, fly wheel, belt drive wheel, rear fenders, large 2" and 1" 12-spoke wheels.....	No Price Found		
KTV20 Truck, "20", 3⅛". Ford?, solid w/s, 2 OW, 3 tanks, VL, HG rear faucet, MWW. Versions w/and w/o driver. Also an UV......	16	24	32
KTV21 Steam tractor, "25", 3". "Case", crew of 2, tow loop, large front, small rear MSW and flywheel. See #71. Also an UV with no name..............	35	52	70
KTV22 Racer, "26", 4". "Bearcat" stripdown, long hood, motometer, 3 intakes, driver, open frame, left exhaust. See #33......................	No Price Found		
KTV23 Separator-thresher, "27", 3". Tow hook, auto-type MSW (not tractor rims), lacquer or enamel. Also UV. See #72...	35	52	70
KTV24 Midget racer, "31", 2⅛". Driver, torpedo tail, VL, HG, HO, MWW, lacquer. Also UV. See #67....................	12	15	18
KTV25 Racer, "33", 3". "Bearcat" stripdown, smaller version of #26 above..................	No Price Found		
KTV26 Coupe, "35", 2¼". Convertible, LI, VL, HG, HO, RM, MWW. Also an UV........	No Price Found		
KTV27 Locomotive-tender, "36", 4⅜". "KT & N RR" 6 MSW, 4 MDW, 0-6-4...............	7	10	14
KTV28 "Pullman" car, "37", 3½". "KT & N RR", 4 MDW.....	No Price Found		
KTV29 Box car, "38", 3¼". "KT & N RR", Union Pacific shield (an early promotional?), 4 MDW	No Price Found		

	C6	C8	C10
KTV30 Tank car, "39", 3⅛". "KT & N RR", ladder, filler, MDW	No Price Found		
KTV31 Caboose, "40", 2¾". "KT & N RR", stack, brakeman's cab, MDS..................	No Price Found		
KTV32 Stock car, "41", "KT & N RR", MDW...............	No Price Found		
KTV33 Dump truck, "42", 3½". Ford?, driver, no cab, diamond emblem on hinged body, VL, HG, SP, MWW.............	35	52	70
KTV34 Steam road roller, "43", 3¼". Driver, SP, boiler, wooden rollers......................	10	15	20
KTV35 Racer. "46", 2⅞". 1929 Golden Arrow record car, driver, large tail fin, MWW..	12	18	24
KTV36 Warehouse tractor, "48", 3". "Caterpillar", "Whoopee", driver, VL, HG, HO, SP, tow loop, MWW. Also an UV....	18	27	36
KTV37 Tour bus, "49", 2⅜". 1928 Pickwick COE "Nite Coach", HG, SP, MDW duals. Also an UV. See #59................	No Price Found		
KTV38 Pickup truck, "51", 2¾". Ford w/cab, VL, HG, tow loop, MDW, lacquer. Also an UV..	No Price Found		
KTV39 Roadster, "54", 2⅜". Buick, driver w/cap, rumble seat, T, plain hood and grille, no headlamps, SM, MWW. Also an UV. See #77................	10	15	20
KTV40 Roadster, "54", 2¼". Same as above, no trunk..........	No Price Found		
KTV41 Truck-semi, "55", 4". Ford, stake trailer, VL, HG, MDW.	No Price Found		
KTV42 Farm tractor, "57", 1¾". Fordson, driver, SP, MDW rear, MSW front. Smaller version of #17. Also an UV............	No Price Found		
KTV43 Sedanette, "58", 2¼". Austin Bantam, unique fighting cock on door panels, 4 OW, HL, VG, RM, MWW............	No Price Found		

	C6	C8	C10
KTV44 Tour bus, "59", 3⅜". 1928 Pickwick COE double-deck night-coach, screen grille. Larger version of #49 above. Also an UV with dual wheels........	No Price Found		
KTV45 Sedan, "60", 3½". 1930 Reo Royale ? or Chrysler 2 dr. brougham, plain hood, vee-VG, square rear deck, MDW, MDWSM. Also an UV with MWW and MWWSM........	24	36	48

Note: The following is a unique towed farm set with several hinged or moving parts, each a different color and large 1¼" spoked tractor wheels.

	C6	C8	C10
KTV46 Planter, "KTN No. 61", 4". V-blade plough with seed hopper. 4 piece incl. wheels and 3 colors......................	35	52	70
KTV47 Disc harrow, "62", 4". 8 discs on same 1⅝" wide frame as #61. 13 pieces, incl. discs and wheels, 4 colors.............	35	52	70
KTV48 Plough, "63", 4". Single blade on same shaft as #61..	No Price Found		
KTV49 Dirt tumble, "64", 4". Adjustable dumping scoop, 1½" wide on same frame as #62. 6 pieces, 4 colors.............	20	30	40
KTV50 Dirt scraper, "65", 3⅝". Blade, 1⅞", adjustable, on same frame as #62................	No Price Found		
KTV51 Coupe, "66", 3½", Streamlined 3-wheeler, 6 OW, MWW, lacquer	No Price Found		
KTV52 Midget racer, "67", 1½". Driver, torpedo-tail, VL, HG, HO, MDW. Smaller version of #31. Also an UV............	44	66	88
KTV53 Fire engine, "70". 2¼". Seagrave ? pumper, driver, VL, HG, MDW	No Price Found		
KTV54 Steam tractor, "71", 2½". Crew of 2, tow-loop. Small version of #25	10	15	20
KTV55 Separator-thresher, "72", 2+". Tow hook for #71	No Price Found		

KTV56 Army tank, "74", 2¼". "US Army", WWI type, high turret, large front, small rear wheels. OD color .... No Price Found

KTV57 Racer, no #, 1". Miniature solid-cast version of #10, moving wheels, charm loop on nose No Price Found

Kansas Toy Racers, top row: KTV1, KTV2
Middle row: KTV14, KTV24, KTV52
Bottom row: KTV35, KTV25
Photo by Fred Maxwell

Kansas Toy Autos, top row: KTV4, KTV5
Middle row: KTV7, KTV7
Bottom row: KTV26, KTV26, KTV43
Photo by Fred Maxwell

Kansas Toy Coupes in two scales KTV9, KTV26
Photo by Fred Zegel

Kansas Toy Bus - KTV12
Photo by Fred Maxwell

KTV13
Drawing courtesy of Deb Eccles

Kansas Toy Vehicles, top row: KTV16, KTV15
2nd row: KTV14, KTV25
3rd row: KTV33, KTV35
Bottom row: KTV36, KTV58
Photo by Fred Maxwell

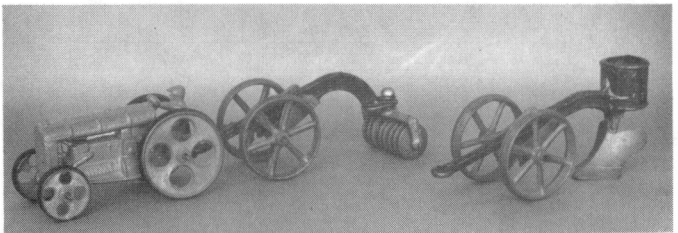

Kansas Toy and Novelty from L to R: KTV17, KTV47, KTV46
Photo by Chic Gast

Kansas Toy Farm Vehicles, top row: KTV17, KTV17
Middle row: KTV23, KTV21
Bottom row: KTV23, KTV17
Photo by Fred Maxwell

Kansas Toy Deere Model D Tractor - KTV19
Photo by Fred Zegel

Kansas Toy Commercial Vehicles, top row: KTV20, KTV33
Middle row: KTV34, KTV36
Bottom row: KTV38, KTV41 (later wheels)
Photo by Fred Maxwell

Kansas Toy, L to R, top: KTV33A, Ralstoy?, KTV38.
Middle: KTV23, KTV21, KTV34
Bottom: KTV46, KTV18, KTV47
Photo by Perry Eichor

Kansas Toy, L to R, top: KTV14, KTV35, KTTV69
Middle: Best "85", KTV52, KTTV71
Bottom: Craftoy? KTV24, Best "97"
Photo by Fred Maxwell

Kansas Toy Vehicles, top row: KTV24, KTV26, KTV37
2nd row: KTV27, KTV29
3rd row: KTV38, KTV40, KTV43
4th row: KTV45, KTV52, KTV53
Bottom row: KTV62 (small version?) KTTV67

Kansas Toy, top row: KTV7, KTV15
Bottom row: KTV45, KTTV67
Photo by Perry Eichor

Three versions of the original Kansas Toy #42 truck:
Top row: Kansas Toy version, KTV33
Bottom row: Ralstoy, RAV1, Earlier version (Ralstoy?)
Photo by Perry Eichor

Kansas Toy: KTV22 (mid 1930s), KTV25 (1920s)
Photo by Perry Eichor

Kansas Toy and Novelty KTV34
Photo by R.F. Sapita

Kansas Toy KTV56
Photo by Perry Eichor

Kansas Toy Towed Implements, top row: KTV46, KTV49
Bottom row: KTV47, KTV50
Photo by Fred Maxwell

Kansas Toy Vehicles with Wood Hubs, top row: KTTV64, KTTV65
Bottom row: KTTV66, KT&N #85
Photo by Fred Maxwell

Kansas Toy Autos with Hard Rubber Wheels, top row: KTTV59,
KTV45
Middle row: KTTV63
Bottom row: KTTV67, KTTV72
Photo by Fred Maxwell

Kansas Toy KTTV64
Photo by Craig A. Clark

Kansas Toy, top row: KTTV66, KTTV63
Middle row: KTTV68, KTV45
Bottom row: KTV43
Photo by Perry Eichor

This is probably an ad for Kansas Toy vehicles. It ran in the April, 1933 Butler Bros. catalog. The numbers have been typed in by Fred Maxwell

KANSAS TOY TRANSITIONAL VEHICLES

	C6	C8	C10
KTTV58 Tractor, "48", 3". "Caterpillar", "Whoopee" same as KTV36 except ¾" grooved metal wheels with rubber track	35	52	70
KTTV59 Tour bus, no #, 3⅜". Pickwick COE, a more streamlined version of #59 above, with 8 open windows	No Price Found		
KTTV60 ? Fire engine, no #, 3¼". Pumper, 2 fireman w/old style helmets, hose reel, HG, MDW. Kansas ?	12	18	24
KTTV61 Army tank, "74", 2¼". "US Army", 2 gun turret, OD color. A different tank than #74 above......................	No Price Found		
KTTV62 Coupe, "75" 4¼". Graham like (Tootsietoy) VG, SM, T, WHRT, 1933 issue ...	No Price Found		
KTTV63 Racer, "76", 4¼". Auburn speedster, low driver, headrest fairing, SP, HG, slanted louvers, large oval fin, kickplates, HWRW or WHRT.	20	30	40
KTTV64 Roadster, "77". 4". Open sport Duesenberg, W/S down, driver, VG, slanted louvers, SM, T, WHRT	16	24	32
KTTV65 Concrete mixer, "78", 3¾". Truck with water tank & mixing barrel, VG, HL, WHRT. Found both with and w/o a bottom pan. Sometimes called a fuel tanker	No Price Found		
KTTV66 Sedan, "79", 4¼". 2 door, Graham like, 4 OW, VG, HL, RM, WHRT w/5 removable tires. Found both with and w/o bottom pan	14	21	28
KTTV67 Coupe, "80", 3½". Convertible, top up, LI, 2 OW, VG, T, MWW w/ MWW SM	20	30	40
KTTV68 Coupe, "80", 3½". Same as above except HRDW w/MDW SM. (a different casting re sidemounts)	No Price Found		

	C6	C8	C10
KTTV69 Racer, "81", 4⅜". Miller FWD, driver, 8 cyl., right exhaust, HG, WHRT, 1933 issue	No Price Found		
KTTV70 Sedan, "82", 4". Pierce Arrow Silver Arrow fastback, 6 OW, HRDW. Also an UV ...	No Price Found		
KTTV71 Indy racer, "83", 4⅝". FWD type, driver, VG, HL, right exhaust, WHRT	No Price Found		
KTTV72 Sedan, "84", 3⅝". Desoto? airflow, 4 OW, HO, HG, HL, HRDW. 1934 issue .	20	30	40

Note: Although not yet certain when the hobo molds changed hands, the higher numbers are described and illustrated under Best Toy and Ralstoy.

Karl Bub Mercedes Limousine, 13½" long, c.1928.
Photo by Bob Smith

Karl Bub Limousine, 14" long, c.1915.
Photo by Bob Smith

KARL BUB

("KBN", Nuremburg, Germany, 1851-1966)
by Bob Smith

Bub had one of the longest reigns in the toy business. He took over the Carette Toy Co. in 1917 after Georges Carette fled to France at the onset of World War I. He also took over the Bing Toy Works in 1932. Bub used much of the technology practiced by Carette. His toys were of the better-quality toys to come out of Germany in the early 1900's. Bub produced many of the fine toys sold by F.A.O Schwarz Co. of New York.

Karl Bub Limousine, 9¾" long.
Photo by Bob Smith

	C6	C8	C10
KARL BUB Limousine. Green/black, 9.75" long. Doors open, front crank c/w motor .	700	1100	1500
Karl Bub Limousine, 14" long, clockwork, c.1920s	1200	1800	2500
KARL BUB Limousine. Red/black, c/w motor, 14" long. Opening doors, hand brake. c.1915....	1200	1800	2500
KARL BUB Mercedes Limousine. Green/black, 13.5" long. Doors open, windshield folds, head lamps, tool box's c/w motor, head lamps, steering. c.1928 .	950	1450	1950

Karl Bub Limousine, 14" long, clockwork, c.1920s.
Courtesy Sotheby's NY

234

KELMET

(Also known as Trumodel and Big Boy)

Kelmet was founded in Chicago in 1925 by several wholesale toy representatives. It was their wish to compete with the large toy steel vehicles of the period. Work was done to at least some extent through A.C. Gilbert. White trucks were a Kelmet staple. The toys were big (about two feet) and heavy (about ten pounds).

	C6	C8	C10
Kelmet Aerial Ladder Truck	800	1250	1700
Kelmet Chemical Truck	900	1400	2000
Kelmet Coal Pocket Loader.....	1200	2000	3000
Kelmet Crane Truck	2500	4000	6000
Kelmet Sand Loader	1000	1700	2400
Kelmet Scissor Dump Truck, 25" long......................	600	950	1400
Kelmet Steam Shovel, Big Boy .	325	488	650
Kelmet Tank Truck, 27" long ..	1000	1700	2400
Kelmet Trumodel Derrick with power hoist and tip bucket ..	1000	1700	2400
Kelmet "U.S. Army" truck, 25" long, canvas cover	400	625	850
Kelmet White Dump Truck, 25" long, No. 501..............	1200	2000	2700
Kelmet White Fire Truck (ladder)	1200	2000	3000

KENTON

Kenton Lock Manufacturing Co. was incorporated in May, 1890, in Kenton, Ohio. In November of 1894, it became the Kenton Hardware Manufacturing Company, and around this period, began producing toys. In 1903 it brought out its first toy auto line, calling them the "Red Devils", since most cars in those days were painted red. The firm was a guild. In 1930 L.S. Bixler, of Jones & Bixler, was its president. Cast iron was its material.

	C6	C8	C10
Kenton Ambulance, 7" long, cast iron.....................	750	1300	1700
Kenton "Army Motortruck 807", 14" long, cast iron	600	950	1300

Kenton Amublance, 7" long, cast iron, driver incorrect. Courtesy Sotheby's NY

Kenton "Army Motor Truck 807", incorrect driver in photo. Courtesy Sotheby's NY

	C6	C8	C10
Kenton Auto, very early, clockwork, tiller, driver in top hat, approx. 4" long	250	400	550
Kenton Auto, 6" long, cast iron	1000	1700	2400
Kenton Auto Dray Truck, black driver, 9" long..............	400	700	1000
Kenton Boat-tail cut-down speedster, 1910, 7" long	120	180	240
Kenton Buckeye Ditcher........	700	1050	1400
Kenton Bus, double-decker, 6" long, 1920s	400	600	800
Kenton Bus, double decker, 1920, 7¼" long................	1100	1650	2200
Kenton Bus, double-decker, 9½" long.....................	1000	1500	2000
Kenton Bus, double-decker, 12" long.....................	500	800	1200
Kenton Bus, 8" long, cast iron .	340	510	680
Kenton Bus, 1920s, 10¾" long .	375	525	750
Kenton Bus, Twin Coach, 8½" long......................	1000	1600	2350

Kenton Bus, double-decker, 9½'' long.
Courtesy Phillips NY

Kenton Buckeye Ditcher, 12½'' long.
Courtesy Sotheby's NY

	C6	C8	C10
Kenton Cattle Truck, 8'' long, cast iron, c.1938	150	225	300
Kenton Cement Mixer	400	600	800
Kenton Circus Truck, 10'' long .	1300	2000	2700
Kenton ''Coal'' dump truck, 8½'' long	140	210	280
Kenton ''Coast-to-Coast'' bus . . .	350	525	700
Kenton ''Contractors'' Dump Wagon, cast iron	250	375	500

Kenton ''Contractors'' Dump Wagon.
Courtesy Sotheby's NY

	C6	C8	C10
Kenton Coupe, 5'' long	230	345	460
Kenton Dump Truck, 6'' long . .	337	505	675
Kenton Emergency Truck, c.1930s, black rubber tires, takes batteries for headlights and spotlight . .	180	270	360
Kenton Fire Apparatus Truck . . .	400	600	800
Kenton Fire Pump truck, early with driver, approx. 10'' long	185	278	350
Kenton Fire Pumper, 11½'' long, 1911	No Price Found		
Kenton Fire Pumper, 14½'' long, 1920s	800	1200	1600
Kenton Fire Pumper, 18'' long, c.1920, has gong	350	525	700

Kenton Fire Pumper, 18'' long, has gong.
Courtesy Mape Auctioneers & Appraisers

	C6	C8	C10
Kenton Fire Truck, 15'' long with pumper	1200	2000	2800
Kenton Franklin, air-cooled, 8½'' long	1300	1950	2600
Kenton ''Hose'' truck, approx. 6¾'' long, open cab, c.1920s, green, driver, rider, hose, ladders	350	525	700
Kenton Ice Truck, tongs and glass ice, 7½''	300	450	600
Kenton Jaeger cement mixer, 6½'' long, iron wheels	350	525	700
Kenton Jaeger cement mixer, 8'' long	1000	1500	2000
Kenton Jaeger ''Mixer'', cast iron cement truck, 9'' long	850	1400	1900

Kenton "Jaeger" cement mixer.
Courtesy Sotheby's NY

Kenton "Jaeger" Cement Mixer Truck, 8" long.
Courtesy HAKE'S Americana & Collectibles

Kenton "Jaeger" Cement Mixer, rubber wheels, 9"?
Courtesy Sotheby's NY

Kenton Ladder Truck, approx. 7½" long. From a 1927 Kenton
catalog.

	C6	C8	C10
Kenton Ladder Truck, approx. 7½" long, cast iron	300	450	600
Kenton Ladder Truck, 9" long, driver, early 1930s	90	135	180
Kenton Ladder Truck, 11½" long	400	600	800
Kenton Ladder Truck, pressed steel ladders, 16" long	500	850	1100
Kenton Ladder Truck, 17¼" long	750	1200	1700
Kenton Ladder Truck, 20" long	1100	1800	2500
Kenton Ladder Truck, 22" long	1500	2400	3500
Kenton Overland Circus cage truck with driver, 7½" long	900	1500	2000
Kenton Overland Circus with lion, 9" long	800	1300	1800
Kenton Overland Circus Calliope Truck, 10" long (Rare)	No Price Found		
Kenton Patrol Wagon, marked "Patrol" on side, c.1920s-1930s	400	600	800
Kenton Phaeton touring car, 12"	350	562	700
Kenton "Pickwick Nite Coach", 14" long, cast iron	1900	2750	3800
Kenton "Pickwick Nite Coach", 11" long	No Price Found		

"Pickwick Nite Coach", 11" long.
Courtesy Phillips NY

	C6	C8	C10
Kenton Pontiac, approx. 4" long	150	225	300
Kenton Pontiac & Trailer, 10" long	350	525	725
Kenton Racer, 7½" long	350	550	750
Kenton Racer, 9" long, early, cast iron	600	1000	1400
Kenton Reo Sedan, 1929, 8" long	No Price Found		
Kenton Road Grader, 5½" long	112	168	225
Kenton Road Grader, 7¼" long, 1950	135	205	275
Kenton Road Grader, cast iron, 7½" long, rubber tires, nickel-plated moveable blade	155	230	310

	C6	C8	C10
Kenton Runabout Auto, 5" long, 1900	170	255	340
Kenton Runabout Auto, cast iron, 7" long, resembles a 1910 Franklin, has driver	700	1050	1400
Kenton Sedan, 4" long	110	165	225
Kenton Sedan, 7" long, late 1930s, rubber tires, take apart body	1400	2100	2800
Kenton Sedan, 8½" long	2000	3000	5000
Kenton "Speed" stake truck, c.1927, 5½" long	50	75	100
Kenton Sprinkler Truck, early, 8"	300	450	600
Kenton Stake Truck, 6" long	337	405	675
Kenton Steam Roller, "Gallon Master", 6½" long	150	225	300
Kenton Steam Shovel, Marion, 7¼" long	600	900	1200
Kenton Tank, cast iron, 2½" long	80	120	160
Kenton Touring Car, open, driver and passenger, 8½" long	650	975	1300
Kenton Tow Auto, 1920s, 9½" long	1600	2400	3200
Kenton Yellow Cab, 1950s, 6⅜" long	300	450	600

Kenton Touring Car, open, driver and passenger, 8½" long (air-cooled Franklin).
Courtesy Sotheby's NY

KEYSTONE

Keystone, of Boston, Massachusetts, had an odd assortment of products; movie projectors, steel trucks, wooden boats and pressed wood forts and garages. Founded in June, 1922 or 1923 by Chester Rimmer and Arthur Jackson, it was first located in a small shop in Malden, Mass. under the name Jacrim, using parts of partners' last names. Rimmer retired in 1958 and sold out to various companies. Address in Boston was 288 A Street. All numbers and descriptions in bold type are Keystone's own.

	C6	C8	C10
Keystone No. ? "Dugan Brothers" "ridem" truck, 27" long	1200	2200	3200
Keystone **No. 41 Dump Truck**, 26½" long	450	750	1100
Keystone **No. 43 American Railway Express**, 26" long	800	1300	2000
Keystone **No. 44 Truck Loader**, 17¾" high	175	263	350
Keystone **No. 45 U.S. Mail Truck**, 26" long	700	1200	1700
Keystone **No. 46 Steam Shovel**, 26" long when arm is extended	125	188	250
Keystone **No. 47 Steam Shovel**, 34½" long when arm is extended	200	300	400
Keystone **No. 48 U.S. Army Truck**, 26" long	650	110	1500
Keystone **No. 49 Fire Truck**, 27½" long	600	1000	1400
Keystone **No. 51 Police Patrol**, 27½" long	700	1200	1700
Keystone **No. 52 Fire Truck**, 27½" long	600	1100	1500
Keystone **No. 53 Sprinkler Truck**, tank 12" long	800	1300	2000
Keystone **No. 54 Koaster Truck**, with skids, hoist cable, windlass, 26" long when skids retracted	800	1350	1825
Keystone **No. 55 Koaster Truck**, without skids and windlass	450	675	900
Keystone **No. 56 Water Pump Tower**, 29" long	600	1000	1400
Keystone **No. 57 Chemical Pump Engine**, 27½" long	700	1200	1600

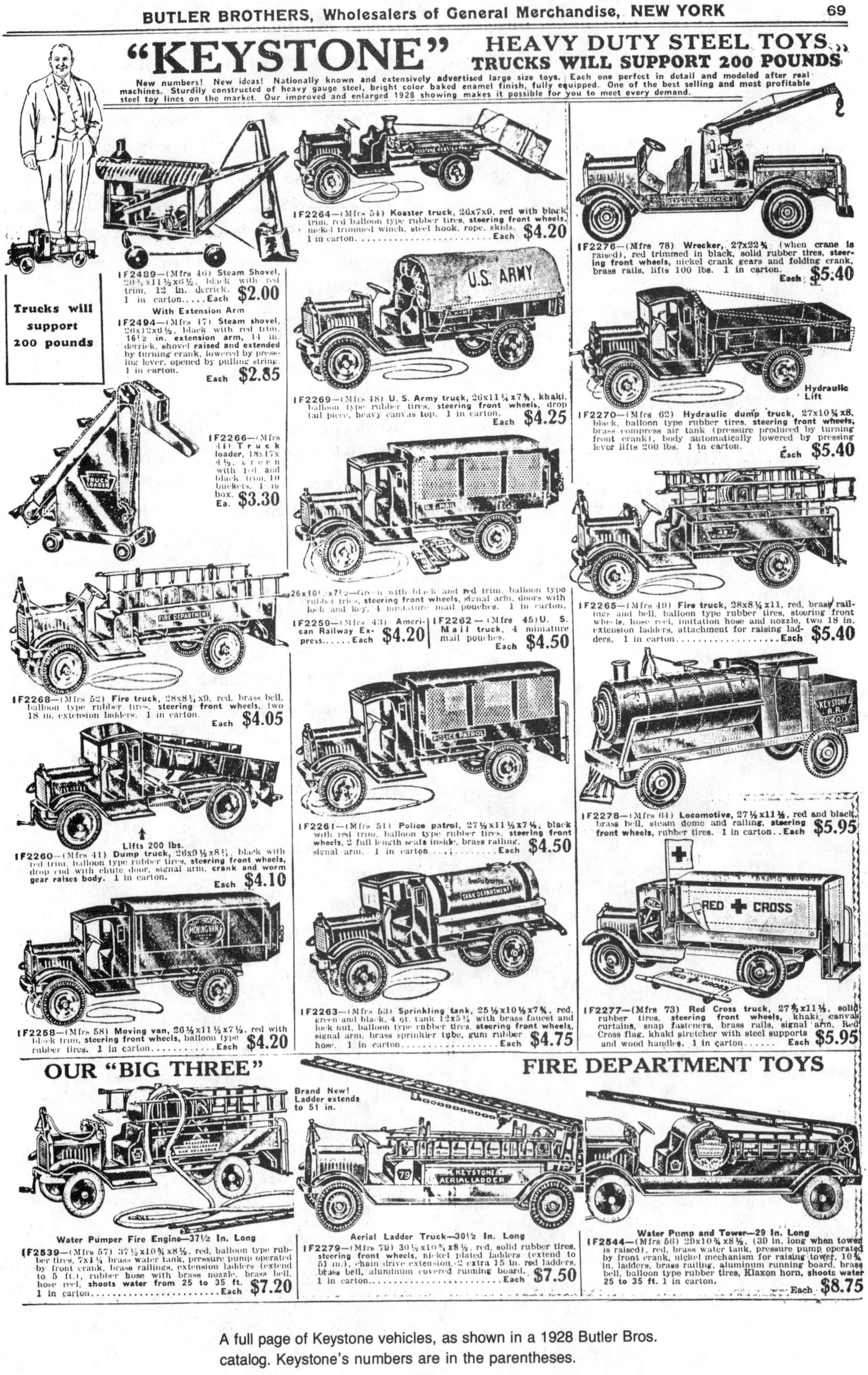

BUTLER BROTHERS, Wholesalers of General Merchandise, NEW YORK 69

"KEYSTONE" HEAVY DUTY STEEL TOYS

TRUCKS WILL SUPPORT 200 POUNDS

New numbers! New ideas! Nationally known and extensively advertised large size toys. Each one perfect in detail and modeled after real machines. Sturdily constructed of heavy gauge steel, bright color baked enamel finish, fully equipped. One of the best selling and most profitable steel toy lines on the market. Our improved and enlarged 1928 showing makes it possible for you to meet every demand.

Trucks will support 200 pounds

1F2489—(Mfrs 46) **Steam Shovel,** 20¾x11½x6½, black with red trim, 12 in. derrick. 1 in carton.....**Each $2.00**

With Extension Arm

1F2494—(Mfrs 47) **Steam shovel,** 26x12x6½, black with red trim, 16½ in. **extension arm,** 14 in. derrick, shovel **raised and extended** by turning crank, lowered by pressing lever, opened by pulling string. 1 in carton. **Each $2.85**

1F2266—(Mfrs 44) **Truck loader,** 18x17x4½, green with red and black trim, 10 buckets. 1 in box. **Ea. $3.30**

1F2268—(Mfrs 52) **Fire truck,** 28x8¼x9, red, brass bell, balloon type rubber tires, **steering front wheels,** two 18 in. extension ladders. 1 in carton. **Each $4.05**

Lifts 200 lbs.

1F2260—(Mfrs 41) **Dump truck,** 26x9½x8¼, black with red trim, balloon type rubber tires, **steering front wheels,** drop end with chute door, signal arm, **crank and worm gear raises body.** 1 in carton. **Each $4.10**

1F2258—(Mfrs 58) **Moving van,** 26½x11½x7½, red with black trim, **steering front wheels,** balloon type rubber tires. 1 in carton............**Each $4.20**

1F2264—(Mfrs 54) **Koaster truck,** 26x7x9, red with black trim, red balloon type rubber tires, **steering front wheels,** nickel trimmed winch, steel hook, rope, skids. 1 in carton..........................**Each $4.20**

1F2269—(Mfrs 48) **U. S. Army truck,** 26x11¼x7¾, khaki, balloon type rubber tires, **steering front wheels,** drop tail piece, heavy canvas top. 1 in carton. **Each $4.25**

26x10½x7½—Green with black and red trim, balloon type rubber tires, **steering front wheels,** signal arm, doors with lock and key, 4 miniature mail pouches. 1 in carton.

1F2259—(Mfrs 43) **American Railway Express......Each $4.20**

1F2262—(Mfrs 45) **U. S. Mail truck,** 4 miniature mail pouches. **Each $4.50**

1F2261—(Mfrs 51) **Police patrol,** 27½x11½x7½, black with red trim, balloon type rubber tires, **steering front wheels,** 2 full length seats inside, brass railing, signal arm. 1 in carton...........**Each $4.50**

1F2263—(Mfrs 53) **Sprinkling tank,** 25½x10½x7¾, red, green and black, 4 qt. tank 12x5¼ with brass faucet and lock nut, balloon type rubber tires, **steering front wheels,** signal arm, brass sprinkler tube, gum rubber hose. 1 in carton.................**Each $4.75**

1F2276—(Mfrs 78) **Wrecker,** 27x22¾ (when crane is raised), red trimmed in black, solid rubber tires, **steering front wheels,** nickel crank gears and folding crank, brass rails, lifts 100 lbs. 1 in carton. **Each $5.40**

Hydraulic Lift

1F2270—(Mfrs 62) **Hydraulic dump truck,** 27x10¾x8, black, balloon type rubber tires, **steering front wheels,** brass compress air tank (pressure produced by turning front crank), body automatically lowered by pressing lever lifts 200 lbs. 1 in carton. **Each $5.40**

1F2265—(Mfrs 49) **Fire truck,** 28x8¼x11, red, brass railings and bell, balloon type rubber tires, steering front wheels, hose reel, imitation hose and nozzle, two 18 in. extension ladders, attachment for raising ladders. 1 in carton.....................**Each $5.40**

1F2278—(Mfrs 64) **Locomotive,** 27½x11⅓, red and black, brass bell, steam dome and railing, **steering front wheels,** rubber tires. 1 in carton..**Each $5.95**

1F2277—(Mfrs 73) **Red Cross truck,** 27½x11½, solid rubber tires, **steering front wheels,** khaki canvas curtains, snap fasteners, brass rails, signal arm, Red Cross flag, khaki stretcher with steel supports and wood handles. 1 in carton...... **Each $5.95**

OUR "BIG THREE" FIRE DEPARTMENT TOYS

Water Pumper Fire Engine—37½ In. Long

1F2539—(Mfrs 57) 37½x10¾x8½, red, balloon type rubber tires, 7x1¼ brass water tank, pressure pump operated by front crank, brass railings, extension ladders (extend to 5 ft.), rubber hose with brass nozzle, brass bell, hose reel, **shoots water from 25 to 35 ft.** 1 in carton...........................**Each $7.20**

Brand New! Ladder extends to 51 in.

Aerial Ladder Truck—30½ In. Long

1F2279—(Mfrs 79) 30½x10¾x8½, red, solid rubber tires, **steering front wheels,** nickel plated ladders (extend to 51 in.), chain drive extension, 2 extra 15 in. red ladders, brass bell, aluminum covered running board. 1 in carton........................**Each $7.50**

Water Pump and Tower—29 In. Long

1F2544—(Mfrs 56) 29x10¾x8½, (30 in. long when tower is raised), red, brass water tank, pressure pump operated by front crank, nickel mechanism for raising tower, 10¾ in. ladders, brass railing, aluminum running board, brass bell, balloon type rubber tires, Klaxon horn, **shoots water 25 to 35 ft.** 1 in carton. **Each $8.75**

A full page of Keystone vehicles, as shown in a 1928 Butler Bros. catalog. Keystone's numbers are in the parentheses.

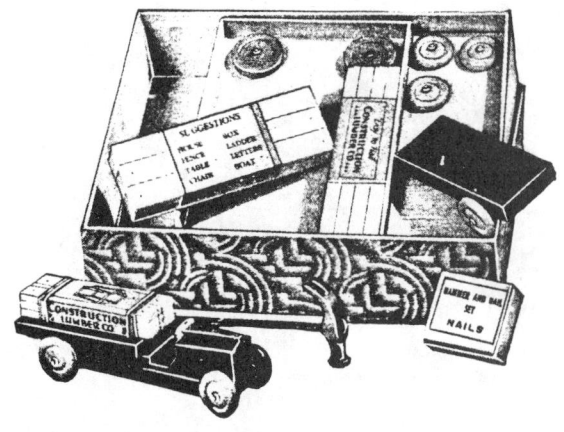

NO. 741—WOOD FIRE DEPARTMENT

This set contains one knock-down fire station; ladder truck with removable ladder and a sound alarm operated by turning wheel on sound box. Packed in an individual display box.

NO. 734—LUMBER SET

A construction set containing one lumber truck equipped with load of construction lumber suitable for the building of many objects. Also contains two packages of building lumber, wheels, axles, block, hammer and nails. Building lumber drilled for easy nailing and may be used many times. Packed in an individual display box.

NO. 752—WOOD TRAFFIC SET

This set contains one knock-down garage, one ice truck and one dumping coal truck. Dumping motion on coal truck operated by lever on side of chassis. Packed in an individual display box.

Keystone wood toys, from a Keystone catalog. The Fire Station, in C6, C8, C10 is worth $85, 128, 170. The Garage in C6, C8, C10 is worth $125, 188, 250. No price found for the Lumber Set, or its "Construction Lumber Co." truck.
Courtesy Ron Fink

Keystone No. ?? Plastic Sedans, 4½" long.
Photo by Terry Sells

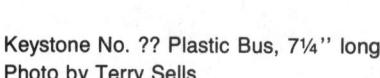

Keystone No. ?? Plastic Bus, 7¼" long.
Photo by Terry Sells

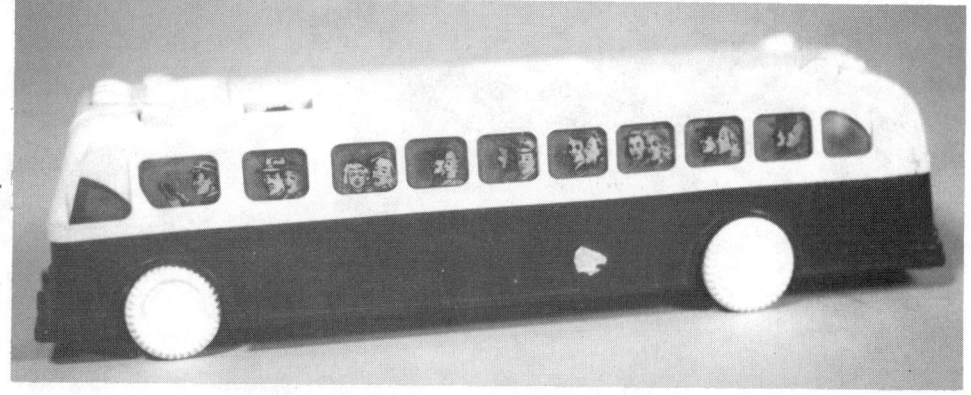

	C6	C8	C10
Keystone **No. 58 Moving Van,** 26'' long	750	1300	1850
Keystone **No. 59** Water Tower..	1300	2100	3000
Keystone No. 60 Riding Steam roller	300	450	600
Keystone **No. 62 Hydraulic Dump Truck,** 26'' long	325	488	650
Keystone **No. 73 Ambulance,** military, 27'' long	725	1275	1800
Keystone **No. 78 Wrecking Car,** 27'' long	700	1200	1600
Keystone **79 Aerial Ladder,** 30½'' long	600	1000	1400
Keystone **No. 84** ''Coast to Coast'' Bus, windup, 31'' long	1500	2700	4000
Keystone No. ?? Ladder Truck, 24'' long	250	385	525
Keystone No. ?? Milk Truck, 27'' long	1400	2300	3300
Keystone Pure Milk Divco, No. D-402, motor drive	150	225	300
Keystone No. ?? Steam Shovel Ride 'Em	500	800	1100
Keystone No. ?? Dump, Cab Over, 25'' long	275	405	550
Keystone No. ?? Plastic Bus, 7¼'' long	No Price Found		
Keystone No. ?? Plastic Sedan, 4½'' long, c.1950, hood lifts, gas tank fills & drains	14	18	22
Keystone No. ?? Steam Roller, red and black, air pressure whistle, brass bell, 20'' long	400	600	800
Keystone No. ?? ''World's Greatest Circus'' Truck, 26'' long, c.1930s	1500	2700	4000

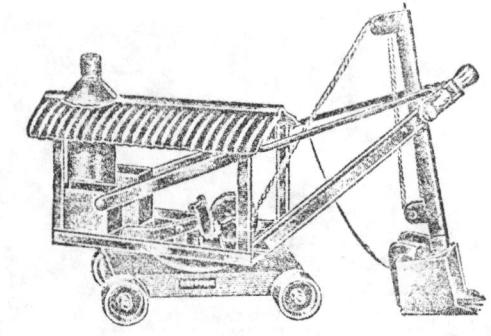
Keystone 47
From the September, 1931 Butler Bros. catalog

Keystone No. 48
Photo by Calvin L. Chaussee

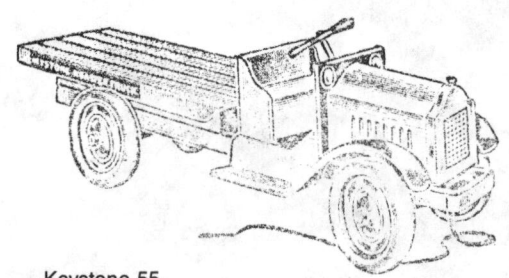
Keystone 55
From the September, 1931 Butler Bros. catalog

Keystone No. 41
Courtesy Sotheby's NY

Keystone 56
From the October, 1932 Butler Bros. catalog

Keystone No. 58
Courtesy Mapes Auctioneers, Vestal, NY

A Keystone tank, wooden, metal firing mechanism, 6'' long, c.WWII.
No Price Found.
Photo by Ed Poole

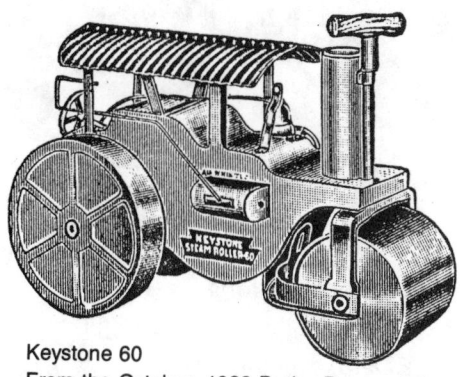

Keystone 60
From the October, 1932 Butler Bros. catalog

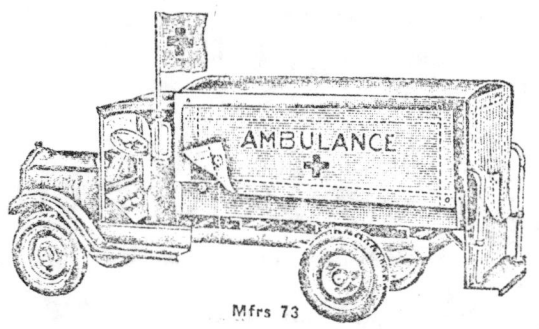

Keystone No. 73 From the September, 1931 Butler Bros. catalog

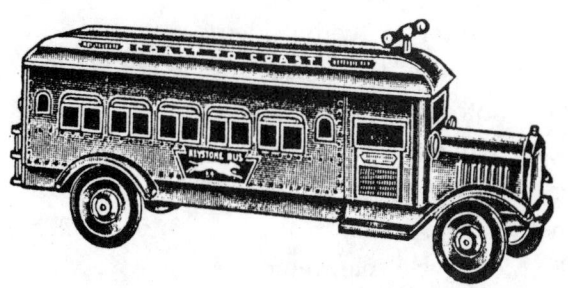

Keystone 84. From the October, 1932 Butler Bros. catalog

KILGORE

Kilgore, of Westerville, Ohio, appears to have begun toymaking in the 1920s. Its toys were cast iron and low-priced, with cap pistols its most popular line. But it also did well with a number of attractive trucks, fire engines and cars, as well as scattered aircraft and ships. Some subsidiary manufacturing was done in Lancaster, Pennsylvania and Canada. In 1937 Kilgore began making plastic cars, trucks, planes and buses, and later added plastic cap pistols, placing it among the first (if not the first) companies to produce plastic toys. Kilgore remained in business until at least 1978. The first owner, a Mr. Kilgore, sold out in 1921.

	C6	C8	C10
Kilgore Arctic Ice Cream Truck, 8'' long	800	1300	1750
Kilgore ''Arctic Ice Cream'' truck, 9'' long	500	750	1000
Kilgore Auto, ''LF 1300A'', with driver	180	270	360
Kilgore Bus, plastic, advertised in 1937, 4''	20	25	30
Kilgore Convertible with Rumble Seat, 7'' long, early 1930s, with driver	160	240	320
Kilgore Coupe, 4'' long, cast iron	60	90	120
Kilgore Coupe, streamlined, plastic, 4'', advertised in 1939	15	20	25

Kilgore, Arctic Ice Cream Truck

Kilgore "Express" Truck, plastic
Photo by Dave Leopard

Kilgore, Coupe, streamlined, plastic.
Photo by Dave Leopard

Kilgore "Fire Chief" sedan, plastic
Photo by Dave Leopard

	C6	C8	C10
Kilgore Dump Truck, cast iron, c.1934, 5¾" long	160	240	320
Kilgore Dump Truck, 7" long, 1930s	180	270	360
Kilgore Dump Truck, 8½" long, cast iron, c.1934	400	600	800

	C6	C8	C10
Kilgore Fire Pumper, 4" long, cast iron	80	120	160
Kilgore Ford Deluxe Sedan, 1934, 7" long	No Price Found		
Kilgore Livestock Truck, 7" long, 1930s	700	1050	1400
Kilgore Livestock Truck, 9" long	600	900	1200
Kilgore Model T Coupe, 5" long	200	300	400

Kilgore Dump Truck, cast iron, c.1934, 8½" long.
Courtesy James S. Maxwell/Virginia Caputo
Photo by Virginia Caputo

	C6	C8	C10
Kilgore "Express" Truck, plastic, 4" advertised in 1937	15	20	25
Kilgore "Fire Chief" sedan, plastic, 4" advertised in 1937	15	20	25
Kilgore Fire Pumper, 5" long, cast iron	88	132	175

KILGORE MOTORCYCLES

(list by Kent M. Comstock)

	C6	C8	C10
(KM1) Motorcycle solo, police, white rubber tires, 4"	75	100	150
(KM2) Motorcycle trike "Special Delivery", white rubber tires, 4¼"	150	225	350
(KM3) Motorcycle with sidecar nickel wheels, 4¼"	125	200	300
(KM4) Motorcycle with sidecar nickel wheels, 5"	175	250	400
(KM5) Motorcycle solo, rubber tires, 5¾"	150	225	350
(KM6) Motorcycle solo, removable rider, rubber tires, 6½"	400	600	1000

Note: All Kilgore MC have cast-in drivers except for #6 which has a removable driver. This is not a complete list, although it is close.

Kilgore Tank, 2½'' long.
Photo by Ed Poole

Kilgore, L to R: KM2, KM4
Photo by Kent M. Comstock

Kilgore ''Taxi''
Photo by Dave Leopard

	C6	C8	C10
Kilgore Open Town Car, plastic, 4'' long	15	20	25
Kilgore Packard Luxury Sedan, 8¼'', take-apart body	800	1200	1600
Kilgore Pierce-Arrow Roadster, 6⅛'' take-apart body	250	375	500
Kilgore Police Car, plastic, 4'' long, 1937	15	20	25
Kilgore Pontiac, 10'' long, cast iron, 1930 (See Stutz)			
Kilgore Roadster, 6'' long, driver, rumble seat	230	345	460
Kilgore Sedan, 3¼'' long	70	105	140
Kilgore Stutz Roadster, 13 parts	1100	1500	2500
Kilgore Tank, 2½'' long, cast iron	30	45	60
Kilgore ''Taxi'', plastic, 4'', advertised in 1937	15	20	25
Kilgore ''Toy Town Delivery'' truck, 6⅛'' long	200	300	400
Kilgore Tractor w/scoop	100	150	200

Kilgore toys, as seen in the November, 1932 Butler Bros. catalog

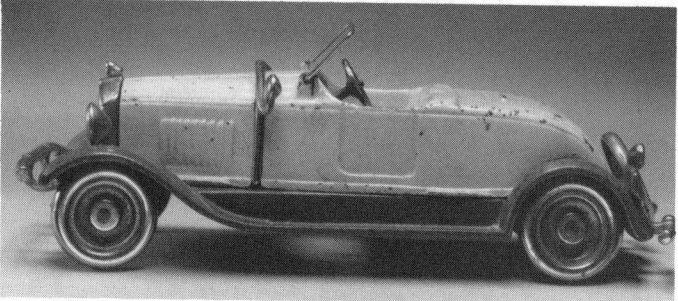

Kilgore Stutz Roadster
Courtesy Sotheby's NY

CONDITION OF A TOY
AND ITS RELATION TO PRICE

CONDITION CODE:

C6 - Good, Evident overall wear, well-played with, but acceptable to many collectors

C8 - Very Good Minor wear overall, very clean

C10 - Mint (like new)

NOTE: Mint in Box commands a high price. Condition below C6 brings considerably lower prices.

This June, 1939 *Playthings* ad shows Kilgore's new plastic toys in the foreground, with the cast iron versions at rear.
Courtesy *Playthings Magazine*

KINGSBURY

Kingsbury had its origins in 1886 in Keene, New Hampshire. Its owner was Harry T. Kingsbury, who bought the Wilkins Toy Company, apparently not changing that firm's name till after World War One. Steel and spring motors characterize Kingsbury's toys, with cars, fire engines, farm equipment and racing cars its primary output. Kingsbury is still in business, but seems to have given up toy production in 1942.

Kingsbury Airflow
Courtesy Mapes Auctioneers & Appraisers

Kingsbury Cannon Truck c.1939, 15" long.
Photo by Orville C. Britton

	C6	C8	C10
Kingsbury Aerial Ladder Truck, pressed steel windup c.1941, 24" long, ladder rises automatically to height of 38 inches when the truck runs into any obstruction, fireman on ladder climbs up and down by turning crank at base of ladder, early version new in 1905 ...	200	300	400
Kingsbury Aerial Ladder Truck, c.1920s	1100	1700	2500
Kingsbury Airflow, c.1934, pressed steel, rubber tires, 14" long..	275	363	550
Kingsbury Airflow, clockwork, 14" long....................	250	375	510
Kingsbury Auto, very early, 9¾" long, steel windup	350	525	700
Kingsbury Bluebird Racer	800	1300	2000
Kingsbury Brougham Sedan, 13" long, pressed steel windup ..	450	800	1200
Kingsbury Bus, 18" long, pressed steel.....................	1500	2500	3500
Kingsbury Cab Over Semi-truck	155	232	310
Kingsbury Cannon Truck, very early, 11" long, clockwork ...	135	205	270
Kingsbury Cannon Truck c.1939, 15" windup................	125	188	250
Kingsbury Caterpillar, 8½" long, wind-up	150	225	300
Kingsbury Cattle Truck, 19" long, 1930s....................	90	135	180
Kingsbury Chemical Ladder Truck, 35" long..................	1300	2200	3000
Kingsbury Combination Chemical Truck, 26" long............	1500	2500	3500
Kingsbury Contractors Tractor ..	150	225	300
Kingsbury Coupe No. 244......	800	1300	1900
Kingsbury Coupe No. 74200....	550	900	1300

	C6	C8	C10
Kingsbury Delivery Stake Truck, 1923, 9" long, driver	225	338	450
Kingsbury DeSoto, 14½" long, pressed steel windup, c.1938 .	275	363	550
Kingsbury Divco U.S. Air Mail Truck......................	250	375	500
Kingsbury Dray Stake Truck, early 1930s	100	150	200
Kingsbury Dump Truck, tin, driver, 10" long.............	225	337	450
Kingsbury Dump Truck, early 1930s, 16" long, clockwork...	350	525	700
Kingsbury Express Truck, late ..	150	225	300
Kingsbury "Fire Chief" coupe, 1930s, 14" long	400	625	900

Kingsbury "Fire Chief" coupe.
Photo by Bob Smith

	C6	C8	C10
Kingsbury Fire Pumper, 9½'' long	200	300	400
Kingsbury Fire Pumper, 11'' long, very early, clockwork, iron and steel......................	300	450	625
Kingsbury Fire Pumper, 1930s, 20'' long.....................	300	450	600

Kingsbury Greyhound Bus, windup, 18'' long, c.1937.
Photo by Bob Smith

Kingsbury Fire Pumper, 1930s, 20'' long.
Photo by Calvin L. Chaussee

	C6	C8	C10
Kingsbury Fire Pumper, 1920s, 23'' long......................	1000	1700	2400
Kingsbury Fire Truck, 18'' long.	220	330	440
Kingsbury Ford Sedan & House Trailer, 1937, 23'' long, pressed steel......................	350	535	700
Kingsbury Golden Arrow Racer, 20'' long, pressed steel wind-up	550	825	1200

	C6	C8	C10
Kingsbury Greyhound Bus, wind-up 18'' long...........	300	475	700
Kingsbury Ladder Truck, 19'' long, early......................	500	900	1300
Kingsbury Ladder Truck, 22'' long, steel, driver................	150	225	300
Kingsbury Ladder Wagon fire truck, tin, rubber tires, 23½'' long......................	75	112	150
Kingsbury Lincoln Zephyr & Travel Trailer, 22½'' long, c.1936	325	500	700
Kingsbury ''Little Jim'' Delivery Truck, 13'' long.............	175	263	350

Kingsbury Lincoln Zephyr & Travel Trailer, 22½'' long, c.1936.
Photo by Bob Smith

Kingsbury Golden Arrow Racer, 20'' long.
Courtesy Wilkinson Collection, Detroit Antique Toy Museum

Kingsbury ''Little Jim'' Delivery Truck, 13'' long.
Photo by Calvin L. Chaussee

Ranlite Singer with original box. Spare wheel is on right side only.
Courtesy Gates Willard. Photo by E. W. Willard.

C.R. Dump Truck,
16" long, circa 1935.
Bob Smith Collection.
Photo by Len Rosenberg.

Left to Right: "Unknown" Vis-A-Vis, Germany, 6 1/2" long, circa 1900; Fischer Touring Car, Germany, 8" long, circa 1912. Bob Smith Collection. Photo by Len Rosenberg.

Bing Model T Fords, 6 1/2" long, circa 1924. Bob Smith Collection. Photo by Len Rosenberg.

Brooklin: The Canadian Issues.
Photo by V. Rosa.

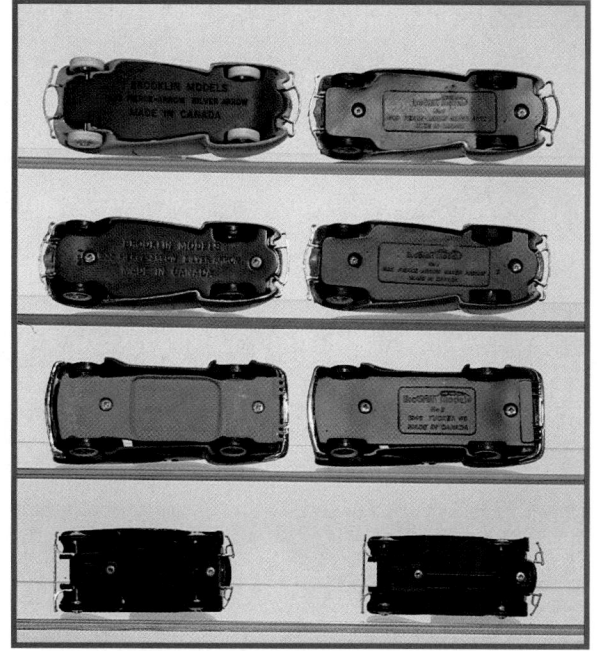

Brooklin: Bases of many variations.
Photo by V. Rosa.

Minic electric-lighted
Sunshine Saloons,
left to right: Rolls,
Daimler, Bentley.
Courtesy Gates Willard.
Photo by E. W. Willard.

Meccano,
left: Early (1932)
No. 2 Constuctor Car.
Right: later (1933-40)
No. 2 Constructor Car.
Courtesy Gates Willard.
Photo by E. W. Willard.

Schieble Fire Truck,
flywheel drive, 11 1/2" long,
circa 1917.
Photo by Bob Smith.

Dayton Armored Car,
11" long, circa 1909.
Photo by Bob Smith.

First hand-made resin
Brooklin model.
Photo by Vincent Rosa.

Acme Curved Dash Olds.
Photo by Bob Smith.

Turner "Yellow Taxicab."
Note passengers.
Photo by Bob Smith.

Savoye SA13.
Photo by Craig A. Clark.

Japanese Tin J103. Photo by Ron Smith.

Marx Racer No.7. Sold from the 1930s into the 1950s. Courtesy Bob & Alice Wagner.

Sun Rubber, **left to right:** ST07, SA01. Courtesy Bob & Alice Wagner.

Keystone No. ??,
World's Greatest
Circus" truck. One of
two variations.
Photo by
Calvin L. Chaussee.

Wyandotte Circus
Truck, WY63.
Courtesy Brian Seligman.

Nylint 1951-52, No. 1600 Payloader.
Photo by Calvin L. Chaussee.

Acme No. 17 Jeep.
Photo by Terry Sells.

Acme, **top:** No. 16.
Bottom: No. 26.
Courtesy Bob & Alice Wagner.

Allied Furniture Moving Van.
Photo by Dave Leopard.

Renwal No. 39. Courtesy
Bob & Alice Wagner.

	C6	C8	C10
Kingsbury "Little Jim" Tow Truck, 11" long	275	363	550
Kingsbury "Little Jim" Tractor..	250	375	500
Kingsbury "Little Jim" Truck...	700	1100	1600
Kingsbury "Panama" Dump Truck, 14" long, clockwork, 1923	750	1000	1400
Kingsbury Phaeton Auto, 1900, rubber slip tires, 9½" long ..	750	1125	1500
Kingsbury Rack Truck, 16" long, pressed steel wind-up	350	525	700
Kingsbury Roadster, 11" long ..	600	1000	1400
Kingsbury Roadster, 13" long, electric headlights, spring motor, luggage rack	500	750	1000
Kingsbury Sand Loader, 12" long	125	188	250

Kingsbury Sand Loader, 12" long.
Photo by Calvin L. Chaussee

	C6	C8	C10
Kingsbury Sedan, two-door, with trailer, 22½" long, 1930s, clockwork	175	262	350
Kingsbury Stake Truck, c.1926, clockwork, 25" long	1900	3100	4400
Kingsbury Studebaker Cannon Truck	110	165	220
Kingsbury Sunbeam Racer, sheetmetal, red with rubber tires on steel wheels, clockwork motor, 19" long	500	750	1050
Kingsbury Tractor, mechanical, 8" with driver	250	375	500

	C6	C8	C10
Kingsbury Tractor and cart, tin, with iron driver, white rubber wheels, c.1930s	110	165	220
Kingsbury Transit Truck, 1930s, 19" long	100	150	200
Kingsbury Truck with C Cap, 10" long, tin	175	262	350
Kingsbury Truck with Crane, 20" long, 1930s	225	338	450

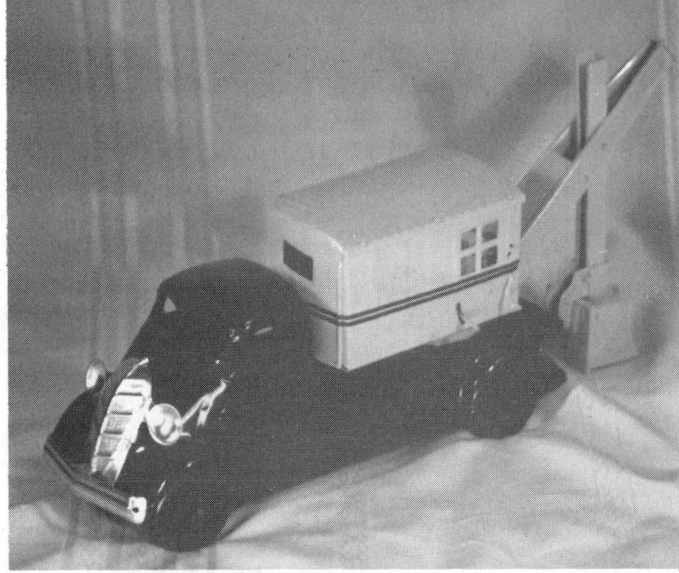

Kingsbury Truck with Crane, 20" long, 1930s.
Photo by Calvin L. Chaussee

	C6	C8	C10
Kingsbury Wind-up Car, curved dash, driver, 9" long	225	337	450
Kingsbury Wrecker, 13" long, pressed steel, wind-up	250	375	500

	C6	C8	C10
Kingston Producers, Kokomo, Indiana, Electricar, 15" long, the Red Arrow, 1930s	150	225	300
Kingston Kokomo Electric Truck	125	188	250

No. 748 AUTO DERRICK
Lower crank swivels crane in complete circle. Upper crank raises and lowers the load.
Length, 14 inches. 1 in box. 1 dozen in case. Weight, 30 lbs.

No. 749 AUTO DELIVERY
No. 749½ with gong.
Length, 10 inches. 1 in box. 1 dozen in case. Weight, 30 lbs.

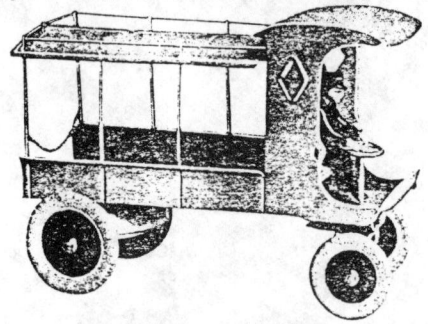

No. 760 AUTO TRANSFER
No. 761 with gong.
Length, 10 inches, 1 in box. 1 dozen in case. Weight, 35 lbs.

Patented May 8, 1917. July 24, 1917.
No. 762 AUTO DUMP TRUCK
No. 763 with gong.
Length, 11½ inches, 1 in box. 1 dozen in case. Weight, 30 lbs.

Some very early-looking Kingsbury trucks. From a 1924 or thereabouts catalog.

CONDITION OF A TOY
AND ITS RELATION TO PRICE

CONDITION CODE:

C6 - Good, Evident overall wear, well-played with, but acceptable to many collectors

C8 - Very Good Minor wear overall, very clean

C10 - Mint (like new)

NOTE: Mint in Box commands a high price. Condition below C6 brings considerably lower prices.

Knapp "Electric Automobile" c.1903, pressed steel, 11" long, battery-activated	C6	C8	C10
	1500	2400	4000

Knapp "Electric Automobile", c.1903
Courtesy Sotheby's NY

Laketoy "John Wanamaker" delivery van, 10½" long, wooden	C6	C8	C10
	180	270	360

LANSING SLIK-TOYS

(Listing and history by Dave Leopard)

Lansing Slik-Toys were made in Lansing, Iowa and sometimes bear the name "Kipp", in addition to the "Lansing" and "Slik-Toy" trademarks. Most Slik-Toys are made of aluminum in a single casting but some were made of hard plastic. All Slik-Toys I have seen bear a 4 digit number beginning with "9". If a toy bears such a number, even if it has no other markings, it is almost surely a Slik-Toy.

	C6	C8	C10
Bulldozer	65	98	130
Combine	150	225	300
Grader, 9½" long	50	75	100

	C6	C8	C10
Oliver 77 Tractor, approx. 7¾" long	200	300	425
Stakebody truck, 11" long, No. 9500	40	50	60
Sedan, fastback, 7" long, No. 9600	25	30	40
Sedan, fastback, 7" long, No. 9600, taxi version	30	40	45
Pickup truck, 7" long, No. 9601	25	30	40
Open Stake Truck, 7" long, No. 9602	25	30	40
Tank truck, 7" long, No. 9603	25	30	40
Sedan, 4 door, 6" long, No. 9604	20	25	35
Pickup truck, 6" long, No. 9605	20	25	35
Firetruck, 6" long, No. 9606	20	25	35
Tank truck, 6" long, No. 9607	20	25	35
Tractor/trailer rig (milk tanker), 8" long, No. 9610	30	35	45
Tractor/trailer rig (grain trailer), 8" long, No. 9611	25	30	40
Tractor/trailer rig (flatbed trailer), 8" long, No. 9613	25	30	40
Tractor/trailer rig (log trailer), 8" long, No. unknown	25	30	40
Wrecker, 5" long, No. 9617	20	25	30
Firetruck, 3½" long, No. 9700	20	25	35
Roadster, 3½" long, No. 9701	20	25	35
Pickup truck, 4" long, plastic, No. 9703	20	25	35
Metro Van, 5" long, No. 9618	25	30	40
Station Wagon, 4", plastic, number 9704	20	25	30
Tank Truck, 4", plastic, No. 9705	20	25	30

LAPIN

(Newark, New Jersey)
Listing by Dave Leopard

	C6	C8	C10
1939 4 door Sedan, 4''........	10	15	20
1939 Coupe, 4''	10	15	20
1939 City Bus, 4''	20	25	30
1949 Cadillac Sedan, 6''........	10	15	20
1949 Cadillac Convertible, 6''...	10	15	20
1949 Cadillac Sedan, 9''........	20	25	30
1949 Cadillac Convertible, 9''...	20	25	30
1947 Chevrolet Stake Truck, 5''.	10	15	20

Lapin Chevrolet Stake Truck.
Courtesy Bob & Alice Wagner

Lapin 1939 Coupe.
Photo by Bob & Alice Wagner

Lapin 1939 4-Door Sedan.
Photo by Bob & Alice Wagner

Lapin 6'' Cadillacs.
Courtesy Bob & Alice Wagner

LEE STOKES INDUSTRIES

Lee Stokes started his firm in 1945 in New Oxford, Pennsylvania. Except for the first three, he created all his own models (31 different types were sold; 6 in 0 Gauge, the rest in HO to take advantage of the post-war interest in HO gauge trains and accessories). The cars were made of a very tough compound of plaster and urea formaldehyde, so that they stand up well. The firm, with eight employees, sold internationally as well as in the U.S. It moved to Bel Air, Maryland, in 1950 and closed in 1955. Stokes died in 1991. Prices average $15-25.

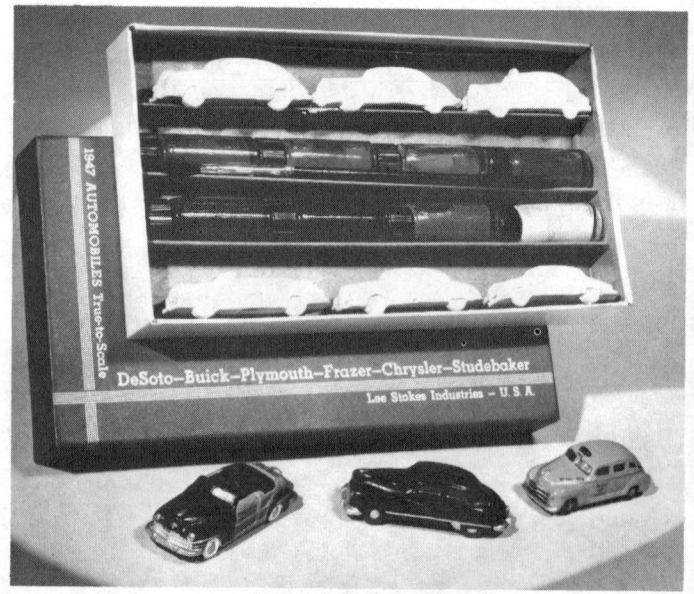

A 1948 Lee Stokes kit.

Lehigh Bitsi-Toys

These are heavy die-cast toys with black rubber tires, produced around 1950. Text and listing by Dave Leopard.

	C6	C8	C10
LV1 Tractor/Trailer, "Modern" decal, c.1948 Reo, 5.5 in.	20	25	30
LV2 1949 Chevrolet Coupe, 2.5 in.	10	15	20

LEHMANN, ERNST PAUL

(Brandenburg, Germany, 1881-present)
by Bob Smith

Lehmann began manufacturing toys in 1881 using the EPL trademark. Its founder passed away in 1934 but the company continued in business under the management of his cousin, Johannes Richter. At the end of WWII Richter moved to West Germany. He opened a new factory in Nuremburg in 1951. The Lehmann Company is still in business making toys.

Lehmann Toys have become a common word among early tin-toy collectors. These wonderful mechanical machines are more sought after than any other wind-up toy, though they usually command a high price. Their value increases more steadily than nearly any other type of collectible. Lehmann toys are always a safe investment for both toy dealers and collectors. The company used many different color variations from year to year on some of its toys, giving the collector a wide variety to choose from. While some Lehmanns are very rare, it is not too difficult to build a collection of them. Most Lehmanns carry a model number for easy reference.

	C6	C8	C10
Lehmann "Aha" delivery van, 5½" long, 1920s tin wind-up	600	900	1200
Lehmann Autobus, tin wind-up	1200	2000	2700
Lehmann "Autohutte" Garage No. 771, 6" long	125	188	250
Lehmann Berolina Car, tin wind-up	1500	2500	3500
Lehmann "Echo" motorcycle No. 725, 1907, 9" long tin wind-up	1000	1600	2200
Lehmann "EHE & Co." open bed tin wind-up	400	600	800
Lehmann Galop racer No. 1, tin wind-up with garage	650	1100	1600

Lehmann Gnom No. 808 "Autohutt", with two No. 807 sedans. Photo by Bob Smith

Lehmann, top, L to R: Gnom Series No. 835, 813. Bottom, L to R: Gnom Series No. 808, 807. Photo by Bob Smith

	C6	C8	C10
Lehmann Gnom series #835 "BV-Aral" Tanker. Blue/gray, 4.5" long, tin litho. C.1938.	200	350	550
Lehmann Gnom series #813 Opel Dump truck, Red/green, 4.5" long, tin litho. c.1935	200	300	500
Lehmann Gnom series #808 Racing Car. Diff. colors, 4.5" long, tin litho. c.1935	200	300	500
Lehmann Gnom series #807 Sedan. Diff. colors, 4.5" long, tin litho. c.1935	200	350	500
Lehmann Gnom #808 "Autohutt" Garage w/two #807 Sedans. Tin litho. c.1935.	500	750	1200
Lehmann "Ito" sedan, 1920s, 6½" long tin wind-up	600	1000	1400
Lehmann Lana Auto tin wind-up	1200	2000	3200
Lehmann "Lehmann's Autobus 590" tin wind-up	1000	1700	2400
Lehmann "Li La" early car, 5½" long tin wind-up	1000	1700	2400

Lehmann Ito
Courtesy Christie's East

Lehmann "Mensa"
Photo by Bob Smith

Lehmann "Lehmann's Autobus 590".
Courtesy Sotheby's NY

Lehmann "Motor Coach"
Courtesy Sotheby's NY

Lehmann "Li La"
Courtesy Sotheby's NY

	C6	C8	C10
Lehmann "Motor Car Kutsche", 1897, 5½" long, tin wind-up.	500	850	1200
Lehmann "Motor Coach", 1920s, 5½" long, tin wind-up	425	638	850
Lehmann "Naughty Boy" tin wind-up	600	900	1200
Lehmann "New Century Cycle", 1907, 5" long tin wind-up	450	675	900
Lehmann "Onkel" tin wind-up.	600	1000	1400
Lehmann "Terra" tin wind-up.	1000	1800	2500
Lehmann "Tut-Tut", man in car with horn, 6¾" long, tin wind-up	650	975	1300
Lehmann "Uhu" amphibious car, tin wind-up	1500	2700	3700

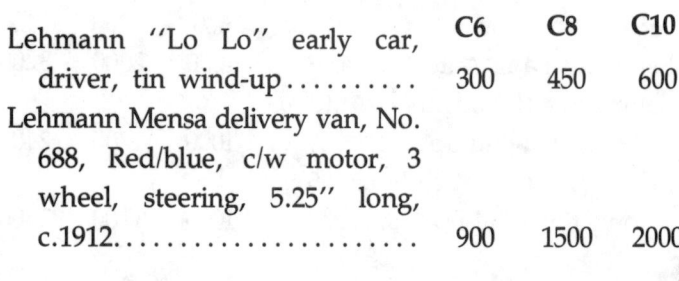

	C6	C8	C10
Lehmann "Lo Lo" early car, driver, tin wind-up	300	450	600
Lehmann Mensa delivery van, No. 688, Red/blue, c/w motor, 3 wheel, steering, 5.25" long, c.1912	900	1500	2000

Lehmann "Naughty Boy"

Lehmann "Uhu"
Courtesy Sotheby's NY

Lehmann "Onkel", from a Lehmann catalog.

Lehmann Tut Tut
Courtesy Christie's East

LIDO

Lido was founded in October 1947 by brothers Seymour and Effrem Arenstein, with the purchase of Elite Toy Co. from David Krotman. Krotman made plastic bubble pipes, scissors and a horn. Since his firm was near the Lido country club, he also used that name. For $6800 the Arensteins bought the molds and the name. They opened Lido at 321 Rider Avenue in the Bronx, and about 1960-61 moved to 1340 Viele Avenue, also the Bronx. Lido's toys were small, always plastic, and eventually the Arensteins were known as the "Louis Marxes of low-end". At peak they employed close to 1000 people. In the years after the 1950s they employed several thousand indirectly in Hong Kong, Japan and Taiwan. They sold out, due to disagreements, to Bala Corporation of Philadelphia, which liquidated a year later. What was left was eventually bought by Gabriel Industries. From 1973-1990 Seymour Arentstein owned Joy Toy.

	C6	C8	C10
Lido Jeep & Trailer	7	11	15

	C6	C8	C10
Limousine, license plate "N.Y. 1918" litho, approx. 6" long, tin windup	200	300	400

Limousine, license plate "N.Y. 1918".
Courtesy James S. Maxwell/Virginia Caputo
Photo by Virginia Caputo

IMPROVED LINCOLN LOGS

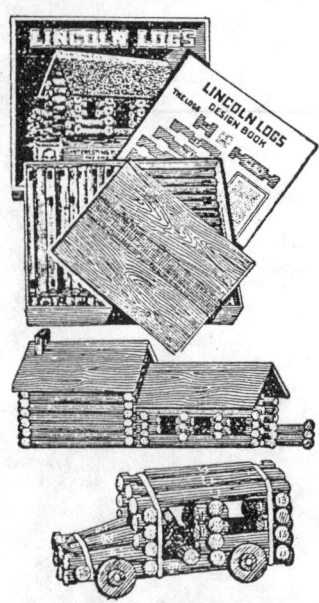

Turned stained wood, each set builds many different models of log cabins, houses, etc., each set in box with instructions.

Many collectors may be unaware that Lincoln Logs briefly advertised that its logs could be turned into vehicles. From a Christmas, 1929 Butler Bros. catalog.

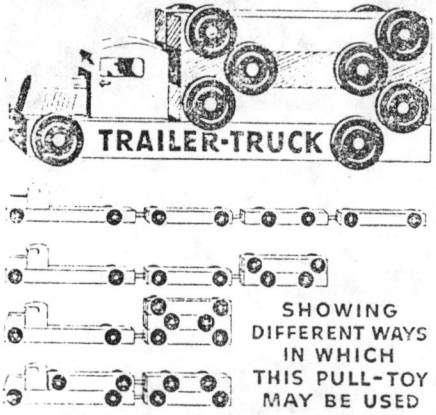

No. 2977 — LINCOLN TRAILER TRUCK. Extreme length 29 inches. Length folded 9¾ inches. All pieces made of hardwood in natural finish with red enamel wheels. A unique presentation of the ever popular truck idea combined with flat cars, which may be arranged in a number of interesting ways. Truck fitted with hook for attaching pull cord. Packed in a box.
Each **$1.32**

For research purposes, here is a Lincoln (Logs?) Trailer Truck as shown in a 1940-41. L. Gould catalog. None found for sale.

LINCOLN TOYS

(Windsor, Ontario, Canada)

	C6	C8	C10
"Allied Van Lines" truck, 23" long	175	275	375
Lincoln Toys Auto Transport, 24" long	110	165	220
Lincoln Toys Coca Cola Truck, 12 cases	300	475	650
Lincoln Toys Dump Truck, 7" long	55	83	110
Lincoln Toys Dunlop Wrecker	60	90	120

Lincoln Toys "Sand Truck" dump, 14" long.
Photo by Bob Smith

	C6	C8	C10
Lincoln Toys "Sand Truck" dump, 14" long	50	85	125
Lincoln Toys Telephone Service Truck	100	150	200

LINCOLN WHITE METAL WORKS

By Fred Maxwell, Slushmold Contributing Editor and Perry Eichor

This Lincoln, Nebraska firm has long been a mysterious pre-war maker of slushmold "orphan toys", so-called when we cannot identify a collectible toy. One might think that with other major lines fairly well documented we could identify Lincoln toys by a process of elimination, but there were too many small makers and homecasters to rely on this. This obscurity is surprising, for Clayton E. Stevenson, the founder, made interesting designs with high quality casting in high volume for a long period - 9 years during the 1930s. What we know came from a Xmas story in the Nebraska State Journal of December 20, 1931 and a good article in the *Antique Toy World* of Jan. 1984.

Stevenson was born in 1896 and raised in Axtell, Kansas. He was an auto mechanic who was associated with Western Diecasting Co. and Kansas Toy & Novelty Co. for several years in the 1920s. He may also have been familiar with C.A.W. Novelty Co. for his style and quality is closer to Charles Wood toys than Kansas toys. He, and his wife, Esther, moved to Lincoln in 1931 and started making toys in his home at 1250 Dakota St. For a new business, he had a rapid rise. In his first season he made "800,000 toys in three months". He was manager, purchaser, worker and salesman.

As his business grew - "30,000 toys a day and 27 to 30 laborers" at one time - he moved to a larger facility at 2204 Y street. In 1935 he was listed at 3433 J street. The toys were sold to Woolworth, Kress, Kresge and Schwartz Paper Co. stores, as well as all over the country, especially California and New York, and even abroad.

The factory was sold in 1940, after 9 years of production, due to shortages of lead and rubber and the rising costs of labor - all due to expansion of war production. (We were not told who bought what, although a few clues point to nearby Ralstoy. Although 1940 is the date given by a family member, I did not find the business listed in Lincoln directories after 1937.)

A variety of toys were made, "tiny airplanes, midget racer, larger speed cars - about 6" long - brilliant sedans, small coupes, tri-motor plane models and miniature sawmills. They range in size from 3 to 7" in length". "Mr. Stevenson, who does the modeling, uses pictures of planes and cars shown in magazines. For his midget racer he used a picture of a Miller Special. His sedan is a replica of the front-drive Cord. His coupe is a Nash model. His trimotor plane is taken from a photo of a Ford product". This in 1931; other patterns were issued later. Early toys used metal wheels and tin propellers and had neat patterned bottom-pans we use as clues. Later toys had rubber wheels. This list below is incomplete; we were dependent on the few toys we have found. Can anyone help with more data?

Lincoln white metal, LWV1, mid 1930s - Other ??
Photo by Perry Eichor

LWV1 Indy Racer, 5⅛". Miller FWD Special, driver, rounded grille, horizontal cooling fins alongside hood, torpedo tail . . . . No Price Found

LWV2 Speed Car, 6". Bluebird record car, driver, V-8 engine with intake ports, triangular fin with wing design embossed . . No Price Found

LWV3 Speed Car, 4". Bluebird, smaller version of above . . . . . No Price Found

LWV4 ? Speed car, 4⅜". A V-12 version of Bluebird with triangular fin. Lincoln? . . . . No Price Found

LWV5 ? Sedan, 3½". Pierce-Arrow Silver Arrow, vertical vee-grille, headlamps and front fenders faired, 6 open windows (OW), divided windshield (W?S), plan pan. Lincoln? . . . . No Price Found

LWV6 Sedan, 3¾". 2 door Chrysler or DeSoto airflow, hood ornament (HO), divided open W/S, horizontal louvers (HL), plain pan . . . . No Price Found

LWV7 ? Sedan, 3⅞". 2 door Pontiac, HO, grid pattern grille, HL, 4 OW, trunk . . . . No Price Found

LWV8 "Wrecker", 3½". High style with chopped top, Graham-like grille, 2 OW, fenders faired bumper to bumper, solid crane with grid pattern and hook, patterned pan "Made in USA" . . . . No Price Found

LWV9 fire engine, 3¾". Pumper with fireman on rear step, Graham-like grille, fenders faired bumper to bumper, patterned pan "Made in USA" . No Price Found

LWV10 Tanker truck, 3¾". COE, 2 OW, 6 tanks, 8 compartments, patterned pan "Made in USA" No Price Found

LWV11 Railcar, 4½". Streamlined No Price Found

Lincoln white metal - Top: LWV2, Bottom: LWV3.
Photo by Perry Eichor

Lincoln white metal - LWV8.
Photo by Perry Eichor

257

Lincoln white metal - Top: LWV10, Bottom: LWV11.
Photo by Perry Eichor

LINDSTROM

The Lindstrom Tool & Toy Company made wind-ups of light pressed steel as well as tin. It was located in Bridgeport, CT., and began making toy cars about 1913. It seems to have ceased production sometime in the 1940s.

	C6	C8	C10
Lindstrom Bumper Car, 6½'' long, tin wind-up	100	150	200
Lindstrom Lumber Truck no. 160, steerable front wheels, tin, with driver, 10'' long	125	187	250
Lindstrom "Parcel Post No. 2" truck, tin wind-up	200	300	400

	C6	C8	C10
Lindstrom Racing Car, 1930s, tin wind-up, 6'' long	90	135	185
Lindstrom "Skeeter Bug", 1930s, (bumper car) 7'' long, tin wind-up	120	180	240
Lindstrom Steam Roller No. 181, mechanical, 12'' long	50	75	100
Lindstrom "U.S. Mail No. 1" truck, early, 7'' long	500	800	1200

"SPEED DEVIL" RACING CARS

8 STYLES—5⅞ in. long, metal, **strong spring motor** propels racer at amazing speed, white rubber tires on wood wheels, detachable key, asst. litho color combinations.
Assortment—Each car in 4-color litho box.
62-5007—1 doz in box......Doz **.92**

Set of 10—5 with motors, 5 without motors, in litho box.
62-5109—⅒ doz sets in box.................Doz sets 8.00

Lindstrom "Speed Devil" racing cars, as shown in the Butler Bros. November/December 1936 catalog. No Price Found.

258

Lionel (Trains) Electric Racing	C6	C8	C10
Automobile set..........	1600	2500	3750

Lionel Electric Racing Automobile Set.
Courtesy Sotheby's NY

Log Truck (Beck), steers via horn on top of cab, late 1940s, large	60	90	120

	C6	C8	C10
6″ size:			
Six-window Sedan.............	No Price Found		
Panel Delivery................	No Price Found		
Canadian Greyhound Bus......	No Price Found		
Thunderbolt Racer............	No Price Found		
Beverage Truck................	20	25	30
Oil Tanker....................	20	25	30
1941 Ford Pickup Truck........	20	25	30
1941 Chevrolet Master Deluxe Coupe....................	20	25	30
Firetruck.....................	20	25	30
City Bus.....................	No Price Found		
Larger Than 6″:			
Tractor and Van Trailer........	60	80	100
Dump Truck..................	No Price Found		
Stake Body Truck.............	No Price Found		
Moving Van (tin body)........	No Price Found		
Car Transporter..............	No Price Found		
Lumber Truck................	No Price Found		

Lumar: See Marx

LONDONTOY

by Dave Leopard

Londontoy die-cast vehicles were produced in London, Ontario for approximately five years (1945-1950). They were also molded in the United States by the Leslie Henry Company, by special arrangement with London toy. The U.S. versions are characterized by the absence of the "Made in Canada" marking and the larger American versions sometimes had a three-dimensional baseplate, which simulated the vehicle drivetrain. The larger versions were sometimes equipped with a heavy flywheel friction motor or a wind-up mechanism. Oil tankers and beverage trucks sometimes bore advertising for actual brandnames. Either motors or advertising would add to the values below: (O'Brien: There is evidence Londontoy made toy soldiers in 1941, suggesting the 1941 vehicles were also produced in that year.)

4″ size:

	C6	C8	C10
1941 Ford Pickup Truck........	15	20	25
Oil Tanker....................	15	20	25
1941 Chevrolet Master Deluxe Coupe....................	15	20	25
Beverage Truck................	15	20	25
1941 Ford Open Cab Firetruck..	15	20	25
City Bus.....................	20	25	30

LUPOR METAL PRODUCTS

New York

	C6	C8	C10
Lupor Ambulance.............	50	75	100
Lupor Fire Chief car...........	55	82	110
Lupor Police Car, 1949 Ford....	95	145	190
Lupor Racer No. 8, 1930s, tin wind-up....................	100	150	200
Lupor Racer, 12″ long, no wind-up	30	45	60
Lupor Trailer Truck...........	25	38	50

M & L TOY CO. INC.

M&L was incorporated October 21, 1947. It was located on Paterson Plank Road in Union City, New Jersey and got its name from the two brothers (or father and son) who owned it, Morris and Louis (last name unknown). The company may have begun in 1946, and lasted till at least 1948. It made vehicles, trains, "jeweled swords", water guns, mechanical toys, and plastic horns. Most or all of its vehicles seem to have been sold unpainted and with plastic wheels. The alloy used in the vehicles was more than 99% zinc, with a smidgen of aluminum added. Most or all of their toys were copies. There were about thirty employees. By 1948 it was at 123-33rd Street in Union City.

M&L (5)   Photo by Bill Conover

M&L (6)   Photo by Bill Conover

M&L (1) Racer.
Photo by Craig A. Clark

Top: M&L Cabin racer, cast headlamps
Bottom: Barclay prototype, rhinestone headlamps missing.
Photo by Perry Eichor

MANOIL

Manoil was owned by two brothers, Jack and Maurice Manoil. Its sole sculptor was Walter Baetz, the man responsible for Manoil's striking seven early vehicles, which were Manoil's first toys, debuting in 1934. The firm, originally located in Manhattan, then Brooklyn, and finally in Waverly, NY, closed down about 1955.

No. 700 - SEDAN

No. 701 - SEDAN

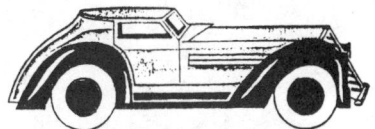

No. 702 - COUPE

No. 703 - WRECKER

MANOIL, circa 1935
Courtesy Peter and Marjorie Ruben

This Fire Pumper and Fire Ladder Truck appear to be from M&L. The ladder truck probably had a bell hanging from the loop. These are probably copies of Barclays.
Photo by Craig A. Clark.

	C6	C8	C10
M&L (1) Racer, 2¾'' long......	10	15	20
M&L (2) Cabin Racer..........	12	18	25
M&L (3) Fire Pumper..........	12	18	25
M&L (4) Fire Ladder Truck	12	18	25
M&L (5) Coupe, 1930s, rubber spare tire post.............	12	18	25
M&L (6) Sedan, streamlined....	12	18	25

	C6	C8	C10
MANOIL 700 *Sedan*, futuristic ..	45	68	90
MANOIL 701 *Sedan*, futuristic ..	45	68	90
MANOIL 702 *Coupe*, futuristic ..	45	68	90
MANOIL 703 *Wrecker*, futuristic .	45	68	90

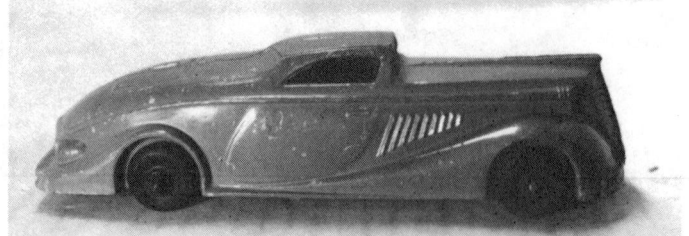

Manoil 704   Courtesy K. Warren Mitchell

MANOIL 704 Roadster, futuristic,	C6	C8	C10
Pat. No. 95791	45	68	90

Manoil 705
Photo courtesy Bob & Alice Wagner

Manoil 706   Courtesy K. Warren Mitchell

MANOIL 705 Sedan, futuristic, Pat.			
No. 95792	45	68	90
MANOIL 706 Rocket, futuristic bus-			
like vehicle, Pat. No. 95793 . .	60	90	120

Manoil 69 cannon, metal wheels, wood wheels, wood wheels variant.
Manoil Vehicles, top row, L to R: 70, 71. Middle row: 71 with variant
on wheel support 72, 73 with front tow loop, 74. Bottom row: 75, 75A
with siren cast separately, 75A siren cast integrally.
Photo by Ed Poole

MANOIL 70 Soup Kitchen, large			
number	9	13	18
MANOIL 70A Soup Kitchen, small			
number	9	13	19

	C6	C8	C10
MANOIL 71 Shell Carrier With Soldier On Shell Box, has loop	11	16	22
MANOIL 71A Same as above, no loop	10	15	20
MANOIL 72 Water Wagon, larger number	10	15	20
MANOIL 72 A Same as above, small number	9	13	18
MANOIL 72 B No. number	9	13	18
MANOIL 73 Tractor, loop front .	11	16	22
MANOIL 73A Tractor, plain front	11	16	22
MANOIL 74 Armored Car with Anti-Tank Gun	17	26	35
MANOIL 75 Armored Car with Anti-Aircraft Gun	27	41	55
MANOIL 75A Armored Car with Siren, siren cast separately . . .	25	38	50
MANOIL 75A Armored Car with Siren, siren cast with vehicle .	32	48	65

L to R: 95, 96, 97, 98

L to R: 103, 104, 105, 200
Photo by Ed Poole

MANOIL 95 Tank	8	12	17
MANOIL 96 Large Shell on Truck	9	13	18
MANOIL 97 Pontoon on Wheels .	18	27	36
MANOIL 98 Torpedo on Wheels . .	10	15	20
MANOIL 103 Gasoline Truck	10	15	20
MANOIL 104 Chemical Truck	12	18	24
MANOIL 105 Five Barrel Gun on Wheels	11	16	22
MANOIL (MC5) Tank, composition	12	18	25

MC5

261

MANOIL Post War Vehicles

Manoil, L to R: 708A, 708.
Photo courtesy Alice & Bob Wagner

	C6	C8	C10
MANOIL *707 Sedan*	25	38	50
MANOIL *708 Roadster*, horizontal radiator	17	26	35
MANOIL *708A Roadster*, vertical radiator	25	38	50
MANOIL *709 Fire Engine*	15	22	30
MANOIL *710 Oil Tanker*	12	18	25
MANOIL *711 Aerial Ladder*	200	300	400
MANOIL *712 Pumper*	200	300	400
MANOIL *713 Bus*	12	18	24
MANOIL *714 Towing Truck*	10	15	20
MANOIL *715 Commercial Truck* . .	10	15	20

712 top
711
Photo by Norbert Schachter
Courtesy Marjorie and Peter Ruben

No. 713   BUS

No. 710 - OIL TANKER

No. 709 - FIRE ENGINE

No. 707 - SEDAN

No. 715 - COMMERCIAL TRUCK has removable panels, as shown above

No. 714 - TOWING TRUCK

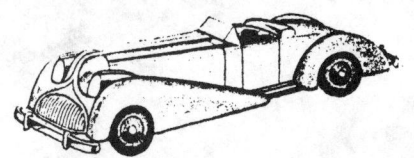

No. 708 - ROADSTER

Manoil Post-War Vehicles
Courtesy Peter and Majorie Ruben

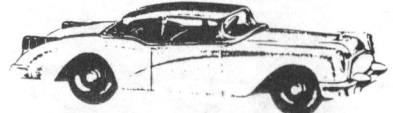

No. 716 · SEDAN

No. 717 · HARD TOP CONVERTIBLE

No. 718 · CONVERTIBLE

No. 719 · SPORT CAR

No. 720 · RANCH WAGON

MANOIL Postwar Vehicles
Courtesy Peter and Marjorie Ruben

	C6	C8	C10
MANOIL 716 Sedan............	10	15	20
MANOIL 717 Hard Top Convertible	12	18	24
MANOIL 718 Convertible	10	15	20
MANOIL 719 Sport Car........	10	15	20
MANOIL 720 Ranch Wagon.....	10	15	20

MANOIL Plastic Vehicles

MANOIL P-7 Roadster.........	8	12	16
MANOIL P-8 Sedan............	8	12	16
MANOIL P-9 Pick-Up..........	8	12	16
MANOIL P-10 Towing Truck....	8	12	16
MANOIL P-11 Road Scraper.....	8	12	16
MANOIL P-12 Tractor.........	8	12	16
MANOIL P-13 Dump Cart......	8	12	16

P-7 ROADSTER

P-8 SEDAN

P-9 PICK-UP TRUCK

P-10 TOWING TRUCK

P-11 ROAD SCRAPER

P-13 DUMP CART

P-12 TRACTOR

MARKLIN VEHICLE CONSTRUCTION SETS

by Gates Willard

Well-known today for currently manufactured toy trains, the German Marklin Company enjoyed a fine reputation for quality toys long before 1933-34 when a series of constructional motor vehicles was introduced. Marklin had been making multi-purpose construction sets similar in concept to Erector in the USA and Meccano in England, but now they were building specialized sets that would appeal to the young automotive engineer. A clever merchandising scheme was developed. You could buy a boxed set of parts to build a complete chassis, but a motor would have to be purchased separately. The body of your choice was still another kit to buy, and up to six types were available by the late 1930's. If you wished to have other types of vehicles, alternative body kits were available. Complete sets with body, motor, and chassis were also sold, and some sets included more than one body, but Marklins were costly, and in the 1930's, many could afford to buy only one piece at a time. The quality of finish is superb, and some pieces were decorated with hand striping.

The group of construction vehicles could be referred to as "The 1100 series". However, there was no 1102. A prototype fire engine exists, and perhaps this was a candidate for that number. In 1991, Marklin made a limited run of fire engines very similar in appearance to the Prototype. Other limited editions included a Postal Van (1990) and a Lorry similar to #1105 but with a canvas cover for the bed bearing the Marklin logo. Copies of the 1133 R and 1133 AL have been made and sold at a German Toy Museum.

The 1100 Series was revived after the war, but 1104P, 1106T, 1108G, 1110B, and 99R were not made again. Marklin phased out the remaining construction vehicles in the mid-1950's.

Marklin 1103 St. Streamlined Coupe
Courtesy Gates Willard
Photo by E.W. Willard

Marklin 1104P Pullman Limousine.
Courtesy Gates Willard
Photo by E.W. Willard

Marklin 1105L Lorry
Courtesy Gates Willard
Photo by E.W. Willard

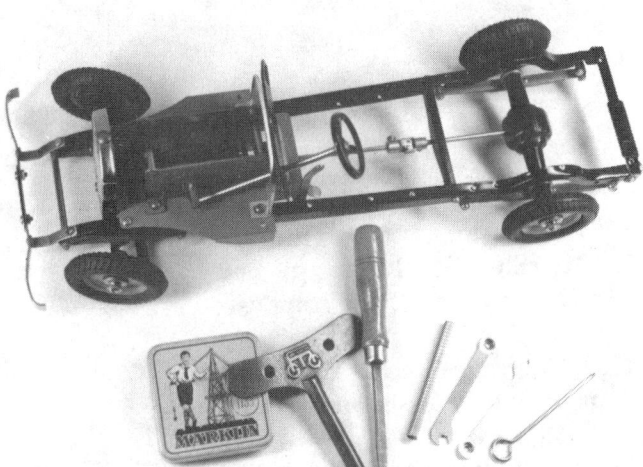

Marklin: Assembled No. 1101C chassis with parts box, cast iron key and tools. 1109M clockwork motor is installed.
Courtesy Gates Willard
Photo by Ed Poole

The following list uses the factory numberings:

1101C Chassis

1103St Streamlined Coupe Body. Early is 2-tone blue, later is all green with brown roof.

1104 Pullman Limousine Body. Early is beige and green. Later is ivory with gray roof.

1105L Lorry (Pick-up) Body. Red/Green.

1106T Tanker Body. Red/Blue.

1107R Racing (Sports Car) body, red/white.

1108G Armored Car Body, camouflaged (more than one pattern).

Marklin 1106T Tanker, shown with original box. Two tinplate cars were included.
Photo by E.W. Willard
Courtesy Gates Willard

Marklin 1107R racing car with original composition 99R driver. Behind the car is the unassembled car in its box.
Courtesy Gates Willard
Photo by E.W. Willard

Marklin 1108G Armored Car.
Photo by E.W. Willard
Courtesy Gates Willard

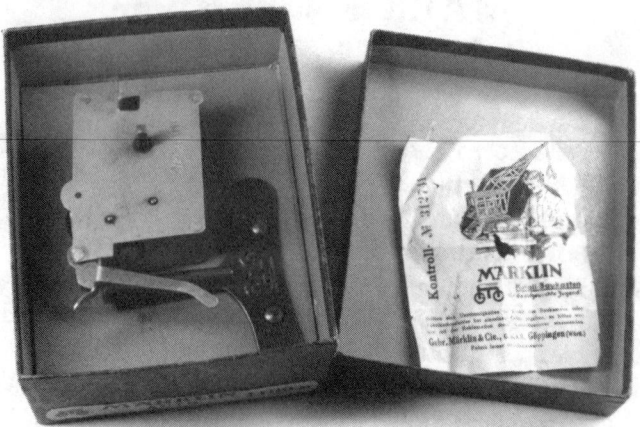

Marklin boxed 1109M Clockwork Motor with cast-iron key.
Courtesy Gates Willard
Photo by E.W. Willard

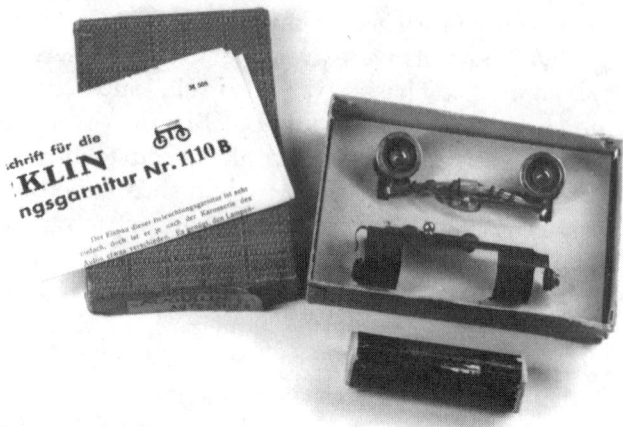

Marklin box 1110B Lighting Set with instructions and original battery.
Courtesy Gates Willard
Photo by E.W. Willard

Marklin 1133R Mercedes Racing Car (smaller scale) with composition driver and cast iron key. Courtesy Gates Willard
Photo by E.W. Willard

1109M Clockwork motor.
1110B Electric Lighting Set
99R Driver (lightweight composition material).
1133R Mercedes Racing Car, complete with chassis and motor. Smaller Scale
1133AL Mercedes Racing Car, aluminum. Complete with chassis and motor. Smaller Scale

Marklin, L to R: Limited editions trucks Postal Van (1990), Fire Engine
(1991) and Lorry (1992). All have working electric headlights.
Courtesy Gates Willard
Photo by E.W. Willard

Marklin Road Working Machine, 3⅝" long.
Courtesy James S. Maxwell Dr./Virginia Caputo
Photo by Virginia Caputo

Marklin Troop Carrier, diecast metal, 4½" long.
Photo by Terry Sells

Marklin Troop Carrier, diecast metal, 5" long.
Photo by Terry Sells

Marklin Kubelwagen, diecast, 3½" long.
Photo by Terry Sells

	C6	C8	C10
Marklin Mercedes Racing Car, 12" long, wind-up	125	188	250
Marklin Road Working Machine, 3⅝" long	100	150	200
Marklin 1108G Armored Car	No Price Found		
Marklin Kubelwagen, die-cast, 3½" long	325	490	650
Marklin Troop Carrier, die-cast metal, 4½" long	325	490	650
Marklin Troop Carrier, die-cast metal, 10 wheels, 5" long	450	675	900

CONDITION OF A TOY
AND ITS RELATION TO PRICE

CONDITION CODE:

C6 - Good, Evident overall wear, well-played with, but acceptable to many collectors

C8 - Very Good Minor wear overall, very clean

C10 - Mint (like new)

*NOTE: Mint in Box commands a high price. Condition below C6 brings
considerably lower prices.*

LES CONSTRUCTIONS AUTOMOBILES

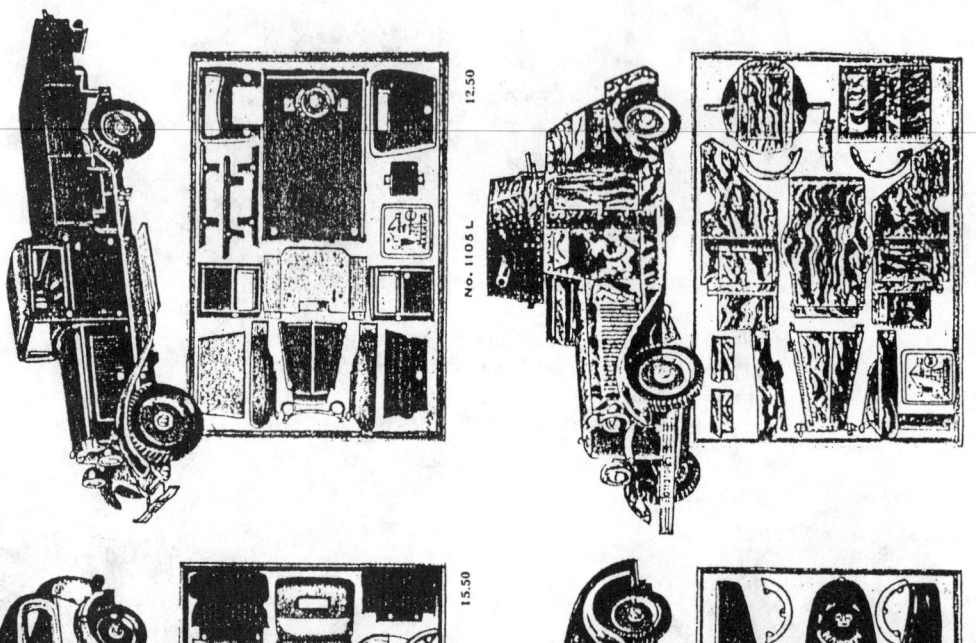

No. 1105 L   12.50

No. 1108 G   17.-

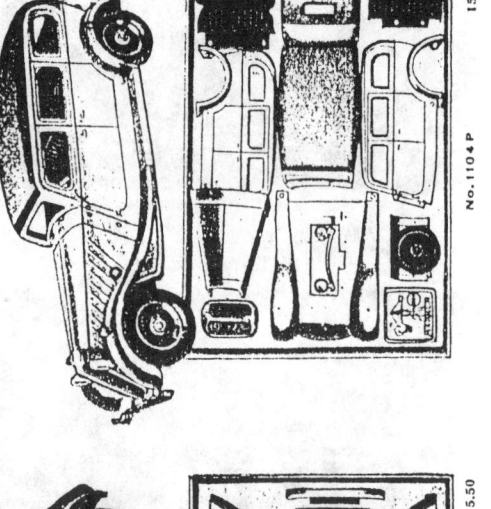

No. 1104 P   15.50

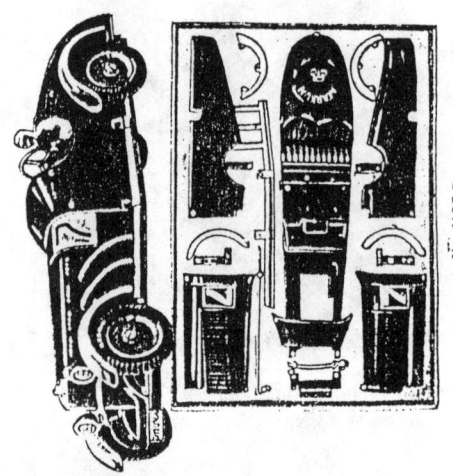

No. 1107 R   11.-

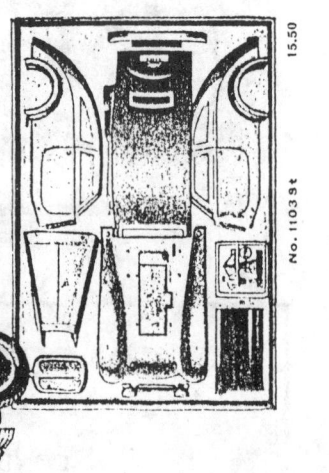

No. 1103 St   15.50

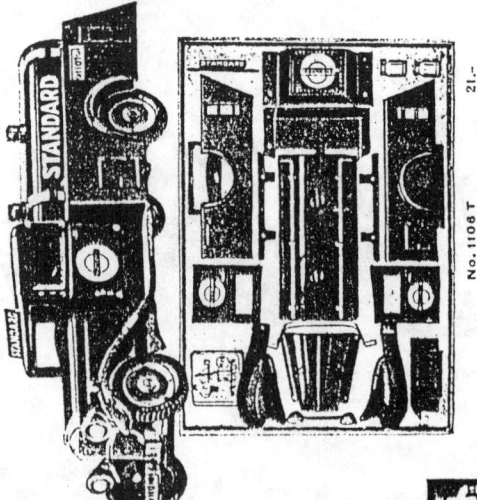

No. 1106 T   21.-

Boîtes Carrosse-ries

pour boîte
«Châssis No. 1101 C

No. 1103 St   15.50
Carrosserie
aérodynamique
verte

No. 1104 P   15.50
Carrosserie–Limousine
— Pullman —
teinté ivoire

No. 1105 L   12.50
Carrosserie–Camion
rouge

No. 1106 T   21.-
Carrosserie
Voiture–Citerne

No. 1107 R   11.-
Carrosserie —
Voiture
de course

No. 110I/07R 25.-
Châssis 1101C
et Carrosserie 1107 R
en une seule boîte,
démontés (sans moteur)

No. 99 R   –.85
Pilote
pour boîte No. 1107 R

No. 1108 G   17.-
Carrosserie
— Auto blindée —
avec canon, obus
caoutchouc
et amorces

Prix en francs suisses

MARKLIN

1939-40 Marklin catalog.
Courtesy Gates Willard

267

Les Constructions Automobiles

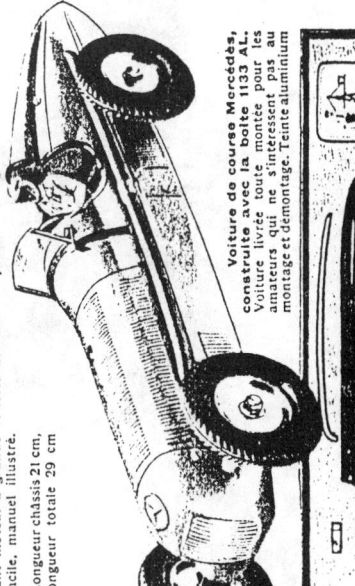

Chassis monté
construit avec la boîte 1101 C
et le bloc-moteur 1109 M

Le châssis achevé, notre puissant bloc-moteur No. 1109 M se monte à l'avant en un tournemain. Les carrosseries illustrées sur page 9 se montent sans difficulté sur le châssis et nos petits amis n'auront que l'embarras du choix, s'ils ne préfèrent confectionner une carrosserie à leur idée

No. 1101 C
Boîte Châssis – boîte fondamentale – contenant toutes les pièces pour construire le châssis ci-dessus (sans moteur). Manuel illustre avec historique de l'auto 16.–

La boîte Châssis No. 1101 C constitue la boîte fondamentale, elle sert de point de départ à toutes les voitures. Cette boîte permet de réaliser un véritable chassis d'automobile de 36 cm de longueur. Toutes les parties sont conformes, le cadre, la suspension, le differentiel, le cardan, la direction etc. Le manuel qui est joint à la boîte, facilite le montage par des descriptions détaillées et de nombreuses illustrations

No. 1110 B 3.–
Phares électriques
avec ampoules 2½ volts
(sans pile-torche)

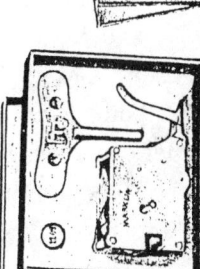

No. 1109 M 6.–
Bloc-Moteur
boîte avec moteur et clef, pour
chassis 1101 C

MÄRKLIN

La fabrique ne livre pas directement aux particuliers

Voiture de course Mercédès

Nouvelle boîte de construction contenant toutes les pièces, y compris le moteur, pour monter la fameuse Mercédès qui a gagné tant de grandes épreuves. Chassis avec roues indépendantes, direction réglable, carrosserie aérodynamique, puissant moteur à grande vitesse. Livrée avec pilote. Montage facile, manuel illustré.

Longueur châssis 21 cm,
longueur totale 29 cm

Voiture de course Mercédès, construite avec la boîte 1133 AL. Voiture livrée toute montée pour les amateurs qui ne s'intéressent pas au montage et demontage. Teinte aluminium

No. 1133 R teinte rouge 21.–   No. 1133 AL teinte aluminium 21.–
Boîte de construction Mercédès
ensemble complet de pièces détachées suivant dessin ci-contre, pour monter la voiture de course ci-dessus. Voir aussi texte en tête de la page.

W 99 Pilote pour voiture de course   –.50

8

1939-40 Marklin catalog.
Courtesy Gates Willard

LOUIS MARX

By the 1950s, Louis Marx was the largest manufacturer of toys in the world; six large factories in the U.S., and ownership of interest in factories in seven other countries. Marx, born in Brooklyn in 1896, was working for "Toy King" Ferdinand Strauss when he was in his teens, and by the age of twenty his energy and enterprise had made him a director of that company. A falling out with Strauss persuaded him to go into business for himself, and in 1921 he and his brother began making their own toys, including some adaptations of items by the now-defunct Strauss. Marx's watchword seems to have been quality at the lowest possible price, and he was such a favorite with toy buyers that he had virtually no need for salesmen or advertising. Marx made virtually every type of toy with the exception of dolls. In April, 1972, he sold his company to the Quaker Oats Company, who in 1976 sold it to Europe's largest toy manufacturer, Dunbee-Combex-Marx. The company went into bankruptcy in 1980. Louis Marx died in 1982 at the age of 85. In 1982 American Plastics bought much of the Marx assets and in 1990 began producing toys from the original molds. In the first Marx break-up, certain rights and molds were retained in Mexico, and these continue.

Marx "Ambulance" with siren, 1930s tin windup.
Courtesy David W. Mapes Auctions

	C6	C8	C10
Marx A&P Truck, 28" long	95	143	190
Marx "Acme Markets" trailer truck, late	125	188	250
Marx Aerial Water Tower truck, 15" long wind-up	275	363	550
Marx Air Force truck, "Air Defense Group" ridem toy, 32" long, No. 3290	125	188	250
Marx Air Force truck, canvas top, 20" long..................	105	158	210
Marx Airport Transport Bus, 6½" long......................	32	48	65
Marx "Allstate Super Trailer" ..	212	318	425
Marx "Ambulance" with siren, 1930s tin wind-up, 14½" long	190	285	380
Marx Ambulance, "M.D. War Dept.", 1930s tin wind-up ...	450	675	900
Marx Ambulance No. 8500, approx. 14" long, 1930s........	112	168	225
Marx Ambulance No. 8600, approx. 14" long, 1930s........	240	360	480

	C6	C8	C10
Marx "American Railroad Express Agency, Inc.", early 1930s, open cab, 7"	120	180	240
Marx "American Railway Express Agency" van, 9" long, closed driver's window, wind-up ...	300	450	600
Marx "American Railway Express Agency" van, Bulldog Mack wind-up	250	375	500
Marx "American Tractor" with implements, 1920s, 10" long, tin wind-up	180	270	360
Marx American Truck Co. No. 65 moving truck, friction........	65	98	130

Marx Amos & Andy Fresh-Air Taxi.
Photo by Bob Smith

	C6	C8	C10
Marx Amos & Andy Fresh-Air Taxi, tin wind-up, 8" long, 1930s	500	800	1100
Marx Anti-Aircraft Unit No. 1 Fire Control Truck, friction, plastic and tin.....................	90	135	180

Marx "Anti-Aircraft Unit No. 12" Civilian Defense Truck. Friction, plastic, 12" long.
Photo by Terry Sells

	C6	C8	C10
Marx "Anti-Aircraft Unit No. 12" Civilian Defense Truck, friction, plastic, 12" long	110	165	220
Marx Armored Truck bank	55	82	110
Marx Armored Trucking Co. tin wind-up	110	165	220

Marx "Army Command Car", 19½" long, friction, tin and plastic.
Photo by Terry Sells

	C6	C8	C10
Marx "Army Command Car", 19½" long, friction, tin and plastic.Siren and flashing signal light	No Price Found		
Marx Army Corps of Engineers, 20" long, canvas top	125	188	250
Marx Army Jeep w/Searchlight Trailer, plastic, 35" long	42	63	85
Marx Army Jeep with Searchlight Trailer, steel	88	132	175

	C6	C8	C10
Marx Army Scout stake truck, c.1940	60	90	120
Marx Army Staff Car, 1930s, tin wind-up	162	243	325
Marx "Army Staff Car", W-601158, with flasher and siren, 11" long, 1940s tin wind-up	225	338	450
Marx Army Staff Car, 9" long, plastic friction	27	41	55
Marx Army Truck, 10" long, cloth cover, 1930s tin wind-up	350	525	700
Marx Army Truck, tin litho, c.early 1930s	85	128	170
Marx Army Truck, cab plastic ..	85	128	170
Marx Army Truck w/cannon, c.1950s	65	98	130
Marx Auto, 4" long, c.1937	27	41	55
Marx Auto Hauler, 1930s, with two Airflows	135	198	270
Marx Auto Hauler, 4 plastic cars	125	188	250
Marx Auto-Laundry Car Wash..	95	143	190
Marx Auto Transport, Mack C-Cab, 12" long wind-up, 3 cars, c.1920s	175	263	350
Marx Auto Transport, 21" long, 3 cars, c.1950s	210	315	420
Marx Auto Transport, 31" long, c.1958, includes 2 Corvettes, 2 T-Birds, everything tin	275	363	550
Marx Auto Transport, 1950s, with two tin litho cars, 34" long ..	120	180	240
Marx "Auto Transwalk" No. T-50447B, 1930s truck with 3 cars	185	278	350

Marx Automatic Fire House.   Photo by Don Hultzman

	C6	C8	C10
Marx "Automatic Fire House", 1950s, Fire Chief Car, 7½" long, Volunteer Fire Dept. Garage, 19" long, tin wind-up	110	165	220

Marx Automatic Garage, comes	C6	C8	C10
with one friction car.........	35	52	70
Marx "Automatic Reversing Road			
Roller", 1925, 9" long tin wind-			
up......................	200	300	400
Marx Baby Wrecker Truck, battery-			
operated...................	50	75	100

Marx Beat It! The Komical Kop.
Courtesy Ed Hyers Antique Toys

Marx Beat It the Komikal Kop,			
1930s tin wind-up..........	250	375	500
Marx Big Boss Car Carrier, 42"			
long......................	80	120	160
Marx Big Job Dump Truck, 28"			
long, plastic................	50	75	100
Marx Big Lizzie Car, early 1930s,			
7¼" long tin wind-up......	150	225	300
Marx "Big Load Van Company",			
13" long wind-up, Bulldog			
Mack.....................	400	700	1000
Marx Big Parade, moving vehicles,			
soldiers, etc., 24" long tin wind-			
up......................	500	900	1200
Marx "Big Shot" Cannon Truck,			
plastic, 22" long, fires cap-			
loaded missiles..............	52	76	105
Marx "Big Silver" Mack Dump			
Truck tin wind-up...........	250	375	500
Marx "Blondie's Jalopy" tin wind-			
up, 16" long..............	1500	2300	3100
Marx Blue Bird Gas Station	150	225	300
Marx Bottom Dump, late.......	40	60	80

Marx Brake Kar with screeching noise.
Courtesy Continental Hobby House

Marx Brake Kar with screeching	C6	C8	C10
noise.....................	105	157	210
Marx "Brightelite Filling Station"	262	395	525

Marx Bulldozer Climbing Tractor.
Courtesy Continental Hobby House

Marx Bulldozer Climbing Tractor,			
caterpillar type, c.1950s, 10½"			
long tin wind-up...........	200	300	400
Marx Bumper Auto, streamlined,			
c.1939, large bumpers, tin wind-			
up......................	120	180	240
Marx "Busy Bridge" tin wind-up	325	488	650
Marx "Busy Parking Station",			
1930s, 17" long, with 2" tin race			
car, wind-up..............	150	225	300
Marx Cadillac Roadster, 13" long,			
trunk w/tools on luggage carrier,			
1930s tin wind-up...........	200	300	400

	C6	C8	C10
Marx Cadillac, Untouchables type	35	55	80
Marx Car Carrier wind-up, carries Airflow	58	85	115
Marx Cargo Truck, 16″ long, post WWII	80	120	160
Marx Carpenter Stakebed Truck with dolly, approx. 14″ long .	100	150	200

Marx Charlie McCarthy in his Benzine Buggy.
Photo by Bob Smith

Marx "Caterpillar" climbing tractor.
Courtesy Continental Hobby House

Marx "City Sanitation Dept."
Photo by Bill Kaufman

	C6	C8	C10
Marx "Caterpillar" Climbing Tractor c.1950s, 10″ long tin wind-up	90	135	180
Marx "Chief-Fire Dept. No. 1", "Friction Drive", c.1948	45	68	90
Marx "Charlie McCarthy and Mortimer Snerd Private Car" tin wind-up	1100	1800	2600
Marx Charlie McCarthy in his Benzine Buggy tin wind-up	425	638	850
Marx "Cities Service Towing Service", 20½″ long	125	188	250
Marx "City Sanitation Dept. Help Keep Your City Clean", c.1940, 12¾″ long	110	165	220
Marx Climbing, Fighting Tank, tin wind-up	175	263	350
Marx Climbing, Fighting Tank, 5½″ long, tin, plastic	22	33	45
Marx Climbing Tractor, sparkling, 1960s, 8½″ long tin wind-up	45	68	90

	C6	C8	C10
Marx "Cloverdale Farms" milk truck	200	300	400
Marx Coal Truck, electric motor and lights, early	190	275	380
Marx Coal Truck, No. 964J	122	183	245
Marx Coal Dump Truck No. 964, 21″ long	180	270	360

Marx Coca-Cola Truck, Linemar, 3″ long, tin friction
Courtesy James S. Maxwell/Virginia Caputo
Photo by Virginia Caputo

	C6	C8	C10
Marx Coca Cola truck, Linemar, 3″ long, friction, tin	50	75	100

Marx Coca-Cola truck, 20" long, Sprite decal.
Photo by Richard MacNary

Marx Convertible, 10" long, plastic windup.
Photo by Terry Sells

Marx Coca Cola truck, 1950s, shelf sidecases.
Photo by Don Hultzman

Marx Coo-Coo Car.
Photo by Don Hultzman

	C6	C8	C10
Marx Convertible Roadster, 1930s, nickel-plated tin. 11" long ...	200	300	400
Marx Convertible, 10" long, plastic wind-up ...	No Price Found		
Marx "Coo Coo Car", 1920s, 7½" long ...	450	700	1000
Marx Cord Convertible, 11" long	250	375	500
Marx Corvette Coupe, plastic friction, 8" long ...	42	63	85
Marx Coupe, steel wind-up, electric headlights, 14" long ...	225	338	450
Marx Crane Truck, approx. 20" long ...	150	225	300
Marx Crazy Dora nodder-head tin wind-up ...	100	150	200

Marx "Coca-Cola" truck, 10½" long, plastic.
Photo by Terry Sells

	C6	C8	C10
Marx Coca Cola truck, 20" long, Sprite decal, stamped steel, late 1940s to early 1950s ...	160	240	320
Marx Coca Cola truck, 1950s, shelf sidecases ...	262	395	525
Marx "Coca Cola" truck, 10½" long, plastic ...	No Price Found		
Marx "Coke Coal City Coal Co." truck, tin wind-up ...	250	375	500
Marx Comicar the Snappy Flivver	275	363	550
Marx "Construction" tractor hauler, 14" long, reverses, has driver ...	175	263	350

Marx "Curtiss Candy Company" truck.
Photo by Gary Linden

	C6	C8	C10
Marx Curtiss Candy Truck, plastic	10	20	30

	C6	C8	C10
Marx "Dagwood the Driver" Crazy Car, 1935, 8" long	500	800	1100
Marx "Dan Dipsy Car", 1950s, 5½" long, plastic nodder, wind-up	138	205	275
Marx "Daredevil Motor Drome", 1930s, 5½" high, 9" diameter, 2" wind-up car	100	150	200
Marx "Day & Nite Service Service Center"	75	112	150
Marx DC Semi Tractor Trailer, late	100	150	200
Marx Delivery Van, plastic	50	75	100
Marx "Delivery" Van, ...	75	112	150
Marx Deluxe Auto Transport, approx. 22" long, 2 plastic cars	200	300	400
Same as above, no cars	100	150	200

Marx "Deluxe Delivery" truck.
Courtesy Thomas G. Nefos, Federal Shipping Network

Marx De Luxe Tractor, 6 wheels, four in treads. C.1932.
Photo by Orville C. Britton

	C6	C8	C10
Marx "Deluxe Delivery" truck ..	100	150	200
Marx "Deluxe Delivery" truck, 1950s 11" long tin wind-up ..	100	150	200
Marx De Luxe Tractor, 6 wheels, 4 in treads, tin wind-up, c.1932	250	375	500
Marx Dick Tracy "Police Station" with 7" long automatic siren car, 1950s	400	600	800

Marx Dick Tracy Squad Car No. 1, 6¾" long.

	C6	C8	C10
Marx Dick Tracy Riot Car, c.1946, 7½" long, friction motor	140	210	280
Marx Dick Tracy Squad Car, convertible, 20" long, c.1948, friction, battery light, Tracy & Sam Catchum in plastic	175	263	350
Marx Dick Tracy Squad Car No.1, 11" long, friction	138	205	275
Marx Dick Tracy Squad Car No. 1, 6¾" long, friction	90	135	180
Marx "Dipsy Doodle Bug" Dodgem car (Dan or Dora) 6" high tin wind-up	250	375	500
Marx "Donald Duck Convertible", 1950s, Linemar, 5" long, tin friction	300	450	600
Marx Donald Duck Crazy Car, 1950s, Linemar, 5½" long wind-up	275	363	550

Donald Duck Dipsy Car.
Photo by Don Hultzman

	C6	C8	C10
Marx Donald Duck Dipsy Car, 1950s, 5¼" long tin wind-up (plastic Mickey or Donald) ...	275	363	550
Marx Donald Duck "Dipsy Car-Donald Duck", 1950s, Linemar wind-up, 6" long	350	525	700

	C6	C8	C10
Marx "Donald Duck Disney Flivver", 1950s, Linemar, 5½" long	250	375	500
Marx "Donald Duck Dump Truck", 1950s, Linemar, 5" long	250	375	500
Marx Donald Duck Fire Chief Crazy Car, Linemar tin wind-up, rubber hat	750	1300	1700
Marx Donald Duck In His Convertible", 1950s, Linemar friction, 6" long	225	338	450
Marx "Donald Duck on Tractor", 1950s, Marx friction, 3½" long, plastic	120	180	240
Marx "Dora Dipsy Car", 1950s, 5½" long plastic nodder, wind-up	155	233	310
Marx "Dottie the Driver", 1950s, 6½" long wind-up	80	120	160

	C6	C8	C10
Marx "Driver Training Car", 1950s, 6" long tin wind-up	105	158	210
Marx "Drive-UR-Self Car", 1950s, 11" long tin wind-up	300	450	600
Marx Dump Truck, 13" long, tin wind-up	200	300	400
Marx Dump Truck, 17" long, No. 695B	75	112	150
Marx Dump Truck, 9½" long, late	22	33	45
Marx Dump Truck, 20" long	88	132	175
Marx Dump Truck, two-color, No. T751, c.1930s	82	124	165
Marx Dump Truck, No. 1084	30	45	60
Marx Dump Truck, 1955 Chevy	62	93	125
Marx Dump Truck, steel wind-up, c.1940	37	56	75
Marx Dump Truck, w/treads, c.1920s	137	205	375

Marx Doughboy Tank, two extending side turrets. From the October, 1932 Butler Bros. catalog.

Marx Doughboy Tank, no extending side turrets.

	C6	C8	C10
Marx Doughboy Tank, two extending side turrets, with top turret, 9¼" long, 1930 tin wind-up, soldier with gun pops out	200	300	400
Marx Doughboy Tank, no extending side turrets, tin wind-up	200	300	400

Marx Dump Truck, steel wind-up, 4½" long. Courtesy James S. Maxwell/Virginia Caputo Photo by Virginia Caputo

	C6	C8	C10
Marx Earth Hauler	62	93	125
Marx Easter Stake Truck, 10½" long, 1938	190	275	380

Marx Electric Combat Tank. Courtesy Heinz Muller, Continental Hobby House

	C6	C8	C10
Marx Electric Combat Tank, battery-operated	100	150	200

	C6	C8	C10
Marx Electric Speedway. Cars, track, transformer	300	450	600
Marx "Electrically Lighted Truck and Trailer Set" No. T-5715 c. 1930s, 15'' long	150	220	300
Marx Falcon with plastic bubble top, black rubber tires	112	168	250
Marx "Fanny Farmer" candy truck, plastic	100	150	200
Marx Farm Tractor, battery operated	40	60	80
Marx Fire Chief Car, c.1920s . . .	175	263	350
Marx Fire Chief Car, 1948 Hudson, 12'' long	162	245	325
Marx Fire Chief Car, friction . . .	50	75	100

Marx Fix-All Motorcycle, 12'' long, plastic.
Photo by Terry Sells

Marx G-Man Pursuit Car.
Courtesy Gary Linden

Marx Fire Chief Car, windup.
Photo by Bill Kaufman

	C6	C8	C10
Marx "Fire Dept. Chief" car, c.1950s, 11'' long tin wind-up	105	158	210
Marx Fire Dept. car	100	150	200
Marx Fire Engine Pumper, friction, late 1920s	275	363	550
Marx Fire Ladder Truck, 6'' long, c.1940	50	75	100
Marx Fire Truck, friction, 25'' long	225	338	450
Marx Fire Truck, plastic, with siren, 1950s	50	75	100
Marx "1st Batt. F.D. Chief's Car", 16'' long, siren, battery headlights, tin wind-up	270	405	540
Marx Fix-All Convertible and Wrecker set	125	188	250
Marx Fix-All Farm Tractor, 1953	112	168	225
Marx Fix-All Hard-top Convertible, w/tools, equipment	88	132	175
Marx Fix-All Motorcycle, 12'' long, plastic	No Price Found		
Marx Fix-It Jaguar, 12'' long, plastic	115	172	230
Marx Ford Convertible, 1951, 11'' long	55	83	110

	C6	C8	C10
Marx "Funny Flivver", c.1925 tin wind-up	450	700	1000
Marx G-Man Pursuit Car, 1930s, tin wind-up	250	375	500
Marx G-Man Pursuit Car No. 7000, 15'' long, 1930s	200	300	400
Marx Gang Buster Car No. 7200, approx. 14'' long, 1930s	550	825	1100
Marx Gas Island, 1930s	100	150	200
Marx General Alarm Fire House	100	150	200

Marx Giant King Racer, "711", as shown in the Christmas, 1929 Butler Bros. catalog.

	C6	C8	C10
Marx "Giant King Racer" c.1930s, "711", tin wind-up	110	165	220
Marx Giant Reversing Tractor Truck with tools, "Hauling", 14'' long, c.1950s tin wind-up	100	150	200
Marx "Gold Star Transfer Company" trailer truck	77	117	155

Marx "Gravel" truck.
Photo by Calvin L. Chaussee

	C6	C8	C10
Marx "Gravel" truck, 13" long.	125	188	250
Marx "Gravel" truck, 9" long..	75	112	150
Marx Grocery Truck, 1950s, 14½" long	62	93	125
Marx Guided Missile Truck No. 4488	220	330	440
Marx "Gulf" Service Station ...	300	450	600
Marx Happitime Service Station	162	243	325
Marx Hauler and Closed Van Trailer, plastic	62	93	125
Marx Hauler and Open Van Trailer, plastic	40	60	80
Marx "Hauling" tractor, wind-up, 14" long, 6-wheel	150	220	300
Marx "Heavy Duty Express" truck, cloth cover	82	123	165
Marx Heavy Duty Hydraulic Dump	72	108	145
Marx Heavy Duty Power Shovel	38	57	75

Marx Highboy Climbing Tractor.
Photo by Don Hultzman

	C6	C8	C10
Marx "Highboy Climbing Tractor", c.1950s, 10½" long tin wind-up	75	112	150
Marx Highboy Tractor, sparkles, c.1950s, 10" long tin wind-up	100	150	200
Marx Hi-Mac Dump Truck & Driver	125	188	250

Marx "Hi-Way Express" truck.
Photo by Calvin L. Chaussee

	C6	C8	C10
Marx "Hi-Way Express" Truck .	125	188	250

Marx "Honeymoon Garage", with the two cars that were sold with it.
Photo by James Apthorpe

	C6	C8	C10
Marx "Home Dairy" truck with bottles	112	168	225
Marx Honeymoon Garage, tin litho, 1930s	55	83	110
Marx Hot Rod "777 Super"	35	52	70
Marx Howard Johnson's truck, 10" long, plastic	75	112	150

Marx Hydraulic Dump.
Courtesy Heinz Mueller, Continental Auctions

	C6	C8	C10
Marx Hydraulic Dump.........	100	150	200
Marx "Ice" truck, c.1941.......	58	87	115
Marx Intercity Delivery, 18" long	100	150	200
Marx International Task Force truck, with soldiers..........	55	82	110
Marx Invasion Force Truck.....	45	68	90
Marx Jalopy Pickup Truck, 7" long tin wind-up.................	80	120	160
Marx Jeep, 11" long...........	100	150	200
Marx Jeep & trailer...........	70	105	140
Marx "Joy-Rider", 1929, 8" long, College Boy driver, tin wind-up	225	338	450
Marx Jumpin' Jeep, c.WWII 6" tin wind-up....................	125	188	250
Marx Kellogg's Express Stake Truck....................	80	120	160
Marx "King Racer", 1930s, 8½" long tin wind-up............	500	800	1100
Marx Landau, 6" long.........	38	58	75
Marx Lazy-Day Dairy Farm Pickup truck and trailer, 22" long	65	98	130
Marx Lazy Day Farms Stake truck 18" long, late..............	95	143	190

Marx "Lifesavers" truck, plastic, 9½" long.
Photo by Terry Sells

	C6	C8	C10
Marx "Lifesavers" truck, plastic, 9½" long..................	No Price Found		
Marx Light Duty Climbing Tractor, 1930s tin wind-up...........	162	243	325
Marx "Limping Lizzie" car, tin wind-up....................	200	300	400

Marx Linemar "Air Defense Pom-Pom Gun".
Courtesy Don Hultzman

	C6	C8	C10
Marx Linemar "Air Defense Pom-Pom Gun", battery operated, 14" long, five action........	120	180	240
Marx Linemar Army Searchlight truck......................	100	150	200
Marx Linemar? "Ferris Wheel Truck", battery operated, four actions, 11" long, c.1950s	140	210	280
Marx Linemar Friction Car, 8½" long.......................	30	45	60
Marx Linemar Mercedes Racer..	138	208	275
Marx Linemar "Military Police Car", 1950s, battery operated, 8½" long, six actions........	90	135	180
Marx Linemar "NBC Television Truck", 1950s, battery operated, five actions, 9" long.........	240	360	480
Marx Linemar "NAR Television Truck", 1950s battery operated, 12" long, four actions, includes six film strip inserts........	280	420	560
Marx Linemar "Old Jalopy", small, 1950s tin wind-up.....	125	188	250
Marx Linemar Police Car, 1954 Chevy, 7½" friction........	60	90	120
Marx Linemar Searchlight Truck, Studebaker.................	90	135	180
Marx Linemar "Steerable Tank", 1950s, 9" long battery operated, 5 actions...................	50	75	100

Marx Linemar Taxi, "Yellow Cab".
Photo by Don Hultzman

Marx Lumar Rocker Dump.
Photo courtesy Heinz Mueller, Continental Auctions

	C6	C8	C10
Marx Linemar Taxi "Yellow Cab", battery-operated, 7½" long, five actions	60	90	120
Marx Linemar "Television Truck", 1950s battery operated, 11" long, 3 actions	200	300	400
Marx Livestock Truck	75	112	150
Marx Loader Dump, 17" long	100	150	200
Marx Lone Eagle Oil company wind-up tank truck, 12" long, Bulldog Mack	700	1100	1600
Marx Lonesome Pine trailer and convertible sedan, 1930s, 19" long	360	540	720
Marx Lumar Aerial Ladder Truck	118	177	235
Marx Lumar Allied Van Lines	41	63	82
Marx Lumar Army Truck	41	63	82
Marx Lumar Army Truck & Electric Searchlight Trailer	100	150	200
Marx Lumar Auto Transport, 28" long	145	218	290
Marx Lumar Carry All Low Boy	32	48	65
Marx "Lumar Contractors" 962 Dump Truck, approx. 17" long	140	210	280
Marx "Lumar Contractors" Steam Shovel	58	88	115
Marx Lumar Contractors Crane	110	165	220
Marx Lumar Dairy Truck	50	75	100
Marx Lumar "Emergency Searchlight Unit", 19" long, tin litho	138	208	275
Marx Lumar Hook & Ladder, 33" long	212	318	425
Marx Lumar Hydraulic Dump	75	112	150
Marx Lumar Police Car, 1954 Chevy, battery operated	68	102	135
Marx Lumar Power Grader	52	78	105

	C6	C8	C10
Marx Lumar Rocker Dump, 18" long	75	112	150
Marx Lumar Scoop-A-Dump	90	135	180
Marx Lumar Searchlight Truck, 19" long	138	208	275
Marx Lumar "U.S. Army" truck, 18½" long, cloth top	62	93	125

Marx Lumar Utility Truck Courtesy Heinz.
Mueller, Continental Hobby House

Marx Lumar Utility Truck w/tools	150	225	300
Marx Lumar Van Lines Trailer Truck	82	124	165
Marx M.D. War Dept. Ambulance, 1930s	650	975	1300
Marx Machinery Moving Truck No. 1016	100	150	200
Marx "Mack Dump Truck", 1930s (City Coal Co.), 13" long tin wind-up	350	525	700
Marx Magic Barn with tractor	112	168	225
Marx "Magic Garage and Car", 1950s, garage 10" long, car 7" long, wind-up	85	128	170
Marx Magnetic Crane, 17"	105	158	210
Marx Magnetic Crane Truck, 8½" long, 1940s	425	640	850
Marx "Main Street" tin wind-up, 1929	150	225	300

	C6	C8	C10
Marx Maintenance Truck, 6'' long, c.1929, 2 ladders at each side of truck	30	45	60
Marx "Mammoth Truck Train" No. T-50-12345, c.1930s, truck with five trailers	175	262	350
Marx "Marbrook Farms" Sparkling Tractor & Trailer Set, c.1950s, 21'' long tin wind-up	75	112	150
Marx Marco Oil Tanker, c.1940 .	150	225	300
Marx Marcrest Dairy stake truck	150	225	300
Marx Marcrest Livestock Semi, 20'' long	75	112	150
Marx Marx-A-Power Giant Bulldozer, battery operated . . .	75	112	150
Marx Mayflower Van, 13'' long.	450	675	900
Marx "Mechanical Roadster", 1950s, 11'' long tin wind-up .	70	105	140
Marx Mechanical Sparkling Tank, late	35	52	70
Marx "Mechanical Speedway Racer" tin wind-up	60	90	120
Marx Mechanical Station Wagon tin wind-up	125	188	250
Marx "Mechanical Taxi Cab", 1950s, 11'' long tin wind-up .	80	120	160
Marx "Mechanical Tractor", 6'' long, c.1930s tin wind-up	110	165	220
Marx "Mechanical Tractor with Earth Grader", 21½'' long, c.1950s tin wind-up	105	158	210
Marx "Merchants Transfer" truck, c.1930s	275	363	550

Marx Mickey Mouse Dipsy Car.
Courtesy Don Hultzman

	C6	C8	C10
Marx Mickey Mouse Dipsy Car, 1950s, 5¼'' long, tin car, plastic Mickey	200	300	400

	C6	C8	C10
Marx "Mickey Mouse Motorcycle", 1950s, Linemar, tin friction, 3½'' long	300	450	600

Marx "Midget Climbing, Fighting Tank".
Courtesy K. Warren Mitchell

	C6	C8	C10
Marx "Midget Climbing Fighting Tank", approx. 5½'' long, c.1935 tin wind-up	75	112	150
Marx Midget Climbing Tractor, 5½'' long, c.1950 tin wind-up	60	90	120
Marx "Midget Racer", 1950s, 6'' long, plastic wind-up	50	75	100
Marx "Midget Special", race car - driver in old headgear and goggles, 5'' long, No. 2 racer, 1930s, tin wind-up	65	98	130

Marx "Midget Special".
Courtesy Scott Smiles.

	C6	C8	C10
Marx "Midget Special" race car driver in old headgear and goggles, 5'' long No. 7 racer, 1930s, tin wind-up	65	98	130
Marx Midtown Service Center . .	112	168	225
Marx Military Power-Mite Bulldozer	45	68	90
Marx Military Power-Mite Dump Truck	45	68	90
Marx Milk Truck, Studebaker type	450	675	910
Marx Milton Berle Car, 1950s tin wind-up	220	330	440
Marx Mobile Crane, c.1940	80	120	160

Marx "Mortimer Snerd's Tricky	C6	C8	C10
Auto", 1939 tin wind-up	438	658	875
Marx Model T Ford, plastic	40	60	80
Marx "Moto-Fix" truck	80	120	160
Marx Motor Market............	170	255	340
Marx Mystery Taxi, c.1930s, press down to operate	82	124	165

Marx Motorcycle Policeman with side-car, "Police", "3".
Courtesy Phillips NY.

Marx Motorcycle Policeman with sidecar, "Police", "3", license plate reads "102D", approx. 8" long, c.1940 tin wind-up.....	188	282	375
Marx "Motorcycle Trooper", 1935 tin wind-up................	125	188	250
Marx "Mystery Police Cycle", 1930s, 4½" long tin wind-up	110	165	220

Marx Mystic Motorcycle.
Courtesy Scott Smiles
Photo by Mike Adams

Marx "Mystic Motorcycle", c.1930s tin wind-up................	75	125	175
Marx Navy Jeep No. 1078......	65	97	130
Marx Navy Jeep with searchlight trailer....................	100	150	200
Marx "New Flivver", 1920s, 7" long tin wind-up...........	200	300	400

Marx "New Rocket Racer", 1930s,	C6	C8	C10
16" long...................	200	300	400
Marx "Newberry's" Semi Truck	120	180	240
Marx North American Van Lines wind-up, 14" long	110	165	220

Marx "Nutty Mads Car"
Courtesy Don Hultzman

Marx Nutty Mad Car, friction, 4" long, c.1965................	70	105	140
Marx "Nutty Mads Car" (Drincar), 1960s, 9¼" long, battery-operated, 3 action	140	210	280
Marx Old-Fashioned Antique Automobile, plastic	20	30	35

Marx "Old Jalopy" large and small.
Courtesy Ed Hyers Antique Toys. (the small is Marx Linemar)

Marx "Old Jalopy" tin wind-up	150	225	300
Marx "P.D." motorcyclist, approx. 4" long tin wind-up.........	120	180	240

Marx "P.D." Police motorcycle w/sidecar.
Courtesy Gary Linden.

	C6	C8	C10
Marx Panel Wagon	40	60	80
Marx "Parcel Post U.S. Mail", 8½" long, early, tin wind-up	225	338	450
Marx Pepsi-Cola truck, 8" long, 1945	47	72	95
Marx Pepsi-Cola truck, 11" long, 1950s	35	52	70

Marx Pepsi-Cola Truck, 7" long, plastic.
Photo by Terry Sells

Marx Pepsi-Cola truck, 7" long, plastic . . . . No Price Found

Marx "PD" motorcycle cop, windup, siren, 8" long, late 1930s. Value in C6, C8, C10: $200, 275, 350.
Courtesy Kent M. Comstock

Marx Pepsi-Cola Truck, 10½" long, plastic.
Photo by Terry Sells

	C6	C8	C10
Marx "P.D." police motorcycle with sidecar, 3½" long 1930s tin wind-up	250	375	500
Marx Paddy Wagon, 5" long, c.1920s	150	225	300

	C6	C8	C10
Marx Pepsi-Cola truck, 10½" long, plastic	No Price Found		
Marx "Pet Shop Delivery", 1950s, 10" long	80	120	160
Marx Peter Rabbit eccentric car, tin wind-up	300	450	600
Marx Pick-up truck, c.1941	65	98	130
Marx "Pinched" tin wind-up, c.1927	450	700	1000

Marx Panel Truck, plastic, 8¼" long.   Photo by Terry Sells

Marx Panel Truck, plastic, 8¼" long . . . . No Price Found

Marx "Polar Ice" Truck, steel, 14" long.
Photo by Terry Sells

	C6	C8	C10
Marx "Polar Ice" truck, steel, 14" long	No Price Found		
Marx Police Car, 1954, Chevy	No Price Found		
Marx "Police Patrol" motorcycle with sidecar, 1935 tin wind-up	150	225	300

Marx Police Car, 1954 Chevy.
Photo by Gary Linden

Marx "Police Siren Motorcycle", 1930s, 8" long tin wind-up	125	188	250
Marx "Police Squad Sidecar", wind-up, 8" long, yellow	200	325	450
Marx Pontiac, friction, late	30	45	60
Marx Popeye "Dippy Dumper" truck	450	675	900

Marx Power Grader.   Courtesy Continental Hobby House

Marx "Power Grader" No. 1759, black or white wheels, 17½" long	55	82	110

	C6	C8	C10
Marx Power House dump truck, late, 25" long	50	75	100
Marx Powerhouse Dump Truck	250	375	500
Marx "Power Snap Caterpillar Climbing Tractor", 1950s, 8" long tin wind-up	80	120	160
Marx Precinct Police Patrol Armored Truck, 10½" long tin wind-up, circa early 1930s	2000	3000	4000
Marx Pure Milk Dairy Truck with glass bottles, pressed steel, tin wheels, c.1940	100	150	200
Marx Racer No. 2, 1930s, 5" long, tin wind-up	44	66	88
Marx Racer No. 3, 1930s, 5" long, tin wind-up	44	66	88
Marx Racer No. 4, 1930s, 5" long tin wind-up	44	66	88
Marx Racer No. 5, 1930s, 5" long tin wind-up	44	66	88
Marx Racer No. 7, 1930s, 5" long tin wind-up	60	100	175
Marx Racer No. 3, plastic wind-up	50	75	100
Marx Racing Car, "12", c.1940, two-man team, tin wind-up	110	165	220
Marx Racing Car, "12", litho, plastic driver, c.1950s, wind-up	300	450	600
Racing Car, "27", litho, plastic driver, c.1950 wind-up	150	225	300
Marx Racing Car "711", 13" long	150	225	300
Marx RCA Panel Truck, 8" long, 1950s, with accessories	200	300	400
Marx REA Express Truck No. 1021	362	544	725
Marx "Reversible Coupe", "The Marvel Car", c.1938 tin wind-up	312	468	625
Marx Reversing Road Roller, tin wind-up	125	188	250
Marx Reversing Tank, 1930s tin wind-up	65	98	130

Marx "Rex" Race Car.
Courtesy Thomas G. Nefos, Federal Shipping Network

	C6	C8	C10
Marx "Rex" race car, 1920s tin wind-up	162	244	325
Marx "Rex Mars Planet Patrol", 1950s tin wind-up, 9½'' long	275	363	550
Marx Ridem Fire Truck, 30'' long	150	225	300
Marx Road Grader, heavy-duty	58	87	115
Marx Road Roller, 8½'' long, c.1930, has driver, tin wind-up	125	188	250
Marx Roadside Rest, 4 pumps, car, garage, 1930	450	700	1000
Marx Rocker Dump No. 1752, 17½'' long	60	90	120
Marx Rocket Racer, 1930s, tin wind-up	150	225	300
Marx "Rookie Cop" with siren, 1930s, 8½'' long tin wind-up	200	325	450

Marx "Rookie Cop", c.1950.
Courtesy Kent M. Comstock

	C6	C8	C10
Marx "Rookie Cop" wind-up, 8'' long, yellow, around 1950	200	275	350

	C6	C8	C10
Marx Royal Bus Line, 10'' long tin wind-up	100	150	200
Marx "Royal Coupe", 1920s, 9'' long	375	563	750

Marx "Royal Van Co."
Courtesy Mapes Auctioneers & Appraisers

	C6	C8	C10
Marx "Royal Van Co.", "We Haul Anywhere", 9'' long tin wind-up	350	525	700
Marx Sabre Car	87	132	175

Marx "Sand" Mechanical Dump Truck c.1939, 9'' long.
Courtesy Charles D. Richards

	C6	C8	C10
Marx "Sand" Mechanical Dump truck c.1939, 9'' long	45	68	90
Marx "Sand & Gravel" dump truck, 10'' long, 1940s	100	150	200
Marx Sand & Gravel dump truck, 21'' long	115	172	230
Marx "Sand and Gravel Truck - Builders Supply Co.", 1920 tin wind-up	100	150	200
Marx Sand Loader	30	45	60
Marx School Bus, 12'' long	55	82	110

	C6	C8	C10
Marx Scoop Dump, 20" long, postwar....................	175	263	350
Marx Searchlight Truck........	100	150	200
Marx Secret Agent Car........	110	165	220
Marx "Service Station", 1929...	300	450	600
Marx "Sheriff Sam & His Whoopee Car", 1950s, 6" long tin wind-up................	180	270	360
Marx "Sheriff Sam & His Whoopee Car", 1960s, 6" long tin wind-up................	88	132	175
Marx Side Dump Truck, four-color No. T-475 c.1940...........	60	90	120
Mack Side Dump Truck and Trailer, No. T-4045, c.1930s..	100	150	200
Marx "Signal Corps" truck, plastic	60	90	120
Marx Silver Streak Racer.......	70	105	140
Marx "Sinclair" truck, steel....	140	210	280
Marx "Single Track Speedway", 1938, 8 track sections, 4" long wind-up car................	60	90	120

Marx "Sparkling Climbing Fighting Tank", cannon recoils.
Courtesy Charles D. Richards

	C6	C8	C10
Marx "Sparkling Climbing Fighting Tank", cannon recoils, tin wind-up......................	100	150	200

Marx "Siren Fire Chief"
Photo by Bob Smith

Marx Sparkling Tank, 4" long.
Courtesy Continental Hobby House.

Marx "Siren Police Patrol".
Photo by Bob Smith

	C6	C8	C10
Marx "Sparkling Climbing Tank", 1939........................	140	210	280
Marx Sparkling Climbing Tractor, 1940s tin wind-up...........	75	112	150
Marx Sparkling Climbing Tractor, 8½" long, c.1950s tin wind-up	100	150	200
Marx "Sparkling Climbing Tractor and Trailer", 16" long, c.1950s tin wind-up................	55	82	110

	C6	C8	C10
Marx "Siren Fire Chief" c.1930, "F.D. 1st Batt.", 15" long...	375	500	700
Marx "Siren Police Patrol", 1930s, 15" long.................	375	500	700
Marx Sparkling Doughboy Tank	175	263	350

	C6	C8	C10
Marx Sparkling Heavy Duty Bulldog Tractor with Road Scraper, c.1950s, 11'' long tin wind-up	125	188	250
Marx "Sparkling Hot Rod Racer", 1950s plastic wind-up, 8'' long	37	56	75
Marx Sparkling Jet Futuristic Car, friction motor, 10'' long	87	132	175
Marx Sparkling Soldier Motorcycle, c.1940 tin wind-up	250	375	500
Marx Sparkling Super Power Tank, c.1950s, 9½'' long tin wind-up	110	165	220
Marx Sparkling Tank, 4'' long tin wind-up	65	98	130
Marx "Sparkling Tractor", tractor with plow blade, 1939 tin wind-up	140	210	280
Marx Sparkling Turn Over Tank, tin wind-up	40	60	80

Marx "Speed Boy Delivery".
Courtesy Kent M. Comstock

	C6	C8	C10
Marx "Speed Boy Delivery" (Motorcycle), 1930s, 9¾'' long, battery lights, tin wind-up . . .	250	375	500
Same as above, no lights	262	393	525
Marx "Speed Boy 4" wind-up, 9½'' long motorcycle	250	375	500
Marx Speedway Coupe, battery lights, 8'' long tin wind-up . .	338	408	675
Marx Sports Coupe, 1930s, 15'' long	200	300	400

	C6	C8	C10
Marx Stake Truck, 4'' long, c.1941	27	41	55
Marx Stake Truck, 6'' long, c.1941	30	45	60
Marx Stake Truck, 12'' long, 1930s, two-color	65	98	130
Marx Stake Truck, No. 1008. . . .	60	90	120
Marx Stake Truck No. E-271, three-color, c.1941	70	105	140
Marx Streamline Convertible, friction	138	207	275
Marx "Streamline Speedway", 1938, tin figure 8 track, 2 wind-up cars, 31'' long	140	210	280
Marx Streamlined Coupe, hard top, no windshield supports, c.1937, steel	30	45	60
Marx Streamlined Coupe, tin wind-up	160	240	320
Marx Studebaker Dump, 1950s .	65	98	130
Marx Stutz Electric Car with driver, 1930, 36'' long tin wind-up	225	338	450
Marx "Sunnyside Service Station", 1930s, complete	400	600	800
Marx Super Hi-Way Service Wrecker	42	63	85
Marx "Super Service" Center . .	175	263	350
Marx "Super Streamline Racer", 1950s, 17'' long tin wind-up .	120	180	240
Marx Superman Rollover Tank, 1940s, 4'' long	450	700	1000

Marx Superman Tank, Linemar, battery-operated, 10¼" long.
Courtesy Christie's East

	C6	C8	C10
Marx "Superman Tank", 1950s, Linemar Co., 10¼" long, battery operated, 3 actions	650	1000	1500
Marx Superman Tank, Linemar, 4" long	500	800	1100
Marx Take-Apart Jaguar, 1950s	115	172	230
Marx Tank No. 4 "U.S. Army" wind-up	100	150	200
Marx Tank, late, machine gun on top of turret	55	82	110
Marx Tank No. 3, 2 machine guns or cannon on top of roof (no turret), tin wind-up	200	300	400
Marx "Tank 392-U.S. Tank Division", 1950s battery operated, 9½" long, 3 actions	60	90	120
Marx Tank Truck, 6" long	42	63	85
Marx Taxi Hauler, 2 cabs, c.1940	150	225	300
Marx Telephone Truck, 11" long, plastic	45	68	90
Marx Tow Truck, 11" long, c.1941	70	105	140
Marx "Toy Town Express Van Lines Deluxe Service" truck	112	168	225
Marx Tractor, 1920s tin wind-up	120	180	240
Marx Tractor, early 1940s tin wind-up	50	75	100

Marx "Toy Town Express Van Lines Deluxe Service" truck.
Courtesy Don Hultzman
Photo by Ron Chojnacki

	C6	C8	C10
Marx Tractor & Trailer set, 1930s, similar to climbing tractor set, but with rounded and radiator front and copper finish metal. Tin plow attaches to front, silver metal trailer attaches to rear; has tin, copper finish and "balloon" tires, wind-up	160	240	320
Earlier version, no balloon tires	125	188	250
Marx Tractor and Trailer, 16½" long, c.1950s tin wind-up	92	138	185
Marx Tractor Service, 1940s, tractor, cardboard garage box, 3 pieces of farm equipment	225	338	450
Marx Tri-City Express Truck	75	112	150
Marx "Tricky Motorcycle", 1930s, 4¼" long, non-fail action with wind-up	125	188	250

287

Marx Tricky Taxi.
Photo by William G. Floyd

Marx Untouchables Rolls Royce.
Photo by Gary Linden

Marx "Tricky Taxi" variation.

Marx Untouchables Touring Car.
Photo by Gary Linden

	C6	C8	C10
Marx "Tricky Taxi", friction, 4½" long	75	112	150
Marx "Tricky Taxi", 1940s, 4½" long tin wind-up	100	150	200
Marx Truck w/Trailer c.1940, 19" overall	88	132	175
Marx Trucking Terminal	90	135	180

	C6	C8	C10
Marx Untouchables Rolls Royce, tin friction	30	50	75
Marx Untouchables Touring Car, tin friction	30	50	75
Marx "U.S. Air Force" truck, cloth top	92	138	185

Marx Turnover Tank No. 3. Photo by Max Heiss.

Marx "U.S. Army" Searchlight Trailer.
Photo by Calvin L. Chaussee

Marx Turn Over Tank No. 3 tin wind-up	175	263	350
Marx Uncle Wiggily Crazy Car, tin wind-up	500	800	1100
Marx "Universal Gas Service Station", 1940s, 6½" high, base 12" long	138	208	275

Marx "U.S. Army" Searchlight Trailer	30	45	60
Marx "U.S. Army" truck with horns, cloth top	60	90	120
Marx "U.S. Army" truck, late, canvas cover	60	90	120

Marx "U.S. Army Truck", 1920s	C6	C8	C10
Mack, cloth cover, 10" long wind-up	90	135	180
Marx "U.S. Army Truck", cloth top, late	75	112	150
Marx "U.S. Army 5th Div." truck with canopy, circa late 1950s	80	120	160

Marx War Tank, as seen in the November, 1932 Butler Bros. catalog.

	C6	C8	C10
Marx War Tank, 5¼" long tin wind-up	100	150	200
Marx Wards Service Station	138	205	275
Marx Western Auto, 25" long trailer truck	47	72	95
Marx Whoopee Car, laughing cows on wheels, driver looks like cowboy, 1929, tin wind-up	225	338	450

Marx "U.S. Mail" truck, 9½" long.
Courtesy Phillips NY

Marx "U.S. Mail" truck, 9½" long			
tin wind-up	200	300	400
Marx "U.S. Mail" truck, 14" long	225	338	450
Marx "U.S. Mobile Guided Missile Squadron" truck	62	93	125
Marx "U.S. Navy Jeep w/search-light, 23" long	112	168	225

Marx "Whoopee Car", "Yale-Princeton" pennants on wheels.
Courtesy Mapes Auctioneers

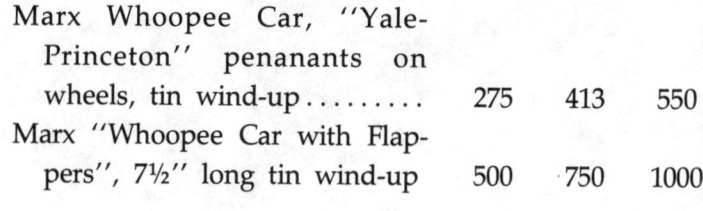

Marx "USA 41573147" Army Truck, 40.
Photo by Bill Kaufman

Marx "USA 4153147" Army Truck,			
c.1952, 13¾" long	100	150	200
Marx "Volunteer Fire Department" tin garage, with 1950s "Chief FD" car	130	195	260
Marx Wacky Taxi tin wind-up	75	112	150
Marx Walt Disney Television Car, 1950s, 7½" long	180	270	360

Marx Whoopee Car, "Yale-Princeton" penanants on			
wheels, tin wind-up	275	413	550
Marx "Whoopee Car with Flappers", 7½" long tin wind-up	500	750	1000

Marx Willys Jeep, steel, c.1940.
Photo by Calvin L. Chaussee

Marx "Yellow Cab". This was Marx's first plastic car. The original has "Made in U.S.A." on the underside of the roof. The 1990s reissue bears a Marx emblem.
Caption and photo courtesy Bob & Alice Wagner

	C6	C8	C10
Marx Willys Jeep, steel, c.1940, 12" long, hood opens, windshield folds down	65	98	130
Marx Willys Jeep & Trailer, c.1940s	95	142	190
Marx Willys Jeepster, plastic wind-up	75	112	150
Marx "Woodie" tin litho wind-up	42	63	85
Marx Woolworth's trailer truck, c.1960s	238	358	475
Marx Wreckage Service Truck, tin, battery lights	75	112	150
Marx Wrecker, 4" long, c.1941 .	27	41	55
Marx Wrecker, 6" long, c.1940 .	42	63	95
Marx Wrecker, 10" long, 1920s .	100	150	200
Marx Wrecker No. T-16, c.1930s	150	225	300

	C6	C8	C10
Marx "Yellow Cab", first Marx plastic car, 4" long. Original has "MADE IN U.S.A." under roof. (1990s reissue has Marx emblem)	9	20	40
Marx "Yellow Cab-LMN 52", 1940s, 6½" long tin wind-up	142	214	285
MASON & PARKER Baby Auto, 1907, 7" long	450	700	1000

MATCHBOX

Matchbox began in London, England, with the partnership of longtime friends Leslie and Rodney Smith, who in 1947 combined portions of their first names to form Lesney Products. Business began in a former pub, and consisted of industrial zinc die-castings. Toys were added as a sideline, and in 1952 England's Woolworth's encouraged the Smiths to expand their toys line. In 1953 the I-75 series began, and in 1954 the firm began using the Matchbox name. Sales to Japan began in 1958, and to the U.S. in 1959. Lesney was acquired by Universal holdings (since 1986 known as Matchbox Toys) in 1982. In 1987 Matchbox, of Moonachie, New Jersey, was one of the top three toy car makers, selling 77 million vehicles. Matchboxes are modeled to a one-sixty-fourth scale. (Moses Kohnstadt was the firm's first agent and sold the toys under his own label, Moko, using portions of his name. Lesney later acquired Moko.) **Prices are for Mint in Box,** since that is how most collectible Matchboxes are sold.

	MIB
No. 1 Diesel Road Roller, 1953 .	175
No. 1 Aveling Barford Road Roller, 1964	25
No. 1 Mercedes Benz Lorry, 1968	15
No. 1 Mod Rod, 1971	13
No. 1 Dodge Challenger, 1976..	10
No. 2 Dumper, 1953	100
No. 2 Muir-Hill Dumper, 1962..	20
No. 2 Mercedes Trailer, 1968	13
No. 2 Hot Rod Jeep, 1971	13
No. 3 Cement Mixer, 1953	50
No. 3 Bedford Ton Tipper, 1961	75
No. 3 Mercedes Benz Ambulance, 1968	18
No. 3 Monteverdi Hai, 1973	11
No. 3 Porsche Turbo, 1978	15
No. 4 Tractor, 1954	95
No. 4 Triumph Motorcycle and sidecar, 1959	95
No. 4 Stake Truck, 1967	15
No. 4 Gruesome Twosome, 1971	6
No. 4 Pontiac Firebird, 1976	7
No. 4 '57 Chevy, 1981	6
No. 5 London Bus, 1954	25
No. 5 Lotus Europea Sports Car, 1969	15

	MIB
No. 5 Seafire, 1976	5
No. 5 U.S. Mail Truck, 1981	12
No. 6 Quarry Truck, 1955	95
No. 6 Euclid 10-wheel Quarry, 1964	50
No. 6 Ford Pick-up, 1969	17
No. 6 Mercedes Tourer, 1974	10
No. 7 Ford Anglia, 1961	25
No. 7 Ford Refuse Truck, 1967 .	15
No. 7 Hairy Hustler, 1971	12
No. 7 VW Golf, 1976	5
No. 8 Caterpillar Tractor, 1955..	125
No. 8 Ford Mustang Fastback, 1966	25
No. 8 Wildcat Dragster, 1971	15
No. 8 De Tomaso Pantera, 1975	8
No. 9 Dennis Fire Engine, 1955	100

Matchbox No. 9 Merryweather Marquis Fire Truck. Courtesy Gary Linden

	MIB
No. 9 Merryweather Marquis Fire Engine, 1959	35
No. 9 Boat & Trailer, 1967	15
No. 9 Javelin, 1972	10
No. 9 Ford Escort RS200, 1978 .	8
No. 10 Mechanical Horse & Trailer, 1955	110
No. 10 Sugar Container Truck, 1961	85
No. 10 Pipe Truck 1967	15
No. 10 Piston Popper, 1973	18
No. 10 Plymouth 'Gran Fury' Police Car, 1980	10

	MIB
No. 11 Petrol Tanker (Esso decal), 1955	95
No. 11 Jumbo Crane (Taylor), 1964	20
No. 11 Scaffolding Truck (Mercedes), 1969	15
No. 11 Flying Bug, 1972	15
No. 11 Car Transporter, 1977	10

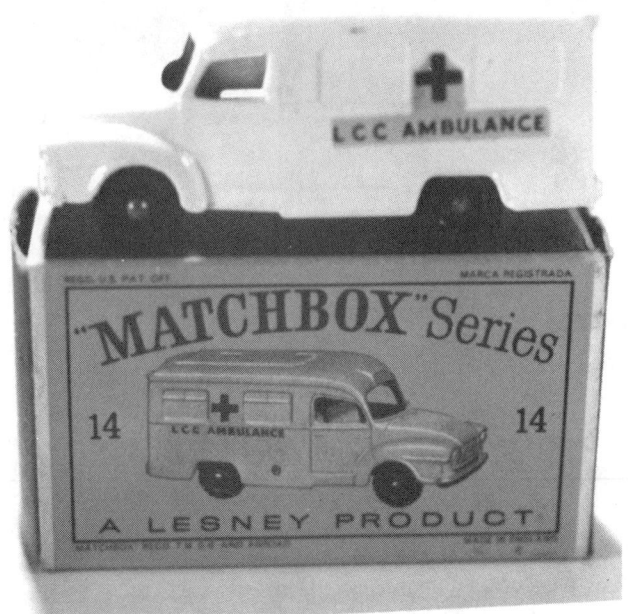

Matchbox No. 14 Bedford Lomas Ambulance.
Courtesy Gary Linden

Matchbox No. 12 Land Rover.
Courtesy Gary Linden

	MIB
No. 12 Land Rover, 1953	20
No. 12 Safari Land Rover, 1965	30
No. 12 Setra Coach, 1971	10
No. 12 Big Bull, 1975	8
No. 12 Citroen CX, 1981	8
No. 13 Bedford Wreck Truck, 1955	No Price Found
No. 13 Thames Wreck Truck (MB Garages), 1959	95
No. 13 Dodge Wreck Truck (BP Label), 1961	30
No. 13 Baja Buggy, 1971	13
No. 13 Snorkel Fire Engine, 1977	6
No. 14 Daimler Ambulance, 1955	85
No. 14 Beford Lomas Ambulance, 1962	20
No. 14 Grifo Sports Car, 1968	15
No. 14 Mini Ha Ha, 1975	10
No. 15 Prime Mover, 1955	50
No. 15 Dennis Refuse Truck, 1963	45
No. 15 Volkswagen 1500 Saloon, 1968	23
No. 15 Fork Lift Truck, 1972	10

	MIB
No. 16 Low-Loading Trailer, 6 wheels, 1955	52
No. 16 Low-Loading Trailer, 8 wheels, 1955	50
No. 16 Scammel Mountaineer Dump with Plow, 1961	28
No. 16 Case Tractor Bulldozer, 1969	30
No. 16 Badger, 1974	10
No. 16 Pontiac, 1981	3
No. 17 Bedford Removal Van, 1955	125
No. 17 Austin Taxi, 1960	90
No. 17 18-Wheel Tipper "Hoveringham", 1964	20
No. 17 Horse Box "Ergomatic Cab", 1969	15
No. 17 Londoner, 1973	12
No. 18 Caterpillar Bulldozer, 1955	60
No. 18 Field Car, 1969	15
No. 18 Hondarora, 1975	10

Matchbox No. 19 MGA, Sports Car.
Courtesy Gary Linden

	MIB
No. 19 MG Midget Sports Car, 1955	95
No. 19 MGA Sports Car, 1959 .	30
No. 19 Aston-Martin F.I., 1961 .	85
No. 19 Lotus Racing Car, 1965 .	15
No. 19 Road Dragster, 1971	10
No. 19 Cement Truck, 1976	10
No. 20 E.R.F. Lorry Truck, 1955	80
No. 20 Taxi Cab (Chevrolet Impala), 1965	20
No. 20 Lamborghini Marzel, 1969	10
No. 20 Police Patrol, 1975	8
No. 21 Long Distance Coach "London To Glasgow", 1955	95
No. 21 Commer Milk Truck, 1961	20
No. 21 Foden Concrete Truck, 1969	15
No. 21 Rod Roller, 1973	10
No. 22 Vauxhall Cresta, 1955 . . .	60
No. 22 Pontiac 'Grand Prix' Sports Coupe, 1964	25
No. 22 Freeman Inter City Commuter, 1970	11
No. 22 Blaze Buster, 1975	10
No. 23 Caravan Trailer, 1956 . . .	15
No. 23 House Trailer Caravan, 1967	25
No. 23 Volkswagen Camper, 1970	15
No. 23 Atlas, 1975	8
No. 24 Excavator, 1956	25

	MIB
No. 24 Rolls Royce Silver Shadow, 1967	15
No. 24 Team 'Matchbox', 1973 .	10
No. 24 Diesel Shunter, 1979	8

Matchbox No. 25 Bedford "Dunlop" Van.
Courtesy Gary Linden

No. 25 Bedford 'Dunlop' Van, 1956	60
No. 25 Volkswagen 1200 Sedan, 1958	95
No. 25 B.P. Tanker, 1960	18
No. 25 Ford Cortina G.T., 1968	15
No. 25 Mod Tractor, 1972	11
No. 25 Flat Car & Container, 1979	5
No. 26 Ready Mix Concrete Truck, 1956	50
No. 26 G.M.C. Tipper Truck, 1968	15
No. 26 Big Banger, 1972	10
No. 26 Site Dumper, 1976	8
No. 27 Bedford Low Loader, 1956	85
No. 27 Cadillac Sedan, 1960	95
No. 27 Mercedes Benz, 230SL, 1965	18
No. 27 Lamborghini Countach, 1974	10

Matchbox No. 28 Bedford Compressor Truck.
Courtesy Gary Linden

	MIB
No. 28 Bedford Compressor Truck, 1956	60
No. 28 Thames Compressor Truck, 1959	85
No. 28 Mark Ten Jaguar, 1964	20
No. 28 Mack Dump Truck, 1968	15
No. 28 Stoat, 1974	10
No. 28 Lincoln Continental, 1980	6
No. 29 Bedford Milk Delivery Van, 1956	50
No. 29 Austin A55 Cambridge, 1961	42
No. 29 Fire Pumper Truck, 1965	25
No. 29 Racing Mini, 1971	15
No. 29 Shovel Nose Tractor, 1976	7
No. 30 Ford Prefect with Towbar, 1956	75
No. 30 German Crane Truck, 1961	45
No. 30 Favin Crane, 8 wheel, 1965	20
No. 30 Beach Buggy, 1971	13
No. 30 Swamp Rat, 1977	6
No. 30 Articulated Truck, 1981	6
No. 31 Ford Customline Station Wagon, 1956	95
No. 31 Ford Fairlane Station Wagon, 1959	95
No. 31 Lincoln Continental, 1964	15
No. 31 Volks Dragon, 1971	15
No. 31 Caravan, 1977	5
No. 32 Jaguar XK 140 Coupe, 1956	75
No. 32 Leyland Tanker, 1968	20

	MIB
No. 32 Excavator, 1981	15
No. 33 Ford Zodiac MKII, 1956	85
No. 33 Ford Zephyr 6 MKIII, 1963	20
No. 33 Lamborghini Muira P400, 1969	12
No. 33 Datsun 126X, 1973	10
No. 33 Police Motorcyclist, 1977	12
No. 34 Volkswagen Microvan 'Matchbox' Express, 1956	60
No. 34 Volkswagen Camper, 1961	30
No. 34 Formula 1 Racing Car, 1971	12
No. 34 Vantastic, 1976	7
No. 34 Chevy Pro Stocker, 1981	8
No. 35 Marschall Horse Box, 1956	65
No. 35 Sno-Trac Tractor, 1961	25
No. 35 Merryweather Marquis Fire Engine, 1970	15
No. 35 Fandango, 1975	8
No. 36 Austin A50 with Towbar, 1956	55

Matchbox No. 36 Lambretta Motorcycle with sidecar.
Courtesy Gary Linden

	MIB
No. 36 Lambretta & Sidecar, 1960	65
No. 36 Opel Diplomat, 1966	15
No. 36 Hot Rod Draguar, 1971	15
No. 36 Formula 5000, 1975	6
No. 36 Refuse Truck, 1981	14

Matchbox No. 37 Coca-Cola Truck.
Courtesy Gary Linden

	MIB
No. 37 Coca-Cola Truck, 1956 ..	200
No. 37 Cattle Truck (Dodge), 1967	15
No. 37 Soopa Coopa, 1973	10
No. 37 Skip Truck, 1976	8

Matchbox No. 38 Carrier Refuse Collector.
Courtesy Gary Linden

No. 38 Darrier Refuse Collector .	85
No. 38 Vauxhall Estate, 1963 . . .	32
No. 38 Honda Motorcycle with Trailer, 1968	20
No. 38 Stingeroo, 1973	10
No. 38 Armored Jeep, 1976	15
No. 38 Camper, 1981	11
No. 39 Ford Zodiac Convertible, 1956	85
No. 39 Pontiac Convertible, 1962	52
No. 39 Ford Tractor, 1967	20
No. 39 Clipper, 1973	12
No. 39 Rolls-Royce Silver Shadow MKII	15

	MIB
No. 40 Bedford 7 Ton Tipper, 1956	95
No. 40 Hay Trailer, 1967	15
No. 40 Leyland 'Royal Tiger' Coach/Long Distance, 1961 . . .	25
No. 40 Guildsman, 1971	10
No. 40 Horse Box, 1977	8
No. 41 'D' Type Jaguar Racing Car, 1956	100
No. 41 Ford G.T. 40 (Sports Racer), 1965	15
No. 41 Siva Spyder, 1972	10
No. 41 Ambulance, 1978	10

Matchbox No. 42 "Bedford Evening News" Van.
Courtesy Gary Linden

No. 42 Bedford 'Evening News' Van, 1956	65
No. 42 Studebaker Lark Wagonaire, 1965	16
No. 42 Iron Fairy Crane, 1969 . .	45
No. 42 Tyre Fryer, 1972	14
No. 42 Container Truck, 1977 . .	13
No. 43 Hillman Minx, 1957	75
No. 43 Aveling-Barford Shovel, 1962	35
No. 43 Pony Trailer, 1968	18
No. 43 Dragon Wheels, 1972 . . .	10
No. 44 Rolls-Royce Silver Cloud, 1957	60
No. 44 Refrigerator Truck, GMC, 1967	15
No. 44 Boss Mustang, 1972	6
No. 44 Passenger Coach, 1978 . .	14
No. 45 Vauxhall Victor, 1957 . . .	35

	MIB
No. 45 Ford Corsair with Green Boat, 1959	18
No. 45 Ford Group Six, 1970 . .	15
No. 45 BMW, 1976	8

Matchbox No. 46 Morris Minor 1000.
Courtesy Gary Linden

	MIB
No. 46 Morris Minor 1000, 1957	85
No. 46 Pickfords Removal Van, 1960	65
No. 46 Mercedes-Benz 300SE, 1968	15
No. 46 Stretcha Fetcha, 1972 . . .	10
No. 46 Ford Tractor. 1978	4

Matchbox No. 47 Trojan "Brooke Bond Tea" van.
Courtesy Gary Linden

	MIB
No. 47 Trojan 'Brooke Bond' Van, 1957	70

	MIB
No. 47 Neilson Ice Cream Van, 1963	30
No. 47 DAF Tipper Container Truck, 1968	15
No. 47 Beach Hopper, 1973	14
No. 48 Sports Boat & Trailer, 1957	25
No. 48 Dodge Dumper Truck, 1967	20
No. 48 Pi-Eyed Piper, 1973	10
No. 48 Sambron Jack Lift, 1977 .	8

Matchbox No. 49 Army Half Track MK III.
Courtesy Gary Linden

	MIB
No. 49 Army Half Track MKIII, 1958	45
No. 49 Mercedes Unimog Truck, 1967	18
No. 49 Chop Suey, 1973	18
No. 49 Crane Truck, 1976	12
No. 50 Commer Pick-up Truck, 1958	75
No. 50 John Deere-Lanz Tractor, 1963	25
No. 50 Ford Kennel Truck, 1969	12
No. 50 Articulated Truck, 1973 .	8
No. 50 Harley Davidson Motorcycle, 1981	6
No. 51 Albion Truck 'Portland Cement', 1958	75
No. 51 Tipping Farm Trailer, 1963	15
No. 51 8 Wheel Tipper truck, 1969	25
No. 51 Citroen SM, 1972	6
No. 51 Combine Harvester, 1979	6
No. 52 Maserati 4 CLT, 1958 . . .	95

	MIB
No. 52 BRM Racing Car, 1965 ..	18
No. 52 Dodge Charger MKIII, 1970	10
No. 52 Police Launch, 1976	10
No. 53 Aston-Martin DB2/4, 1959	85
No. 53 Mercedes-Benz 220SE, 1968	35
No. 53 Ford Zodiac MKIV, 1968	15
No. 53 Tanzara, 1972	12
No. 53 C.J. 6 Jeep, 1977	8

Matchbox No. 55 Ford Police Car.

Matchbox No. 54 Army Saracen Personnel Carrier.

Matchbox No. 56 Fiat 1500.

	MIB
No. 54 Army Saracen Personnel Carrier, 1959	50
No. 54 Cadillac Ambulance, 1965	20
No. 54 Ford Capri, 1971	10
No. 54 Personnel Carrier, 1976 .	10
No. 54 Mobile Home, 1981.....	10
No. 55 D.U.K.W. (Army Amphibian), 1959	65
No. 55 Ford Police Car, 1963...	26
No. 55 Mercury Parkland Police Car, 1969	11
No. 55 Mercury Police Car (Station Wagon), 1970	20
No. 55 Hell Raiser, 1975	12
No. 55 Ford Cortina, 1980	6
No. 56 London Trolley Bus, 1959	85
No. 56 Fiat 1500, 1965	15
No. 56 BMC 1800 Pininfarina, 1970	10
No. 56 Hi Trailer, 1975	10
No. 56 Mercedes 450SEL, 1980 .	8
No. 57 Wolseley 1500, 1959	60
No. 57 Chevrolet Impala, 1966 .	70

	MIB
No. 57 Eccles Caravan, 1970 ...	30
No. 57 Wild Life Truck, 1973...	13
No. 58 British European Airways Coach, 1959	85
No. 58 Drott Excavator, 1963 ...	55
No. 58 DAF Girder Truck, 1968	15
No. 58 Woosh-N-Push, 1972....	12
No. 58 Faun Dumper, 1976	8

Matchbox No. 59 Ford "Singer" Van.
Courtesy Gary Linden

	MIB
No. 59 Ford 'Singer', Van, 1959	100
No. 59 Ford Fairlane Fire Car, 1964	25
No. 59 Fire Chief Car, 1966	13
No. 59 Planet Scout, 1975	10
No. 59 Porsche 928, 1981	8

Matchbox No. 60 Morris Omnitruck J-2 pick-up.
Courtesy Gary Linden

No. 60 Morris Omnitruck J2 Pick-up	65
No. 60 Truck with Site Office, 1967	15
No. 60 Lotus Super Seven, 1971	12
No. 60 Holden Pick-up, 1977 . . .	8
No. 61 Military Scout Car (Ferret), 1959	65

	MIB
No. 61 Alvis Stalwart, 1967	35
No. 61 Blue Shark, 1971	6
No. 61 Wreck Truck, 1978	6
No. 62 General Army Lorry, 1959	75
No. 62 TV Service Van, 1964 . . .	30
No. 62 Mercury Cougar, 1969 . .	15
No. 62 Rat Rod Dragster, 1971 .	12
No. 62 Renault 17TL, 1974	12
No. 62 Chevrolet Corvettte, 1980	8

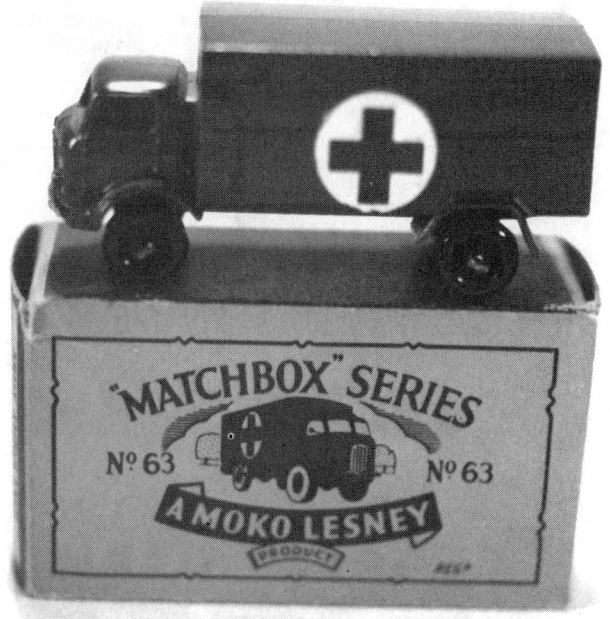

Matchbox No. 63 Army Ambulance.
Courtesy Gary Linden

No. 63 Army Ambulance, 1959 .	35
No. 63 Airport Fire Fighting Crash Tender, 1964	35
No. 63 Dodge Crane Truck, 1968	15
No. 63 Freeway Gas Tanker, 1973	10
No. 64 Scammell Army Wreck Truck, 1959	85
No. 64 MG 1100, 1966	15
No. 64 Slingshot Dragster, 1971	15
No. 64 Fire Chief Car, 1976	14
No. 64 Caterpillar Tractor, 1981 .	8
No. 65 Jaguar 3.4 Litre Saloon, 1959	75
No. 65 Claas Combine Harvester, 1968	15
No. 65 Saab Sonnet, 1973	10
No. 65 Airport Coach, 1977	20
No. 66 Citroen DS19, 1959	75
No. 66 Harley Davidson Motorcycle & Sidecar, 1963	125

Matchbox No. 64 Scammel Army Wreck Truck.
Courtesy Gary Linden

	MIB
No. 66 Greyhound Bus, 1967...	15
No. 66 Mazda RX500, 1972.....	10
No. 66 Ford Transit, 1977......	8
No. 67 'Saladin' Armored Car, 1959......................	30
No. 67 Volkswagen 1600 T.L., 1968	15
No. 67 Hot Rocker, 1973.......	10
No. 67 Datsun 260Z, 1978......	8

Matchbox No. 68 Army Austin MK II Radio Truck.
Courtesy Gary Linden

No. 68 Army Austin MKII Radio Truck, 1959.................	55

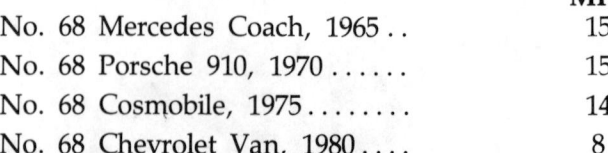

	MIB
No. 68 Mercedes Coach, 1965..	15
No. 68 Porsche 910, 1970......	15
No. 68 Cosmobile, 1975........	14
No. 68 Chevrolet Van, 1980....	8

Matchbox No. 69 Commer 30 CWT. Van "Nestle's".
Courtesy Gary Linden

No. 69 Commer 30 Cwt. Van 'Nestles', 1959.............	100
No. 69 Hatra Tractor Shovel, 1965	35
No. 69 Rolls-Royce Silver Shadow, 1970......................	15
No. 69 Turbo Fury, 1973.......	10
No. 69 Wells Fargo Security, 1978	8
No. 70 Ford Thames Estate Car, 1959......................	42
No. 70 Atkinson Grit-Spreading Truck, 1965................	13
No. 70 Dodge Dragster, 1971...	15
No. 70 S.P. Gun, 1977........	7
No. 70 Ferrari, 1981...........	8
No. 71 Army Water Truck, 1959	85
No. 71 Jeep Pick-up Truck, 1964	55
No. 71 Ford Heavy Wreck Truck, 1968......................	40
No. 71 Cattle Truck, 1976......	10
No. 72 Fordson Tractor (Power Major), 1959................	65
No. 72 Standard Jeep, 1967....	16
No. 72 Bomag Road Roller, 1980	7

Matchbox No. 73 R.A.F. 10 ton Pressure Refueler Tanker.
Courtesy Gary Linden

	MIB
No. 73 RAF 10-Ton Pressure Refueler Tanker, 1959	85
No. 73 Ferrari Racing Car, 1963	30
No. 73 Mercury Station Wagon (Commuter), 1969	15
No. 73 Weasel, 1974	10
No. 73 Model 'A' Ford, 1981 . . .	8
No. 74 Mobile Refreshment Bar (Canteen), 1959	80
No. 74 Daimler Bus, 1966	20
No. 74 Toe Joe, 1972	6
No. 74 Cougar Villager, 1978 . . .	8
No. 75 Ford Thunderbird, 1959 .	100
No. 75 Ferrari Berlinetta, 1965 . .	15
No. 75 Alfa Carabo, 1971	10
Y-1 1936 Jaguar SS 100, 1977 . . .	15
Y-2 1911 'B' Type London Bus, 1955	75
Y-2 1911 Renault 2-Seater, 1963 .	30
Y-2 Prince Henry Vauxhall, 1970	18
Y-3 1907 London 'E' Class Tramcar, 1955	100
Y-3 1910 Benz Limousine, 1965 .	45
Y-3 1934 Riley MPH, 1972	18
Y-4 Sentinel Steam Wagon, 1955	100
Y-4 1909 Opel Coupe, 1966	25
Y-4 1930 Dusenberg Model J, 1976	8
Y-5 1929 LeMans Bentley, 1955 .	65
Y-5 1929 Supercharged 4:1/2 Litre Bentley, 1960	25
Y-5 1907 Peugeot, 1968	30

Matchbox Y-5 Talbot Van.
Courtesy Gary Linden

	MIB
Y-5 1927 Talbot Van, 1978	11
Y-6 1916 A.E.C. "Y" type Lorry Truck, 1955	60
Y-6 1926 Type "35" Bugatti, 1961	75

Matchbox Y-6 1913 Cadillac.
Courtesy Gary Linden

	MIB
Y-6 1913 Cadillac, 1967	30
Y-6 1920 Rolls-Royce Fire Engine, 1978	13
Y-7 1914 4-Ton Leyland, 1955 . .	110
Y-7 1913 Mercer Raceabout Sportcar, 1961	9
Y-7 1912 Rolls-Royce, 1967	40
Y-8 1926 Morris Cowley "Bullnose", 1955	60
Y-8 1914 Sunbeam Motorcycle with Sidecar, 1962	95
Y-8 1914 Stutz Roadster, 1968 . .	30
Y-8 1945 MGTC Sports Car, 1978	9
Y-9 1924 Fowler "Big Lion" Showman Engine, 1955	150
Y-9 1912 Simplex, 1967	45
Y-10 1908 Grand Prix Mercedes Racing Car, 1957	25

	MIB
Y-10 1928 Mercedes-Benz, 36/220, 1963	45
Y-10 1906 Rolls-Royce Silver Cloud, 1968	15
Y-11 1920 Aveling & Porter Steam Roller, 1957	85
Y-11 1912 Packard Landaulet, 1963	35
Y-11 1938 Lagonda Drophead Coupe, 1972	16
Y-12 1899 Horse-Bus (London), 1957	90
Y-12 1909 Thomas Flyabout, 1967	35

	MIB
Y-16 1928 Mercedes SS, 1971 . . .	16
Y-17 1938 Hispano Suiza, 1972 .	16
Y-18 1937 Cord 812, 1979	18
Y-19 1935 Auburn 851, 1980	20
Y-20 1938 Mercedes 540K, 1981 .	16
Y-21 1929 Woody Wagon, 1981 .	9
Y-22 Model A Van	8

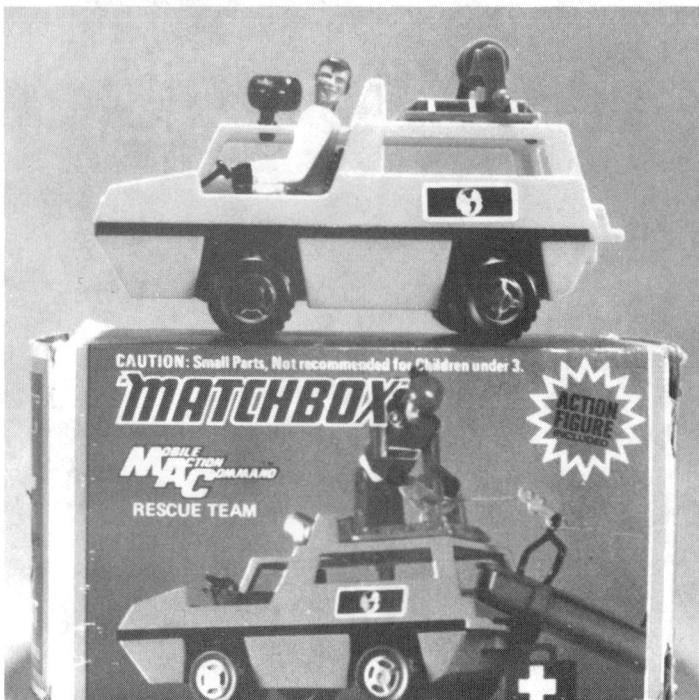

Matchbox Mobile Action Command, value in C6, C8, C10: $5, $10, $20.
Photo by Gary Linden

Matchbox Y-12 1912 Model T Ford.
Courtesy Gary Linden

	MIB
Y-12 1912 Model "T" Ford, 1979	14
Y-13 1911 Daimler, 1965	50
Y-13 1918 Crossley Truck, 1972 .	20
Y-14 1911 Maxwell Roadster, 1965	22

Matchbox Y-14, 1931 Stutz Bearcat.
Courtesy Gary Linden

	MIB
Y-14 1931 Stutz Bearcat, 1972 . . .	13
Y-15 1907 Rolls-Royce "Silver Ghost", 1960	40
Y-15 1930 Packard Victoria, 1969	14
Y-16 1904 Spyker Veteran Automobile, 1961	40

CONDITION OF A TOY
AND ITS RELATION TO PRICE

CONDITION CODE:

C6 - Good, Evident overall wear, well-played with, but acceptable to many collectors

C8 - Very Good Minor wear overall, very clean

C10 - Mint (like new)

NOTE: Mint in Box commands a high price. Condition below C6 brings considerably lower prices.

MATTEL'S HOT WHEELS

1968-1979

by Ron Smith

Whoda thunkit. But these little under-a-buck gems are the fastest-selling toys at flea markets and toy shows. It all started in 1968 when the Mattel company issued the original 16 metallic colored toy cars. Today most toy discount stores will have at least a four-foot section of space devoted to this fast-turnover line of toy vehicles. Listed are issues from 1968 to 1979 through the red line era. These are the most sought after by toy collectors especially if they are still in their original blister package (C-10). Most are found, however, in used condition (C-6).

Note: Asterisk denotes re-release with some probable change in color.

	C6	C8	C10
HW 1, A-OK	3	6	10
HW 2, Alive SS*	10	20	45
HW 3, Ambulance	8	15	30
HW 4, American Victory*	4	6	15
HW 5, American Hauler	4	6	15
HW 6, American Tipper	4	6	15
HW 7, AMX/2	10	20	35
HW 8, Army Funny Car	4	6	15
HW 9, Auburn 852	2	5	10
HW 10, AW Shoot	3	8	15
HW 11, Backwoods Bomb*	8	15	30
HW 12, Baja Breaker	2	5	10
HW 13, Baja Bruiser	4	10	25
HW 14, Beatnik Bandit	2	6	12
HW 15, Boss Hoss*	8	15	30
HW 16, Brabham Repco F1	2	4	10
HW 17, Breakaway Bucket	4	12	28
HW 18, Bubble Gunner	2	4	8

	C6	C8	C10
HW 19, Bugeye	3	10	24
HW 20, Buzz Off	3	8	20
HW 21, Bye Focal	8	14	45
HW 22, Bywayman	2	5	10
HW 23, Carabo	10	15	30
HW 24, California Crusin	3	6	10
HW 25, Captain America*	3	6	10
HW 26, Cement Mixer	4	8	15
HW 27, Chapparel 2G	2	3	5
HW 28, Chevy Monza 2+2	5	12	25
HW 29, Chevy 1957	3	5	10
HW 30, Chiefs Special 442	25	40	65
HW 31, Classic Cord	45	65	95
HW 32, Classic Nomad	8	12	25
HW 33, Classic 31 Woody	6	10	20
HW 34, Classic 32 Ford Vicky	6	10	20
HW 35, Classic 57 Bird	6	10	20
HW 36, Classic 36 Ford Coupe	6	12	25
HW 37, Cockney Cab	8	15	30
HW 38, Continental MKIII	8	12	20
HW 39, Cool One*	8	15	30
HW 40, Corvette Stingray	10	18	30
HW 41, Custom AMX	10	20	35
HW 42, Custom Barracuda	15	40	65
HW 43, Custom Camero	15	40	65
HW 44, Custom Charger	20	45	65
HW 45, Custom Corvette	10	20	35
HW 46, Custom Couger	10	20	30
HW 47, Custom Eldorado	10	20	40
HW 48, Custom Firebird	10	20	40
HW 49, Custom Fleetside	12	18	30
HW 50, Custom Mustang	10	20	50
HW 51, Custom T-Bird	10	20	50
HW 52, Custom Volkswagen	8	15	25
HW 53, Deora	12	25	45

L to R: HW34, HW31, HW33
Photo by Ron Smith

L to R: HW36, HW32, HW35
Photo by Ron Smith

L to R: HW41, HW42, HW46
Photo by Ron Smith

L to R: HW51, HW44, HW38
Photo by Ron Smith

L to R: HW48, HW50, HW45
Photo by Ron Smith

	C6	C8	C10		C6	C8	C10
HW 54, Doozie '31	2	4	8	HW 62, Evil Weevil	8	20	35
HW 55, Double Header	12	30	55	HW 63, Exploder	8	15	30
HW 56, Double Vision	12	25	50	HW 64, Ferrari 312P ***	4	10	15
HW 57, Dumpin' A	2	4	8	HW 65, Ferrari 512S	8	20	35
HW 58, Dumptruck	10	20	45	HW 66, Firechief Cruiser	4	10	20
HW 59, Dune Daddy	8	15	40	HW 67, Fire Chaser	2	4	8
HW 60, Elray Special	8	15	40	HW 68, Fire Eater	2	4	8
HW 61, Emergency Squad	4	8	15	HW 69, Fire Engine	8	20	45

L to R: HW49, HW176, HW53
Photo by Ron Smith

	C6	C8	C10		C6	C8	C10
HW 70, Flat Out 442	2	3	6	HW 94, Inferno	6	15	30
HW 71, Ford J Car	2	3	9	HW 95, Inside Story	2	3	5
HW 72, Ford MK IV	2	4	8	HW 96, Jack Rabbit Special	2	6	13
HW 73, Formula P.A.C.K.*	2	6	16	HW 97, Jaguar XJS	2	4	8
HW 74, Formula 5000	2	3	10	HW 98, Jet Threat	4	10	20
HW 75, Fuel Tanker	25	40	55	HW 99, Jet Threat II	4	10	20
HW 76, Funny Money**	20	35	50	HW 100, King Kuda*	6	12	25
HW 77, GMC Motor Home	2	4	8	HW 101, Khaki Kooler	6	10	20
HW 78, Grasshopper*	8	20	40	HW 102, Large Charge*	5	10	18
HW 79, Greased Gremlin	2	6	10	HW 103, Letter Getter	2	5	10
HW 80, Gremlin Grinder	6	12	20	HW 104, Lickety Six	3	6	12
HW 81, Gun Bucket	2	6	12	HW 105, Light My Firebird	8	15	22
HW 82, Gun Slinger	2	6	15	HW 106, Lola GT 70	2	4	7
HW 83, Hairy Hauler	4	10	20	HW 107, Lotus Turbine	2	3	9
HW 84, Hare Splitter	2	4	8	HW 108, Lowdown*	5	12	25
HW 85, Heavy Chevy***	6	15	30	HW 109, Mantis	3	6	11
HW 86, Hi-Tail Hauler '56	2	5	10	HW 110, Maserati Mistral	4	10	22
HW 87, Hiway Patrol	3	8	15	HW 111, Maxi Taxi 442	15	22	35
HW 88, Hiway Robber	12	25	50	HW 112, MC Laren M VI A	2	3	6
HW 89, Hot Bird	2	5	10	HW 113, Mercedes Benz C 111	5	10	18
HW 90, Hot Heap	3	8	15	HW 114, Mercedes Benz 280 SL	4	9	17
HW 91, Human Torch	2	5	10	HW 115, Mighty Maverick XXX	10	20	30
HW 92, Ice T**	4	12	25	HW 116, Mod Quad	3	6	10
HW 93, Indy Eagle	2	5	10	HW 117, Mongoose Funny Car	15	20	30

L to R: HW138, HW133, HW66
Photo by Ron Smith

L to R: HW171, HW27, HW93
Photo by Ron Smith

L to R: HW64, HW112, HW141
Photo by Ron Smith

L to R: HW90, HW136, HW159B
Photo by Ron Smith

	C6	C8	C10		C6	C8	C10
HW 118, Mongoose Dragster ...	15	25	35	HW 131, Open Fire	40	60	90
HW 119, Monte Carlo Stocker*.	8	12	20	HW 132, P-911*	3	8	15
HW 120, Moto Cross	9	15	25	HW 133, Paddy Wagon*	3	8	15
HW 121, Moto Cross Van......	8	12	20	HW 134, Packin Pacer	2	4	8
HW 122, Moving Van	9	15	25	HW 135, Paramedic...........	3	8	15
HW 123, Mustang Stocker****..	20	30	40	HW 136, Peepin Bomb........	2	6	12
HW 124, Mutt Mobile	10	18	26	HW 137, Poisen Pinto	3	8	15
HW 125, Neet Streeter.........	3	6	12	HW 138, Police Cruiser	5	12	25
HW 126, Nitty Gritty Kitty.....	12	20	30	HW 139, Police Cruiser 442	30	40	55
HW 127, Noodle Head.........	9	15	30	HW 140, Pitcrew Car	30	45	65
HW 128, Odd Job	20	30	50	HW 141, Porsche 917	2	6	12
HW 129, Odd Rod*	8	12	25	HW 142, Power Pad...........	4	15	30
HW 130, Olds 442.............	50	75	100 +	HW 143, Prowler*	4	12	25

305

L   to   R: HW198,   HW184,   HW198
Photo by Ron Smith

L to R: HW-83, HW215, HW20
Photo by Ron Smith

L to R: HW19, HW136, HW109
Photo by Ron Smith

L to R: HW170, HW173, HW203
Photo by Ron Smith

L to R: HW144, HW14, HW160
Photo by Ron Smith

L to R: HW175, HW163, HW76
Photo by Ron Smith

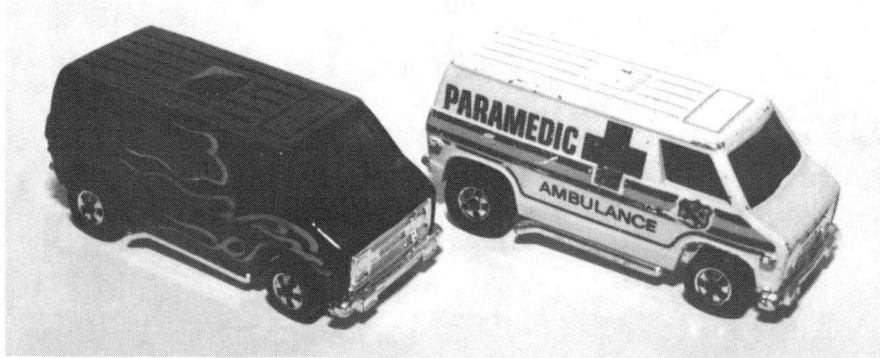

L to R: HW195, HW135
Photo by Ron Smith

	C6	C8	C10		C6	C8	C10
HW 144, Python	2	3	6	HW 154, Red Baron*	4	8	15
HW 145, Race Bait 308	2	3	5	HW 155, Road King Truck	50	70	90
HW 146, Racer Rig	30	45	65	HW 156, Rock Buster	4	8	16
HW 147, Ramblin' Wrecker	5	10	20	HW 157, Rocket Bye Baby	5	10	20
HW 148, Ranger Rig	6	12	25	HW 158, Rodger Dodger	6	12	25
HW 149, Rash 1	8	20	40	HW 159, Royal Flash	2	3	6
HW 150, Rear Engine Mongoose (drag)	50	70	90	HW 159B, Rolls Royce Silver Shadow	6	14	30
HW 151, Rear Engine Mongoose (funny)	50	70	90	HW 160, Sand Crab	3	6	10
HW 152, Rear Engine Snake (drag)	50	70	90	HW 161, Sand Drifter	6	12	22
				HW 162, Sand Witch	8	20	40
HW 153, Rear Engine Snake (funny)	50	70	90	HW 163, S' Cool Bus	40	60	85
				HW 164, S' Cooper	30	40	55

307

L to R: HW216, HW23, HW154
Photo by Ron Smith

L to R: HW7, HW115, HW114
Photo by Ron Smith

	C6	C8	C10
HW 165, Science Friction......	2	3	5
HW 166, Sea Sider............	20	30	45
HW 167, Second Wind	6	12	25
HW 168, Show Hoss II*.......	6	12	20
HW 169, Show Off...........	8	20	40
HW 170, Short Order.........	10	20	40
HW 171, Shelby Turbine.......	5	10	20
HW 172, Six Shooter.........	8	15	30
HW 173, Silhouette...........	2	4	8
HW 174, Side Kick...........	5	10	20
HW 175, Sir Rodney Roadster..	6	12	25
HW 176, Sky Show Fleetside...	40	60	100 +
HW 177, Snake..............	40	60	100 +
HW 178, Snake Dragster.......	30	40	50
HW 179, Snorkel.............	30	40	50
HW 180, Space Van..........	6	12	25
HW 181, Spacer Racer........	2	4	7
HW 182, Special Deliveries.....	10	20	30
HW 183, Spider-Man*........	6	10	15
HW 184, Splittin Image........	3	6	10
HW 185, Spoiler Sport........	2	4	8
HW 186, Staff Car 442........	75 +	90 +	100 +
HW 187, Stagefright...........	3	6	9
HW 188, Steamroller..........	8	18	27
HW 189, Street Eater.........	5	10	20

	C6	C8	C10
HW 190, Street Rodder........	2	4	8
HW 191, Street Snorter........	12	25	50
HW 192, Strip Teaser..........	8	15	30
HW 193, Sugar Caddy.........	6	12	25
HW 194, Super-fine Turbine....	75 +	90 +	100 +
HW 195, Super Van*..........	10	20	30
HW 196, S.W.A.T. Van........	8	15	30
HW 197, Sweet 16...........	9	18	35
HW 198, Swinging, Wing*.....	3	7	14
HW 199, T-4-2..............	8	15	30
HW 200, T-Bird 57...........	2	3	6
HW 201, T-Totaller...........	4	8	15
HW 202, Team Hauler.........	15	30	60
HW 203, The Demon..........	4	8	15
HW 204, The Hood...........	5	10	20
HW 205, The Incredible Hulk*.	4	8	10
HW 206, The Thing...........	4	8	15
HW 207, Thor...............	4	8	15
HW 208, TNT Bird...........	5	10	20
HW 209, Top Eliminator*......	9	18	35
HW 210, Torero..............	4	8	15
HW 211, Torino Stocker*......	7	15	25
HW 212, Tough Customer.....	2	5	10
HW 213, Tow Truck...........	6	12	25
HW 214, Tri Baby............	5	10	20
HW 215, Turbo Fire...........	2	3	6

L to R: HW85, HW15, HW100
Photo by Ron Smith

L to R: HW208, HW105, HW126
Photo by Ron Smith

	C6	C8	C10		C6	C8	C10
HW 216, Twin Mill	2	4	8	HW 223, Warpath	4	8	15
HW 217, Twin Mill II	2	4	8	HW 224, Waste Wagon	10	20	40
HW 218, Up Front 924	2	3	6	HW 225, What 4	10	20	40
HW 219, Volkswagen	8	15	30	HW 226, Whipped Creamer	5	10	20
HW 220, VW Beach Bomb	8	15	30	HW 227, Winnipeg	12	25	50
HW 221, Vega Bomb	8	15	30	HW 228, Z Whiz	6	21	25
HW 222, Vetty Funny	6	8	12				

Assorted tin & plastic pins valued at $1 ea.

309

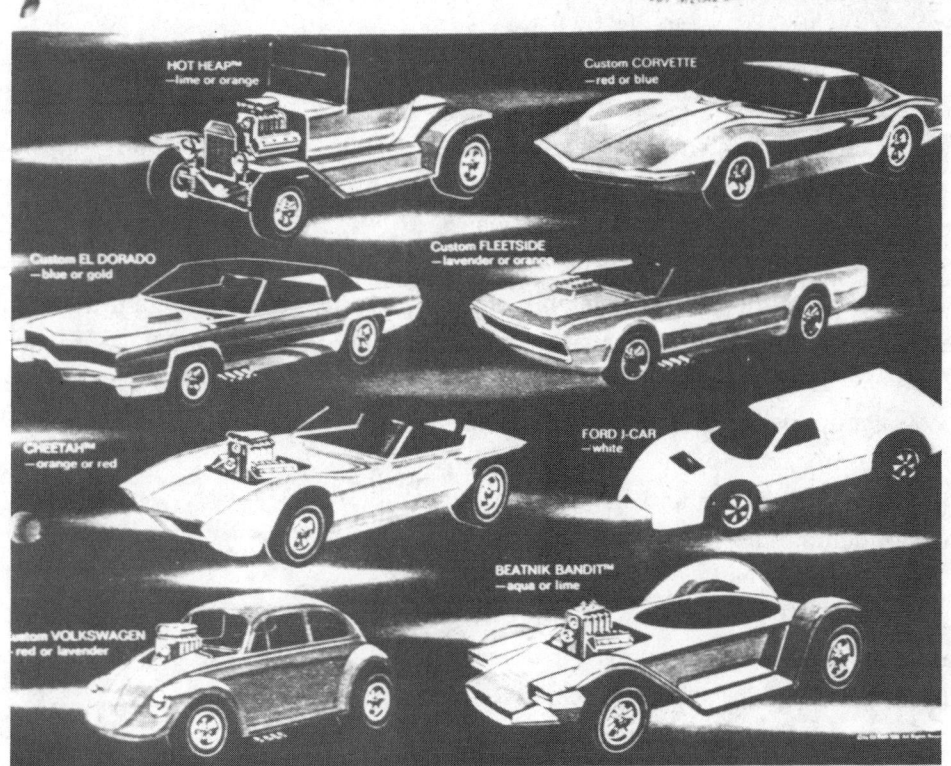

Punched-hole blister card.
5¾" x 6".

NEW! HOT WHEELS ASSORTMENT
NO. 1 #A6221

12 each of 8 metal cars, shown at the
left, on set-up wire rack display with
header card. 96 total cars plus laminated
Collector's Catalog.
Std. Pack: 1 ea. (1 carton)   Wt:14Lbs.

NEW! HOT WHEELS BASIC
ASSORTMENT NO. 1 #A6231

Same contents as #A6221, without wire
rack and Collector's Catalog.
Std. Pack: 1 ea. (1 carton)   Wt: 7 Lbs.

NEW! HOT WHEELS ASSORTMENT
NO. 2 #A6222

12 each of 8 metal cars, shown at the
right, on set-up wire rack display with
header card. 96 total cars.
Std. Pack: 1 ea. (1 carton)   Wt:12Lbs.

NEW! HOT WHEELS BASIC
ASSORTMENT NO. 2 #A6232

Same contents as #A6222, without wire
rack
Std. Pack: 1 ea. (1 carton)   Wt: 7 Lbs.

A page from Mattel's initial 1968 "Hot Wheels" catalog.

310

MECCANO CARS

by Gates Willard

The Meccano Company closed its doors at the Liverpool, England factory on November 30, 1979. It was a sad ending to the great company founded by Frank Hornby early in the 20th century. His construction sets had become very popular by the time the first specialized Meccano car constructor appeared in time for Christmas, 1932. The largest of the three cars to be made, it was later dubbed the No. 2 Motor Car Constructor Outfit. In 1933, the smaller No. 1 outfit became available at a much lower price. At about the same time, an accessory electric lighting set was made available for the No. 2 car only. The two-seater sports car (sometimes called the non-constructional car) probably appeared in 1934. It is in scale with the No. 1 constructor and has the same wheels, but it is nondemountable and was sold fully assembled. The two constructional cars were marketed in the USA, but the 2-seater sports car was imported in very small numbers, if at all. In any case, it is rare in the USA and scarce in England. Meccano cars went out of production forever in 1940. A wooden garage was made, but few were sold. A beautiful miniature Kaye Oil car made of copper and brass is a much-sought-after accessory.

The French Meccano Factory also manufactured both car constructor sets, and these are identified by decals stating that they were made in France. Earlier models appear to be the same as their English counterparts, but the tires of the French No. 1 car can be marked Hutchinson instead of Dunlop. Later French No. 1 cars continued to have demountable tires on stamped steel wheels while the English No. 1 cars changed to solid rubber wheels with metal discs on the outside only. The last French No. 1 cars retained the original chassis and wheels, but all of the sheet metal and radiator were revised to create a more modern appearance.

Recognizing that a complete construction set in a large box could be a bit formidable for a youngster whose manual dexterity, reading ability, and/or availability of funds might be limited, Meccano produced some lower-priced, factory-assembled constructional cars in both sizes. The box was big enough only for one assembled car with no extra alternative pieces. Individually boxed assembled cars are identical to those sold in the larger sets. They were not very popular, and individually boxed constructor cars are rare today.

How To Identify Approximately When an English Meccano Car Was Made:

(Note that over the years, parts can get substituted and moved around)

English No. 1 Meccano Car Constructor
EARLY (1933-34)

Demountable Rubber tires on stamped steel wheels; yellow opaque headlight lenses, large oval decal (hood).

LATER (1934-40)

Solid Rubber Wheels with metal discs; translucent gray headlight lenses, small round decal (hood).

COLOR COMBINATIONS

Fenders: Yellow
Body: Green
Fenders: Cream
Body: Blue
Fenders: Red
Body: Cream
Fenders: Red
Body: Black
Fenders: Blue
Body: Red

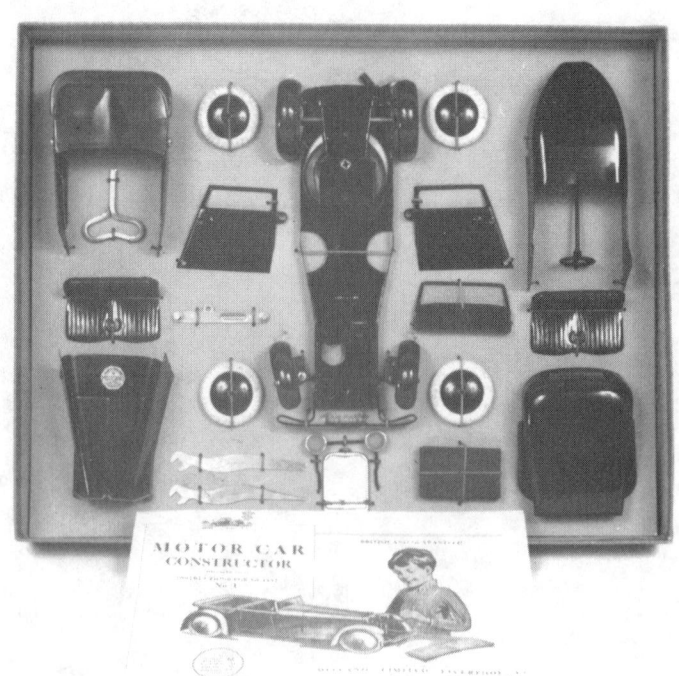

No. 1 car Constructor as purchased in the store.
Photo by E.W. Willard
Courtesy Gates Willard

311

Five ways of assembling the No. 1 Car, in front of original box.
Photo by E.W. Willard
Courtesy Gates Willard

Factory-assembled No. 1 car with original box.
Courtesy Gates Willard
Photo by E.W. Willard

Left: Early (1933) No. 1 car.
Right: Later (1933-40) No. 1 car
Courtesy Gates Willard
Photo by E.W. Willard

Left: Late French No. 1 car. Right: Late English No. 1 car
Courtesy Gates Willard
Photo by E.W. Willard

Left: Late French No. 1 car, Right: Late English No. 1 car.
Courtesy Gates Willard
Photo by E.W. Willard

English No. 2 Meccano Car Constructor

EARLY (1932-33)

Soft alloy wheels, Dunlop tires, Rubber spare tire, No holes in seat or dashboard.

Tall handbrake lever. Opaque yellow headlight lenses split pin steering mechanism assembly, large oval decal (rear body sections).

Smaller box

Colors: All had cream fenders. Body was painted red, blue, or green.

LATER (1933-1940)

Hard die-cast wheels (very subject to metal fatigue) Dunlop (more commonly) or Firestone tires. Soft alloy cast metal tire cover. Holes in seat and dashboard for figure and switch for lighting set.

Short handbrake lever. Gray translucent headlight lenses, Simplified steering assembly, round decal (rear body sections).

Larger box.

Colors:

Fenders: yellow   Body: green
Fenders: cream   Body: blue
Fenders: red   Body: cream
Fenders: red   Body: black
Fenders: blue   Body: red

No. 2 Car assembled and placed on a store display stand. Original box in background.
Courtesy Gates Willard
Photo by E.W. Willard

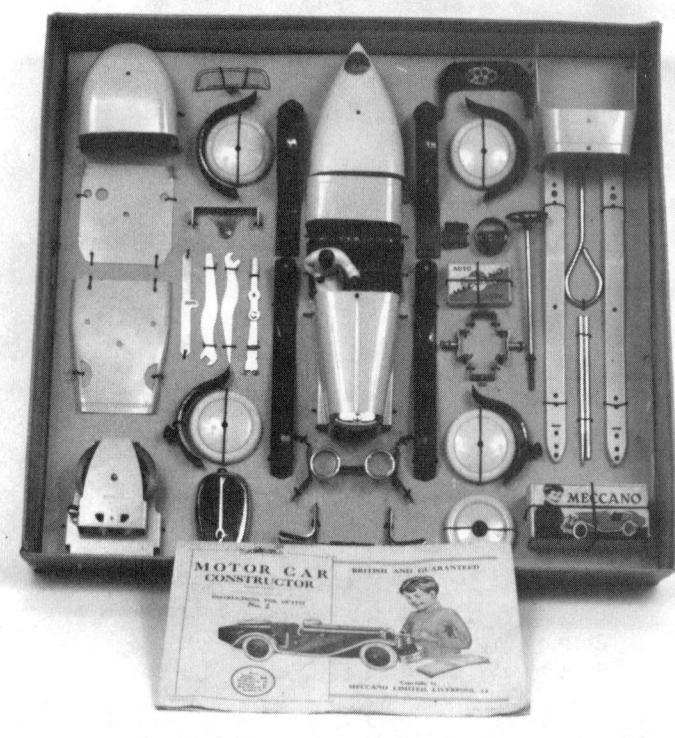

No. 2 Car Constructor shown as purchased at the store.
Courtesy Gates Willard
Photo by E.W. Willard

Left: Early (1932) No. 2 Constructor Car.
Right: Late (1933-40) No. 2 Constructor Car.
Courtesy Gates Willard
Photo by E.W. Willard

Left: Miniature K (oil can) can be compared with a real one. Center: Electric Lighting Set with instructions. No. 2 car is present to give concept of scale.
Courtesy Gates Willard
Photo by E.W. Willard

313

Tires for No. 2 car, left Firestone, right Dunlop (more common)
Courtesy Gates Willard
Photo by E.W. Willard

Size Comparison of No. 1 and No. 2 Constructor Cars.
Courtesy Gates Willard
Photo by E.W. Willard

Left: No. 1 Constructor Car. Right: 2-seater Sports Car (non-constructional).
Courtesy Gates Willard
Photo by E.W. Willard

	C6	C8	C10
Meccano No. 1 open Touring Car	800	1400	2100

Two-Seater Sports Car

EARLY

Opaque yellow headlight lenses.

Colors: Same as No. 1 and No. 2 constructor cars (two-tone) except green and yellow combination was never used.

Picture on box lid shows a red car with cream fenders, but the reverse of this combination was actually made. All had hand painted black running boards.

LATE

Translucent gray headlamp lenses.

Colors: The last cars were painted single colors: all blue with slightly darker blue wheel discs and all red with maroon wheel discs. Hand painting of running boards black was phased out. Cost savings was passed on to the buyer. Prices were slightly reduced.

No picture label on box lid.

Left: Early two-seater Sports Car with box. Right: Later two-seater Sports Car with box.
Courtesy Gates Willard   Photo by E.W. Willard

September, 1935, Meccano Magazine
Courtesy Gates Willard

METAL CAST PRODUCTS COMPANY

by Fred Maxwell

Metal Cast Products, an outgrowth in 1929 of a venerable toy soldier company, S. Sachs, made hand-operated slushcasting molds for small businesses and hobbyists, what some have called the homecasting industry. Since identical molds were sold to many franchises we cannot identify the actual makers unless they engraved their names on their products. One who did was Fred Green Toys, whose name is found prominently on their toys.

Metal Cast offered full support services to its franchisees, including marketing, printing, publishing and parts.

A variety of wheels may be found on its vehicles: metal disk wheels, metal spoke wheels, wood wheels w/rubber tires, and white or black rubber wheels.

We see many homecast lead soldiers and novelties, but the production of toy vehicles has not left much of a mark. Perhaps it was the Great Depression, perhaps it was the lack of identity; demand today seems weak. However, collectors of the unusual should find many collectibles; most of those I have seen were well designed and professionally finished.

Metal Cast No. 61

Metal Cast Products, Top row: No. 01-02, Middle row: No. 01-03, Bottom row: No. 40

Photo by Perry Eichor

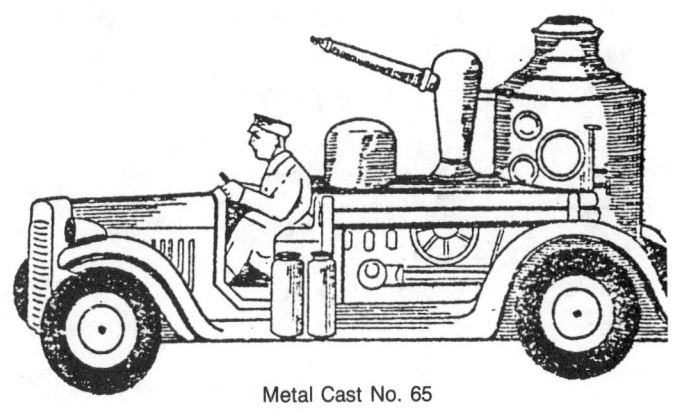

Metal Cast No. 65

	C6	C8	C10
Metal Cast Van Truck, #01-02, 6''. COE cab, semi-trailer moving van. Trailer also found in a ''FRED GREEN'' version.....	No Price Found		
Metal Cast Tank Truck, #01-03, 6''. Same COE cab, semi-fuel tanker. My version is 5¾'', ''FRED GREEN TOYS'' ''Made in USA''....................	4	6	8
Metal Cast Open Rack Truck, #01-04, 6''. COE cab, stake semi-trailer......................	8	12	16
Metal Cast War Tank, #08, 4''. Early heavy Sherman tank......	33	49	66
Metal Cast Cadillac Sedan, #40, 5¼''. 2 door	No Price Found		
Metal Cast Packard Convertible, #41, 5¼''. 2 door, top down.	10	15	20

	C6	C8	C10
Metal Cast Dump Truck, #42, 5¼''. COE chassis, dump body mechanism..................	No Price Found		
Metal Cast Streamline Sedan, #60, 4''. De Soto ? Airflow, 8 open windows, spoke wheels, rubber tires	10	15	20

Metal Cast Products, Top row: Greyhound Bus, No. 62, Middle row: No. 40 Limousine, No. 60, Bottom row: No. 64

Photo by Perry Eichor

	C6	C8	C10
Metal Cast Fire Engine, #61, 4½''. Hook and ladder truck, crew of 2	6	10	14
Metal Cast Racer, #62, 4½''. Bluebird type record car, driver	No Price Found		
Metal Cast Coupe, #63. Convertible, 2 open windows, side-mounts, trunk	No Price Found		
Metal Cast Truck, #64, 4¼'', Dodge? stake-body, 1920s 2 OW	No Price Found		
Metal Cast Fire Engine, #65, 4''. Steam pumper w/watercannon, driver	No Price Found		
Metal Cast Fire Engine, no #, 3⅞''. Similar to #65 without water-cannon	6	10	14

METAL MASTERS

(listing by Dave Leopard)

MM01 Roadster, c.1938, 7'' long	20	30	40
MM02 Bus, c.1938, 7¼'' long	20	30	40
MM03 Pick-up truck, c.1938, 7'' long	20	30	40
MM04 Firetruck version of pick-up, c.1938, 7'' long	30	40	50
MM05 Tow Truck version of pick-up, c.1938, 7'' long	30	40	50
MM06 Jeep, c.1947, 5½'' long	20	25	30
MM07 Station Wagon, c.1940, 8½'' long	40	50	65
MM08 Station Wagon, c.1940, 8½'' long, wind-up motor	45	55	70
MM09 Station Wagon, c.1940, 8½'' long, ambulance version	45	55	70
MM10 Tow Truck, c.1940, 10'' long, ''ABC Towing Service''	40	50	65
MM11 Tow Truck, c.1940, 10'' long, wind-up motor	45	55	70
MM12 Firetruck, c.1940, 10'' long, removable ladders	50	60	75
MM13 Firetruck, c.1940, 10'' long, ladders, wind-up motors	50	65	80
MM14 Tractor w/driver, 5'' long	55	82	110

METALCRAFT

Metalcraft, of St. Louis, Missouri, began producing its pressed steel trucks in 1928. About a million were sold, most as "advertising toys". In 1937, defeated by the Depression, Metalcraft shuttered.

	C6	C8	C10
Metalcraft BFG Wrecker........	300	450	600
Metalcraft "Bordens Milk" truck	225	338	450

Metalcraft "Borden's Milk" truck.
Photo by Calvin L. Chaussee

	C6	C8	C10
Metalcraft "Bunte Candies" 12" truck	175	262	350
Metalcraft "Buster Brown Shoes"	300	450	600
Metalcraft Coca Cola Truck, 11" long, pressed steel, rubber tires, circa late 20s-early 30s, 10 bottles in rack, "Every Bottle Sterilized"	500	800	1100
Metalcraft Coca Cola Truck, 10 bottles, 10½" long, 1930s	350	525	700
Metalcraft Coca Cola Truck, 12" long, 10 bottles, late 1930s, long nose, stamped metal	450	675	900
Metalcraft Coca Cola Truck, c.1928, with bottles in racks	500	800	1100
Metalcraft CW Coffee Dump Truck, 10¾" long	350	525	700
Metalcraft CW Coffee wrecker ..	300	450	600
Metalcraft Delivery Truck Van, 11" long, steel	200	300	400
Metalcraft Dump Truck, 24" long, electric headlights	200	300	400

Metalcraft Coca-Cola Truck, 11" long.
Courtesy Wilkinson Collection, Detroit Antique Toy Museum

Metalcraft Coca-Cola Truck, late 1930s, 12'' long.
Courtesy Richard L. MacNary

Metalcraft CW Coffee Dump Truck.
Photo by Orville C. Britton

	C6	C8	C10
Metalcraft ''Kroger Food Express'', 11'' long..................	300	450	600
Metalcraft ''Krug Bakery'' truck.	450	675	935
Metalcraft ''Machinery Hauling''	500	800	1200
Metalcraft ''Meadow Gold Butter'' truck 13'' long, battery lights	500	800	1200
Metalcraft ''Plee-zing Quality Products'' Delivery Van 11'' long, c.1928	300	450	600
Metalcraft ''Sand-Gravel'' dump	175	263	350
Metalcraft ''Shell Motor Oil'' truck	370	555	740
Metalcraft ''St. Louis'' truck, 11'' long, c.1930	250	375	500
Metalcraft Steam Shovel........	115	172	230
Metalcraft ''Sunshine Biscuits'' truck	275	363	550
Metalcraft ''Towing & Repairs''.	250	375	500
Metalcraft ''Werks Tag Soap'' truck	225	338	450

Metalcraft, L to R: Coca-Cola truck, ''Heinz'' truck.
Courtesy Phillips NY

	C6	C8	C10
Metalcraft Esso Stake Truck with barrels (very rare)	No Price Found		
Metalcraft ''Goodrich Silvertone Tires'' wrecker, with 3 spare tires	250	375	500
Metalcraft ''Heinz'' truck, c.1932 ''Baked Beans, Bottled Vinegar'', ''Rice Flakes'', 12'' long.......................	350	525	700

	C6	C8	C10
Metalcraft ''Weston's English Biscuits'' truck	250	375	500
Metalcraft ''White King Delivery'' truck 12'' long	425	638	850

Metalcraft "Plee-Zing Quality Products" Delivery Van, 11" long, c.1928.
Photo by Bob Smith

Metalcraft "Machinery Hauling"
Photo by Calvin L. Chaussee

Heavy Gauge Steel
Toy Trucks—2 Styles

Metalcraft, L to R: "Shell Motor Oil" and "Goodrich Silvertone Tires"
trucks as shown in the October 1932 Butler Bros. catalog.

Metalcraft Steam Shovel.
Photo by Calvin L. Chaussee

CONDITION OF A TOY
AND ITS RELATION TO PRICE

CONDITION CODE:

C6 - Good, Evident overall wear, well-played with, but acceptable to many collectors

C8 - Very Good Minor wear overall, very clean

C10 - Mint (like new)

NOTE: *Mint in Box commands a high price. Condition below C6 brings considerably lower prices.*

METALGRAF COMPANY

Milan, Italy - Est. 1910-1939
by Bob Smith

Metalgraf Company manufactured toys from 1920 until 1939. They are still in business today, but have not produced toys for many years. A Metalgraf car is seldom found offered for sale. They are considered rare and are especially hard to find in the U.S.

	C6	C8	C10
Metalgraf Touring Car, Gray/black litho, c/w motor, steering, 10" long, c.1922	1150	1700	2500

METTOY

	C6	C8	C10
Mettoy Motorcycle, c.1940	425	638	850
Mettoy Racer, "7"	900	1600	2100
Mettoy Rolls Royce, 14" long	500	800	1200
Mettoy Sedan, 14" long, c.1930	300	450	600
Mettoy Steam Roller, clockwork	100	150	200

Metalgraf Touring Car, 10" long, c.1922.
Photo by Bob Smith

MIDGETOY

Midgetoy was created in 1946 by brothers Alvin and Earl Herdklotz, who from 1943, as A&E Tool and Gauge Co. had produced precision tooling for defense. Their intention with Midgetoy was to produce low cost diecast vehicles that were both sturdy and precisely detailed. Midgetoys run from 2 to 9 inches in length and were an immediate hit with five and tens, and later, discount chains such as Walmart. There were about 200 different models and one hundred full-time employees. Midgetoy stopped producing its toys about 1984. Prices seem to run from about $5 to $15 in mint unboxed condition.

Some Military Vehicles by Midgetoy, Rockford, IL. Tootsietoy soldier added for scale is 1½" high.
L to R - Back Row: Turreted Assault Gun, Truck towing Fieldpiece, Halftrack towing trailer, Van, Sherman Tank, Tracked Assault Gun.
Front row: Firetruck, Tank-Truck, tiny Jeep, Jeep, Staff Car, Ambulance, Modern Jeep.
Note: All but van & ambulance (same casting) imprinted with manufacturer's name.
Photo by Ed Poole

MILITARY VEHICLES
(IDs and Miscellaneous)

1/24 ID Models sell for $30 to $100 in mint, unboxed
condition. 1/36 ID Models also sell for the same price.

1/24th scale metal identification models WWII
(Manoil 3¼" GI for scale)
Back row - L to R: Amphibian Tractor, 105mm
S.P. (illegible) M7", Half-trak car. M2.
Front row: Jeep (some of these movable wheel
versions are also marked "Dale"), "4X4 Ton
Truck-Jeep" (fixed wheel version)", "Cletrac"
(bulldozer).
Photo by Ed Poole

1/36 Scale Metal Identification models - WWII
British (Britains 54mm 'Tommy' for scale). L to
R - Back Row: "Infantry Tank MKIV Comet NY"
(Churchill Tank), "Humber MKII Comet NY" (ar-
moured car), "Cruiser MKV" (Covenanter Tank),
"UK Cruiser MKVI Crusader Comet NY".
"Universal Carrier" (Bren Gun)
Front row: "Universal Carrier" (Bren Gun Car-
rier), "MKIII UK Cruiser Comet NY" (Valentine
Tank), "UK Infantry Tank MKIIA Comet NY"
(Matilda II Tank), "MKI Daimler Comet NY" (ar-
moured car), "Carden Lloyd Carrier"
Photo by Ed Poole

1/36 Scale Metal Identification models (cont'd) - WWII Japanese (Bri-
tains Ltd. 54mm Soldier added for scale)
Decals not original.
L to R - Back row: "Japanese Medium Tank - Cometal", "Japanese
Cruiser Tank - Cometal", "Japanese Heavy Medium Tank -
Cometal".
Front row: "Japanese Amphibian Tank", "Japanese 1938 Tankette",
"Japanese L.M. Tank M2595 Cometl", "Japan. Tankette M2592 -
1932 Cometl".
Photo by Ed Poole

1/36 Scale Metal Identification Models (cont'd) WWII German (Jones
54mm Soldier included for scale)
L to R - Back row: "Ger. Light Tank P.Z.K.W.1 Maybach 1936", "Ger
Light Tank (P) Z.K.1 Command Tank", "Ger. Light Tank PZ:KW:2",
"Ger. Light Med. Tank PZ.KW.3 Type 'C'."
Photo by Ed Poole

1/36 Scale Metal Identification Model (cont'd) WWII German (Jones 54mm soldier included for scale).
L to R - Back row: "Ger. Light med. tank C.K.D.V.8.H.".
Front row: "German Light Amphibian Tank C.K.D.F.4.H.E.", "Ger. Light Arm. car Horch 1936 SD:K 223", "Ger. Heavy 8 wheeled armor, car".
Photo by Ed Poole

1/36 Scale Metal Identification Models (cont'd) WWII U.S. (Britains Ltd. GI included for scale) L to R - Back row: "Heavy Tank M-6", "Med. Tank, M4-2" (Turret Revolves), "Med. Tank M-4", "Med. Tank M-3".
Front row: "Light Tank M-3", "Light Tank M-3" (turret revolves), "3" Gun Car. M-5", "105 MM Howitzer Motor T32 My M7 Priest M-7".
Photo by Ed Poole

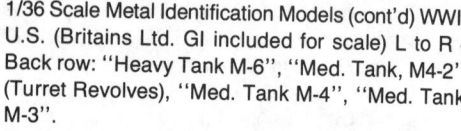

1/36 Scale Metal Identification Models - WWII U.S. (cont'd) (Britains Ltd. GI included for scale) L to R - Back row: "Half TRK Car M2", "Half TRK pers. car - M3", "75 MM Gun Car. M-3 Half Track Car M2" (decal not original but AAF Acceptance tag dated "Jul 3 1946" is), "Scout Car M-3 A-1".
Front row: "Armoured Car T-17", "Duck" (1/48th scale), "37MM Gun Car. M6".
Photo by Ed Poole

Movable Wheel Versions of 1/36 Scale Metal Identification Models - WWII U.S. (Britains Ltd. 54mm GI included for scale)
L to R - Back row: "Med. Tank M4", "General Sherman" (turret rotates), "105 MM Howitzer Motor T32 M7 Priest M7".
Front row: "Armored Car T-17 Dale model Co. Chicago" "75MM Gun Car M3 Dale - Model Co. Chicago", "Stuart M5". (Company Name & City imprinted on hubs' of wheeled vehicles - other data on hulls).
Photo by Ed Poole

Some contemporary Russian diecasts. Dinky soldiers added for scale is 30mm tall
L to R - Back row: 76mm Gun, T34-85 Tank & 100mm Gun in 1/43 scale by UEHA (?).
Front row: T34 Tank by ?, Two YA3-469 Cars in 1/43 scale by Schelano B CCCP
Photo by Ed Poole

Some Military Vehicles by Miscellaneous British manufacturers (Skybird soldier shown for scale is 30mm tall).

L to R - Back row: **Lone Star** Bren Gun Carrier towing Gun, **Skybirds** Artillery Tractor towing Howitzer, **TriAng Mini-Toys** Jeep, **Lledo Days Gone** Ambulance.

Front Row: **Charbens** Armoured Car, **Crescent** Armoured Car towing Limber & Gun **Corgi Major**. International (6X6 Truck, **Corgi Toys Hong Kong** King Tiger Tank, **Lone Star** Jeep.

Photo by Ed Poole

Die-cast Military Vehicles from Various Countries (Starlux soldiers shown are 30mm tall) L to R - Back row: "Henschel Bau J 1926 Made in W. Germany" (maker unknown); Mercedes Benz 1937 Cabriolet Feuhrerwagen and Fiat Antocarro Militaire 1914 by RIO (Italy); Military truck, Radar Truck and Ambulance by TEKNO (Denmark).

Front row: Liasson Car by Brumm (Italy) "Dodge 6X6 Made in France (marked FJ within a geared wheel); three tanks by Play Art (Hong Kong): Tiger I, Panther and Sherman; Two jeeps - front by Play Art and behind by Fun Ho! (New Zealand); Zylmex "King Tiger" (Hong Kong).

Photo by Ed Poole

Miniature metal military vehicles as Souvenirs (Heyde soldier 50mm tall) L to R - Back row: Renault Tank Inkwells - "G.B.W. © 1919...Carton Steel Company" (Turret hinges back to uncover inkpot); "G.B.W. © 1919...Renault Constructeur" (Turret Cupola unstoppers. Piece repainted & gun replaced); "Depose S.R. Tour Eiffel" (Turret hinges to left. Like Mignot but lacks recessed wheels.

Front row: Ashtray Decorations Fourth tank from left bears soldered plaque, State Capital Columbus Ohio.

Photo by Ed Poole

1/108 Scale Metal Identification Models - WWII British. Numbering is that of the manufacturer Comet/Authenticast but a Denzil Skinner model is substituted for number 5012. Authenticast GI by Holger Eriksson is 23mm tall.

L to R - Back row: 5000 Convenanter IV, 5001 Churchill MKV, 5002 Universal Carrier, 5003 Humber Armoured Car, 5004 Carden Loyd Carrier.

Middle row: 5005 Valentine, 5006 Matilda, 5007 Crusader, 5009 Cromwel!

Front row: 5008 Daimler Armoured Car, 5010 Churchill MKVII 5011 Sherman VC 5012 Centurion.

Photo by Ed Poole

Miscellaneous Small metal AFVs. Comet GI is 20mm tall. L to R - Back row: HR Products WWI Rhomboidal and Renault FT tanks, Quality Castings Desert War 2018 Stuart 'Honey', 2019 MKVI light tank and 2020 Cruiser MK IV.
Front: Denzil Skinner (England): British tank Series BZ Centurion, B25 Vickers MKVI and MKIII Medium; British Armoured Car Series BII Daimler, B23 Rolls Royce and Armoured Truck (number unknown).
Photo by Ed Poole

Miscellaneous small metal AFVs (cont'd). Comet GI is 20mm tall. L to R - Back Row: Crescent (England) Russian Tank, British Cruiser Tank and Humber Armoured Car. Daimler Ambulance and tank by unknown makers.
Front: Series by Unknown Maker - Patton Tank, Sherman Tank, Armored car, Tank and Amphibian. U.S. Markings by imprinted "JAPAN".
Photo by Ed Poole

Miscellaneous small die-cast military vehicles. Comet GI 20mm tall. L to R - Back row: Mattel "Hot Wheels Gun Bucket", Corgi Junior (England) Daimler Scout Car, Lesney "Matchbox Rolamatics" No. 73 Weasel, Sherman Tank (made in Hong Kong, pencil sharpener aft!)
Front row: Efsi (Holland) T-Ford 1919 Ambulance, Budgie Toy (England) Tank Transporter, 25pdr Gun Howitzer (maker unknown).
Photo by Ed Poole

This Dale 1/36 ID model bought in an Army "PX" post WWII, mailing label already attached to box to send home as souvenir.
Photo by Ed Poole

Prime Mover (after Barclay) and Howitzer (after Tootsietoy) from Junior Caster Mold No. E45. Homecast
Courtesy Ron Eccles
Photo by Ed Poole

Lledo (U.K.): Three Battle of Britain 50th Anniversary Commemorative sets. Vehicles each about 8cm in length.
Photo by Ed Poole

Home castings from Ever-Ready Mould No. ML21 (American Craft Manufacturing company, Chicago), "Big Bertha in Action", Gun barrel 11.5cm long.
Photo by Ed Poole

Arnold (Germany) Jeep with Five and Dime Corps troops and mascot. Jeep 17cm long.
Photo by Ed Poole

Five and Dime Corps HQ troops with TriAng Jeep (England), 16cm long
Photo by Ed Poole

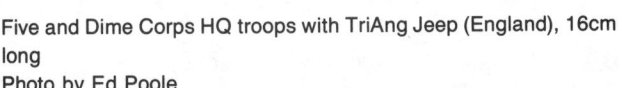

MINIATURE VEHICLE CASTINGS INC.

Though these appear to be toys from the 1930s, they were first produced in 1985. The models were carved and cast by owner Robert E. Wagner. Made of die-cast lead from silicone molds, they were sold for $21 apiece, and at least 3500 have been sold. Some are beginning to appear at toy shops and on dealer lists. The average length is about 4½'', and the N.J. firm's name is visible (sometimes dimly) on a piece of tin soldered to the bottom. The toys today seem to sell at slightly more than double their original price.

Following is a list of Miniature Vehicle Castings: 1937 Ford 2-door Sedan; 1938 Ford Standard Sedan Del; 1934 Olds 2-door Humpback; 1936 Olds 4-door Humpback; 1937 Hudson Terraplane 2-door; 1938 Dodge Step Van; 1937 Plymouth 5-window Coupe; 1937 Dodge 2-door Humpback; 1938 Plymouth 2-door sedan; 1941 Ford C.O.E. Truck (flatbed or dump); 1935 Hudson 2-door sedan; 1937 Studebaker 3-window coupe; 1936 Plymouth 4-door sedan; 1936 Plymouth 4-door Taxi; 1935 Pontiac 3-window Coupe; 1940 Dodge 2-door Sedan; 1939 Dodge 2-door Sedan; 1941 Divco Milk Truck (Sunrise Dairy). In 1993 Wagner was planning four new cars, to differ somewhat from the preceding in wheels, tires and frame so that the new series could be told from the old: 1934 Dodge 2-door sedan, 1935 Pontiac 2-door sedan, 1936 Plymouth Pick-up, 1938 Hudson Coupe.

Miniature Vehicle Castings, L to R: 1934 Olds, 1936 Olds.
Courtesy Bob & Alice Wagner

Miniature Vehicle Castings, L to R: 1941 Ford C.O.E. Truck, 1937 Studebaker 3-window Coupe, 1936 Plymouth Taxi.
Courtesy Bob & Alice Wagner

Miniature Vehicle Castings 1938 Dodge Step Van.
Courtesy Bob & Alice Wagner

Miniature Vehicles Castings, L to R: 1937 Hudson Terraplane, 1935 Hudson.
Courtesy Bob & Alice Wagner

Miniature Vehicle Castings, L to R: 1938 Plymouth 2-door Sedan, 1937 Plymouth Coupe, 5 windows; 1937 Dodge 2-door Humpback.
Courtesy Bob & Alice Wagner

CONDITION OF A TOY
AND ITS RELATION TO PRICE

CONDITION CODE:

C6 - Good, Evident overall wear, well-played with, but acceptable to many collectors

C8 - Very Good Minor wear overall, very clean

C10 - Mint (like new)

NOTE: Mint in Box commands a high price. Condition below C6 brings considerably lower prices.

MINIC (Pre-war Tri-ang Minic)

by Gates Willard

Established by George Lines in the 1870's, the original Lines company of England made wooden rocking horses. Brother Joseph joined the firm and ultimately bought out George's share. After the first world war, three of Joseph's sons formed a company called Lines Bros., Ltd., and their logo was a triangle....made up of three lines! Later their products came to be known as Tri-ang Toys. By the mid 1930's, they were making prams, cycles, pedal cars, stamped steel trucks, wooden toys, doll houses, and many other kinds of playthings.

In 1935, the Tri-ang Minic Miniature Clockwork Vehicles were introduced. Only 14 models were available that first year. Three to seven inches in length, they were robustly made of heavier gauge steel than that used by competing German manufacturers. They had brightly plated radiators and wheels. The trucks and some of the cars even had plated fenders! Painting was done by a dipping and baking process with runs as well as thick and thin areas, but the finishes were durable. Subtle shades of red, blue, green, beige, orange, and yellow plus black and chrome were tastefully combined to make some unusually attractive color schemes. The road vehicles had white rubber tires, and each Minic came with a stamped steel key and a little color folding catalogue inside the box.

The first Minics must have sold well, for in 1936 many new types were added, and a few had electric lights. A miniature Shell gasoline can appeared on the left running board of most cars and trucks. By early September, 1939 England was at war, and the Shell can had been deleted. The white tires were replaced with black, and the plated trunk rack on the ordinary cars was replaced by a decal number plate and a plain rear bumper. Since 1935, many new models were added and none discontinued. The factory claimed that more than 70 types were available. However, by 1940, some vehicles were painted in army camouflage, while others, such as the electric unglazed types, were phased out. The non-military vehicles had some parts chemically blackened instead of plated. Steering wheels were later attached with miniature split pins instead of being pressed onto a brass column.

After hostilities ended, Minics were rushed into production. The British economy required exports, and large quantities of Minics were sent to the USA which was starved for metal toys. Minics seem to have been available in many areas of this country, whereas there had been very few outlets before the war. The first post-war Minics often had leftover pre-war parts and boxes. Stronger colors were used (Mostly bright red, dark blue, and shades of green) and the quality of finish was below the pre-war standard. Tooling was wearing out, and the stampings often lacked definition. In time, quite a few new types and variations were produced before the company ceased operations in the 1970's.

In addition to the vehicles, various garages, service stations and even a fire station were made pre-war and post-war.

The numbering system used below was instituted about 1938-39. In general, the lower the number, the cheaper the item. However, new toys announced 1939-1940 were tacked on to the end of the existing list (65M-79M). Some of this last group were never put into production before toy manufacturing ended during World War II.

Gates Willard with a Triang Minic Double-Deck Bus. The date was February 1, 1941.

Gates Willard became a toy collector at the age of nine, but gave away his carefully preserved collection when he was married in 1952. About 1965 he met an adult automotive toy collector and became motivated to build a second collection. He's still working on it. From 1946-89 he owned restored real cars, but nowadays it's toys only. "They require little maintenance, they don't break down and it is possible to own many at a time". He has a B.A. and M.S. in geology and had a career in that field before becoming a science teacher, assistant principal and principal of a public school from which he retired in 1983.

Comments

Use the following numerical reference for the numbers appearing in the listings, usually preceding the date.

1 - Scarce

2 - Rare

3 - None Made After World War II

4 - Made Only 1939-40

5 - Headlights, Radiator, Bumper stamped in one piece (Same for cars and trucks)

6 - Small number made post-war. New tooling for radiator, matte black baseplate

7 - Headlights riveted to bar held in place by radiator. Most post-war headlights are soldered to bar.

8 - No front bumper (pre-war only)

9 - No decals first year made (1935)

10 - Cataloged but never made

11 - Cataloged pre-war but not made until post-war

12 - Painted glossy dark green

13 - Electric headlamps

14 - A special issue (not numbered) Brockhouse promotional made about 1937. Rare

15 - Actually had ten wheels

16 - Number on box is 70M

17 - Number on box is 71M

18 - Number on box is 75M

Minic Fords, L to R: Light Van, Royal Mail Van, Saloon, Camouflaged Saloon.
Courtesy Gates Willard   Photo by E.W. Willard

Minic, Left: Sports Saloon. Right: Limousine.
Photo by E.W. Willard
Courtesy Gates Willard

Minic L: Learner's Car. R: Racing Car.
Courtesy Gates Willard
Photo by E.W. Willard

	C6	C8	C10
1M Ford Saloon (Sedan), 1936..	75	112	150
1MCF Ford Saloon, Camouflaged 1, 3, 4, 1940	No Price Found		
2M Ford Light Van, 1936	75	112	150
3M Ford Royal Mail Van, 1936.	No Price Found		
4M Sports Saloon (2 window sedan) 3, 5, 1935	75	112	150
5M Limousine (3 window sedan) 3, 5, 1935	No Price Found		
6M Cabriolet (Coupe) 6 ?, 5, 1935	100	150	200
7M Town Coupe (town car) 6, 5, 1935	No Price Found		
8M Open Touring Car 6, 5, 1935	No Price Found		
9M Streamline Saloon (airflow sedan), 1935	No Price Found		
10M Delivery Lorry (pick-up truck) 5, 1935	110	165	220
11M Tractor 7, 1935	35	52	70
11MCF Tractor, Camouflaged 2,3, 1940	No Price Found		
12M Learner's Car 1, 5, 1936	No Price Found		
13M Racing Car, 1936	No Price Found		
14M Streamline Sports, 1935	No Price Found		

Minic, L to R: Town Coupe, Cabriolet (early type without Shell can),
Open Tourer.
Courtesy Gates Willard   Photo by E.W. Willard

Minic Caravan Sets, L: Limousine with unlighted caravan. R: Tourer
with Passengers and Caravan with Electric Light.
Courtesy Gates Willard   Photo by E.W. Willard

Minic, L to R: Late Pre-War car with plain bumper and number plate;
Earlier car with luggage rack and shell can.
Courtesy Gates Willard
Photo by E.W. Willard

Minic, L: Streamline Saloon. R: Streamline Sports.
Courtesy Gates Willard
Photo by E.W. Willard

Minic Vauxhalls, L to R: Open Tourer, Town Coupe, Cabriolet,
Camouflaged Cabriolet.
Courtesy Gates Willard
Photo by E.W. Willard

Minic, L to R: Rolls, Bentley and Daimler with electric headlights,
Rolls, Daimler and Bently, non-electric.
Courtesy Gates Willard   Photo by E.W. Willard

Minic: Four Sedancas. The Rolls and Daimler on left have electric
lights. The Rolls and Daimler on the right are non-electric. Bentley
Sedancas were never made.
Courtesy Gates Willard
Photo by E.W. Willard

Minic: The two Sedancas on the left have electric lights. The battery is inside the opening trunk. A turn screw operated the lamps.
The two cars on the right are non-electric, and there is no separate
trunk lid. All Post-War Rolls, Bentleys and Daimlers have an opening trunk, but they are non-electric.
Courtesy Gates Willard
Photo by E.W. Willard

Minic, L to R: Four Tourers - Rolls, Daimler and Bentley, non-electric (electric versions never made), electric-lighted Bentley Tourer. Note that Battery Box displaces the rear sets.
Photo by E.W. Willard   Courtesy Gates Willard

	C6	C8	C10		C6	C8	C10
15M Petrol Tank Lorry (Oil Tanker) 5, 1936	88	132	175	30M Mechanical Horse and Pantechnicon 5, 9, 14, 1935 . .	No Price Found		
15MCF Petrol Tank Lorry, camouflaged 1, 3, 5, 1940	No Price Found			31M Mechanical Horse and Fuel Oil Tanker, 5, 1936	No Price Found		
16M Caravan, Non Electric (House Trailer), 1937	No Price Found			32M Dust Cart (Garbage Truck), 5, 1396	70	105	140
17M Vauxhall Tourer, 7, 1937 . .	85	128	170	33M Steam Roller, 1935	55	83	110
18M Vauxhall Town Coupe, 7, 1937	No Price Found			34M Tourer with Passengers 1, 3, 5, 1937	No Price Found		
19M Vauxhall Cabriolet, 7, 1937	100	150	200	35M Rolls Tourer, Non-electric, 1, 7, 8, 1937	No Price Found		
19MCF Vauxhall Cabriolet, camouflaged, 1, 3, 7, 1940 . . .	No Price Found			36M Daimler Tourer, Non-electric, 1, 7, 1937	No Price Found		
20M Light Tank 3, 12, 1935	No Price Found			37M Bentley Tourer, Non-electric, 1, 7, 1938	No Price Found		
20MCF Light Tank, camouflaged 2, 3, 1940	No Price Found			38M Caravan Set (Limousine and Non-electric caravan), 2, 1937	No Price Found		
21M Transport Van, 5, 9, 1935 .	No Price Found			39M Taxi (Production Delayed until 1938), 1, 1937	80	120	160
21MCF Transport Van, camouflaged, 1, 3, 5, 1940 . . .	No Price Found			40M Mechanical Horse and Trailer with cases 1, 5, 1936	No Price Found		
22M Carter Paterson Van, 5, 1936	110	165	220	41ME Caravan with electric light 1, 3, 1937	No Price Found		
23M Tip Lorry (Dump Truck) 5, 1936	95	142	190	42M Rolls Sedanca, Non-electric, 1, 7, 8, 1937	No Price Found		
24M Luton Transport Van (moving van) 5, 1396	125	188	250	43M Daimler Sedanca, Nonelectric, 1, 7, 1937	No Price Found		
24MCF Luton Van, camouflaged 3, 1940	No Price Found			44M Traction Engine, 1, 1938	No Price Found		
25M Delivery Lorry with cases, 5, 1936	No Price Found			45M Bentley Sunshine Saloon, (Sunroof Sedan), Non-electric, 2, 7, 1938	No Price Found		
26M Tractor and trailer with cases, 1936	88	132	175				
27M, 28M - Numbers not used	No Price Found			46M Daimler Sunshine Saloon, non-electric, 2, 7, 1938	No Price Found		
29M Traffic Control Car (Police Car), 7, 1938	75	112	150				

Minic non-electric Sunshine Saloons, L to R: Rolls, Daimler and Bentley.
Courtesy Gates Willard
Photo by E.W. Willard

Minic, L to R: Fire Engine with electric headlamps and attachments (hoses are in an opening compartment); Taxi; Traffic Control Car.
Courtesy Gates Willard
Photo by E.W. Willard

Minic, L to R: Double-Deck Bus, Single-Deck Bus. Produced in red and beige or two-tone green. All four were separately numbered in the trade catalog.
Courtesy Gates Willard
Photo by E.W. Willard

Minic Luton Vans, L to R: Camouflaged; Civilian version.
Courtesy Gates Willard
Photo by E.W. Willard

Minic, L to R: Breakdown Lorry; Camouflaged Breakdown Lorry; Searchlight Lorry; Camouflaged Searchlight Lorry. Note original battery for Electric Searchlight.
Courtesy Gates Willard   Photo by E.W. Willard

	C6	C8	C10
47M Rolls Sunshine Saloon, Non-electric 2, 7, 1938	No Price Found		
48M Breakdown Lorry (Wrecker truck), 5, 1936	135	202	270
48MCF Breakdown Lorry, Camouflaged 2, 3, 5, 1940 . . .	No Price Found		

	C6	C8	C10
49ME Searchlight Lorry, 3, 5, 1936	No Price Found		
49MECF Searchlight Lorry, camouflaged 2, 3, 5, 1940	No Price Found		
50ME Rolls Sedanca, Electric, 2, 3, 8, 13, 1936	No Price Found		

Minic Vans, L to R: 1936-38 type with Shell can, Carter Paterson,
early wartime version with black radiator and black tires, Camouflaged
Van.
Courtesy Gates Willard   Photo by E.W. Willard

Minic Mechanical Horse and Pantechnicon. L: typical 1936-38 ver-
sion. R: rare Brockhouse promotional.
Courtesy Gates Willard
Photo by E.W. Willard

Minic late Pre-War issues, L to R: Mechanical Horse and Milk Tanker;
Log Lorry.
Courtesy Gates Willard
Photo by E.W. Willard

Minic, L to R: Tanker, Wartime Pool Tanker, Mechanical Horse and
Fuel Oil Tanker, Wartime Pool Articulated Tanker.
Courtesy Gates Willard
Photo by E.W. Willard

	C6	C8	C10
51ME Daimler Sedanca, Electric, 2, 3, 13, 1937	No Price Found		
52M Single Deck Bus, Red, 1936	No Price Found		
53M Single Deck Bus, Green, 1936	No Price Found		
54M Traction Engine and Trailer, 2, 1939	92	138	185
55ME Bentley Tourer, Electric, (production probably delayed) 2, 3, 13, 1938	No Price Found		
56ME Rolls Sunshine Saloon, Electric, 2, 3, 13, 1938	No Price Found		

	C6	C8	C10
57ME Bentley Sunshine Saloon Electric, 2, 3, 13, 1938	No Price Found		
58ME Daimler Sunshine Saloon Electric, 2, 3, 13, 1938	No Price Found		
59ME Caravan Set, tourer with passengers and caravan with electric light, 2, 3, 1937	No Price Found		
60M Double Deck Bus, red, 1935	230	345	460
61M Double Deck Bus, green, 2, 3, 1395	140	210	280

334

Minic, rear, L to R: Lorry with Cases, Mechanical Horse and Trailer with Cases. Front, L to R: Lorry, Tip Lorry.
Courtesy Gates Willard
Photo by E.W. Willard

Minic, L to R: Steam Roller, Camouflaged Tractor, Tractor and Trailer with cases.
Courtesy Gates Willard
Photo by E.W. Willard

Minic, late Pre-War issues, L to R: Farm Lorry, Timber Lorry, Mechanical Horse and Lorry with barrels.
Courtesy Gates Willard
Photo by E.W. Willard

Minic, L to R: Dust Cart, Traction Engine with Trailer.
Courtesy Gates Willard
Photo by E.W. Willard

Minic, L to R: Canvas Tilt Lorry; Camouflaged Canvas Tilt Lorry; 6-wheel Army Lorry; Camouflaged 6-wheel Army Lorry.
Courtesy Gates Willard
Photo by E.W. Willard

	C6	C8	C10
62ME Fire Engine, 13, 1936	138	208	275
63M No. 1 Presentation Set 3, 1397	No Price Found		
64M No. 2 Presentation Set, 3, 1937	No Price Found		
65M Construction Set 1, 3, 1936	No Price Found		
66M Six Wheel Army Lorry 1, 3, 5, 12, 15, 1939	No Price Found		
66MCF Six Wheel Army Lorry, Camouflaged, 1, 3, 4, 5, 1940	No Price Found		
67M Farm Lorry, 2, 3, 4, 5, 1939	No Price Found		

	C6	C8	C10
68M Timber Lorry, 2, 5, 1939 ..	No Price Found		
69M Canvas Tilt Lorry (Enclosed Army Truck) 2, 3, 4, 5, 12, 15, 1939.......................	No Price Found		
69MCF Canvas Tilt Lorry, Camouflaged, 2, 3, 4, 5, 15, 1940	No Price Found		
(70M) (Coal Lorry NOT MADE), 10, 1939	No Price Found		
71M Mechanical Horse and Milk Trailer, 2, 5, 16, 1939........	125	188	250

Minic, L to R: Camouflaged Tanker, Camouflaged Light Tank, Light Tank.
Courtesy Gates Willard
Photo by E.W. Willard

Minic, L to R: Fire Station, small 00 Service Station.
Courtesy Gates Willard
Photo by E.W. Willard

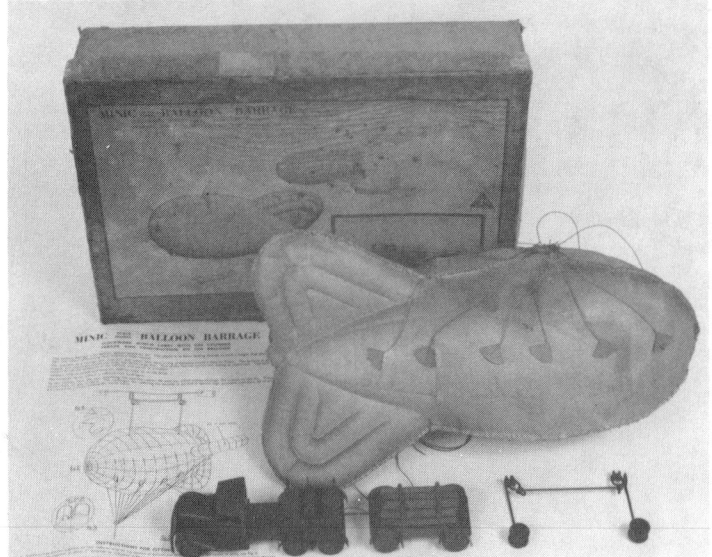

Minic Balloon Barrage.
Courtesy Gates Willard
Photo by E.W. Willard

Minic Construction Set: Everything needed to assemble and paint six vehicles.
Courtesy Gates Willard   Photo by E.W. Willard

Some Pre-War Minic boxes. Every Minic was sold with a box that also contained a folding color catalog and a steel key (as shown in front of the boxes).
Courtesy Gates Willard
Photo by E.W. Willard

	C6	C8	C10
72M Mechanical Horse and Lorry with Barrels, 2, 5, 17, 1939 ..	150	225	300
(73M) (Cable Lorry (Pre-war) **Not Made**), 11, 1939			
74M Log Lorry, 2, 5, 18, 1939 ..	No Price Found		
(75M) (Ambulance (Pre-war) **Not Made**), 11, 1939			
76M Balloon Barrage Wagon and Trailer production delayed until 1940 made in camouflage only. Should have been numbered 76 MCF	No Price Found		
77M Double Deck Trolley Bus (**Not Made**), 10, 1939			
78M Pool Tanker, 2, 3, 4, 5, 1940	No Price Found		
79M Mechanical Horse and Pool Tanker, 2, 3, 4, 5, 1940	No Price Found		

Tri Ang Minic (U.K.) M101 Armoured Car (16cm long) with Box. One of the 15 vehicles in the Advanced Airfield Maintenance Wing and Armoured Brigade Headquarters Squadron Series.
Photo by Ed Poole

LOOKS LIKE A REAL ROAD DOESN'T IT?

Though it's difficult to believe, the traffic jam in this photograph is actually made up of MINIC scale model clockwork toys.

This unique clockwork series will contain almost every vehicle to be seen on the roads. Each model is true to scale so that the bus is exactly the right amount larger than the lorry and the limousine in the right proportion to the open tourer.

These MINIC vehicles are wonderfully built and have reliable long-running clockwork; they are most reasonably priced too, the smaller ones costing only 1/- each. They have a front wheel drive, so that they will run on carpet and can be used in any room.

Start collecting your road full now.

MINIC scale model LIMOUSINE
Strong construction, with powerful long-running clockwork motor. Colours: Dark Green, plated guards; Ivory, Red guards; New Blue, Ivory guards. Radiator and bumpers plated, also wheels, with rubber tyres. Length, 4¾ in. Price 1/-

MINIC scale model STREAMLINE CLOSED.
Strong construction, with powerful long-running clockwork motor. Colours: Red, Ivory, New Blue. Plated bumpers, radiator, also wheels, with rubber tyres. Length, 5 in. Price 1/-

MINIC scale model STREAMLINE OPEN.
Strong construction, with powerful long-running clockwork motor. Colours: Ivory, Red hood; Red, Ivory hood; or Light Green, Ivory hood. Plated radiator, bumpers, also wheels, with rubber tyres. Length, 5 in. Price 1/-

MINIC scale model SPORTS SALOON.
Strong construction, with powerful long-running clockwork motor. Colours: Ivory, New Blue, Primrose, with plated mudguards, radiator, bumpers, also wheels, with rubber tyres. Length, 4¾ in. Price 1/-

MINIC scale model TRACTOR.
Strong construction, with powerful long-running clockwork mechanism. Colours: Green with Red wheels, or Red with Green wheels. Length, 3 in. Price 1/-

MINIC scale model TOWN COUPÉ.
Strong construction, with powerful long-running clockwork motor. Colours: New Blue, plated mudguards; Light Brown, Black mudguards; or Ivory, Red mudguards. Plated radiator, bumpers, also wheels, with rubber tyres. Length, 4¾ in. Price 1/-

MINIC scale model CABRIOLET.
Strong construction, with powerful long-running clockwork motor. Colours: Ivory and Green with plated mudguards, or Red with Ivory mudguards. Radiator, bumpers, plated, also wheels, with rubber tyres. Length, 4¾ in. Price 1/-

MINIC scale model OPEN SPORTS TOURER.
Strong construction, with powerful long-running clockwork motor. Colours: Green, plated mudguards, Ivory hood; Red, Ivory mudguards and hood; Ivory, Red mudguards and hood. Plated bumpers, radiator, also wheels, with rubber tyres. Length, 4¾ in. Price 1/-

MINIC
Regd. Trade Mark

CLOCKWORK TOYS ALL TO SCALE
Obtainable from all good Toy Shops and Stores
Made by Lines Bros. Ltd., Tri-ang Works, Merton, S.W.19

The first Minic advertisement.
Courtesy Gates Willard

MINIC Regd. Trade Mark

ALL TO SCALE CLOCKWORK TOYS

Almost every type of vehicle on the road represented; some with **ELECTRIC LIGHTS**. Strongly constructed and fitted with powerful, long-running mechanism, they will run anywhere, **EVEN ON THE CARPET.** Each model is beautifully finished in a variety of colours, and packed singly in an attractive box.

MINIC Ford £100 Saloon
LENGTH 3¼ ins.   Price 6d.

MINIC Racing Car
LENGTH 5½ ins.   Price 1/-

MINIC Luton Transport Van
LENGTH 5½ ins.   Price 1/6

MINIC Breakdown Lorry
with Mechanical Crane
LENGTH 5½ ins.   Price 3/6

MINIC Mechanical Horse and
Fuel Oil Trailer
LENGTH 7 ins.   Price 2/-

MINIC Dust Cart
LENGTH 5½ ins.   Price 2/-

MINIC Steam Roller
LENGTH 5½ ins.   Price 1/6

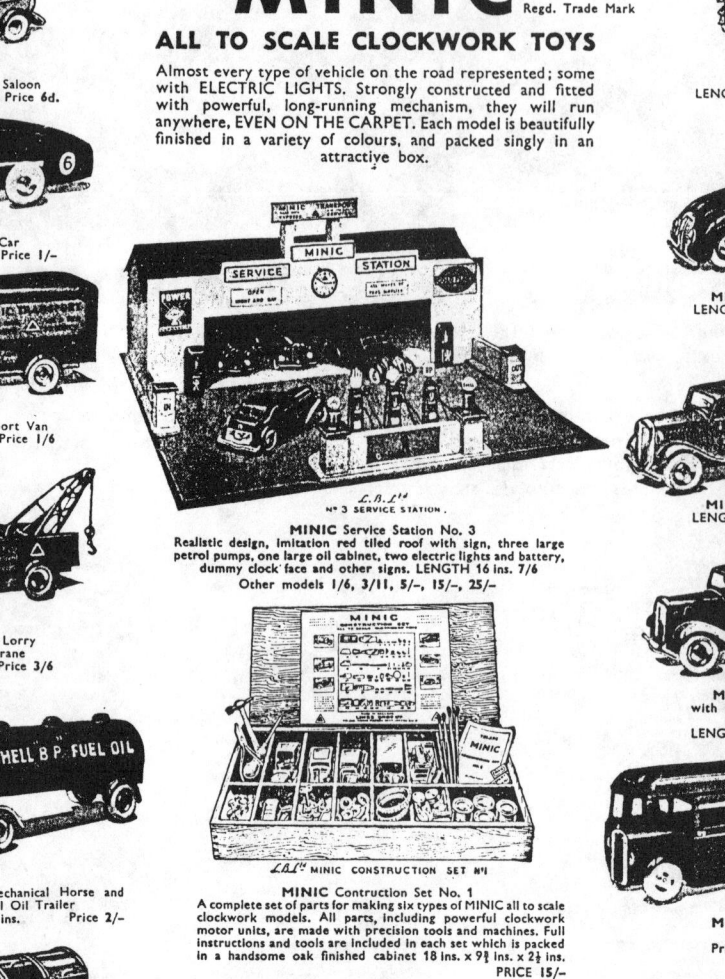

N° 3 SERVICE STATION.

MINIC Service Station No. 3
Realistic design, imitation red tiled roof with sign, three large petrol pumps, one large oil cabinet, two electric lights and battery, dummy clock face and other signs. LENGTH 16 ins. 7/6
Other models 1/6, 3/11, 5/-, 15/-, 25/-

L.B.L. MINIC CONSTRUCTION SET N°1

MINIC Contruction Set No. 1
A complete set of parts for making six types of MINIC all to scale clockwork models. All parts, including powerful clockwork motor units, are made with precision tools and machines. Full instructions and tools are included in each set which is packed in a handsome oak finished cabinet 18 ins. x 9⅞ ins. x 2½ ins.
PRICE 15/-

MINIC Caravan Trailer.
LENGTH 4½ ins.
COMPLETE WITH ELECTRIC LIGHT AND BATTERY 3/6
CAR NOT INCLUDED, BUT CAN BE OBTAINED PRICE 1/-

There are thirty-four models to choose from; some with **ELECTRIC LIGHTS.**

Ask your dealer to show you the complete range, also the **MINIC** Service Stations.

TRI-ANG TOYS
OBTAINABLE AT ALL GOOD TOY SHOPS AND STORES

MINIC Light Tank
LENGTH 3¼ ins.   Price 1/6

MINIC Streamline Saloon
LENGTH 5 ins.   Price 1/-

MINIC Petrol Tank Lorry
LENGTH 5½ ins.   Price 1/-

MINIC Searchlight Lorry
with Electric Searchlight and
Battery
LENGTH 5½ ins.   Price 3/6

MINIC Single Deck Bus
LENGTH 7¼ ins.
Price 3/6. Red or green.

MINIC Lorry with cases
LENGTH 5½ ins.   Price 1/6

MINIC Tip Lorry
LENGTH 5½ ins.   Price 1/3

Made in England by

LINES BROS. LTD., Tri-ang Works, Morden Rd., London, S.W.19

The Minic line was getting more sophisticated.
Courtesy Gates Willard

MINIC Regd. Trade Mark
ALL TO SCALE CLOCKWORK TOYS

Almost every type of vehicle on the road represented; some with ELECTRIC LIGHTS. Strongly constructed and fitted with powerful, long-running mechanism, they will run anywhere, EVEN ON THE CARPET. Each model is beautifully finished in a variety of colours, and packed singly in an attractive box.

MINIC Ford £100 Saloon
LENGTH 3¼ ins.
Price 6d.

MINIC Ford Royal Mail Van
LENGTH 3¼ ins.
Price 6d.

MINIC VAUXHALL TOURER
LENGTH 4¾ ins.   Price 1/3

MINIC VAUXHALL CABRIOLET
LENGTH 4¾ ins.   Price 1/3

MINIC DAIMLER TOURER
LENGTH 5¼ ins.   Price 2/-

MINIC DAIMLER SEDANCA
With Electric Headlamps and Battery
LENGTH 5¼ ins.   Price 3/6

BOYS!
Learn the Principles of Engineering Mechanics

A complete set of parts for making six types of MINIC all to scale clockwork models. All parts, including powerful clockwork motor units, are made with precision tools and machines. Full instructions and tools are included in each set which is packed in a handsome oak finished cabinet 18 ins. × 9½ ins. × 2¼ ins.
PRICE 15/-

MINIC Racing Car
LENGTH 5¼ ins.   Price 1/-

MINIC Streamline Saloon
LENGTH 5 ins.
Price 1/-

SERVICE STATIONS
Specially Designed for Your Minics

MINIC Luton Transport Van
LENGTH 5¼ ins.
Price 1/6

MINIC Dust Cart
LENGTH 5¼ ins.
Price 2/-

MINIC Service Station No. 3
Realistic design, imitation red tiled roof with sign, three large petrol pumps, one large oil cabinet, two electric lights and battery, dummy clock face and other signs. LENGTH 16 in. 9/11   Other models from 1/- to 32/6

MINIC Steam Roller
LENGTH 5¼ ins.
Price 2/-

MINIC Breakdown Lorry
with Mechanical Crane
LENGTH 5¼ ins.
Price 3/6

MINIC Fire Engine
with Electric Headlamps and Battery
LENGTH 6¼ ins.
Price 6/6

MINIC Single Deck Bus
LENGTH 7¼ ins.
Price 3/6

MINIC Mechanical Horse and
Fuel Oil Trailer LENGTH 7 ins.
Price 2/-

ASK YOUR DEALER TO SHOW YOU THE MINIC RANGE
OBTAINABLE AT ALL GOOD TOY SHOPS AND STORES

Made in England by
LINES BROS. LTD. *Makers of the famous* TRI-ANG TOYS
TRI-ANG WORKS, MORDEN ROAD, LONDON, S.W.19

TRI-ANG   TRI-ANG

Sept. 1937 Meccano Magazine.
Courtesy Gates Willard

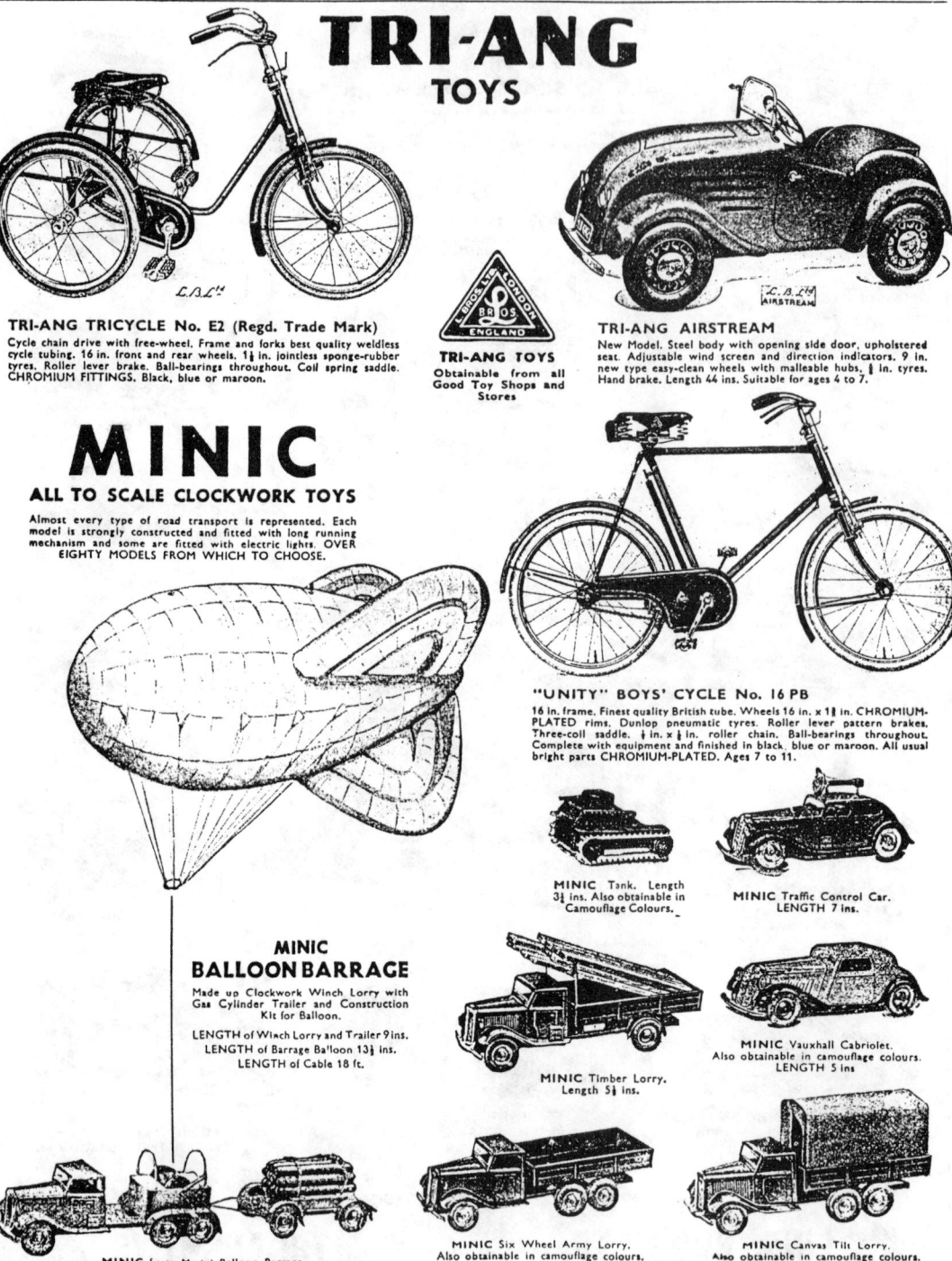

TRI-ANG
TOYS

TRI-ANG TRICYCLE No. E2 (Regd. Trade Mark)
Cycle chain drive with free-wheel. Frame and forks best quality weldless cycle tubing. 16 in. front and rear wheels. 1¼ in. jointless sponge-rubber tyres. Roller lever brake. Ball-bearings throughout. Coil spring saddle. CHROMIUM FITTINGS. Black, blue or maroon.

TRI-ANG TOYS
Obtainable from all Good Toy Shops and Stores

TRI-ANG AIRSTREAM
New Model. Steel body with opening side door, upholstered seat. Adjustable wind screen and direction indicators. 9 in. new type easy-clean wheels with malleable hubs, ⅝ in. tyres. Hand brake. Length 44 ins. Suitable for ages 4 to 7.

MINIC
ALL TO SCALE CLOCKWORK TOYS

Almost every type of road transport is represented. Each model is strongly constructed and fitted with long running mechanism and some are fitted with electric lights. OVER EIGHTY MODELS FROM WHICH TO CHOOSE.

"UNITY" BOYS' CYCLE No. 16 PB
16 in. frame. Finest quality British tube. Wheels 16 in. x 1⅜ in. CHROMIUM-PLATED rims. Dunlop pneumatic tyres. Roller lever pattern brakes. Three-coil saddle. ⅜ in. x ⅛ in. roller chain. Ball-bearings throughout. Complete with equipment and finished in black, blue or maroon. All usual bright parts CHROMIUM-PLATED. Ages 7 to 11.

MINIC Tank. Length 3¼ ins. Also obtainable in Camouflage Colours.

MINIC Traffic Control Car. LENGTH 7 ins.

MINIC BALLOON BARRAGE

Made up Clockwork Winch Lorry with Gas Cylinder Trailer and Construction Kit for Balloon.

LENGTH of Winch Lorry and Trailer 9 ins.
LENGTH of Barrage Balloon 13½ ins.
LENGTH of Cable 18 ft.

MINIC Timber Lorry. Length 5¼ ins.

MINIC Vauxhall Cabriolet. Also obtainable in camouflage colours. LENGTH 5 ins.

MINIC Scale Model Balloon Barrage

MINIC Six Wheel Army Lorry. Also obtainable in camouflage colours. LENGTH 5¼ ins.

MINIC Canvas Tilt Lorry. Also obtainable in camouflage colours. LENGTH 5¼ ins.

Made by LINES BROS. LTD., Tri-ang Works, LONDON S.W.19

At Last - The Balloon Barrage! England had been at war for a year.
Courtesy Gates Willard

	C6	C8	C10
Modern Toys Convertible, 9'' long	125	188	250
Modern Toys Mobilgas Tanker..	80	120	160
Mohawk Toy Blue Bird Taxi, windup, 6'' long.................	188	282	375
Mohawk Toy ''Yellow Taxi'' ...	275	363	550

MOKO TOYS

(Moses Kohnstam-Furth, Germany, 1875-1959)
by Bob Smith

Moses Kohnstam not only manufactured toys, he also ran a large wholesale house and had his toys made to order by toy companies such as Guntermann, Distler and Fischer. He became a distributor for Gama, Tippco, Levy, Carette and other Companies. Most special order toys carried the ''MOKO'' logo. Moses died in 1912 leaving the business to his sons, Willi & Emil. His other son, Julius had opened a branch office in England before 1900. The company was shut down in 1933 as were many other Jewish businesses in Germany before WWII. Emil fled to England while Willi stayed in Germany. Willi died a year later. Emil joined his brother Julius to help run the English firm. Julius died in 1935. However, the MOKO Company survived and is still in business today.

''Moxie'' Horse Car
Courtesy Sotheby's NY

	C6	C8	C10
''Moxie'' Horse car (based on the actual promotional vehicle) tin litho, 8'' long..............	750	1125	1500

MURRAY

	C6	C8	C10
MURRAY Camaro Pedal Car, 1968	88	132	175
Murray Champion Pedal Car ...	750	1300	1800
Murray Comet Pedal Car, 1956 .	250	375	500
Murray Country Squire Station Wagon Pedal Car, 1955......	325	488	650
Murray Earth Mover Pedal Car, 1959......................	450	750	1000
Murray ''Fire Chief'' Pedal Car .	500	800	1100
Murray Pontiac Station Wagon, 1948 Pedal Car..............	950	1500	2200
Murray Racer No. 8, 1960 Pedal Car........................	215	322	430
Murray Suburban Pedal Car, 1950	550	850	1200
Murray Tee Bird Pedal Car, 1961	175	263	350
Murray Tractor Pedal Car, c.1950	300	450	600

MOKO Six-Cylinder Limousine, 9½'' long, c.1927.

	C6	C8	C10
MOKO Six-Cylinder Limousine. Green/black, 9.5'' long. c/w motor runs car in forward & reverse, as pistons on top of engine move up & down. Also has opening doors and hood. c.1927	650	900	1600
''Moko'' Kohnstam Four-Cylinder Sedan. Green/black, 8'' long, smaller version of above car, c.1928	500	700	1100

NEFF-MOON TOY COMPANY

Neff-Moon, of Sandusky, Ohio was owned by William Moon and Charles Neff. Production of their pressed steel toys began in 1923, with the firm, which seems to have been located above a grocery, apparently an early victim of the Depression.

	C6	C8	C10
Neff-Moon Groceries Van	175	262	350
Neff-Moon Tow Truck, 16", c.1925	200	300	400
Neff-Moon No. 14 Set, "10 Toys in 1"	900	1350	1800

NIFTY

Nifty "Skidoodle"
Courtesy PB84

Nifty "Speedy Felix"
Courtesy Phillips NY

	C6	C8	C10
"Nifty Bus" tin wind-up	1200	2000	2700
Nifty "Skidoodle" tin wind-up .	1800	1900	4000
Nifty "Speedy Felix" Felix the Cat car	425	635	850

NOMA

	C6	C8	C10
NOMA Low Boy, wooden	100	150	200
Noma Steam Shovel, wooden . .	90	135	180
Noma Truck, wooden, 1940s . . .	45	68	90

NORTH & JUDD

Research by collector C.B.C. Lee suggests that this company, located at the time in New Britain, Connecticut, made cast iron toys for only one year, probably 1930, for S.H. Kress. Their original designs appear to have been marked with the company's name, but their toys for the most part are unmarked. The company is still in business, making quality hardware.

Austin Convertible, open top, marked "North & Judd" . . . .   No Price Found
Austin Sedan, two-door, marked "North & Judd" . . . .   No Price Found
Bus, looks like Dent, 4.667" long   No Price Found
Ford Model A Coupe, looks like Arcade, length of left cab 1.528", has driver in window, trunk at rear . . . .   No Price Found
Ford Model T stake truck, like Arcade's, but marked "Anchor Truck Co." (an anchor is North & Judd's trademark) . . . .   No Price Found
Motorcycle cop, like Hubley's "Cop", separate nickeled driver is held by mushrooms at front of handle-bars and on driver's feet . . . .   No Price Found

North & Judd semi-trailer stake truck.
Photo by Terry Sells

Semi-Trailer Stake Truck, marked "North & Judd" . . . .   No Price Found
Tractor, looks like Arcade, but has nickeled driver, 2.988" long . .   No Price Found

NOSCO PLASTICS

Nosco Plastics was located in Erie, PA. It made a variety of plastic toys, including several planes and trains. Some of its toys appear in a 1952-53 Toy Year Book.

Nosco Fire Truck

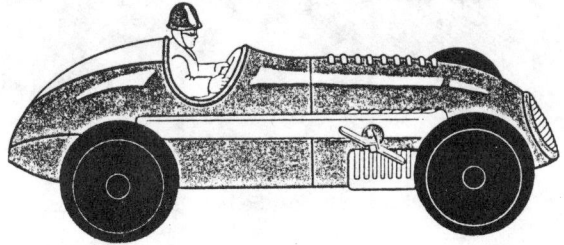

Nosco Ace Racer

Nosco Hot 'See Hot Rod'
Photo by Terry Sells

	C6	C8	C10
Nosco Ace Racer, 8" long, No. 6390	60	100	160
Nosco Bus, "Nosco Lines"	No Price Found		

Nosco Cop-Cycle   Photo by Terry Sells

Nosco Pokey Joe

Nosco Doodle-Bug   Photo by Terry Sells

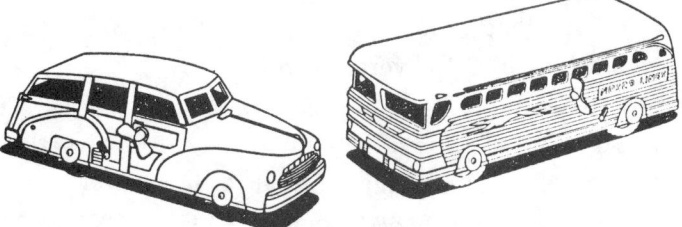

Nosco Station Wagon & Bus

Nosco Cop-Cycle, 5½" long, friction, No. 6357 . . . . No Price Found

Nosco Doodle-Bug, No. 6381, 9½" long wind-up 70   110   180

	C6	C8	C10
Nosco Fire Truck No. 6386, 7½" long	No Price Found		
Nosco Hot 'See Hot Rod No. 6490, 10¼" long, friction	70	110	180
Nosco Pokey Joe fire pumper, No. 6430, 10½" long	No Price Found		
Nosco Station Wagon	No Price Found		

Nosco Vizy Vee   Courtesy Alice & Bob Wagner

Nosco Vizy Vee Stockar Racer, No.	C6	C8	C10
6565, 9¼″ long	70	110	180

NYLINT

The Nylint Tool and Manufacturing Company was formed in 1937 by Bernard C. Klint and David Nyberg (thus its name) in Rockford, Illinois. Toy production began in the spring of 1946. Since 1950, the firm has concentrated on the production of heavy duty scale reproductions, in steel, of earth-moving equipment and over-the-road trucks. The early part of this list was prepared by Calvin L. Chaussee.

1947 Nylint Fork Lift	75	112	150
1949 Nylint No. 100 Amazing Car (Turns-Parks-Corners), 13¾″ long	120	180	240
Nylint No. 800 Scootcycle (wind-up), 7¼″ long	250	375	500
Nylint No. 1000 Deliverall (wind-up), 10″ long	300	450	600
1950			
Nylint No. 1100 Elgin Street Sweeper (wind-up), 8¼″ long	135	200	270
Nylint No. 1200 Pump Mobile (wind-up) 8⅝″ long	120	180	240
1951-52			
Nylint No. 1300 Tourna Rocker, 18″	75	112	150
Nylint No. 1400 Roadgrader, 19¼″ long	80	120	160
Nylint No. 1500 Tournahopper,			

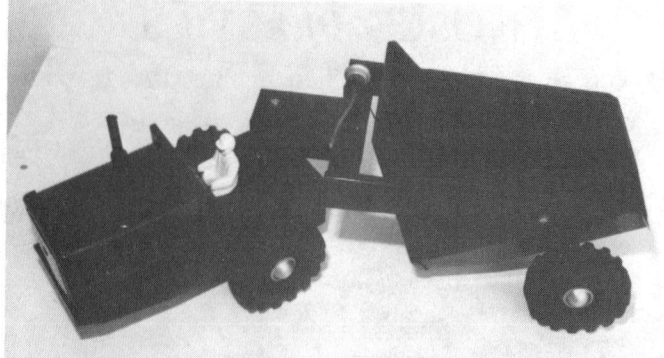

Nylint (1951-52) No. 1300 Tournarocker
Courtesy Thomas G. Nefos, Federal Shipping Network

Nylint 1951-52 No. 1600 Payloader
Courtesy Continental Hobby House

	C6	C8	C10
22½″	70	105	140
Nylint No. 1600 Payloader, 18″ long	50	75	100
1953-54			
Nylint No. 1700 Tourna Hauler, 30¼″ long	100	150	200

Nylint 1953-54 No. 1800 Traveloader
Courtesy Thomas G. Nefos, Federal Shipping Network

Nylint No. 1800 Traveloader, 30″ long	100	150	200
Nylint No. 1900 Tourna Tractor-Dozer, 14¾″	110	165	220

Nylint 1955 No. 2000 Speed Swing
Courtesy Thomas G. Nefos, Federal Shippng Network

Nylint 1958 No. 2800 Guided Missile Carrier.
Photo by Calvin L. Chaussee

Nylint 1955 No. 2200 Michigan Shovel.

1955	C6	C8	C10
Nylint No. 2000 Speed Swing, 19''	92	140	185
Nylint No. 2100 Tournadozer, 20'' long	125	188	250
Nylint No. 2200 Michigan Shovel, 31½'' long	100	150	200

Nylint 1956 No. 2400 Electric Cannon.
Calvin L. Chaussee

1956			
Nylint No. 2300 Elgin Sweeper, 8¾'' long, battery-operated	100	150	200
Nylint No. 2400 Electric Cannon, 22½'' long	75	112	150
Nylint No. 2500 Telescoping Crane, 27''	100	150	200
Nylint No. 2600 Missile Launcher, 31½''	150	225	300

1958	C6	C8	C10
Nylint No. 2500 Telescoping Crane, 35¾''	160	240	320
Nylint No. 2600 Missile Launcher	150	225	300
Nylint No. 2700 Uranium Hauler, 22½'' long	105	158	210
Nylint No. 2800 Guided Missile Carrier, 15½'' long	140	210	280
1959			
Nylint No. 2900 Junior Jack Hammer, 19½''	75	112	150
Nylint No. 3000 Grader-Loader, 23¾''	150	225	300
Nylint No. 3100 Payloader Tractor-Shovel, 17⅝''	120	180	240
Nylint No. 3200 Power and Light Lineman Truck, 35¾''	130	195	260
Nylint No. 3300 Power and Light Truck, Posthole Digger, 35¾'' long	180	270	360
Nylint No. 3400 Highway Emergency Truck, 18⅝'' long	85	128	170
Nylint No. 3500 Count Down Rocket Launcher, 21''	75	112	150
1960			
Nylint No. 3600 Ford Rapid Delivery, 18¼'' long	125	188	250
Nylint No. 3700 Street Sprinkler Truck, 18'' long	140	210	280
Nylint No. 3800 Ford Sales and Service, 13⅝'' long	70	105	140
Nylint No. 3900 Ford Platform Tilt Truck, 15¾''	87	131	175
Nylint No. 4000 Ford Speedway Truck with Racer, 24¾''	150	225	300

Nylint 1961 No. 4100 U-Haul Truck
Courtesy Thomas G. Nefos, Federal Shipping Network

1961

	C6	C8	C10
Nylint No. 4100 U-Haul Truck and Trailer, 22'' long	90	135	180
Nylint No. 4200 Bulldozer, 14'' long	90	135	180
Nylint No. 4400 Camper on Pick-up, 13½'' long	55	82	110

Nylint 1961 No. 4500 Truck
Courtesy Thomas G. Nefos, Federal Shipping Network

Nylint No. 4500 Ranch Truck, 14'' long	60	90	120
Nylint No. 4600 Construction 4 wheel Platform Dump, 15¾'' long	150	225	300
Nylint No. 4700 Happy Acres truck with Horses, 14''	100	150	200
Nylint No. 4800-A U-Haul Rental Trailer (Van type)	50	75	100
Nylint No. 4900-A U-Haul Rental Trailer (Open type)	50	75	100

1962

Nylint No. 5000 Dump Truck w/Cement Mixer, 20½'' long . . .	35	52	70

	C6	C8	C10
Nylint No. 5100 Dump Truck, 13½'' long	37	56	75
Nylint No. 5200 Pick-up Truck (Econoline), 11¼'' long	60	90	135
Nylint No. 5300 Custom Camper on above, 12½'' long	52	78	105
Nylint No. 5400 Custom Camper on above with boat, 23½'' long	150	225	300

Nylint 1962 No. 5500 ''Pepsi'' truck, Ford Cab-Over, 16½'' long, 1962?   Photo by Bob Smith

Nylint No. 5500 Pepsi Truck, 16½'' long	95	135	195

1963

Nylint No. 5800 Ford Econoline Van, 12'' long	45	68	90

Nylint 1963 No. 6000 Ford Econoline Tow Truck, 11'' long.
Photo by Bob Smith

Nylint No. 6000 American Oil Emergency Truck, 11¼'' long . . .	65	98	130
Nylint No. 6100 Hudraulic Dump Truck, 13½'' long	75	112	150
Nylint No. 6200 Kennel Truck with dogs, 11½'' long	48	72	95
Nylint No. 6300 Horse Van, 23½'' long	70	105	140
Nylint No. 6500 Payloader, added crank hoist	90	135	180

1964

	C6	C8	C10
Nylint No. 5900 Race Team, 21″	120	180	240
Nylint No. 6000 American Emergency Unit	65	98	130

1964

	C6	C8	C10
Nylint No. 6600 Mobile Home, Semi Type, 30″ long	80	120	160
Nylint No. 6700 Ambulance, 12″ long	85	128	170
Nylint No. 6800 Jalopy, 9⅝″ long	32	48	65
Nylint No. 6900 Airport Courtesy Van, 12″ long	250	375	500
Nylint No. 7000 Lawn and Garden Service Truck, 20″ long, 12 piece set	170	255	340
Nylint No. 7100 Fun on Farm Econoline Truck, 11¼″ long, 29 pieces	190	285	380

1965

	C6	C8	C10
Nylint No. 1100 Digger Power Shovel, 27″ long	90	135	180
No. 4100 Truck & U-Haul Rental Trailer, Twin I-Beam Suspension	75	112	150
Nylint No. 6801 Jalopy w/top, 9⅝″ long	50	75	100
Nylint No. 7300 Army Ambulance, 12″ long	66	99	132
Nylint No. 7800 Race Team set .	120	180	240
Nylint No. 7900 Road Grader, 15″ long	36	54	72
Nylint No. 8000 Pony Farm Van, 11¼″ long, 7 piece set	100	150	200
Nylint No. 8100 Suburban Fire Pumper, 12½″ long	85	128	170
Nylint No. 8200 Bronco, 12½″ long	30	45	60
Nylint No. 8300 Texaco Service Van, 12″ long	85	128	170

No date known

	C6	C8	C10
Nylint Austin Western crane . . .	100	150	200
Nylint Brinks truck	48	72	95

Nylint Chase & Sanborn Stake Truck, 14½″ long.
Photo by Bob Smith

Nylint Ford Cab-Over Tow Truck, 17″ long.
Photo by Bob Smith

	C6	C8	C10
Nylint Chase & Sanborn, stake sides	85	125	185
Nylint Fire Truck (1970), 20″ long	27	41	55
Nylint Ford Cab-over Tow truck, 17″ long	75	110	160
Nylint Harley Davidson Tanker, 25″ long	100	150	200
Nylint Hot Rod and Trailer	60	90	120
Nylint 4125 Rhino Pick-up	22	33	45

OH BOY

(Kiddies Metal Toys Inc., Plainfield, New Jersey)

$8.25 Doz "OH BOY" STEEL PULL TOYS

Sturdily constructed of heavy gauge metal, bright enamel finishes.
All with disc wheels and imitation balloon tires. Each in box.

1F2474—(Mfrs 100) Dump truck, 19½x7½x6½, red with black trim, crank for raising body. ⅙ doz. in pkg.................Doz **$8.25**

1F2486—(Mfrs 125) Wrecker, 19x7x6½, orange with black trim. ½ doz. in pkg. Doz **$8.25**

1F2479—(Mfrs 115) Ice truck, 19½x7x6½, green chassis and body, stenciled "ice." ½ doz. in pkg. Doz **$8.25**

1F2484—(Mfrs 120) Delivery truck, 19½x7x6½, red with black trim. ½ doz. in pkg. Doz **$8.25**

1F2478—(Mfrs 110) Racer, 19¾x7x7½x6¾, red body, imitation aluminum windshield, radiator and hood. ½ doz. in pkg....................Doz **$8.25**

1F2476—(Mfrs 105) Bus, 19½x7x6½, blue with black, pink and yellow trim. ½ doz. in pkg. Doz **$8.25**

1F2487—(Mfrs 130) Fire truck, 21x7x6½, red body, aerial and 2 orange side ladders, lever for raising aerial ladder. ½ doz. in pkg. Doz **$8.25**

1F2476

1F2488—(Mfrs 135) Fire engine, 19½x8½x6¾, red body, orange boiler with brass trim. ½ doz. in pkg. Doz **$8.25**

1F2487

Oh Boy toys, as shown in a c.1928 Butler Bros. catalog. Manufacturer's numbers in parentheses.

(photo of truck)

Oh Boy "American Express Truck", 22" long, c.1920s.
Photo by Bob Smith

	C6	C8	C10
Oh Boy "American Express Truck" No. 205, 22" long...	750	1200	1900
Oh Boy "Ice" Truck No. 115, 19½" long.................	250	375	500
Oh Boy Racer "No. 110", tin, 19" long.....................	100	150	200

OHIO ART

Ohio Art was started in October, 1908 by a dentist, H.S. Winzeler. Originally its intent was to make metal picture frames (thus its name), but in 1917 the firm bought C.E. Carter (Erie Toy Plant) and began producing metal toys, including a climbing monkey on a string for Ferdinand Strauss. Winzeler later sold the plant to Louis Marx, but continued making tin toys, while Marx, according to Ohio Art history, used the former Carter plant as the foundation of his own company. Ohio Art is still making toys in Bryan Ohio.

Photo by Don Hultzman

Ohio Art "Tank Bank" No. 15, 1941.......................	30	45	60
Ohio Art "Traffic Control", 1950s, tin wind-up cars, 3½" long, base 19x13".................	40	60	80

OHLSON & RICE

(Los Angeles)

	C6	C8	C10
Ohlsson & Rice Midget Racer, aluminum body, rubber tires, c.1940s	238	358	475
Ohlsson & Rice Pusher Racer . .	210	315	420

OROBR TOY WORKS

Brandenburg, Germany
1900-1922
by Bob Smith

Orobr Toy Works was founded by three partners, Neil, Muller, and Blechschmidt. The company produced numerous lower end toy vehicles, many of them made for the U.S. market. Even though a large amount of toy vehicles are found with the Orobr mark, there is not much information in print about the company. Orobr made some toys that do carry a fair value and they make a nice accent to any collection.

Orobr Six-Window Mercedes Pullman Limousine, 9½'' long.
Photo by Bob Smith

No. 24 Orobr Six Window Mercedes Pullman Limousine. Three tone green/red/white litho. 9.5'' long, electric lights, c/w motor, 4 opening doors, driver, c.1920 . . . . 800 1200 1600

Orobr Touring Car, 8¾'' long, c.1918.
Photo by Bob Smith

No. 25 Orobr Touring Car. Red/gray, 8.75'' long, c/w motor, fold down rear seats, c.1918. 400 600 800

Orobr, top: Model T Ford Sedan, 6'' long. Bottom, L to R: Model T Ford Sedan, 7¾'' long; Model T Ford Touring Car, 7¾'' long. Photo by Bob Smith

	C6	C8	C10
No. 26 Orobr Model T Ford Sedan. Black, 6'' long, c/w motor. c.1920s. Add $200 for color . .	300	450	650
No. 27 Orobr Model T Ford Sedan. Black, 7.75'' long, c/w motor, full interior, c.1920s	450	650	875
No. 28 Orobr Model T Ford Touring Car. Black/gray, 7.75'' long, c/w motor, c.1920s	500	700	925

P & F DIE WORKS

Located in Dayton, Ohio. They made plastic cars that may have been cereal giveaways.

P & F, L to R: No. 2 Highway Patrol, Police Ambulance.
Photo by Gary Linden

P&F No. 2 Highway Patrol State Police Car, 3½'' long		No Price Found	
P&F Police Ambulance, 3½'' long		No Price Found	
PAGCO Racer with motor	80	120	160

Parker Bros. Toy Town Garage.
Courtesy Heinz Muller, Continental Hobby House

PARKER BROS. Toy Town	**C6**	**C8**	**C10**
Garage, 3 litho tin penny cars,			
paper litho garage, c.1910....	600	900	1200

PETER-MAR TOYS
by Mary Gaeta

Ralph Lohr was the owner of Peter Products Manufacturing. He was an entrepreneur, artist and musician. He operated a music store in the early 1920's. In 1941 he started manufacturing wooden kitchen items, such as clothes racks, stools, ladders and ironing boards.

When WWII broke out lumber was limited to government contracts. Mr. Lohr was faced with closing his business. It was then he found he could purchase scrap lumber from government contractors and he started to design toys. The first of these were military vehicles. Farm toys were very popular, so he began making tractors, hay racks, trailers and wagons. These toys were very much in demand and continued to be much sought after. Other toys were Noah's Ark, Humpty Dumpty, Lucky Dog, Village Smitty, Old Woman in a Shoe, trolley cars, Carousel and Ferris Wheel.

Mr. Lohr had a son, Peter and his colleague, Clifford Hakes, had a daughter, Mary, hence the name Peter-Mar was chosen for the toys.

After over fifty years these toys are still popular and very much sought after. When these toys are found in antique stores the prices for arks and tractors in mint condition are $300.00 and $250.00 respectively. The Village Smitty, a pound a peg type toy has been sold for as much as $65.00. These toys are very well constructed and quite durable.

Peter-Mar's address was 708 E. Fourth St., Muscatine, Iowa.

Mary Gaeta is a lifetime resident of Muscatine; she graduated from Saint Mathias School and Muscatine Community College. She has been active in family business, has enjoyed a life long interest in antiques and has managed an antique consignment business for many years.

All kinds of { sales, eye-appeal, play-value, safety-value } Power!

PETER-MAR TOYS SELL THEMSELVES - *It's the craftsmanship!*

These attractive toys are not a substitute made necessary by wartime restrictions — these are quality toys that will have a ready market in peacetime as well. These well-built miniature farm toys are made by experienced craftsmen. They are doweled and glued — they are attractively designed and finished — they are made from HAY RACK (removable platform)____10 inches high — 21 inches long.

selected, well-seasoned woods. Special lubricated, hardwood axles.

Peter-Mar Toys have Eye Appeal — Safety Appeal — Play Value — All of which adds up to more SALES POWER for you. A sample order will convince you that Peter-Mar Toys . . . SELL THEMSELVES!

TRACTOR _____ 8 inches high — 12 inches long.

An original Peter-Mar flier, Courtesy Mary Gaeta

	C6	C8	C10
Peter-Mar Jeep, wood.........	No Price Found		
Peter-Mar Tractor, wood.......	125	188	250
Peter-Mar Trailer, wood........	125	188	250
Plasticville Gas Station........	4	6	8
Plasticville Sedan.............	No Price Found		
PLAYBOY Delivery Truck, "Playboy Trucking Co." 21" long......................	300	450	600
Playboy Dump Truck, 22" long	150	225	300
Playboy "Intercity Bus", 23½" long, cream color............	300	450	600
Playboy Tow Truck, "Playboy Trucking Co.", white, 22" long	250	400	650

Playboy Delivery Truck, "Playboy Trucking Co."
Photo by Calvin L. Chaussee

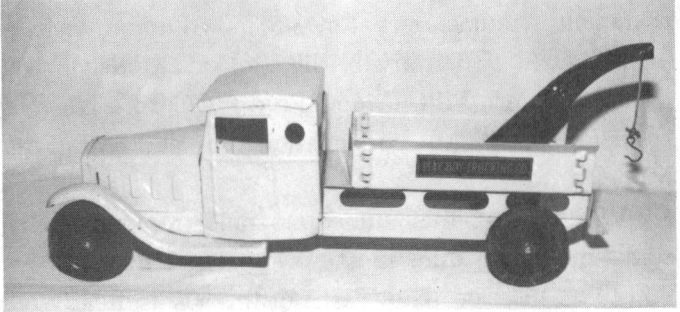

Playboy Tow Truck "Playboy Trucking Co." tow truck, white, 22" long, c.1930s.
Photo by Bob Smith

PLAYWOOD PLASTICS was a WWII era company that employed wood composition. It was a subsidiary of Transogram and its factory was at 133 Floyd Street in Brooklyn, NY.

Playwood Plastics, L to R: 438 or 436?; 407?a.

	C6	C8	C10
Playwood 407? "Dispatch Rider on Cycle"	7	11	14
Playwood 407?a As above, round base, head higher	7	11	14
Playwood 438 or 436? Motorcyclist, leather-type helmet (probably post-WWII)	No Price Found		
Pressman Ambulance, plastic	45	68	90

PROMOTIONALS

by Ron Smith

Promos are very accurately-produced reproductions of the full-size cars sitting on your car dealer's show room floor. They are almost always produced in 1/25th scale plastic or pot metal. Most of the pot metal (like a lead dimestore soldier) were discontinued by the very early 1950s. Molded in factory colors, they were sold to car dealers, who passed them out to the children of customers so Junior could have one just like dad. This price guide deals mostly with those produced up to 1972. They are still being made today, but in reduced numbers. In recent years as few as three or four different models were produced, whereas in the mid-sixties as many as fifty different models were produced. The most popular full-size cars are usually the popular promo. The most dominant manufacturers were AMT ("Aluminum Model Toys"), BAN (Banthrico), JH (JoHan Models), MC (Master Caster), MPC (Model Products Corp.), NP (National Products), PM (Product Miniatures) and SMP (Scale Model Products).

When using this guide one must remember that sometimes even mint in the original box may not get you the C10 price. The plastic of the 50s and early 60s had a tendency to warp, and each car had a specific place where the warpage occurred. In addition, the plating on the grille or bumpers might be flaking or dull. Something as small as a missing hood ornament or a cracked vent window post can reduce your C10 to a C6.

	C6	C8	C10
AMX 2 dr. hardtop, 1969 JH	20	30	60
AMX 2 dr. hardtop, 1970 JH	20	40	70
Aero Willys 4 dr. sedan, 1953 BIR	80	170	340
Aerocar convertible, 1953 GLA	40	80	160
Barracuda 2 dr. fastback, 1965 AMT	20	50	100
Barracuda 2 dr. fastback, 1966 AMT	20	40	80
Barracuda 2 dr. hardtop, 1967 AMT	20	40	80
Barracuda 2 dr. hardtop, 1968 MPC	40	80	150
Barracuda 2 dr. hardtop, 1969 MPC	30	50	110
Barracuda 2 dr. hardtop, 1970 MPC	70	150	290
Barracuda 2 dr. hardtop, 1971 MPC	90	180	360
Buick 4 dr. sedan, 1947 NP	40	80	160
Buick 4 dr. sedan, 1948 NP	30	70	140
Buick sedan 1950 NP	30	60	120
Buick 4 dr. sedan, 1952 BAN	30	60	120
Buick sedan, 1953 BAN	30	50	110
Buick 2 dr. hardtop, 1954 BAN	20	40	90
Buick Skylark convertible 1954 AMT	40	80	150
Buick 4 dr. sedan, 1954 AMT	20	40	90
Buick 2 dr. hardtop, 1955 BAN	20	40	80
Buick 4 dr. sedan, 1955 AMT	20	40	70
Buick convertible, 1955 AMT	20	40	80
Buick 4 dr. hardtop, 1956 BAN	30	50	100
Buick Roadmaster 4 dr. hardtop, 1956 AMT	20	40	80
Buick Century convertible, 1956 AMT	30	60	120
Buick Roadmaster convertible, 1957 AMT	30	60	120
Buick Roadmaster 2 dr. hardtop, 1957 AMT	30	60	120
Buick Roadmaster convertible, 1958 AMT	20	50	100
Buick Roadmaster 2 dr. hardtop, 1958 AMT	20	50	100
Buick Invicta convertible, 1959 AMT	20	50	90
Buick Invicta 2 dr. hardtop, 1959 AMT	20	40	80

	C6	C8	C10
Buick Invicta 2 dr. hardtop, 1960 AMT	30	60	120
Buick Invicta convertible, 1960 AMT	30	60	120
Buick Special station wagon, 1961 AMT	20	30	70
Buick Invicta convertible, 1961 AMT	30	60	120
Buick Invicta 2 dr. hardtop, 1961 AMT	20	40	90
Buick Electra 225 convertible, 1962 AMT	30	50	100
Buick Special station wagon, 1962 AMT	10	30	60
Buick Electra 225 2 dr. hardtop, 1962 AMT	20	50	100
Buick Electra 225 2 dr. hardtop, 1963 AMT	20	50	100
Buick Riviera 2 dr. hardtop, 1963 AMT	30	70	140
Buick Electra 225 convertible, 1963 AMT	30	70	130
Buick Wildcat 2 dr. hardtop, 1964 AMT	60	120	240
Buick Riviera 2 dr. hardtop, 1964 AMT	20	50	100
Buick Riviera 2 dr. hardtop, 1965 AMT	50	90	180
Buick Wildcat convertible, 1965 AMT	60	120	240
Buick Wildcat 2 dr. hardtop, 1965 AMT	60	130	260
Buick Skylark 2 dr. hardtop, 1966 AMT	40	90	180
Buick Wildcat 2 dr. hardtop, 1966 AMT	20	40	80
Buick Riviera 2 dr. hardtop, 1966 AMT	20	30	70
Buick Riviera 2 dr. hardtop, 1967 AMT	20	30	60
Buick Riviera 2 dr. hardtop, 1968 AMT	30	50	110
Buick Riviera 2 dr. hardtop, 1969 AMT	20	40	80
Buick Wildcat 2 dr. hardtop, 1969 AMT	10	30	60
Buick Wildcat 2 dr. hardtop, 1970 AMT	10	20	40

	C6	C8	C10
Cadillac 4 dr. sedan, 1952 BAN	30	60	120
Cadillac, 4 dr. sedan, 1954 BAN	30	60	130
Cadillac, 2 dr. hardtop, 1955 AMT	20	50	100
Cadillac, 4 dr. sedan, 1955 BAN	40	70	140
Cadillac Eldorado, 2 dr. hardtop, 1956 BAN	30	70	140
Cadillac 62, 2 dr. hardtop, 1956 AMT	20	40	80
Cadillac 60 S, 4 dr. sedan, 1958 JH	10	30	60
Cadillac Fleetwood, 4 dr. 1959 JH	20	40	90
Cadillac Fleetwood, 4 dr. hardtop, 1960 JH	20	50	90
Cadillac Fleetwood, 4 dr. hardtop, 1961 JH	20	40	90
Cadillac Fleetwood, 4 dr. hardtop, 1962 JH	20	50	90
Cadillac convertible, 1963 JH	10	30	60
Cadillac 2 dr. hardtop, 1963 JH	10	30	60
Cadillac convertible, 1964 JH	20	40	80
Cadillac 2 dr. hardtop, 1964 JH	20	40	80
Cadillac 2 dr. hardtop, 1965 JH	20	40	80
Cadillac convertible, 1965 JH	20	40	80
Cadillac 2 dr. hardtop, 1966 JH	20	40	80
Cadillac convertible, 1966 JH	20	40	90
Cadillac Eldorado, 2 dr. hardtop, 1967 JH	20	40	80
Cadillac 2 dr. hardtop, 1967 JH	20	30	70
Cadillac convertible, 1967 JH	20	40	80
Cadillac convertible, 1968 JH	10	20	50
Cadillac 2 dr. hardtop, 1968 JH	10	20	50
Cadillac Eldorado 2 dr. hardtop, 1968 JH	10	30	50
Cadillac 2 dr. hardtop, 1969 JH	10	30	50
Cadillac Eldorado 2 dr. hardtop, 1969 JH	10	30	50
Cadillac 2 dr. hardtop, 1970 JH	10	20	40
Cadillac Eldorado 2 dr. hardtop, 1970 JH	20	30	60
Cadillac Eldorado 2 dr. hardtop, 1971 JH	10	30	60
Cadillac Eldorado 2 dr. hardtop, 1972 JH	10	20	40
Camaro convertible, 1967 AMT	40	80	150
Camaro convertible pace, 1967 AMT	130	250	500
Camaro 2 dr. hardtop, 1967 AMT	40	80	170
Camaro convertible, 1968 MPC	50	90	190

	C6	C8	C10
Camaro convertible, 1969 AMT	40	90	180
Camaro convertible pace, 1969 AMT	80	160	320
Camaro 2 dr. hardtop, 1969 AMT	40	80	160
Camaro 2 dr. hardtop, 1970 AMT	30	60	120
Camaro 2 dr. hardtop, 1971 MPC	20	40	80
Camaro 2 dr. hardtop, 1972 MPC	20	50	90
Chevelle station wagon, 1964 AMT	20	40	90
Chevelle 2 dr. hardtop, 1964 AMT	30	50	110
Chevelle Malibu station wagon, 1965 AMT	30	50	100
Chevelle Malibu SS, 2 dr. hardtop, 1965 AMT	20	40	80
Chevelle 2 dr. hardtop, 1969 AMT	30	60	130
Chevelle convertible, 1969 AMT	40	80	160
Chevelle SS convertible, 1970 AMt	30	70	140
Chevelle SS 2 dr. hardtop, 1970 AMT	30	70	140
Chevelle 2 dr. hardtop, 1971 MPC	20	50	100
Chevelle SS 2 dr. hardtop, 1972 MPC	20	50	100
Chevrolet Fleetline 2 dr., 1947 NP	40	80	160
Chevrolet Fleetline 2 dr., 1948 NP	40	80	160
Chevrolet Stlyline 4 dr. sedan, 1949 BAN	30	70	140
Chevrolet convertible, 1949 BAN	40	90	180
Chevrolet Fleetline 2 dr., 1949 BAN	40	80	160
Chevrolet Fleetline 4 dr., 1949 BAN	40	80	160
Chevrolet Styline 2 dr., 1949 BAN	30	70	140
Chevrolet 2 dr. coupe, 1949 BAN	60	130	260
Chevrolet 2 dr. coupe, 1950 BAN	30	70	130
Chevrolet Bel Air 2 dr. hardtop, 1950 BAN	30	70	140
Chevrolet convertible, 1950 BAN	40	80	160
Chevrolet Fleetline 4 dr., 1950 BAN	30	70	130
Chevrolet Styline 4 dr. sedan, 1950 BAN	30	60	120
Chevrolet Styline 2 dr. sedan, 1950 BAN	30	60	120
Chevrolet Fleetline 2 dr., 1950 BAN	40	70	150
Chevrolet Styline 4 dr. sedan, 1951 PMC	30	70	140
Chevrolet convertible, 1951 PMC	60	120	240
Chevrolet Bel Air 2 dr. hardtop, 1951 PMC	30	70	140
Chevrolet Styline 2 dr. sedan, 1951 PMC	30	70	140

Chevrolet Styline 4 dr. Sedan 1951.
Photo by Ron Smith

	C6	C8	C10
Chevrolet 2 dr. coupe, 1951 PMC	30	70	130
Chevrolet Fleetline 2 dr., 1951 PMC	40	80	160
Chevrolet Fleetline 4 dr., 1951 PMC	40	80	170
Chevrolet Styline 2 dr. sedan, 1952 PMC	40	70	150
Chevrolet Styline 4 dr. sedan, 1952 PMC	30	70	130
Chevrolet Fleetline 2 dr., 1952 PMC	40	80	160
Chevrolet 2 dr. coupe, 1952 PMC	40	70	150
Chevrolet convertible, 1952 PMC	60	120	240
Chevrolet Bel Air 2 dr. hardtop, 1952 PMC	30	70	130
Chevrolet 210 2 dr. sedan, 1953 PMC	30	60	130
Chevrolet Bel Air 4 dr. sedan, 1953 PMC	30	60	120
Chevrolet 150 4 dr. sedan, 1953 PMC	30	60	130
Chevrolet Bel Air 2 dr. hardtop, 1953 PMC	30	70	140
Chevrolet Bel Air 2 dr. sedan, 1953 PMC	30	70	130
Chevrolet 210 4 dr. sedan, 1953 PMC	30	60	120
Chevrolet 150 2 dr. sedan, 1953 PMC	30	60	130
Chevrolet convertible, 1953 PMC	40	80	160
Chevrolet Bel Air 2 dr. hardtop, 1954 PMC	40	80	160
Chevrolet 210 4 dr. sedan, 1954 PMC	30	60	120

	C6	C8	C10
Chevrolet Bel Air convertible, 1954 PMC	40	80	160
Chevrolet 210 2 dr. sedan, 1954 PMC	40	80	160
Chevrolet Bel Air 2 dr. sedan, 1954 PMC	30	70	140
Chevrolet 150 2 dr. sedan, 1954 PMC	40	80	160
Chevrolet Bel Air 4 dr. sedan, 1954 PMC	40	70	140
Chevrolet 150 4 dr. sedan, 1954 PMC	40	80	160
Chevrolet 2 dr. hardtop, 1955 PMC	30	70	140
Chevrolet 4 dr. sedan, 1955 PMC	30	70	140
Chevrolet 2 dr. hardtop, 1955 BAN	40	70	150
Chevrolet 4 dr. hardtop, 1956 PMC	30	70	140
Chevrolet Cameo pick-up, 1956 PMC	40	70	140
Chevrolet 4 dr. sedan, 1956 PMC	30	70	130
Chevrolet 2 dr. hardtop, 1956 PMC	30	60	110
Chevrolet station wagon, 1956 PMC	20	50	90
Chevrolet 2 dr. hardtop, 1956 BAN	40	70	140
Chevrolet station wagon, 1957 SMP	30	70	130
Chevrolet 4 dr. hardtop, 1957 PMC	30	60	130
Chevrolet 2 dr. hardtop, 1957 SMP	30	70	140
Chevrolet convertible, 1957 SMP	40	70	140
Chevrolet pick-up, 1957 PMC...	30	60	130
Chevrolet 2 dr. hardtop, 1958 AMT	30	60	120
Chevrolet convertible, 1958 AMT	30	60	120
Chevrolet station wagon, 1958 PMC	20	50	90
Chevrolet 4 dr. hardtop, 1958 PMC	20	40	80
Chevrolet pick-up, 1958 AMT ..	40	90	180
Chevrolet pick-up, 1959 PMC...	40	90	170
Chevrolet station wagon, 1959 SMP	20	40	90
Chevrolet convertible, 1959 SMP	30	70	140
Chevrolet 2 dr. hardtop, 1959 SMP	20	40	80
Chevrolet pick-up, 1960 SMP...	50	90	180
Chevrolet Impala 2 dr. hardtop, 1960 SMP	20	30	70
Chevrolet Impala 4 dr. hardtop, 1960 SMP	30	60	120

Chevrolet El Camino Pick-Up 1960.
Photo by Ron Smith

	C6	C8	C10
Chevrolet El Camino pick-up, 1960 AMT	30	60	120
Chevrolet Nomad station wagon, 1960 SMP	20	40	90
Chevrolet Impala convertible, 1960 SMP	30	60	110
Chevrolet Impala convertible, 1961 AMT	50	100	200
Chevrolet Impala 4 dr. hardtop, 1961 AMT	60	120	240
Chevrolet Apache pick-up, 1961 AMT	40	80	160
Chevrolet pick-up, 1962 AMT ..	60	120	240
Chevrolet Impala convertible, 1962 AMT	50	100	200
Chevrolet Impala 2 dr. hardtop, 1962 AMT	70	150	300

Chevrolet Impala 2 dr. HT 1963.
Photo by Ron Smith

	C6	C8	C10
Chevrolet Impala convertible, 1963 AMT	70	140	290
Chevrolet Impala 2 dr. hardtop, 1963 AMT	50	100	210
Chevrolet pick-up, 1963 AMT ..	60	130	260
Chevrolet El Camino pick-up, 1964 AMT	30	70	130

	C6	C8	C10
Chevrolet Impala convertible, 1964 AMT	40	70	150
Chevrolet Impala 2 dr. hardtop, 1964 AMT	40	70	140
Chevrolet Fleetside pick-up, 1965 AMT	40	80	160
Chevrolet El Camino pick-up, 1965 AMT	40	70	140
Chevrolet Impala SS 2 dr. hardtop, 1965 AMT	30	60	110
Chevrolet Impala SS convertible, 1965 AMT	30	70	140
Chevrolet Impala SS Budget Rent-A-Car, 1966 AMT	40	80	160
Chevrolet Impala SS 2 dr. hardtop, 1966 AMT	30	60	130
Chevrolet Impala convertible, 1966 AMT	30	60	120
Chevrolet Fleetside pick-up, 1966 AMT	50	90	190
Chevrolet Impala 2 dr. hardtop, 1967 AMT	30	70	130
Chevrolet Fleetside pick-up, 1967 AMT	30	70	130
Chevrolet Impala convertible, 1967 AMT	40	70	140
Chevrolet Impala 2 dr. hardtop, 1968 MPC	30	70	130
Chevrolet Fleetside pick-up, 1968 MPC	30	60	120
Chevrolet Impala convertible, 1968 MPC	40	80	170
Chevrolet Impala convertible, 1969 AMT	20	40	80
Chevrolet Fleetside pick-up, 1969 AMT	30	70	140
Chevrolet Impala 2 dr. hardtop, 1969 AMT	20	40	80
Chevrolet Impala convertible, 1970 AMT	20	40	80
Chevrolet Impala 2 dr. hardtop, 1970 AMT	20	40	70
Chevrolet Monte Carlo 2 dr. hardtop, 1970 AMT	20	40	80
Chevrolet Fleetside pick-up, 1970 AMT	30	70	130
Chevrolet Fleetside pick-up, 1971 MPC	30	50	110

	C6	C8	C10
Chevrolet Monte Carlo 2 dr. hardtop, 1971, AMT	30	60	110
Chevrolet Impala 2 dr. hardtop, 1971 MPC	20	40	90
Chevrolet Impala convertible, 1971 MPC	20	40	90
Chevrolet Impala 2 dr. hardtop, 1972 MPC	20	30	70
Chevrolet Monte Carlo 2 dr. hardtop, 1972 MPC	20	50	100
Chevrolet Fleetside pick-up, 1972 MPC	30	50	100
Chevrolet Nova 2 dr. hardtop, 1962 AMT	40	90	180
Chevrolet Nova convertible, 1962 AMT	30	60	120
Chevrolet Nova convertible, 1963 AMT	50	100	210
Chevrolet Nova station wagon, 1963 AMT	20	40	90
Chevrolet Nova 2 dr. hardtop, 1963 AMT	30	60	120
Chevrolet 11 2 dr. hardtop, 1965 AMT	30	60	110
Chrysler 2 dr. hardtop, 1953 BAN	30	50	100
Chrysler 4 dr. hardtop, 1957 JH	20	30	60
Chrysler New Yorker 4 dr., 1958 JH	20	40	80
Chrysler New Yorker 4 dr. hardtop, 1959 JH	10	30	60
Chrysler New Yorker 2 dr. hardtop, 1960 JH	10	30	60
Chrysler New Yorker 2 dr. hardtop, 1961 JH	10	30	60
Chrysler 300 convertible, 1962 JH	20	40	90
Chrysler 300 2 dr. hardtop, 1962 JH	20	40	90
Chrysler 300 convertible pace, 1963 JH	70	140	280
Chrysler 300 convertible, 1963 JH	40	70	150
Chrysler 300 2 dr. hardtop, 1963 JH	30	60	130
Chrysler convertible, 1964 JH . . .	40	70	150
Chrysler 2 dr. hardtop, 1964 JH	20	40	80
Chrysler Turbine 2 dr. hardtop, 1964 JH.	10	30	60
Chrysler 300 convertible, 1965 JH	30	70	140
Chrysler 300 2 dr. hardtop, 1965 JH	50	100	210
Chrysler 300 convertible, 1966 JH	20	40	80
Chrysler 300 2 dr. hardtop, 1966 JH	40	80	160
Chrysler 300 2 dr. hardtop, 1967 JH	10	20	40

	C6	C8	C10
Chrysler 300 convertible, 1967 JH	10	20	50
Chrysler 300 convertible, 1968 JH	10	30	50
Chrysler 300 2 dr. hardtop, 1968 JH	10	20	50
Chrysler 4 dr. sedan, 1950 BAN	30	60	120
Chrysler 4 dr. sedan, 1948 NP .	20	40	90
Chrysler 4 dr. sedan, 1954 BAN	30	50	100
Comet 4 dr. sedan, 1960 AMT .	10	20	40
Comet 2 dr. sedan, 1961 AMT .	10	20	50
Comet 2 dr. sedan, 1962 AMT .	10	30	60
Comet convertible, 1963 AMT ..	10	30	60
Comet 2 dr. hardtop, 1964 AMT	60	130	260
Comet Cyclone GT pace car (white), 1966 AMT	50	90	190
Comet Cyclone GT pace car (red), 1966 AMT	50	100	190
Comet 2 dr. sedan, 1971 JH....	10	20	30
Continental Mark II 2 dr. hardtop, 1956 AMT	40	80	150
Continental Mark II 2 dr. hardtop, 1957 AMT	40	80	150

Continental MK III 4 dr. HT 1958.
Photo by Ron Smith

	C6	C8	C10
Continental MK III 4 dr. hardtop, 1958 AMT	10	30	60
Continental MK IV convertible, 1959 AMT	20	40	70
Continental MK IV 2 dr. hardtop, 1959 AMT	20	40	70
Continental MK V 2 dr. hardtop, 1960 AMT	10	20	50
Continental MK V convertible, 1960 AMT	10	30	50
Continental convertible, 1961 AMT	20	40	80
Continental 4 dr. sedan, 1961 AMT	20	40	80
Continental 4 dr. convertible, 1962 AMT	30	60	110
Continental 4 dr. sedan, 1962 AMT	30	60	110
Continental 4 dr. sedan, 1963 AMT	20	30	60

	C6	C8	C10
Continental 4 dr. convertible, 1963 AMT	20	30	70
Continental 4 dr. sedan, 1964 AMT	40	90	180
Continental 4 dr. convertible, 1964 AMT	20	40	90
Continental 4 dr. convertible, 1965 AMT	10	20	40
Continental 4 dr. sedan, 1965 AMT	30	50	100
Continental 4 dr. sedan, 1966 AMT	20	50	90
Continental 4 dr. sedan, 1967 AMT	20	50	100
Continental 4 dr. sedan, 1968 AMT	10	20	50
Corvair 4 dr. sedan, 1960 AMT .	20	40	80
Corvair Monza coupe, 1961 AMT	20	40	90
Corvair 700 4 dr. sedan, 1961 AMT	20	50	90
Corvair Monza 2 dr. hardtop, 1962 AMT	50	100	200
Corvair Monza 2 dr. hardtop, 1963 AMT	30	60	120
Corvair Monza convertible, 1963 AMT	30	70	130
Corvair Monza 2 dr. hardtop, 1964 AMT	40	90	170
Corvair Monza convertible, 1964 AMT	40	90	170
Corvair Corsa convertible, 1965 AMT	30	70	130
Corvair Corsa 2 dr. hardtop, 1965 AMT	40	80	160
Corvair Corsa convertible, 1966 AMT	20	30	70
Corvair Corsa 2 dr. hardtop, 1966 AMT	30	70	140
Corvair Monza 2 dr. hardtop, 1967 AMT	30	60	120
Corvette convertible (orig.), 1954 BAN	20	50	100
Corvette convertible, 1954 PMC.	110	220	440
Corvette convertible, 1958 AMT .	90	180	360
Corvette convertible, 1959 AMT .	80	170	340
Corvette convertible, 1960 AMT .	110	220	440
Corvette conv. w/hardtop, 1961 AMT	60	120	240
Corvette convertible, 1961 SMP.	150	300	600
Corvette convertible, 1962 AMT .	150	300	600
Corvette Sting Ray convertible, 1963 AMT	70	150	300
Corvette Sting Ray coupe, 1963 AMT	150	300	610

	C6	C8	C10		C6	C8	C10
Corvette Sting Ray coupe, 1964 AMT	120	250	500	Dodge pick-up, 1950 NP	30	70	130
Corvette Sting Ray convertible, 1964 AMT	130	260	530	Dodge stake truck, 1950 NP	30	60	130
Corvette Sting Ray coupe, 1965 AMT	140	280	560	Dodge 4 dr. sedan, 1950 BAN	20	50	100
				Dodge 4 dr. sedan, 1951 BAN	20	50	90
Corvette Sting Ray convertible, 1965 AMT	130	260	520	Dodge 4 dr. sedan, 1953 BAN	20	50	100
Corvette Sting Ray coupe, 1966 AMT	220	440	880	Dodge 4 dr. sedan, 1954 BAN	20	40	90
Corvette Sting Ray convertible, 1966 AMT	230	460	920	Dodge Lancer 2 dr. hardtop, 1955 BAN	20	30	70
Corvette Sting Ray coupe, 1967 AMT	250	510	1020	Dodge Lancer 4 dr. hardtop, 1956 AMT	30	50	100
Corvette Sting Ray convertible, 1967 AMT	220	440	880	Dodge Custom Royal 2 dr. hardtop, 1958 JH	20	30	60
Corvette Sting Ray convertible, 1968 MPC	100	200	400	Dodge Custom Royal 2 dr. hardtop, 1959 JH	10	30	60
Corvette Sting Ray coupe, 1968 MPC	20	50	100	Dodge Phoenix 2 dr. hardtop, 1960 JH	20	40	70
Corvette Sting Ray convertible, 1969 AMT	100	200	400	Dodge Phoenix 2 dr. hardtop, 1961 JH	20	30	70
Corvette Sting Ray coupe, 1969 AMT	150	300	600	Dodge police car, 1961 JH	20	50	100
				Dodge Dart 2 dr. hardtop, 1962 JH	10	30	60
Corvette Sting Ray coupe, 1971 MPC	100	200	400	Dodge Dart police car, 1962 JH	60	120	240
Corvette Sting Ray coupe, 1972 MPC	90	180	360	Dodge Dart convertible, 1962 JH	20	30	70
				Dodge Polara convertible, 1963 JH	20	40	80
Cougar 2 dr. hardtop, 1968 AMT	10	30	60	Dodge Polara 2 dr. hardtop, 1963 JH	30	50	100
Covette Sting Ray coupe, 1970 AMT	90	180	350	Dodge Polara 2 dr. hardtop, 1964 JH	30	50	100
Covette Sting Ray convertible, 1970 AMT	90	190	380	Dodge Polara convertible, 1964 JH	30	50	110
Desoto sedan, 1948 NP	20	40	80	Dodge Custom 880 convertible, 1965 MPC	40	80	160
Desoto 4 dr. sedan, 1955 JH	20	30	60	Dodge Monaco 2 dr. hardtop, 1965 MPC	30	70	130
Desoto 4 dr., 1956 JH	20	30	70	Dodge Coronet 500 2 dr. hardtop, 1965 MPC	50	100	210
Desoto Sportsman 4 dr. hardtop, 1957 JH	20	40	80	Dodge Coronet 500 convertible, 1965 MPC	40	90	180
Desoto Fireflight 4 dr. hardtop, 1958 JH	20	30	60	Dodge Charger 2 dr. hardtop, 1966 MPC	40	80	160
Desoto Fireflight 4 dr. hardtop, 1959 JH	10	30	60	Dodge Polara 500 convertible, 1966 MPC	40	80	160
Desoto Adventurer 2 dr. hardtop, 1960 JH	20	30	60	Dodge Monaco 500 2 dr. hardtop, 1966 MPC	40	70	150
Diamond T semi-truck, 1956 PMC	20	40	90	Dodge Charger 2 dr. hardtop, 1967 MPC	50	90	190
Diamond T dump truck, 1956 PMC	20	40	80	Dodge Charger 2 dr. hardtop, 1968 MPC	70	140	270
Divco milk truck, 1951 AMT	70	130	260	Dodge Coronet 2 dr. hardtop, 1968 MPC	60	130	260
Dodge 4 dr. sedan, 1948 NP	20	50	100				

	C6	C8	C10
Dodge Charger R/T 2 dr. hardtop, 1969 MPC	60	110	230
Dodge Coronet convertible, 1969 MPC	50	110	220
Dodge Coronet 2 dr. hardtop, 1969 MPC	50	100	210
Dodge Challenger 2 dr. hardtop, 1970 MPC	60	120	240
Dodge Charger RT 2 dr. hardtop, 1970 MPC	50	110	220
Dodge Charger 2 dr. hardtop, 1971 MPC	70	140	270
Dodge Challenger 2 dr. hardtop, 1971 MPC	50	100	200
Dodge Challenger 2 dr. hardtop, 1972 MPC	30	70	130
Dodge Charger 2 dr. hardtop, 1972 MPC	30	60	130

Edsel Convertible 1958
Photo by Ron Smith

	C6	C8	C10
Edsel convertible, 1958 AMT	50	100	190
Edsel 2 dr. hardtop, 1958 AMT	50	90	190
Edsel Corsair convertible, 1959 AMT	40	90	180
Edsel Corsair 2 dr. hardtop, 1959 AMT	40	80	170
Edsel Ranger convertible, 1960 AMT	30	70	130
Edsel Ranger 2 dr. hardtop, 1960 AMT	30	60	120
Euclid quarry dump truck, 1950 PM	20	50	100
Euclid dump truck, 1958 BAN	20	30	60
Euclid dump truck, 1965 BAN	10	30	60

	C6	C8	C10
F-85 station wagon, 1961 JH	10	20	40
F-85 convertible, 1964 JH	30	60	120
F-85 2 dr. hardtop, 1964 JH	30	60	120
F-85 Cutlass convertible, 1962 JH	20	40	70
F-85 Cutlass 2 dr. sedan, 1962 JH	20	30	60
F-85 442 2 dr. hardtop, 1968 JH	20	40	80
Fairlane 2 dr. sedan, 1962 AMT	20	30	70
Fairlane 2 dr. hardtop, 1963 AMT	20	40	80
Fairlane 500 2 dr. hardtop, 1964 AMT	20	40	90
Fairlane 2 dr. hardtop, 1965 AMT	20	30	70
Fairlane 2 dr. hardtop, 1966 AMT	30	60	110
Fairlane Cobra 2 dr. hardtop, 1970 AMT	10	30	60
Falcon 2 dr. sedan, 1960 AMT	20	30	60
Falcon Ranchero pick-up, 1961 SMP	20	40	70
Falcon 2 dr. sedan, 1961 AMT	10	20	50
Falcon Futura 2 dr. sedan, 1962 AMT	10	20	50
Falcon convertible, 1963 AMT	30	60	120
Falcon Sprint convertible, 1964 AMT	20	40	90
Falcon Sprint 2 dr. hardtop, 1964 AMT	20	40	80
Falcon convertible, 1965 AMT	20	30	70
Falcon 2 dr. hardtop, 1965 AMT	20	40	80
Falcon Futura 2 dr. 1966 AMT	20	40	80
Falcon 2 dr. hardtop, 1969 AMT	10	20	40
Fiord Torino Cobra hardtop, 1969 AMT	20	40	90
Firebird convertible, 1967 MPC	40	80	160
Firebird 2 dr. hardtop, 1967 MPC	20	40	80
Firebird convertible, 1968 MPC	60	120	240
Firebird 2 dr. hardtop, 1968 MPC	40	90	170
Firebird convertible, 1969 MPC	30	70	130
Firebird 2 dr. hardtop, 1969 MPC	30	70	130
Firebird 2 dr. hardtop, 1970 MPC	20	50	100
Firebird 400 2 dr. hardtop, 1971 MPC	20	30	70
Firebird 400 2 dr. hardtop, 1972 MPC	20	40	70
Ford 4 dr. sedan, 1948 AMT	30	60	120
Ford 2 dr. sedan, 1948 MC	30	60	120
Ford 4 dr. sedan, 1950 BAN	30	60	130
Ford pick-up, 1950 NP	40	80	160
Ford 2 dr. sedan, 1950 MC	30	70	140
Ford 4 dr. sedan, 1950 AMT	20	40	80

	C6	C8	C10
Ford stake truck, 1951 NP	20	40	80
Ford pick-up, 1951 NP	20	50	100
Ford 4 dr. sedan, 1951 AMT . . .	20	40	80
Ford panel truck, 1951 NP	20	40	90
Ford 4 dr. sedan, 1953 BAN . . .	20	50	100
Ford 4 dr. sedan, 1953 AMT . . .	20	40	80
Ford pick-up, 1953 BAN	40	80	160
Ford 4 dr. sedan, 1954 AMT . . .	20	40	80
Ford convertible, 1954 AMT	20	50	100
Ford station wagon, 1955 PMC .	30	50	100
Ford station wagon, 1956 PMC .	20	50	90
Ford 4 dr. sedan, 1956 AMT . . .	30	60	120
Ford station wagon, 1957 PMC .	20	40	80
Ford station wagon, 1958 PMC .	20	40	80
Ford station wagon, 1959 AMT .	20	40	80
Ford station wagon, 1960 HUB .	20	40	80
Ford pick-up, 1960 AMT	30	70	130
Ford station wagon, 1961 HUB .	20	40	80
Ford station wagon, 1962 HUB .	20	40	80
Ford Custom 4 dr. sedan, 1952 AMT	20	40	70
Ford Pace Car convertible, 1953 AMT	70	150	290
Ford Ford Sunliner, convertible, 1955 AMT	40	80	160
Ford Victoria 2 dr. hardtop, 1955 BAN	20	50	100
Ford Victoria 4 dr. sedan, 1955 BAN	30	60	120
Ford Sunliner convertible, 1956 AMT	20	40	80
Ford Victoria 4 dr. sedan, 1956 AMT	20	40	90
Ford Fairlane convertible, 1957 AMT	30	50	110
Ford Custom 300 2 dr. sedan, 1957 AMT	70	140	280
Ford Fairlane 2 dr. hardtop, 1957 AMT	20	50	90
Ford Fairlane convertible, 1958 AMT	30	60	110
Ford Fairlane 2 dr. hardtop, 1958 AMT	20	30	70
Ford Galaxie 2 dr. hardtop, 1959 AMT	20	50	100
Ford Galaxie convertible, 1959 AMT	30	50	100
Ford Ranchero pick-up, 1959 PMC	20	40	70

	C6	C8	C10
Ford Galaxie 4 dr. hardtop, 1960 AMT	20	40	80
Ford Starliner hardtop, 1960 AMT	20	50	90
Ford Sunliner convertible, 1960 AMT	20	50	100
Ford Fairlane 4 dr. sedan, 1960 HUB	20	40	70
Ford Fairlane 4 dr. sedan, 1961 HUB	20	40	70
Ford Starliner hardtop, 1961 AMT	20	40	80
Ford F-100 pick-up, 1961 AMT .	40	70	150
Ford Galaxie 2 dr. hardtop, 1961 AMT	20	40	70
Ford, Sunliner convertible, 1961 AMT	20	50	100
Ford F-100 pick-up, 1962 AMT .	30	60	110
Ford Galaxie 2 dr. hardtop, 1962 AMT	20	50	90
Ford Galaxie convertible, 1962 AMT	30	50	110
Ford Galaxie 2 dr. hardtop, 1963 AMT	20	40	70
Ford Galaxie convertible, 1963 AMT	20	40	70
Ford Galaxie 500XL 2 dr. hardtop, 1964 AMT	20	40	90
Ford Galaxie 500XL convertible, 1964 AMT	20	40	90
Ford Cobra roadster, 1964 AMT	10	30	50
Ford Galaxie convertible, 1965 AMT	20	30	60
Ford Galaxie 2 dr. hardtop, 1965 AMT	10	30	60
Ford Galaxie 500 2 dr. hardtop, 1966 AMT	20	40	70
Ford Galaxie 500 convertible, 1966 AMT	20	40	80
Ford Galaxie 2 dr. hardtop, 1967 AMT	20	30	60
Ford Galaxie 2 dr. hardtop, 1968 AMT	20	30	70
Ford LTD 2 dr. hardtop, 1969 AMT	10	30	60
Ford LTD 4 dr. hardtop, 1970 AMT	20	30	60
Ford Grand Torino 2 dr. hardtop, 1972 JH	10	20	50
Ford Torino 2 dr. hardtop, 1969 AMT	30	60	120

	C6	C8	C10
GMC pick-up, 1950 NP	30	50	110
GMC dump truck, 1950 NP	30	50	110
Henry J 2 dr. sedan, 1951 AMT	40	80	150
Hornet 2 dr. sedan, 1970 JH . . .	10	20	40
Hudson 4 dr. sedan, 1948 MC .	50	100	200
Hudson sedan, 1950 MC	40	80	160
Hudson 4 dr. sedan, 1951 MC .	30	60	120
Imperial convertible, 1958 AMT .	20	40	90

Imperial 2 dr. HT 1958
Photo by Ron Smith

	C6	C8	C10
Imperial 2 dr. hardtop, 1958 AMT	20	40	90
Imperial convertible, 1959 SMP .	20	40	80
Imperial 2 dr. hardtop, 1959 SMP	20	40	80
Imperial convertible, 1960 SMP .	10	30	60
Imperial 2 dr. hardtop, 1960 SMP	10	30	60
Imperial 2 dr. hardtop, 1961 AMT	40	70	140
Imperial convertible, 1961 AMT .	30	50	100
Imperial convertible, 1962 AMT .	20	40	80
Imperial 2 dr. hardtop, 1962 ATM	20	40	80
Imperial 2 dr. hardtop, 1963 AMT	50	100	200
Imperial convertible, 1963 AMT .	20	40	80
Imperial Crown 2 dr. hardtop, 1964 AMT	50	100	200
Imperial convertible, 1964 AMT .	50	100	200
Imperial 2 dr. hardtop, 1965 AMT	20	40	80
Imperial convertible, 1965 AMT .	50	100	200
Imperial convertible, 1966 AMT .	60	120	250
Imperial 2 dr. hardtop, 1966 AMT	60	120	240
Imperial 2 dr. hardtop, 1967 AMT	40	70	140
Imperial 2 dr. hardtop, 1968 JH	10	20	50
International pick-up, 1947 PMC	50	100	190
International telephone tk, 1947 NP	30	70	140
International pick-up, 1950 PMC	40	70	150
International semi-truck, 1951 PMC	30	50	110
International pick-up, 1951 PMC	40	80	160
International dump truck, 1951 PMC	30	60	120
International stake truck, 1951 PMC	30	60	130

	C6	C8	C10
International semi (plain) 1953 PMC	20	50	90
International stake truck 1953 PMC	20	50	100
International semi "Mayflower", 1953 PMC	20	40	80
International dump truck, 1953 PMC	20	50	100
International tilt cab semi, 1955 PMC	20	40	70

International Pick-Up 1956
Photo by Ron Smith

	C6	C8	C10
International pick-up, 1956 PMC	20	40	90
International pick-up, 1957 PMC	20	50	100
International 4 dr. sedan, 1958 PMC	10	20	50
International dump truck, 1958 PMC	10	20	40
International Scout convertible, 1965 ESK	20	30	70
Javelin 2 dr. hardtop, 1968 JH . .	10	30	60
Javelin 2 dr. hardtop, 1969 JH . .	10	30	60
Javelin 2 dr. hardtop, 1970 JH . .	20	30	70
Javelin/AMX 2 dr. hardtop, 1971 JH	10	30	50
Javelin/AMX 2 dr. hardtop, 1972 JH	10	20	40
Jeep station wagon, 1950 AUT . .	40	90	180
Kaiser 4 dr. sedan, 1953 BAN . .	80	160	320
Lincoln Cosmopolitan 4 dr. sedan, 1950	110	220	440
Lincoln 4 dr. sedan, 1951 BAN .	30	50	100
Lincoln 4 dr. sedan, 1953 BAN .	20	50	100
Lincoln 2 dr. hardtop, 1954 BAN	20	50	90
Mack tanker truck, 1950 NP	30	60	120
Maverick 2 dr. sedan, 1969 JH .	10	20	40
Mercedes 300 SL coupe, 1958 HUB	20	40	80

	C6	C8	C10
Mercedes 300 SL convertible, 1958 HUB	20	50	90
Mercury 4 dr. sedan, 1951 BAN	30	60	120
Mercury 4 dr. sedan, 1953 BAN	20	50	100
Mercury 2 dr. hardtop, 1954 BAN	20	50	90
Mercury 2 dr. hardtop, 1955 BAN	30	60	130
Mercury Park Lane 2 dr. hardtop, 1959 AMT	20	40	80
Mercury Park Lane convertible, 1959 AMT	20	40	70
Mercury Park Lane 2 dr. hardtop, 1960 AMT	20	40	80
Mercury Park Lane convertible, 1960 AMT	20	40	80
Mercury Monterey convertible, 1961 AMT	20	50	100
Mercury Monterey 2 dr. hardtop, 1961 AMT	120	20	50
Mercury Monterey 2 dr. hardtop, 1962 AMT	30	70	130
Mercury Monterey convertible, 1962 AMT	30	70	140
Mercury Monterey convertible, 1963 AMT	20	40	80
Mercury Monterey 2 dr. hardtop, 1963 AMT	20	40	80
Mercury Park Lane convertible, 1964 AMT	20	50	90
Mercury Park Lane 2 dr. hardtop, 1964 AMT	20	30	70
Mercury Breezeway 2 dr. hardtop, 1964 AMT	20	40	80
Mercury Park Lane 2 dr. hardtop, 1965 AMT	10	20	50
Mercury Park Lane 2 dr. hardtop, 1966 AMT	10	30	60
Meteor Custom 2 dr. sedan, 1962 AMT	40	80	160
Meteor 2 dr. hardtop, 1963 AMT	30	60	120
Metro panel trk. (sgl.), 1952 PMC	20	30	60
Metro panel trk. (dbl.), 1952 PMC	20	30	70
Metropolitan convertible, 1958 HUB	70	150	300
Metropolitan 2 dr. hardtop, 1958 HUB	70	140	280
Mustang 2 dr. hardtop, 1964 AMT	30	60	110
Mustang convertible pace, 1964 AMT	50	100	200

	C6	C8	C10
Mustang 2 dr. convertible, 1964 AMT	30	60	120
Mustang convertible, 1965 AMT	30	50	100
Mustang 2 dr. fastback, 1965 AMT	30	50	100
Mustang 2 dr. hardtop, 1965 AMT	20	40	80
Mustang 2+2 2 dr. hardtop, 1966 AMT	50	110	220
Mustang 2 dr. hardtop, 1966 AMT	30	60	120
Mustang convertible, 1966 AMT	20	50	90
Mustang 2+2 2 dr. hardtop, 1967 AMT	60	110	220
Mustang Mach I 2 dr. fastback, 1969 AMT	60	120	240
Mustang Mach I 2 dr. fastback, 1971 AMT	40	80	160
Mustang Mach I 2 dr. hardtop, 1972 AMT	30	60	120
Nash 4 dr. sedan, 1950 NP	20	40	70
Nash 4 dr. sedan, 1953 PMC	20	50	100
Nash 4 dr. sedan, 1954 PMC	30	50	100
Nash Golden Airflight 4 dr., 1952 PMC	30	50	100
Oldsmobile 4 dr. sedan, 1953 BAN	30	50	100
Oldsmobile 2 dr. hardtop, 1954 BAN	20	40	90
Oldsmobile 2 dr. hardtop, 1955 BAN	20	40	90
Oldsmobile 4 dr. hardtop, 1956 JH	20	40	80
Oldsmobile 98 4 dr. hardtop, 1957 JH	20	50	90
Oldsmobile 4 dr. hardtop, 1958 JH	20	30	60
Oldsmobile 98 4 dr. hardtop, 1959 JH	20	40	80
Oldsmobile 98 2 dr. hardtop, 1960 JH	10	30	60
Oldsmobile 88 4 dr. hardtop, 1961 JH	20	30	70
Oldsmobile Starfire convertible, 1962 JH	20	40	80
Oldsmobile 88 4 dr. hardtop, 1962 JH	20	40	90
Oldsmobile Starfire convertible, 1963 JH	10	30	60
Oldsmobile Starfire 2 dr. hardtop, 1963 JH	10	30	60
Oldsmobile 88 2 dr. hardtop, 1965 AMT	20	50	100

	C6	C8	C10
Oldsmobile 88 convertible, 1965 AMT	30	50	110
Oldsmobile Toronado 2 dr. hardtop, 1966 JH	10	30	60
Oldsmobile Toronado 2 dr. hardtop, 1969 JH	10	30	60
Oldsmobile 442 2 dr. hardtop, 1969 JH	20	40	80
Oldsmobile Toronado 2 dr. hardtop, 1970 JH	10	20	40
Oldsmobile 442 2 dr. hardtop, 1970 JH	20	40	70
Oldsmobile 442 2 dr. hardtop, 1971 JH	20	40	70
Oldsmobile Toronado 2 dr. hardtop, 1971 JH	20	30	70
Oldsmobile Toronado 2 dr. hardtop, 1972 JH	10	20	40
Opel sedan, 1959 PMC	10	20	40
Opel GT 1900 coupe, 1969 AMT	20	40	90
Packard convertible, 1948 MC	30	60	120
Packard Henesey ambulance, 1951 AMT	70	150	300
Packard 4 dr. sedan, 1953 BAN	40	70	140
Packard 4 dr. sedan, 1954 BAN	30	60	120
Pinto 2 dr. sedan, 1971 AMT	10	20	30
Pinto Runabout 2 dr. sedan, 1972 AMT	10	20	30
Plymouth sedan, 1948 NP	30	60	120
Plymouth 4 dr. sedan, 1950 AMT	20	40	90
Plymouth 4 dr. taxi, 1953 PMC	20	40	90
Plymouth 4 dr. sedan, 1953 BAN	30	60	120
Plymouth 4 dr. sedan, 1953 PMC	20	40	80
Plymouth station wagon, 1954 PMC	30	60	110
Plymouth 4 dr. sedan, 1954 PMC	20	40	80
Plymouth sedan, 1955 BAN	20	50	90
Plymouth 4 dr. sedan, 1955 JH	20	50	100
Plymouth Belvedere 4 dr., 1956 JH	20	40	90
Plymouth 2 dr. sedan, 1956 BAN	20	50	90
Plymouth Belvedere 2 dr. hardtop, 1957 JH	20	40	80
Plymouth taxi, 1957 JH	40	70	150
Plymouth Fury 2 dr. hardtop, 1958 JH	30	60	120
Plymouth Belvedere 2 dr. hardtop, 1958 JH	10	30	60
Plymouth taxi, 1958 JH	40	70	150
Plymouth Fury 2 dr. hardtop, 1959 JH	20	40	80
Plymouth Fury taxi, 1959 JH	10	30	60
Plymouth Fury 2 dr. hardtop, 1960 JH	20	40	70
Plymouth Fury taxi, 1960 JH	30	70	140
Plymouth station wagon, 1960 JH	10	30	60
Plymouth Fury 2 dr. hardtop, 1961 JH	20	40	90
Plymouth taxi, 1961 JH	30	70	140
Plymouth police car, 1961 JH	20	50	100
Plymouth Fury convertible, 1963 JH	20	40	90
Plymouth Fury 2 dr. hardtop, 1963 JH	20	50	100
Plymouth Fury convertible, 1964 JH	20	40	80
Plymouth 2 dr. hardtop, 1964 JH	30	70	140
Plymouth Fury III convertible pace, 1965 JH	60	130	260
Plymouth Fury III driver's training, 1965 JH	20	40	90
Plymouth Fury III 2 dr. hardtop, 1965 JH	30	60	120
Plymouth Fury III convertible, 1965 JH	30	70	140
Plymouth Fury III convertible, 1966 JH	20	40	80
Plymouth Fury III driver's training, 1966 JH	30	50	110
Plymouth Fury III 2 dr. hardtop, 1966 JH	20	40	80
Plymouth Fury 2 dr. hardtop, 1967 JH	10	30	60
Plymouth Fury convertible, 1967 JH	20	30	60
Plymouth Fury III convertible, 1968 JH	20	30	60
Plymouth Fury III 2 dr. hardtop, 1968 JH	10	30	50
Plymouth GTX 2 dr. hardtop, 1969 JH	20	40	90
Plymouth GTX 2 dr. hardtop, 1970 JH	20	50	100
Plymouth Duster 2 dr. hardtop, 1971 MPC	20	50	100

	C6	C8	C10
Plymouth Roadrunner 2 dr. hardtop, 1971 MPC	30	70	140
Plymouth Roadrunner 2 dr. hardtop, 1972 MPC	30	60	120
Plymouth Duster, 1972 MPC	30	60	120
Plymouth "Cuda" 2 dr. hardtop, 1972 MPC	50	90	180
Plymouth Fury police car, 1962 JH	40	80	160
Plymouth Fury taxi, 1962 JH	50	110	220
Plymouth Fury 2 dr. hardtop, 1962 JH	30	50	100
Plymouth Fury convertible, 1962 JH	30	50	110
Pontiac 4 dr. sedan, 1947 NP	40	70	150
Pontiac 4 dr. sedan, 1948 NP	30	70	130
Pontiac 4 dr. sedan, 1951 AMT	20	40	80
Pontiac 4 dr. sedan, 1952 AMT	20	50	100
Pontiac 2 dr. sedan, 1953 AMT	20	50	100
Pontiac sedan, 1953 BAN	30	50	100
Pontiac 2 dr. sedan, 1954 AMT	20	40	90
Pontiac sedan, 1955 BAN	20	40	80
Pontiac 4 dr. sedan, 1955 JH	20	40	80
Pontiac 2 dr. sedan, 1955 JH	20	40	80
Pontiac 4 dr. hardtop, 1956 JH	20	40	80
Pontiac Star Chief 4 dr. hardtop, 1957 AMT	30	70	140
Pontiac Star Chief convertible, 1957 AMT	40	90	180
Pontiac Bonneville convertible, 1958 AMT	30	70	140
Pontiac Bonneville 2 dr. hardtop, 1958 AMT	20	40	80
Pontiac Bonneville convertible, 1959 AMT	20	40	90
Pontiac Bonneville 2 dr. hardtop, 1959 AMT	30	60	110
Pontiac Bonneville 2 dr. hardtop, 1960 AMT	20	40	80
Pontiac Bonneville convertible, 1960 AMT	20	40	80
Pontiac Bonneville 2 dr. hardtop, 1961 AMT	30	60	120
Pontiac Bonneville convertible, 1961 AMT	30	60	120
Pontiac Bonneville 2 dr. hardtop, 1962 AMT	40	80	170
Pontiac Bonneville convertible, 1962 AMT	70	140	280

	C6	C8	C10
Pontiac Bonneville convertible, 1963 AMT	40	80	160
Pontiac Bonneville 2 dr. hardtop, 1963 AMT	30	50	100
Pontiac Bonneville 2 dr. hardtop, 1964 AMT	30	60	130
Pontiac Bonneville 2 dr. hardtop, 1964 AMT	40	70	140
Pontiac Bonneville convertible, 1964 AMT	40	70	150
Pontiac Grand Prix 2 dr. hardtop, 1965 AMT	40	80	160
Pontiac Bonneville convertible, 1965 AMT	40	70	150
Pontiac Bonneville 2 dr. hardtop, 1965 AMT	40	80	160
Pontiac Bonneville convertible, 1966 MPC	40	70	140
Pontiac Bonneville 2 dr. hardtop, 1966 MPC	40	80	160
Pontiac Bonneville convertible, 1967 MPC	30	60	120
Pontiac Bonneville 2 dr. hardtop, 1967 MPC	30	60	120
Pontiac Bonneville 2 dr. hardtop, 1968 MPC	20	40	80
Pontiac Bonneville convertible, 1968 MPC	30	50	110
Pontiac Bonneville 2 dr. hardtop, 1969 MPC	20	40	80
Pontiac Grand Prix 2 dr. hardtop, 1969 MPC	20	40	80
Pontiac Bonneville convertible, 1969 MPC	20	40	80
Pontiac Grand Prix 2 dr. hardtop, 1970 MPC	20	40	80
Pontiac Bonneville 2 dr. hardtop, 1970 MPC	10	30	60
Pontiac Bonneville 2 dr. hardtop, 1970 MPC	20	40	70
Pontiac GTO 2 dr. hardtop, 1970 MPC	30	50	110
Pontiac GTO 2 dr. hardtop, 1971 MPC	20	50	100
Pontiac Grand Prix 2 dr. hardtop, 1971 MPC	20	40	70
Pontiac GTO 2 dr. hardtop, 1972 MPC	20	50	100

	C6	C8	C10
Pontiac Grand Prix 2 dr. hardtop, 1972 MPC	20	40	80
Rambler convertible, 1951 NP . . .	30	60	120
Rambler 2 dr. hardtop, 1952 BAN	30	60	110
Rambler sedan, 1953 BAN	20	50	100
Rambler 2 dr. hardtop, 1954 BAN	30	70	140
Rambler station wagon, 1959 JH	10	30	50
Rambler station wagon, 1960 JH	10	30	60
Rambler American 2 dr. sedan, 1961 JH	10	20	40
Rambler Cross Country station wagon, 1961 JH	10	30	60
Rambler Unit construction demo, 1961 JH	10	20	40
Rambler Classic 4 dr. sedan, 1962 JH	10	20	50
Rambler American 2 dr. sedan, 1962 JH	10	20	40
Rambler American convertible, 1962 JH	10	20	50
Rambler Classic station wagon, 1962 JH	10	20	50
Rambler Classic station wagon, 1963 JH	10	30	50
Rambler Classic 4 dr. sedan, 1963 JH	10	30	60
Rambler American convertible, 1963 JH	10	30	50
Rambler Classic station wagon, 1964 JH	10	20	40
Rambler Classic 4 dr. sedan, 1964 JH	10	20	40
Rambler American convertible, 1964 JH	10	20	40
Rambler American 2 dr. hardtop, 1964 JH	10	20	50
Rambler Classic 4 dr. sedan, 1965 JH	10	20	40
Rambler Marlin 2 dr. fastback, 1965 JH	20	30	70
Rambler Classic convertible, 1965 JH	10	20	50
Rambler Marlin 2 dr. fastback, 1966 JH	20	40	80
Rambler American convertible, 1966 JH	10	20	50
Rambler American 2 dr. hardtop, 1966 JH	10	30	50
Rambler Ambassador 2 dr. hardtop, 1966 JH	10	30	50
Rambler Ambassador 2 dr. hardtop, 1967 JH	10	20	40
Rambler Ambassador convertible, 1967 JH	10	20	40
Rambler Ambassador convertible, 1968 JH	10	20	40
Rambler Ambassador 2 dr. hardtop, 1968 JH	10	20	40
Rambler Ambassador 2 dr. hardtop, 1969 JH	10	20	40
Rambler C.C. station wagon, 1966 JH	10	20	50
Rambler Dauphine 4 dr., 1958 HUB	10	20	40
Rambler Rolls Royce Silver Ghost 4 dr. sedan, 1958 HUB	20	40	80
Studebaker 2 dr. sedan, 1947 NP	40	80	160
Studebaker 2 dr. sedan, 1948 NP	30	70	130
Studebaker stake truck, 1950 NP	90	180	360
Studebaker 2 dr. sedan, 1950 AMT	30	60	110
Studebaker 2 dr. sedan, 1951 AMT	30	60	120
Studebaker 2 dr. sedan, 1952 AMT	20	50	100
Studebaker Starliner coupe, 1953 BAN	20	50	90
Studebaker Starliner coupe, 1953 AMT	20	50	90
Studebaker Starliner coupe, 1954 AMT	20	50	100
Studebaker 2 dr. hardtop, 1955 AMT	20	40	80
Studebaker Golden Hawk 2 dr., 1956 AMT	20	50	90
Studebaker Lark 2 dr. hardtop, 1959 JH	10	30	60
Studebaker Lark 2 dr. hardtop, 1960 JH	10	30	60
Studebaker Lark 2 dr. hardtop, 1961 JH	10	30	60
Studebaker Lark convertible, 1962 JH	20	30	70
Studebaker Lark 2 dr. hardtop, 1962 JH	20	30	70
Tempest 4 dr. sedan, 1961 AMT	20	30	70
Tempest Lemans 2 dr. sedan, 1962 AMT	20	40	70

	C6	C8	C10
Tempest LeMans convertible, 1962 AMT	20	40	80
Tempest LeMans convertible, 1963 AMT	30	70	130
Tempest LeMans 2 dr. sedan, 1963 AMT	40	70	140
Tempest LeMans 2 dr. hardtop, 1964 AMT	30	60	130
Tempest GTO 2 dr. hardtop, 1964 AMT	20	30	60
Tempest LeMans convertible, 1964 AMT	30	60	120
Tempest GTO 2 dr. hardtop, 1965 AMT	70	150	300
Tempest GTO convertible, 1965 AMT	70	150	300
Tempest GTO 2 dr. hardtop, 1966 MPC	80	160	320
Tempest GTO convertible, 1966 MPC	60	130	260
Tempest GTO 2 dr. hardtop, 1967 MPC	70	140	280
Tempest GTO convertible, 1967 MPC	70	140	290
Tempest GTO convertible, 1968 MPC	40	90	180
Tempest GTO 2 dr. hardtop, 1968 MPC	20	40	90
Tempest GTO 2 dr. hardtop, 1969 MPC	40	90	180
Tempest GTO convertible, 1969 MPC	50	100	200
Thunderbird convertible, 1956 AMT	40	80	170
Thunderbird convertible, 1954 AMT	30	60	120
Thunderbird convertible, 1955 AMT	40	80	160
Thunderbird convertible, 1957 AMT	40	70	140
Thunderbird 2 dr. hardtop, 1958 AMT	20	40	80
Thunderbird convertible, 1959 AMT	20	40	80
Thunderbird 2 dr. hardtop, 1959 AMT	20	40	80
Thunderbird 2 dr. hardtop, 1960 AMT	20	40	80

	C6	C8	C10
Thunderbird convertible, 1960 AMT	20	50	100
Thunderbird convertible, 1961 AMT	30	70	140
Thunderbird 2 dr. hardtop, 1961 AMT	20	50	100
Thunderbird 2 dr. hardtop, 1962 AMT	30	60	120
Thunderbird convertible 1962 AMT	50	110	210
Thunderbird 2 dr. hardtop, 1963 AMT	20	40	80
Thunderbird convertible, 1963 AMT	50	100	210
Thunderbird 2 dr. hardtop, 1964 AMT	20	40	80
Thunderbird convertible 1964 AMT	30	60	120
Thunderbird 2 dr. hardtop, 1965 AMT	20	40	70
Thunderbird convertible, 1965 AMT	20	40	80
Thunderbird convertible, 1966 AMT	20	30	70
Thunderbird 2 dr. hardtop, 1966 AMT	20	30	60
Thunderbird 2 dr. hardtop, 1967 AMT	10	30	60
Thunderbird 2 dr. hardtop, 1968 AMT	10	20	50
Thunderbird 2 dr. hardtop, 1969 AMT	10	30	60
Thunderbird 2 dr. hardtop, 1970 AMT	10	30	60
Thunderbird 2 dr. hardtop, 1971 AMT	10	30	60
Torino Cobra 2 dr. hardtop, 1971 AMT	10	30	60
Triumph TR-3A hardtop, 1958 HUB	10	20	50
Triumph TR-3A convertible, 1958 HUB	10	20	50
Valiant 4 dr. sedan, 1960 AMT	10	20	50
Valiant 4 dr. sedan, 1961 AMT	10	20	50
Valiant 2 dr. hardtop, 1961 AMT	10	20	40
Valiant Signet 800 2 dr. hardtop, 1962 AMT	30	70	130
Valiant Signet 800 2 dr. hardtop, 1963 AMT	10	30	60

	C6	C8	C10
Valiant Signet 200 2 dr. hardtop, 1964 AMT	40	80	160
Valiant 2 dr. hardtop, 1965 AMT	20	30	70
Valiant 2 dr. hardtop, 1966 AMT	90	180	360
Vega Hatchback 2 dr. hardtop, 1971 MPC	10	20	30
Valiant Hatchback 2 dr., 1972 MPC	10	20	30
Volkswagen Karmann Ghia convertible, 1959 PM	10	20	40
Volkswagen sedan, 1959 PM	10	20	30
White c.o.e. truck, 1950 NP	50	100	200
Willys Jeep FC pick-up, 1961 AUT	30	50	100
Willys Jeep FC stake truck w/plow, 1961 AUT	30	60	120
Willys Jeep "Jolly" 1961 AUT	20	50	100
Willys Jeep stake truck, 1961 AUT	30	50	110
Willys Jeepster 1968 MPC	10	20	30
Willys ¾ ton army truck, 1969 BAN	20	40	80

PYRO

(1939-1969)
by Terry Sells

Pyro is probably best known for its plastic model kits produced in the '50's and '60's. But it did produce a nice line of toy vehicles in the 1950's.

The originals of these were probably military vehicles made around the time of the Korean War. There were two sizes of vehicles, moulded in khaki, o.d. and grey (for Navy and Marine) plastic. They were heat stamped with stars and other identifying marks.

Lionel used the large Pyro military vehicles as loads for its Navy and Marine trains. The loads were all grey and had no figures glued in place.

After the war came the inevitable decline in sales of war toys. The vehicles were issued in civilian roles (i.e. Horse Transport) and specialty roles (i.e. Coca Cola Truck). Also, Pyro produced a wide range of toys and trinkets for Planters Peanuts.

Specialty advertising issued included at least one political truck. An "Elect Marvin Griffin for Governor - Get On The Griffin Bandwagon" truck. Griffin was governor of Georgia 1954-58.

Military sets continued in production into the mid to late '50's. A 1956 Pyro advertisement in "Toys & Novelties" magazine declared: "Military Toys Are Hot Again!" The ad pictured boxed military sets C-242, C-243 & C-244.

Toys gradually faded behind Pyro's growing line of model kits. The company went out of business in 1969. It was located in Pyro Park, Union City, New Jersey, and at its height had 400 employees.

Terry Sells was born and raised in the Atlanta, GA area. He is a graphic artist who works with Music and Entertainment accounts. He cartoons for fun and collects all manner of Plastic and Celluloid toys.

He started collecting in 1972 when his wife innocently gave him a toy car for his birthday. He mostly collects toys from the 1945-1960 period.

His wife, Patti, shares his interest in toys and also collects Disney and childrens' books. They have two "daughters", Birdie and Jinkie.

	C6	C8	C10
Pyro Army Tank P-1020	No Price Found		
Pyro Bulldozer, front loader	35	70	100

Pyro "City Builders" truck, 5½". Photo by Terry Sells

Pyro "City Builders" truck, 5½" long	No Price Found

Pyro "Coca-Cola" truck, 5½". Photo by Terry Sells

Pyro "Coca-Cola" truck, 5½" long	No Price Found

Pyro "Design-A-Car" set, builds 14 models.
Photo by Terry Sells

Pyro "Mr. Peanut's Peanut Wagon", 5½".
Photo by Terry Sells

	C6	C8	C10
Pyro "Design-A-Car" set, builds 14 models	No Price Found		

	C6	C8	C10
Pyro "Mr. Peanut's Peanut Wagon", 5½" long	No Price Found		
Pyro Mobile Anti-Aircraft Truck P-1015	No Price Found		
Pyro Mobile Radar Truck, P-957	No Price Found		
Pyro Mobile Searchlight Truck P-958	No Price Found		
Pyro Mobile Sound Truck P-956			
Pyro Motorcycle	25	40	60

Pyro "Elect Marvin Griffin Governor", "Get On the Griffin Bandwagon" truck, 5½".
Photo by Terry Sells

Pyro "Elect Marvin Griffin Governor", "Get On the Griffin Bandwagon" truck, 5½" long No Price Found

Pyro "Planter's Peanuts" semi w/trailer, 5½".
Photo by Terry Sells

Pyro "Planters Peanuts" semi w/trailer, 5½" long .... No Price Found

Pyro "Ice & Coal" truck, 5½".
Photo by Terry Sells

Pyro "Ice & Coal" truck, 5½" long	No Price Found		
Pyro Lumber Loader	20	35	50

Pyro "Planters Peanuts" stake truck, semi, 5½".
Photo by Terry Sells

Pyro "Planters Peanuts" stake truck, semi, 5½" long .... No Price Found

Pyro "Pyro Ranch Horse Transport", 5½".
Photo by Terry Sells

	C6	C8	C10
Pyro "Pyro Ranch Horse Transport", 5½" long	No Price Found		
Pyro Race Car, 4" long	20	30	40
Pyro Range Patrol Truck	10	15	20
Pyro 6 U.S. Army Mobile Units Set	No Price Found		
Pyro Soldier Transport P-955 ...	No Price Found		
Pyro Steam roller	12	18	25
Pyro 21-Piece U.S. Army Set ...	No Price Found		
Pyro Twin 40MM Mobile Gun P-1087	No Price Found		
Pyro "U.S. Army" truck	10	15	20
Pyro "U.S.M.C." truck	10	15	20
Pyro "U.S. Navy" truck	10	15	20

Pyro toys, as advertised in a December, 1951 Woolworth's comic-book catalog.

RAINBOW

(Butler, PA)

The following list, with its codings, was compiled by David Leopard. Vehicles are broken down by types.

Rainbow RA01
Photo by Dave Leopard

	C6	C8	C10
RA01 '35 Oldsmobile Coupe, 3¾" long	35	40	55
RA02 '35 Oldsmobile 4 door sedan, 3¼" long	35	40	55
RA03 '35 Oldsmobile 4 door sedan, 5" long	50	60	75

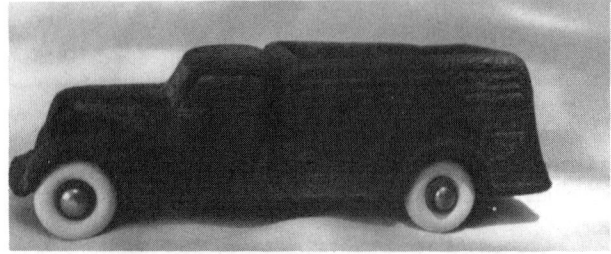

Rainbow RT01
Photo by Dave Leopard

RT01 '35 Studebaker (?) stake side pick-up, 5¼" long	35	45	55
RR01 Open Racer, tapered tail, 4" long	30	40	50

CONDITION OF A TOY
AND ITS RELATION TO PRICE

CONDITION CODE:

C6 - Good, Evident overall wear, well-played with, but acceptable to many collectors

C8 - Very Good Minor wear overall, very clean

C10 - Mint (like new)

NOTE: Mint in Box commands a high price. Condition below C6 brings considerably lower prices.

RALSTOY

(Ralston Toy and Novelty Company)
by Fred Maxwell and Ferd Zegel with Assistance of Alice Shooter and the Ralston Archives

Ralston Toy & Novelty Co. was founded in July 1939 to manufacture slushmold toys and novelties. It was formed by Dr. Felix Despecher, former mayor of Ralston, Nebraska, A.M. Erickson and Henry C. Nestor to acquire the assets of Best Toy Co. of Manhattan, Kansas and the surviving molds of Kansas Toy Co. of Clifton, Kansas. These assets included the temporary services of John M. Best, his molder Conrad Morsch and about 140 molds from these pioneering slushmold vehicle toy companies. The new enterprise was located in a building formerly occupied by the American Legion at 7632 Burlington St. This continued a low-cost toy line familiar to collectors since Kansas Toy was founded in 1923.

With the death of its founder, Dr. Despecher, about a year later the young company was forced into reorganization. Paul Massey, a lawyer, reorganized the company but had to give up production of potmetals soon thereafter due to the war's need for lead. To survive he turned to making wooden toys, including a replica of the famous Army Jeep of which about 2 million copies were sold through the Dime Stores, mainly Woolworth and Kresge. Other wooden toys included an Army tank, a Navy PT boat and a (rumored) DUKW amphibious landing craft. These toys were completely made in Ralston except for Jeep wheels which were made in Omaha by the blind. When war-time labor became short handicapped workers were hired.

After the war the company turned to die-casting toys and novelties. As the business expanded it moved to 5707 So. 77th St., where it is today producing a well-known line of promotional trucks under Art Massey. But the post-war history is for other researchers.

By now the history of those migrating molds "with the numbers" is getting confusing. Although market values will depend on other factors than the actual makers we will mention some clues to assist collectors. Ralstoy did label a few of its toys. They liked bottom pans, introduced by Best to increase rigidity of these fragile toys; this provided a surface to emboss "Ralstoy" and "Made in USA". Military olive drab colors reflected the growing war consciousness. Wheels are not a good clue, even when the latest fad, black rubber wheels, were used.

Ralstoy probably reproduced many pieces from their acquired molds, but there is no practical way to know who made them when they are not labeled. (See Best Toy Co. and Kansas Toy Co. in this book). The toys described below are mostly new issues.

Ralstoy, Top: RAV4 Middle: RAV2A, RAV2B metal wheels Bottom: Ralstoy field gun
Photo by Perry Eichor

	C6	C8	C10

RAV1 Dump Truck, "42", 3⅜". International ? COE, 2 open windows (OW), hinged tin dump body. Different casting than Kansas Toy dump truck #42 . No Price Found

RAV2 Tractor, "48", 3" "Caterpillar" tractor, "Whoopee", driver in different color, grooved wood ¾" wheels with rubber tracks on Kansas Toy body .. No Price Found

Ralstoy, L to R - Top: RAV5 - Transporter with tank #74,, Cannon #34, Aircraft #32 ?; Middle: RAV6 - Anti-aircraft unit, RAV8 - Railway? cannon, Bottom: RAV7 - Tank #107, Cannon.
Photo by Ed Poole

RAV3 Army tank, "74", 2¼". "US Army", 2 gun turret. Entirely different tank than Kansas Toy #74 .... 13 20 26

RAV4 Tanker truck, "No. 102", 6¾". "Ralstoy" International ? sleeper cab, 3⅜", 2 OW, vertical grille with "Gasoline" semi-trailer, "No. 102", 4", 4 tanks, 4 storage compartments 14 21 28

	C6	C8	C10

RAV5 Large transporter, 9". "Ralstoy" cab unit in RAV4 above, steel semi-trailer with #74 tank, #34 muzzle loading cannon and #32 aircraft, olive drab color. Not known if Ralstoy issued them as a set. (Some stamped "No. 108", some No. 101) 20 45 60

RAV6 Large gun truck, 5⅝". "US Army Anti-aircraft Unit", 3 axle carrier, AA gun, searchlight and crew of 3 . . . . 28 42 56

Ralstoy RAV7
Courtesy K. Warren Mitchell

RAV7 Army tank, "107", 3⅛". "US Army", wood grooved ¾" tracklaying wheels, 2 gun turret, larger version of #74 above. Also version w/black rubber wheels 13 20 26

RAV8 Railway ? gun, "108", 3¼". Version of #23 *muzzle-loading cannon on wheeled platform with hook and loop connectors. Perhaps addition to #3600 toy train* 12 18 25

RAV10 Army Jeep. Wooden, WWII issue 20 30 40

Ralstoy RAV11
Photo by Ed Poole

RAV11 Army tank. Wooden, "USA W356", "Ralstoy" on bottom, WWII issue 37 56 75

Ralstoy RAV12
Photo by Fred Maxwell

	C6	C8	C10

RAV12 Large sedan, "2R", 5⅝". Die-cast, Cadillac ?, "Ralstoy", "Made in USA", 4 open vent windows, divided open windshield, 3 open rear windows, long fenders, rear-wheel skirts, bumper guards, black rubber wheels. Early post-war issue? No Price Found

Ralstoy Ford Tractor, 1948, with trailer, 9" overall 30 45 60

Ralstoy Mayflower Moving Van, 8½" long 15 22 30

Ralstoy Phillips 66 Tanker 37 56 75

RANLITE
by Gates Willard

Whatever happened to Automobiles (Geographical) Limited of Halifax, Yorkshire, England? Except for the Ranlite Toys made 1931-32, there is no information about the company and what else it may have manufactured. The only advertising known is in the December, 1931 issue of the Meccano Magazine. It is possible that the company was yet another Depression casualty. Ranlite toys were quite expensive for their time, and it is unlikely that they were a marketing success. Certainly very few have survived.

Complex in design, Ranlites were quite different from other toys made in the 1930's. Bodies and wheels were molded in Bakelite, a hard and brittle plastic commonly used to make control knobs and radio cases. The chassis and fenders of the two cars were stamped out of heavy gauge steel. The large clockwork motor powers the rear axle. The front wheels are steerable. At extra cost, a remote cable control kit was available so that the vehicle could be wound up and steered around obstacles. Wheels can be removed and re-installed with the small hub nut wrench provided. The hollow Dunlop "Semi

Pneumatic'' tires are demountable. The boxes are made of heavy cardboard, but the maroon paper covering tends to fade badly.

Two popular English saloons (sedans) were modeled rather realistically. Body and chassis are identical for the Singer and the Austin, but the radiator and hood are unique to each. The Austin has more wire spokes per wheel than the Singer. Both cars have a sliding sunroof. Upper and lower body sections were cast separately, allowing for variations in color schemes. The Austin has a rear mounted spare wheel and luggage rack but no bumpers. The Austin name appears on a diagonal bar across the radiator, and the bonnet (hood) has vertical louvers. The Singer has a small letter 's' at the top front of the radiator, and the bonnet louvers are horizontal. The Singer has double-bar spring-steel bumpers front and rear, resulting in a total length of ten and ¾'', whereas the bumperless Austin is ten inches long. Of the two cars, the Singer is scarcer. The foldaway key wind is permanently attached underneath so the body is not spoiled by having a visible key hole. No headlamps were fitted. The die-cast key wind, differential gears, and front axle are subject to metal fatigue which has often destroyed them.

The Golden arrow racing car is 16½'' long, and it is a beautifully proportioned model of the famous Seagrave Record Car. Except for the tires, it does not share parts with the two passenger cars. The key is separate and not attached to the motor. It has steerable front wheels, and a remote control cable was also available at extra cost.

The petrol (gasoline) pump is made of Bakelite. It has a flexible hose made of a tightly coiled spring and is a good model of a contemporary English Hammond pump.

	C6	C8	C10
Ranlite Austin Saloon		No Price Found	
Ranlite Golden Arrow Racing Car		No Price Found	
Ranlite Singer Saloon		No Price Found	
Ranlite Hammond Petrol Pump .		No Price Found	

Ranlite Austin with original box. Sunroof is in open position.
Courteys Gates Willard
Photo by E.W. Willard

Ranlite, L to R: Singer, Austin, with Hammond Petrol Pump in between.
Courtesy Gates Willard
Photo by E.W. Willard

Ranlite, L to R: Singer, Austin.
Courtesy Gates Willard
Photo by E.W. Willard

Underside of Ranlite Singer. At left:
Hub Nut Wrench and Envelope.
Courtesy Gates Willard
Photo by E.W. Willard

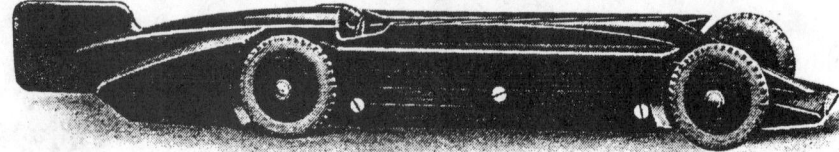
The only known Ranlite ad, from the December, 1931 Meccano
Magazine.
Courtesy Gates Willard

REALISTIC

by Dave Leopard

Realistic toys were made in Freeport, Illinois during the late '40's - early '50's. They used some original Arcade molds to produce cast-aluminum vehicles. Realistic seemed to specialize in buses, and produced varieties of both Greyhound and Trailways buses. Their bus models were often sold as souvenirs at bus terminals.

	C6	C8	C10
RV1 1939 Studebaker President Yellow Cab, 8.25 in.	60	75	100
RV2 Greyhound Bus, Silversides, 8.75 in.	60	75	100
RV3 Trailways Bus, 8.75 in.	60	75	100
RV4 Trailways Bus, 8.75 in.	60	75	100
Rehrberger "David" Moving Van, c.1924, 7¼" long	1500	2250	3000

RELIABLE

Canada

Reliable Bus, 6¼" long.
Photo by Terry Sells

Reliable Lowboy w/Crane, 6½".
Photo by Terry Sells

Reliable Bus, 6¼" long, plastic . No Price Found
Reliable Lowboy w/crane, 6½" long, plastic . . . . No Price Found

Reliable Super Deluxe Mechanical Sedan, wind-up, 6" long, plastic   No Price Found
Reliable Tractor-Trailer, 6¼" long, plastic . . . . No Price Found

Reliable Super Deluxe Mechanical Sedan, wind-up, 6".
Photo by Terry Sells

Reliable Tractor-Trailer, 6¼".
Photo by Terry Sells

RELIANCE MOLDED PLASTICS, INC.

(335 Barton St., Pawtucket, R.I.)

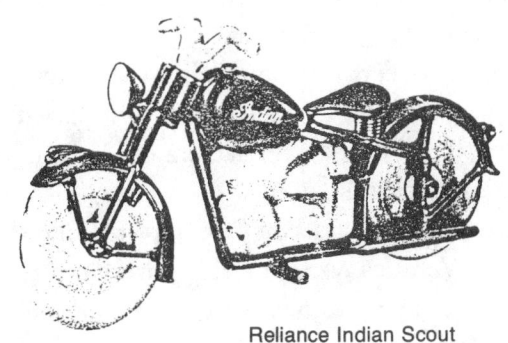

Reliance Indian Scout

Reliable Indian Scout Motorcycle, movable handle bars, revolving wheels, plastic, sold for 29¢ c.1948 . . . . No Price Found

376

REMCO

(Harrison, New Jersey)

Remco Electronic Mobile Loudspeaker & Signal System.

	C6	C8	C10
Remco Bulldog Tank	57	87	115
Remco Electronic Mobile Loudspeaker & Signal System, 24" long, 1955	65	98	130
Remco Flying Dutchman Antique Car	36	48	72
Remco "Movieland Drive-In Theatre", battery-operated, 1959, 14" long, includes 6 small cars, ad cards, filmstrips	100	150	200
Remco Old-Timer Convertible, 22" long	50	75	100
Remco Shark Racer	55	82	110
Remco U-Drive Auto w/driver	36	54	72

RENWAL

Accounts vary as to whether Renwal Manufacturing Company was founded in 1939 by Irving Rosenblum or Irving Lawner. What is indisputable is that Lawner spelled backward is Renwal.

The firm seems to have begun as a manufacturer of a glass knife. A plastic knife replaced it, and presumably led to the manufacture of plastic toys, which went on sale at least as early as August, 1945. Its initial line consisted of World War Two airplanes and doll house furniture. Vehicles were probably introduced in late 1946 or 1947 (the earliest known Renwal catalog is from 1948). The firm's early ads proclaimed it was "Famous for toys and houseware products".

In 1945 Renwal's showroom and factory were at 902 Broadway, New York City. An additional showroom at 200 Fifth Avenue seems to have been given up by 1946. In 1950 Renwal moved to Toyland Park, Mineola, New York. It seems to have remained there till the end (circa the 1970s). When it went out of business its tooling was sold to Chein, which in turn sold it to Revell. (Years in parentheses indicate the earliest known year of production).

	C6	C8	C10
No. 23 Motorcycle & Side Car with Passenger, 5¼" long. Handlebars steer (1949)	50	75	100

Renwal No. 39
Photo by Terry Sells

	C6	C8	C10
No. 39 Convertible Sedan with Driver, 6½" long, doors open, top slides back, trunk opens (1948)	35	65	100

Renwal No. 46
Photo by Terry Sells

	C6	C8	C10
No. 46 Coal Truck with Driver, 7½" long, doors open, body raises (1948)	45	65	90

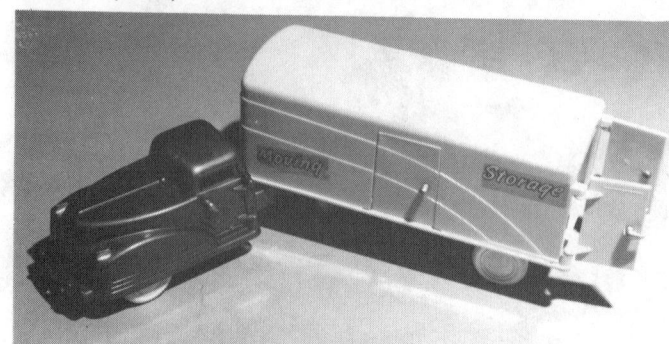

Renwal No. 48
Courtesy Bob & Alice Wagner

	C6	C8	C10
No. 48 Transport Truck with Driver, 10¾" long, doors open, body swings (1948)	75	100	125

Renwal No. 49
Courtesy Bob & Alice Wagner

	C6	C8	C10
No. 49 Gasoline Truck with Driver, 7¾'' long, doors open, tank holds water (1948)	40	65	125
No. 49 Like above, but top reads "Super-X", working faucet inside rear door (1950)	40	65	125

Renwal No. 50
Photo by Terry Sells

	C6	C8	C10
No. 50 Dump truck with driver, 7½'' long, doors open, body raises (1948)	45	68	90

Renwal No. 56
Courtesy Bob & Alice Wagner

	C6	C8	C10
No. 56 Cement Mixer Truck, 7¼'' long, mixer revolves, rear cap comes off, tank raises (1948)	50	75	100

	C6	C8	C10
No. 57 Fire Truck with Three Firemen, 7'' long, 8'' high when ladder extended (1948)	35	60	100
No. 58 Racing Car, 6⅜'' long, marked "Speed King" (1948)	30	50	70
No. 59 Sedan, 4¼'' long (1948)	7	11	14
No. 60 Coupe, 4¼'' long (1948)	No Price Found		
No. 61 Racer, 4³⁄₁₆'' long (1948)	7	11	14
No. 62 Truck (pick-up) 4¼'' long (1948)	No Price Found		
No. 79 Auto Carrier Truck with Driver, 4 autos. 13'' long, cab turns, doors open, elevator raises cars for upper level (1949)	50	100	175
No. 86 Steam Shovel Truck with truck driver and steam shovel operator, 19'' long. Doors open, cab swings, shovel can be raised, lowered, extended via handle on side of cab (1949)	45	68	90
No. 88 Racer, 4⅜'' long (1950)	No Price Found		

Renwal No. 90
Courtesy Bob & Alice Wagner

	C6	C8	C10
No. 90 2-door Sedan with Driver, 6½'' long, doors and trunk open (1949)	45	60	95
91 Taxicab with Driver, 6½'' long, cab doors and trunk open (1949)	45	70	95
No. 92 Plastic Garage, 6½'' long (1949)	25	38	50
No. 93 Panel Truck, "Delivery", 4¼'' long (1949)	No Price Found		
No. 94 Gasoline Truck, "Gasoline", 4¼'' long (1949)	8	12	16
No. 99 Stake Wagon (8⅜'' long). gates removable, tongue hinged (1950)	No Price Found		

	C6	C8	C10
No. 101 Stake Truck, with driver, 7¾'' long, doors open, gates removable (1950)	No Price Found		
No. 102 Coupe, 4¼'' long (1950)	8	10	15
No. 103 Sedan, 4¼'' long (1950)	7	11	14
No. 104 Convertible, 4¼'' long (1950)	8	10	15
No. 105 Fire Engine, 4¼'' long, with ladder (1950)	10	12	20
No. 106 Friction Motor Convertible with driver, 9½'' long (1950)	50	75	150
No. 107 Speed King Friction Motor Racer with Driver, 10¼'' long (1950)	No Price Found		
No. 110 Auto Jack, base 3¾'' long. Raises cars 1½'' (1950)	5	8	10

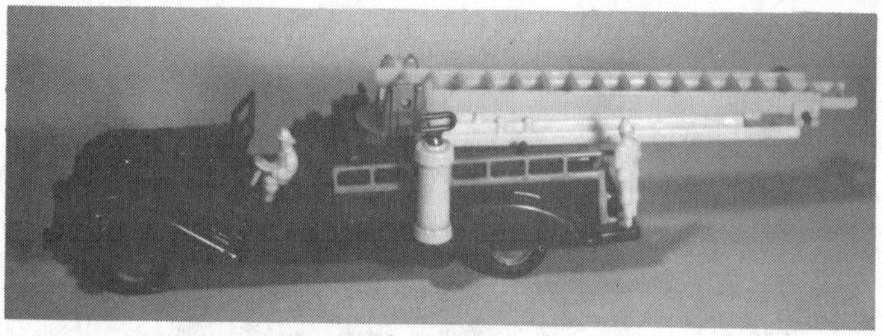

Renwal No. 113
Photo by Terry Sells

	C6	C8	C10
No. 113 Friction Motor Fire Truck with driver and 2 firemen, 11½'' long, 16' high when ladder extended. Has water tank, pump, unwinding hose, nozzle with water release, siren, gear-controlled ladder (1950)	No Price Found		
No. 123 School Bus, 4$\frac{7}{16}$'' long, new in 1950	10	20	30
No. 124 City Bus, 4$\frac{7}{16}$'' long, new in 1950	10	20	30

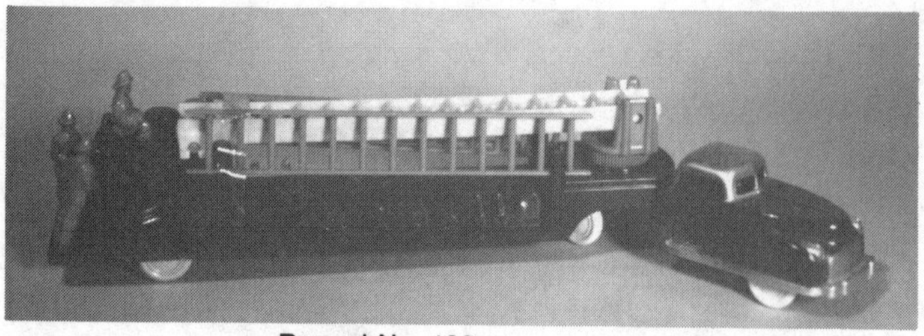

Renwal No. 126
Photo by Terry Sells

	C6	C8	C10
No. 126 Hook & Ladder Truck with drivers. 15¾'' long, 16'' high when ladder extended. Cab turns, doors open, rear wheels turn (1950)	60	80	100

	C6	C8	C10
No. 131 Cement Mixer, 9⅞'' long. Crank turns mixer, mixer revolves, tilts. Can be filled & emptied. Doors open (1951)	50	70	90

Renwal No. 132
Photo by Terry Sells

	C6	C8	C10
No. 132 Gasoline Truck, 12'' long, ''Gas Oil'', rear & cab doors open. Tank can be filled & emptied through plastic hose, which folds up inside rear doors (1951)	No Price Found		
No. 133 Heavy Duty Tow Truck with Driver, 11'' long. Adjustable crane, windlass clicks, doors open (1951)	50	70	90
No. 134 Heavy Duty Dump Truck with Driver, 10⅞'' long, crank operates hoist, cab doors & tailgate open (1951)	50	70	90

Renwal No. 135
Photo by Terry Sells

	C6	C8	C10
No. 135 Heavy Duty Coal Truck with driver, 10¾'' long, crank operates hoist, load divider, unloading chute, cab doors open (1951)	50	70	90
No. 143 Sedan, 3⅛'' long, new in 1950	6	9	12
No. 144 Coupe, 3$\frac{1}{16}$'' long, new in 1950	6	9	12
No. 145 Fire Truck, 3¼'' long, new in 1950	6	9	12

Renwal No. 8008
Photo by Terry Sells

	C6	C8	C10
No. 146 Hook & Ladder, 3¼" long, new in 1950	6	9	12
No. 147 Convertible, 3⅛" long, new in 1950	6	9	12
No. 148 Gasoline Truck, 3⅛" long, new in 1950	6	9	12
No. 149 Pick-up Truck, 3³⁄₁₆" long, new in 1950	6	9	12
No. 150 Racer, 3¼" long, new in 1950	10	12	15
No. 151 Fire Chief Coupe, 4¼" long (1950)	No Price Found		
No. 152 Police Coupe, 4¼" long (1950)	No Price Found		
No. 153 Taxi, 4¼" long (1950) .	No Price Found		
No. 167 Fire Truck Builder Kit (1953), truck 7" long. Has ladder, hose reel, crank, firemen, driver	No Price Found		
No. 168 Auto-Boat (1954), 6½" long, auto on one side, boat on other	20	30	50
No. 173 Speedway Racer, 9½" long (1953) with driver	No Price Found		
No. 174 Cadillac Convertible with driver, 5½" long, top goes up and down (1953)	20	30	50
No. 175 Motorcycle with Sidecar Construction Kit (1953), cycle 5¼" long	No Price Found		
No. 176 2-door Sedan Construction Kit (1953), 6½" long with driver and spare wheel; doors, trunk open	No Price Found		
No. 177 Taxicab Construction Kit (1953), cab 6½" long, with driver, spare; doors, trunk open	No Price Found		
No. 178 Fire Truck, 15" long (1953), ladder extends to 16", turns, 2 firemen	No Price Found		

	C6	C8	C10
No. 179 Fire Truck, 7½" long, 2 firemen, 8" high with ladder up (1953)	No Price Found		
No. 186 Tractor, 5¼" long with driver (1953)	No Price Found		
No. 187 Tractor & Trailer (1953), tractor is No. 186	No Price Found		
No. 188 Motorcycle Cop, 9" long (1953)	17	26	35
No. 189 Motorcycle Cop. Same as No. 188 but 3¾" long (1953)	No Price Found		
No. 191 Trailer Truck with load of 2 boats, 13¼" long (1953)	No Price Found		
No. 192 Trailer Truck with 8 logs, 13¼" long (1953)	No Price Found		
No. 195 Two-car garage with 2 cars (1954), 4⅛" x 3⅝" x 2¼", doors open	20	30	40
No. 196 Pick-up Truck, 11" long (1953)	No Price Found		
No. 201 Old Fashioned Car, 8½" long. Open top, with driver (1954)	No Price Found		
No. 206 Convertible (1952), like No. 106, but no motor	No Price Found		
No. 207 Racer (1952), like No. 107 but no motor	90	135	180
No. 210 Take-Apart Hot Rod (1954), 10½" long	No Price Found		
No. 213 Fire Engine (1952), like No. 113, but no motor	No Price Found		
No. 216 Champion Racer, 10⅜" long, friction motor (1954), dome over driver, siren	No Price Found		
No. 218 Toytown Service Garage Set (1955), 7 x 5 x 2⅞", five 3¼" cars	No Price Found		
No. 220 Take-Apart Racer, 10½" long (1954)	No Price Found		
No. 221 Coal Truck Kit, truck 7½" long (1954)			
No. 222 Dump Truck Kit (1954), truck 7½" long	No Price Found		
No. 223 Transport Kit (1954), truck 10¾" long	No Price Found		
No. 224 Gasoline Truck Kit (1954), truck 7¾" long	No Price Found		
No. 226 Cement Mixer Kit (1954), truck 7¼" long	No Price Found		

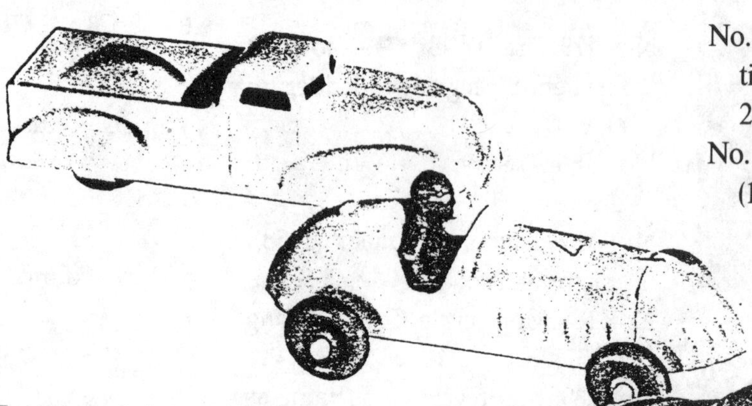

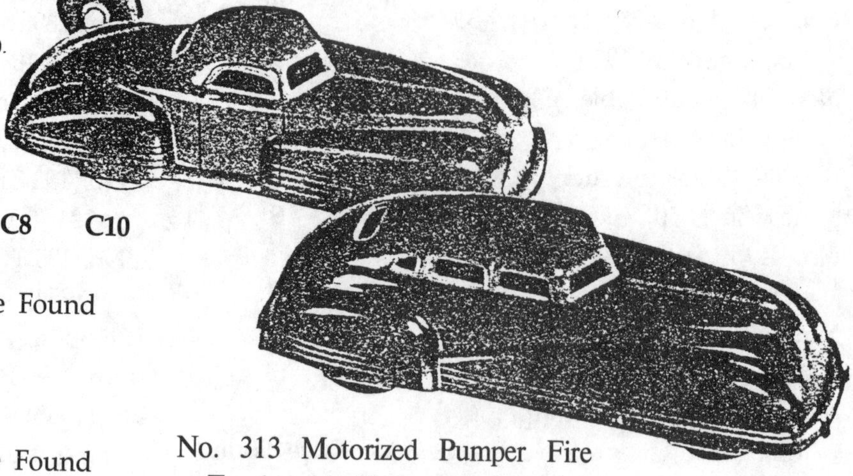

Renwal, top to bottom: No. 62, No. 61, No. 60, No. 59.
Ad brochure c.1948 courtesy Islyn Thomas

	C6	C8	C10
No. 235 Motorized Fuel Truck (1954), 7½'' long, friction, driver, doors open, body raises, rear door opens to slide out chute	No Price Found		
No. 236 Motorized Sand Truck (1954), 7½'' long, friction, doors open, body raises, rear gate opens	No Price Found		
No. 237 Motorized Tank Truck (1954), 7¾'' long, friction, doors open, tank cap opens for filling, rear door opens to faucet	No Price Found		
No. 238 Motorized Ready-Mix Concrete Truck (1954), 7⅛'' long, friction, driver. Doors open, mixer revolves as truck moves, raises, rear cap comes off	No Price Found		
No. 239 Motorized Moving Van (1954), 10⅝" long, friction, driver; cab, trailer doors open	No Price Found		
No. 243 Racer, 9½" long (1954), with driver	No Price Found		
No. 248 Motorized Fire Truck with Siren (1955), 15" long, friction, driver, 2 firemen, ladder extends to 16"	No Price Found		
No. 259 Engine Running Racer (1955), 10½" long, transparent engine block shows action	No Price Found		
No. 260 TV Mobile (1956). Truck, camera, spotlight, microphone, cable. "Renwal-TV" on side	75	112	150
No. 270 Steam Shovel Construction Kit (1953), truck 8⅛" long	No Price Found		

	C6	C8	C10
No. 271 Hook & Ladder Construction Kit (1953), truck 15¾" long. 2 drivers, firemen	No Price Found		
No. 301 Customized Service Truck (1964), 1/32 scale	No Price Found		
No. 313 Motorized Pumper Fire Truck with Siren and extension ladder (1955), 11½" long, friction, throws water through plastic hose. Driver, 2 firemen	No Price Found		
No. 621 Truck (1951), 4¼" long, same as No. 62	No Price Found		
No. 813 Visible Auto. Chassis over 3 feet long. Circa early 1960s . .	No Price Found		
No. 2039 Convertible with Driver, 6½" long (1952), same as No. 39 but has "simulated chrome trim"	No Price Found		
No. 2057 Fire Truck (1952). Same as No. 57, but with "simulated chrome trim"	No Price Found		
2061 Racer (1952). Same as No. 61, but with "simulated chrome trim"			
No. 2088 Racer (1952). Same as No. 88 but with chrome trim	No Price Found		
No. 2090 Sedan, with driver, 6½" long (1952). Same as No. 90 but with "simulated chrome trim" . .	No Price Found		
No. 2091 Taxicab (1952). Same as No. 91, but with "simulated chrome trim"	60	90	120
No. 2093 Delivery Truck (1952). Same as No. 93 but with chrome trim	10	15	20

	C6	C8	C10
No. 2094 Gasoline Truck (1952). Same as No. 94 but with chrome trim	10	15	20
No. 2102 Coupe (1952) Same as No. 102 but with chrome trim	10	15	20
No. 2103 Sedan (1952). Same as No. 103, but with chrome trim	10	15	20
No. 2104 Convertible (1952). Same as No. 104, but with chrome trim	10	15	20
No. 2621 Truck (1952), Same as No. 62, but with chrome trim	10	15	20
No. 8001 Ferrari Racer, metal (1955), 9¼" long, motorized	100	150	200
No. 8002 Maserati Racer, metal (1955), 9¼" long, motorized	No Price Found		
No. 8003 Pontiac Convertible, metal (1955), 8¼" long, motorized	60	90	120
No. 8004 Plymouth Convertible, metal (1955), 7⅞" long, motorized	No Price Found		
No. 8005 Chevrolet Sedan, metal (1955), 7⅞" long, motorized	No Price Found		
No. 8006 Ford Sedan, metal (1955), 7⅞" long, motorized	No Price Found		
No. 8007 Sedan, metal (1955), 6" long	No Price Found		
No. 8008 Gasoline Truck, metal (1955), 6" long	40	50	70
No. 8009 Racer, metal (1955), 7" long	No Price Found		
No. 8010 Delivery truck, metal (1955), 6" long	40	50	70
No. 8011 Pick-up truck, metal (1955), 6" long	30	45	60

	C6	C8	C10
No. 8012 Hot Rod, metal (1955), 6½" long	No Price Found		
No. 8013 Jeep, metal (1955), 5⅝" long	No Price Found		
No. 8014 Fire Truck, metal (1955), 6" long	No Price Found		
No. 8015 Convertible, metal (1955), 6" long	No Price Found		
No. 8028 Citroen, metal (1955), 6" long	No Price Found		
No. 8029 Porsche, metal (1955), 5¾" long	No Price Found		
No. 8030 Pegasa, metal (1955), 6" long	No Price Found		
8031 Lancia, metal (1955), 6" long	No Price Found		
No. 8032 Rolls Royce, metal (1955), 6⅛" long	No Price Found		
No. 8033 Jaguar, metal (1955), 6⅛" long	No Price Found		
No. 8034 MG, metal (1955), 6" long	No Price Found		
No. 8035 Mercedes-Benz, metal (1955), 5⅞" long	No Price Found		
No. 8036 Kaiser-Darrin, metal (1955), 6⅛" long	No Price Found		
No. 8037 Austin-Healey, metal (1955), 6" long	No Price Found		
No. 8853 3½" metal replicas of Renwal's plastic convertible, sedan, coupe, pick-up truck, gasoline truck, fire truck, hook & ladder, racer (1955)	No Price Found		
No. 8854 4¼" - 4½" metal replicas of Renwal's plastic convertible, coupe, gasoline truck, city bus (1955)	No Price Found		

CONDITION OF A TOY
AND ITS RELATION TO PRICE

CONDITION CODE:

C6 - Good, Evident overall wear, well-played with, but acceptable to many collectors

C8 - Very Good Minor wear overall, very clean

C10 - Mint (like new)

NOTE: Mint in Box commands a high price. Condition below C6 brings considerably lower prices.

HIGH GLOSS INFRA-RED BAKED ENAMEL
FINISHES...*safe, non-toxic!*

A page from a 1955 Renwal catalog.

8007 Sedan.

8009 Racer

8015 Convertible

AN INFINITE CAPACITY FOR TAKING PAINS . . . that's what goes into your finished Renwal toy . . . from careful polishing of dies before they are hardened to the final application of enamel to a casting. Your customers will show their appreciation by buying the WORLD'S FINEST TOYS . . . toys by Renwal!

8013 Jeep

8012 Hot Rod

14

FINEST FINISHES ON ANY METAL TOYS . . . ON WORLD'S FINEST TOYS BY Renwal

REPUBLIC TOOL PRODUCTS CO.

Dayton, Ohio c.1922-32
by Bob Smith

Charles Black received a patent for a unique cover to protect the friction mechanism from dirt and moisture. The patent date, November 1, 1921, is stamped on this cover, which sits between the rear wheels of their "Republic Toy" cars and trucks. Black had been employed at the Dayton Toy Works until 1922, when he left the company to form a partnership with Elijah Miller, another ex-Dayton employee. The company ceased making "Republic Toys" in 1932. Although Republic toys were produced for a mere ten years, they have become an important part of American toy manufacturing history.

	C6	C8	C10
Republic Bus, 28" long, 1920s ..	700	110	1700

Republic Cargo Truck, friction drive, 13" long, c.1922.
Photo by Bob Smith

	C6	C8	C10
Republic Cargo Truck, friction drive, green, 13" long, c.1922	250	375	550
Republic Coupe	1500	2500	3500

Republic/Dayton Racer, spring-wind, 11" long, c.1910 or 1922.
Photo by Bob Smith

	C6	C8	C10
Republic/Dayton Racer. Operates on large spring-wind motor cranked from front of car. Gray/Blue/Red, 11" long, c.1910 or 1922	300	450	650
Republic Ladder Truck, 24" long, friction	400	600	800
Republic Ladder Truck, 17" long	237	356	475

Republic Limousine, friction drive, 11" long, c.1922.
Photo by Bob Smith

	C6	C8	C10
Republic Limousine, friction drive, blue, 11" long, c.1922	225	350	500
Republic Momentum Dump Truck, pat. 11/1/21, driver, 20" long	400	600	800

Republic Roadster, friction drive, 11" long, c.1922.
Photo by Bob Smith

	C6	C8	C10
Republic Roadster, friction drive, red, 11" long, c.1922	225	350	500
Republic Taxi Cab with driver, sheet-metal, friction, c.1926 ...	200	300	400

REUHL PRODUCTS, INC.

2609 Monroe St., Madison, Wisconsin

	C6	C8	C10
Reuhl Caterpillar D-7, T-4000 . . .	312	468	625
Reuhl Caterpillar Grader No. 12	800	1300	1800
Reuhl Caterpillar Ripper	188	282	375
Reuhl Caterpillar Scraper No. 70, 16″ long, plastic, S-4500	325	488	650
Reuhl Cedar Rapids Rock Crusher	500	800	1100
Reuhl Cedar Rapids Paver	75	112	150
Reuhl DW-10	350	525	700
Reuhl Farmall Cub T-3000, 1950, 6¼″ long	No Price Found		
Reuhl Lorain Shovel	600	1000	1425
Reuhl Massey Harris Combine . .	188	282	375

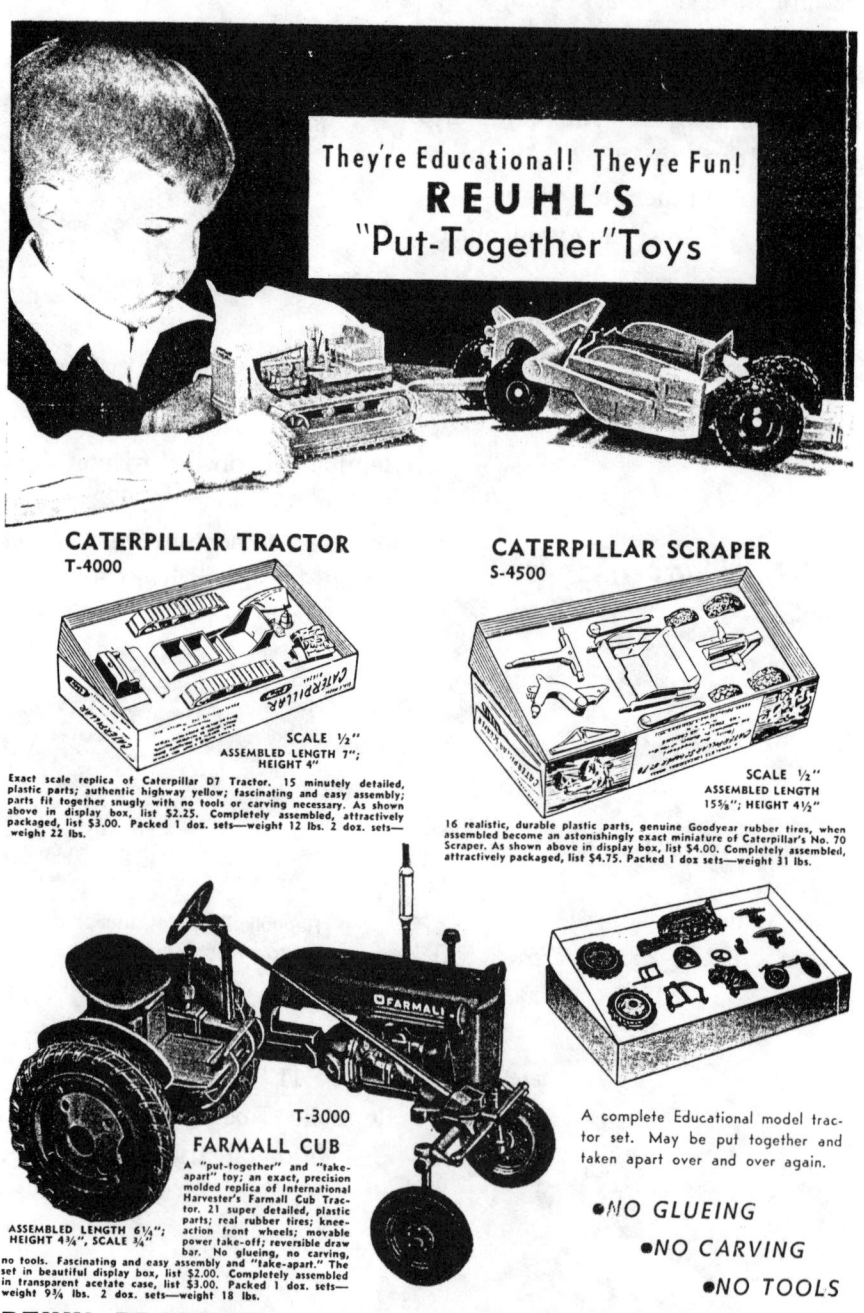

A Reuhl flier from Jan. 1950.
Courtesy Ray Funk

385

REVELL

Revell seems to have begun in 1951, and soon produced more cars a year than Ford, General Motors and Chrysler put together. Located in Venice, California, the firm was founded by Lewis H. Glaser.

	C6	C8	C10
Revell Backfiring Hot Rod......	42	63	85
Revell Grader	11	16	22
Revell Maxwell Auto, c.1950-51.	No Price Found		
Revell Jr. Mechanic Gift Set....	No Price Found		
Revell Plumbing Service Truck w/tools	35	52	70

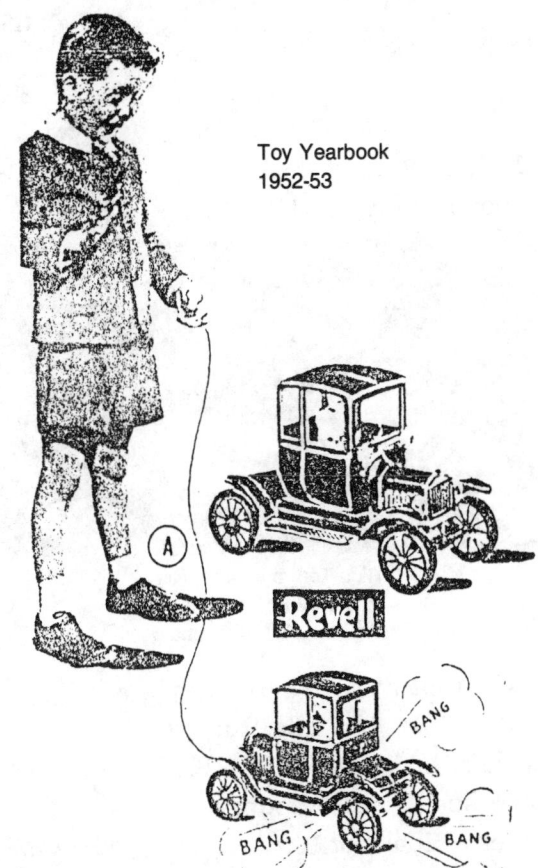

Revell Back-Firing Ford. Constructed of durable plastic, this is an authentic replica of the famous 1917 model "T" Closed Coupe. It runs along freely as a pull toy but when the trigger is squeezed, the engine backfires with a loud BANG! The clever metal backfiring mechanism takes any standard roll of caps. $3.00

REVELL "HIGHWAY PIONEERS" CONSTRUCTION KITS provide the basis for an absorbing and practical hobby. Each kit includes complete equipment and instructions for building authentically detailed, historically accurate model autos, complete with whimsical drivers. No special tools needed. Plastic parts are pre-cut, scaled ⅜" to 1 ft. In addition to the models shown, youngsters may build a 1904 Oldsmobile Delivery Wagon, 1907 Sears Touring "Buggy," 1911 Rolls Royce Town Car and 1904 Nash Rambler. 89c* each. (Other "Revell" kits, 69c* each.)

Prices Approximate—See Page Six

Revell Antique Autos, as shown in the Toy Yearbook from 1953-54.

Revell Maxwell Auto. This seems to have been Revell's first toy.
Courtesy Charles D. Richards

	C6	C8	C10
Rich Toy Texaco Gas Station, 16'' x 22''	205	308	410
Richard Toys "Heavy Transport", 32'' long Ridem, steel	225	338	450
Richmond Dump Truck, 12'' long	75	112	150

Rico Tom and Jerry Car
Photo by Ron Chojnacki
Courtesy Don Hultzman

	C6	C8	C10
Rico Co. (Spain) "Tom and Jerry Car", 1960s, 13'' long, battery operated, 3 actions	400	600	800
"Robot Bus" - see Woodhaven.			
"Rocket" Pedal Car	450	675	900

RUBBER VEHICLES

Unknown Manufacturers

The following list, with its codings, was compiled by Dave Leopard. Vehicles are broken down by types. The gaps in the numbering indicate vehicles that have been identified since the list was first made up.

	C6	C8	C10
UA05 '35 Pontiac 2 door slantback sedan, 4'' long (Rainbow?)	50	60	75
UA06 '35 DeSoto 4 door Airflow Sedan, 5'' long	40	50	65
UA07 '35 Chrysler 4 door Airflow Sedan, rear spare, 4¾'' long, ad on roof	No Price Found		
UA08 '35, Chrysler 2 door Airflow Sedan, 5⅛'' long	40	50	65
UA08A '35 Plymouth 4-door Sedan, 4⅞'' long	No Price Found		
UA09 '36 Plymouth 4 door trunkback sedan, 4⅞'' long	No Price Found		
UA10 '37 Plymouth 4 door trunkback sedan, 4⅞'' long	No Price Found		

Rubber Vehicles UA11
Photo by Dave Leopard

	C6	C8	C10
UA11 '46 Nash, 2 door Fastback Sedan, hollow, molded tires, 4'' long	12	15	20
UA12 c.'35 LaFayette (?) Sedan, fastback, solid, w/tires, 4'' long	30	40	50
UA13 '35 Ford 2 door slantback sedan, 5'' long	No Price Found		
UT04 '34 Dodge Rack Truck, 4⅞'' long	No Price Found		
UR01 Open Racer, left side Header pipes, solid rubber, 3½'' long	No Price Found		
UR02 Open Racer, V-8, solid, large tires on wood hubs, 4'' long	No Price Found		
UR03 Open Racer, solid, rubber tires on wood hubs, 6''	No Price Found		

SAUNDERS TOOL & DIE CO.

Aurora, Illinois

Saunders "Fire Chief"
Courtesy Continental Auctions

Saunders Military Police Car
Photo by Terry Sells

	C6	C8	C10
Saunders "Fire Chief" car wind-up, 10" long	75	112	150
Saunders Fire Truck, 12" long wind-up	70	105	140
Saunders Hot Rod, 7" long friction	40	100	150
Saunders Jaguar, 8" long	40	100	150
Saunders Ladder Truck	55	82	110

Saunders, L to R: Hot Rod, Stock Car Racer.
Courtesy Bob & Alice Wagner

	C6	C8	C10
Saunders Semi Trailer, 16" long, 1960s	88	132	175
Saunders Semi Van	32	48	65
Saunders Stock Car Racer with removable hood, friction, 8" long	60	125	175
Saunders Super Searchlight Fire Truck, battery, bulb, on/off switch, 12" long	No Price Found		

Saunders Marvelous Mike
Photo by Don Hultzman

	C6	C8	C10
Saunders Marvelous Mike, 1950s battery operated, 17" long, four actions	190	275	380
Saunders Military Police Car, 9" long, friction	No Price Found		
Saunders Police Car	27	41	55
Saunders Race Car wind-up	37	56	75
Saunders Race Car	16	24	32
Saunders Sedan	32	40	65

SAVOYE PEWTER TOY COMPANY

Savoye was incorporated August 1930. In 1931 Savoye Pewter Toy Co., manufacturer of "pewter toys" (pewter was often the word used for lead alloy or potmetal) was listed in a directory at 69 Paterson Plank Road in North Bergen, New Jersey, with six male and three female employees. The names of the owners may have been Selma and Joseph Wigh. In 1934 at the same address the workforce was seven males and two females. Slushmold toys were probably their only product. Savoye was in the 1936 phonebook, and out of the February, 1937 directory.

Collectors identify vehicle toys as Savoye if they have a somewhat coarse appearance, heavy slushmold body and white rubber tires on oversized red wooden hubs that are smooth on the outside surface (no axle showing); but whether this is simply lore is not known at present. The son of one of the owners of Tommy Toy Co. thinks some Savoye-looking vehicles were made by Tommy Toy. If so, it's possible Savoye sold its molds to nearby Tommy Toy.

The following was contributed by Fred Maxwell:

Those big red hubs and rubber tires are consistent with industry styles of the early 1930s, but the style of some of the vehicles is from an earlier era (see SA17 & SA19 whose metal wheels suggest an earlier beginning of the Savoye-Tommy Toy-Barclay dynasty).

Savoye, top: SA1, SA2   Middle: SA7, SA3   Bottom: SA9
Photo by Fred Maxwell

Savoye SA5
Photo by Al Lane

Savoye, L to R: SA7, SA18, SA20
Photo by Craig A. Clark

	C6	C8	C10
SA1 Roadster, 3½''. Driver, open rumble seat, silver vertical grille, (VG, reminiscent of Tootsietoy Graham), vertical louvers (VL)	No Price Found		
SA2 Roadster, 3½''. Similar to above; different casting	No Price Found		
SA3 Coupe, 3⅜''. 2 open windows (OW), silver VG, (Graham like), VL	20	30	40
SA4 ? Coupe, 3⅜''. Similar to above (Savoye or copy ?). Slanted louvers, fantasy grille and large black rubber wheels (original ?)	14	21	28
SA5 Van, 3¼''. ''Milk Grade A'', 2 OW, sidemounts (SM)	20	30	40
SA6 Van, 4''. ''Police Patrol'', policeman on rear step, 6 OW, gilt trim, SM	24	36	48

Savoye SA13
Photo by Craig A. Clark

Savoye SA21
Photo by Bill Conover

389

	C6	**C8**	**C10**

SA7 Bus, 4¾". Heavy 5th Ave. sight-seeing bus, open overhanging upper deck, 12 OW, gilt or silver trim 62 93 125

SA8 Bus, 3⅜". Cross-country bus, partial upper deck, 12 OW, rear-mount spare 20 30 40

SA9 Bus, 7½". Tour bus; Mack cab, 3½", 2 OW; "Motor Coach", 5¼", dual-axle semi-trailer, 12 OW, gilt trim ..... No Price Found

SA10 Truck, 4⅜". Heavy "Beer Truck", 6 wood barrels set in cast depressions 40 60 80

SA11 Truck, 4½". Stake body.. 12 18 24

SA12 Truck, 5¾". Stake body, hinged tailgate w/chains ..... No Price Found

SA13 Truck, c.4". Tow truck, SA3 - like coupe cab, chain & hook on crane................... No Price Found

SA14 Truck, 5¾". Heavy tow truck, oversized crane, wire hook .... No Price Found

SA15 Fire truck, 4¼". Driver and steersman w/high style gilt helmets, bell on hood, 2 ladders (glued on), oversized wheel wells, oversized tires .... No Price Found

SA16 Fire truck, 3¾". Driver & fireman w/high style gilt helmets, 2 detachable ladders on high rack, oversized wheel wells, oversized tires .... No Price Found

SA17 ? Fire Engine, 3¾". Steam pumper, driver & fireman w/high style gilt helmets, large 10-spoke metal wheels. An early Savoye ? in the style of the fire trucks above; large wheels would explain over-sized wheel wells in SA15 & SA16 above No Price Found

SA18 Tractor, 2¾". Caterpillar? tractor w/stack 10 15 20

SA19 ? Tractor, 3". Same as above w/large 10 spoke metal wheels. An early Savoye? (same casting as Tommy Toy but longer wheelbase than Barclay #7)... No Price Found

Savoye, top: SA10, SA15 Middle: SA7, SA6 Bottom: SA14, SA12
Photo by Fred Maxwell

Savoye SA17 ?
Photo by Fred Maxwell

Savoye SA19?
Photo by Fred Maxwell

	C6	**C8**	**C10**

SA20 Tank car set, 10¼". Tow cab shorter version of SA13, 3¼"; 2 tank cars 3½", "Oil" "Cap. 80,000" (RR type). Not known whether Savoye sold these as a set; no known Savoye train, either...................... 40 60 80

SA22 Pickup truck

SA23 Moving Van

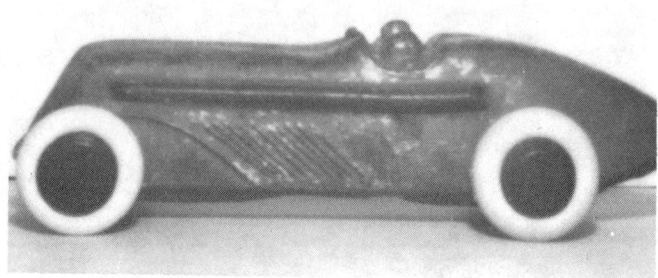

SA24 Racer

SCHIEBLE TOY & NOVELTY CO.

Dayton, Ohio, c.1909-1931
by Bob Smith

William E. Schieble was a partner in D.P. Clark & Co. for nearly ten years. In 1909, after some disagreements with Clark, he broke up the partnership and became the sole owner. At this time, Schieble changed the name of the company to "Schieble Toy & Novelty". Things went well during the 1920's. But as did many other manufacturing companies, Schieble had to declare bankruptcy in 1931.

	C6	C8	C10
Schieble Coupe...............	412	618	825

Schieble Fire Engine Pumper, flywheel drive, 11¾" long, c.1917.
Photo by Bob Smith

	C6	C8	C10
Schieble Fire Engine Pumper, flywheel drive, red/gold, 11¾" long, c.1917.................	275	400	600

Schieble, L to R: large driver, small driver. Each Fire Ladder Trucks, flywheel drive, 21½" long, c.1909.
Photo by Bob Smith

	C6	C8	C10
SA21 Gun Truck, 3¼". Army, driver & gunner. (Angular rear deck distinguishes it from similar gun trucks)	No Price Found		
SA22 Pick-up truck	20	30	40
SA23 "Moving Van", six wheels	No Price Found		
SA24 Racer, 4¼" long, driver and co-pilot	No Price Found		
SA25 "Ambulance" (same as the Tommy Toy, who probably bought the molds)..........	16	24	32
SA26 Open Convertible with Driver in Cap (like Tommy Toy's TTV7; probably from the same mold)	10	15	20

Schieble Racer, team, 12'' long.
Courtesy Wilkinson Collection, Detroit Antique Toy Museum

Schieble Mack Semi Dump Truck, 22'' long, c.1925.
Photo by Bob Smith

	C6	C8	C10
Schieble Fire Ladder Truck, flywheel drive, white/red, 21½'' long, c.1909, small driver	300	450	600
Schieble Fire Ladder Truck, flywheel drive, white/red, 21½'' long, c.1909, large driver	375	525	750
Schieble Fire Truck, flywheel drive, red/gold, 11½'' long, c.1917 . .	250	375	575
Schieble Mack Semi Dump Truck, 22'' long, c.1925 (Chein lookalike)	300	550	800
Schieble Pick-up Truck	300	450	600
Schieble Racer, team, 12'' long, c.1910, steel windup	450	675	900
Schieble Roadster, 18¼'' long, spare tire on back	350	525	700
Schieble Sedan, 17'' long	400	600	800

	C6	C8	C10
Schoenhut ''Every Boy Auto Build 5 in 1 Toy'' wood set to build, boxed	45	67	90
Schoenhut Stutz Racer, 10'' long	135	202	270

SCHUCO

by Don Hultzman

Schuco was founded in 1912 by Heinrich Muller and Herr Schreyer which was later called Schreyer and Co., and adopted the name ''Schuco'' as its trademark. Schuco toys are noted for their ingenious mechanisms, and were produced in the 1930s-1950s, and marked either ''Germany'' or ''U.S. Zone - Germany''. Other markings are reissues.

	C6	C8	C10
''Akustico 2002'', 1940s, 5½'' long	80	120	160
''Anno 2000'', 1940s, 5½'' long .	80	120	160
Buick No. 5311, 9'' long	200	300	400
''Cadillac DeVille Convertible 5505'', 1960s, 11'' long, plastic	80	120	160
''Dalli 1011'', 1950s, 6½'' long, tin car & plastic driver	80	120	160
''Elektro Ingenico 5311'', 1950s, 8½'' long, remote control	220	330	440

Schuco Examico 4001
Photo by Ron Chojnacki
Courtesy Don Hultzman

	C6	C8	C10
"Examico 4001", 1950s, 6" long, 5 speed BMW	120	180	240
"Fex 1111", 1950s, 6" long	60	90	120
"Gas Station 3054", 1950s, 8" long	60	90	120
"Grand Prix Racer 1070", 1950s, 6" long	90	135	180
"Jaguar 1250", 1940s, 5½' long.	160	240	320
"Lasto 3042", 1950s, 4½" long truck	60	90	120

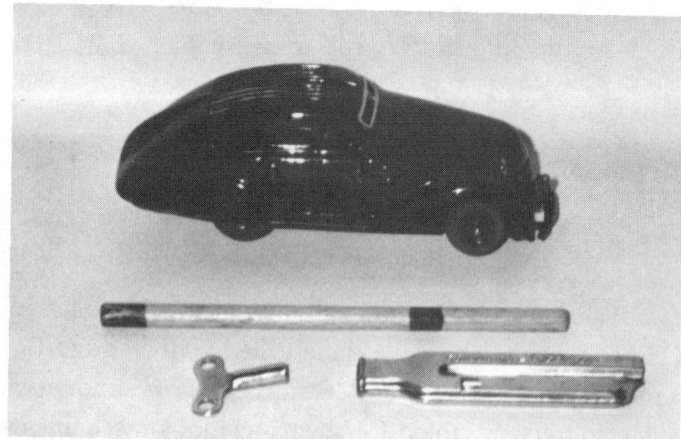

Schuco Magico Auto 2008
Photo by Don Hultzman

"Magico Auto 2008", 1950s, 5½" long, responds to blowing	140	210	280
"Magico Car and Garage", 1950s, 6" long	120	180	240
"Mercedes 190SL, 2095", 1950s, 8" long	150	225	300
"Mercedes TYP SSK 1928", 1950s, 4" long	100	150	200
"Mercer Auto 1225", 1950s, 7½" long	90	135	180

	C6	C8	C10
"Micro Racer 101", 1950s, 3½" long, Porsche style	90	135	180
"Micro Racer 102", 1950s, 3½" long, Indy style	90	135	180
"Micro Racer 104", 1950s, 3½" long, Indy style	90	135	180
"Micro Racer 1036", 1950s, 4½" long	100	150	200

Schuco Micro Racer 1040
Photo by Don Hultzman

"Mirco Racer 1040", 1950s, 4" long	100	150	200
"Micro Racer 1041", 1950s, 4" long	100	150	200
"Micro Racer 1042", 1950s, 4" long	100	150	200
"Micro Racer 1043", 1950s, 4" long	100	150	200
"Micro Racer '57 Ford 1045", 1950s, 4" long	80	120	160
"Micro Racer Alpha Romeo 1048", 1950s, 4" long	90	135	180
"Micro Racer Go Kart 1035", 1950s, 4" long	100	150	200
"Micro Racer Hotrod 1036", 1950s, 4" long	80	120	160
"Mirco Racer - Mercedes Benz 1038", 1950s, 4" long	90	135	180
"Micro Racer - Mercedes Benz 1044", 1950s, 4" long	110	165	220
"Micro Racer Mercer 1036/1", 1950s, 4" long	100	150	200
"Micro Racer Porsche 1047", 1950s 4" long	110	165	220
"Micro Racer Rally 1034", 1950s, 10'6" long - 8 three lane tracks	60	90	120
"Micro Racer Stake Truck 1049", 1950s, 4" long	90	135	180
"Micro Racer Volkswagen 1046", 1950s, 4" long	90	135	180
"Micro Racer Volkswagen Polizei 1039", 1950s, 4" long	100	150	200

	C6	C8	C10
"Mirakocar 1001", 1950s, 4½" long, non-fall action	80	120	160
"Monkey Car", 1930s, 6" long, orange-black, smiling monkey	1400	2100	2800

Schuco Motodrill Clown 1007
Photo by Don Hultzman

	C6	C8	C10
"Motodrill Clown 1007", 1950s, 5" long, composition head	400	600	800
"Mystery Car 1010", 1950s, 5½" long, non-fall action	90	135	180
"Radio 4012", 1950s, 6" long, musical car	200	300	400
"Station Car 3118", 1950s, 4½" long.	60	90	120

Schuco Studio Racer 1050
Photo by Don Hultzman

	C6	C8	C10
"Studio Racer 1050", 1950s, 5½" long, includes tools	120	180	240
"Synchromatic 5700", 1950s, 11" long - resembles Packard Hawk	500	750	1000
"Telesteering 3000 Limo", 1950s, 4" long.	50	75	100

	C6	C8	C10
"Varianto 3010", 1950s, tin cars are 4½" long, two car playset . . .	100	150	200
"Varianto 3010 Super", 1950s, service station with two 4½" tin cars	170	225	340
"Varianto 3041 Limo", 1950s, 4" long.	50	75	100
"Varianto 3064", 1950s 8" long, all plastic	30	45	60
"Varianto Box 3010/30", (tin garage and 3041 Limo, 1950s, 4½" long	110	165	220
"Varianto Bus 3044", 1950s, 4" long.	60	90	120
"Varianto Electro 3112", 1950s, 4" long truck	60	90	120
"Varianto Electro 3112u", 1950s, 4½" long truck	60	90	120
Scientific Forklift	67	100	135

SEIBERLING RUBBER

Compiled by Dave Leopard

	C6	C8	C10
GA01 '35 Ford 2 door slantback sedan, 5" long	40	50	65
GA02 '35 Ford 2 door slantback sedan, 4" long	30	40	50

Seiberling GA01
Photo by Dave Leopard

Seiberling GA02
Photo by Dave Leopard

SHARRON

by Dave Leopard

Sharron toys are die-cast aluminum, with two-piece construction similar to cast iron vehicles from the 30's. Sharron toys were made for a brief time at the Eastern Mennonite College in Harrisonburg, Virginia during the Depression era. The molds were designed by a craftsman from Hubley and the toys were made at the school from melted-down scrap aluminum. The toys are not marked in any way, but the originals bore a small paper tag that read "Indestructable Aluminum Toys". Manufacture of the toys was part of the work-study program at the school and they apparently landed some large orders with chain stores. Julian Thomas now owns the plates, which produced 8 of the smaller cars in one pouring.

Sharron SV-2 (with mold).
Photo by Perry Eichor
Courtesy Dave Leopard

	C6	C8	C10
SV1 1933 Pierce-Arrow Silver Arrow, 6 in.	125	175	225
SV2 1934 Rohr, 5 in.	100	150	200
SV3 Open Racer, 6 in.	75	100	125
SV4 Trolley Car	No Price Found		

Skippy Pedal Car, 54" long, Chrysler Airflow; 1936. Asking price in 1992, $25,000.

Slik-Toys - See Lansing Slik-Toys

SMITH-MILLER (SMITTY)

Smith-Miller (later, Miller-Ironson) of Santa Monica, California, was founded in 1945. The firm's plan was to produce, in two price ranges, duplicates of trucks and tractors in cast metal and aluminum. The lower-priced items weren't exact replicas; the higher-priced were. The prices were extremely high for the day; $6.95 to $27.85 (for an aerial ladder truck). According to Smitty expert Ray Funk, the trucks had "one terrible flaw, namely their wheels", which were "simple and poorly produced". Despite this flaw, Smith-Miller-Ironsons are highly collectible, and custom reproductions are being made by Fred Thompson. The original firm closed its doors in 1954.

(Thanks to Dennis C. Bellesfield for his help on this section.)

	C6	C8	C10
Smitty (Smith-Miller) No. 201-L Lumber Truck, 60 boards, 6 wheel, 14" long	350	525	700
Smitty No. 202-M Material Truck, 3 barrels, 3 cases, 18 boards, 4 wheels, 14" long	450	675	900
Smitty No. 203-H Heinz Grocery Truck, 6 wheels, 14" long	237	355	475
Smitty No. 204-A Arden Milk Truck, 12 milk cans, 4 cases, 4 wheels, 14" long	150	250	325
Smitty No. 205-P Oil Truck, 4 drums, 6 wheels, 14" long	225	338	450

Smitty No. 206-C Coca-Cola Truck.
Photo by Dick MacNary

	C6	C8	C10
Smitty No. 206-C Coca-Cola Truck, 16 Coca-Cola cases, 4 wheels, 14" long	450	675	900
Smitty No. 208-B Bekins Vanliner, 14 wheels, 22½" long	1000	1500	2000
Smitty No. 209-T Timber Giant, 3 logs, 14 wheels, 23½" long	162	243	325

	C6	C8	C10
Smitty No. 210-S Stake Truck, 14 wheels, 23½" long	250	375	500
Smitty No. 211-L Sunkist Special, 14 wheels, 23½" long	150	250	375
Smitty No. 212-R Red Ball, 14 wheels, 23½" long	150	250	375
Smitty No. 301-W GMC Wrecker, 4 wheeler	125	188	250
Smitty No. 302-M GMC Materials Truck, 4 barrels, 3 timbers ...	200	300	400
Smitty No. 303-R GMC Rack Truck, 6 wheels	175	263	350
Smitty No. 304-K GMC Kraft Foods, 4 wheels	300	450	600
Smitty, No. 305-T GMC Triton Oil, 3 drums	175	263	350
Smitty No. 306-C GMC Coca-Cola, 4 wheels, 16 Coke cases	450	675	900
Smitty No. 307-L GMC Redwood Logger Tractor-Trailer, 3 logs .	500	800	1100
Smitty No. 308-V GMC Lyon Van Lines Tractor-Trailer, 14 wheels	325	488	650
Smitty No. 309-S GMC Super Cargo Tractor-Trailer, 14 wheels, ten barrels	200	300	400
Smitty No. 310-H GMC Hi-Way Freighter Tractor-Trailer, 14 wheels	150	225	310
Smitty No. 311-E GMC Silver Streak Express Tractor Trailer, 14 wheels	275	363	550

Smitty Catalog illustrations of Models 402, 401.
Courtesy Ray Funk

Smitty catalog illustration of models 406 and 405.
Courtesy Ray Funk

Smitty No. 312-P GMC Pacific Intermountain Express ("P.I.E.").
Photo by Calvin L. Chaussee

	C6	C8	C10
Smitty No. 312-P GMC Pacific Intermountain Express ("P.I.E.") Tractor-Trailer	300	450	600
Smitty No. 401 Tow Truck, 15" long	125	188	250
Smitty No. 402 Dump Truck, 11½" long	175	263	350
Smitty No. 403 Scoop Dump, 14" long	110	165	225
Smitty No. 404 Lumber Truck, 19" long	375	563	750
Smitty No. 404T Lumber Trailer, 17" long	150	225	310
Smitty No. 405 Silver Streak 6-wheel tractor, 28" long	170	255	340
Smitty No. 406 Bekins Van, 29" long, six-wheel tractor and four-wheel trailer	325	488	650

Smitty catalog illustrations of models 408, 404 and 404T.
Courtesy Ray Funk

Smitty #409 Pacific Intermountain Express.
Photo by Ray Funk

Smitty catalog illustrations of models 407, 403, 409.
Courtesy Ray Funk

Smitty catalog illustration of Model 410.
Courtesy Ray Funk

Smitty No. 401-W GMC Wrecker.
Photo by Calvin L. Chaussee

	C6	C8	C10
Smitty No. 407 Searchlight Truck, 18½'' long, ''Hollywood Filmad''	150	225	300
Smitty No. 408 Blue Diamond 10-wheel dump truck, 18½'' long.	700	1200	1700
Smitty No. 409 Pacific Intermountain Express (P.I.E.) six-wheel tractor semi with eight wheel aluminum trailer, 29'' long . . .	450	675	900

	C6	C8	C10
Smitty No. 410 Aerial Ladder semi, six-wheel tractor and four-wheel trailer, 36'' long, ''SMFD'' . . .	400	600	800
Smitty No. 401-W GMC Wrecker, 6 wheels.	225	336	450
Smitty No. 402-M GMC Material Truck, 4 barrels, 2 timbers . . .	200	300	400
Smitty No. 403-R GMC Rack Truck, 6 wheels	125	188	250
Smitty No. 404-B GMC Bank of America, lock and key, 4 wheels	200	300	400
Smitty No. 405-T GMC Triton Oil, 6 wheels, 3 drums	188	282	375

Smitty No. 402-M GMC Material Truck.
Photo by Calvin L. Chaussee

Smitty No. 404-B GMC Bank of America truck.
Photo by Calvin L. Chaussee

Smitty No. 407-V GMC Lyon Van Lines tractor trailer, 10 wheels.
Photo by Bob Smith

Smitty No. 409G Mobil gas tanker.
Photo by Calvin L. Chaussee

Smitty No. 412-P GMC P.I.E. 14 wheels.
Photo by Bob Smith

	C6	C8	C10
Smitty No. 406-L GMC Lumber Tractor-Trailer, 14 wheels, eight timbers	215	322	430
Smitty No. 407-V GMC Lyon Van Tractor-Trailer, 10 wheels	325	475	650
Smitty No. 408-H GMC Machinery Hauler, 13 wheels	750	1200	1700
Smitty No. 409-G GMC Mobilgas Tanker, 14 wheels, 2 hoses . .	250	375	500
Smitty No. 410-F GMC Transcontinental Tractor-Trailer, 14 wheels	165	255	370
Smitty No. 411-E GMC Silver Streak Tractor-Trailer, 14 wheels	240	360	480
Smitty No. 412-P GMC P.I.E. 14 wheels	300	450	625
Smitty "B" Mack "Associated Truck Lines", 14 wheels	No Price Found		
Smitty "B" Mack Jr. Fire Truck, warning light, battery-operated, 4 wheels	400	650	950
Smitty "B" Mack Orange Dump, 10 wheels	750	1350	1800
Smitty "B" Mack P.I.E., 18 wheels	400	625	850

CONDITION OF A TOY
AND ITS RELATION TO PRICE

CONDITION CODE:

C6 - Good, Evident overall wear, well-played with, but acceptable to many collectors

C8 - Very Good Minor wear overall, very clean

C10 - Mint (like new)

NOTE: Mint in Box commands a high price. Condition below C6 brings considerably lower prices.

Smitty No. 404-T "B" Mack Lumber Truck & Trailer, 12 wheels. Courtesy Bob & Alice Wagner

Smitty GMC Searchlight Truck, "Hollywood Film-Ad", with trailer. Photo by Bob Smith

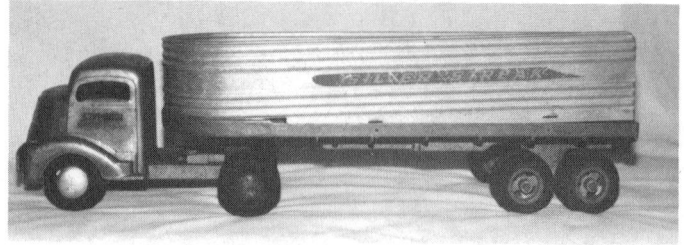

Smitty No. 311-E GMC "Silver Streak", 14 wheels. Photo by Bob Smith

	C6	C8	C10
Smitty Chevy Bekins Van, 14 wheels, plain tires, hubcaps..	260	340	530
Smitty Chevy Coca-Cola, 4 wheels, plain tires, early.............	400	625	850
Smitty Chevy Flatbed Tractor-Trailer, 14 wheels, unpainted wood trailer, plain tires, hubcaps, early..................	150	250	350
Smitty Chevy Milk Truck, 4 wheels, plain tires, hubcaps, early, 1945-46..............	180	300	400
Smitty Ford Bekins Van, 14 wheeler, plain tires, hubs. Earliest Smitty?, 1944........	180	300	400
Smitty Ford Coca-Cola, 4 wheels, wood soda cases, 1944.......	400	650	900
Smitty GMC Be Mac 14 wheel T-Trailer, 1949................	165	250	370
Smitty GMC Coca-Cola Truck, 24 plastic bottles in 6 cases, 4 wheels, 1954-55..............	425	675	925

	C6	C8	C10
Smitty GMC "Drive-O" Steerable Dump, 6 wheels, cable with hand control, 1949..........	225	350	500
Smitty GMC "Furniture Mart" Pick-up, 4 wheels, 1953......	150	225	310
Smitty GMC Heinz Grocery Truck	180	300	400
Smitty GMC Machinery Hauler, 10 wheels.....................	150	250	335
Smitty GMC Marshall Field & Company Tractor-Trailer, 10 wheel T-Trailer..............	225	350	460
Smitty GMC Peoples First National Bank and Trust Company armored truck; lock and key, 1951	225	400	525
Smitty GMC Rexall Drug, 4 wheels	200	350	450
Smitty GMC Searchlight Truck, "Hollywood Film Ad" with trailer, 1953................	400	575	800
Smitty GMC U.S. Treasury Truck armored truck, with lock and key, 1952....................	175	275	375
Smitty "L" Mack Aerial Ladder, "SMFD", 8 wheels..........	425	675	950

Smitty GMC "Drive-O" Steerable dump, 6 wheels. Photo by Bob Smith

Smitty "L" Mack Aerial Ladder Truck, "S.M.F.D."
Photo by Bob Smith

Smitty "L" Mack Army Materials Truck, 7-piece cargo load, 10 wheel.
Photo by Bob Smith

Smitty "L" Mack Army Personnel Carrier, 10 wheels.
Photo by Bob Smith

	C6	C8	C10
Smitty "L" Mack Army Materials Truck, 3 barrels, 2 boards, 1 large crate, 1 small, 10 wheels	400	600	850
Smitty "L" Mack Army Personnel Carrier, 10 wheels	400	600	850
Smitty "L" Mack Bekins Van, all white, 10 wheels	1000	1700	2300
Smitty "L" Mack Blue Diamond Dump, 10 wheels	500	850	1200
Smitty "L" Mack International Paper Co., 10 wheels	500	800	1100
Smitty "L" Mack Lyon Van, 6 wheels	450	750	1000
Smitty "L" Mack Material Truck, 2 barrels, 6 timbers, 6 wheels	350	550	750
Smitty "L" Mack Merchandise Van, 6 wheels	250	400	550
Smitty "L" Mack Merchandise Van & Trailer, 12 wheels	750	1100	1700
Smitty "L" Mack Mobile Tandem Tanker, 12 wheels	700	1100	1500
Smitty "L" Mack Orange Hydraulic Dump, 10 wheels	350	550	800
Smitty "L" Mack Orange Material Truck, 10 wheels, 3 barrels, 2 boards, one large crate, one small	450	750	1000
Smitty "L" Mack Orange Utility Truck, 4 wheels (rare)	325	550	775
Smitty "L" Mack P.I.E., 14 wheel	300	500	700
Smitty "L" Mack "Sibley's" Van, 6 wheels (rare)	400	650	900

Smitty "L" Mack Material Truck, minus 2 barrels, 6 timbers.
Courtesy R.F. Sapita

Smitty "L" Mack Merchandise Van & Trailer, 12 wheels.
Photo by Bob Smith

Smitty MIC Aerial Ladder
Courtesy Ray Funk

Smitty MIC Lift Gate Truck, 6 wheels.
Photo by Bob Smith

Smitty MIC Tow Truck "Official Tow Car", 6 wheels.
Photo by Bob Smith

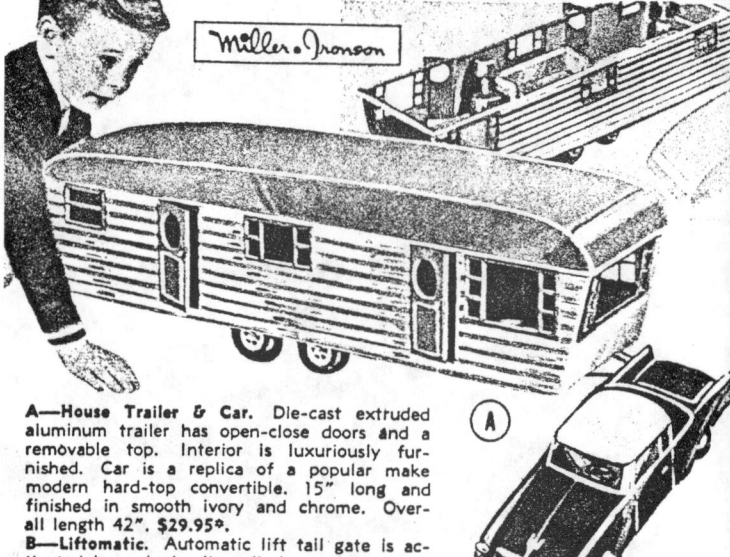

A—House Trailer & Car. Die-cast extruded aluminum trailer has open-close doors and a removable top. Interior is luxuriously furnished. Car is a replica of a popular make modern hard-top convertible. 15" long and finished in smooth ivory and chrome. Overall length 42". $29.95*.
B—Liftomatic. Automatic lift tail gate is activated by a hydraulic cylinder and closes at top to protect load of barrels (included). Cab has full 45-degree steering ability. Doors open and close. 19¾" long. $17.95*. (Also recommended: Tow Truck, $14.95*; Hydraulic Dump, $17.95*; Freuhauf, $19.95*.)

*Prices Approximate—See Page 8ix

MILLER-IRONSON TOYS are designed and built to exemplify perfection. Their unusual play features give them distinction which is positively unique.

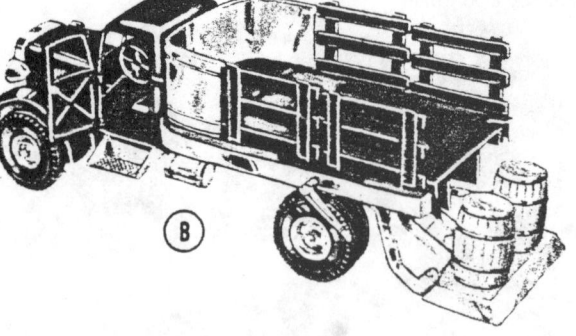

Smitty, Top: MIC House Trailer and MIC Lincoln Capri. Bottom: MIC Lift Gate Truck (Liftomatic).
From The Toy Yearbook, 1953-54

	C6	C8	C10
Smitty "L" Mack Tandem Timber, 6 wheel, 18 or 24 timbers (varies)	400	650	900
Smitty "L" Mack Telephone Truck, 6 wheels	600	1000	1400
Smitty "L" Mack West Coast Transport, 6 wheel	800	1300	1800
Smitty MIC Aerial Ladder	300	500	650
Smitty MIC "Fruehauf Road Star" tractor-trailer, 14 wheels	250	385	550
Smitty MIC House Trailer	350	650	800
Smitty MIC Hydraulic Dump, 10 wheels	400	700	1000
Smitty MIC Lift Gate Truck, 6 wheels, 2 barrels	375	550	800

	C6	C8	C10
Smitty MIC Lincoln Capri (for MIC House Trailer), steerable	375	600	850
Smitty MIC Lumber Truck, 6 wheels, 9 timbers	400	700	1000
Smitty MIC P.I.E. Tractor-Trailer, 14 wheels.	500	800	1200
Smitty MIC ''Teamsters'' Hydraulic Dump, 10 wheels. .	650	1000	1500
Smitty MIC ''Teamsters'' Tow Truck, 6 wheels	No Price Found		
Smitty MIC ''Teamsters'' Tractor-Trailer, 14 wheels	750	1100	1700
Smitty MIC Tow Truck, ''Official Tow Car'', 6 wheels.	400	575	825
Smitty MIC Tow Truck, 6 wheels, unpainted, polished	400	575	825
Smitty MIC Tractor-Trailer, polished aluminum trailer, no decals, 14 wheels.	375	600	850

SOLIDO

Solido (France) No prices were found for civilian Solido vehicles. Their military line seems to sell for between $20-$30 in mint condition.

Solido (France) Military Vehicles. 30mm Starlux Soldier at left and 54mm Britains Ltd. Gunner at right added for scale.
L to R, back row: 200 Combat Car M20, 202 Patton Tank, 203 Renault 4X4 truck, 204 Antiaircraft Gun.
Front row: 205 105mm Howitzer, 206 250mm Howitzer, 207 Russian PT-76 Tank.
Photo by Ed Poole

Late ''Solido'' Military Models and Box (253 'General Lee' U.S. Tank and, on right, 245 GMC 6X6 U.S. truck). Decals were supplied and left to buyers' imagination where to apply. Officer is French Starlux 30mm tall.
Photo by Ed Poole

Early ''Solido'' Military Model and Box (M-20 U.S. Armored Car in French markings) Crewman is a 30mm Starlux, also made in France.
Photo by Ed Poole

Solido Vehicles (continued). Starlux soldiers are 30mm tall.
L to R, back row: 222 Tiger Tank, 226 German Armored Car (radio aerial missing), 231 Sherman Tank, 232 M10 Tank Destroyer.
Front row: Renault R35 Tank, 234 Somua S35 Tank, 237 Panzer IV Tank, 241 German Half-Track   Photo by Ed Poole

Solido Vehicles Starlux GI's are 30mm tall.
L to R, back row: 242 Dodge 6X6 truck, 244 Half-Track M-3, 245 GMC 6X6 M-34 Truck, 252 M7BI ''Priest'' Assault Gun.
Front Row: 253 General Lee Tank, 253 Jeep & Trailer, GMC Truck (?) Air Compressor and Dodge Ambulance (numbers unknown).
Photo by Ed Poole

	C6	C8	C10
"Sonicon Bus"	55	83	110
Sonny Army Truck "U.S.A. 1120"	375	600	850
Sonny Dump, 26" long........	350	575	800
Sonny Moving Van..........	400	700	1000
Sonny Parcel Post Van........	650	1000	1500

Sonny "Railway Express Co." truck, 26" long, c.1920s.
Photo by Bob Smith

	C6	C8	C10
Sonny "Railway Express Co." truck, 26" long, c.1920s......	800	1200	2000
Sonny "USA 1120" Anti-Aircraft Truck, 24" long	500	800	1100
Sonny "US 1120" Artillery Truck, 26" long..................	325	480	650

Sonny trucks, as shown in a 1928 Butler Bros. catalog.

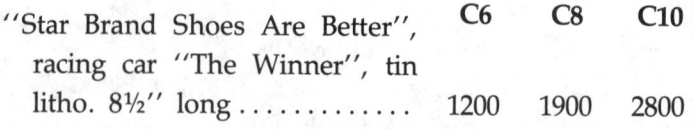

	C6	C8	C10
"Star Brand Shoes Are Better", racing car "The Winner", tin litho. 8½" long	1200	1900	2800

STEELCRAFT

Murray-Ohio Co.

	C6	C8	C10
Steelcraft Army Truck, Mack, c.1930, 22" long.............	650	1000	1450

Steelcraft "Bloomingdale's" delivery truck, 25" long, c.1930s.
Photo by Bob Smith

	C6	C8	C10
Steelcraft "Bloomingdale's" delivery truck, 25" long	450	650	900
Steelcraft "City Delivery" truck, 19" long...................	350	525	750

Steelcraft "City Ice Co." Mack truck, as shown in a September, 1934 Butler Bros. catalog.

	C6	C8	C10
Steelcraft "City Ice Co." Mack truck, 24" long	250	375	500
Steelcraft "City Milk Co.", 18" long......................	400	600	800
Steelcraft Coca-Cola truck, 12 bottles on side	400	600	800

"Star Brand Shoes Are Better" racing car.
Courtesy Sotheby's NY

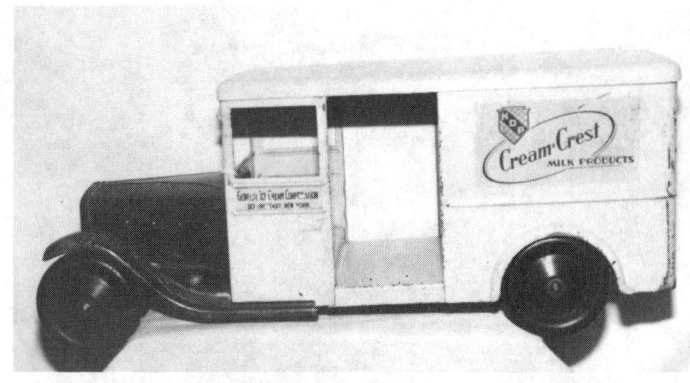

Steelcraft "Cream Crest" truck, 18" long.
Photo by Bob Smith

	C6	C8	C10
Steelcraft "Cream Crest" truck, 18" long	375	650	900
Steelcraft Dump Truck, Airflow	1500	2500	3500
Steelcraft Dump Truck, Mack, 26" long	450	700	1000
Steelcraft Dump Truck, Mack, 20" long, 1930s	150	225	300
Steelcraft Fire Truck, 25" long	750	1100	1500
Steelcraft Fire Hook & Ladder, Airflow pedal truck	1600	2700	3800
Steelcraft "Fro-Joy" Ice Cream Truck, c.1930s	350	525	700
Steelcraft GMC Scissor Dump Truck, 26" long	500	800	1250
Steelcraft GMC Trailer Truck	1500	2500	4600
Steelcraft Inter City, 24" long	350	525	700
Steelcraft Lincoln Zephyr, 1941 pedal car	1400	2500	4000
Steelcraft Little Jim Fire Truck	600	900	1200

Steelcraft "Little Jim" Mack Dump Truck, sold by J.C. Penney's Dept. Store, c.1928.
Photo by Bob Smith

	C6	C8	C10
Steelcraft "Little Jim" Mack Dump Truck, red/black, c.1928 (Little Jims were sold by J.C. Penney's)	600	900	1400
Steelcraft Mack Ladder Truck, 26" long	450	675	900

	C6	C8	C10
Steelcraft Mack Pedal Car	No Price Found		
Steelcraft Mack Police Patrol, 25" long	1400	2500	4000
Steelcraft Mandrel Bus Van	450	700	1000
Steelcraft Marion Steam Shovel	200	300	400
Steelcraft Model T Roadster pedal car, 50" long, Lic. # 65-287	450	675	900
Steelcraft New York Trucking Co., 25" long, headlights work, 1930s	450	700	950
Steelcraft Racer pedal car, 1941	800	1300	1800
Steelcraft Railway Express Truck, 26" long	1100	1600	2600
Steelcraft Richfield Oil Tanker	800	1300	1800

Steelcraft Road Roller, 16½" long. From a November, 1932 Butler Bros. catalog.

	C6	C8	C10
Steelcraft Road Roller, 16½" long	150	225	300
Steelcraft Shell Motor Oil truck with oil barrels	300	450	600
Steelcraft Steam Shovel, 26" long	225	338	450
Steelcraft Tank truck, sheet metal, 25½" long	1000	1700	2350

Steelcraft "U.S. Mail"   Photo by Calvin L. Chaussee

	C6	C8	C10
Steelcraft "U.S. Mail", 27¼" long, c.1928	1150	1725	2300
Steelcraft Van	450	700	1000

STRAUSS

Ferdinand Strauss was an immigrant from Alsace. He began as a toy importer in the early 1900s, and by 1914 had four New York toy shops. When war disrupted imports of toys, he began manufacturing them. In 1918 he was located in East Rutherford, New Jersey, with fifty employees. Eventually Strauss was known as "The Founder of the Mechanical Toy Industry in America". Strauss seems to have been wholly or partially out of business in the late 1920s, and then resumed turning out wind-ups and other toys until at least 1941-42. He is also famous for having given employment to the very young Louis Marx.

Strauss Interstate Double-Decker Bus, 10½'' long.

	C6	C8	C10
Strauss Big Show Circus Truck.	1500	2250	3000
Strauss "Bus Deluxe", 1920s, 12'' long	500	750	1000
Strauss Check-A-Cab	450	675	900

Strauss Circus Wagon, containing lion and tamer.
Courtesy Sotheby's NY

	C6	C8	C10
Strauss Circus Wagon, containing lion and tamer, 8½'' long, no engine compartment	420	630	840
Strauss Circus Wagon, 10'' long, has engine compartment	1250	1875	2500
Strauss "Haul Away Truck" No. 22, dump body	240	360	480
Strauss Hooligans Hack	300	450	600
Strauss Interstate Double Decker Bus	500	750	1000
Strauss "Kraka Jack Car", 1920s, 5½'' long	150	225	300
Strauss "Leaping Lena"	262	395	525
Strauss "Long Haulage Truck".	350	525	700

	C6	C8	C10
Strauss "Old Jalopy, The", 4 college kids	100	150	200
Strauss "Red Star Van"	400	600	800
Strauss "Standard Oil Truck 73"	325	488	650
Strauss "Trikauto", No. 53	225	338	450
Strauss "Water Sprinkler" truck	450	675	900
Strauss "What's It?" Car, No. 53, 1925, 9½'' long	600	900	1200
Strauss "Yell-o Taxi"	675	1012	1350

STRUCTO

Structo, or Freeport, Illinois, was founded in 1908 by three men: brothers Louis and Edward Strohacker and C.C. Thompson. They initially manufactured Erector Construction Kits, and about 1919 they started making toy vehicles. In 1935 J.G. Cokey bought a majority of the business, and when he died in 1975, the toy patents and designs were taken over by the Ertl Company. (Numbered Structos are found at the end of this listing.)

	C6	C8	C10
Structo Aerial Ladder Truck, 33'' long	100	150	200
Structo Army Ambulance No. 416, 17'' long	175	263	350
Structo Army Searchlight Cannon	88	132	175
Structo Army Tank No. 4120	60	90	120
Structo Army Tank, like 4120 but lights up, winds up, 13'' long	150	225	300

Structo Army Truck with canvas top, 18'' long, 1920s.
Photo by Calvin L. Chaussee

	C6	C8	C10
Structo Army Truck with canvas top, 21'' long	155	233	310
Structo Army Truck with canvas top, 18'' long, 1920s	350	525	700
Structo Army Van, 17½'' long, presed steel and canvas, No. 415	170	255	340
Structo Auto Haul-Away w/cars	70	105	140
Structo Auto Transport, 1950s	77	116	155
Structo Barrel Truck, wind-up	135	202	270
Structo Bearcat Racer, 12¼'' long, clockwork	400	600	800
Structo Camper with cloth top, 12'' long	50	75	100
Structo Caterpillar Tractor with Trailer, heavy spring clockwork motor, steel treads, No. 46	200	300	400

''Structo Cattle Farms'' truck, 22'' long.
Photo by Calvin L. Chaussee

	C6	C8	C10
''Structo Cattle Farms'' truck, 22'' long	62	94	125
Structo Cement Mixer, 20'' long, c.1950s	82	124	165
Structo Cletrac Crawler, wind-up	212	318	425

	C6	C8	C10
Structo Communications Center truck, 21'' long	70	105	140
Structo Corvair Pick-up	60	90	120
Structo Coupe, convertible, 1920s	160	240	320
Structo Delivery Truck, tin electric lights	150	225	300
Structo Dump Truck, 21'' long, c.1930s	138	208	275

Structo Dump Truck, 20'' long, 1930s.
Photo by Calvin L. Chaussee

Structo Dump Truck, 19'' long, 1940s.
Photo by Calvin L. Chaussee

Structo Dump Truck, 18'' long, open cab, 1920s, levers on each side of cab.
Photo by Calvin L. Chaussee

Structto Dump Truck, 18" long, open cab, 1920s, no levers at cab.
Photo by Calvin L. Chaussee

Structo Dump Truck, 14" long, 1959.
Photo by Calvin L. Chaussee

	C6	C8	C10
Structo Dump Truck, 20" long, 1930s	150	225	300
Structo Dump Truck, 19" long, 1940s	138	206	275
Structo Dump Truck, 18" long, open cab, 1920s, levers on each side of cab, No. 405	175	263	350
Structo Dump Truck, 18" long, open cab, 1920s, no levers at cab	175	263	350
Structo Dump Truck, 14" long, 1959	40	60	80
Structo Dump Truck, 1950s	100	150	200
Structo Fire Dept. Emergency Patrol Truck, red bubble light, 12" long, 1950s	75	112	150
Structo Garbage Truck, 21" long	75	112	150
Structo Gasoline Truck No. 912, 1950s, 13" long	75	112	150
Structo Grader, 18" long	75	112	150
Structo Guided Missile Launcher, No. 906, 13" long, with wood & vinyl missiles	70	105	140

	C6	C8	C10
Structo Hook & Ladder Fire Truck, early	262	394	525
Structo Hook & Ladder Fire Truck, No. 251, 1939	150	225	300
Structo Horse Van, late	75	112	150
Structo Ladder Truck, 1950s	75	112	150
Structo Ladder Truck, 1930s	225	338	450
Structo Loboy & Shovel	105	158	210

Structo Machinery Hauler.
Photo by Calvin L. Chaussee

	C6	C8	C10
Structo Machinery Hauler	75	112	150
Structo Moving Van, 16" long, open cab, c.1929, No. 427	175	265	350
Structo North American Van Lines	85	128	170

"Structo Package Delivery" truck, 12" long.
Photo by Calvin L. Chaussee

	C6	C8	C10
"Structo Package Delivery" truck, 12" long	100	150	200

Structo Pick-Up Truck, 17" long, 1940s.
Photo by Calvin L. Chaussee

	C6	C8	C10
Structo Pick-up Truck, 17" long, 1940s	130	195	260

Structo "Police Patrol" truck No. 426.
Photo by Thomas G. Nefos, National Toy Connection

"Structo Ready-Mix" concrete truck, c.1960s.
Photo by Bob Smith

	C6	C8	C10
Structo Police Patrol Truck, 17" long, No. 426	250	375	500
Structo "Popeye" truck, early	1700	2800	4200
Structo Pumper, late	125	188	250

	C6	C8	C10
Structo "Pumper", 22" long, 1920s	275	363	550
Structo "Ready-Mix" cement truck, 14" long	100	150	200
"Structo Ready-Mix" concrete truck, c.1960s	50	75	135
Structo Renault Tank, clockwork, green with red turret	260	390	520
Structo Road Builder Set, c.1950s	100	150	200
Structo Roadster, 16" long, 1920s, clockwork	500	800	1200
"Structo Rocker", 23½" long	130	195	265

Structo "Pumper", 22" long, 1920s.
Photo by Calvin L. Chaussee

"Structo Rocker", 23½" long.
Photo by Calvin L. Chaussee

"Structo Ready-Mix" cement truck, 14" long.
Photo by Calvin L. Chaussee

"Structo Sanitation Dept." garbage truck, c.1960s.
Photo by Bob Smith

	C6	C8	C10
Structo Sand Loader, 12" high, c.1928	44	66	88
"Structo Sanitation Dept." garbage truck, c.1960s, 17" long	50	75	135
Structo Searchlight Truck, truck metal, light and generator plastic, uses batteries, has rubber tires	62	93	125
Structo Speedster, 1920s	400	600	800
Structo Steam Shovel, 14"x11"	68	102	135
Structo Steam Shovel, 16"	58	88	115
Structo Steam Shovel, 21"x18"	105	158	210
Structo Steel Hauler, cast cab	44	66	88

Structo "Structo Telephone Co."
Photo by Bill Kaufman

	C6	C8	C10
Structo "Structo Telephone Co.", 12" long, c.1948	67	101	135

Structo Tank, 11" long, No. 48.
Courtesy Mapes Auctioneers & Appraisers.

	C6	C8	C10
Structo Tank, 11" long, #48	225	338	450
Structo Tank, olive drab with orange turret, ten metal wheels, 12½" long	300	450	600
Structo Texaco Tanker, 25" long	50	75	100
Structo Tow Truck, early	200	300	400

Structo "Toyland Construction Company" elevated dump, 12" long.
Photo by Calvin L. Chaussee

	C6	C8	C10
Structo "Toyland Construction Company" elevated dump, 12" long	125	188	250
Structo Toyland Oil Co.	175	263	350
Structo Toyland Tow Truck	40	60	80
Structo Tractor 8½" long with cast iron driver, early, caterpillar type	250	375	500
Structo Trailer Truck, 24" long, early	600	1000	1400
Structo Truck Assortment No. 317: Dump truck, blue, Stake truck, Lumber truck. Each 9" long, 3½" wide, 3½" tall. Heavy gauge metal, rubber wheels, original box folds to form garage. 1920s. Price per set	150	225	300
Structo U.S. Army Road Grader	45	68	90

Structo "U.S. Hi-Way Maintenance Service Truck".
Courtesy Thomas G. Nefos, National Toy Connection.

	C6	C8	C10
Structo "U.S. Hi-Way Maintenance Service Truck"	45	68	90

	C6	C8	C10
Structo U.S. Mail Delivery Truck, 17″ long, No. 428	325	488	650
Structo Van Lines, 20″ long, 1960s	45	68	90
Structo Whippet Tank, 12″ long, heavy spring clockwork motor enameled green, red and black, may read ''Patented 1920'', on sale in 1929, No. 48	200	300	400
Structo Yuba Tractor, copyright 1924	450	675	900
Structo No. 601 Motor Express stake truck, early 1950s	110	175	230
Structo No. 603 Package Delivery, early 1950s	80	120	160
Structo No. 605 Shovel Dump, early 1950s	150	225	300
Structo No. 607 Machinery Truck, early 1950s	170	255	340
Structo No. 609 Barrel Truck, early 1950s	140	210	280
Structo No. 700 Transport Trailer, early 1950s	150	225	300
Structo No. 702 Steel Cargo Trailer, early to mid-1950s	300	450	600
Structo No. 704 Overland Freight Trailer, early 1950s	140	210	280

	C6	C8	C10
Structo No. 704 Grain Trailer, early and mid-1950s (replaced Freight Trailer)	100	150	200
Structo No. 706 Auto Transport Trailer, sold 1953-54, with cars	125	188	250
Structo No. 708 Cattle Trailer	90	135	180
Structo No. 811 Barrel Truck windup early 1950s	600	900	1200
Structo No. 822 Wrecker Truck, wind-up, early-mid 1950s	80	120	160
Structo 844 Hi-Lift Dump, wind-up, early 1950s	90	135	180
Structo 866 Gasoline Truck, wind-up, early 1950s	260	390	520
Structo 902 Aerial Ladder Truck	88	132	175
Structo 940 Log Truck	75	112	150

Structo 940 Log Truck
Courtesy Thomas G. Nefos, National Toy Connection

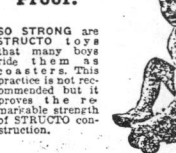

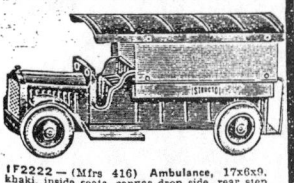

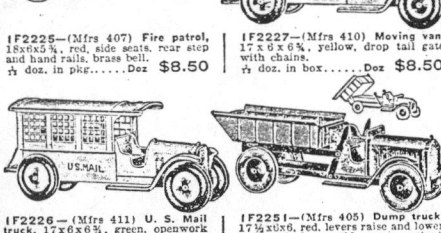
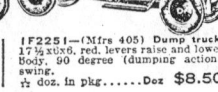

Structo vehicles (mfr. # in parentheses) as shown in the Xmas, 1929 Butler Bros. catalog.

	C6	C8	C10
Sturdibilt Logging Truck (Oregon)	325	510	650

STURDITOY

The Sturdy Corporation of Providence and Pawtucket, Rhode Island, manufactured its steel toy trucks from about 1929-1933.

	C6	C8	C10
Sturditoy Ambulance, 26" long, open cab, c.1926	2000	3500	5000
Sturditoy American Railway Express Truck, c.1920s, 26" long	1000	1500	2200
Sturditoy Armored Truck, 24" long	2200	3700	5500
Sturditoy Coal Truck, 26" long	1400	2300	3200
Sturditoy Coal Truck, high-sided, 27" long	1200	2000	2800
Sturditoy Dairy Truck, 25" long	600	1000	1400
Sturditoy Dump Truck, 1920s, 25" long	800	1300	1800
Sturditoy Dump Truck, 1920s, 26½" long	500	800	1200
Sturditoy Huckster Truck, 27" long	450	700	1000
Sturditoy Oil Tanker, 27" long	1700	3000	4000

Sturditoy Police Patrol.
Photo by Calvin L. Chaussee

	C6	C8	C10
Sturditoy Police Patrol, 26" long	1100	1800	2500
Sturditoy Pumper, 26" long, c.1930	1100	1800	2500
Sturditoy Sand & Gravel Truck	900	1600	2000
Sturditoy Steam Shovel, 26" long	162	243	325
Sturditoy Tanker, 15" long	1500	2500	3500
Sturditoy Traveling Store	1000	1700	2200
Sturditoy "U.S. Army" truck, 26" long	550	850	1300
Sturditoy U.S. Mail Screenside Truck	1100	1800	2500
Sturditoy Water Tower	1500	2500	3500

SUN RUBBER

Sun Rubber of Barberton, Ohio was founded in 1923. Toymaking started in 1924 and autos were introduced in April, 1935. Owner was Tom W. Smith Jr. (List by Dave Leopard).

	C6	C8	C10
SA01 Coupe, external exhaust pipes, from 1936, 4" long, No. 515	20	25	35

Sun Rubber SA02
Photo by Dave Leopard

SA02 '34 DeSoto Airflow, four door sedan, 4" long No. 500	20	25	35

Sun Rubber, L to R: SA03, SA07
Courtesy Alice & Bob Wagner

Sun Rubber SA04
Photo by Dave Leopard

SA03 '40 Dodge, 4 door sedan, 4½" long No. 12001	20	25	35
SA004 c.1936 "Teardrop" Sedan, 5½" long, No. 1010 (1936)	25	35	45

	C6	C8	C10
SA05 Art Deco Housetrailer, fits SA04, 4⅜″ long, No. 1025 ...	No Price Found		
SA06 Town Car, Brewster type limo, exposed driver, 5⅜″ long, No. 1015	30	40	55
SA07 Station Wagon, woody, mid-30s. 3¾″ long, No. 12007	20	25	35

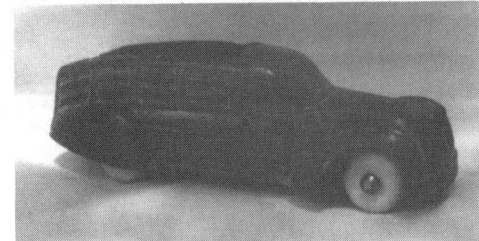

Sun Rubber ST01
Photo by Dave Leopard

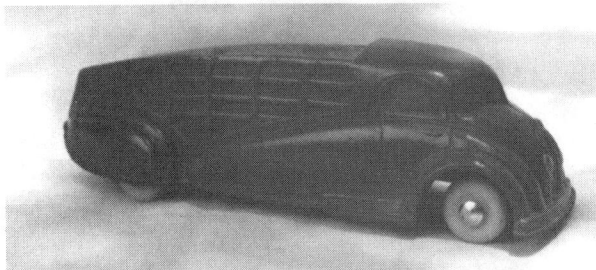

Sun Rubber ST02
Photo by Dave Leopard

Sun Rubber ST03
Photo by Dave Leopard

Sun Rubber, L to R: ST04, ST05
Photo by Dave Leopard

	C6	C8	C10
ST01 Pick-up Truck, stake sides, streamlined, 4½″ long, No. 510	20	25	35
ST02 Open Truck, stake sides, streamlined (White?), 5¼″ long No. 1005	25	30	40
ST03 Tractor/trailer, one-piece, 3 axles, futuristic, 5⅛″ long, No. 12013	25	30	40
ST04 Open Truck, futuristic, 4½″ long, No. 12003	20	25	35
ST04A as above, "U.S. Army".	25	30	40
ST05 Open "Master" truck, futuristic, 5⅝″ long, No. 12111	25	30	40
ST06 Open "Master" truck, futuristic, 6⅝″ long, No. 12011, may not exist.			
ST07 '36 White Bus, streamlined, 4¼″ long, No. 520 (1936)	20	25	35

Sun Rubber ST08
Photo by Dave Leopard

Sun Rubber, L to R: STO8, ST04A
Photo by Ed Poole

Sun Rubber SR01
Photo by Dave Leopard

	C6	C8	C10
ST08 Ambulance, c.late 1930s, 3¾″ long, No. 12006	20	25	35
ST08A Ambulance, military paint	25	30	40
SR01 Open racer, 2 drivers, 4⅜″ long, No. 505 (1936)	20	25	35

Sun Rubber SR02
Photo by Dave Leopard

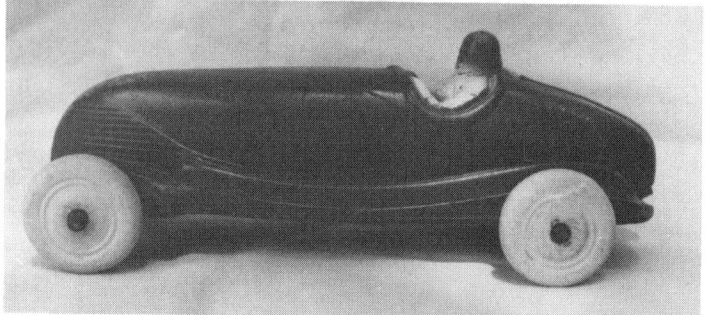

Sun Rubber SR03
Photo by Dave Leopard

Sun Rubber SD01

Sun Rubber SD02

	C6	C8	C10
SR02 Open racer, full fenders on rear, 6½'' long, No. 1000 (1936)	30	40	55
SR03 Open racer, boat tail, "Super" racer, 6¾'' long, No. 12012	25	30	40

Sun Rubber, L to R: SM02, SM01
Photo by Ed Poole

Sun Rubber SD03
Photo by Dave Leopard

	C6	C8	C10
SM01 Tank, revolving turret and gunner, 6'' long, No. 12015 (1946)	30	35	50
SM02 Scout Car, 4 gunners, 6¾'' long, No. 12014 (1946)	30	35	50
SD01 Mickey Mouse and Donald Duck Fire Truck, No. 12017	55	82	110
SD02 Mickey Mouse Tractor No. 12020	60	90	120
SD03 Donald Duck Roadster, with Pluto	68	102	135

	C6	C8	C10
Superior Dump Truck	40	60	80

	C6	C8	C10		C6	C8	C10
Technofix Motorcycle	125	188	250	Thimble Drome Racer	150	225	300
Technoflex (Germany) Scooter, wind-up	250	375	500	Thimble Drome Racer No. 25	188	282	375
Thimble Drome (Roy Cox) Champion Racer	200	300	400	Thimble Drome Racer with Engine	275	363	550
Thimble Drome Prop Rod	105	158	210	Thimble Drome Special wind-up	188	282	375

303-C THIMBLE DROME CHAMPION
Polished Radiator Grille. Chrome Exhaust Pipe. Polished Disc Wheels. Non-Skid Rubber Tires. Clutch Lever and Pressure Pump. In 6 Solid-Colors—Contrasting Numerals.
May 1 delivery as ready

L 9¾" W 4¼" H 3¾"
Individually Boxed. Approx. 1¼ Lb. Each

Roy Cox
THIMBLE DROME
Race Car

Roy Cox
THIMBLE DROME
Race Car

304-CT THIMBLE DROME CHAMPION TETHER MODEL. Same as CHAMPION Racer, equipped and Ten Feet of Control Line

Each

THIMBLE DROME DE LUXE. Sensational Seller, Chrome Exhaust Pipe. Polished Disc Wheels. Rubber Tires, 6 Color Combination, contrasting numerals.

L 8" W 4" H 3"
Individually Boxed. 1 lb. Each

THIMBLE DROME STANDARD. Same Aluminum Body and Detail less Solid Colors instead of 2 combination.

L 8" W 4" H 3"
Individually Boxed. 1 lb. Each

THOMAS TOYS

Thomas Toys was owned from first to last by Islyn Thomas (5/27/12 -), who founded the company in 1944 after leaving his post as general manager of the Ideal Toy Company. According to Thomas, its first toys - jeeps, planes and vinyl dolls - were produced that year.

The firm was located from first to last at 80 Clinton Street, Newark, New Jersey. It made only toys, and at its peak had 350 employees. It was also tied to Acme, in the sense that Acme's Ben Shapiro was a financial partner, and Islyn Thomas made up toys at his request with the Acme imprint substituted for that of Thomas. When Thomas sent the author his company's order sheets, some were printed in Acme's name, with Thomas indicating in handwriting to the author that they were Thomas' as well. In addition, on at least one Thomas page, ''Acme'' can be clearly seen on the hoods of two trucks. Acme and Thomas sometimes, perhaps always, shared the same catalog art. Sometimes, but not always, even their order numbers coincided.

The company's molds, and perhaps some of its sculpting, were provided by Richard Koegl (perhaps Koegel), whose Koegl stampworks were in Newark. Sculpting of some of Thomas' finer-detailed toys, such as its lines of small babies, dolls and civilians, were done by a Mr. Kaiser. In 1960 Thomas, aware of the impending impact of new, low-priced Japanese imports, sold out to Banner Plastics. Thomas then became an international plastics consultant, which remains his profession.

Islyn Thomas was made a member of the Plastics Hall of Fame in 1977 (the presentation made by President Ford). He was also made an Officer of the British Empire by Queen Elizabeth. He had served as chief engineer for the plastic parts in the Spitfire's Merlin engine (which was made in the U.S.) and in the immediate post-War period, heading Thomas Engineering Company, he had helped restore the ravaged European community by setting up a number of companies in England and the Continent. One of these was the toy company Popular Playthings in Wales, of which he was half owner for a while. This was founded in 1945 and continues in business today. Thomas is also the author of the books *Our Welsh Heritage, Injection Molding of Plastics* (Reinhold Publishing Corp.) and many technical articles.

The following listing was prepared by the author from the order sheets sent him by Islyn Thomas. It is not necessarily complete. Thomas had at least three different numbering systems over the years, with the same items having their numbers changed as time went on. All of the items have been listed in numerical order, with an alphabetical code preceding them where it applies. Those with a TMC preceding the number appear to be the earliest, those with a T next, and those without a code the latest. Where toys appeared on dated sheets, the date is given in parentheses.

Islyn Thomas

	C6	C8	C10
TMC-9 Streamlined truck, 5'' long (1949)	10	12	14
TMC-10 Jeep, 4¼'' long (1949) .	10	12	14
TMC-10 Jeep & Driver, driver is khaki soldier, jeep red, blue or green	12	14	16
TMC-13 Trailer, 4'' long, for jeep (1949)	4	6	8
TMC-17 Same as T-17			
T-17 Streamlined Buick Sedan, 4⁵⁄₁₆'' long, appears in 1949 as TMC-17 and in 1947 Acme catalog sheet	11	13	15
T-18 Wrecker, 5'' long	12	14	16

416

T-17 STREAMLINED BUICK SEDAN

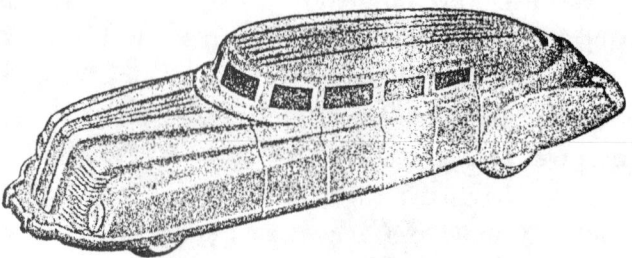

TMC-19 AIRLINE LIMOUSINE

No. 19 JEEP & TRAILER (with Driver)

No. 19 JEEP & TRAILER (with Driver)

THE Tommy-Car Line for '49 | 4 smart models—2 utility trailers—sold individually and in combination units

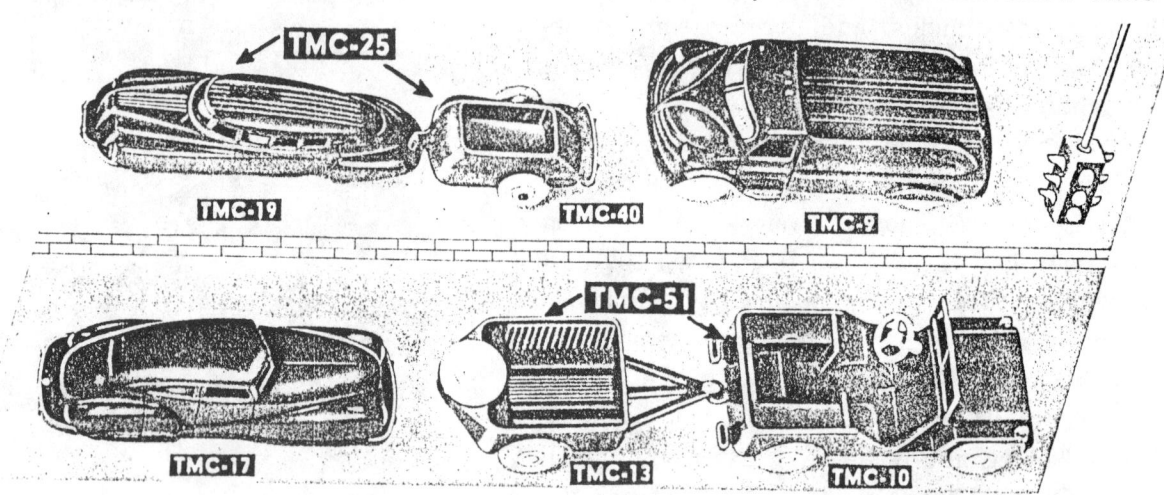

No. 77 CONVERTIBLE COUPE & DRIVER

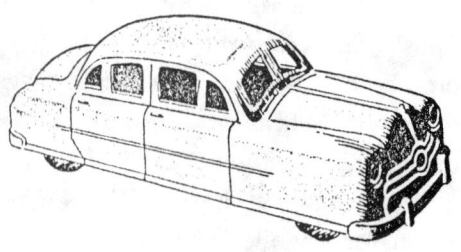

No. 77S STREAMLINED SEDAN

	C6	C8	C10
No. 18 Same as TMC-9, listed in 1955 as No. 18			
TMC-19 Airline Limousine, 4½" long (1949)	8	10	12
No. 19 Jeep & Trailer, 8⅜" long, with yellow driver in GI helmet (1954)	14	16	18
No. 19 Jeep & Trailer, 8⅜" long, yellow civilian driver, otherwise same as above	14	16	18
No. 24 Sport Convertible & Sedan, each 4¼" long (1955), set consists of numbers 77 and 77S.	20	24	28
TMC-25 Limousine (TMC-19) & Trailer (TMC-40), 6¾" long (1949)	12	14	16
No. 25 Sedan w/Canoe & Polyethylene House Trailer, overall length 9½" (1955)	30	35	40
No. 26 Truck Wrecker, 5" long	12	14	16
No. 30 Coupe & House Trailer, 8¼" long	20	22	24
TMC-32 Dump Truck, 5" long (also in 1947 Acme order sheet)	12	14	16
TMC-40 Utility Trailer, 2½" long (1949)	6	8	10
No. 40 Texaco Gas Truck, 4" long	8	10	12
No. 41 Delivery Truck, 4" long	8	10	12
No. 43 Esso Gas Truck (Acme's 1947 numbering. Doesn't turn up in known Thomas order sheets, but presumably was sold by Thomas Toys)	No Price Found		
TMC-51 Jeep (TMC-10) and Trailer (TMC-13), (1949), 8½" long	14	16	18
TMC-53 Truck (TMC-9) & Trailer (TMC-13), (1949), 9" long overall	14	16	18
T66 Same as No. 67.			
No. 67 Police-Fire Chief Radio Car, each 4½" long, price per each	11	13	15
No. 72 Plastic Motorcycle & Rider, 4" long	20	25	30
No. 74 Merry-Go-Round Truck, 4¾" long	20	25	30
No. 77 Convertible Coupe & Driver, 4½" long (1953, 1954)	11	13	15

	C6	C8	C10
No. 77C Same as No. 77. Sold with or without driver under the same number			
No. 77S Streamlined Sedan, 4½" long	11	13	15
T-79 Convertible Coupe (or Sedan), 4½" long (Same as No. 77 and No. 77S)			
T-89, Same as No. 74			
No. 107 Military Policeman & Motorcycle (with detachable Policeman), 4" long	20	25	30
T-110 Same as No. 168, but plated	No Price Found		
T-114 Road Roller (Self Winding), 4½" long, with ivory driver (1953)	No Price Found		
No. 125 Same as No. 168, but plated	No Price Found		
No. 126 Same as T-114			
No. 128 Taxi, 4½" long (1953)	22	33	45
No. 131 Car & House Trailer, overall length 9½"	25	30	35
No. 132 Truck & Racer, 4" long	No Price Found		
No. 134 Same as No. 257			
No. 135 Repair Truck (with detachable ladder), (1953), 4" long	No Price Found		
No. 139 Same as T-148			
T-140 Same as No. 131			
T-141 Same as No. 132			
T-144 Same as No. 257			
T-145 Same as No. 135 (both 1953)			
T-148 Tow Truck, 4" long, 1953	8	10	12
No. 148 Truck & Air Compressor, 8½" long	14	16	18
T-152 (1953) Same as No. 148			
No. 160 International Racer, 5" long (1955), sold with & without driver, same number	No Price Found		
No. 162 Servi-Car (Driver not included), 4½" long	25	30	35
No. 168 Solo Motorcycle (Driver not included), 4" long	20	25	30
No. 170 Motorcycle & Side-Car with passenger 4" long (yellow girl passenger, no driver)	No Price Found		
T-171 Same as No. 162			
T-174 Large Tow Truck, 5½" long	12	14	16

	C6	C8	C10
No. 175-6 Police & Fire Chief Radio Cars, each 4½″ long, price per each	11	13	15
No. 177 Large Tow Truck, 5½″ long	12	14	16
T-179 Motorcycle, 4″ long	20	25	30
No. 183 Army Jeep and Trailer (with Driver), 8¾″ long	14	16	18
No. 184-5 Army Radar & Tow Trucks, each 4″ long (may be the same as T-192/3), price per each	No Price Found		
No. 188 Military Police Jeep w/3 MPs (1955, 1956), 4¼″ long	16	18	20
No. 189 Maintenance Truck, 5½″ long, with detachable ladders	No Price Found		
T-192/3 Army Radar & Tow Trucks, each 4″ long, olive drab (may be the same as No. 184-5)	No Price Found		
No. 196 Army Road Roller (self-winding), 4½″ long	No Price Found		
T-205 Army Jeep & Driver. Same as T-10, but all khaki	No Price Found		
T-209 Same as No. 189 (1953)			
T-209 Army Maintenance Truck (with detachable ladders), 5½″ long, olive drab (crane may differ from No. 189's)	No Price Found		
No. 212 Plated Two-Tone Racer with Driver, 5″ long (same as No. 160 except top half is Special Silver Metal Plated)	No Price Found		
T-215 Army Road Roller (same as No. 196)			
No. 222 Mobile Searchlight Unit, 15½″ overall length, uses batteries	90	115	135
No. 222 Mobile Searchlight Unit with Friction Motor, overall length 15½″, uses batteries (1954). Same number as above, but also slight variations	90	115	135
T-223 Same as No. 77 (both in 1953)			
No. 234 Gas & Delivery Trucks with Trailers, overall length 6¼″, per each	14	16	18

	C6	C8	C10
No. 237 Motorcycle & Side-Car, 4″ long (1955) same as No. 170, but no passenger	No Price Found		
T-242 Same as non-friction-motor No. 222			
No. 245 Limousine & Trailer w/luggage & rack, assembly kit (1955)	No Price Found		
No. 254 Polyethylene TV Truck w/ladder, 4″ long (1955)	No Price Found		
No. 257 Polyethylene Sound Truck, 4″ long, (1955)	No Price Found		
No. 261 Vespa Motor Scooter, 4″ long (1955)	No Price Found		
No. 267 Truck & Polyethylene Trailer, 6¼″ long overall (1955)	No Price Found		
No. 289 Jet Hot Rod, 5½″ long (1955)	No Price Found		
No. 299 Searchlight Truck w/Friction Motor Assembly Kit (1955)	No Price Found		
No. 303 Ferguson Tractor Assembly Kit (1955)	No Price Found		
No. 334 Electronic Airport Traffic Control Set (1956), contains plane, "Flash" Truck with Signal Light, "Radar" Truck with Signal Buzzer, remote control Morse Code Unit	No Price Found		
No. 360 Indianapolis Speed Race, 2 racers with drivers, spring-action mechanism, (1956)	No Price Found		
No. 369 Radar Signal Set - 4 radar vehicles (1956)	No Price Found		
No. 449 Lumberyard Express, trailer has retractable wheels	No Price Found		
No. 457 Jet Car	No Price Found		
No. 519 Sport Car Transport, 23½″ long when boxed, four sports cars included from Jaguar, Mercedces-Benz, Thunderbird, Alfa Romeo, Talbot, Corvette	No Price Found		
No. 520 Overland Express Van, 21⅝″ when boxed	No Price Found		
No. 521 Cabin Cruiser and Trailer, 22⅞″ long when boxed, 56 put-together parts	No Price Found		

No. 457 THOMAS' Jet Car

Thomas Toys No. 457 Jet Car.
Courtesy Islyn Thomas

	C6	C8	C10
No. 522 Jeep & Horse Trailer Set, 18⅞'' long when boxed, includes doll family, pet, table and bench	No Price Found		
No. 524 Animal Transport, 21⅛'' long when boxed. No animals included	No Price Found		
No. 545 Speed Boat, Jeep & Trailer, with boat driver. Outboard motor is rubber-band propelled	No Price Found		
No. 558 Auto and Horse Trailer, 7½'' long bagged	No Price Found		
No. 566 Military Set. Jeep, Howitzer, 4 Soldiers	No Price Found		
No. 572 Assorted 6'' Sport Cars. Pkg. 5⅛'' x 9''	No Price Found		

No. 576 International Sport Cars, same as No. 581, except packed 3 dozen in plain box

	C6	C8	C10
No. 579 Authentic 8'' Jeep. Spare tire, moveable windshield, no driver	No Price Found		
No. 580 8'' Jeep and Driver, moveable windshield, spare tire	No Price Found		
No. 581 Chest of Sport Cars. Contains 6 Dozen ''All-Poly Cars'' in 6 styles: Jaguar, Mercedes-Benz, Thunderbird, Talbot, Corvette, Alfa Romeo	No Price Found		
No. 592 Stake Trailer Truck, 24½'' long when bagged (probably the same as No. 524)	No Price Found		
No. 597 Van Trailer Truck, 24½'' long when bagged	No Price Found		

No. 604 Same as T-114.

	C6	C8	C10
No. 607 Auto Transport, 24½'' long when bagged. Trailer loaded with any four of these Sports Cars; Jaguar, Mercedes-Benz, Thunderbird, Alfa Romeo, Talbot, Corvette	No Price Found		
No. 614 Assortment of 8'' Authentic All-Poly Ack-Ack & Searchlight Jeeps, Price per each	No Price Found		
No. 635 Sight-Seeing Bus	No Price Found		

No. 638 Same as No. 25, but in blister pack

CONDITION OF A TOY
AND ITS RELATION TO PRICE

CONDITION CODE:

C6 - Good, Evident overall wear, well-played with, but acceptable to many collectors

C8 - Very Good Minor wear overall, very clean

C10 - Mint (like new)

NOTE: Mint in Box commands a high price. Condition below C6 brings considerably lower prices.

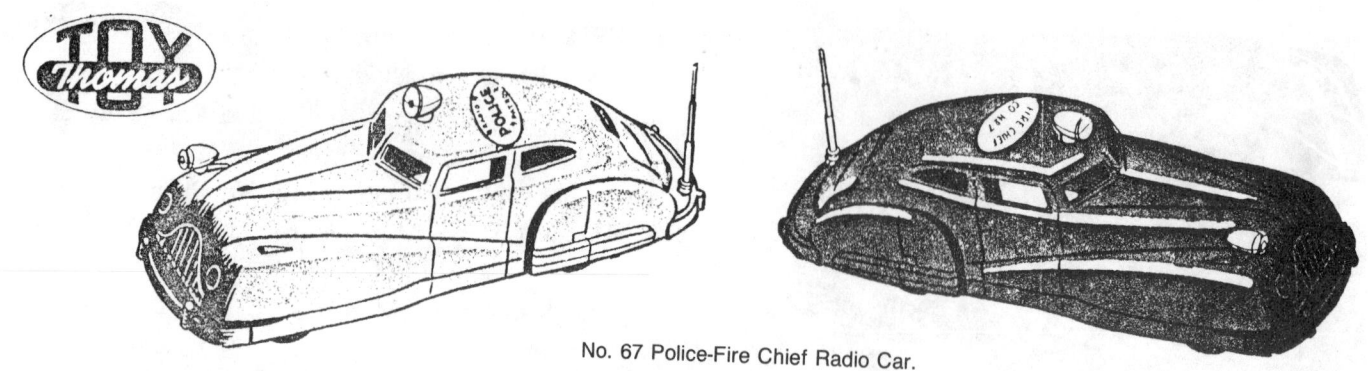

No. 67 Police-Fire Chief Radio Car.

No. 128 Taxi

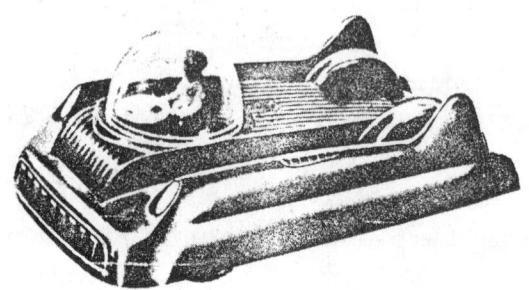

No. 289 Jet Hot Red

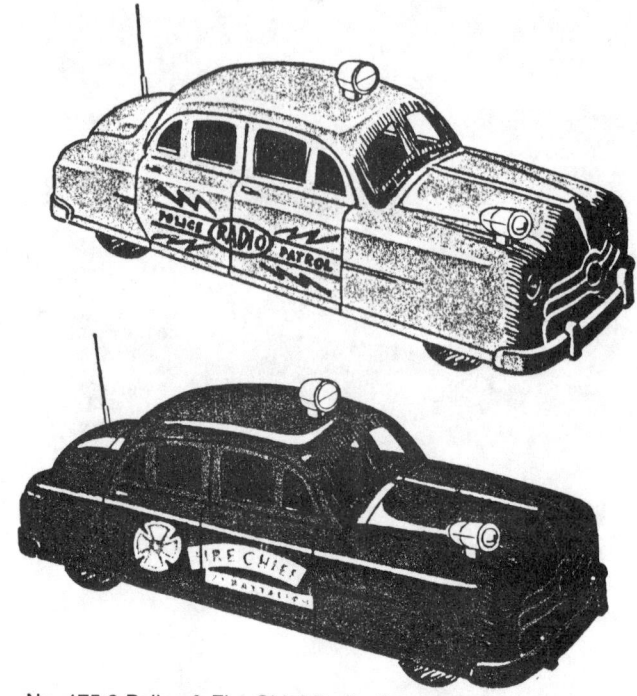

No. 175-6 Police & Fire Chief Radio Cars (50% each model).

No. 572

No. 576 (New)

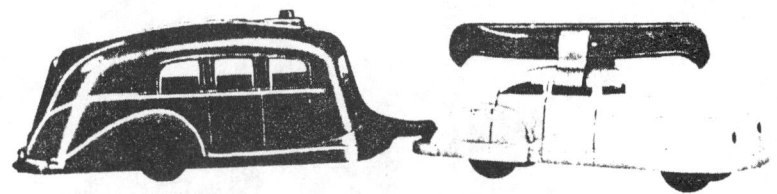

No. 25 Sedan w/Canoe & Polyethylene House Trailer.

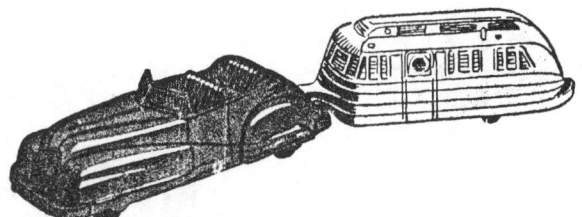

No. 30 Coupe & House Trailer

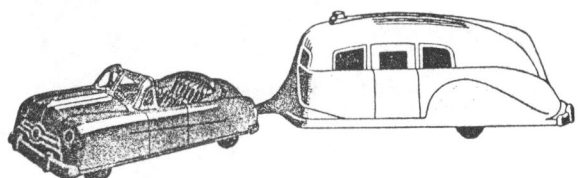

No. 131 Car & House Trailer

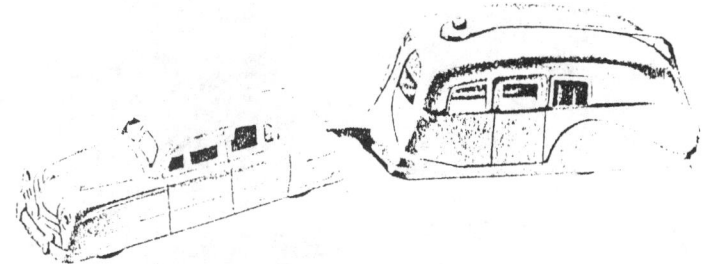

T-140 Car & House Trailer

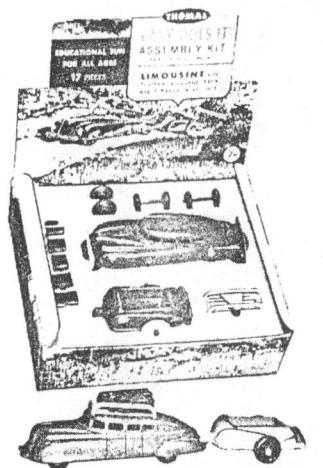

No. 245 Limousine & Trailer w/luggage
& rack (Boxed).

No. 558

No. 522
Jeep and House Trailer Set

No. 72 Plastic Motorcycle & Rider.

No. 107 Motorcycle & Policeman.

No. 162 Servi-Car (Driver not included)

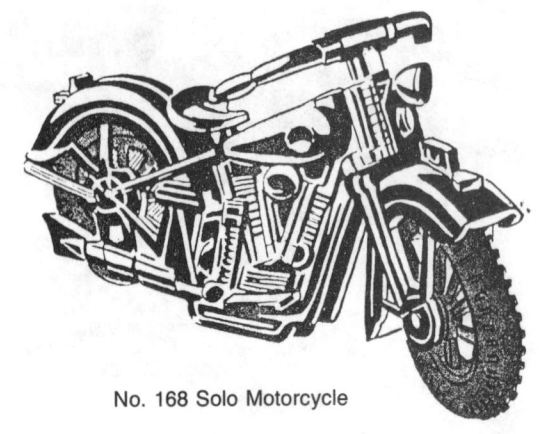

No. 168 Solo Motorcycle

No. 170 Motorcycle & Side-Car with passenger
4'' long, 3½'' wide, 2'' high. Asst Colors: Metallic Silver and Blue,
Red with Yellow Wheels and Yellow Girl Passenger.

T-179 Motorcycle

No. 237 Motorcycle & Sidecar

No. 261 Vespa Motor Scooter

No. 132 Truck & Racer

No. 160 International Racer & Driver

No. 360

No. 635 (New)

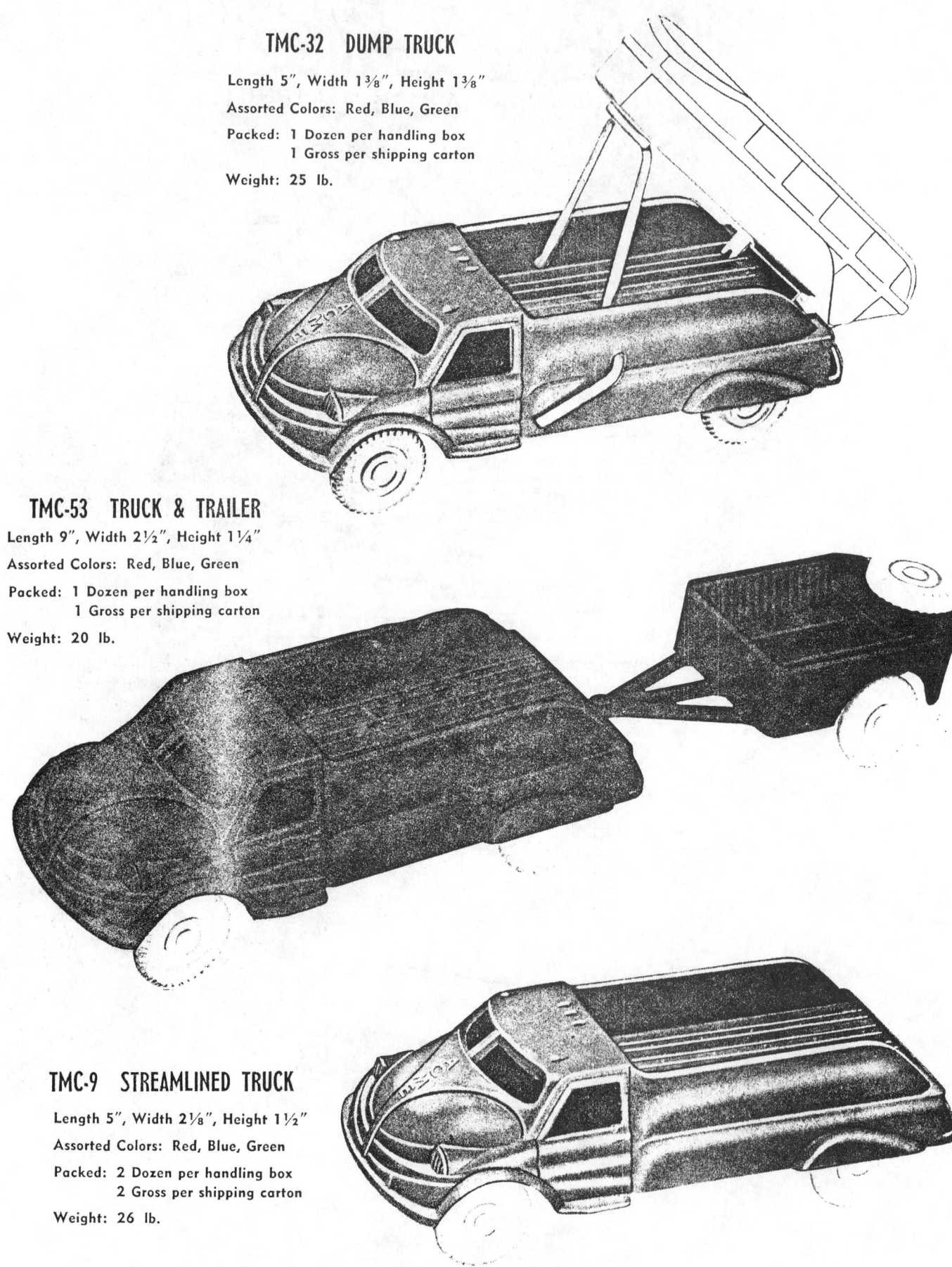

TMC-32 DUMP TRUCK

Length 5", Width 1⅜", Height 1⅜"

Assorted Colors: Red, Blue, Green

Packed: 1 Dozen per handling box
1 Gross per shipping carton

Weight: 25 lb.

TMC-53 TRUCK & TRAILER

Length 9", Width 2½", Height 1¼"

Assorted Colors: Red, Blue, Green

Packed: 1 Dozen per handling box
1 Gross per shipping carton

Weight: 20 lb.

TMC-9 STREAMLINED TRUCK

Length 5", Width 2⅛", Height 1½"

Assorted Colors: Red, Blue, Green

Packed: 2 Dozen per handling box
2 Gross per shipping carton

Weight: 26 lb.

This is a Thomas Toys order sheet but note the "Acme" marking
on the hoods.

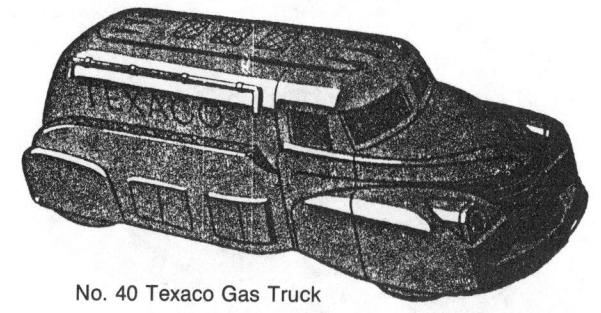

No. 40 Texaco Gas Truck

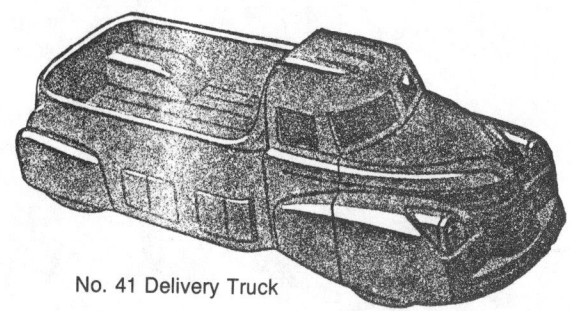

No. 41 Delivery Truck

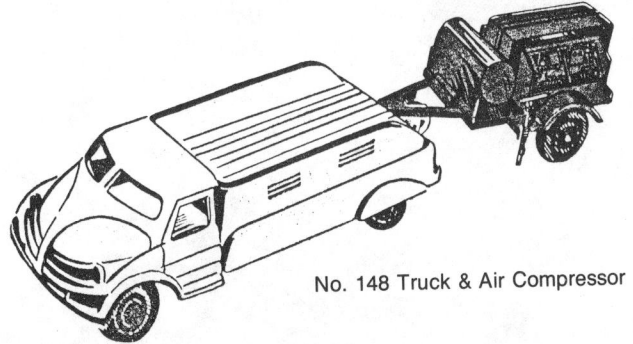

No. 148 Truck & Air Compressor

No. 234 Gas & Delivery Trucks with trailers.

No. 267 Truck & Polyethylene Trailer

No. 257 Polyethylene Sound Truck

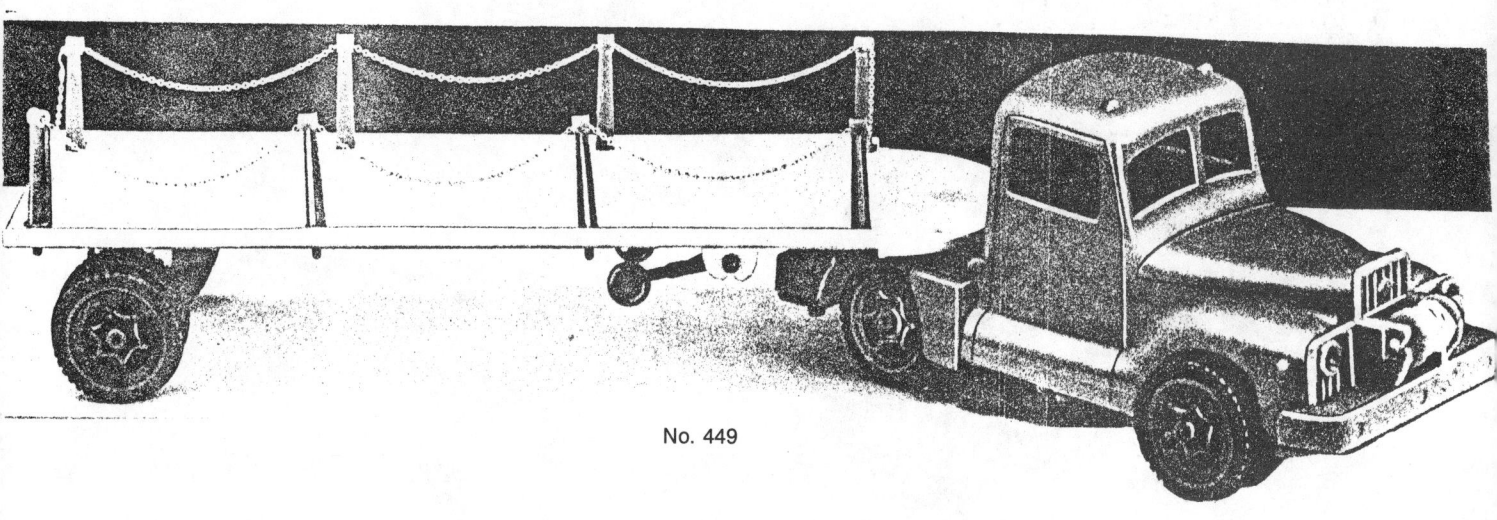

No. 449

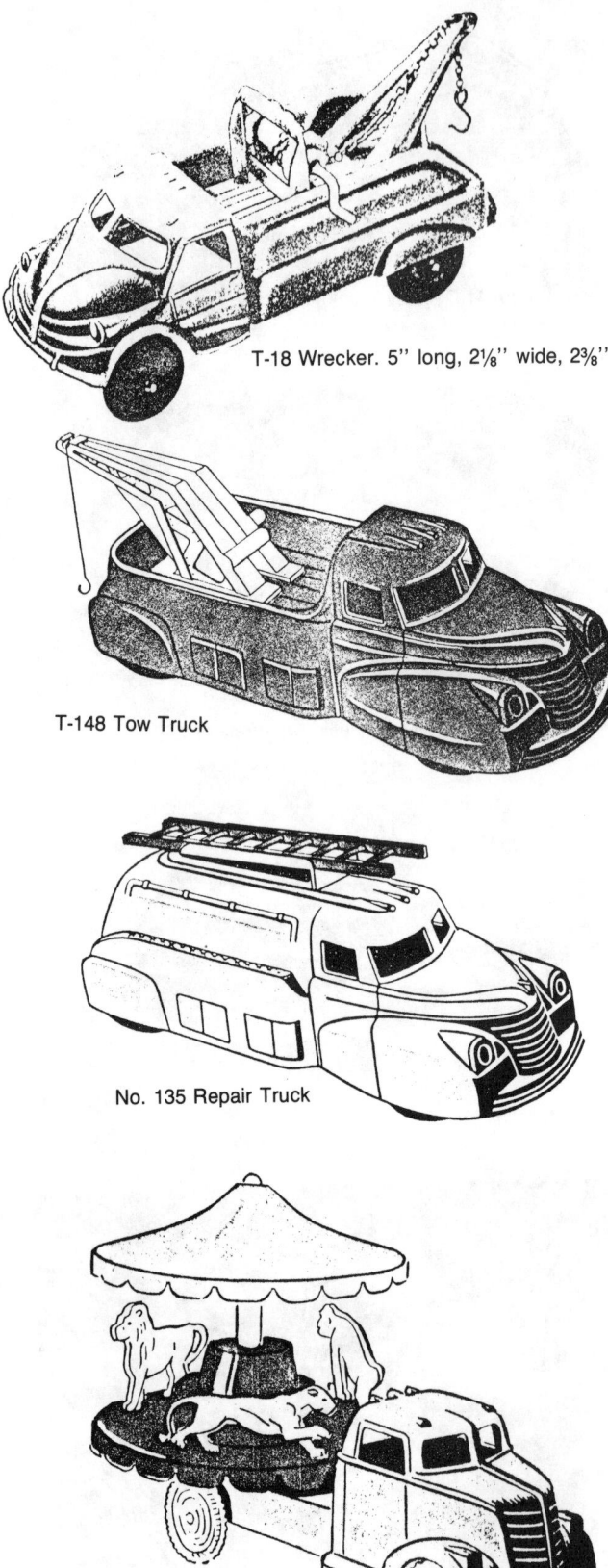

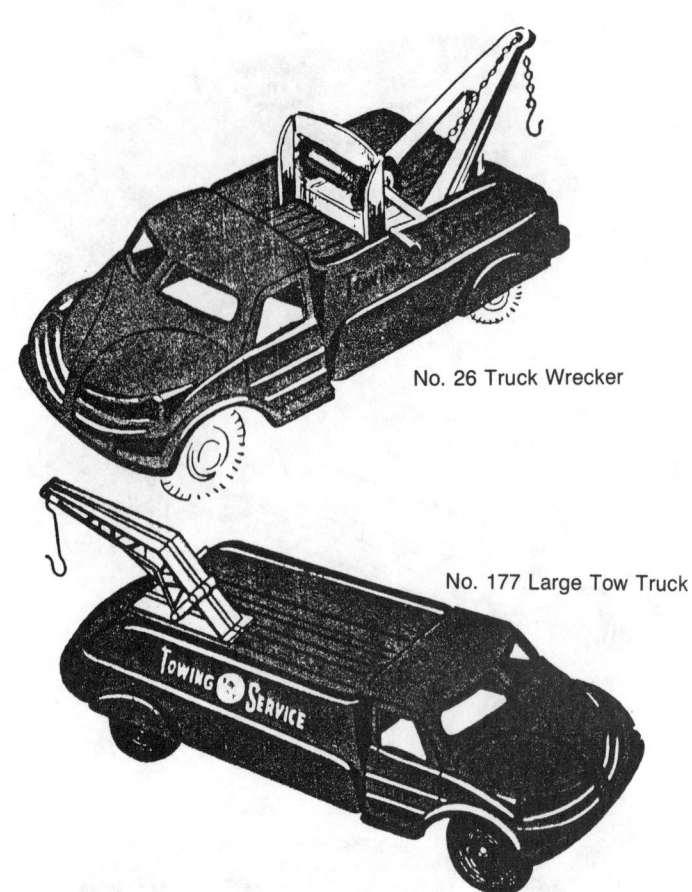

T-18 Wrecker. 5'' long, 2⅛'' wide, 2⅜'' high

No. 26 Truck Wrecker

T-148 Tow Truck

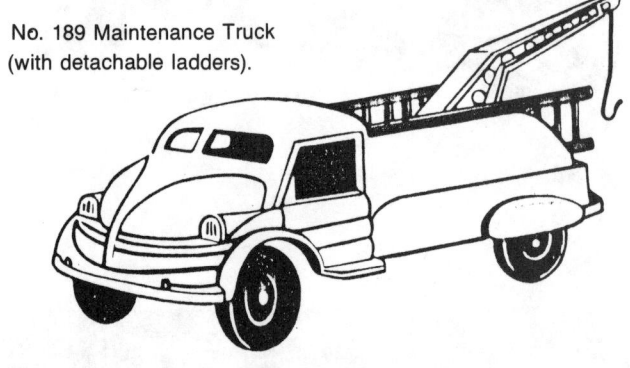

No. 177 Large Tow Truck

No. 135 Repair Truck

No. 189 Maintenance Truck
(with detachable ladders).

No. 74 Merry-Go-Round Truck

No. 254 Polyethylene TV Truck w/ladder

No. 222 Mobile Searchlight Unit (Boxed)

No. 222 Mobile Searchlight Unit with Friction Motor (Boxed).

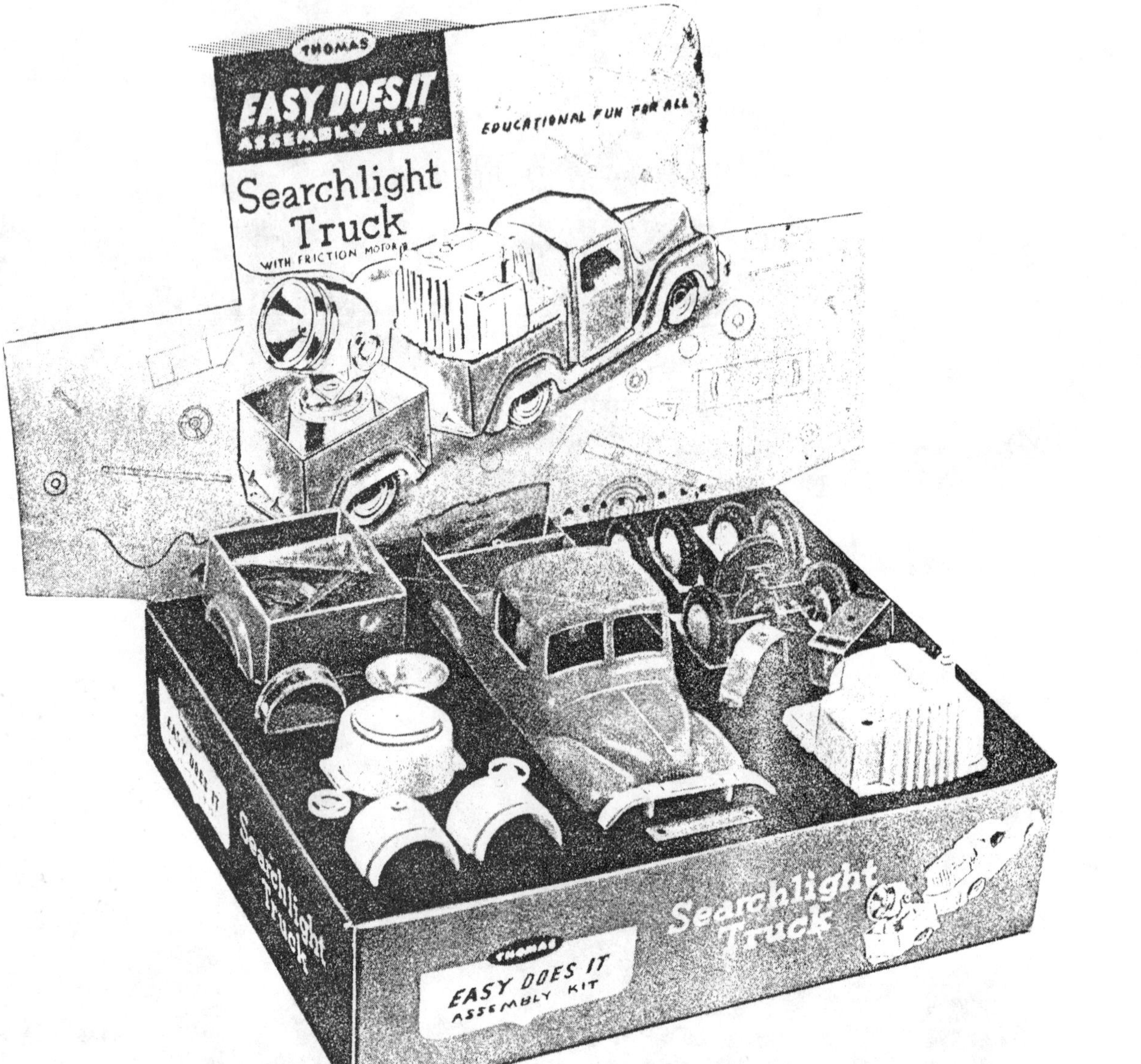

No. 299 "Easy Does It" Searchlight Truck Construction Kit.

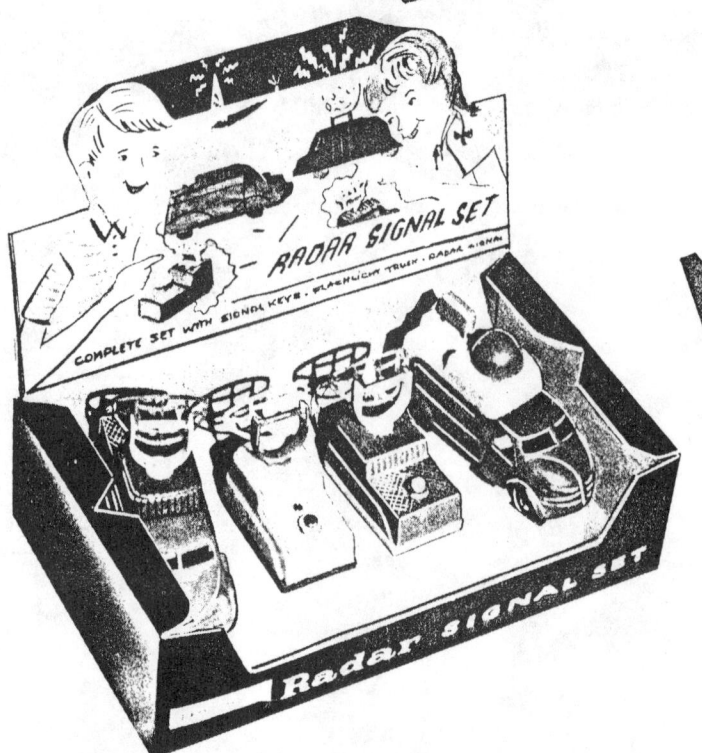

NEW !

RADAR SIGNAL SET
(Boxed)
Item No. 369
Size: 12" x 7" x 3" overall
Packed: 1 dozen to carton
Weight: 10 bs.   l
Suggested retail: $1.98

Inspired by America's Playtime "Pilots"

SUGGESTED **$2⁹⁸** RETAIL

- BIG 13" SUPER CONSTELLA-TION with both Signal Light Flasher and Code Buzzer.
- "FLASHER" TRUCK WITH SIGNAL LIGHT.
- "RADAR" TRUCK WITH SIGNAL BUZZER.
- BATTERY POWERED REMOTE CONTROL UNIT.
- INTERNATIONAL MORSE CODE.

THOMAS' ELECTRONIC AIRPORT TRAFFIC CONTROL SET

Here's an intriguing new action toy by THOMAS that's really different. There may be other toy planes, but only THOMAS' Replica of the Lockheed Super Constellation has electronic code signalling "flashing" light and "radar" buzzer.

There may be other "communication" trucks, but only THOMAS' mobile units have electronic code "flashing" light and "radar signalling buzzer.

And to top it off — nobody but THOMAS has a battery powered remote control unit for secret code communication between plane and trucks.

Yes, this new item, another THOMAS educational toy for children 4 to 12, is extraordinary in ACTION . . . PLAY APPEAL . . . and VALUE.

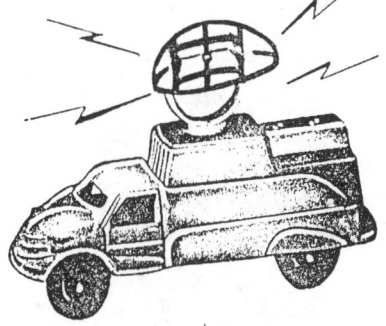

ORDER NOW!
ITEM NO. 334

(Boxed)
SIZE: 12" x 19" x 2½" overall
PACKED: 1 dozen to carton
WEIGHT: 25 lbs.

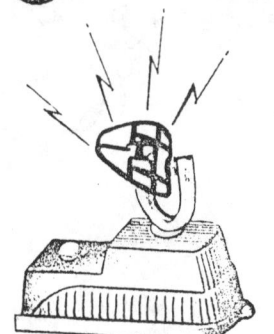

It's a THOMAS Toy!

MARK OF QUALITY

THOMAS
MANUFACTURING CORP.
80 CLINTON STREET, NEWARK 5, N. J.
Showroom: 200 Fifth Avenue, New York 10, N. Y.

Export Sales Agents: GUITERMAN COMPANY INC.
35 S. William Street, New York 4, New York, U.S.A.

No. 334

No. 520

No. 524

No. 519

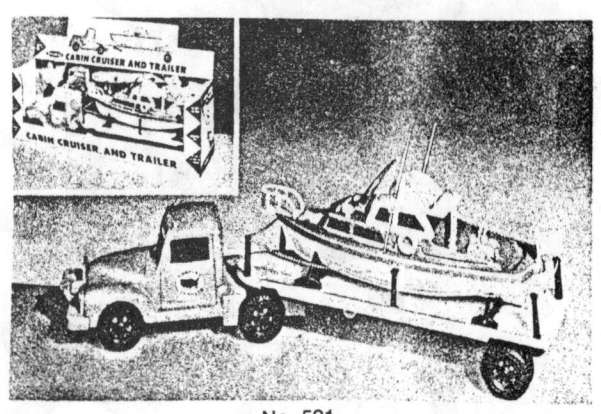

No. 521

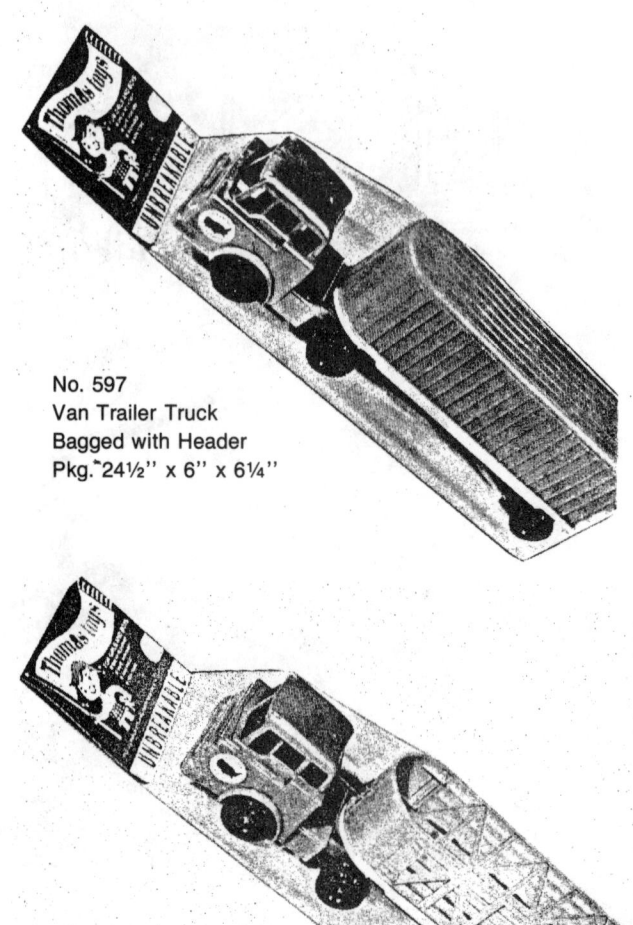

No. 597
Van Trailer Truck
Bagged with Header
Pkg. 24½'' x 6'' x 6¼''

No. 592
Stake Trailer Truck
Bagged with Header
Pkg. 24½'' x 6''x 5¾''

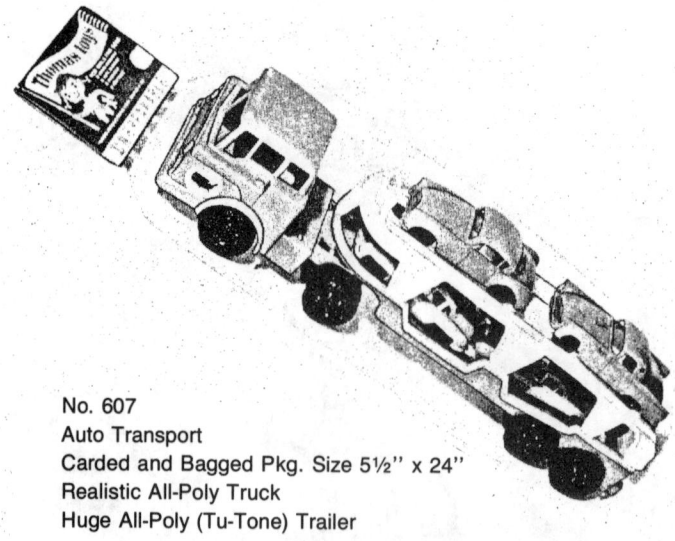

No. 607
Auto Transport
Carded and Bagged Pkg. Size 5½'' x 24''
Realistic All-Poly Truck
Huge All-Poly (Tu-Tone) Trailer

T-114 Road Roller

No. 303 Ferguson Tractor (Boxed)

No. 545 Speed Boat, Jeep & Trailer

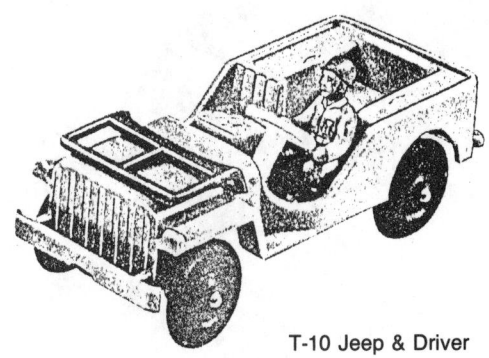

T-10 Jeep & Driver

No. 107 Military Policeman & Motorcycle (with detachable Policeman).

No. 183 Army Jeep and Trailer (with driver).

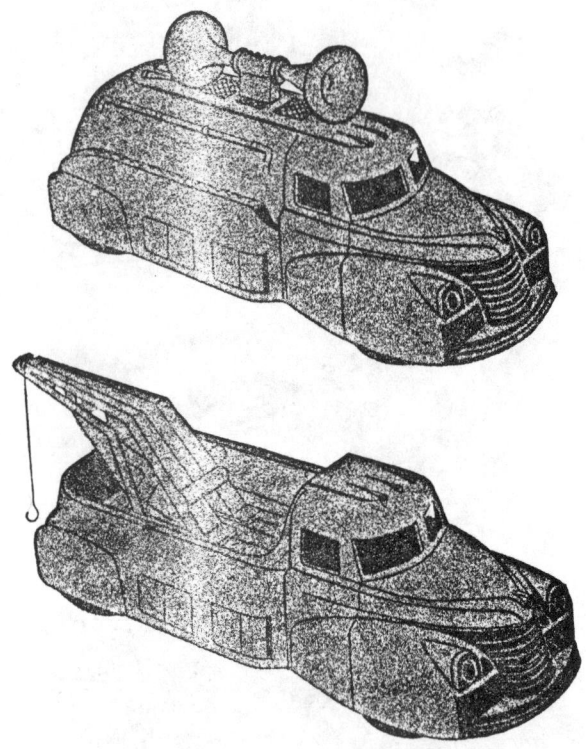

No. 188 Military Police Jeep w/3 MP's.

No. 184-5 Army Radar & tow trucks.

No. 189 Army Maintenance Truck (with detachable ladders).

T-192/3 Army Radar & Tow Trucks

No. 196 Army Road Roller (Self-Winding).

T-209 Army Maintenance Truck (with detachable ladders).

THOMAS TOYS

No. 566 Military Set

No. 579
Authentic 8" Jeep
Bulk
- Assorted Red and Blue
- All-Poly Jeep with Realistic Plastic Wheels on Free-Running Steel Axles
- Spare Tire and Movable Windshield

Retail .... 59¢

No. 580
8" Jeep and Driver
Bagged with Header
Pkg.: 4¼" x 11"
- Assorted Red and Blue Poly Jeeps with Driver at Wheel
- Plastic Wheels on Free-Running Steel Axles
- Spare Tire on Back of Jeep
- Movable Windshield

Retail .... 69¢

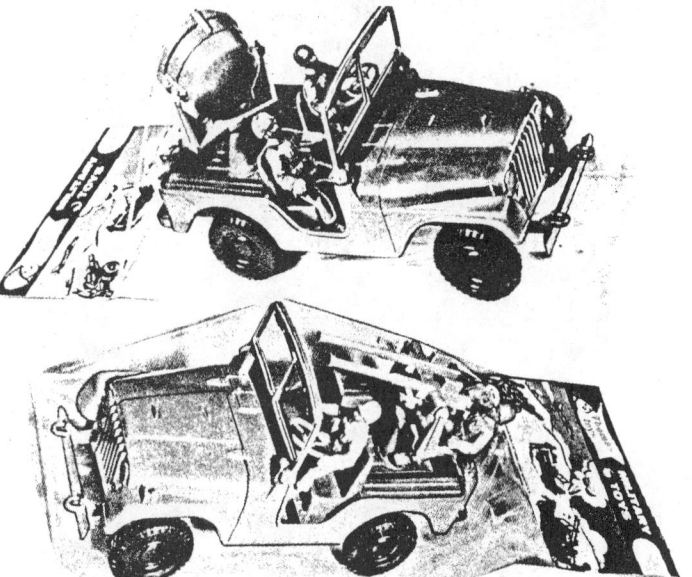

No. 614
Assortment of 8" Authentic All-Poly Ack-Ack & Searchlight Jeeps
Bagged with Header — Pkg.: 4½" x 4½" x 11"
- Movable Windshield
- Spare Tire Attached
- Black Poly Wheels on Free-Running Steel Axles
- Guns and Searchlight Swivel and Elevate
- Realistic Lens in Searchlight
- 2 Action Soldiers
- 1 Doz. Each Style — 75% Flaming Red and 25% Thomas Blue to the 2 Doz. Carton

Retail .... 98¢

	C6	C8	C10
Timmee Army Tow Truck, hard plastic, 9'' long	12	18	25

TIP TOP TOY CO.

The Tip Top Toy Co. was located in San Francisco, and produced slush cast vehicles through most of the 1920s and 30s. The firm embossed its name inside some of its toys, but not all. (List by C.B.C. Lee and Craig A. Clark)

	C6	C8	C10
Tip Top Coupe, 1923 Dodge, 3⅛'' long	16	24	32
Tip Top Tanker, marked "Gasoline", 3½'' long		No Price Found	
Tip Top Tow Truck, 3⁵⁄₁₆'' long, with trailer, 5¼'' overall	16	24	32
		No Price Found	
Tip Top Pick-up truck with tailgate, 3³⁄₁₆'' long		No Price Found	
Tip Top Bus, 3⅜'' long		No Price Found	
Tip Top Coupe, 3³⁄₁₆'' long		No Price Found	
Tip Top Coupe 1935 Hupmobile, 3¼'' long		No Price Found	
with trailer		No Price Found	
Tip Top Small tanker, 2¹¹⁄₁₆'' long		No Price Found	
Tip Top Small tanker with bumpers		No Price Found	
Tip Top "Parcel Delivery" panel truck, 2⅛'' long		No Price Found	
Tip Top Small coupe, 2⅛'' long		No Price Found	
Tip Top Studebaker Sedan, 1935, 2⁹⁄₁₆'' long		No Price Found	
Tip Top Stake truck, four or six wheels, 5⁵⁄₁₆'' long		No Price Found	
Tip Top Airflow, smaller		No Price Found	
Tip Top Airflow, larger		No Price Found	

These are a rare make of toy, evidently manufactured through most of the twenties and thirties in San Francisco by the Tip Top Toy Co. Photo by C.B.C. Lee.

	C6	C8	C10
Tippco (Germany) Aerial Ladder Fire Truck, early	350	525	700
Tippco Stake Truck, c.1930, 10'' long, wind-up	135	198	270
Tippco "Silver Racer" wind-up motorcycle, 7½'' long	500	750	1000

Tippco "Silver Racer".
Courtesy Kent M. Comstock

	C6	C8	C10
Tipper Fire Ladder Truck	400	600	800

TOLEDO METAL WHEEL COMPANY

("Blue Streak")

The Toledo Metal Wheel Company was located in Toledo, Ohio during at least the early and late 1920s. It manufactured a large range of pedal cars as well as toy trucks. Its trade name for its products was "Blue Streak".

	C6	C8	C10
Toledo No. 45 "Bull Dog" Truck, 26'' long, open cab	500	1000	1500
Toledo No. 46 "Bull Dog" Dump Truck, 26½'' long	600	1000	1475
Toledo No. 47 "Bull Dog" Sprinkler Truck, 27½'' long . .	600	1100	1510
Toledo No. 48 "Bull Dog" Moving Van, 26'' long	550	1050	1550
Toledo No. 50 "Bull Dog" Coal Truck, 25'' long	800	1350	1875

	C6	C8	C10
Toledo Fire Chief Pedal Car for sale in 1992 for $10,000			
Toledo Fire Pumper Car, red-painted, 59'' long	1250	1875	2500

TOMMY TOY

The following vehicles have been identified by Charles E. Weldon Jr., son of one of the owners of Tommy Toy. He is sure these are Tommy Toy, but admits there is always a chance he could be mistaken on some. Certainly the Cannon Truck, aside from the hubs, looks just like Barclay's, which was produced in the same years. Some others resemble Metal Cast, Savoye and other companies' vehicles. However, since slush molds did tend to change hands, production of a vehicle by one company would not preclude later manufacture of the same toy by another company. American Alloy is known to have produced copies of Tommy Toy's soldiers using new molds. The only vehicle known to bear the Tommy Toy trademark is the 810 Cord (TTV8).

	C6	C8	C10
TTV1 Aerial Ladder Truck (like Savoye), late 20s type	20	30	40
TTV2 Airflow type auto (like Kansas Toy), c.1935	32	48	65
TTV3 ''Ambulance'', late 20s-early 30s type	16	24	32
TTV4 ''Beer truck'' with wooden barrels, late 1930s	14	21	28
TTV5 Cannon Truck, mid-30s (like Barclay; Barclay's had wooden hubs).....................	17	25	34
TTV6 Convertible no driver, mid-late 30s	8	12	16
TTV7 Convertible with driver, mid-late 30s, 1935 Oldsmobile	10	15	20
TTV8 Cord, 810 (1935)	40	60	80
TTV9 ''Delivery Deluxe'' delivery truck (like Savoye), late 30s ..	18	27	36
TTV10 Double-Decker Bus, closed top, early 30s	16	24	32

	C6	C8	C10
TTV11 Double-Decker Bus, open top, extended hood (like Savoye), late 1920s	35	52	70
TTV12 Double-Decker Bus, open top, no hood (like Barclay),'late 1930s	16	24	32
TTV13 Dump Truck, late 1930s (resembles Kansas Toy, Best Toy, Manhattan Toys)	16	24	32
TTV14 ''General Trucking'' late 30s	12	18	25
TTV15 Ladder Truck, mid 30s ..	20	30	40
TTV16 ''Milk'' truck, late 1930s .	20	30	40
TTV17 ''Milk Truck'', grilled window circa late 1930s	20	30	40
TTV18 ''Milk Truck'', smooth window, circa late 30s	20	30	40
TTV19 ''Motorcoach'', mid-30s (like Savoye)	No Price Found		
TTV20 ''Oil'' tanker, ''Cap 80000'' (like Metal Cast, which has different capacity number), 1930s, attaches to Tommy Toy Towing Car Coupe..................	8	12	16

L to R: TTV23, TTV22, TTV3

L to R, top: TTV31, TTV33, TTV13
Bottom: TTV9, TTV29, TTV30

L to R, top: TTV18, TTV17, TTV14, TTV16
Bottom: TTV10, TTV11, TTV12

L to R, top: TTV27, TTV28
Bottom: TTV2, TTV30, TTV32

Tommy Toy "Tourist" - TTV30
Photo by Perry Eichor

L to R, top: TTV24, TTV1, TTV15
Bottom: TTV25, TTV26

TTV19

L to R, top: TTV20, TTV5, TTV7, TTV21
Bottom: TTV4, TTV18, TTV6

Tommy Toy TTV8
Photo by Perry R. Eichor

	C6	C8	C10
TTV21 "Packard", coupe, mid-30s	17	26	35
TTV22 "Police Patrol", open windows, late 20s-early 30s type .	70	105	140
TTV23 "Police Patrol", solid windows, late 20s-early 30s type .	35	52	70
TTV24 Pumper, mid 1930s	12	18	23
TTV25 Pumper, large, red hubs, late 30s	11	16	22
TTV26 Pumper, small, late 30s .	8	12	16
TTV27 Racing Car, large, circa mid-30s	16	24	32
TTV28 Racing Car, small, circa mid-30s	12	18	25
TTV29 Sedan, four-door, c.1935 .	17	26	35
TTV30 Sedan towing "Tourist" trailer, c.1936-37	20	30	40
TTV31 Towing Car Coupe (like Savoye), early 30s type	16	24	32
TTV32 Tractor	12	18	25
TTV33 Wrecker, late 1930s	10	15	20

TONKA

(by Don & Barb DeSalle)

Tonka toys began production in the basement of a small schoolhouse in Mound, Minnesota, a suburb of Minneapolis, MN. Mound Metalcraft Company was founded by Lynn E. Baker, Avery Crounse and Alvin Tesch. During the first year of production, the tooling for a steam shovel was purchased from the L.E. Streeter Company. Mound Metalcraft Company refined the tooling and produced the first two Tonka toys for 1947, the #100 steam shovel and the #150 crane and clam. The crane and steam shovel were displayed at the New York Toy Show in 1947 and were well received. The small staff of employees manufactured a total of 37,000 of the two metal toys.

In 1948 Mound Metalcraft Company produced the #200 power lift and trailer. In 1949 began the production of the cab over trucks. 1954 marked the introduction of the "round fendered cab" Ford trucks. In 1958, the "square fendered cab" trucks were introduced. Trucks produced after 1961 are referred to as "generic" as they no longer resembled any particular truck.

Don and Barb DeSalle, authors of the book *Collector's Guide to Tonka Toys*. The DeSalles are avid Tonka collectors.

1947	C6	C8	C10
Tonka No. 50 Steam Shovel, 20¾" long	135	202	270
Tonka No. 150 Crane and Clam, 24" long	88	132	175

1948			
Tonka No. 200 Lift Truck and Cart	100	150	300

1949			
Tonka No. 100 Steam Shovel Deluxe, 22" long	100	150	200

	C6	C8	C10
Tonka No. 120 Tractor and Carry-All Trailer with No. 50 Steam Shovel	155	280	350
Tonka No. 125 Tractor & Carry-All Trailer with No. 100 Steam Shovel	150	250	350
Tonka No. 130 Tractor-Carry-All Trailer, 30½" long	100	150	250
Tonka No. 140 "Tonka Toy Transport Van", 22¼" long	150	225	300

Tonka 1949 No. 140 "Tonka Toy Transport" Van. Photo by Calvin L. Chaussee

	C6	C8	C10
Tonka No. 170 Tractor & Carry-All Trailer with No. 150 Crane & Clam	200	300	400
Tonka No. 180 Dump Truck, 12" long	100	150	240
Tonka No. 190 Loading Tractor, 10½" long	No Price Found		
Tonka No. 250 Wrecker Truck, 12½" long	100	150	250

1951 *(1950 almost identical to 1949 line with minor color and decal changes).*

	C6	C8	C10
Tonka No. 145 Street Carrier Semi, 22" long	125	188	250
Tonka No. 175 Utility Hauler, 12" long	100	150	200
Tonka No. 400 Allied Van Lines Semi, 23½" long	175	260	350

Tonka 1951? No. 400 Allied Van Lines. Photo by Calvin L. Chaussee

438

1952	C6	C8	C10
Tonka No. 500 Livestock Hauler Semi, 22¼" long............	90	135	180
Tonka No. 550 Grain Hauler Semi, 22¼" long.................	125	188	250

1953			
Tonka No. 575 Logger semi, 22¼" long......................	125	188	250
Tonka No. 575 Logger Semi, wood flat bed....................	125	150	250
Tonka No. 600 Road Grader, 17" long.......................	50	75	100
Tonka No. 650 Green Giant Transport Semi, 22¼" long..	150	225	350
Tonka Wrecker...............	110	150	250
Tonka No. 675 Trailer Fleet Set, two tractors (five interchangeable trailers), per set..	350	580	775

1954 *(Newer Style Trucks - Rounded Fenders)*

	C6	C8	C10
Tonka No. 580 Pick-up Truck ..	75	125	250
Tonka No. 700 Aerial Ladder Semi Fire Truck, 32½" long.......	175	260	350
Tonka No. 725 Minute Maid Delivery Van, 14½" long	250	350	550
Tonka No. 725 Star Kist Van, 14½" long.................	250	375	550
Tonka No. 750 Carnation Milk Step Van, 11¾" long........	200	300	400
Tonka No. 750 Parcel Delivery Van, 11¾" long.............	200	300	400
Tonka Steel Carrier Truck......	90	135	180

Tonka 1954 Steel Carrier Truck.
Courtesy Continental Hobby House

	C6	C8	C10
Tonka Wrecker...............	90	135	250
Tonka Utility Truck...........	112	168	225
Tonka No. 775 Road Builder Set - 5 pc. set - Road Grader (Semi T&T Crane and Dump Truck)	350	525	700

1955	C6	C8	C10
Tonka No. 725 Minute Maid Orange Juice Van...........	275	350	550
Tonka No. 750 Carnation Milk Delivery Van.................	150	225	300
Tonka No. 880 Pick-up Truck ..	125	180	250
Tonka 0850 Lumber Truck, 6 wheel	175	263	350
Tonka No. 0860 Stake Truck, 6 wheel.....................	80	120	160
Tonka Allied Van Lines........	85	128	170
Tonka Dump..................	70	105	140
Tonka Freighter	90	135	180
Tonka Hook & Ladder.........	100	200	300
Tonka Livestock Truck........	110	165	220
Tonka Loboy & Shovel	150	225	300
Tonka Rescue Van............	100	200	300
Tonka Wrecker...............	100	150	200
Tonka No. 65 Trailer, Stake Side	30	45	60
Tonka No. 600 Grader........	40	80	100

1956			
Tonka No. 120 Shovel & Carry-All (Loboy), 33" long total	188	282	375
Tonka No. 180 Dump Truck, 13" long......................	60	90	120
Tonka No. 600 Road Grader, 17" long......................	45	80	100
Tonka No. 700 Aerial Ladder, 32½" long.................	100	200	350
Tonka No. 880 Pick-up Truck, 13¾" long.................	100	250	400
Tonka No. 950 Pumper, 17" long	150	225	300

Tonka 1956 No. 950 Pumper.
Photo by Calvin L. Chaussee

	C6	C8	C10
Tonka No. 980 Hi-Way Dump Truck, 13" long.............	130	180	265
Tonka No. 990 Suburban Pumper, 17" long.................	200	300	400

	C6	C8	C10
Tonka No. 991 Farm Stake Truck, 13'' long	80	120	160
Tonka No. 992 Aerial Sand Loader Set, Loader and Dump Truck	175	260	350

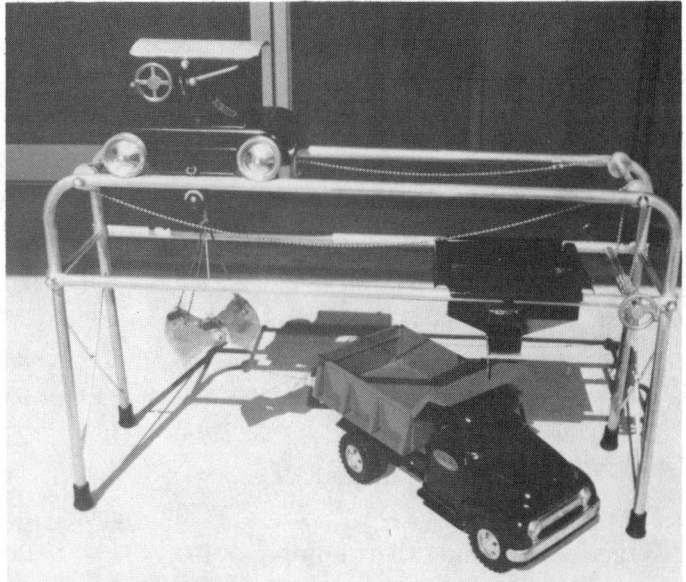

Tonka 1956 No. 992 Aerial Sand Loader Set.
Courtesy Thomas G. Nefos, Federal Shipping Network

	C6	C8	C10
Tonka No. 994 Sand Loader Set, Loader and Dump Truck	125	188	250

Tonka 1956 No. 994 Sand Loader.
Courtesy Thomas G. Nefos, Federal Shipping Network

	C6	C8	C10
Tonka No. 996 Wrecker (white color) (AAA) 12'' long	200	300	400
Tonka No. 998 Lumber Truck, 18¾'' long	80	120	160
Tonka Rescue Squad Van, 11¾'' long	115	173	230
Tonka Green Giant Semi Reefer	155	250	400

1957	C6	C8	C10
Tonka Aerial Ladder Truck	200	300	400
Tonka Big Mike Dual Hydraulic Dump Truck, 14'' long	325	488	650
Tonka Farms Stake Truck	190	275	380
Tonka Gasoline Truck, 15'' long	350	525	700
Tonka Hook & Ladder	150	225	300
Tonka Parcel Delivery Van, 12'' long	200	300	400
Tonka Pick-up w/Stake Trailer, 20½'' long	100	150	300
Stake Trailer alone	30	45	75
Tonka Stock Rack Truck with Animals, 16¼'' long	175	263	350
Tonka 3 in 1 Hi-way Service Truck, w/2 snowblades, 13'' long	200	300	400
Tonka Thunderbird Express Semi, 24'' long	150	250	350
Tonka Wrecker	100	150	250

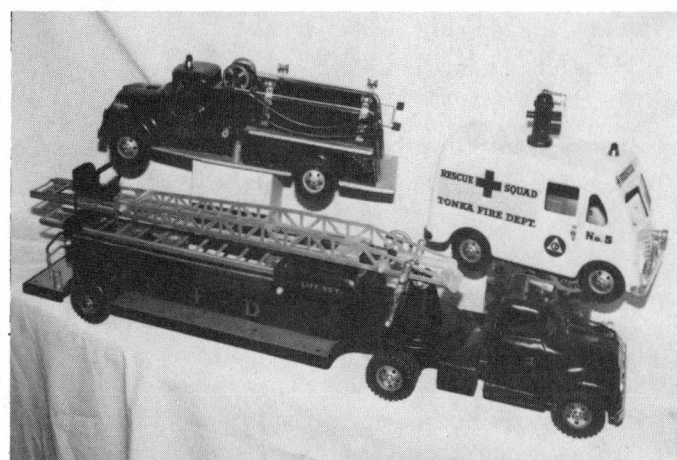

Tonka Fire Truck Set, c.1957. Rescue Squad, Ladder Truck, Pumper, Hydrant. Value in C6, C8, C10: $400, 625, 850
Photo by Bob Smith

1958 *Next Generation Cars*	C6	C8	C10
Tonka No. 02 Pick-up Truck	60	90	120
Tonka No. 03 Utility Truck	92	138	185
Tonka No. 04 Farm Stake Truck	65	98	130
Tonka No. 05 Sportsman Pick-up with topper, 12¾'' long	70	125	200
Tonka No. 06 Dump Truck	80	120	160
Tonka No. 12 Road Grader	75	112	150
Tonka No. 18 Wrecker Truck	100	150	200
Tonka No. 20 Hydraulic Dump Truck	132	198	265

	C6	C8	C10
Tonka No. 28 Pick-up with Stake Trailer & Animal............	100	150	200
Tonka No. 29 Sportsman truck with Box Trailer.............	150	225	300
Tonka No. 32 Stock Rack truck.	112	168	225
Tonka No. 33 "Gasoline" truck, hinged back door, hose & nozzle.....................	250	300	450
Tonka No. 34 Deluxe Sportsman with Boat Trailer, 22¾" long.	150	225	300
Tonka No. 35 Farm Stake with 2-Horse Trailer, 21¾" long...	125	188	250
Tonka No. 36 Livestock Van ...	175	263	350
Tonka No. 37 Thunderbird Express	150	250	350
Tonka No. 39 Nationwide Moving Van, 24¼" long............	250	375	500
Tonka No. 41 Hi-Way Service Truck.....................	70	105	140
Tonka No. 43 Shovel & Carry-All Trailer....................	190	275	380
Tonka No. 45 Big Mike Dual Hydraulic Dump Truck w/Snow Plow.....................	275	375	550
Tonka No. 46 Surburban Pumper	175	260	350
Tonka No. 48 Hydraulic Aerial Ladder....................	100	150	250

1959

	C6	C8	C10
Tonka No. 01 Service Truck, 12¾" long......................	75	112	150
Tonka No. 05 Sportsman.......	40	60	80
Tonka No. 14 Dragline, 20" long	75	112	150
Tonka No. 16 Air Express......	150	225	300
Tonka No. 22 Deluxe Sportsman	150	225	300
Tonka No. 30 Tandem Platform Stake, 28¼" long..........	140	210	280
Tandem No. 36 Tandem Air Express, with trailer, 24¾" long	225	338	450
Tandem No. 40 Car Carrier	44	66	88
Tandem No. 41 Boat Transport, 38" long..................	150	250	350
Tandem No. 42 Hydraulic Land Rover, 15" long............	350	525	700
Tonka No. 44 Dragline & Trailer, 26¼" long	112	168	225
Tonka Sanitary Truck (Square back)......................	250	350	500

1960 *(Two Center Ribs on Truck Cabs Replaced by One Rib)*

	C6	C8	C10
Tonka No. 01 Service Truck....	75	112	150
Tonka No. 02 Pick-up	60	100	175
Tonka No. 04 Farm Stake Truck	50	75	125
Tonka No. 05 Sportsman.......	75	112	150
Tonka No. 06 Dump Truck	55	82	110
Tonka No. 08 Logger	150	225	300
Tonka No. 18 Wrecker, white sidewalls..................	85	128	170
Tonka No. 20 Hydraulic Dump .	45	75	100
Tonka No. 22 Deluxe Sportsman	70	105	140
Tonka No. 28 Pick-up & Trailer	100	150	200
Tonka No. 35 Farm Stake & Horse Trailer....................	125	188	250
Tonka No. 37 Thunderbird Express	150	250	350
Tonka No. 40 Car Carrier	75	125	250
Tonka No. 41 Boat Transport, 38" long....................	150	250	350
Tonka No. 46 Suburban Pumper	100	150	200
Tonka No. 48 Aerial Ladder....	125	188	250
Tonka No. 100 Bulldozer, 8⅞" long, (plated roller wheels only in 1960)	40	60	80
Tonka No. 105 Rescue Squad, 13¾" long.................	90	150	250
Tonka No. 110 Fisherman Pick-up with Sportsman, cover, 14" long	50	75	100
Tonka No. 115 Power Boom Loader (1960 only), 18½" long	225	350	450
Tonka No. 120 Cement Mixer, 15½" long.................	100	150	200
Tonka No. 125 Lowboy and Bulldozer, 26¼" long........	190	275	380
Tonka No. 130 Deluxe Fisherman (also new boat & trailer).....	150	225	300
Tonka No. 135 Mobile Dragline.	100	150	250
Tonka No. 140 Sanitary Truck..	250	350	500
Tonka No. 145 Tanker (first Tonka with major use of plastic), 28" long......................	100	150	250
Tonka Ford Falcon (from set)...	50	75	100
Tonka "Jolly Green Giant" Special, white, green stake racks	175	250	350
Tonka "Standard" Oil Company Wrecker Special..............	200	300	500

Tonka 1960 No. 01 Service Truck.
Photo by Calvin L. Chaussee

Tonka 1960 No. 06 Dump Truck.
Courtesy Thomas G. Nefos, Federal Shipping Network

Tonka 1960 No. 08 Logger. Missing timbers.
Photo by Calvin L. Chaussee

	C6	C8	C10
Tonka No. 39 Allied Van	112	168	225
Tonka No. 40 Car Carrier	100	150	250
Tonka No. 41 Boat Transport Truck	150	250	350
Tonka No. 48 Aerial Ladder	125	188	250
Tonka No. 116 Dump Truck with Sandloader, 23¼'' long total .	80	120	160
Tonka No. 117 Boat Service Truck (1961 only)	75	150	250
Tonka No. 118 Giant Dozer, 12½'' long	50	75	100
Tonka No. 120 Cement Mixer . .	100	150	200
Tonka No. 130 Deluxe Fisherman	100	150	250
Tonka No. 134 Grading Service Truck, trailer & bulldozer, 25½'' long total	100	150	250
Tonka No. 135 Mobile Dragline .	100	150	250
Tonka No. 136 Houseboat Set, 29'' long total	200	300	400
Tonka No. 140 Sanitary Truck (never made)			
Tonka No. 142 Mobile Clam, 27¼'' long	100	150	200
Tonka No. 145 Tanker	100	150	250

1962 (*New Tonka logo; Tonka above wavy line, Mound, Minnesota below*)

	C6	C8	C10
Tonka No. 200 Jeep Dispatcher, 9¾'' long	40	60	80
Tonka No. 201 ''Serv-I-Car'', 9⅛'' long	50	75	100
Tonka No. 249 Jeep Universal . .	25	50	75
Tonka No. 250 Tractor, 8⅝'' long	50	75	100
Tonka No. 300 Bulldozer	50	75	100
Tonka No. 301 Utility Dump, 12½'' long (revised Golf Club Tractor, 1961 only)	100	150	200
Tonka No. 302 Pick-up	35	50	100
Tonka No. 308 Stake Pick-up, 12⅝'' long	50	75	100
Tonka no. 350 Jeep Survey, fringe top, 10½'' long	50	75	100
Tonka No. 402 ''Loader'', yellow & green	40	60	80
Tonka No. 404 Farm Stake Truck	50	75	100
Tonka No. 405 Sportsman	55	82	110
Tonka No. 406 Dump Truck . . .	60	90	120
Tonka No. 410 ''Jet Delivery'' truck, 14'' long (1962 only) . .	100	150	250

1961 (*''T'' Eliminated in Grill's Center*)

	C6	C8	C10
Tonka No. 02 Pick-up	60	90	120
Tonka No. 04 Farm Stake	35	52	70
Tonka No. 05 Sportsman	65	98	130
Tonka No. 06 Dump	55	82	110
Tonka No. 12 Road Grader, yellow	50	75	100
Tonka No. 14 Dragline, yellow .	62	93	125
Tonka No. 18 Wrecker	100	150	200
Tonka No. 20 Hydraulic Dump .	75	112	150
Tonka No. 22 Deluxe Sportsman	No Price Found		
Tonka No. 35 Farm Stake Truck & Horse Trailer	70	105	140

	C6	C8	C10
Tonka No. 420 Airlines Luggage Service, 16⅝" long	100	150	200
Tonka No. 512 Road Grader . . .	45	68	90
Tonka No. 514 Dragline	150	225	300
Tonka No. 516 Jeep Runabout, trailer, boat, 25⅝" long, total.	75	112	150
Tonka No. 518 Wrecker	45	75	125
Tonka No. 520 Hydraulic Dump	60	90	120
Tonka No. 524 Dozer Packer, 18¼" long total, Packer has 11 tires, sold only in 1962	75	150	200
Tonka No. 528 Pick-up & Trailer	50	75	100
Tonka No. 530 Camper, 14" long	50	100	150
Tonka No. 616 Dump Truck & Sand Loader	70	105	140
Tonka No. 618 Giant Dozer	100	150	200
Tonka No. 620 Cement Mixer . .	85	150	200
Tonka No. 735 Farm Stake & Horse Trailer	50	75	125
Tonka No. 739 Allied Van	112	168	225
Tonka No. 834 Grading Service Truck	70	100	150
Tonka No. 840 Car Carrier	100	150	200
Tonka No. 926 Pumper Truck . .	100	150	200
Tonka No. 942 Mobile Clam . . .	80	150	220
Tonka No. 1348 Aerial Ladder . .	100	150	250

1963 *(Faceted Headlights introduced)*

	C6	C8	C10
Tonka No. 50 Mini-Tonka Jeep pick-up, 9¼" long	35	52	70
Tonka No. 56 Mini-Tonka Stake Truck, 9¼" long	35	52	70
Tonka No. 60 Mini-Tonka Dump, 9¾" long	75	112	150
Tonka No. 68 Mini-Tonka Wrecker, 9½" long	30	45	60
Tonka No. 70 Mini-Tonka Camper, 9⅝" long	75	112	150
Tonka No. 200 Jeep Dispatcher .	No Price Found		
Tonka No. 201 "Servi-I-Car" . . .	55	82	110
Tonka No. 250 Tractor, yellow with red seat	75	112	150
Tonka No. 251 Military Jeep Universal, 10½" long	25	38	50
Tonka No. 300 Bulldozer	55	82	110
Tonka No. 302 Pick-up	35	52	70
Tonka No. 308 Stake Pick-up . . .	35	52	70

	C6	C8	C10
Tonka No. 350 Jeep Surrey	50	75	100
Tonka No. 352 Loader	40	60	80
Tonka No. 354 Style-Side Pick-up, 14" long	40	60	80
Tonka No. 404 Farm Stake Truck	60	90	120
Tonka No. 406 Dump Truck . . .	45	68	90
Tonka No. 422 Back Hoe, 17⅛" long	65	98	130
Tonka No. 425 Jeep Pumper, 10¾" long	80	120	160
Tonka No. 512 Road Grader, red clearance lights	No Price Found		
Tonka No. 514 Dragline	60	90	120
Tonka No. 516 Jeep Runabout, trailer & boat	60	90	120
Tonka No. 518 Wrecker	25	38	50
Tonka No. 520 Hydraulic Dump Truck	45	68	90
Tonka No. 522 Style-Side Pick-up & Stake Trailer, 22¾" long total	No Price Found		
Tonka No. 524 Dozer Packer, yellow	200	300	400
Tonka No. 530 Camper	25	38	50
Tonka No. 534 Trencher, 18¼" long	32	48	65
Tonka No. 536 Giant Dozer	112	168	225
Tonka No. 616 Dump Truck & Sand Loader, yellow	67	100	135
Tonka No. 620 Cement Mixer . .	75	112	150
Tonka No. 625 Stake Pick-up & Horse Trailer, 21¾" long overall	100	150	200
Tonka No. 640 Ramp Hoist, 19¼" long, red & white	175	263	350
Tonka No. 720 Terminal Train, 33⅝" long, total, 15 suitcases	105	158	210
Tonka No. 739 Allied Van	118	175	235
Tonka no. 840 Car Carrier	42	63	85
Tonka No. 926 Pumper	60	90	120
Tonka No. 942 Mobile Clam . . .	75	112	150
Tonka No. 1001 Trencher & LoBoy, 28½" long total	75	112	150
Tonka No. 1348 Aerial Ladder Truck	100	150	200
Tonka No. 2100 Airport Service Set	150	225	300

1964 *(Futuristic Cab introduced)*

	C6	C8	C10
Tonka No. 77 Mini-Tonka Mixer, 9″ long	50	75	100
Tonka No. 86 Mini-Tonka Van, 16″ long	36	54	72
Tonka No. 90 Mini-Tonka Livestock Van, 16″ long	50	75	100
Tonka No. 96 Mini-Tonka Car Carrier, 18½″ long, 2 cars	50	75	150
Tonka No. 250 Military Tractor, black seat	55	70	100
Tonka No. 251 Military Jeep Universal	35	55	75
Tonka No. 304 Jeep Commander, canvas top, 10½″ long	30	45	60
Tonka No. 315 Dump Truck, 13½″ long	40	60	90
Tonka No. 375 Jeep Wrecker, 11″ long	50	75	150
Tonka No. 380 Troop Carrier, 14″ long	70	120	175
Tonka No. 384 Military Jeep & Box Trailer, 19⅜″ overall	50	75	150
Tonka No. 404 Stake Truck, red	70	120	170
Tonka No. 425 Jeep Pumper, black steering wheel	100	150	250
Tonka No. 504 Stake Pick-up & Trailer, 21⅝″ long	50	75	100
Tonka No. 525 Jeep & Horse Trailer, 19¼″ long total, 2 horses	45	68	90
Tonka No. 526 Shovel, 20″ long	No Price Found		
Tonka No. 616 Dump Truck & Sandloader, orange & yellow	75	125	175
Tonka No. 640 Ramp Hoist, park green & white, very rare	200	350	600
Tonka No. 739 Allied Van Lines, black knob on door	75	125	175
Tonka No. 900 Mighty Tonka Dump Truck (Most Popular Tonka of all: 9,655,000 sold between 1964 & 1983)	65	98	130
Tonka No. 942 Mobile Clam, yellow	50	75	100
Tonka No. 998 Aerial Ladder, 2 auxillary ladders	50	75	100

Tonka 1968 No. 2252 Air Force Jeep. Value in mint $45.
Photo by Calvin L. Chaussee

Tonka 1968 No. 2306. "Life Guard" Jeep, minus raft and raft supports. Value in mint $220.
Photo by Calvin L. Chaussee

Tonka 1968 No. 2435 Jeep Wrecker & Plow. Value in Mint $100.
Photo by Calvin L. Chaussee.

TOOTSIETOY

by John Gibson

Tootsietoy began in 1876 as Dowst & Company, publishers of the National Laundry Journal. Using the "Linotype" machine purchased at the 1893 World's Fair, Samuel Dowst began turning out die-cast novelties and eventually toys. His first significant success occurred with the production of a small limousine. The Tootsietoy trade name was registered in 1924 and in 1926 the company was sold to Nathan Shure who merged it with his Cosmo toy and novelty company. With the acquisition of the Strombecker Company in 1961, the company was renamed to Strombecker and is still in business today producing toy cap guns, die-cast and plastic vehicles, wood pre-school toys, plastic action figures, easter egg dyes and other novelties.

John Gibson has always been a collector of sorts, from antique firearms to the Arts & Crafts Movement, to art nouveau, to art deco, to advertising tins, to vintage posters and to pin up art. While antique hunting in 1989, he discovered a mint, boxed set of Deluxe Grahams and has been actively involved with Tootsietoys ever since. He also repairs and restores them for fellow collectors. Born in Montpelier, Vermont, he graduated from the University of Wisconsin and is self-employed in the Washington, D.C. area. He is currently researching and writing a pre-war book on Tootsietoys.

PRE-WAR TOOTSIETOYS:

	C6	C8	C10
4528 Limousine	16	24	30
4570 Ford, Model T, open tourer	33	50	65
4610 Ford Model T pick-up truck	30	50	70
4629 (Yellow Cab) sedan	15	23	30
4630 (Federal) "Grocery" delivery van	38	57	75
4631 (Federal) "Bakery" delivery van	50	80	105
4632 (Federal) "Market" delivery van	35	55	70

	C6	C8	C10
4633 (Federal) "Laundry" delivery van	35	60	75
4634 (Federal) "Milk" delivery van	25	35	50
4635 (Federal) "Florist" delivery van	90	135	175
4636 Buick Coupe	23	34	45
4638 Mack stake truck,	23	34	45
4639 Mack coal truck	23	34	45
4640 Mack tank truck	23	34	45
4641 Buick touring car	28	42	55
4642 Long Range Cannon	13	18	25
4643 Mack Anti-aircraft Gun	25	38	50
4644 Mack searchlight truck	27	41	55
4645 Mack "US Mail - Airmail Service"	38	57	75
4646 Caterpillar tractor	18	27	35
4647 Renault tank	20	30	40
4648 Steamroller	65	95	125
4651 Fageol safety coach	27	41	55
4652 Fire Engine - hook and ladder	30	45	60
4653 Fire Engine - water tower	38	56	75
4654 Farm Tractor	35	53	70
4655 Ford, Model A Coupe	20	30	40

Tootsietoy, L to R: 4665, 5655, unnumbered "U.S. Mail" (sold only in sets), 0716 "Doodlebug".
Courtesy Phillips New York.

	C6	C8	C10
4656 Buick Coupe in tinplate garage	60	90	115
4657 Buick sedan in tinplate garage	60	90	115
4658 Mack Insurance Patrol in tinplate garage	85	125	165
4665 Ford Model A Sedan	20	30	40
4666 Bluebird I Daytona record car	23	34	45
4670 Mack tractor and two semi-trailers, "A&P", "American Express"	95	145	190
4680 "Overland Bus Lines"	45	65	85
23 Racer with driver	33	50	65
190 Mack auto transport with 3 Buicks	75	115	150
190 Mack auto transport with 4 Buicks	115	170	225

Tootsie Toy, L to R: 4670, 4680, 4651, 4634
Courtesy Phillips NY

					C6	C8	C10
191 Contractors tipper set	90	130	175	6105 Cadillac Touring car, GM series	48	71	95
5101 Andy Gump Roadster, standard	175	265	350	6106 Cadillac Screenside Delivery truck, GM series	48	71	95
5101 Andy Gump Roadster, articulated	225	340	450	6201 Chevrolet Roadster, GM series	33	50	65
5102 Uncle Walt Roadster, standard	175	265	350	6202 Chevrolet Coupe, GM series	33	50	65
5102 Uncle Walt Roadster, articulated	225	340	450	6203 Chevrolet Brougham, GM series	33	50	65
5103 Smitty motorcycle, standard	175	265	350	6204 Chevrolet Sedan, GM series	33	50	65
5103 Smitty motorcycle, articulated	200	320	425	6205 Chevrolet Touring car, GM series	35	53	70
5104 Moon Mullins police wagon, standard	150	225	300	6206 Chevrolet Screenside Delivery truck, GM series	35	53	70
5104 Moon Mullins police wagon, articulated	185	285	375	6301 Oldsmobile Roadster, GM series	35	53	70
5105 Kayo ice wagon, standard.	150	225	300	6302 Oldsmobile Coupe, GM series	35	53	70
5105 Kayo ice wagon, articulated	185	285	375	6303 Oldsmobile Brougham, GM series	35	53	70
5106 Uncle Willie rowboat, standard	135	210	275	6304 Oldsmobile Sedan, GM series	35	53	70
5106 Uncle Willie rowboat, articulated	175	265	350	6305 Oldsmobile Touring car, GM series	50	75	100
6001 Buick Roadster, GM series	30	45	60	6306 Oldsmobile Screenside Delivery truck, GM series	50	75	100
6002 Buick Coupe, GM series	28	41	55	6-01 No Name Roadster, GM series	55	83	110
6003 Buick Brougham, GM series	28	41	55	6-02 No Name Coupe, GM series	55	83	110
6004 Buick Sedan, GM series	28	41	55	6-03 No Name Brougham, GM series	55	83	110
6005 Buick Touring car, GM series	30	45	60	6-04 No Name Sedan, GM series	55	83	110
6006 Buick Screenside Delivery truck, GM series	35	53	70	6-05 No Name Touring Car, GM series	75	113	150
6101 Cadillac Roadster, GM series	40	60	80	6-06 No Name Screenside Delivery truck, GM series	75	113	150
6102 Cadillac Coupe, GM series	40	60	80	---- Ford Model A Van marked "U.S. Mail", sold only in sets	38	56	75
6103 Cadillac Brougham, GM series	40	60	80				
6104 Cadillac Sedan, GM series	40	60	80				

	C6	C8	C10
4654 Farm Tractor for Army Field Battery Set No. 5071	58	86	115
---- Box Trailer and Roadscraper Raker, sold only in boxed set Farm Tractor No. 7003	135	205	275
6665 Ford Model A Sedan	25	38	50
101 Buick Coupe	10	15	20
102 Buick Roadster	13	19	25
103 Buick Sedan	10	15	20
104 Mack Insurance Patrol	18	26	35
105 Mack Tank Truck	18	26	35
108 Caterpillar Tractor	13	19	25
109 Ford Pick-up truck	20	30	40
110 Bluebird Daytona record car	20	30	40
0192 Mack Tootsietoy Dairy, 1 pc cab, 3 trailers	75	113	150
0192 Mack Tootsietoy Dairy, 2 pc cab, 3 trailers	115	165	225
0198 Mack Auto Transport, 1 pc cab, 3 35' Fords	125	185	245
0198 Mack Auto Transport, 2 pc cab, 3 34' Fords	215	320	425
0801 Mack "Express" stake semi-trailer, 1 pc cab	55	80	105
0801 Mack "Express" stake semi-trailer, 2 pc cab	63	95	125
0802 Mack "Domaco" tank semi-trailer, 1 pc cab	60	90	120
0802 Mack "Domaco" tank semi-trailer, 2 pc cab	65	98	130
0803 Mack "Long Distance Hauling" semi-trailer, ...	70	105	140
0804 Mack "City Fuel" coal truck, 10 wheel	80	120	155
0804 Mack "City Fuel" coal truck, 4 wheel	100	150	200
0805 Mack "Tootsietoy Dairy" semi-trailer truck	60	90	120
0806 Graham Wrecker	62	95	125
0807 Delivery Motorcycle adapted from 5103	125	185	250
0808 Graham "Tootsietoy Dairy"	62	95	125
0809 Graham Ambulance	65	98	130
---- Graham "Commercial Tire & Supply"	100	150	200
0810 Mack "Railway Express Co." truck with "Wrigleys Gum" ad, 1 pc cab	65	95	125

Tootsietoy 0192
Courtesy Phillips NY

Tootsietoy No. 04638
Courtesy Phillips NY

Tootsietoy 0802
Photo by Bill Kaufman
Courtesy Good Old Days Store

Tootsietoy No. 804 "City Fuel Co.", 100mm 10-wheel version, issued 1933, in catalog 1933-35.
Courtesy The Graham Werkes

Tootsietoy No. 0804 "City Fuel Co.", rarer 4-wheel version - issued 1936, in catalog 1936-38.
Courtesy The Graham Werkes

Tootsietoy 0805
Photo by Bill Kaufman
Courtesy Good Old Days Store

Tootsietoy 0806
Courtesy Phillips NY

	C6	C8	C10
0810 Mack "Railway Express Co." truck with "Wrigleys Gum" ad, 2 pc cab	75	115	150
0511 Graham Roadster, 5 wheel	75	115	150
0512 Graham Coupe, 5 wheel	60	90	120
0513 Graham Sedan, 5 wheel	60	90	120
0514 Graham Convertible coupe, 5 wheel	65	100	135
0515 Graham Convertible sedan, 5 wheel	65	100	135
0516 Graham Town Car, 5 wheel	75	115	150
0611 Graham Roadster, 6 wheel	75	115	150
0612 Graham coupe, 6 wheel	60	90	120
0613 Graham Sedan, 6 wheel	60	90	120
0614 Graham Convertible Coupe, 6 wheel	65	100	135
0615 Graham Convertible sedan, 6 wheel	65	100	135
0616 Graham Towncar, 6 wheel	65	100	135
---- Graham Roadster, 4 wheel, Bild-A-Car	75	115	150
---- Graham Coupe, 4 wheel, Bild-A-Car	60	90	120
---- Graham Sedan, 4 wheel, Bild-A-car	60	90	120
0712 LaSalle Coupe	133	200	265
0713 LaSalle Sedan	133	200	265
0714 LaSalle Convertible Coupe	143	214	285
0715 LaSalle Convertible Sedan	143	214	285

	C6	C8	C10
0716 Briggs Lincoln prototype, "Doodlebug"	55	85	115
6015 Lincoln Zephyr (plain version)	145	215	285
6015 Lincoln Zephyr (wind-up)	225	335	450
6016 Lincoln Wrecker (plain version)	185	285	375
6016 Lincoln Wrecker (wind-up)	275	415	550
0111 1934 Ford V8 Sedan	30	45	60
0111 1935 Ford V8 Sedan	15	23	30
0112 1934 Ford V8 Coupe	33	49	65
0112 1935 Ford V8 Coupe	18	26	35
0113 1934 Ford V8 Wrecker	38	56	75
0113 1935 Ford V8 Wrecker	23	34	45
0114 1934 Ford V8 Convertible Coupe	40	60	80
0115 1934 Ford V8 Convertible Sedan	40	60	80
0116 Ford V8 Roadster	18	26	35
0117 Zephyr Railcar	38	56	75
0118 DeSoto Airflow Sedan	23	34	45
0120 Oil Tank Truck	23	34	45
0121 Ford Pick-up Truck	18	26	35
0123 Ford "Special Delivery" "camelback van	25	38	50
0123 Ford "Wieboldt's" camelback van	125	185	250
0123 Ford "Lewis's" camelback van	100	150	200
0123 Ford "Miller & Rhoads" camelback van	125	185	250
0123 Ford "McLeans" camelback van	125	185	250
0123 Ford "Shepards" camelback van	125	185	250
180 Lincoln Zephyr & Roamer House Trailer without wind-up motor	420	630	835
180 Lincoln Zephyr & Roamer House Trailer with wind-up motor	500	750	1000
187 Mack Auto Transport with up-tilted trailer & 3 vehicles	235	350	465
4634 Army Supply Truck	33	49	65
4635 Armored Car	23	34	45
1006 "Standard" Oil Truck	33	49	65
1007 "Sinclair" Oil Truck	33	49	65
1008 "Texaco" Oil Truck	33	49	65
1009 "Shell" Oil Truck	35	53	70

TOOTSIETOY

Tootsietoy No. 1040 Hook & Ladder, 139mm, issued 1937, in catalog 1937-41.
Courtesy The Graham Werkes

Tootsietoy No. 1010 Wrigley's truck, 114mm long, issued 1940, reissued post war 4''.
Courtesy The Graham Werkes

Tootsietoy No. 1011 Massey-Ferguson farm tractors in only known colors: green/silver; red/silver. Issued in 1941. 4'' long considered rare.
Courtesy The Graham Werkes

Tootsietoy No. 1046 Station Wagon, 113mm, issued 1940, reissued postwar.
Courtesy The Graham Werkes

	C6	C8	C10
1010 "Wrigley" Box Van	43	64	85
1011 "Massey-Ferguson" Farm Tractor	185	285	375
1016 Auburn Roadster, jumbo torpedo	23	34	45
1017 Jumbo torpedo Coupe	20	30	40
1018 Jumbo torpedo Sedan	20	30	40
1019 Jumbo torpedo Pick-up Truck	20	30	40
1027 Jumbo torpedo Wrecker	22	33	45
1040 Fire Engine, Hook & Ladder	35	50	70
1041 Fire Engine, Hose Car	35	55	75
1042 Fire Engine, Insurance Patrol, open end	25	35	50
1042 Fire Engine, Insurance Patrol with single ladder & rear fireman	35	50	65
1043 No. 111 Ford Sedan & small House Trailer	30	45	60
1044 Roamer House Trailer with door	275	415	550
1045 Greyhound deluxe Bus	35	50	70
---- Transamerica bus (sold only in sets)	90	130	175

	C6	C8	C10
1046 Station Wagon	25	40	55
230 LaSalle Sedan	15	20	30
231 Coupe	15	20	30
232 Open Touring Coupe	15	20	30
233 Boat-Tail Roadster	15	20	30
234 Box Van	15	20	30
235 Oil Tank Truck	13	18	25
236 Fire Engine, Hook & Ladder	20	30	40
237 Fire Engine, Insurance Patrol	15	25	35
238 Fire Engine, Hose Wagon	20	30	40
239 Station Wagon	15	20	30

CONDITION OF A TOY
AND ITS RELATION TO PRICE

CONDITION CODE:

C6 - Good, Evident overall wear, well-played with, but acceptable to many collectors

C8 - Very Good Minor wear overall, very clean

C10 - Mint (like new)

NOTE: Mint in Box commands a high price. Condition below C6 brings considerably lower prices.

IMPROVED 1933 "TOOTSIETOYS"

Modeled after 1933 autos with the latest streamline bodies. Some with rubber tires.

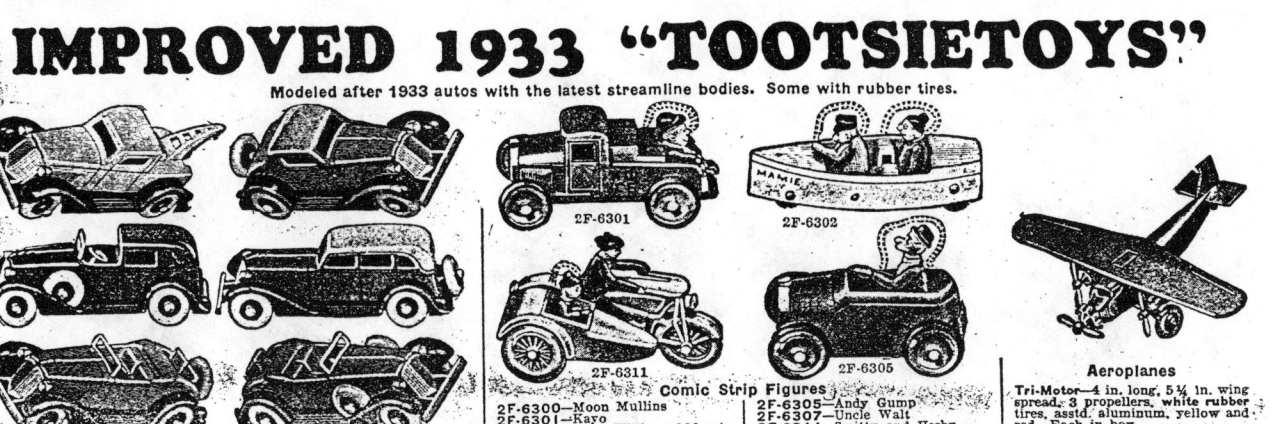

10 Styles Autos
3¾ in. long, 1¼ in. wide, sloping radiator and wind break mudguards, white rubber tires, asstd. color combinations.
2F-6316—10 in box.................................Box **67c**

2F-6301

2F-6302

2F-6311

2F-6305

Comic Strip Figures
2F-6300—Moon Mullins
2F-6301—Kayo
2F-6302—Uncle Willie and Mamie
2F-6305—Andy Gump
2F-6307—Uncle Walt
2F-6311—Smitty and Herby
Aver. 3¼ in. long, asstd. color combinations, action figures. 1 doz in box. ....Doz **80c**

Aeroplanes
Tri-Motor—4 in. long, 5¼ in. wing spread, 3 propellers, white rubber tires, asstd. aluminum, yellow and red. Each in box.
2F-6313—1 doz.
in carton...........Doz **84c**

Tootsietoys shown in the April, 1933 Butler Bros. catalog.

POST-WAR TOOTSIETOYS

	C6	C8	C10
1954 American LaFrance Pumper, 3'',	10	15	20
1956 Austin-Healy 100-6 4-passenger roadster, 6''	18	26	35
1955 Austin-Healy 100-6, 9'', unassembled kit & box	150	225	300
1954 Buick Century Estate Wagon, 6''	18	26	35
1951 Buick LeSabre Experimental Roadster, 6''	23	34	45
1949 Buick Roadmaster 4 door Sedan, 6''	25	38	50
1954 Buick Experimental Coupe, 6''	18	26	35
1947 Buick Special Fastback, 4''	18	26	35
1948 Buick Super Estate Wagon, 6''	38	56	75
1938 Buick Y Experimental Roadster, 4''	18	26	35
1948 Cadillac Special 4 door Sedan, 6''	18	26	35
1954 Cadillac 62 4 door Sedan, 6''	18	26	35
1956 Caterpillar Bulldozer, 6''	18	26	35
1956 Caterpillar Bulldozer with blade, 6''	20	30	40
1956 Caterpillar Roadscraper, 6''	18	26	35
1950 Chevrolet Ambulance, 4''	13	19	25
1955 Chevrolet Bel Air 4 door sedan, 3''	10	15	20

	C6	C8	C10
1956 Chevrolet Cameo Pick-up, 4''	13	19	25
1947 Chevrolet Coupe, 4''	13	19	25
1950 Chevrolet Deluxe Panel Truck, 4''	13	19	25
1950 Chevrolet Deluxe Panel Truck, 3''	10	15	20
1960 Chevrolet El Camino with camper/boat, 6''	68	102	135
1960 Chevrolet El Camino, 6''	18	26	35
1950 Chevrolet Fleetline 2 door fastback Sedan, 3''	10	15	20
1959 Chevrolet Semi Cab only:	63	94	125
with ''Mobile'' Trailer	80	120	160
with Hook and Ladder	93	139	185
with Log Trailer	75	113	150
with Boat Trailer	78	116	155
with 3 car transport	78	116	155
with Army flatbed	80	120	160
with ''Dean Van Lines''	75	113	150
1953 Chrysler New Yorker 4 door Sedan, 6''	18	26	35
1955 Chrysler Regent 2-door hard-top, 6'', may not have been produced	No Price Found		
1942 Chrysler Thunderbolt Experimental Roadster, 6''	23	34	45
1941 Chrysler Windsor Convertible, 4''	14	21	28
1950 Chrysler Windsor Convertible, 6''	50	75	100
1960 Chrysler Windsor Convertible, 4''	13	19	25

Tootsietoy Dodge D100 Panel Truck from 1956 and a No. 1008 Texaco Oil Truck (1939-41).
Courtesy Mapes Auctioneers

	C6	C8	C10
1954-55 Corvette Roadster, 4″ ..	13	19	25
1956 Dodge D100 Panel Truck, 6″	20	30	40
1950 Dodge Pick-up truck, 4″ ..	13	19	25
1956 Ferrari Racer, 6″	28	41	55
1931 Ford B Hot Rod, 3″	8	11	15
1956 Ford C600 Oil Tanker, 3″ .	9	14	18
1962 Ford C600 Truck, 6″......	18	26	35
1959 Ford Country Sedan Station Wagon, 6″..................	18	26	35
1960 Ford Country Sedan Station Wagon, 6″..................	13	19	25
1949 Ford Custom Convertible, 3″	11	16	22
1949 Ford Custom 4 door Sedan, 3″	11	16	22
1955 Ford Custom V8 2 door Sedan, 3″	11	16	22
1962 Ford Econoline Pick-up, 6″	15	23	30
1949 Ford F1 Pick-up, 3″	8	11	15
1949 Ford F6 Oil Tanker,. 6″ ...	30	45	60
1949 Ford F6 Oil Tanker, 4″ ...	10	15	20
1949 Ford F6 Stake Truck (Pick-up), 4″..................	13	19	25
1957 Ford F100 Styleside Pick-up with rear window, 3″.......	8	11	15
1957 Ford F100 Styleside Pick-up w/o rear window, 3″........	8	11	15
1956 Ford F600 Army Gun Truck, 6″..................	18	26	35
1955 Ford F600 Stake Truck with tin cover, 6″..............	30	45	60

	C6	C8	C10
1957 Ford Fairlane 500 Convertible, 3″	8	11	15
1960 Ford Falcon 2 door Sedan, 3″	8	11	15
1956 Ford Farm Tractor, 6″	25	38	50
1960 Ford LTD 2 door hardtop, 4″	13	19	25
1952 Ford Mainline 4 door Sedan, 3″	8	11	15
1954 Ford Ranch Wagon, 4″ ...	13	19	25
1940 Ford Special Deluxe Convertible, 6″	28	41	55
1940 Ford V8 Hot Rod, 6″	18	26	35
1948 GMC 3751 Greyhound Bus, 6″	23	34	45
1957 Greyhound Scenicruiser Bus, 6″	23	34	45
1040 Hook & Ladder, 4″.......	18	26	35
1041 Hose Car, 4″............	18	26	35
1941 International K1 Panel Truck, 4″	20	30	40
1946 International K-11 Oil Tanker, 6″	18	26	35
1960 International Metro Step Van, 6″	88	131	175
1955 International RC180, 6″:			
with rocket launcher; army version	45	68	90
with grain trailer	20	30	40
with oil tanker, no decals	25	38	50
with moving van	25	38	50
with boat transport	23	34	45

	C6	C8	C10
with car transport............	23	34	45
with gooseneck trailer........	23	34	45
1957 Jaguar type D, 3''........	8	11	15
1954 Jaguar XK120 Roadster, 3''	10	15	20
1956 Jaguar XK140 Coupe, 6''..	18	26	35

Tootsietoy Jeep CJ3, 3'', 1950.
Photo by Ed Poole

	C6	C8	C10
1950 Jeep CJ3, Army version, 3''	8	11	15
1950 Jeep CJ3, Civilian version, 3''	8	11	15
1950 Jeep CJ3, Civilian version, 4''	13	19	25
1960 Jeep CJ5, Civilian version, 6''	18	26	35
1960 Jeep CJ5, Army version, 6''	18	26	35
1960 Jeep CJ5, Snowplow version, 6''................	38	56	75
1947 Jeepster, 3''..............	9	14	18
1947 Kaiser Sedan, 6''.........	20	30	40
1956 Lancia Racer, 6''..........	38	56	75
1952 Lincoln Capri 2 door hardtop, 6''......................	18	26	35
1955 Mack B Line Cement Mixer, 6''......................	20	30	40
1955 Mack B Line Hook & Ladder, 6''......................	38	56	75
1955 Mack B Line Moving Van (w/ or w/o doors), 6''..........	43	64	85
1955 Mack B Line Log Trailer, 6''	43	64	85
1955 Mack B Line Oil Tanker, 6''	23	34	45
1955 Mack B Line Open Stake Truck, 6''..................	63	94	125
1947 Mack L Line Dump Truck, 6''	18	26	35
1947 Mack L Line Fire Pumper, 6''	43	64	85
1947 Mack L Line Fire (Ladder) Trailer, 6''................	43	64	85
1947 Mack L Line Log Truck, 6''	43	64	85
1947 Mack L Line Moving Van, 6''	25	38	50
1947 Mack L Line Closed Side Stake, 6''..................	20	30	40
1947 Mack L Line Stake Trailer, 6''	63	94	125

	C6	C8	C10
1947 Mack L Line ''Tootsietoys Coast to Coast'', 6''	43	64	85
1947 Mack L Line Towtruck, 6''	20	30	40
1956 Mercedes 190SL, 6''......	18	26	35
1955 Mercedes 300SL Gullwing (doors intact), 9''...........	150	225	300
1952 Mercury Custom Sedan, 4 door, 4''..................	13	19	25
1949 Mercury Fire Chief car, 4''	14	21	28
1949 Mercury Sedan, 4 door, 4''	13	19	25
---- Metro Van, HO Series.....	8	11	15
1954 MG TF Roadster, 6''......	21	32	42
1954 MG TF Roadster, 3''......	10	15	20
1954 Nash Metropolitan Convertible, 3''..................	30	45	60
1947 Offenhauser Hill Climber Racer, 3''..................	9	13	18
1949 Oldsmobile 88 Convertible, 4''	15	23	30
1959 Oldsmobile Dynamic 88 Convertible, 6''...............	13	19	25
1955 Oldsmobile 98 Holiday 2 door hardtop, 4''..............	13	19	25
1955 Oldsmobile 98 Holiday 2 door hardtop, 4'' Army version...	13	19	25
1956 Packard Patrician 4 door Sedan, 6''..................	18	26	35
1957 Plymouth Belvedere 2 door hardtop, 3''................	8	11	15
1950 Plymouth Special Deluxe 4 door Sedan, 3''.............	8	11	15
1950 Pontiac Chieftan Deluxe Coupe Sedan, 4''..........	13	19	25
1950 Pontiac Chieftan Fire Chief Coupe Sedan, 4''..........	18	26	35
1955 Pontiac Safari Station Wagon, 9''......................	100	150	200
1959 Pontiac Star Chief 4 door Sedan, 4''.................	13	19	25
1956 Porsche Spyder Roadster, 6''	18	26	35
1960 Rambler Super Cross Country Station Wagon, 4''.......	15	23	30
---- School Bus, HO Series.....	10	15	20
1947 Studebaker Champion 5 window Coupe, 3''.............	25	38	50
1960 Studebaker Lark Convertible, 3''......................	8	11	15
1955 Thunderbird Coupe, 4''...	11	17	22

	C6	C8	C10
1955 Thunderbird Coupe, 3″ ...	8	11	15
1956 Triumph TR3 Raodster, 3″	9	14	18
1950 Twin Coach Bus, 3″	23	34	45
1960 Volkswagen Beetle, 6″	18	26	35
1960 Volkswagon Beetle, 3″	5	8	10
1941 White Army Half Track, 4″	18	26	35

Trailer Co. (L.A.) Traveleer Land
   Coach Traveler, 1927 180   270   360
Triumph Station Wagon, plastic
   wind-up .... No Price Found

Triumph Station Wagons.
Photo by Dave Leopard

TRU-SCALE INTERNATIONAL TRUCKS

by Bob Smith

Early in the 1940s, Joseph Carter founded the Carter Machine Company. After WWII, Carter began to manufacture a line of toys. At first, Carter's toy line mainly consisted of International and John Deere farm tractors and implements. In the 1950s Carter began his new line of 1/16th scale trucks under the "Tru-Scale" trade mark. Carter felt that the International truck model would be the best choice because International had been building trucks since 1907. The first Tru-Scale model would be the "S" series. This was the model then in production by the International Truck Company. The models marked with the I.H. logo on the doors were sold by International Harvester outlets only. Any models marked Tru-Scale on the doors would have been sold

through other retail outlets. As the International Truck Co. re-designed their body style, Carter would follow this design with their comparable model. While thought of as a toy, one must consider the fine detail and workmanship that went into the Tru-Scale models. Their paint colors were correct, the grill styling and fender lines followed the real truck body lines and they were very well detailed for a pressed-steel toy. After the "S" series the "A" series, "B" series, and "C" series trucks followed, in respective order. The models were made as pick-up trucks, service trucks with tool boxes, dump trucks with single or dual axle, semi-tractor trailer trucks with open or enclosed trailers, and also as grain trucks. The dump trucks came with either a hydraulic cylinder or manual control, depending on which model or year it was produced. The later "C" series came with plasitc windows and white-wall tires with full hub caps. Another feature was the finger-tip steering that worked by applying pressure on the front of the cab to steer the front wheels. Tru-Scale also produced some Private Label trucks, such as Ryerson Steel and Yale Trucking.

In 1971 Carter Tru-Scale sold the business to Ertl, who used parts of the Tru-Scale line for the new Ertl die-cast International "Loadster" series. Ertl did not continue with the Tru-Scale line of International trucks. (Info. Bob Smith)

	C6	C8	C10
No. 1 Tru-Scale "S" series International Service Truck Green/white. c.1953	175	275	425
No. 2 Tru-Scale "A" series International Service Truck. Red/white. c.1957	175	275	425
No. 2a Tru-Scale "S" series International Pick-up truck light blue/white. c.1953	125	225	350
No. 3 Tru-Scale "B" series International Service Truck. Red/white. c.1959	125	225	350
No.4 Tru-Scale "C" series International Service Truck. Orange/white, w/w tires, windshield. c.1961	150	250	375
No. 5 Tru-Scale "A" series International Pick-up truck. Red/cream. c.1957	150	250	375
No. 6 Tru-Scale "C" series International Pick-up truck. Red/white, T/S decal, c.1961.	100	175	275

Tru-Scale (#1)
Photo by Bob Smith

Tru-Scale (#4)
Photo by Bob Smith

Tru-Scale, top to bottom: (#2), (#2a)
Photo by Bob Smith

Tru-Scale (#5)
Photo by Bob Smith

Tru-Scale (#3)
Photo by Bob Smith

Tru-Scale, top to bottom: (#6), (#6a)
Photo by Bob Smith

	C6	C8	C10
No. 6a Tru-Scale "C" series International Pick-up truck. Blue/white, I/H decal. c.1961	100	175	275
No. 7 Tru-Scale "A" series International Grain truck. Blue, I.H. decal. c.1957	150	250	375
No. 7a Tru-Scale "B" series International Grain truck. Green. I/H decal. c.1959.	100	175	275
No. 8 Tru-Scale "S" series International 10-wheel Hydraulic Dump Truck. Orange/white. c.1953	175	275	400
No. 9 Tru-Scale "A" series International 10-wheel Hydraulic Dump truck. Orange. c.1957 .	175	275	400
No. 10 Tru-Scale "B" series 6-wheel Manual Dump truck. Orange. c.1959	150	250	375
No. 11 Tru-Scale "B" series 10-wheel Hydraulic Dump truck. Orange. c.1959	125	200	300
No. 12 Tru-Scale "C" series 6-wheel International Dump truck. Red/white. c.1961	125	200	300
No. 13 Tru-Scale "B" series Semi-Tractor & Van Trailer. Red/white. c.1959	200	300	425
No. 14 Tru-Scale "C" series Semi-Tractor & Van Trailer. Green/white. "Yale Trucking". c.1961	225	325	450
No. 15 Tru-Scale "B" series Semi-Tractor Hydraulic Dump truck. Dark red. c.1959	125	225	350
No. 15a Tru-Scale "C" series Semi-Tractor Stake Truck. Red/yellow. "Ryerson Steel". c.1961	150	250	375
No. 16 Tru-Scale/Ertl, Ertl Int'l. Fleetstar Cab w/Tru-Scale Dump Trailer. White/green, c.1971. "Anderson Payload"	125	225	350
No. 16a Tru-Scale International "C" series Semi-Tractor Hydraulic Dump Truck. Orange/yellow. c.1961.	125	225	350

Tru-Scale (#7)
Photo by Bob Smith

Tru-Scale (#7a)
Photo by Bob Smith

Tru-Scale (#8)
Photo by Bob Smith

Tru-Scale (#9)
Photo by Bob Smith

Tru-Scale (#14)
Photo by Bob Smith

Tru-Scale (#10)
Photo by Bob Smith

Tru-Scale, top to bottom: (#15), (#15a)
Photo by Bob Smith

Tru-Scale (#11)
Photo by Bob Smith

Tru-Scale, top to bottom: (#16), (#16a)
Photo by Bob Smith

Tru-Scale (#12)
Photo by Bob Smith

Tru-Scale (#13)   (Model in photo restored)
Photo by Bob Smith

TURNER, JOHN C.

by Bob Smith

John Turner began in the trade working first with D.P. Clark and later with the Schieble Toy Co. He went off on his own in 1915 and within two years he was producing a line of friction cars. In 1925 Turner was issued a patent for a new flywheel design made of metal disks, giving the appearance of large flat washers fitted together. The Turner flywheel is noticeably different from other manufactorers' mechanisms. Turner was located in Dayton and Wapkoneta, Ohio, c.1915-1940s.

	C6	C8	C10
Turner Bulldog Mack closed cab dump truck, red and green steel, 23'' long	400	600	800
Turner Car Hauler	425	638	850
Turner Crane Truck, 22'' long	300	450	600
Turner Delivery Van, 12½'' long, c.1920s	900	1500	2200
Turner Dump, friction, 15½'' long, circa early 1930s	240	360	480
Turner Dump, 17'' long, 1930s	65	98	130
Turner Dump, 22'' long, C-Cab	400	600	800
Turner Dump, 26'' long	250	375	500
Turner Dump, 28'' long, Dodge	100	150	200
Turner Fire Engine Pumper, 15'' long	750	1400	1800
Turner Fire Engine Pumper, 26'' long, early	275	363	550
Turner Hook & Ladder, 15'' long, c.1930s	250	375	500
Turner Ladder Truck, 1940	160	240	320
Turner Lincoln Sedan, 26'' long	2000	3500	5000
Turner Mack Ladder Truck	250	375	500
Turner "Overland Bus", pressed steel	No Price Found		
Turner Packard Roadster, 16½'' long, 1920s	800	1300	1850
Turner Packard (?) Roadster, 26'' long, friction	900	1500	2200
Turner Panel Truck, early 13'' long	250	375	500
Turner Speedster, 1920s, 17'' long, circa late 1920s, early 1930s	500	750	1000

	C6	C8	C10
Turner Stake Truck, C-Cab, 22'' long	188	282	375
Turner Steam Shovel, 14'' long	105	158	210
Turner Tow Truck	250	375	500
Turner Water Truck, copper tank	150	225	300
Turner "Yellow Taxicab", flywheel drive, orange/black, 9¾'' long, four riders, c.1927	275	400	600

Turner Crane Truck, 22'' long.
Photo by Calvin L. Chaussee

Turner Dump, 26'' long
Photo by Calvin L. Chaussee

Turner "Overland Bus"
Courtesy James Apthorpe

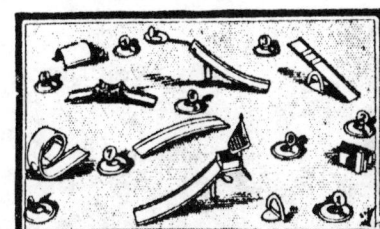

Turner trucks, as shown in the June, 1931 *Toys and Novelties* magazine.

UNIQUE ART MFG. CO.

Unique Art Mfg. Co. was in business from 1916, when it introduced its Merry Juggler and Charlie Chaplin. In 1931 it was located at Waverly and Peshine Avenues in Newark, New Jersey. Its president was Wm. Marbe, and there were 28 male employees (no females listed). In 1934 employees numbered 110 male and 165 female (same address). In a 1946-47 directory the address was 200 Waverly Avenue, Newark and the president was Samuel Burger (this last name may be incorrect; the handwriting in my notes is hard to read). Employees were equally divided: 125 male and 125 female. Unique was still manufacturing toys, mainly wind-ups, in 1952. Little else is known about the company, except that at some date, Louis Marx bought it.

	C6	C8	C10
Unique Artie the Clown in his Crazy Car	238	358	475
Unique "Capitol Hill Racer", 1930s, 17½" long with 2" tin racing car...................	165	248	330
Unique "Daredevil Motor Cop", 8½" long, 1940s	250	375	500
Unique "G.I. Joe and His Jouncing Jeep", post WWII, 7" ...	150	225	300
Unique Krazy Kar, new in 1921	210	315	420
Unique "Lincoln Tunnel", moving vehicles, cop, 1935, 24" long .	300	450	600
Unique "Motorcycle Cop", 1930s, 9" long...................	220	330	440

Unique G.I. Joe & His Jouncing Jeep.
Courtesy Mapes Auctioneers

Germany, Horseless Carriage, tin litho, clockwork motor, driver &
passenger, 6" long, c.1903. Prices in C6, C8, C10: $700, 1200, 1800.
Photo by Bob Smith

Unique "Daredevil Motor Cop".
Courtesy Kent M. Comstock

	C6	C8	C10
Unique Rodeo Joe Crazy Car...	225	338	450
Unique "Rollover Motorcycle Cop", 1935	200	300	400

UNKNOWNS: These are vehicles
whose manufacturer has yet to
be established.

Germany, Vis-a-vis, tin litho, clockwork motor, steering, rubber tires,
6½" long, c.1900. (Possibly Carette and marketed by MOKO). Prices
in C6, C8, C10: $1700, 2200, 2800.
Photo by Bob Smith

Germany, white hand-painted tin, clockwork motor, 9" long, hand
brake, doors open, rubber tires, lamps, cast seats. C.1911. (Possibly
Carette) Prices in C6, C8, C10: $1450, 1950, 2700. Photo by Bob Smith

Germany, tin litho, green, gray, red, clockwork motor, 9'' long, rear doors open, c.1915. (Possibly Carette).
Prices in C6, C8, C10: $1300, 1800, 2400.
Photo by Bob Smith

German Bulldog Mack, maker unknown, c.1950s, 7'' long. Value of each in C6, C8, C10: $15, 25, 50. Courtesy Bob & Alice Wagner

Mack Trucks, and a fire engine by an unknown maker. Plastic, 4½'' long. Values in C6, C8, C10: $6, 15, 25. The maker may possibly be Greyshaw of Georgia, Inc. C.1940s-50s.
Photo and caption courtesy Bob & Alice Wagner

Unusual 30s steel coupe. No Price Found.
Photo by Calvin L. Chaussee

Wood and fibreboard tank, no maker known. 7¾'' long, makes ''rat-a-tat'' noise. C.WWII. Value about $35 in mint.
Courtesy Roger Johnson

L to R: Wooden ''Ambulance'' and ''Supply Co. 123rd Field Artillery'' truck. Both probably Tillicum (Milton Bradley).
Courtesy Roger Johnson and Charles Breslow

Bronzed slush metal souvenir tanks, two to four inches long. No Price Found. The tank at right was attached to an ashtray. L to R: MI2, MI3, MI4.
Photo by Ed Poole

Renault FT tank, slush-cast, 3'' long. Worth about $25 in mint. Maker is unknown.
Photo by Ed Poole

Three 3½-4" long composition tanks, mfrs. unknown. No Price Found.
Top: MI1
Bottom, L to R: MI2, MI3.
Photo by Ed Poole

"Whelan's" steel truck, c. the 1930s. Possibly Marx or Wyandotte. No Price Found.
Photo by Calvin L. Chaussee

Scale model autos!

No. 2473

Ford Sedan has accurate detail, really astonishing down to the last touch. In HO scale. Various colors. Carton — 36 assorted. List, each............ 10¢

No. 2474

Ford Pickup is another Varney plastic triumph. Rolls freely. Great on train layouts. Assorted colors. List, ea....10¢

No. 2475

Ford Panel Truck, like the above, comes 36 to the carton, assorted colors. Really ingenious HO models. List, ea... 10¢

Varney Scale Models, as advertised in the May, 1954 Hobby Merchandiser.

	C6	C8	C10
Viking (Ohio) Dump Truck, 27" long........................	550	850	1300

VARNEY SCALE MODELS (4401

Ponce de Leon, Coral Gables, Florida)

Varney No. 2473 Ford Sedan, HO scale......................	No Price Found		
Varney No. 2474 Ford Pick-up..	No Price Found		
Varney No. 2475 ford Panel Truck, HO Scale...................	No Price Found		

VINDEX

Vindex of Belvidere, Illinois, was in business as a toymaker from about 1928-1932. Its products were cast iron. Vindex was a division of National Sewing Machine Co.

	C6	C8	C10
Vindex Coast to Coast Bus, cast iron, c.1930, 12" long	1250	1875	2500
Vindex Hay Loader...........	1600	2400	3200

461

Vindex Hay Loader, from a c.1932 Vindex catalog.

Vindex VM2. From a c.1932
Vindex catalog.

VINDEX MOTORCYCLES

list by Kent M. Comstock

	C6	C8	C10
(VM1) Motorcycle with detachable cop, "Henderson", 9", red or green	1000	1500	2500
(VM2) Motorcycle with sidecar, 2 detachable cops, "Henderson" 9", red or green	1200	1800	3000
(VM3) Motorcycle with package truck, "Henderson PDQ Delivery" with detachable blue rider, 9" red or green	1800	2500	3500
Vindex "P&H" power shovel, cast iron, 12" (17" extended), wheels in caterpillar base, handle revolves rig	2000	3000	4000
Vindex Pick-up Truck, cast iron, 7½" long	300	450	600
Vindex Racer, cast iron, "2" 11½" long, c.1920s	900	1400	2100

Vindex VM3. From a c.1932
Vindex catalog.

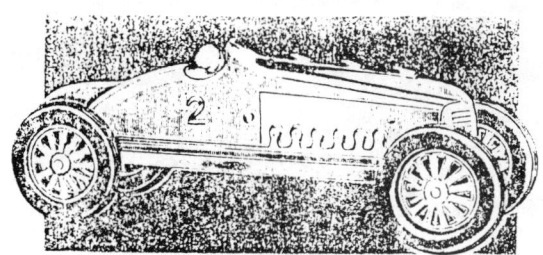

Vindex Racer, cast iron, "2". From a c.1932 Vindex catalog.

	C6	C8	C10
Wannatoy Cadillac, 9" long, plastic	7	11	15
Wannatoy Convertible, 6" long	7	11	14
Wannatoy Delivery truck, 4" long	3	4	6
Wannatoy Tank Truck, 5" long	7	11	14
Wannatoy Tow Motor w/trailer	7	11	14

Vindex VM1
Photo by Kent M. Comstock

462

WARREN

Warren, of New York City, was a toy soldier company owned by John Warren Jr., from about 1936-39. Its two vehicles were conversions of toys made by Kenton, and are of particular interest to toy soldier collectors.

	C6	C8	C10
Warren (W173) Scout Car	300	450	600
Warren (W174) Staff Car	300	450	600

Weeden Auto, Live Steam, 8¾" long, early.
Courtesy Sotheby's NY

W174 and W175

Warren L to R: W173, 174.
Courtesy Phillips NY

	C6	C8	C10
Wellmade Doll & Toy Co. Jeep, composition, 7½" long	37	56	75
Wellmade Doll & Toy Co. Jeep, composition, 3½" long	No Price Found		

The 7½" long composition jeep is by New York's Wellmade Doll & Toy Co. Presumably the 3½" copy is too.
Photo by Ed Poole

WEEDEN

Weeden was founded in 1882 by William N. Weeden, in New Bedford, Massachusetts. In 1884 he invented his first toy steam engine. His toys included engines, vehicles, and boats. Weeden toys were produced into at least the 1940s.

Weeden Auto, live steam, 8¾" early	1500	3000	4500
Weeden Steam Fire Pumper	1200	2000	3000
Weeden Steam Road Roller, 1920s, 7" long, brass, tin, cast iron, steam toy fired by alcohol	250	375	500
Weeden Steam Tractor, 9"	250	375	500

A variation of Wellmade Doll & Toy company's Jeep. Possibly by the same firm. 7½" long, No Price Found.
Photo by Ed Poole

	C6	C8	C10
Wen-Mac Automite Racer	47	71	95
Wen-Mac Texaco Tanker	42	64	85

Wilkins Aerial Ladder Truck, c.1910, 18'' long.
Courtesy Phillips NY

WILKINS TOY COMPANY

Wilkins, of Keene, New Hampshire, was begun by James S. Wilkins as the Triumph Wringer Company. But the tiny model Wilkins produced to promote his product proved so intriguing to prospective customers and their children that requests for them poured in. The real thing was quickly forgotten as Wilkins turned to toymaking. Its toys were generally cast-iron and steel. The firm was acquired in 1894 by Kingsbury, which is still in business, though now as a tool and die maker.

	C6	C8	C10
Wilkins Aerial Ladder Truck, 1910, 18'' wind-up	500	750	1000
Wilkins Automobile Racer, silver, clock-work motor, light stamped steel, 10'' long, c.1905	750	1000	1400
Wilkins Fire Engine, c.1900, with driver, steam boiler	125	188	250
Wilkins Hook & Ladder, early, 14½'' long	600	900	1250
Wilkins Hook & Ladder open truck, steel, wind-up motor, 9¼'' long	150	225	300
Wilkins Ladder Truck, 15'' long, wind-up, early	450	695	925
Wilkins ''Panama'' Dump Truck. Gray, c.1919, 14'' long, light stamped steel, clock-work motor (also made as Kingsbury in 1923, different wheels, same value)	650	850	1200
Wilkins Runabout, 1911, with driver	650	1000	1500
Wilkins Truck, open cab, 11'' long, very early, clock-work	450	675	900

Wilkins Automobile Racer, 10'' long.
Photo by Bob Smith

Wilkins Hook and Ladder open truck, steel, windup motor, 9¼'' long.
Courtesy Phillips NY

Wilkins ''Panama'' Dump Truck, 14'' long, clockwork, c.1919.
Photo by Bob Smith

464

A.C. WILLIAMS

A.C. Williams was founded in 1886 when Adam Clark Williams (1/22/1848-6/15/32) bought the J.W. Williams Company from his father. After a fire the firm was moved in 1893 from Chagrin Falls, Ohio to Ravenna. Toy production began about this time. Small cast iron toys were Williams' specialty, with banks, cars and aircraft predominant. A.C. Williams retired in 1919, but the firm continued to make toys until 1938, after which it continued in business in a non-toys capacity. Williams marked few, if any, of its toys. Two clues to an A.C. Williams toy are turned steel hubs and starred axle peens.

	C6	C8	C10
Williams Austin for Car Carrier.	150	225	300
Williams Car Carrier, with 3 Austins, 12½" long, 1920....	500	800	1200
Williams "Coast to Coast Cartage Co." stake trailer truck......	200	300	400

A.C. Williams "Coast to Coast" Cartage Co. stake trailer truck. Photo by Bill Kaufman

	C6	C8	C10
Williams Coupe, 3" long, 2-piece body, 1936..............	70	105	140
Williams Coupe, 4½" long.....	75	112	150
Williams Coupe, rumble seat, 6¾" long, side mounts, 1930.....	175	263	350
Williams Delivery Van, 8" long	350	525	700
Williams Dump Truck, 7" long.	112	168	225
Williams Fire Pumper, 5" long, interchangeable..............	350	525	700
Williams four-casting nickeled radiator car, approx. 4" long.	75	112	150
Williams Laundry Truck, 8" long	400	600	800
Williams Lincoln Touring Car, 7" long.......................	350	525	700

	C6	C8	C10
Williams Lincoln Touring Coupe, 8¾" long..................	900	1500	2200
Williams Mack Gas Tank Truck, 3¾" long..................	45	68	90
Williams Mack Gas Tank Truck, 5⅛" long..................	65	98	130
Williams Mack Gas Tank Truck, 7¼" long..................	140	210	280
Williams Mack Stake Truck, 3½" long.......................	45	68	90

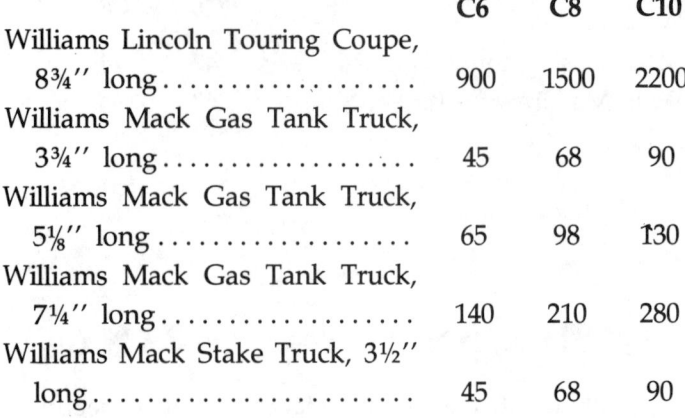

Williams Mack Stake Truck, 3½" long. (1932 ad).

	C6	C8	C10
Williams Mack Stake Truck, 4¼'' long	80	120	160
Williams Mack Stake Truck, 5⅛'' long	112	170	225
Williams Mack Stake Truck, 7'' long	150	225	300
Williams Mack Stake Truck, 8½'' long	200	300	400
Williams Mack Truck, 3½'' long	45	68	90
Williams Mack Truck, 4¾'' long	55	82	110
Williams Mack Truck, 6¾'' long	100	150	200
Williams Model T Coupe, 6'' long	125	187	250
Williams Phaeton, driver, lady passenger, open, 12'' long, c.1921	No Price Found		
Williams Racer, 8½'' long, driver, tail fin	200	300	400
Williams Racer, 6½'' long, boat-tailed	125	188	250
Williams Sedan, approx 3½'' long, c.1920s	200	300	400
Williams Sedan, 4'' long, c.1920	170	255	340
Williams Sedan, 5'' long	118	176	235
Williams Racer, boat-tailed, 6½'' long	175	262	350
Williams Sedan, c.1930, cast iron, 6½'' long, streamlined rear fender	225	337	450

Williams Sedan, c.1930, cast iron, 6½'' long.
Courtesy Phillips NY

	C6	C8	C10
Williams Sedan, 6¾'' long, c.1931, cast iron, interchangeable body	300	450	600
Williams Stake Truck 7'' long, c.1931, interchangeable body	170	225	340
Williams Steamroller 5½'', 1930s	75	112	150
Williams Studebaker, c.1933-34, approx. 4'' long, two-tone sedan	110	165	220
Williams Tank, 4'' long	67	101	135

Williams Tank, 4'' long.
Photo by Ed Poole

A.C. Williams Touring Car, 11¾'' long, c.1917, two riders not pictured.
Photo by Bob Smith

	C6	C8	C10
Williams Touring Car, 9½'' long, cast iron	450	675	900
Williams Touring Car, 11¾'' long, c.1917, with two riders	500	800	1100
Williams Wrecker, 7¾'' long	375	562	750

1F-2833—
3¾ In. Racer

1F-2834—
3½ In. Bus

1F-2838—
8½ In. Dump Car Trailer

1F-2866—
4 In. Wrecker

1F-2839—
8¾ In. Austin Coupe

1F-2867—
3⅝ In. Roadster

1F-2831—
3¾ In. Fire Engine

1F-2868—
3⅝ In. Coupe

1F-2836—
8½ In. Mack Truck

1F-2869—
3¾ In. Moving Van

Williams vehicles, as shown in the November, 1932 Butler Bros. catalog. Each sold for a dime.

WOLVERINE

Wolverine, of Pittsburgh, Pa., was founded in 1903 by B.F. Bain. The company got its name from Bain's Michigan hometown. In later years Wolverine became a subsidiary of Spang Industries, and in 1970 moved to Boonville, Arkansas. The "Sandy Andy," in all its variations, was probably Wolverine's most successful and famous toy. The firm's name is now Today's Kids.

	C6	C8	C10
Wolverine "Autolift", 1930s, 10¼" high, includes 2½" tin car and four sections of track	150	225	300
Wolverine Dump Truck, 12" long, white	112	168	225
"Wolverine Express Bus", 14" long, "Mystery Motor"	125	188	250
Wolverine "Loop-A-Loop", 1930s, 19" long, includes small car No. 30	125	188	250
Wolverine Motorcycle Rabbit, 1930s, 9½" long	90	135	180
Wolverine "Mystery Car"	150	225	300
Wolverine "Mystery Car" and Trailer, press down to make car move, c.1953	250	375	500

Wolverine Mystery Car & Trailer.
Photo by Calvin L. Chaussee

Wolverine Sky View Taxi	115	172	230
Wolverine Speeding Bus "5 Via Main St." tin litho, driver and occupants, 14" long, "19302", press down on rear to move	105	158	210
Wolverine "Sunny Andy" Tank, 14" long	130	195	260

Wolverine "Sunny Andy Tank" From a December, 1929 Butler Bros. catalog.

Wolverine Taxi, 13" long, tin	180	270	360
Wolverine "U.S.A. Transport" army truck	150	225	300
Wolverine "White Mustang" dump truck, 14" long	80	120	160
Wolverine White Stake Truck	102	153	205

Wolverine "U.S.A. Transport" army truck.
Photo by Terry Sells

WYANDOTTE (All Metal Products)

by Brian Seligman

Wyandotte Toys began in the Fall of 1921 when William Schmidt and George Stallings decided that instead of making steel parts for the automobile industry they would make toys. All Metal Products initially became well known for their large line of toy guns, rifles, and water pistols but also would be increasingly known for pressed steel vehicles and air planes, mechanical toys and games, target sets, musical tops, doll carriages and other sturdy toys for boys and girls to spend hours of good and safe fun.

Arthur Edwards bought into the growing company and became its President and General Manager, running the company until his death in 1932. He was succeeded by his son C. Lee Edwards.

By the mid 1930's, Wyandotte toys was a major mid-price contender in the toy business. It was not unusual for "Wyandotte" to issue different sizes of the same toy. One might find the same stake truck in four sizes, ranging from 4½" to 15". Additionally, the baked enamel toys came in many colors and color combinations, with special color runs for the Easter holidays. Lithographed toys also figured prominently, and with the Wyandotte Circus #503 truck and trailer of 1936 reached the pinnacle of lithography.

During WWII, Wyandotte made clips for the M-1 rifle and was able to offer a reduced toy line of all-wood toys but it would not be until after the war that they would get back to major toy production.

In April, 1947 long-time employee William Wenner was elected President. In 1950, Wyandotte bought Hafner Manufacturing Company with the thought of increasing market penetration by marketing their toy train line.

In 1951, C. Lee Edwards, Mary Reberdyand, and the estate of his late father sold their interests to a new set of owners. The new directors hoped to reorganize the company successfully. It was during this time one plant was moved to Martin's Ferry, Ohio, another to Pequa, Ohio, and one to the McCord Corporation for its gasket division.

The year 1955 saw both C. Lee Edwards and William Wenner retiring and selling their stock that was acquired as part of the 1951 reorganization. The company was also undergoing financial problems at the time. It has been reported that Louis Marx, of Marx Toys, in order to assume a larger market share for his own company, purchased some of the Wyandotte and Haffner toy lines and sent them to his Mexican operations.

All Metal Products (Wyandotte Toys) filed for bankruptcy November 6, 1956, thereby closing this chapter in toy history.

Brian Seligman was first introduced to collecting by his mother, an antique collector/dealer in Vermont. He thought that nothing was better than going to an old farm estate auction until in 1989 he picked up his first toy, a Steelcraft riding road roller, because it looked "neat".

While researching the history of the toy he purchased he became hooked.

Originally the collector started with large pressed steel pieces like Buddy L and Keystone but as he was drawn deeper and deeper into the hobby (compulsion) he began to pick up many of the more reasonably priced examples of pressed steel, Marx, Girard and Wyandotte.

What has now transpired is a growing collection of Wyandotte vehicles and airplanes. By no means an expert, Brian is currently trying to fill in the spaces of his collection as well as acquiring as much research material to further knowledge of Wyandotte. A series of articles entitled "Why not Wyandotte?" is being prepared for publication in U.S. *Toy Collector Magazine*.

Brian is a real estate developer in South Florida, has a wife, three kids, one dog, five box turtles, a house, two cars, and a mortgage. All in all a typical toy collector, except during the month of February, when he goes toy hunting every weekend and during the Summer when he tries to hit the Rochester and Macungie toy shows, as well as any other antique flea markets he can find while he visits his wife as she works the Summer as an assistant director of a summer camp in Pennsylvania.

Abbreviations

brt - black rubber tires

bpw - black plastic wheels

bww - black wood wheels

eww - embossed wood wheels

lmw - litho metal wheels

pmw - pressed steel wheels

wrt - white rubber tires

www - white wood wheels

yww - yellow wood wheels

e/l - electric lights

trk - truck

" " - lettering on vehicle

TRUCKS

Advertising

Army truck

(B), 9½", 1942, bww, "Army
Supply", all wood const..... 75 100 150

(W), 11¾", 1941, brt, "Army
Supply Corp", cloth top..... 45 75 105

(W), 17½", 1941, brt, "Army
Engineer Corp No. 42" cloth top 60 90 130

(W), 21" long, 1940/41, brt, "Army Corps", canvas cover.... 65 95 135

(M), 21" long, 1941, brt,
"Engineers Corp USA"...... 65 95 135

Auto transport

WY93, 10¼", 1940's, brt, plastic
cab, "Wyandotte" on side... 50 70 145

(WY) - 15" long, 193?, yww, w/3
cars...................... 65 150 250

WY99, 21⅝", 193?, yww, w/4 cars 75 150 275

(WO), 22" long, 1952/54, pmw,
w/4 cars + ramp........... 55 75 135

Auto Transport, WY93
Courtesy Brian Seligman

Auto Transport, WY99
Courtesy Brian Seligman

Baggage truck

(W) 11¾", 1941, brt, "Baggage",
w/freight trk................ 45 75 105

Bank truck

WY19, 6⅜", 1936/40, bww,
portholes on side, rear hatch,
#375 w/key................. 40 60 75

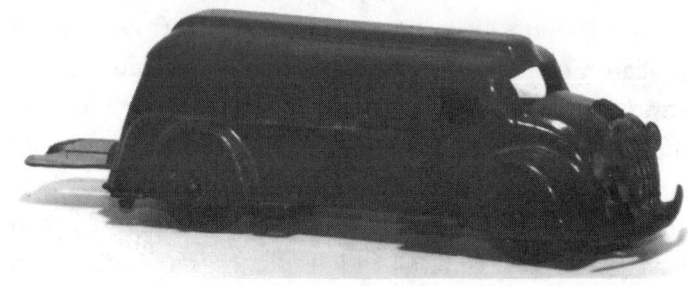

Bank Truck, WY19
Courtesy Brian Seligman

Buses

WY20, 6⅜", 1936/40, bww, #371 40 60 75

WY60, 6⅜", 1939, bww, #233 .. 40 60 75

(B), 21" long, 1938, bww, roof
rack, rear door.............. 90 135 200

(M), 21" long, 1938, bww, no roof
rack, rear door, "Coast to Coast
Bus Line"................... 90 135 200

(B), 21" long, 1939/40, bww, no
roof rack, rear door, "Coast to
Coast Bus Line", #1002 HD
Motor Bus.................. 90 135 200

(B) 21" long, 1941, brt, no roof
rack, rear door "Coast to Coast
Bus Line"................... 90 135 200

Bus WY20
Courtesy Brian Seligman

Bus WY60
Courtesy Brian Seligman

Contractor truck	C6	C8	C10
(W), 11¼'', 1941, bww, ''Contractor Truck''	45	70	105

Circus truck - w/wo trailer

	C6	C8	C10
( ), 10¾'', 1936 - eww #503, short nose	150	350	500
( ), ?, 193?, eww, #503, long nose	150	350	500
WY63, 19¼'', 1936, eww, #503, short nose w/trailer	200	750	1000
( ), ?, 193?, eww, #503, long nose w/trailer	200	750	1000

Wyandotte Circus Truck, WY63, missing trailer.
Courtesy Mapes Auctions

Dairy/Milk truck

	C6	C8	C10
(W), 11½'', 1938/39, bww, w/2 milk bottles, #349	50	80	115
(W), 11¾'', 1941, brt, ''Sunny Dairy'', ''Drink More Milk'', w/1 milk bottle	60	85	120

Delivery Van truck	C6	C8	C10
(W), 11⅜'', 1938/39, bww, ''City Delivery'', #345	60	75	100
(W), 16'' long, 1938, brt/ws hub, spring motor key attached ...	80	95	120
(W), 16⅜'', 1938/39, wd whls...	60	75	100

Wyandotte Delivery Van, 11'' long.
Photo by Bob Smith

Dump Body, WY2
Courtesy Brian Seligman

Dump Body

	C6	C8	C10
WY2, 4¾'', 1934, wrt	40	65	80
WY1, 5⅝'', 1932, bww	20	35	55

Dump Body, WY1
Courtesy Brian Seligman

Dump Body, WY3
Courtesy Brian Seligman

Dump Body, WY5
Courtesy Brian Seligman

	C6	C8	C10
WY3, 6'' long, 1934/37, wrt, rooster comb hood orn	40	65	80
(B), 6'' long, 1938, bww	40	65	80
WY9, 6'' long, 1939/41, bpw, #222	20	35	50
WY10, 6'' long, 1939/41, bpw, #222	20	35	50
WY5, 7'' long, 1933, eww	50	70	95
WY4, 7'' long, 1934, wrt	40	60	85
WY85, 7'' long, 1934, wrt	40	60	85

Dump Body, WY4
Courtesy Brian Seligman

Dump Body, WY9
Courtesy Brian Seligman

Dump Body, WY85
Courtesy Brian Seligman

Dump Body, WY10
Courtesy Brian Seligman

	C6	C8	C10
WY6, 10'' long, 1934, brt, rooster comb hood orn	40	60	85
(B), 11¼'', 1938/41, bww, #343c, w/5¼ wheelbarrow	60	80	100
WY88, 12¼'', 1941, bww, side lever rear dump, w/wheelbarrow	45	60	75
WY37, 12¾'', 1934, wrts/red hubs	65	85	115
(B), 13¼'', 1942, bww, ''Highway Dept. Dump'', all wood const.	75	100	150
WY44, 15'' long, 1933/34, wrt/red hubs - e/l	55	95	165

Dump Body, WY6
Courtesy Brian Seligman

Dump Body, WY51
Courtesy Brian Seligman

Dump Body, WY88
Courtesy Brian Seligman

	C6	C8	C10
WY51, 15¼", 1934/37, brt/red hubs	65	95	135
(B), 16" long, 1938/39, bww, mech. w/attached key, #381	65	95	140
(B), 16" long, 1938/39, bww, came with shovel	50	75	100
(B), 17⅜", 1939/41, bww, side dump	45	70	110
(W), 21" long, 1938/40, bww, HD dump truck #101, w/shovel	65	105	135
(?), 21" long, 1941, brt/wd hubs	45	70	100
(WO) 21" long, 1953/54, brt, "Giant", w/12" shovel	60	75	115

Dump Body, WY37
Courtesy Brian Seligman

Wyandotte Dump Truck, electric lights. Value in C6, C8, C10: $90, 130, 190.
Photo by Bob Smith

Dump Body, WY44
Courtesy Brian Seligman

Dump w/wood rear dual wheels

	C6	C8	C10
WY7, 9⅝", 1931/32, yww, side lever, slide track dump	60	80	95
WY8, 9⅝", 1931/32, yww, side catch	60	80	95
WY41, 15¼", 1931/32, yww, side catch	75	150	225

Dump, wood dual rear wheels, WY8.
Courtesy Brian Seligman

Dump, wood dual rear wheels, WY41.
Courtesy Brian Seligman

Dump Body, "Arrow Truck Lines", value in C6, C8, C10: $55, 95, 145.
Photo by Bob Smith

Dump Body, "Wyandotte Construction Co." Value in C6, C8, C10:
$65, 105, 155.
Photo by Bob Smith

	C6	C8	C10
Dump truck, Easter Style			
(W), 6'' long, 1937, bww, rooster comb hood orn, pastel colors, # E318, w/chicken on side	40	60	75
Express			
Fire Truck			
(W), 11¾'', 1941, bww, bell plus 2, 7½'' ladder	50	70	150
(W), 17½'', 1941, bww, bell plus 2 ladders	50	70	150
(W) 27½'', 1940, 6 bww trs, Hook and Ladder, 29'' ladder plus bell	50	70	150
Ice truck			
(W), 11½'', 1938/39, bww, 2 ice cubes/1 ice tong, #348	45	70	120
(W), 11¾'', 1941, brt, 1 ice cube/1 ice tong, "Toy Town Ice Co." "Crystal Clear"	45	70	120
Medical truck			
(W), 11¾'', 1941, bww, "Medical Corps plus Red Cross", white cloth top	45	70	130
Moving truck			
Oil/Gas Tanker			
WY18, 6⅜'', 1936/38, wrt, top hatches, rear hatch, #376	20	35	65
WY76, 6⅜'', 1939, bww, top hatches, rear hatch, #225	20	35	65
WY78, 6⅜'', 1939, bww, top hatches, rear hatch, #225	20	35	65
WY21, 10½'', 1936, wrt, top hatches, rear hatch, fin hood detail	65	90	125
WY82, 10½'', 1937, brt, top hatches, rear hatch, fin hood detail	65	90	125
WY77, 10½'', 1937, brt, top hatches, rear hatch, fin hood detail	65	90	125
(W), 21'' long, 1939/40, brt, rear hatch, HD Gas trk #1003	60	95	125

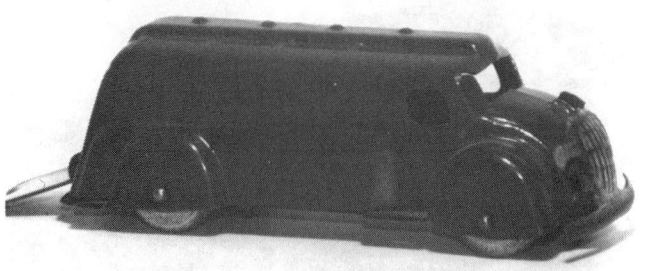

Oil/Gas Tanker, WY18
Courtesy Brian Seligman

Oil/Gas Tanker, WY77
Courtesy Brian Seligman

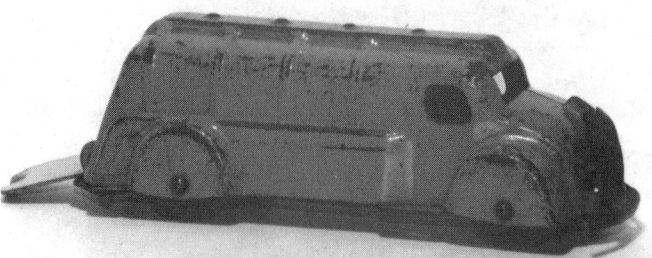

Oil/Gas Tanker, WY76
Courtesy Brian Seligman

Pick-up truck	C6	C8	C10
Railway express			
WY96, 6½'', 19??, brt, REA litho	35	50	65
(W), 12½'', 1952, brt, REA litho	60	90	135

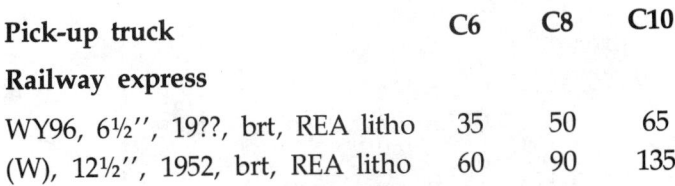

Oil/Gas Tanker, WY78
Courtesy Brian Seligman

Railway Express, WY96
Courtesy Brian Seligman

Oil/Gas Tanker, WY21
Courtesy Brian Seligman

Riding trk

	C6	C8	C10
(?), 16¼'', 1935, brt, fin hood orn	50	75	135
WY57, 16¼'', 1936, brt/red hubs, fin hood orn	50	75	135
(WO), 32½'', 1952/56, brt, fire trk, e/l/siren	75	105	150

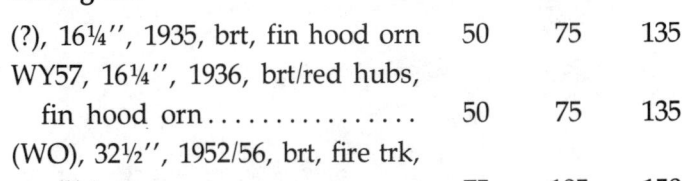

Oil/Gas Tanker, WY82
Courtesy Brian Seligman

Riding Truck, WY57
Courtesy Brian Seligman

Sand and gravel	C6	C8	C10
School bus			
Stake body			
WY45, 4⅝'', 1934, wrt	40	65	80
WY54, 5⅝'', 1934/37, wrt/bww, rooster comb hood orn	40	55	75
WY55, 6'' long, 1939/41, brt/bpw, ''Wyandotte Toys'' emb on driver's side	20	35	50
WY89, 6'' long, 1939/41, brt/bpw, ''Wyandotte Toys'' emb on driver's side	20	35	50
WY56, 6'' long, 1939/41, brt/bpw, ''Wyandotte Toys'' emb on driver's side	20	35	50
WY46, 6⅝'', 1934, wrt	50	75	85
WY75, 9⅝'', 1931, wrt/metal spokes	60	85	175
WY), 11½'', 19??, pww, ''Pickwick Pastures''	35	50	75

Stake Body, WY55
Courtesy Brian Seligman

Stake Body, WY89
Courtesy Brian Seligman

Stake Body, WY45
Courtesy Brian Seligman

Stake Body, WY46
Courtesy Brian Seligman

Stake Body, WY54
Courtesy Brian Seligman

Stake Body, WY75
Courtesy Brian Seligman

Stake Body, WY92
Courtesy Brian Seligman

Stake Body, WY49
Courtesy Brian Seligman

	C6	C8	C10
WY92, 12″ long, 1938/39, bww, w/5¾″ hand trk, #342C	65	75	105
WY48, 12⅛″, 1935, wrt	75	150	220

	C6	C8	C10
WY53, 12¼″, 1940/41, bww	50	75	95
WY43, 15″ long, 1933/34, wd whls, e/l.........................	60	95	150
WY49, 15¼″, 1934/37, wrt/red hubs, e/l, rooster comb hood orn.......................	75	105	150
WY50, 15¼″, 1934/37, brt/red hubs, e/l, rooster comb hood orn.......................	75	105	150

Stake Body, WY48
Courtesy Brian Seligman

Stake Body, WY50
Courtesy Brian Seligman

Stake Body, WY53
Courtesy Brian Seligman

Stake Body, WY52
Courtesy Brian Seligman

	C6	C8	C10
WY52, 16″ long, 1938/39, bww or brt/red hubs, with hand trk ..	60	95	135
(W), 16″ long, 1938/39, wrt/wd hubs, spring motor key attached, #380....................	65	90	130
(W), 21″ long, 1939/40, brt, w/hand trk, #1000...........	65	105	135

Stake Body, WY43
Courtesy Brian Seligman

	C6	C8	C10
(W), 21″ long, 1941, brt, w/hand trk, "Express", #1000	65	105	135

Stake body w/wood dual rear wheels

WY47, 9⅝″, 1931/32, yww	50	75	105

Stake Body, wood dual rear wheels, WY47.
Courtesy Brian Seligman

Stake Body, "Wyandotte Truck Lines". Plastic cab. Value in C6, C8, C10: $85, 125, 175.
Photo by Bob Smith

Stake body, Easter Style

	C6	C8	C10
(W), 6″ long, 1937, bww, rooster comb hood orn, pastel colors, rabbit on side, #E317	35	65	80
(W), 10″ long, 1937, lmw, rooster comb hood orn, pastel colors, rabbit on side, #E325Z	45	75	95

Tractor (Semi) Trailer

WY95, 7¾″, 19??, brt, "Wyandotte Van Lines" "Coast to Coast" "Moving Packing Storage" . . .	50	70	105

Tractor (Semi) Trailer, WY95
Courtesy Brian Seligman

Tractor (Semi) Trailer, WY94
Courtesy Brian Seligman

	C6	C8	C10
WY94, 7⅞″, 19??, brt, "Produce Van" "Refrigerated Cargo" "Coast to Coast"	50	70	105
( ), 8½″, 19??, brt, "Valley Farms Livestock Produce"	50	70	105
(WO), 17″ long, 1952/53, pmw, side dump w/shovel	45	70	145
(W), 17⅜″, 1939/41, brt, "Highway Freight", rear door, #392	55	80	115

Tractor (Semi) Trailer, WY69
Courtesy Brian Seligman

WY69, 17⅜″, 1939/41, brt, side dump, #391	65	95	140

Tractor (Semi) Trailer, WY68
Courtesy Brian Seligman

WY68, 17⅜'', 1939/41 brt, ''Wyandotte Express Co.'', #390 .... 50 75 100
(WO), 22'' long, 1952/54, brt,
  ''Wyandotte Van Lines'' 95 130 175
(WO), 23'' long, 1952, brt, ''Deluxe
  Highway Express'', plastic cab 65 80 105
( ), 24'' long, 195?, brt, ''Grey
  Lines''...................... 90 150 225
(W), 25'' long, 1941, 6 brt/wd
  hub/metal inserts, rear door
  w/spare tire, 3 front/2 rear
  reflectors ''Van Truck'', #1500 60 105 150
(W), 25'' long, 1941, 6 brt/wd
  hub/metal inserts, spare tire on
  rear, mini tarpaulin, ''Highway
  Freight'' 60 105 150

Tractor (Semi) Trailer, ''Shady Glen Stock Ranch'' cattle truck. Value
in C6, C8, C10: $70, 95, 140.
Photo by Bob Smith

Tow trk	C6	C8	C10
(W), 11¾'', 1941, bww, ''Official Service Car'', rear hoist	50	90	130
(WO), 15'' long, 1953/54, brt, ''24 hr'' ''Emergency'' ''Auto Service'' ''W'', w/tools and spare tires, plastic cab............	65	105	145

Tow Truck Wyandotte ''Emergency Auto Service'', plastic cab, 15''
long.
Photo by Bob Smith

	C6	C8	C10
(WO), 15'' long, 1956, brt, ''Towing Service'', w/tools and spare tires, roof light.............	65	105	145
(W), 17½'', 1941, ? whls, ''Service + Wrecker'' ''Toy Town Only 24 hr Service'', rear hoist .	50	90	130
(W), 22½'', 1940, brt/wd hubs, ''AAA Service'', hoist.......	50	90	130
(W), 22½'', 1941, brt/wd hub, ''W'', hoist	50	90	130

Wyandotte ''Towing'' truck, 14'' long. Value in C6, C8, C10: $60,
100, 150.
Photo by Bob Smith

Wyandotte "Dot Towing Service Nite/Day" radio-dispatched towcar.
Value in C6, C8, C10: $65, 105, 155.
Photo by Bob Smith

Boat tail racer	C6	C8	C10
WY16, 5⅞″, 1934, wrt	40	50	75
WY81, 5⅞″, 1934, wrt	40	50	75
WY17, 8⅝″, 1934, wrt, e/l	60	95	125

Boat Tail Racer, WY16
Courtesy Brian Seligman

Truck sets

CARS

Air flows

Ambulance	C6	C8	C10
(B), 6⅜″, 1938, wrt, side ports .	40	65	80
(W), 6⅜″, 1939, bww, side ports, #224	35	50	75
(WO), 9½″, 1952/53, brt, "Fire Dept. Rescue Squad Truck", friction	35	50	75
WY42, 11¼″, 1936/39, bww, #340, rear hatch, with stretchers ...	65	85	105

Boat Tail Racer, WY81
Courtesy Brian Seligman

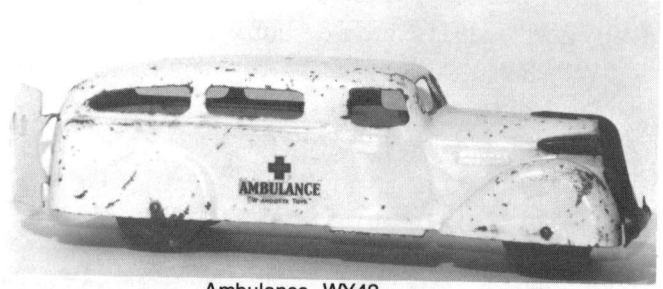

Ambulance, WY42
Courtesy Brian Seligman

Boat Tail Racer, WY17
Courtesy Brian Seligman

Army

	C6	C8	C10
(B), 9″ long, 1942, bww, "Jeep", all wood const	75	100	150

WYANDOTTE

Convertible	C6	C8	C10
WY29, 4⅜'', 1937/40, wrt/www, also came as set with coupe and garage 1938/40	10	25	35
( ), 19??, brt, regular	70	150	225
( ), 19??, brt, town and country	70	150	225
( ), Woody Convertible, 12'' long, top converts	70	105	140

Cord, WY36
Courtesy Brian Seligman

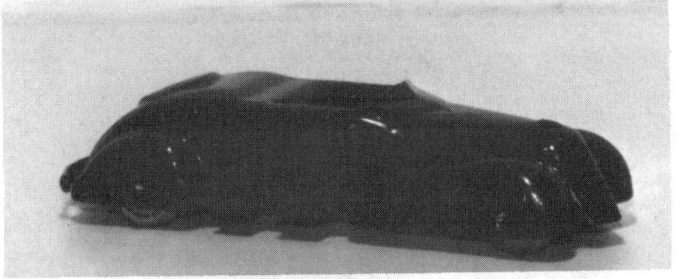

Convertible, WY29
Courtesy Brian Seligman

Woody Convertible
Photo by Calvin L. Chaussee

Cord

	C6	C8	C10
( ), 13⅜'', 1936/37, brt/wood hubs, rev. wind-up motor	125	350	550
( ), 13⅜'', 1938/39, bwws.	75	275	425
WY36, 13⅜'', 193?, bww, attached key wind-up, fire dept w/brass bell, bell sounds	125	300	475
(W), 13⅜'', 193?, brt, ''Zephyr'' no wind spring motor fire dept w/brass bell, bell sound	125	300	475
(W), 17¼'', 1938/39, brt, fire dept w/brass bell	100	300	525
(W), 17⅜'', 1939, #384, whls?, fire dept w/brass bell, bell sounds, attached key wind-up motor .	125	325	575

Cord and Trailer Set	C6	C8	C10
WY24, 23½'', 1938/39, bww, trailer door, #363	100	300	450

Cord & Trailer Set, WY24
Courtesy Brian Seligman

Coupes

	C6	C8	C10
WY86, 4⅜'', 1937/40, wrt/www, green, also came in set w/2 cars and garage, 1938/40	10	25	40

Coupe, WY86
Courtesy Brian Seligman

Coupe, WY14
Courtesy Brian Seligman

Coupe, WY26
Courtesy Brian Seligman

Coupe, WY58
Courtesy Brian Seligman

	C6	C8	C10
WY14, 4½'', 1934, wrt, rear spare	35	50	70
WY87, 4½'', 1934, wrt, rear spare	35	50	70
WY38, 4⅞'', 1932, yww	60	75	90
WY26, 6'' long, 1935/38, wrt, #309	35	50	75
WY58, 6⅜'', 1934, eww	35	50	70
WY39, 8¼'', 1932, yww, rumble seat	55	95	135
WY40, 8¼'', 1933, wrt, e/l	55	99	135

Coupe, WY87
Courtesy Brian Seligman

Coupe, WY39
Courtesy Brian Seligman

Coupe, WY38
Courtesy Brian Seligman

Coupe, WY40
Courtesy Brian Seligman

Coupes with trailers/Land Cruiser (mini)

	C6	C8	C10
WY27, 11¾'', 1936/38, bww	60	105	145
WY90, 11¾'', 1936/38, wrt	60	105	145

Coupe w/Trailer, WY27
Courtesy Brian Seligman

Coupe w/Trailer, WY90
Courtesy Brian Seligman

Garage Set

(W), 3¾'' x 4¾'' metal gar., 1938/39, 2 4⅜'' cars w/wrt, #7603 /#501	50	75	115

Garage Set, ''2 Car Garage''.
Courtesy Brian Seligman

La Salle

	C6	C8	C10
(w), 15'' long, 1936/39, wrt.....	65	125	190
(w), 15'' long, 1939, wrt, e/l, hood opens	75	130	210

La Salle and Trailer Set

WY22, 26½'', 1936/38, wrt	145	275	425

LaSalle & Trailer Set, WY22.
Photo by Bob Smith

Sedan, WY15
Courtesy Brian Seligman

Sedan, WY100
Courtesy Brian Seligman

Sedans, 4 dr.

WY15, 4½'', 1934, wrt, rear spare	35	50	70
WY100, 5'' long, 19??, yww	45	60	75
(W), 6'' long, 1938, wd whls, sm hood orn..................	30	50	75

Sedan, WY34
Courtesy Brian Seligman

Sedan, WY83
Courtesy Brian Seligman

Sedan, WY79
Courtesy Brian Seligman

Sedan, WY84
Courtesy Brian Seligman

Sedan, WY59
Courtesy Brian Seligman

	C6	C8	C10
WY34, 6'' long, 1939/41, bpw, touring sedan, #220	30	50	75
WY79, 6'' long, 1939/41, bpw, touring sedan #220	30	50	75
WY59, 6¼'', 1934, eww	30	50	75
WY33, 9'' long, 1934, wrt, e/l rooster comb hood orn	65	80	110
WY83, 9'' long, 1934, wrt, e/l rooster comb hood orn	65	80	110
WY84, 9'' long, 1934, wrt, e/l rooster comb hood orn.......	65	80	110
(B), 9⅛'', 1938, wd whls	65	80	110
(W), 9¾'', 1938, lmw, #344	65	80	110
(W), 11'' long, 1939, pmw, town sedan #425	65	105	150
(W), 15¾'', 1938, brt, key attached spring motor	75	150	190

Sedan with trailer

WY30, 11¾'', 1938, bww, #7625	60	105	145
WY80, 11¾'', 1938, bww, #7625	60	105	145

Sedan, WY33
Courtesy Brian Seligman

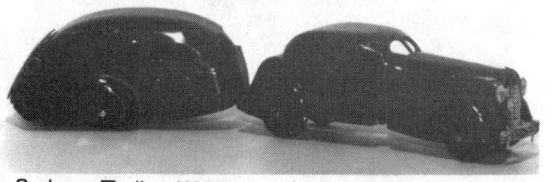

Sedan w/Trailer, WY30   Courtesy Brian Seligman

483

Sedan w/Trailer, WY80
Courtesy Brian Seligman

Speedster, WY13
Courtesy Brian Seligman

Soap Box Derby Racer	C6	C8	C10
(W), 6¼'', 1941, brt, "Soap Box Derby" "Thunderbird 226", w/driver	75	150	195

Speedster

	C6	C8	C10
WY11, 6¾'', 1937, bww, w/wo two figures	40	60	100
WY12, 10'' long, 1938, bww, w/roof like cord	60	75	125
WY13, 10'' long, 1937, bww, rev wind-up motor	60	100	140

Town car

Toytown

	C6	C8	C10
( ), 194?, ? trs, delivery	No Price Found		
(W), 21'' long, 1941, brt/wd hubs, estate station wagon litho of family	75	125	215
(W), 21'' long, 1941, brt/wd hubs, Grocer Wagon, "Meats plus Groceries", litho driver	70	125	215
( ), 1941, Ice Co.	70	125	215

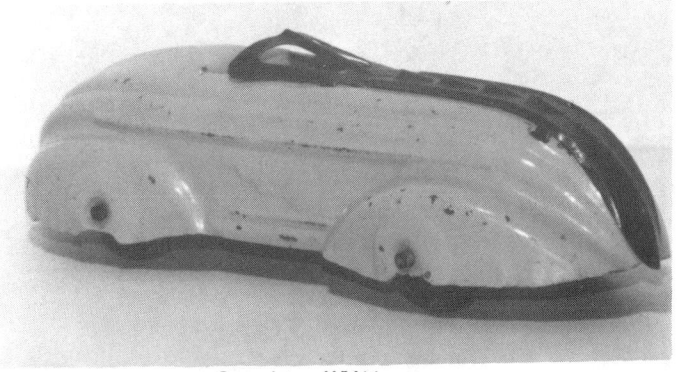

Speedster, WY11
Courtesy Brian Seligman

Toytown Estate Station Wagon, door missing.
Photo by Calvin L. Chaussee

Speedster, WY12
Courtesy Brian Seligman

Construction

Riding Steam Shovel

Steam shovel

Steam roller

Cement mixer

Construction Equipt.

	C6	C8	C10
WY97, 22¼'', 19??, Flatbed and steam shovel	50	75	125

Construction WY97
Courtesy Brian Seligman

Rocket Racer, WY61
Courtesy Brian Seligman

Construction WY110
Courtesy Brian Seligman

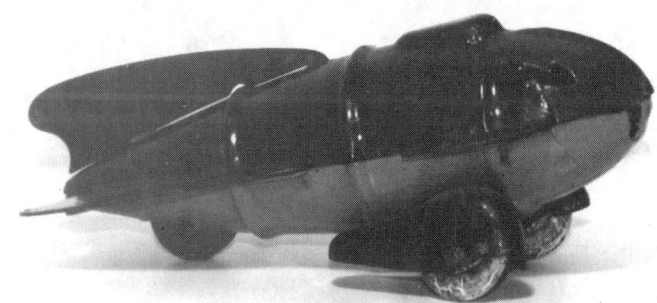

Rocker Racer, WY62
Courtesy Brian Seligman

	C6	C8	C10
WY110, 193?, Sand loader and crane	50	80	100
(WO), 20½'', 1952/53, Scale Model Earth Mover	55	85	105
(WO), 19'' long, 1952/53, Scale Model Road Grader	55	85	105

Rocket Racer

	C6	C8	C10
WY61, 6¼'', 1935/36, wrt/wd rear whl, #319	60	75	115
WY62, 6¼'', 1935/36, wrt/wd rear whl, #319	60	75	115

TOY SHOWS

There are hundreds of toy shows across the United States every year. The best way to find out about them is through such periodicals as *Antique Toy World* and *Toy Shop* (see below). However, to get the novice started, here are a few of the more prominent:

ALLENTOWN - November. (1-800) 392 TOYS.

ROCHESTER - June and November. Bob Smith (716) 377-8394.

DALLAS - July, November. Don Maris (817) 261-8745.

CHICAGO - April, June, October. (312) 725-0633.

NEW YORK & NEWARK - September, June. Bob Bostoff (516) 791-4858.

DAYTON - May. (513) 233-8381.

TOLEDO - July, October. John Carlisle, Old Toyland Shows, Bewley Bldg., Rm. 409, Lockport, NY 14094.

ATLANTA - November (404) 987-2773.

PASADENA - January (213) 656-1266.

PERIODICALS

There are many periodicals devoted wholly or partially to toys. The three following are probably the most important to readers of this book. *Antique Toy World* tends to run articles and ads on the older vehicles, *Toy Shop* tends to run ads on the newer ones, and *U.S. Toy Collector* concentrates, in text and ads, almost exclusively on vehicles.

Antique Toy World. Monthly. $25 a year. P.O. Box 34509 Chicago, IL 60634. *Toy Shop*. Monthly. $23.95 a year. 700 E. State St. Iola, WI 54990. *U.S. Toy Collector*. Monthly. $18 a year. P.O. Box 4244 Missoula, MT 59801.

TOY REPAIRERS AND RESTORERS

There are a number of experts in this area. Some of them do it full time and even have full-time employees. Most or all advertise in the publications above. But for the beginner, here are some of the leading names:

New Era Toy Restorations. Pressed steel. (609) 397-2113.

Portell Restorations. Pedal Cars. (314) 937-8192.

Castings. Walter Allen. (508) 283-2988.

Decals. Bob Gerrity (206) 941-6055.

Arnie Prince. Cast Iron. (209) 334-6101.

Paint & Rust Removal. (914) 359-1736 and (914) 937-3354.

Plastic Parts Reproductions. Toy Surgeon, 6528 Cedarbrook, New Albany, Ohio, 43054.

Buddy L, etc. parts, accessories, decals. (215) 838-6505.

Don Hultzman. Repairs of battery-operated and tin wind-ups. 5026 Sleepy Hollow Road, Medina, Ohio 44256.

Tin Toy Works. Missing Parts and Complete Restoration. (215) 439-8268.

Julian Thomas. Iron or Tin repairs. Wind-ups, decals. SASE to Thomas Toys, P.O. Box 405, Fenton, MI 48430.

SOME LEADING COLLECTORS & DEALERS

(It's suggested that, when writing to any of the following, you enclose a stamped, self-addressed envelope, known to hobbyists as an SSAE or SASE.)

EDWARD K. POOLE
1/36 scale ID vehicles and
old wooden military vehicle kits
926 Terrace Mt. Drive
Austin, TX 78746

DON HULTZMAN
Tin wind-up and battery-operated, also repairs, restorations
5026 Sleepy Hollow Road
Medina, OH 44256

RON SMITH
Tin, Hot Wheels, Promos, Die-Cast Cars, Trucks, Planes.
33005 Arlesford
Solon, Ohio 44139
(216) 248-7066

VINCENT ROSA
Brooklins (sells the Brooklin Book & Collector's Guide)
Model Cars & Trains Unlimited
28 Arthur Ave.
Blue Point, NY 11715
(516) 363-2134

GATES WILLARD
1925-40 Automotive Toys
233 Manhasset Ave.
Manhasset, NY 11030

BRIAN SELIGMAN
Wyandotte, Marx, Girard
910 NW 199th Terrace
Pembroke Pines, FL 33029
(305) 431-6942

BOB SMITH
Old Toys, buy, sell, trade, appraise.
Toy Shows.
62 West Ave.
Fairport, NY 14450
(716) 377-8394

THOMAS G. NEFOS
Hess, Investment quality transportation toys.
Publisher of National Toy Connection.
National Toy Connection
P.O. Box 615
Brigantine, NJ 08203-0615
(609) 266-6155

WILLIAM KILBORN
Military Dinky, etc.
P.O. Box #614
St. Mary's, Ontario
N4X, 1B4 Canada

DAVID M. LEOPARD
Old toy cars and trucks
2507 Feather Run Trail
West Columbia, SC 29169-4915

JOE & SHARON FREED
Vehicles
6209 Sandy Forks Rd.
Raleigh, NC 27609

GARY J. LINDEN
Marx and other plastic toys
P.O. Box 5243
River Forest, IL 60305

KENT M. COMSTOCK
Motorcycles of every type.
507 Vine Street
Ashland, Ohio 44805

CALVIN L. CHAUSSEE
Antique Toy Buyer - Any Quantity
Box 22
Calhan, CO 80808
(719) 347-2000
FAX: (719) 347-2780

BILL LANGO
Barclay vehicles, animals and soldiers
from original and new molds - Send for flyer
127 74th Street
North Bergen, NJ 07047

FRED MAXWELL - COLLECTOR-RESEARCHER
Slush mold cars, planes, novelties, literature, toys
4722 No. 33 Street
Arlington, VA 22207

RAY FUNK
Toy, Bicycles
P.O. Box 5019
Upland, CA 91785

SCOTT SMILES
Tin wind-ups, etc.
848 S. Atlantic Dr., E.
Lantana, FL 33462

CONTINENTAL HOBBY HOUSE
Toys and Trains, Regular catalogs
P.O. Box 193
Sheboygan, WI 53082

FRED THOMPSON
New designs of Smitty vehicles
Smith-Miller Inc.
P.O. Box 139
Canoga Park, CA 91305

ECCLES BROTHERS
Vehicles from original molds
Catalog $3.00
R.R. 1, Box 253-D
Burlington, IA 52601

JAMES S. MAXWELL - VIRGINIA CAPUTO
Old toys, all types, buy and sell
Box 367
Lampeter, PA 17537

SECOND CHILDHOOD
Antique Toys
283 Bleecker Street
New York, NY

JOHN MURRAY
Fisher-Price
Box 29
Eden, NY 14057

RICHARD MacNARY
Coca-Cola vehicles
4727 Alpine Drive
Lilburn, GA 30247

BILL HELLIE
ALL AMERICAN TOY COMPANY
American Toy Company parts and
limited editions; buy, sell, restore antique toys
P.O. Box 4266
Salem, OR 97302

JOHN D. (JACK) MATTHEWS
World War II toys, etc.
13 Bufflehead Drive
Kiawah Island, SC 29455

ROBERT & ALICE WAGNER
Toy vehicles of all types.
58 S. Main St.
Wharton, NJ 07885

DON COVIELLO
Collector and produces Die-cast Police Car
replicas.
Box 283
Purchase, NY 10577

LEN ROSENBERG
Advertising Photographer and Collector
2077 Clinton Ave. S.
Rochester, NY 14618

BLYSTONE'S
The leading dealer in collector books,
especially toys.
2132 Delaware Ave.
Pittsburgh, PA 15218
Phone: (412) 371-3511   FAX: (412) 244-8028

TUTTLE & SPICE GENERAL STORE & MUSEUM
Section on toys
I-81 Exit 269
Shenandoah Caverns, VA 22847
1-800-635-4599

ROD CARNAHAN
Classic cast iron toys, etc.
541 El Paso St.
Jacksonville, TX 75766

WAYNE FREESE
Sells many toy catalogs, originals & Xeroxes.
RD1 Dogwood Lane
Chester Spring, PA 19425

LLOYD L. LAUMANN
Tonka expert. Sells catalog Xeroxes, etc.
6980 Co. Rd. 10, North
Waconia, MN 55387-9643

JEFF BUB
Auctioneer, Appraisals
1658 Barbara Drive
Brunswick, OH 44212
(216) 225-1110

CHICAGO ANTIQUE TOY AUCTIONS
by JUST RIGHT, INC.
6582 R.F.D.
Long Grove, IL 60047
(708) 949-0059

OEI ENTERPRISES, LTD.
Buys, Sells, Trades, Restores old toys
241 Rowayton Ave.
Rowayton, CT 06853-1227
(203) 866-2470

MAPES AUCTIONEERS & APPRAISERS
1600 Vestal Parkway West
Vestal, NY 13850
(607) 754-9193

HAKE'S AMERICANA & COLLECTIBLES
Mail Auctions
Sample catalog $3.00
P.O. Box 1444N
York, PA 17405
(717) 848-1333

LLOYD W. RALSTON
Auctions
173 Post Road
Fairfield, CT 06430
(203) 255-1233

CONTINENTAL AUCTIONS (Mail)
P.O. Box 193
Sheboygan, Wisconsin 53082

JOHN A. GIBSON
Tootsietoy Restoration, Parts & Services
The Graham Werkes
P.O. Box 40054
Washington, D.C. 20016

BARB & DON DESALLE
Tonka, especially Private Label trucks
5106 Knollwood
Anderson, IN 45011
1-800-392-TOYS

COLLECTING TOY TRAINS
Identification and Value Guide
by Richard O'Brien

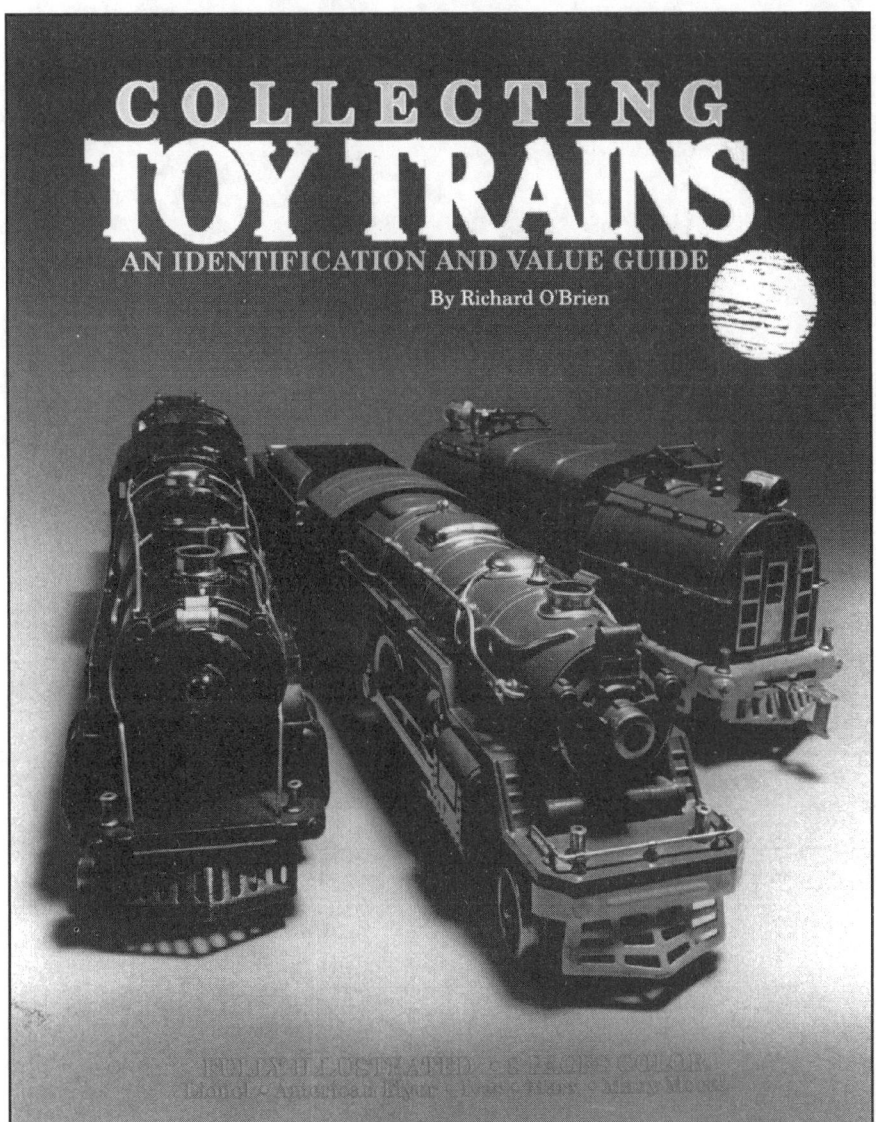

$22.95

This 3rd edition has added hundreds of new photos and listings.
LIONEL, MARX, AMERICAN FLYER, IVES, BUDDY L, plus others.
This guide includes engines, cars and accessories with descriptions, prices and photos.
Richard O'Brien (Collecting Toys No. 6) has had the aid of the top train collectors
from across the country.
Now in large format (8½" x 11"), 352 pages, 8 in color, softcover.

ISBN 0-89689-084-8

COLLECTING TOY SOLDIERS
Identification and Value Guide
by Richard O'Brien

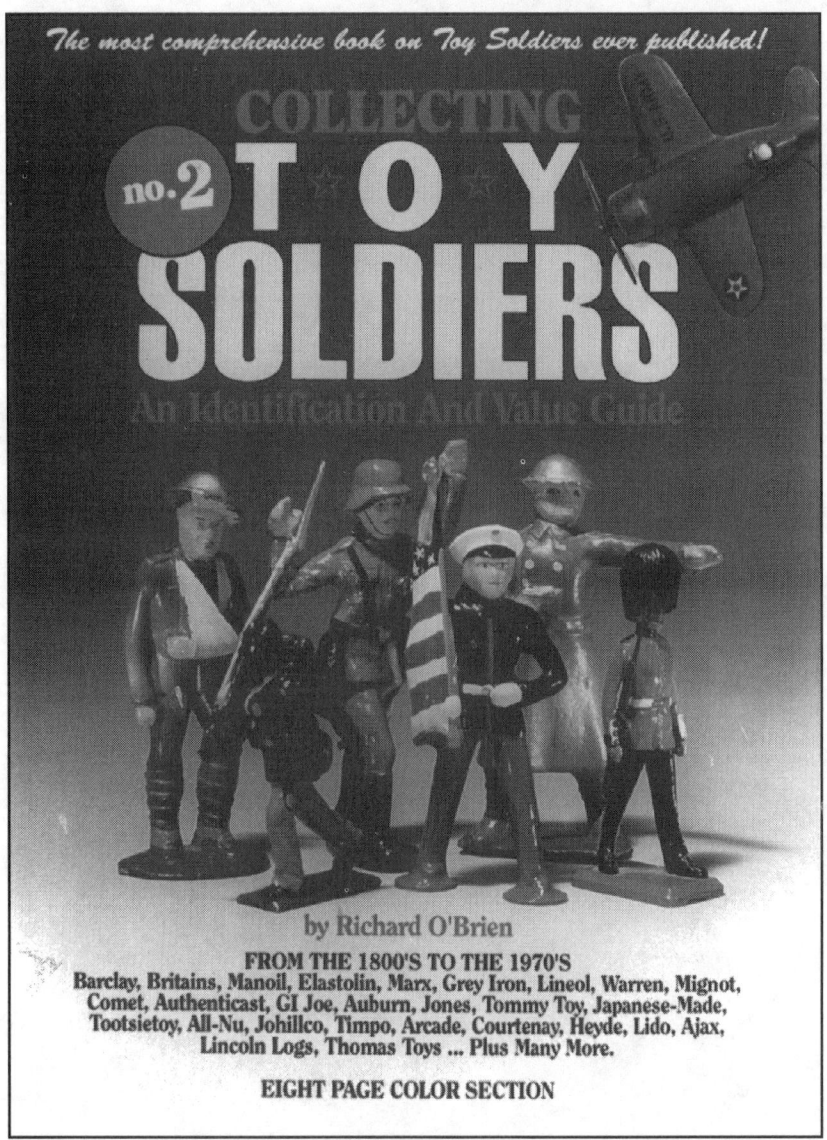

The most comprehensive book on Toy Soldiers ever published!

COLLECTING
no.2 **T O Y**
SOLDIERS
An Identification And Value Guide

by Richard O'Brien
FROM THE 1800'S TO THE 1970'S
Barclay, Britains, Manoil, Elastolin, Marx, Grey Iron, Lineol, Warren, Mignot,
Comet, Authenticast, GI Joe, Auburn, Jones, Tommy Toy, Japanese-Made,
Tootsietoy, All-Nu, Johillco, Timpo, Arcade, Courtenay, Heyde, Lido, Ajax,
Lincoln Logs, Thomas Toys ... Plus Many More.

EIGHT PAGE COLOR SECTION

$29.95

Former sections have been expanded and many new ones added.
Major expansions include BRITAINS, JOHILLCO, MARX AND OTHER PLASTIC.
Many newly-discovered early American makers have been added,
with their soldiers shown in depth. Other additions include Japan's Minikin, Danish-made soldiers
and French "dimestore" figures. In the American dimestore area, many new finds are
shown, as well as such "new" companies as Wilton, H.B. Toys and Paul Paragine.
Hundreds of related toys: Vehicles, Airplanes, Tanks, Ships, etc.
640 Heavily - Illustrated Pages, Including Eight Pages of Color

8½" x 11", Softcover   ISBN 0-89689-089-9

An Identification & Value Guide To
COLLECTING TOYS # 6
by Richard O'Brien

A COLLECTOR'S IDENTIFICATION & VALUE GUIDE

Collecting no.6
TOYS
Richard O'Brien

NEW LISTINGS INCLUDE:
MATCHBOX, JAPANESE TIN, ACTION FIGURES, AURORA FIGURE KITS

$22.95

This book is the favorite of toy collectors worldwide, but whether you are a collector or not, this book is just plain fun reading. 520 pages loaded with illustrations, many in full color, paperback. 8½ x 11. ISBN 0-89689-094-5